Lecture Notes in Computer Science 1963

Edited by G. Goos, J. Hartmanis and J. van Leeuwen

Springer

Berlin
Heidelberg
New York
Barcelona
Hong Kong
London
Milan
Paris
Singapore
Tokyo

Václav Hlaváč   Keith G. Jeffery
Jiří Wiedermann (Eds.)

SOFSEM 2000:
Theory and Practice
of Informatics

27th Conference on Current Trends
in Theory and Practice of Informatics
Milovy, Czech Republic, November 25 – December 2, 2000
Proceedings

 Springer

Series Editors

Gerhard Goos, Karlsruhe University, Germany
Juris Hartmanis, Cornell University, NY, USA
Jan van Leeuwen, Utrecht University, The Netherlands

Volume Editors

Václav Hlaváč
Czech Technical University, Department of Cybernetics
Karlovo nám. 13, 121 35 Prague, Czech Republic
E-mail: hlavac@vision.felk.cvut.cz

Keith G. Jeffery
CLRC RAL, Information Technology Department
Chilton, Didcot, Oxfordshire, United Kingdom
E-mail: K.G.Jeffery@rl.ac.uk

Jiří Wiedermann
Academy of Sciences of the Czech Republic, Insitute of Computer Science
Pod vodárenskou věží 2, 182 07 Prague, Czech Republic
E-mail: wieder@cs.cas.cz

Cataloging-in-Publication Data applied for

Die Deutsche Bibliothek - CIP-Einheitsaufnahme

Theory and practice of informatics : proceedings / SOFSEM 2000, 27th Conference
on Current Trends in Theory and Practice of Informatics, Milovy, Czech Republic,
November 25 - December 2, 2000. Václav Hlavác ... (ed.). - Berlin ; Heidelberg ;
New York ; Barcelona ; Hong Kong ; London ; Milan ; Paris ; Singapore ; Tokyo :
Springer, 2000
   (Lecture notes in computer science ; Vol. 1963)
   ISBN 3-540-41348-0

CR Subject Classification (1998): D, F, H.1-3, I.2, C.2, G.2

ISSN 0302-9743
ISBN 3-540-41348-0 Springer-Verlag Berlin Heidelberg New York

Springer-Verlag Berlin Heidelberg New York
a member of BertelsmannSpringer Science+Business Media GmbH
© Springer-Verlag Berlin Heidelberg 2000
Printed in Germany

Typesetting: Camera-ready by author, data conversion by DA-TeX Gerd Blumenstein
Printed on acid-free paper   SPIN: 10781064   06/3142   5 4 3 2 1 0

Preface

The international conference on current trends in the theory and practice of informatics SOFSEM 2000 was held 25 November – 2 December 2000 in the conference facilities of the Devět Skal (Nine Rocks) Hotel, Milovy, Czech-Moravian Highlands, the Czech Republic. It was already the 27th annual meeting in the series of SOFSEM conferences organized in either the Czech or the Slovak Republic.

Since its establishment in 1974, SOFSEM has gone through a long development in parallel with the entire field of informatics. Currently SOFSEM is a wide-scope, multidisciplinary conference, with stress on the interplay between the theory and practice of informatics. The SOFSEM scientific program consists mainly of invited talks which determine the topics of the conference. Invited talks are complemented by short refereed talks contributed by SOFSEM participants. The topics of invited talks are chosen so as to cover the span from theory to practice and to bring interesting research areas to the attention of conference participants. For the year 2000, the following three streams were chosen for presentation by the SOFSEM Steering Committee:

- Trends in Algorithmics
- Information Technologies in Practice
- Computational Perception

The above streams were covered through 16 invited talks given by prominent researchers. There were 18 contributed talks also presented, chosen by the international Program Committee from among 36 submitted papers. The program also included a panel on lessons learned from the Y2K problem. For the first time in SOFSEM history, the conference was also accompanied by a workshop on soft computing.

The present volume contains invited papers (including the keynote talk by Dines Bjørner), the workshop opening plenary talk and all contributed papers.

We are grateful to the members of both the SOFSEM Advisory Board and the SOFSEM Steering Committee for their proposals for the conference scientific program and for their cooperation in recruiting the invited speakers. We also wish to thank everybody who submitted a paper for consideration, all Program Committee members for their meritorious work in evaluating the papers, as well as to all subreferees who assisted the Program Committee members in the selection process. We are deeply indebted to all authors of invited and contributed papers who prepared their manuscripts for presentation in this volume. A special thanks goes to Petr Hájek who organized the scientific part of the workshop on soft computing and set up a special volume of the journal *Neural Network World* containing the selected papers presented at the workshop.

The secretary of the Program Committee, Aleš Křenek, did a great job in maintaining the SOFSEM program agenda. Moreover, he prepared, with the appreciated help of Zdeněk Salvet, the camera-ready version of the proceedings manuscript and took the responsibility for its final LATEX typesetting.

Many thanks are due to the members of the Organizing Committee who did an excellent job in preparing and conducting SOFSEM 2000, as usual. Jan Staudek was a very efficient conductor of his Organizing Committee orchestra. We also thank all institutions and scientific societies that cooperated in organizing SOFSEM 2000 and all sponsors who, through financial support, permitted the invited speakers and Ph.D. students to participate. The assistance of Springer-Verlag in the preparation of the volume is highly appreciated. Last but not least, we thank the editorial board of the journal *Neural Network World*, where the papers from the soft computing workshop were presented.

September 2000   Václav Hlaváč, Tokyo
                                                    Keith G. Jeffery, Didcot
                                                 Jiří Wiedermann, Prague

▮▬ Advisory Board

Dines Bjørner	Technical University of Denmark, Lyngby, Denmark
Manfred Broy	Technical University Munich, Germany
Michal Chytil	ANIMA Prague, Czech Republic
Peter van Emde Boas	University of Amsterdam, The Netherlands
Georg Gottlob	Vienna University of Technology, Austria
Keith G. Jeffery	CLRC RAL, Chilton, Didcot, Oxon, UK
Maria Zemánková	NSF, Washington D. C., USA

▮▬ Steering Committee

Jiří Wiedermann, *chair*	Academy of Sciences, Prague, Czech Republic
Miroslav Bartošek, *secretary*	Masaryk University, Brno, Czech Republic
Keith G. Jeffery	CLRC RAL, Chilton, Didcot, Oxon, UK
František Plášil	Charles University, Prague, Czech Republic
Igor Prívara	INFOSTAT, Bratislava, Slovak Republic
Branislav Rovan	Comenius University, Bratislava, Slovak Republic
Jan Staudek	Masaryk University, Brno, Czech Republic
Gerard Tel	Utrecht University, The Netherlands

▮▬ Program Committee

Václav Hlaváč, *chair*	Czech Technical University, Prague, Czech Republic
Keith G. Jeffery, *co-chair*	CLRC RAL, Chilton, Didcot, Oxon, UK
Jiří Wiedermann, *co-chair*	Academy of Sciences, Prague, Czech Republic
Aleš Křenek, *secretary*	Masaryk University, Brno, Czech Republic
Vasco Brattka	University of Hagen, Germany
Luboš Brim	Masaryk University, Brno, Czech Republic
Peter van Emde Boas	University of Amsterdam, The Netherlands
Anna Gambin	Warsaw University, Poland
Damas Gruska	Comenius Univeristy, Bratislava, Slovak Republic
Bořivoj Melichar	Czech Technical University, Prague, Czech Republic
Aleš Mičovský	Softec, s.r.o., Bratislava, Slovak Republic
Jan Pavelka	DCIT Ltd., Prague, Czech Republic
Jaroslav Pokorný	Charles University, Prague, Czech Republic
Jiří Polák	Deloitte & Touche, Prague, Czech Republic
Peter Ružička	Comenius Univeristy, Bratislava, Slovak Republic
Robert Sablatnig	Vienna University of Technology, Austria
Sebastian Seibert	RWTH Aachen, Germany
Milan Šonka	University of Iowa, Iowa City, USA
Gerard Tel	Utrecht University, The Netherlands
Petr Tůma	Charles University, Prague, Czech Republic
Ulrich Ultes-Nitsche	University of Southhampton, UK
Thomas Worsch	University of Karlsruhe, Germany

⦂≡ Subreferees

Peter Borovanský
Michael Butler
David R. Gilbert
Dušan Guller
Neil Henderson
Juraj Hromkovič
Petr Klán
Ralf Klasing
Ivan Kopeček
Dariusz Kowalski
Mojmír Křetínský

Antonín Kučera
Adam Malinowski
Luboš Popelínský
Zdenko Staníček
Ján Šturc
Miroslav Tůma
Walter Unger
Pavol Voda
Jana Zvárová

⦂≡ Organization

SOFSEM 2000 is organized by

CLRC RAL, Chilton, Didcot, Oxon, UK
Czech Technical University, Prague, Czech Republic
Czech Society for Computer Science
Faculty of Informatics, Masaryk University, Brno, Czech Republic
Institute of Computer Science, Academy of Science, Prague, Czech Republic
Institute of Computer Science, Masaryk University, Brno, Czech Republic

in cooperation with

Czech ACM Chapter
Czechoslovak Chapter of the IEEE Computer Society
Slovak Society for Computer Science

⦂≡ Organizing Committee

Jan Staudek, *chair*
Miroslav Bartošek
Petr Hanáček
Dana Komárková
Zdeněk Malčík

Tomáš Pitner
Jaromír Skřivan
Petr Sojka
Tomáš Staudek

⦂≡ Sponsoring Institutions

ApS Brno, s.r.o.
Compaq Computer, s.r.o.
ERCIM, the European Research Consortium for Informatics and Mathematics
Hewlett Packard, s.r.o.
IBM Czech Republic, s.r.o.
Oracle Czech, s.r.o.

Table of Contents

Computational Perception

Soft Computing

CONTRIBUTED PAPERS

Domain Engineering:
A Software Engineering Discipline
in Need of Research

Dines Bjørner

Department of Computer Science & Technology, Technical University of Denmark,
DK–2800 Lyngby, Denmark
db@it.dtu.dk

Abstract. Before software can be developed its requirements must be
stated. Before requirements can be expressed the application domain
must be understood. In this invited paper we outline some of the basic
facets of domain engineering.

Domains seem, it is our experience, far more stable than computing
requirements, and these again seem more stable than software designs.
Thus, almost like the universal laws of physics, it pays off to first develop
theories of domains.

But domain engineering, as in fact also requirements engineering, really
is in need of thoroughly researched development principles, techniques
and tools. The aim of this invited paper is to advocate: that researchers
study these development method components, and that universities focus
their education on basing well-nigh any course on the use of formal techniques: Specification and verification, and that software engineers take
heed: Start applying formal techniques. A brief example of describing
stake-holder perspectives will be given — on the background of which we
then proceed to survey the notions of domain intrinsics, domain support technologies, domain management & organisation, domain rules
& regulations, domain human behaviour, etc. We show elsewhere how
to "derive" requirements from domain descriptions. Domain requirements: by domain projection, instantiation, extension and initialisation;
interface requirements: multi-media, dialogue, etc.; and machine requirements: performance, dependability (reliability, availability, accessability,
safety, etc.), and maintainability (adaptability, perfectability and cor-
rectability).

The current paper presents *work-in-progress*. The text of the paper is
therefore very schematic.

1   Introduction

In this introduction we briefly "define"[1] the concepts of computer and computing
sciences and that of software engineering as consisting of domain engineering,

---

[1] By double, tongue-in-cheek, quoting the term 'define' we wish to express that certain
ideas should not be fully and formally defined — rather the "definition" is a characterisation.

V. Hlaváč, K. G. Jeffery, and J. Wiedermann (Eds.): SOFSEM 2000, LNCS 1963, pp. 1–17, 2000.

requirements engineering and software design. We also "define" the concepts of method and methodology.

1.1 Computer vs. Computing Science

Computing science, or, as we also refer to it, programming methodology, seems far from being sufficiently studied and propagated. Software engineering, "walking the bridge" between computing science and software technology, likewise seems a stepchild of most computer/computing science departments.

In this invited paper we shall highlight these claims and this problem.

I was asked, specifically, to take the opportunity to voice some, perhaps controversial, personal observations.

Clever "boys and girls" dig themselves into deep holes — of so-called theoretical computer science — and produce wondrous results. Perhaps it is not so easy: One really only has to "master" a narrow field. It seems that breadth, as well as depth, and in particular contemplation, is needed to contribute, with clearly identifiable results, to programming methodology.

Computing science (i. e. programming methodology) deals with studying directions as to how people proceed in making software. That may be a reason why it takes other skills.

1.2 The Two Sciences and One Engineering

1.2.1 Computer Science. *Computer science* is the study and knowledge of the *properties* of the phenomena that can exist inside computers, data and processes, and includes: Automata theory and formal languages; algebraic, axiomatic, denotational and structural operational semantics; computational models; proof theories; algorithmic complexity theory; cryptography; etc.

> **Challenges:** Is this postulated borderline — between computer science and computing science — just a meaningless distinction, or, if not, is the borderline "just" the borderline between 'what' and 'how'? And if so, what do we mean by "just"?

1.2.2 Computing Science. *Computing science* is the study and knowledge of *how to construct* those devices, data and processes, and includes: Functional, imperative, logic, parallel and algebraic programming; algorithmics: Algorithms & data structures; domain, requirements and software specification: Abstraction and modelling: Hierarchies and configurations, contexts and states, looseness and underspecification, etc.; refinement calculi and property verification: Theorem proving and model checking; systems: real-time embedded systems, distributed systems, compiler systems, operating systems, database systems, etc.

1.2.3 Software Engineering. *Software engineering* is, to us, a triptych:

Domain engineering. Engineering an understanding of the *domain* of applications — void of any reference to computing. Constituent development principles, techniques and tools involve: Designations, definitions and refutable assertions; static and dynamic (inert, autonomous, biddable, programmable, reactive) attributes; intrinsic, support technology, management & organisation, rules & regulations, human behaviour, etc., facets; tangible and intangible attributes; discrete, continuous and chaotic attributes; etc.

Requirements engineering. Engineering *requirements* to software for computing applications in the support of operations of the domain: Domain requirements (projection, instantiation, extension initialisation, etc.); interface requirements (multi-media, man-machine dialogues, etc.) and machine requirements (performance, dependability [reliability, safety criticality, availability, accessability, etc.], [perfective, adaptive and corrective] maintainability, development and operational platforms, etc.).

> **Challenges:** Are these the only requirements aspects, facets and attributes? We need more research here. We must understand better methodological relations between domain and requirements specifications.

Software design. Engineering the *design* of that software: Architecture (implementing domain requirements); program organisation (implementing machine requirements); object/module design; ... ; code.

> **Challenges:** We have far from understood relations between domain requirements and architecture; between machine requirements and program organisation; and what of interface requirements fit with architecture, what with program organisation.

1.3   Methods & Methodology

By a method we here understand a set of principles for efficiently analysing and constructing, using techniques and tools, efficient software. And: By methodology we understand the study and knowledge about a set of methods.

All of the above is, obviously w. r. t. the deployment of formal techniques: Such which are based on sound mathematics.

> **Challenges:** We claim: Not enough proposed principles, techniques and tools are put forward, and even less study is done of what has been proposed. The question really is: Are these proper ways of characterising the terms 'method' and 'methodology'? And, if so, or anyway, which are the principles, techniques and tools alluded to? This invited paper will outline some, but not really discuss, more thoroughly, the 'method' concept.

2   Example: Resource Management

We now turn to a set of examples in order to illustrate the issues of principles and techniques — the tools — here — mainly being those of informal, respectively formal description languages.

2.1   Synopsis and Narrative

The scope is that of resources and their management. The span is that of strategic, tactical and operations management and of actual operations. Strategic resource management is about acquiring ("expanding, upgrading") or disposing ("down-sizing, divesting") resources: Converting one form of resource to another. Tactical resource management is about allocating resources spatially and scheduling them for general, temporal availability. Operations resource management is about allocating resources to tasks and scheduling them for special, time interval deployment.

These three kinds of resource management reflect rather different perspectives: Strategic resource management is the prerogative and responsibility of executive management. Tactical resource management is the prerogative and responsibility of line ("middle level") management. Operations resource management is the prerogative and responsibility of operations (i. e. "ground level") management. And: Strategic resource management can, at best, be specified in such a way, that at most grossly incomplete decision support is possible. Tactical resource management can, somewhat better, be specified such that improved, but still only decision support is possible. Operations resource management, however, be increasingly algorithmitised.

2.2   Formalisation: Resources and Their Handling

We divide this part on formalisation into four sub-parts: First we just present the formalisation of the signature of the domain: The "data" and function types. Then their annotation. We normally go through several "motions" of rough sketching, analysis and narration before embarking on the formalisation. See [1] for the "story" on development of informative, descriptive and analytical documents: Synopses, rough sketches, analyses, narratives, validations, formalisations and verifications. Then the formalisation of the resources management and enterprise operation functions, followed by their annotation.

We remind the reader that the whole point of this example is to serve as an introductory exercise on the background of which we will later discuss intrinsic, support technology, management & organisation, rules & regulation, and human behaviour facets of domains; but before that we discuss stake-holder perspectives.

2.2.1   Formalisation: Resources

type R, Rn, L, T, E, A
  RS = R-**set**
  SR = T $\overrightarrow{m}$ RS,   SRS = SR-**infset**
  TR = (T×T) $\overrightarrow{m}$ R $\overrightarrow{m}$ L,   TRS = TR-**set**
  OR = (T×T) $\overrightarrow{m}$ R $\overrightarrow{m}$ A

  A = (Rn $\overrightarrow{m}$ R-**set**) $\overset{\sim}{\to}$ (Rn $\overrightarrow{m}$ R-**set**)

value
  srm: RS → E×E $\overset{\sim}{\to}$ E × (SRS × SR)
  trm: SR → E×E $\overset{\sim}{\to}$ E × (TRS × TR)
  orm: TR → E×E $\overset{\sim}{\to}$ E × OR

  p: RS × E → **Bool**

  ope: OR → TR → SR → (E×E×E×E) → E × RS

2.2.2   Resource Formalisation — Annotation.

R, Rn, L, T, E and A stand for resources, resource names, spatial locations, times, the enterprise (with its estimates, service and/or production plans, orders on hand, etc.), respectively tasks (actions). SR, TR and OR stand for strategic, tactical and operational resource views, respectively. srm, trm and orm stand for strategic, tactical, respectively operations resource management. p is a predicate which determines whether the enterprise can continue to operate (with its state and in its environment, e), or not.

To keep our model "small", we have had to resort to a "trick": Putting all the facts knowable and needed in order for management to function adequately into E! Besides the enterprise itself, E, also models its environment: That part of the world which affects the enterprise.

There are, accordingly, the following management functions: *Strategic resource management,* srm(rs)(e,e'''') = (e',(srs,sr)), proceed on the basis of the enterprise (e) and its current resources (rs), and "ideally estimates" all possible strategic resource possibilities (srs), and selects one, desirable (sr). The "estimation" is heuristic. Too little is normally known to compute sr algorithmically. *Tactical resource management,* trm(sr)(e,e'''') = (e'',(trs,tr)), proceed on the basis of the enterprise (e) and one chosen strategic resource view (sr) and "ideally calculates" all possible tactical resource possibilities (trs), and selects one, desirable (tr). *Operations resource management,* orm(tr)(e,e'''') = (e''',or), proceed on the basis of the enterprise (e) and one chosen tactical resource view (tr) and effectively decides on one operations resource view (or). We refer to [2] for details on the above and below model.

Actual enterprise operation, ope, enables, but does not guarantee, some "common" view of the enterprise: ope depends on the views of the enterprise, its state and environment, e, as "passed down" by management; and ope applies, according to prescriptions kept in the enterprise state, actions, a, to named (rn:Rn) sets of resources. The above account is, obviously, rather "idealised". But, hopefully, indicative of what is going on. To give a further abstraction of the "life cycle" of the enterprise we "idealise" it as now shown:

2.2.3   Formalisation: Resource Handling

value
    enterprise: RS $\xrightarrow{\sim}$ E $\xrightarrow{\sim}$ **Unit**
    enterprise(rs)(e) $\equiv$
      if p(rs)(e) **then**
        let (e$'$,(srs,sr)) = srm(rs)(e,e$''''$),
              (e$''$,(trs,tr)) = trm(sr)(e,e$''''$),
              (e$'''$,or) = orm(tr)(e,e$''''$),
              (e$''''$,rs$'$) = ope(or)(tr)(sr)(e,e$'$,e$''$,e$'''$) **in**
        let e$'''''$:E • p$'$(e$''''$,e$'''''$) **in**
        enterprise(rs$'$)(e$'''''$) **end end**
      else stop end

    p$'$: E × E → **Bool**

The enterprise re-invocation argument, rs', a result of operations, is intended to reflect the use of strategically, tactically and operationally acquired, spatially and task allocated and scheduled resources, including partial consumption, "wear & tear", loss, replacements, etc.

    An imperative version of enterprise could be:

value
    enterprise(rs)(e) $\equiv$
      variable ve:E := e;
      while p(ve) **do**
        let (e$'$,(srs,sr)) = srm(rs)(ve,e$''''$),
              (e$''$,(trs,tr)) = trm(sr)(ve,e$''''$),
              (e$'''$,or) = orm(tr)(ve,e$''''$),
              (e$''''$,rs$'$) = ope(or)(tr)(sr)(ve,e$'$,e$''$,e$'''$) **in**
        let e$'''''$:E • p$'$(e$''''$,e$'''''$) **in**
        ve := e$'''''$ **end end end**

Only the program flow of control recursion has been eliminated. The **let** e$'''''$:E • p$'$(e$''''$,e$'''''$) **in** ... shall model a changing environment.

2.2.4   Resource Handling — Annotation.
Thus there were two forms of recursion at play here: The simple tail-recursive, next step, day-to-day recursion, and the recursive "build-up" of the enterprise state e$''''$. The latter is the

interesting one. Solution, by iteration towards some acceptable, not necessarily minimal fixpoint, "mimics" the way the three levels of management and the "floor" operations change that state, "pass it around, up-&-down" the management "hierarchy". The operate function "unifies" the views that different management levels have of the enterprise, and influences their decision making.

We remind the reader that — in the previous example — we are "only" modelling the domain! That model is, obviously, sketchy. But we believe it portrays important facets of domain modelling and stake-holder perspectives.

We are modelling a domain with all its imperfections: We are not specifying anything algorithmically; all functions are rather loosely, hence partially defined, in fact only their signature is given. This means that we model well-managed as well as badly, sloppily, or disastrously managed enterprises. We can, of course, define a great number of predicates on the enterprise state and its environment (e:E), and we can partially characterise intrinsics — facts that must always be true of an enterprise, no matter how well or badly it is managed.

If we "programme-specified" the enterprise then we would not be modelling the domain of enterprises, but a specifically "business process engineered" enterprise. And we would be into requirements engineering — we claim. So let us take now, a closer view of the kind of things we can indeed model in the domain!

Challenges: We need more research into what characterises the spectrum from incomplete specifications — which, however, allow some form of computerised decision support, to algorithmically tractable specifications.

Challenges: And we need understand, for example, which decomposition into recursive equations reflect which organisational principles, and which solutions to the recursive equations designate which management principles.

---

3   Stake-Holder Perspectives

There are several kind of domain stake-holders. For a typical enterprise we can enumerate: Enterprise stake-holders: (i) owners, (ii) management: (a) executive, (b) line, and (c) "floor" managers, (iii) workers, (iv) families of the above. Non-enterprise stake-holders: (v) clients (customers), (vi) competitors, (vii) resource providers: (a) IT resource providers, (b) non-IT/non-finance resource providers, and (c) financial service providers, (viii) regulatory agencies, (ix) local and state authorities, (x) politicians, and the (xi) "public at large". For each stake-holder there usually is a distinct domain perspective: A partial specification. The example shown earlier illustrated, at some level of abstraction, the interaction between, hence the perspectives of, enterprise managers and workers, and, at a higher level of abstraction, interaction with the environment, incl. all other stake-holders. For infrastructure components — such as the health care sector — the above enumeration is "multiplied" by the variety of "enterprises" — vis.: clinics, hospitals, pharmacies, test laboratories, etc.

> **Challenges:** We need research relations between pragmatic classifications of stake-holders into classes and the semantic (i. e. specification) ramifications: Do certain specification compositions etc. designate management principles that are different from todays'?

4   Domain Facets

We shall sketch the following facets:

Domain intrinsics. That which is common to all facets.

Domain support technologies. That in terms of which several other facets (intrinsics, management & organisation, and rules & regulations) are implemented.

Domain management & organisation. That which constrains communication between enterprise stake-holders.

Domain rules & regulations. That which guides the work of enterprise stake-holders as well as their interaction and the interaction with non-enterprise stake-holders.

Domain human behaviour. The way in which domain stake-holders despatch their actions and interactions w. r. t. enterprise: dutifully, forgetfully, sloppily, yes even criminally.

We shall briefly characterise each of these facets. We venture to express "specification patterns" that "most closely capture" essences of the facet.

4.1   Intrinsics

Atomic rail components are called units, U. Units are either linear, switch, crossover, etc., units. Units have connectors. Certain pairs of unit connectors determine paths through units. A unit state, $\sigma{:}\Sigma$, is a set of (open) paths. A unit state may range over a set of states, $\omega{:}\Omega$

type U, C
  P = C $\times$ C, Σ = P-set, Ω = Σ-set
value
  obs_Cs: U $\rightarrow$ C-set
  is_Linear, is_Switch, is_Crossover: U $\rightarrow$ **Bool**

The intrinsics of a rail switch is that it can take on a number of states. A simple switch $\left(^{c_|}Y_c^{c_/}\right)$ has three connectors: $\{c, c_|, c_/\}$. c is the connector of the common rail from which one can either "go straight" $c_|$, or "fork" $c_/$.

$$\omega_{g_s} : \{ \, \{\},$$
$$\{(c, c_|)\}, \{(c, c_|), (c_|, c)\}, \{(c_|, c)\},$$
$$\{(c, c_/)\}, \{(c, c_/), (c_/, c)\}, \{(c_/, c)\},$$
$$\{(c, c_/), (c_|, c)\}, \{(c, c_/), (c_/, c), (c_|, c)\}, \{(c_/, c), (c_|, c)\} \, \}$$

ω_{g_s} ideally models a general switch. Any particular switch ω_{p_s} may have $\omega_{p_s} \subset \omega_{g_s}$. Nothing is said about how a state is determined: Who sets and resets it, whether determined solely by the physical position of the switch gear, or also by visible signals up or down the rail away from the switch. The intrinsics of a domain is a partial specification. Amongst many relevant specification patterns the following is typical.

type
 Γi, Σ_i, Syntax, VAL_i
value
 I: Syntax $\rightarrow$ Γi $\overset{\sim}{\rightarrow}$ Σ_i $\overset{\sim}{\rightarrow}$ Σ_i
 V: Syntax $\rightarrow$ Γi $\overset{\sim}{\rightarrow}$ Σ_i $\overset{\sim}{\rightarrow}$ VAL
 E: Syntax $\rightarrow$ Γi $\overset{\sim}{\rightarrow}$ Σ_i $\overset{\sim}{\rightarrow}$ Σ_i $\times$ VAL_i
 D: Syntax $\rightarrow$ Γi $\overset{\sim}{\rightarrow}$ Σ_i $\overset{\sim}{\rightarrow}$ Γi $\times$ Σ_i
 C: Syntax $\rightarrow$ Γi $\overset{\sim}{\rightarrow}$ Σ_i $\overset{\sim}{\rightarrow}$ Γi $\times$ Σ_i $\times$ VAL_i

Γi, Σ_i stands for context, respectively state spaces. Together they form a configuration space.

 Other specification patterns, for example centered around [concurrent] processes, hence having "result" type **Unit,** are also likely.

 Intrinsics descriptions emphasise looseness and non-determinism.

> **Challenges:** We need better understand the concept of 'intrinsics'.

4.2   Support Technologies

An example of different technology *stimuli:* A railway switch, "in ye olde days" of the "childhood" of railways, was *manually "thrown";* later it could be mechanically controlled from a distance by *wires and momentum "amplification";* again later it could be electro-mechanically controlled from a further distance by *electric signals that then activated mechanical controls;* and today switches are usually *controlled in groups that are electronically interlocked.*

Example 1 (Probabilistic Rail Switch State Machine). An aspect of supporting technology includes the recording of state-behaviour in response to external stimuli. Figure 1 on the following page indicates a way of formalising this aspect of a supporting technology.

Example 2 (Air Traffic Radar). Air traffic (iAT), intrinsically, is a total function over some time interval, from time (T) to monotonically positioned (P) aircrafts (A).

 A conventional air traffic radar "samples", at regular intervals, the intrinsic air traffic. Hence a radar is a partial function[2] from intrinsic to sampled air traffics (sAT).

---

[2] This example is due to my former MSc Thesis student Kristian M. Kalsing.

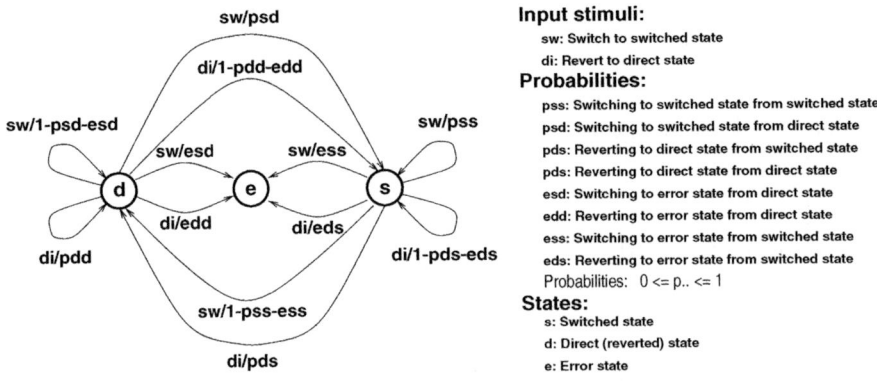

Fig. 1. Probabilistic State Switching

type
    iAT = T → (A $\overrightarrow{m}$ P), sAT = T $\overrightarrow{m}$ (A $\overrightarrow{m}$ P)
value
    radar: iAT $\xrightarrow{\sim}$ sAT, close: P × P → **Bool**
axiom
    ∀ iat:iAT •
        let sat = radar(iat) **in** ∀ t:T • t ∈ **dom** sat •
            t ∈ **dom** iat ∧ ∀ a:A • a ∈ **dom** iat(t) ⇒
                a ∈ **dom** sat(t) ∧ close((iat(t))(a),(sat(t))(a)) **end**

An axiom relates intrinsic air traffic to radar sampled air traffic. The axiom thus characterises this support technology.

Support technologies thus "implement" intrinsic contexts and states: γ_i:Γ_i, σ_i:Σ_i in terms of "actual" contexts and states: γ_a:Γ_a, σ_a:Σ_a.

type
    Syntax,
    Γ_i, Σ_i, VAL_i, Γ_a, Σ_a, VAL_a,
    ST = Γi × Σ_i $\xrightarrow{\sim}$ Γ_a × Σ_a
value
    sts:ST-**set**
    I: Syntax → Γ_a $\xrightarrow{\sim}$ Σ_a $\xrightarrow{\sim}$ Σ_a
    V: Syntax → Γ_a $\xrightarrow{\sim}$ Σ_a $\xrightarrow{\sim}$ VAL_a
    E: Syntax → Γ_a $\xrightarrow{\sim}$ Σ_a $\xrightarrow{\sim}$ Σ_a × VAL_a
    D: Syntax → Γ_a $\xrightarrow{\sim}$ Σ_a $\xrightarrow{\sim}$ Γ_a × Σ_a
    C: Syntax → Γ_a $\xrightarrow{\sim}$ Σ_a $\xrightarrow{\sim}$ Γ_a × Σ_a × VAL_a
axiom
    ∀ st:ST • st ∈ stst ⇒ ...

Support technology is not a refinement, but an extension. Support technology typically introduces considerations of technology accuracy, failure, etc. Axioms characterise members of the set of support technologies sts.

> **Challenges:** We need research the concept of support technology: When is something a support technology, how to model it, etc.?

4.3   Management & Organisation

People staff the enterprises, the components of infrastructures with which we are concerned: For which we develop software. The larger these enterprises, these infrastructure components, are, the more need there is for management and organisation. The rôle of management is roughly, for our purposes, twofold: To make strategic, tactical and operational policies — including rules & regulations, cf. Section 4.4 — and see to it that they are followed, and to react to adverse conditions: Unforeseen situations, and decide upon their handling, i.e. conflict resolution.

Policy setting should help non-management staff operate normal situations — for which no management interference is thus needed, and management "backstops" problems: Takes these problems off the shoulders of non-management staff. To help management and staff know who's in charge w.r.t. policy setting and problem handling, a clear conception of the overall organisation is needed: Organisation defines lines of communication within management and staff and between these. Whenever management and staff has to turn to others for assistance they follow the command line: The paths of organigrams — the usually hierarchical box and arrow/line diagrams.

Management is a set of predicates, observer and generator functions which parameterise other, the operations functions, that is: Determine their behaviour. Organisation is a set of constraints on communication behaviours.

type
    Msg, Ψ, Σ, Sx
channel
    { ms[i]:Msg | i:Sx }
value
    sys: **Unit** $\rightarrow$ **Unit**
    mgr: Ψ $\rightarrow$ **in,out** { ms[i] | i:Sx } **Unit**
    stf: i:Sx $\rightarrow$ Σ $\rightarrow$ **in,out** ms[i] **Unit**
    sys() $\equiv$ || { stf(i)(iσ) | i:Sx } || mgr(ψ)
    mgr(ψ) $\equiv$
        let ψ' = ... ;
            (|| { ms[i] ! msg ; f_m(msg)(ψ) | i:Sx })
            []
            ([] { **let** msg$'$ = ms[i] ? **in** g_m(msg$'$)(ψ) **end** | i:Sx }) **in**
        mgr(ψ') **end**
    stf(i)(σ) $\equiv$

let $\sigma' = ...$;
 $((\textbf{let } msg = ms[i] \ ? \ \textbf{in } f\_s(msg)(\sigma) \ \textbf{end})$
 $[]$
 $(ms[i] \ ! \ msg' \ ; \ g\_s(msg')(\sigma)))$ **in**
stf(σ') **end**
f_m,g_m: Msg $\rightarrow \Psi \rightarrow \Psi$, f_s,g_s: Msg $\rightarrow \Sigma \rightarrow \Sigma$

The example of Section 2 illustrated another management & organisation description pattern. It is based on a set of, in this case, recursive equations. Any way of solving these equations, finding a suitable fix point, or an approximation thereof, including just choosing and imposing an arbitrary "solution", reflects some management communication. The syntactic ordering of the equations — in this case: a "linear" passing of enterprise "results" from "upper" equations onto "lower" equations — reflects some organisation.

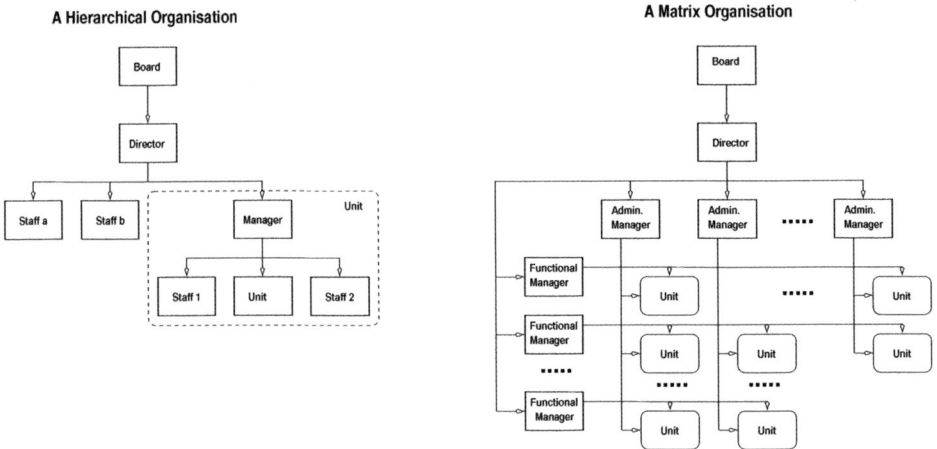

Fig. 2. Organisational Structures

"Hierarchical", rather than "linear", and "matrix" structured organisations can also be modelled as sets (of recursively invoked sets) of equations.

We refrain, in this case from showing the two forms of specification patterns that here characterise management & organisation. The examples should suffice.

Challenges: We need research varieties of management & organisation principles and, through formal modelling, characterise these and relate them to classical and novel "business school" dogmas about management & organisation.

4.4 Rules & Regulations

Rules & regulations are set by enterprises, enterprise associations, [government] regulatory agencies, and by law.

(i) In China arrival and departure of trains at, respectively from railway stations are subject to the following regulation: In any three minute interval at most one train may either arrive or depart.
(ii) In many countries railway lines (between stations) are segmented into blocks or sectors. The purpose is to stipulate that if two or more trains are moving — obviously in the same direction — along the line, then there must be at least one free sector (i. e. without a train) between any two such trains.
(iii) In the United States of America personal checks issued in any one state of the union must be cleared by the sending and receiving banks, if within the same state, then within 24 hours, and else within 48 or 72 hours, depending on certain further stipulated relations between the states.

There may be two kinds of syntax involved here: The syntax (Syntax_rr) describing the rules & regulations. And the syntax (Syntax_cmd) of [always current] system "input". A rule or regulation is, semantically, a predicate over [current] system input (i:Syntax_cmd) and current and next system configuration (context and state). We omit treatment of [current] system "input", hence choose RR rather than RR' below:

type
    Syntax_cmd, Syntax_rr
    $RR' = \text{Syntax\_cmd} \rightarrow (\Gamma \times \Gamma) \rightarrow (\Sigma \times \Sigma) \rightarrow$ **Bool**
    $RR = (\Gamma \times \Gamma) \rightarrow (\Sigma \times \Sigma) \rightarrow$ **Bool**
    $RRS = RR\text{-set}$
value
    interpret: $\text{Syntax\_rr} \rightarrow \Gamma \rightarrow \Sigma \rightarrow RRS$

    valid: $RRS \rightarrow (\Gamma \times \Gamma) \rightarrow (\Sigma \times \Sigma) \rightarrow$ **Bool**
    $valid(rrs)(\gamma,\gamma')(\sigma,\sigma') \equiv \forall\ rr:RR \bullet rr \in\ rrs \Rightarrow rr(\gamma,\gamma')(\sigma,\sigma')$

The need to express rules & regulations results in later requirements that special, domain-specific *Rules & Regulation Script Languages* be designed.

> **Challenges:** We need experimentally & exploratively research varieties of script languages: Which attributes they must possess in relation to attributes of rules & regulations, etc.

4.5   Human Behaviour

Some people try their best to perform actions according to expectations set by their colleagues, customers, etc. And they usually succeed in doing so. They are therefore judged reliable and trustworthy, good, punctual professionals (b_p) of their domain. Some people set lower standards for their professional performance: Are sometimes or often sloppy (b_s), make mistakes, unknowingly or even knowingly. And yet other people are outright delinquent (b_d) in the despatch of their work: Couldn't care less about living up to expectations of their colleagues and customers. Finally some people are explicitly criminal (b_c) in the conduct of what they do: Deliberately "do the opposite" of what is expected, circumvent rules & regulations, etc. And we must abstract and model, in any given situation where a human interferes in the "workings" of a domain action, any one of the above possible behaviours!

We often model the "arbitrariness", the impredictability, of human behaviour by internal non-determinism:

$$... \; b\_p \; \lceil \rceil \; b\_s \; \lceil \rceil \; b\_d \; \lceil \rceil \; b\_c \; ...$$

The exact, possibly deterministic, meaning of each of the b's can be separately described. In addition we can model human behaviour by the arbitrary selection of elements from sets and subsets of sets:

let x:X • s ∈ xs **in** ... **end**
let xs':X-**set** • xs' ⊆ xs **in** ... **end**

The above shows just fragments of formal descriptions of those parts which reflect human behaviour.

Commensurate with the above, humans interpret rules & regulations differently, and not always "consistently" in the sense of repeatedly applying the same interpretations. Our final specification pattern is therefore:

type
    Action $= \Gamma \xrightarrow{\sim} \Sigma \xrightarrow{\sim} \Gamma \times \Sigma$
value
    interpret: Syntax_rr $\rightarrow \Gamma \rightarrow \Sigma \rightarrow$ RRS-**infset**

    human_behaviour: Action $\rightarrow$ Syntax_rr $\rightarrow \Gamma \xrightarrow{\sim} \Sigma \xrightarrow{\sim} \Gamma \times \Sigma$
    human_behaviour(α)(srr)$(\gamma)(\sigma)$ **as** (γ',σ')
       post
          $\alpha(\gamma)(\sigma) = (\gamma',\sigma') \wedge$
          let rrs:RRS • rrs $\in$ interpret(srr)$(\gamma)(\sigma)$ **in**
             $\forall$ rr:RR • rr $\in$ rrs $\Rightarrow$ rr$(\gamma,\gamma')(\sigma,\sigma')$ **end**

We have taken some liberties in expressing the action part, but the idea should be clear: Humans determine next configurations based on arbitrary interpretation of rules & regulations.

> **Challenges:** We need further propose models for human behaviour.

4.6   Discussion

We have sketched some domain facets: Intrinsics, support technologies, management & organisation, rules & regulations, and human behaviour. For each we attempted a characterising specification pattern. There are, undoubtedly other facets and other patterns. Much work needs to be done.

Elsewhere ([1,3]) we detail other facets. (I) Along one axis is abstraction & modelling facets: (i) Model — and property-oriented specifications, (ii) representational and operational abstractions, (iii) functional, imperative, logic and concurrent models, (iv) hierarchical and compositional developments and presentations, (iv) denotational and computational semantics, (v) configurations: context and state models, (vi) time and space, and (vii) determinacy and looseness. (II) Along another axis are the domain attributes: (viii) Discrete, continuous and chaotic domain, (ix) static and dynamic (inert, active [autonomous, biddable, programmable], and reactive) domain [4], and (x) tangible and intangible domain [4]. (III) And along an altogether different axis there are the domain frames (Jackson: [4,5]): (xi) algebraic structures (languages), (xii) reactive systems, (xiii) information systems ("databases"), (xiv) work flows (flexible manufacturing, health care, office automation, etc.), (xv) workpieces (CAD, word processing, administration forms, etc.) (xvi) connectors, &c.

Whether these "axes of description" are comprehensive remains to be seen, but they seem sufficient to characterise: Transportation (road, rail, air, ship), financial services (bank, insurance, securities exchange, portfolio management, clearing, etc.), manufacturing (flexible, etc., and producer, supplier, trader and consumer), public government (health care, social welfare, ministry of finance, etc.), and other enterprises and infrastructure components.

Challenges: We need find out whether the above classification of facets is applicable across different problem frames, whether they are the only ones, etc.

---

5   Conclusion

We have presented work-in-progress.

The work reported here is part of an endeavour to understand *"What is a method?"*. We have "scratched" a surface: Shown some principles of stakeholder and facet specification and techniques for their description. And we have posed some 'method' research challenges.

One can formalise certain techniques and one can base certain tools on such formal techniques. Among the most common application of formal techniques and tools in software development is specification and analysis (incl. verification). Methods cannot be formal: Human ingenuity, which principles are chosen in relation to others, cannot be formalised.

One serious problem with the current invited paper is its total lack of any reference to knowledge engineering, certainly a close "ally" to what is being done here. This omission is acknowledged and some comparative study is made elsewhere [1].

Acknowledgements

I am grateful for the inspiration drawn from the work of Michael Jackson on requirements and software specification. I am grateful to my other colleagues in IFIP WG 2.2 for like inspiration. And I am grateful to my recent students: Asger Eir and Kristian M. Kalsing.

Bibliographical Notes

This document being an invited paper currently lacks proper citations. I do, however, strongly confess my delight in having studied Jackson's [4,6,7,8,9].

To support the implied claims made in the present document we refer to the following own reports and publications: [1,2,3,5,10,11,12,13].

References

1. Dines Bjørner. Domain Engineering, Elements of a Software Engineering Methodology — Towards Principles, Techniques and Tools — A Study in Methodology. Research report, Dept. of Computer Science & Technology, Technical University of Denmark, Bldg. 343, DK–2800 Lyngby, Denmark, 2000. One in a series of summarising research reports [14,15]. 4, 15, 16, 17
2. Dines Bjørner. Domain Modelling: Resource Management Strategics, Tactics & Operations, Decision Support and Algorithmic Software. In J. C. P. Woodcock, editor, *Festschrift to Tony Hoare*. Oxford University and Microsoft, September 13–14 1999. 5, 16
3. Dines Bjørner. Domains as Prerequisites for Requirements and Software &c. In M. Broy and B. Rumpe, editors, *RTSE'97: Requirements Targeted Software and Systems Engineering*, volume 1526 of *Lecture Notes in Computer Science*, pages 1–41. Springer-Verlag, Berlin Heidelberg, 1998. 15, 16
4. Michael A. Jackson. *Software Requirements & Specifications: a lexicon of practice, principles and prejudices*. ACM Press. Addison-Wesley Publishing Company, Wokingham, nr. Reading, England; E-mail: ipc@awpub.add-wes.co.uk, 1995. ISBN 0-201-87712-0; xiv + 228 pages. 15, 16
5. Dines Bjørner, Souleymane Koussoube, Roger Noussi, and Gueorgui Satchok. Jackson's Problem Frames: Domain, Requirements and Design. In Shaoying Liu, editor, *International Conference on Formal Engineering Methods: ICFEM'97*, Washington D. C., USA, 12–14 November 1997. IEEE Computer Science Press; IEEE sponsored conference, Hiroshima, Japan. 15, 16
6. Michael A. Jackson. Problems, methods and specialisation. *Software Engineering Journal*, pages 249–255, November 1994. 16
7. Michael A. Jackson. Problems and requirements (software development). In *Second IEEE International Symposium on Requirements Engineering (Cat. No.95TH8040)*, pages 2–8. IEEE Comput. Soc. Press, 1995. 16
8. Michael A. Jackson. The meaning of requirements. *Annals of Software Engineering*, 3:5–21, 1997. 16
9. Pamela Zave and Michael A. Jackson. Four dark Corners of Requirements Engineering. *ACM Transactions on Software Engineering and Methodology*, 6(1):1–30, January 1997. 16

10. Dines Bjørner. Pinnacles of Software Engineering: 25 Years of Formal Methods. *Annals of Software Engineering*, 2000. Eds. Dilip Patel and Wang Yi. 16
11. Dines Bjørner. A Triptych Software Development Paradigm: Domain, Requirements and Software. Towards a Model Development of A Decision Support System for Sustainable Development. In ErnstRüdiger Olderog, editor, *Festschrift to Hans Langmaack*. University of Kiel, Germany, October 1999. 16
12. Dines Bjørner. Where do Software Architectures come from ? Systematic Development from Domains and Requirements. A Re–assessment of Software Engneering ? *South African Journal of Computer Science*, 1999. Editor: Chris Brink. 16
13. Dines Bjørner and Jorge R. Cuéllar. Software Engineering Education: Rôles of formal specification and design calculi. *Annals of Software Engineering*, 6:365–410, 1998. Published April 1999. 16
14. Dines Bjørner. Requirements Engineering, Elements of a Software Engineering Methodology — Towards Principles, Techniques and Tools — A Study in Methodology. Research report, Dept. of Computer Science & Technology, Technical University of Denmark, Bldg. 343, DK–2800 Lyngby, Denmark, 2000. One in a series of summarising research reports [1,15]. 16, 17
15. Dines Bjørner. Software Design: Architectures and Program Organisation, Elements of a Software Engineering Methodology — Towards Principles, Techniques and Tools — A Study in Methodology. Research report, Dept. of Computer Science & Technology, Technical University of Denmark, Bldg. 343, DK–2800 Lyngby, Denmark, 2000. One in a series of summarising research reports [1,14]. 16, 17

Exhaustive Search, Combinatorial Optimization and Enumeration: Exploring the Potential of Raw Computing Power

Jürg Nievergelt

ETH, 8092 Zurich, Switzerland
jn@inf.ethz.ch

Abstract. For half a century since computers came into existence, the goal of finding elegant and efficient algorithms to solve "simple" (well-defined and well-structured) problems has dominated algorithm design. Over the same time period, both processing and storage capacity of computers have increased by roughly a factor of a million. The next few decades may well give us a similar rate of growth in raw computing power, due to various factors such as continuing miniaturization, parallel and distributed computing. If a quantitative change of orders of magnitude leads to qualitative advances, where will the latter take place? Only empirical research can answer this question.

Asymptotic complexity theory has emerged as a surprisingly effective tool for predicting run times of polynomial-time algorithms. For NP-hard problems, on the other hand, it yields overly pessimistic bounds. It asserts the non-existence of algorithms that are efficient across an entire problem class, but ignores the fact that many instances, perhaps including those of interest, can be solved efficiently. For such cases we need a complexity measure that applies to problem instances, rather than to over-sized problem classes.

Combinatorial optimization and enumeration problems are modeled by state spaces that usually lack any regular structure. Exhaustive search is often the only way to handle such "combinatorial chaos". Several general purpose search algorithms are used under different circumstances. We describe reverse search and illustrate this technique on a case study of enumerative optimization: enumerating the k shortest Euclidean spanning trees.

1 Catching Up with Technology

Computer science is technology-driven: it has been so for the past 50 years, and will remain this way for the foreseeable future, for at least a decade. That is about as far as specialists can extrapolate current semiconductor technology and foresee that advances based on refined processes, without any need for fundamental innovations, will keep improving the performance of computing devices. Moreover, performance can be expected to advance at the rate of "Moore's law",

V. Hlaváč, K. G. Jeffery, and J. Wiedermann (Eds.): SOFSEM 2000, LNCS 1963, pp. 18–35, 2000.
© Springer-Verlag Berlin Heidelberg 2000

the same rate observed over the past 3 decades, of doubling in any period of 1 to 2 years. An up-to-date summary of possibilities and limitations of technology can be found in [12].

What does it mean for a discipline to be *technology-driven*? What are the implications?

Consider the converse: disciplines that are demand-driven rather than technology-driven. In the 60s the US stated a public goal "to put a man on the moon by the end of the decade". This well-defined goal called for a technology that did not as yet exist. With a great national effort and some luck, the technology was developed just in time to meet the announced goal — a memorable technical achievement. More often than not, when an ambitious goal calls for the invention of new technology, the goal remains wishful thinking. In such situations, it is prudent to announce fuzzy goals, where one can claim progress without being able to measure it. The computing field has on occasion been tempted to use this tactic, for example in predicting "machine intelligence". Such an elastic concept can be re-defined periodically to mirror the current state-of-the-art.

Apart from some exceptions, the dominant influence on computing has been a technology push, rather than a demand pull. In other words, computer architects, systems and application designers have always known that clock rates, flop/s, data rates and memory sizes will go up at a predictable, breath-taking speed. The question was less "what do we need to meet the demands of a new application?" as "what shall we do with the newly emerging resources?". Faced with an embarassment of riches, it is understandable that the lion's share of development effort, both in industry and in academia, has gone into developing bigger, more powerful, hopefully a little better versions of the same applications that have been around for decades. What we experience as revolutionary in the break-neck speed with which computing is affecting society is not technical novelty, but rather, an unprecedented penetration of computing technology in all aspects of the technical infrastructure on which our civilization has come to rely. In recent years, computing technology's outstanding achievement has been the *breadth* of its impact rather than the originality and depth of its scientific/technical innovations. The explosive spread of the Internet in recent years, based on technology developed a quarter-century ago, is a prominent example.

This observation, that computing technology in recent years has been "spreading inside known territory" rather than "growing into new areas", does not imply that computing has run out of important open problems or new ideas. On the contrary, tantalizing open questions and new ideas call for investigation, as the following two examples illustrate:

1. A challenging, fundamental open problem in our "information age", is a scientific definition of information. Shannon's pioneering information theory is of unquestioned importance, but it does *not* capture the notion of "information" relevant in daily life ("what is your telephone number?") or in business transactions ("what is today's exchange rate"). The fact that we process information at all times without having a scientific definition of what we are processing is akin to the state of physics before Newton: humanity

has always been processing energy, but a scientific notion of energy emerged only three centuries ago. This discovery was a prerequisite of the industrial age. Will we ever discover a scientific notion of "information" of equal rigor and impact?

2. Emerging new ideas touch the very core of what "computing" means. Half a century of computing has been based on electronic devices to realize a von Neumann architecture. But computation can be modeled by many other physical phenomena. In particular, the recently emerged concepts of quantum computing or DNA computing are completely different models of computation, with strikingly different strengths and weaknesses.

The reason fundamentally new ideas are not receiving very much attention at the moment is that there is so much to do, and so much to gain, by merely riding the wave of technological progress, e. g. by bringing to market the next upgrade of the same old operating system, which will surely be bigger, if not better. Whereas business naturally looks for short-term business opportunities, let this be a call to academia to focus on long-term issues, some of which will surely revolutionize computing in decades to come.

2   "Ever-Growing" Computing Power: What Is It Good for?

Computer progress over the past several decades has measured several orders of magnitude with respect to various physical parameters such as computing power, memory size at all hierarchy levels from caches to disk, power consumption, physical size and cost. Both computing power and memory size have easily grown by a factor of a million. There are good reasons to expect both computing power and memory size to grow by the same two factors of a million over the next couple of decades. A factor of 1000 can be expected from the extrapolation of Moore's law for yet another dozen years. Another factor of 1000, in both computing power and memory size, can be expected from increased use of parallel and distributed systems — a resource whose potential will be fully exploited only when microprocessor technology improvement slows down.

With hindsight we know what these two factors of a million have contributed to the state of the art — the majority of today's computer features and applications would be impossible without them. The list includes:

- graphical user interfaces and multimedia in general,
- end-user application packages, such as spreadsheets,
- data bases for interactive, distributed information and transaction systems,
- embedded systems, for example in communications technology.

Back in the sixties it was predictable that computing power would grow, though the rapidity and longevity of this growth was not foreseen. People speculated what more powerful computers might achieve. But this discussion was generally limited to applications that were already prominent, such as scientific computing.

The new applications that emerged were generally not foreseen. Evidence for this is provided by quotes from famous pioneers, such as DEC founder Ken Olsen's dictum "there is no reason why anyone would want a computer in his home" ([9] is an amusing collection of predictions).

If past predictions fell short of reality, we cannot assume that our gaze into the crystal ball will be any clearer today. We do not know what problems can be attacked with computing power a million times greater than available today. Thus, to promote progress over a time horizon of a decade or more, experimenting is a more promising approach than planning.

3   Uneven Progress in Algorithmics

After this philosophical excursion into the world of computing, let us now consider the small but important discipline of algorithmics, the craft of algorithm design, analysis and implementation. In the early days of computing, algorithmics was a relatively bigger part of computer science than it is now — all computer users had to know and program algorithms to solve their problem. Until the seventies, a sizable fraction of computer science research was dedicated to expand and improve our knowledge of algorithms.

The computer user community at large may be unaware that the progress of algorithmics can be considered spectacular. Whereas half a century ago an algorithm was just a prescription to be followed, nowadays an algorithm is a mathematical object whose properties are stated in terms of theorems and proofs. A large number of well-understood algorithms have proven their effectiveness, embedded in program libraries and application packages. They empower users to work with techniques that they could not possibly program themselves. Who could claim, for example, to know and be able to program all the algorithms in a symbolic computation system, or in a computational geometry library?

Asymptotic complexity analysis has turned out to be a surprisingly effective technique to predict the performance of algorithms. When we classify an algorithm as running in time $O(\log n)$ or $O(n \log n)$, generously ignoring constant factors, how could we expect to convert this rough measure into seconds? It's easy: you time the program for a few small data sets, and extrapolate to obtain an accurate prediction of running times for much larger data sets, as the measurements in Table 1 illustrate.

By and large, the above claim of spectacular success is limited to algorithms that run in polynomial time, said to be in the class P. We have become so used to asymptotic complexity analysis that we forget to marvel how such a simple formula such as "$\log n$" yields such accurate timing information. But we may marvel again when we consider the class of algorithms called NP-hard, which presumably require time exponential in the size n of the data set.

For these hard problems, occasionally called *intractable*, we have a theory that is not nearly as practical as the theory for P, because it yields overly pessimistic bounds. Our current theory of NP-hard problems is modeled on the same approach that worked so successfully for problems in P: prove theorems

Table 1. Running times of Binary Search

n	$\log n$	t bin search	$t/\log n$
1	0	0.60	
2	1	0.81	0.81
4	2	0.91	0.45
8	3	1.08	0.36
16	4	1.26	0.32
32	5	1.46	0.29
64	6	1.66	0.27
128	7	1.88	0.27
256	8	2.08	0.26
512	9	2.30	0.26
1024	10	2.51	0.25
2048	11	2.71	0.25
4096	12	2.96	0.25
8192	13	3.23	0.25
16384	14	3.46	0.25

that hold for an entire class $C(n)$ of problems, parametrized by the size n of the data. What is surprising, with hindsight, is that this ambitious sledge-hammer approach almost always works for problems in P! We generally find a *single* algorithm that works well for all problems in C, from small to large, whose complexity is accurately described by a simple formula for all values of n of practical interest.

If we aim at a result of equal generality for some NP-hard problem class $C(n)$, the outcome is disappointing from a practical point of view, for two reasons:

1. Since the class $C(n)$ undoubtedly contains many hard problem instances, a bound that covers all instances will necessarily be too high for the relatively harmless instances. And even though the harmless instances might be a minority within the class $C(n)$, they may be more representative of the actual problems a user may want to solve.
2. It is convenient, but not mandatory, to be able to use a single algorithm for an entire class $C(n)$. But when this approach fails in practice we have another option which is more thought-intensive but hopefully less compute-intensive: to analyze the specific problem instance we want to solve, and to tailor the algorithm to take advantage of the characteristics of this instance.

In summary, the standard complexity theory for NP-hard problems asserts the non-existence of algorithms that are efficient across an entire problem class, but ignores the possibility that many instances, perhaps including those of interest, can be solved efficiently.

An interesting and valuable approach to bypass the problem above is to design algorithms that efficiently compute approximate solutions to NP-hard problems. The practical justification for this approach is that an exact or optimal solution is often not required, provided an error bound is known. The limitation of approximation algorithms is due to the same cause as for exact algorithms for NP-hard problems: that they aim to apply to an entire class $C(n)$, and thus cannot take advantage of the features of specific instances. As a consequence, if we insist on a given error bound, say 20 %, the approximation problem often remains NP-hard.

There is a different approach to NP-hard problems that still insists on finding exact or optimal solutions. We do not tackle an entire problem class $C(n)$; instead, we attack a challenging problem instance, taking advantage of all the specific features of this individual instance. If later we become interested in another instance of the same class C, the approach that worked for the first instance will have to be reappraised and perhaps modified. This approach changes the rules of algorithm design and analysis drastically: we still have to devise and implement clever algorithms, but complexity is not measured asymptotically in terms of n: it is measured by actually counting operations, disk accesses, and seconds.

4   Exhaustive Search and Enumeration: Concepts and Terminology

One of the oldest approaches to problem solving with the help of computers is brute-force enumeration and search: generate and inspect all data configurations in a large state space that is guaranteed to contain the desired solutions, and you are bound to succeed — if you can wait long enough. Although exhaustive search is conceptually simple and often effective, such an approach to problem solving is sometimes considered inelegant. This may be a legacy of the fact that computer science concentrated for decades on fine-tuning highly efficient polynomial-time algorithms. The latter solve problems that, by definition, are said to be in P. The well known class of NP-hard problems is widely believed to be intractable, and conventional wisdom holds that one should not search for exact solutions, but rather for good approximations. But the identification of NP-hard problems as *intractable* is being undermined by recent empirical investigation of extremely compute-intensive problems. The venerable *traveling salesman problem* is just one example of a probably worst-case hard problem class where many sizable instances turn out to be surprisingly tractable.

The continuing increase in computing power and memory sizes has revived interest in brute-force techniques for a good reason. The universe of problems that can be solved by computation is messy, not orderly, and does not yield, by and large, to the elegant, highly efficient type of algorithms that have received the lion's share of attention of the algorithms research community. The paradigm shift that may be changing the focus of computational research is that *combinatorial chaos* is just as interesting and rewarding as well-structured problems. Many "real" problems exhibit no regular structures to be exploited, and that leaves exhaustive enumeration as the only approach in sight. And even though we look in vain for order of magnitude asymptotic improvements due to "optimal" algorithms, there are order of magnitude improvements waiting to be discovered due to program optimization, and to the clever use of limited computational resources. It is a game of algorithm design and analysis played according to a new set of rules: forget asymptotics and see what can be done for some specific problem instance, characterized by some large value of n. The main weapon in attacking instances of NP-hard problems, with an invariably irregular structure, is always *search and enumeration*.

The basic concepts of search algorithms are well known, but the terminology used varies. The following recapitulation of important concepts serves to introduce our terminology.

State space S. Discrete, often (but not necessarily) finite. Modeled as a graph, $S = (V, E)$ where V is the set of vertices or nodes, E the set of edges (or perhaps arcs, i.e. directed edges). Nodes represent states, arcs represent relationships defined by given operators.

One or more **operators,** $o: S \to 2^S$, the powerset of S. An operator transforms a state s into a number of neighboring states that can easily be computed given s. In the frequently occuring *symmetric case*, an operator o is *its own inverse* in the following sense: $s' \in o(s)$ implies $s \in o(s')$.

Distinguished states, e.g. starting state(s), goal or target state(s). The latter are usually defined by some target predicate $t: S \to \{true, false\}$.

Objective function, cost function $f: S \to Reals$. Serves to define an optimization problem, where one asks for any or all states s that optimize (minimize or maximize) $f(s)$.

Search space. Often used as a synonym for state space. Occasionally it is useful to make a distinction: a state space defines the problem to be solved, whereas different search algorithms may traverse different subsets of S as their search space.

Traversal. Sequentialization of the states of S. Common traversals are based on imposing tree structures over S, called search tree(s) or search forest.

Search tree. A rooted, ordered tree superimposed on S. The children $s_1 \ldots s_f$ of a node s are obtained by applying to s one of the operators defined on S, and they are ordered (*left-to-right order* when drawn). The number f of children of a node is called its *fan-out*. Nodes without children are called *leaves*.

Search DAG. It is commonly the case that the same state s will be encountered along many different paths from the root of a search tree towards its leaves. Thus, the same state s may generate many distinct nodes of the same search tree. By identifying (merging) all the tree nodes corresponding to the same state s we obtain a directed acyclic graph, the search DAG.

DFS, BFS, etc. The most common traversal of S w.r.t. a given search tree over S is *depth-first search* (DFS) or *backtrack*. DFS maintains at all times a single path from the root to the current node, and extends this path whenever possible. *Breadth-first search* (BFS) is also common, and can be likened to wave-propagation outwards from a starting state. BFS maintains at all times a frontier, or wave-front, that separates the states already visited from those yet to be encountered. Several other traversals are useful in specific instances, such as best-first search, or iterative deepening.

Search structures. Every traversal requires data structures that record the current state of the search, i. e. the subspace of S already visited. DFS requires a stack, BFS a queue. The entire state S may require a mark (e. g. a bit) for each state to distinguish states already visited from those not yet encountered. The size of these data structures is often a limiting factor that determines whether or not a space S can be enumerated with the memory resources available.

Enumeration. A sequential listing of all the states of S, or of a subset $S|t$ consisting of all the target states s for which $t(s) = true$.

Output-sensitive enumeration algorithm. It is often difficult to estimate a priori the size of the output of an enumeration. An appropriate measure of the time required by an enumeration is therefore output-sensitive, whereby one measures the time required to produce and output one state, the next in the output sequence.

Search. The task of finding one, or some, but *not necessarily all*, states s that satisfy some constraint, such as $t(s) = true$ or $f(s)$ is optimal.

Exhaustive search. A search that is guaranteed to find all states s that satisfy given constraints. An exhaustive search need not necessarily visit all of S in every instance. It may omit a subspace S' of S on the basis of a mathematical argument that guarantees that S' cannot contain any solution. In a worst case configuration, however, exhaustive search is forced to visit all states of S.

Examples of exhaustive search. Searching for a key x in a hash table is an exhaustive search. Finding x, or determining that x is not in the table, is normally achieved with just a few probes. In the worst case, however, collisions may require probing the entire table to determine the status of a key. By contrast, binary search is not exhaustive; when the table contains 3 or more keys, binary search will never probe all of them. Common exhaustive search algorithms include backtrack, branch-and-bound, and sieves, such as Erathostenes' prime number sieve.

5   Reverse Search

The more information is known a priori about a graph, the less book-keeping data needs to be kept during the traversal. Avis and Fukuda [2] present a set of conditions that enable graph traversal without auxiliary data structures such as stacks, queues, or node marks. The amount of memory used for book-keeping is constant, i. e. independent of the size of the graph. Their *reverse search* is a depth-first search (DFS) that requires neither stack nor node markers to be stored explicitly — all necessary information can be recomputed on the fly. Problems to which reverse search applies allow the enumeration of finite sets much larger than would be possible if a stack and/or markers had to be maintained. Such enumeration is naturally time-consuming. But computing time is an elastic resource — you can always wait "a little bit longer" — whereas memory is inelastic. When it is full, a stack or some other data structure will overflow and stop the search. Thus, exhaustive search is often memory-bound rather than time-bound.

Three conditions enable reverse search to enumerate a state space $S = (V, E)$:

1. There is an *adjacency operator* or *"oracle"* $A: S \to 2^S$, the powerset of S. A assigns to any state s an ordered set $A(s) = [s_1, \ldots, s_k]$ of its neighbors. Adjacency need not be symmetric, i.e. $s' \in A(s)$ does not imply $s \in A(s')$. The pairs (s, s') with $s' \in A(s)$ define the set E of directed edges of S.

2. There is a *gradient function* $g: S \to S \cup \{nil\}$, where nil is a fictitious state (a symbol) not in S. A state s with $g(s) = nil$ is called a *sink* of g. g assigns to any state s a unique successor $g(s) \in S \cup \{nil\}$ subject to the following conditions:
   - for any state s that is not a sink, i.e. $g(s) \neq nil$, the pair $(g(s), s) \in E$, i.e. $s \in A(g(s))$,
   - g defines no cycles, i.e. $g(g(\ldots g(s) \ldots)) = s$ is impossible — hence the name *gradient*.

   Notice that when A is not symmetric, g-trajectories point in the opposite direction of the arcs of E. The *no cycles* condition in a finite space S implies that g superimposes a forest, i.e. a set of disjoint trees, on S, where tree edges are a subset of E. Each sink is the root of such a tree.

3. It is possible to efficiently *enumerate all the sinks* of g before exploring all of S.

The motivation behind these definitions and assumptions lies in the fact that A and g together provide all the information necessary to manage a DFS that starts at any sink of g. The DFS tree is defined by A and g as follows: The children $C(s) = [c_1, \ldots, c_f]$ of any node s are those nodes s' culled from the set $A(s) = [s_1, \ldots, s_k]$ for which $g(s') = s$. And the order $[c_1, \ldots, c_f]$ of the children of s is inherited from the order defined on $A(s)$.

A DFS usually relies on a stack for walking up and down a tree. An explicit stack is no longer necessary when we can call on A and on g. Walking up the DFS tree towards the root is accomplished simply by following the gradient function g. Walking down from the root is more costly. Calling the adjacency oracle from any node s yields a superset $A(s)$ of the children of s. Each s' in $A(s)$ must then be checked to see whether it is a child of s, as determined by $g(s') = s$.

Similarly, no data structure is required that marks nodes already visited. The latter can always be deduced from the order defined on the set $C(s)$ of children and from two node identifiers: the current state and its immediate predecessor in the DFS traversal.

We explain how reverse search works on a simple example where every step can be checked visually. Fig. 1 shows a hexagon (drawn as a circle) with vertices labeled $1 \ldots 6$. Together with all 9 interior edges it makes up the complete graph K_6 of 6 vertices shown at the top left. The other 14 copies of the hexagon, each of them with 3 interior edges, show all the distinct triangulations of this

labeled hexagon. The double-tipped arrows link each pair of states that are
neighbors under the only operator that we need to consider in this problem:
a *diagonal flip* transforms one triangulation into a neighboring one by exchanging one edge for another. This, and the term *diagonal*, will be explained after we
introduce the notation for identifying edges and triangulations.

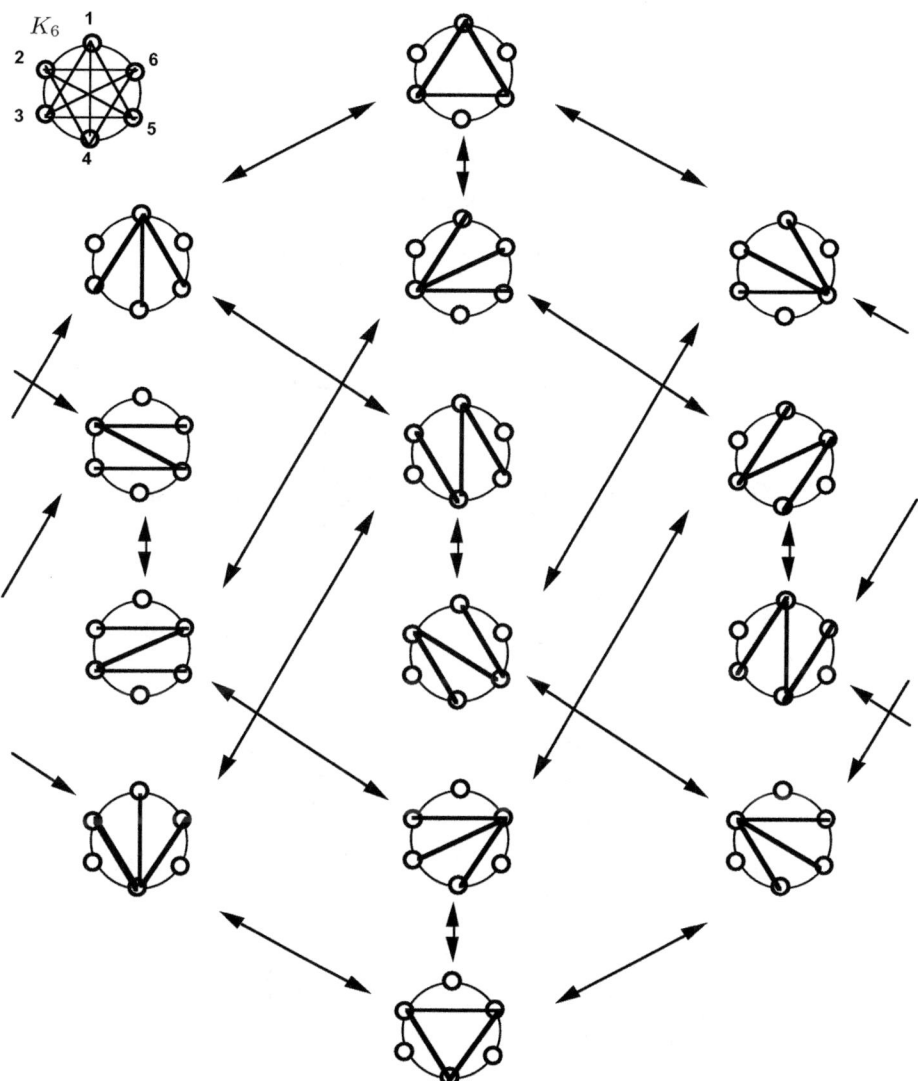

Fig. 1. The state space S of triangulations of a labeled hexagon

The second ingredient required to implement reverse search is a suitable gradient function g. We obtain this by imposing an arbitrary total order on the state space S, accepting the fact that it breaks the elegant symmetry of Fig. 1. Label an edge (i, j) with the ordered digit pair ij, $i < j$. We label the 3 interior edges x, y, z of a triangulation with the triple $x.y.z$ of edge labels (digit pairs) ordered as $x < y < z$. This labeling scheme assigns to each triangulation of the labeled hexagon a unique identifier $x.y.z$. As shown in Fig. 2, we order the 14 triangulations lexicographically. When $x.y.z$ is interpreted as an integer, lexicographic and numerical order coincide.

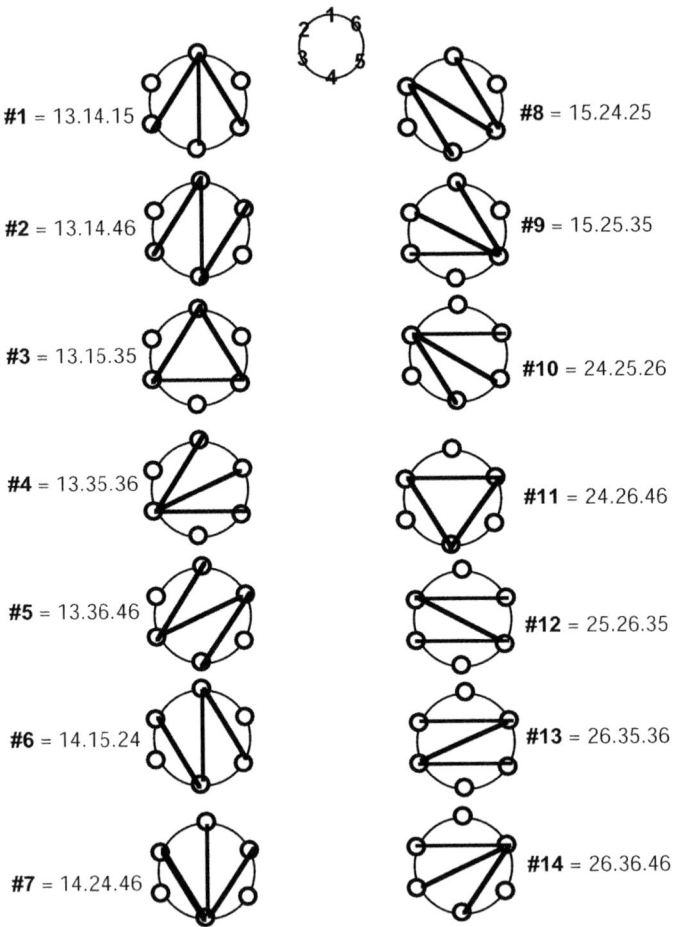

Fig. 2. The state space S sequenced by lexographic order

To understand the operator *diagonal flip*, observe that in every triangulation, each interior edge is the *diagonal* of a quadrilateral, i.e. a cycle of length 4. In triangulation #1 = 13.14.15, for example, 13 is the diagonal of the quadrilateral with vertices $1, 2, 3, 4$. By flipping diagonals in this quadrilateral, i.e. replacing 13 by its diagonal mate 24, we obtain triangulation #6 = 14.15.24. Thus, each of the 14 triangulations has exactly 3 neighbors under the operator *diagonal flip*. The 14 triangulations as vertices and the $14 * 3/2 = 21$ neighbor relations as edges define the state space $S = (V, E)$ of this enumeration problem.

Based on the total order shown in Fig. 2, define the gradient function g as follows: $g(s)$ is the "smallest" neighbor s' of s in lexicographic order, provided $s' < s$. g is defined on all states of s except on triangulation #1 = 13.14.15, which has no smaller neighbor. In order to handle this case we define $g(\#1) = s_0$, where s_0 is the "sentinel" introduced in the definition $g: S \to S \cup \{s_0\}$. This gradient function g defines the search tree shown in Fig. 3.

The third ingredient required by reverse search, an efficient way to construct all the sinks of g, is trivial in this example. The triangulation 13.14.15 contains the three *smallest* interior edges; it is therefore the smallest triangulation and the sink of all g-trajectories. We construct triangulation #1 and start a DFS traversal at this root of the search tree.

Consider the typical case when DFS arrives at node #4. The adjacency oracle returns #4's three neighbors: #3, #5 and #13. The gradient function applied to these three neighbors identifies #13 as #4's only child. DFS must now decide to either descend to its child #13 or to backtrack to its parent $\#3 = g(\#4)$. How can we tell?

In addition to the current node #4, DFS retains the identifier of the immediate predecessor node in the traversal. If the predecessor is #3, then DFS is on its way down and proceeds to visit child #13. If, on the other hand, the predecessor is #13, then DFS is on its way back up and proceeds to re-visit its parent #3. A similar logic lets DFS take its next step in every case. Consider the case when DFS is currently at the root, vertex #1. If the predecessor is *nil*, i.e. our fictitious sentinel s_0, DFS knows that it is just starting its traversal. If the predecessor is #3, DFS has to visit its next child, in order, i.e. #6. If the predecessor is #6, i.e. the last child of the root, DFS is done.

6 Best Euclidean Spanning Trees: A Case Study in Geometry, Combinatorics and Enumerative Optimization

Problems about discrete spatial configurations involve a challenging interaction between the continuum characteristic of geometry and the discreteness of combinatorics. Each of these disciplines has evolved its characteristic techniques that exploit the nature of the objects treated, continuous or discrete. When used together to attack a geometric-combinatorial problem, surprises lurk beneath the surface. A seemingly minor change in a geometric specification may clash

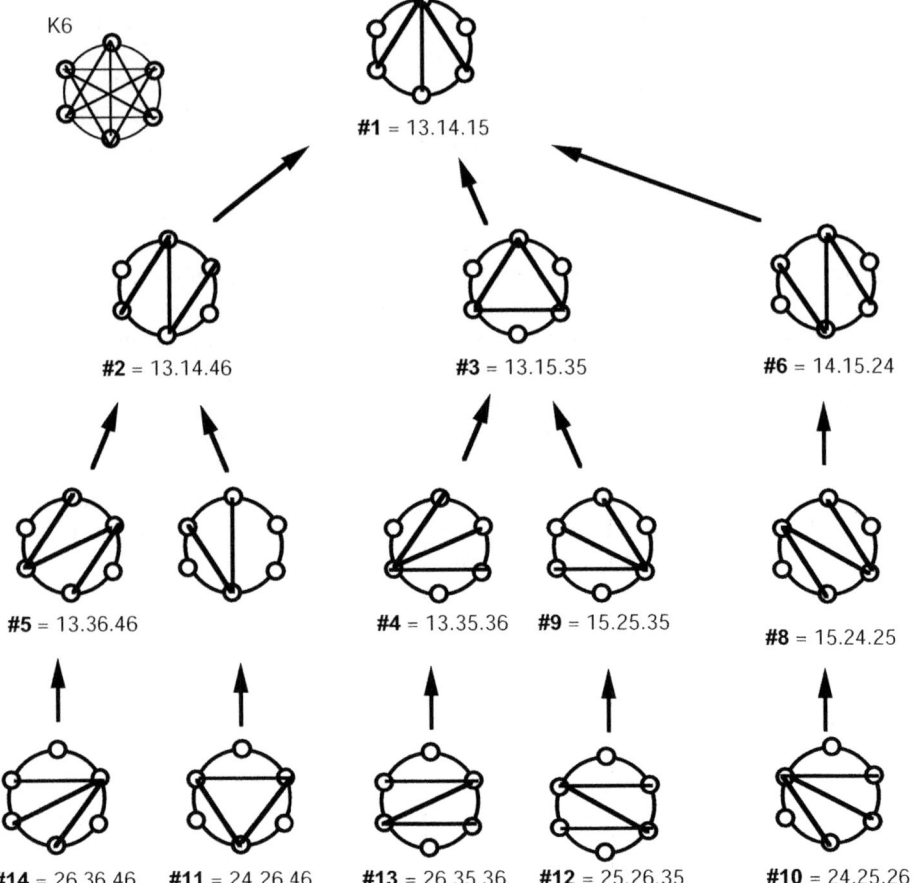

Fig. 3. Search tree defined by the gradient function g

with combinatorial assumptions, and vice versa. This interaction between geometric and combinatorial constraints makes it difficult to predict, on an intuitive basis, which problems are amenable to efficient algorithms, and which are not.

The difficulties mentioned are exacerbated when we aim at enumerating all spatial configurations that meet certain specifications, not in any arbitrary order convenient for enumeration, but rather in a prescribed order. Search techniques impose their own restrictions on the order in which they traverse a search space, and these may be incompatible with the desired order.

We present an example of a simple geometric-combinatorial search and enumeration problem as an illustration of issues and techniques: the enumeration of plane spanning trees over a given set of points in the plane, i.e. those trees constructed with straight line segments in such a manner that no two edges intersect [8]. [2] present an algorithm for enumerating all plane spanning trees, in some uncontrolled order that results from the arbitrary labeling of points. We attack this same problem under the additional constraint that these plane spanning trees are to be enumerated according to their total length (i. e. the sum of the lengths of their edges), from short to long. We may stop the enumeration after having listed the k shortest trees, or all trees shorter than a given bound c. Fig. 4 lists the 10 shortest plane spanning trees among the 55 on the particular configuration of 5 points with coordinates $(0, 5), (1, 0), (4, 4), (5, 0), (7, 3)$.

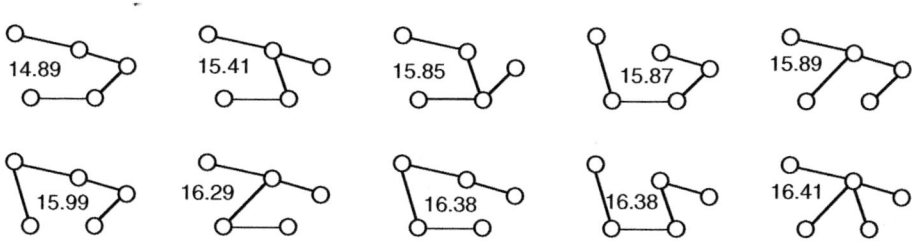

Fig. 4. The 10 shortest plane spanning trees over five given points, in order of increasing length

In trying to apply reverse search to a "k best problem" we face the difficulty that the goal is not just to enumerate a set in some arbitrary, convenient order, as we did in Section 5. In the case of enumerative optimization the goal is to enumerate the elements of S from best to worst according to some objective function f defined on S. One may wish to stop the enumeration after the k best elements, or after having seen all elements s with $f(s) \leq c$.

6.1   The Space of Plane Spanning Trees on a Euclidean Graph

Consider a graph $G = (V, E, w)$ with n vertices $p, q, r, \ldots$ in V, weighted edges $e = (p, q)$ in E, and a weight function $w \colon E \to Reals$. The set of spanning trees over G has a well-known useful structure that is exploited by several algorithms, in particular for constructing a minimum spanning tree (MST). The structure is based on an exchange operator, an *edge flip*, and on a monotonicity property.

Let T be any spanning tree over G, e' an edge not in T, $Ckt(e', T)$ the unique path P in T that connects the two endpoints of e', and e any edge in P. The edge flip $T' = T - e + e'$ that deletes e from T and replaces it by e' creates a new spanning tree T' that is *adjacent to* T. If $w(e) > w(e')$ this edge flip is profitable in the sense that $|T'| < |T|$, where $|T|$ denotes the total length of T. The remarkable fact exploited by algorithms for constructing a minimum spanning tree (MST) is that in the space of all spanning trees over G, any local minimum is also a global minimum. This implies that any greedy algorithm based on profitable edge flips or on accumulating the cheapest edges (e. g. Prim, Kruskal) converges towards an MST.

In this paper we study *Euclidean* graphs and *plane* spanning trees. A Euclidean graph is a complete graph whose vertices are points in the plane, and whose edge weights are the distances between the endpoints of the edge. For $p, q \in V$ and $e = (p, q)$, let $|(p, q)|$ denote the length of edge e. For a Euclidean graph it is natural to consider "plane" or non-crossing spanning trees, i. e. trees no two of whose edges cross. It is well known and follows directly from the triangle inequality that any MST over a Euclidean graph is plane, i. e. has no crossing edges.

In the following section, we define a search tree for enumerating all plane spanning trees, in order of increasing total length, over a given point set in the plane. This search tree is presented in such a form that standard tree traversal techniques apply, in particular reverse search [2]. Specifically, we define a unique root R which is an MST; and a monotonic gradient function g that assigns to each tree $T \neq R$ a tree $g(T)$ with $|g(T)| \leq |T|$. The gradient function g has the property that, for any $T \neq R$, some iterate $g(\ldots g(T))$ equals R, i. e. R is a sink of g; hence g generates no cycles. For efficiency's sake, both g and its inverse can be computed efficiently.

For simplicity of expression we describe the geometric properties of the search tree as if the configuration of points was non-degenerate in the sense that there is a unique MST, and that any two distinct quantities (lengths, angles) ever compared are unequal.

Unfortunately, the space of *plane* spanning trees over a Euclidean graph does not exhibit as simple a structure as the space of *all* spanning trees. It is evident that if T is a plane tree, an edge flip $T' = T - e + e'$ may introduce cross-overs. Thus, the geometric key issue to be solved is an efficient way of finding edge flips that shorten the tree and avoid cross-over. We distinguish two cases:

6.1.1   Flipping edges in the Gabriel Graph.

Consider any set C of non-crossing edges over the given point set V, and any plane tree T contained in C. Trivially, any edge flip limited to edges in C cannot introduce any cross-over. We seek a set C, a *skeleton of G*, that is dense enough so as to contain a sufficient number of spanning trees, and has useful geometric properties. Among various possibilities, the Gabriel Graph of V will do.

Definition 1. The Gabriel Graph $GG(V)$ over a point set V contains an edge (p, q) iff no point r in $V - \{p, q\}$ is in the closed disk $Disk(p, q)$ over the diameter (p, q).

The useful geometric properties mentioned include:

1. $GG(V)$ has no crossing edges.
2. Consider any point x (not in V) that lies inside $Disk(p, q)$. Then $|(x, p)| < |(p, q)|$, $|(x, q)| < |(p, q)|$, $\angle(p, x, q) > 90°$.
3. Any MST over V is contained in $GG(V)$.
   (*Proof:* consider any edge e of an MST. If there was any point $p \in V$ inside $Disk(e)$, e could be exchanged for a shorter edge.)

These geometric properties lead to a first rule.

Rule 1. Let T be a spanning tree over V that is not the (uniquely defined) MST R. If T is contained in $GG(V)$, let $g(T) = T - e + e'$, where e' is the lexicographically first edge of R not in T, and e is the longest edge in $Ckt(e', T)$.

Obviously, $g(T)$ is closer to R than T is, and if the MST is unique, then $|g(T)| < |T|$.

6.1.2 Flipping edges not in the Gabriel Graph.

As a planar graph, the Gabriel Graph $GG(V)$ has a sparse set of edges. Thus, the vast majority of spanning trees over V are not contained in $GG(V)$, and hence Rule 1 applies mostly towards the end of a g-trajectory, for spanning trees near the MST R. For all other spanning trees, we need a rule to flip an edge (p, r) not in $GG(V)$ in such a way that the spanning tree gets shorter, and no cross-over is introduced.

Consider a tree T not contained in $GG(V)$, and hence is not an MST. Among all point triples (p, q, r) such that (p, r) is in T, select the one whose $\angle(p, q, r)$ is maximum. The properties of the Gabriel Graph imply the following assertions: $\angle(p, q, r) > 90°$, (p, r) is not in $GG(V)$, $|(p, q)| < |(p, r)|$ and $|(q, r)| < |(p, r)|$.

Rule 2. With the notation above, let $g(T) = T - (p, r) + e'$, where e' is either (p, q) or (q, r), chosen such that $g(T)$ is a spanning tree.

As mentioned, $|g(T)| < |T|$. Fig. 5 illustrates the argument that this edge flip does not introduce any crossing edges. At left, consider the possibility of an edge e one of whose endpoints u lies in the triangle (p, q, r). This contradicts the assumption that $\angle(p, q, r)$ is maximum. At right, consider the possibility of an edge $e = (u, v)$ that crosses both (p, q) and (q, r). Then $\angle(u, q, v) > \angle(p, q, r)$, again a contradiction. Thus, neither (p, q) nor (q, r) cause a cross-over if flipped for (p, r).

These two rules achieve the goal of finding edge flips that

- shorten the tree, and
- avoid cross-over.

Thus, after a problem-specific detour into geometry, we are back at the point where a general-purpose tool such as reverse search can take over.

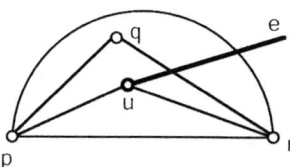 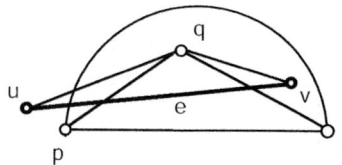

Fig. 5. The assumption of new cross-overs contradicts the choice of "angle(p,q,r) is maximum"

7   The Craft of Attacking Hard Problem Instances

Exhaustive search is truly a creation of the computer era. Although the history of mathematics records amazing feats of paper-and-pencil computation, as a human activity, exhaustive search is boring, error-prone, exhausting, and never gets very far anyway. As a cautionary note, if any is needed, Ludolph van Ceulen died of exhaustion in 1610 after using regular polygons of 2^{62} sides to obtain 35 decimal digits of p—they are engraved on his tombstone.

With the advent of computers, *experimental mathematics* became practical: the systematic search for specific instances of mathematical objects with desired properties, perhaps to disprove a conjecture or to formulate new conjectures based on empirical observation. Number theory provides a fertile ground for the team *computation + conjecture*, and Derrick Lehmer was a pioneer in using search algorithms such as sieves or backtrack in pursuit of theorems whose proof requires a massive amount of computation [6]. We make no attempt to survey the many results obtained thanks to computer-based mathematics, but merely recall a few as entry points into the pertinent literature:

- the continuing race for large primes, for example Mersenne primes of form $2^p - 1$,
- the landmark proof of the "four-color theorem" by Appel and Haken [1],
- more recent work in Ramsey theory or cellular-automata [5].

For such cases we need a complexity measure that applies to problem instances, rather than to over-sized problem classes. Counting individual operations and measuring the running time of numerous procedures is a laborious exercise. Again we marvel at the surprising practical effectiveness of the asymptotic complexity analysis of algorithms—nothing of comparable elegance is in sight when we attack hard problem instances.

The algorithm designer faces different challenges when attacking an instance as compared to inventing an algorithm that solves a problem class. For the second case we have many paradigms such as divide-and-conquer, greedy algorithms, or randomization. The designer's problem is to discover and prove mathematical properties that greatly reduce the number of operations as compared to a brute-force approach. When attacking a problem instance we expect a priori that there is nothing much cleverer than brute-force, and that we will use one of half a dozen general purpose search algorithms. The main difficulty is algorithm and program optimization.

Unfortunately, the discipline of algorithm and program optimization so far has resisted most efforts at systematization. Several recent Ph. D. thesis' have attempted to extract general rules of how to attack compute-intensive problem instances from massive case studies [4,3,7]. Data allocation on disk is a central issue, trying to achieve some locality of data access despite the combinatorial chaos typical of such problems. In problems involving retrograde analysis (e. g. [11,13]), where every state (e. g. a board position in a game) in the state space is assigned a unique index in a huge array, construction of a suitable index function is critical. Since such computations may run for months and generate data bases of many GigaBytes, independent verification of the result is a necessity. Some of the experience gained is summarized in [10].

Attacking computationally hard problem instances has so far never been near the center of algorithm research. It has rather been relegated to the niche of puzzles and games, pursued by a relatively small community of researchers. The experience gained is more a collection of individual insights rather than a structured domain of knowledge. As computing power keeps growing and people attack harder problems, we will often encounter problems that must be tackled as individual instances, because no algorithm that applies to a large class will be feasible. Thus, it is a challenge to the computing research community to turn individual insights into a body of knowledge, and to develop a complexity theory of problem instances.

References

1. K. Appel and W. Haken. The Solution of the Four-Color-Map Problem. *Scientific American*, pages 108–121, October 1977. 34
2. D. Avis and K. Fukuda. Reverse Search for Enumeration. *Discrete Apllied Mathematics*, 65:21–46, 1996. 25, 31, 32
3. A Bruengger. *Solving hard combinatorial optimization problems in parallel. Two case studies.* PhD thesis, ETH Zurich, 1997. 34
4. R. Gasser. *Harnessing computational resources for efficient exhaustive search.* PhD thesis, ETH Zurich, 1995. 34
5. J. Horgan. The Death of Proof. *Scientific American*, pages 74–82, 1993. 34
6. D. H. Lehmer. The machine tools of combinatorics. In E. F. Beckenbach, editor, *Applied combinatorial mathematics*, chapter 1, pages 5–31. Wiley, NY, edition, 1964. 34
7. A Marzetta. *ZRAM: A library of parallel search algorithms and its use in enumeration and combinatorial optimization.* PhD thesis, ETH Zurich, 1998. 34
8. A. Marzetta and J. Nievergelt. Enumerating the k best plane spanning trees. In *Computational Geometry — Theory and Application*, 2000. To appear. 31
9. H. Maurer. Forecasting: An impossible necessity. In *Symposium Computer and Information Technology*, http://www.inf.ethz.ch/latsis2000/, Invited Talk. ETH Zurich. 2000. 21
10. J. Nievergelt, R. Gasser, F. Mäser, and C. Wirth. All the needles in a haystack: Can exhaustive search overcome combinatorial chaos? In J. van Leeuwen, editor, *Computer Science Today*, Lecture Notes in Computer Science LNCS 1000, pages 254–274. Springer, 1995. 35
11. K. Thomson. Retrograde analysis of certain endgames. *ICCA J.*, 9(3):131–139, 1986. 34
12. H. van Houten. The physical basis of digital computing. In *Symposium Computer and Information Technology*, http://www.inf.ethz.ch/latsis2000/, Invited Talk. ETH Zurich. 2000. 19
13. C. Wirth and J. Nievergelt. Exhaustive and heuristic retrograde analysis of the KPPKP endgame. *ICCA J.*, 22(2):67–81, 1999 34

The Incompressibility Method[*]

Tao Jiang[1], Ming Li[2], and Paul Vitányi[3]

[1] Department of Computer Science, University of California,
Riverside, CA 92521, USA
jiang@cs.ucr.edu
[2] Computer Science Department, University of California,
Santa Barbara, CA 93106, USA
mli@cs.ucsb.edu
[3] CWI and University of Amsterdam,
Kruislaan 413, 1098 SJ Amsterdam, The Netherlands
paulv@cwi.nl

Abstract. Kolmogorov complexity is a modern notion of randomness dealing with the quantity of information in individual objects; that is, pointwise randomness rather than average randomness as produced by a random source. It was proposed by A. N. Kolmogorov in 1965 to quantify the randomness of individual objects in an objective and absolute manner. This is impossible for classical probability theory. Kolmogorov complexity is known variously as 'algorithmic information', 'algorithmic entropy', 'Kolmogorov-Chaitin complexity', 'descriptional complexity', 'shortest program length', 'algorithmic randomness', and others. Using it, we developed a new mathematical proof technique, now known as the 'incompressibility method'. The incompressibility method is a basic general technique such as the 'pigeon hole' argument, 'the counting method' or the 'probabilistic method'. The new method has been quite successful and we present recent examples. The first example concerns a "static" problem in combinatorial geometry. From among $\binom{n}{3}$ triangles with vertices chosen from among n points in the unit square, U, let T be the one with the smallest area, and let A be the area of T. Heilbronn's triangle problem asks for the *maximum* value assumed by A over all choices of n points. We consider the *average-case*: If the n points are chosen independently and at random (uniform distribution) then there exist positive c and C such that $c/n^3 < \mu_n < C/n^3$ for all large enough n, where μ_n is the expectation of A. Moreover, $c/n^3 < A < C/n^3$ for almost all A, that is, almost all A are close to the expectation value so that we determine the area of the smallest triangle for an arrangement in "general position". Our second example concerns a "dynamic" problem in average-case running time of algorithms. The question of a nontrivial general lower bound (or upper bound) on the *average-case* complexity of Shellsort has been open for about forty years. We obtain the first such lower bound.

[*] The first and second authors were supported in part by NSERC and CITO grants, and UCR startup grants, the third author was supported in part by the European Union via the NeuroCOLT II Working Group and the QAIP Project. The second author is on leave from the University of Waterloo.

V. Hlaváč, K. G. Jeffery, and J. Wiedermann (Eds.): SOFSEM 2000, LNCS 1963, pp. 36–53, 2000.
© Springer-Verlag Berlin Heidelberg 2000

1   Introduction

The incompressibility of individual random objects yields a simple but powerful proof technique: *the incompressibility method*. This method is a general purpose tool that can be used to prove lower bounds on computational problems, to obtain combinatorial properties of concrete objects, and to analyze the average complexity of an algorithm. Since the middle 1980's, the incompressibility method has been successfully used to solve many well-known questions that had been open for a long time and to supply new simplified proofs for known results. A survey is [20]. The incompressibility method is based on Kolmogorov complexity, and seems especially suited for average-case analysis. We illustrate the versatility of this form of application of Kolmogorov complexity by its use to obtain two recent results, one result from the world of combinatorics dealing with "static" structures, and one result from the world of algorithmics dealing with "dynamic" structures. The first one is a new average-case result in geometric combinatorics (related to half-century old problem of the determination of the Heilbronn triangle constant) [15], and the second one gives the first advance in forty years on general bounds on the average-case complexity of sorting by the Shellsort algorithm [14]. For press articles, see [22,23,24]. The aim of this survey is to help the reader appreciate the beauty of the incompressibility method and to stimulate its use to solve the reader's favorite problems. The coding and information approach appears quite universal. For example, the development of a Kolmogorov complexity version of quantum information [42,2], is driven by the hope that it can perhaps be used to similarly obtain lower bounds on the new quantum mechanical algorithms [21].

1.1   Kolmogorov Complexity

We give some definitions to establish notation. For introduction, details, and proofs, see [20]. We write *string* to mean a finite binary string. Other finite objects can be encoded into strings in natural ways. The set of strings is denoted by $\{0,1\}^*$. The length of a string x is denoted by $l(x)$, distinguishing it from the cardinality $|A|$ of a finite set A.

Let $x, y, z \in \mathcal{N}$, where $\mathcal{N}$ denotes the natural numbers. Identify $\mathcal{N}$ and $\{0,1\}^*$ according to the correspondence

$$(0, \epsilon), (1, 0), (2, 1), (3, 00), (4, 01), \ldots .$$

Here ϵ denotes the *empty word* '' with no letters. The *length* $l(x)$ of x is the number of bits in the binary string x. For example, $l(010) = 3$ and $l(\epsilon) = 0$.

The emphasis is on binary sequences only for convenience; observations in any alphabet can be so encoded in a way that is 'theory neutral'.

1.1.1   Self-delimiting Codes. A binary string x is a *proper prefix* of a binary string y if we can write $x = yz$ for $z \neq \epsilon$. A set $\{x, y, \ldots\} \subseteq \{0,1\}^*$ is *prefix-free* if for any pair of distinct elements in the set neither is a proper prefix of the other.

A prefix-free set is also called a *prefix code*. Each binary string $x = x_1 x_2 \ldots x_n$ has a special type of prefix code, called a *self-delimiting code*,

$$\bar{x} = 1^n 0 x_1 x_2 \ldots x_n.$$

This code is self-delimiting because we can determine where the code word $\bar{x}$ ends by reading it from left to right without backing up. Using this code we define the standard self-delimiting code for x to be $x' = \overline{l(x)}x$. It is easy to check that $l(\bar{x}) = 2n + 1$ and $l(x') = n + 2\log n + 1$.

Let $\langle \cdot, \cdot \rangle$ be a standard one-one mapping from $\mathcal{N} \times \mathcal{N}$ to $\mathcal{N}$, for technical reasons chosen such that $l(\langle x, y \rangle) = l(y) + l(x) + 2l(l(x)) + 1$, for example $\langle x, y \rangle = x'y = 1^{l(l(x))} 0 l(x) xy$.

1.1.2 Kolmogorov Complexity.

Informally, the Kolmogorov complexity, or algorithmic entropy, $C(x)$ of a string x is the length (number of bits) of a shortest binary program (string) to compute x on a fixed reference universal computer (such as a particular universal Turing machine). Intuitively, $C(x)$ represents the minimal amount of information required to generate x by any effective process [17]. The conditional Kolmogorov complexity $C(x|y)$ of x relative to y is defined similarly as the length of a shortest program to compute x if y is furnished as an auxiliary input to the computation. The functions $C(\cdot)$ and $C(\cdot|\cdot)$, though defined in terms of a particular machine model, are machine-independent up to an additive constant, and acquire an asymptotically universal and absolute character through Church's thesis, from the ability of universal machines to simulate one another and execute any effective process. Formally:

Definition 1. Let $T_0, T_1, \ldots$ be a standard enumeration of all Turing machines. Choose a universal Turing machine U that expresses its universality in the following manner:

$$U(\langle \langle i, p \rangle, y \rangle) = T_i(\langle p, y \rangle)$$

for all i and $\langle p, y \rangle$, where p denotes a Turing program for T_i and y an input. We fix U as our *reference universal computer* and define the *conditional Kolmogorov complexity* of x given y by

$$C(x|y) = \min_{q \in \{0,1\}^*} \{l(q) : U(\langle q, y \rangle) = x\},$$

for every q (for example $q = \langle i, p \rangle$ above) and auxiliary input y. The *unconditional Kolmogorov complexity* of x is defined by $C(x) = C(x|\epsilon)$. For convenience we write $C(x, y)$ for $C(\langle x, y \rangle)$, and $C(x|y, z)$ for $C(x|\langle y, z \rangle)$.

1.2 Incompressibility

Since there is a Turing machine, say T_i, that computes the identity function $T_i(x) \equiv x$ it follows that $C(x) \le l(x) + c$ for fixed $c \le 2\log i + 1$ and all x.[1]

---

[1] In what follows, "log" denotes the binary logarithm.

It is easy to see that there are also strings that can be described by programs much shorter than themselves. For instance, the function defined by $f(1) = 2$ and $f(i) = 2^{f(i-1)}$ for $i > 1$ grows very fast, $f(k)$ is a "stack" of k twos. Yet for every k it is clear that $f(k)$ has complexity at most $C(k) + O(1)$. What about incompressibility? For every n there are 2^n binary strings of length n, but only $\sum_{i=0}^{n-1} 2^i = 2^n - 1$ descriptions in binary string format of length less than n. Therefore, there is at least one binary string x of length n such that $C(x) \geq n$. We call such strings *incompressible*. The same argument holds for conditional complexity: since for every length n there are at most $2^n - 1$ binary programs of length $< n$, for every binary string y there is a binary string x of length n such that $C(x|y) \geq n$. "Randomness deficiency" measures how far the object falls short of the maximum possible Kolmogorov complexity. For every constant δ we say a string x is has *randomness deficiency* at most δ if $C(x) \geq l(x) - \delta$. Strings that are incompressible (say, with small randomness deficiency) are patternless, since a pattern could be used to reduce the description length. Intuitively, we think of such patternless sequences as being random, and we use "random sequence" synonymously with "incompressible sequence".[2] Since there are few short programs, there can be only few objects of low complexity: the number of strings of length n that have randomness deficiency at most δ is at least $2^n - 2^{n-\delta} + 1$. Hence there is at least one string of length n with randomness deficiency 0, at least one-half of all strings of length n have randomness deficiency 1, at least three-fourths of all strings of length n have randomness deficiency 2, and at least the $(1 - 1/2^\delta)$-th part of all 2^n strings of length n have randomness deficiency at most δ. In general:

Lemma 1. *Let δ be a positive integer. For every fixed y, every finite set A contains at least $(1 - 2^{-\delta})|A| + 1$ elements x with $C(x|A, y) \geq \lfloor \log |A| \rfloor - \delta$.*

Proof. There are $N = \sum_{i=0}^{n-1} 2^i = 2^n - 1$ binary strings of length less than n. A fortiori there are at most N elements of A that can be computed by binary programs of length less than n, given y. This implies that at least $|A| - N$ elements of A cannot be computed by binary programs of length less than n, given y. Substituting n by $\lfloor \log |A| \rfloor - \delta$ together with Definition 1 yields the lemma.   □

Lemma 2. *If A is a set, then for every y every element $x \in A$ has complexity $C(x|A, y) \leq \log |A| + O(1)$.*

Proof. The lemma holds since x can be described by first describing A in $O(1)$ bits and then giving the index of x in the enumeration order of A.   □

As an example, set $A = \{x : l(x) = n\}$. Then is $|A| = 2^n$. Since $C(x) \leq n + \delta$ for some fixed c and all x in A, Lemma 1 demonstrates that this trivial estimate is quite sharp. If we are given A as an explicit table then we can simply enumerate

---

[2] It is possible to give a rigorous formalization of the intuitive notion of a random sequence as a sequence that passes all effective tests for randomness, see for example [20].

its elements (in, say, lexicographical order) using a fixed program not depending on A or y. Such a fixed program can be given in $O(1)$ bits. Hence the complexity $C(x|A, y) \leq \log |A| + O(1)$.

Incompressibility Method. In a typical proof using the incompressibility method, one first chooses an incompressible object from the class under discussion. The argument invariably says that if a desired property does not hold, then in contrast with the assumption, the object can be compressed. This yields the required contradiction. Applying the *incompressibility method* one uses the fact that both absolutely and relative to any fixed string y, there are incompressible strings of every length, and that *most* strings are nearly incompressible, by *any* standard. Since most objects are almost incompressible, the desired property usually also holds for almost all objects, and hence on average.

2   Average-Case Area of Heilbronn-Like Triangles

From among $\binom{n}{3}$ triangles with vertices chosen from among n points in the unit circle, let T be the one of least area, and let A be the area of T. Let Δ_n be the maximum assumed by A over all choices of n points. H. A. Heilbronn (1908–1975) [3] asked for the exact value or approximation of Δ_n. The list [1,3,4,6,9,10,18,19,25,29,30,31,32,33,34,38,39,40,41] is a selection of papers dealing with the problem. Obviously, the value of Δ_n will change only by a small constant factor for every unit area convex shape, and it has become customary to consider the unit square [33]. A brief history is as follows. Heilbronn observed the trivial upper bound $\Delta_n = O(1/n)$ and conjectured that $\Delta_n = O(1/n^2)$, and P. Erdős proved that this conjecture — if true — would be tight since $\Delta_n = \Omega(1/n^2)$ [29]. The first nontrivial result due to K. F. Roth in 1951 established the upper bound $\Delta_n = O(1/(n\sqrt{\log \log n}))$ [29], which was improved in 1972 by W. M. Schmidt to $O(1/(n\sqrt{\log n}))$ [34] and in the same year by Roth first to $O(1/n^{1.105\cdots})$ [30] and then to $\Delta_n = O(1/n^{1.117\cdots})$ [31]. Roth simplified his arguments in 1973 and 1976 [32,33]. Exact values of Δ_n for $n \leq 15$ were studied in [9,39,40,41]. In 1981, J. Komlós, J. Pintz, and E. Szemerédi [18] improved Roth's upper bound to $O(1/n^{8/7-\epsilon})$, using the simplified arguments of Roth. The really surprising news came in 1982 when the same authors [19] derived a lower bound $\Omega(\log n/n^2)$, narrowly refuting Heilbronn's original conjecture. Some believe that this lower bound is perhaps the best possible [7,8]. In 1997 C. Bertram-Kretzberg, T. Hofmeister, and H. Lefmann [4] gave an algorithm that finds a specific set of n points in the unit square whose A (defined above) is $\Omega(\log n/n^2)$ for every fixed n, using a discretization of the problem. In 1999 G. Barequet [1] derived lower bounds on d-dimensional versions of Heilbronn's problem where $d > 2$. All of this work concerns the *worst-case* value of the minimal triangle area.

---

[3] The webpage http://www.mathsoft.com/asolve/constant/hlb/hlb.html is devoted exclusively for Heilbronn's triangle problem.

Results. Here we consider the *expected* value: If the n points are chosen independently and at random (uniform distribution) then there exist positive c and C such that $c/n^3 < \mu_n < C/n^3$ for all large enough n, where μ_n is the expectation of the area A of the smallest triangle formed by any three points. Moreover, with probability close to one, $c/n^3 < A < C/n^3$. This follows directly from Corollaries 2 and 4 of Theorems 1 and 2. Our technique is to discretize the problem and show that all Kolmogorov-random arrangements (see below) of n points in the unit square satisfy this range of area of the smallest triangle, where the constants c, C are functions of the "randomness deficiency" of the arrangement — that is, how far the Kolmogorov complexity of the arrangement falls short of the maximum attainable Kolmogorov complexity. A Kolmogorov-random arrangement is a rigorous way to say that the arrangement is in "general position" or "typical": there are no simple describable properties that can distinguish any such arrangement from another one [20]. As a consequence, every arrangement in which the smallest triangle has area outside this range — smaller or larger — cannot be Kolmogorov random. According to a recent article [22], this result can act as a mathematical guarantee of the afficacy of certain pseudo Monte Carlo methods to determine the fair market value of derivatives (on the stock market). For use in geometrical modeling see [1].

2.1   Grid and Pebbles

In the analysis of the triangle problem we first consider a discrete version based on an equally spaced $K \times K$ grid in the unit square U. The general result for the continuous situation is then obtained by taking the limit for $K \to \infty$. Call the resulting axis-parallel $2K$ lines *grid lines* and their crossing points *grid points*. We place n points on grid points. These n points will be referred to as *pebbles* to avoid confusion with grid points or other geometric points arising in the discussion.

There are $\binom{K^2}{n}$ ways to put n *unlabeled* pebbles on the grid where at most one pebble is put on every grid point. We count only distinguishable arrangements without regard for the identities of the placed pebbles. Clearly, the restriction that no two pebbles can be placed on the same grid point is no restriction anymore when we let K grow unboundedly.

Erdős [29] demonstrated that for the special case of $p \times p$ grids, where p is a prime number, there are necessarily arrangements of p pebbles with every pebble placed on a grid point such that no three pebbles are collinear. The least area of a triangle in such an arrangement is at least $1/(2p^2)$. This implies that the triangle constant $\Delta_n = \Omega(1/n^2)$ as $n \to \infty$ through the special sequence of primes. We now give some detailed examples — used later — of the use of the incompressibility method.

By Lemma 1, for every integer δ independent of K, every arrangement $X_1, \ldots, X_n$ (locations of pebbles) out of at least a fraction of $1 - 1/2^\delta$

of all arrangements of n pebbles on the grid satisfies

$$C(X_1, \ldots, X_n | n, K) \geq \log \binom{K^2}{n} - \delta. \tag{1}$$

Lemma 3. *If (1) holds with n fixed and K is sufficiently large, then no three pebbles can be collinear, and so the area of a smallest triangle is at least $1/(2(K-1)^2)$.*

Proof. Place $n-1$ pebbles at positions chosen from the total of K^2 grid points — there are $\binom{K^2}{n-1}$ choices. Choose two pebbles, P and Q, from among the $n-1$ pebbles — there are $\binom{n-1}{2}$ choices. Choose a new pebble R on the straight line determined by P, Q. The number of grid points $< K$ on this line between P (or Q) and R identifies R uniquely in $\leq \log K$ bits. There is a fixed algorithm that, on input n and K, decodes a binary description consisting of the items above — each encoded as the logarithm of the number of choices — and computes the posititions of the n pebbles. By (1) this implies

$$\log \binom{K^2}{n-1} + \log \binom{n-1}{2} + \log K + O(1) \geq \log \binom{K^2}{n} - \delta.$$

Using the asymptotic expression

$$\log \binom{a}{b} - b \log \frac{a}{b} \to b \log e - \frac{1}{2} \log b + O(1) \tag{2}$$

for b fixed and $a \to \infty$, one obtains $3 \log n \geq \log K - \delta + O(1)$, which is a contradiction for K sufficiently large. □

Lemma 4. *If (1) holds with n fixed and K is sufficiently large, then no two pebbles can be on the same (horizontal) grid line.*

Proof. Place $n-1$ pebbles at positions chosen from the total of K^2 grid points — there are $\binom{K^2}{n-1}$ choices. Choose one pebble P from among the $n-1$ pebbles — there are $n-1$ choices. Choose a new pebble R on the (horizontal) grid line determined by P — there are $K-1$ choices. There is a fixed algorithm that, on input n and K, reconstructs the positions of all n pebbles from a description of these choices. By (1) this implies

$$\log \binom{K^2}{n-1} + \log(n-1) + \log K + O(1) \geq \log \binom{K^2}{n} - \delta.$$

Using (2) with fixed n and $K \to \infty$ we obtain $2 \log n \geq \log K - \delta + O(1)$, which is a contradiction for large enough K. □

2.2   Lower Bound

Let P, Q, R be three points in the two-dimensional plane with Euclidean metric. With some abuse of notation we use $|PQ|$ to denote the *length* of the line segment PQ, and $|PQR|$ to denote the *area* of the triangle on the points P, Q, R.

Theorem 1. *If (1) holds and n and K are large enough then there is a positive c_1 such that the least area of some triangle formed by three pebbles on the grid is at least $c_1/(2^\delta n^3)$.*

Proof. Place n pebbles at positions chosen from the total of K^2 grid points — there are $\binom{K^2}{n}$ choices. Choose three pebbles, P, Q and R, from among the n pebbles — there are $\binom{n}{3}$ choices. Without loss of generality, let the triangle PQR have PQ as the longest side. Center the grid coordinates on $P = (0,0)$ with $Q = (q_1, q_2)$ and $R = (r_1, r_2)$ in units of $1/(K-1)$ in both axes directions. Then R is one of the grid points on the two parallel line segments of length $L = |PQ| = \sqrt{q_1^2 + q_2^2}/(K-1)$ at distance $H = |q_2 r_1 - q_1 r_2|/((K-1)\sqrt{q_1^2 + q_2^2})$ from the line defined by P, Q. The number of grid points on each of these line segments (including one endpoint and excluding the other endpoint) is a positive integer $g = \gcd(q_1, q_2)$ — the line $q_2 x = q_1 y$ has g integer coordinate points between $(0,0)$ and (q_1, q_2) including one of the endpoints. This implies that f defined by $LH(K-1)^2 = fg$ is a positive integer as well.

Enumerating the grid points concerned in lexicographical order, the index of R takes at most $\log(2gf) = \log(2g) + \log f = \log(4|PQR|(K-1)^2)$ bits, where $|PQR|$ denotes the area of the triangle PQR. By (1) it follows that

$$\log\binom{K^2}{n} + \log\binom{n}{3} + \log(4|PQR|(K-1)^2) + O(1) \geq \log\binom{K^2}{n} - \delta.$$

Thus, by (2) with n fixed, $\log|PQR| + O(1) \geq -3\log n - \delta + O(1), K \to \infty$. Consequently, there exists a positive constant c_1, independently of the particular triangle PQR, such that $|PQR| > c_1/(n^3 2^\delta)$ for all large enough n and K. Since this holds for every triangle PQR it holds in particular for a triangle of least area A.   □

By Lemma 1 the probability concentrated on the set of arrangements satisfying (1) is at least $1 - 1/2^\delta$:

Corollary 1. *If n points are chosen independently and at random (uniform distribution) in the unit square, and A is the least area of a triangle formed by three points, then there is a positive c_1 such that for every positive δ we have $A > c_1/(2^\delta n^3)$ with probability at least $1 - 1/2^\delta$.*

In the particular case of $\delta = 1$ the probability concentrated on arrangements satisfying (1) is at least $\frac{1}{2}$ which immediately implies:

Corollary 2. *If n points are chosen independently and at random (uniform distribution) in the unit square, then there is a positive c such that the least area of some triangle formed by three points has expectation $\mu_n > c/n^3$.*

2.3 Upper Bound

Every pair of pebbles out of an incompressible arrangement of n pebbles on a $K \times K$ grid defines a distinct line by Lemma 3. If A is the least area of a triangle formed by three pebbles, then every line defines a strip extending at least $2A/\sqrt{2}$ to each side of the line where no pebbles can be placed. Our strategy is to show that $n/2$ of the pebbles define many lines where the associated forbidden strips don't overlap. As a consequence the number of choices left to place the remaining $n/2$ pebbles gets restricted to the point that the description of the arrangement can be compressed too far.

Theorem 2. *If (1) holds with $\delta < (2 - \epsilon) \log n$ for some positive constant ϵ, then there is a positive C_4 such that the least area of some triangle formed by three pebbles on the grid is at most $C_4 \delta / n^3$, for fixed n with $K \to \infty$.*

Proof. Choose n pebbles at postions chosen from the total of K^2 grid points such that (1) is satisfied. Divide the unit square by a horizontal grid line into an upper and a lower half each of which contains $n/2 \pm 1$ pebbles — there are no grid lines containing two pebbles by Lemma 4. We write *upper line* for a line determined by two pebbles in the upper half that intersects the bottom horizontal grid line (between the outermost grid points).

Lemma 5. *There is a positive constant C_1 such that there are at least $C_1 n^2$ upper lines.*

Proof. Take the top half to be the larger half so that it has area at least $1/2$. Divide the top half into five vertical strips of equal width of $1/5$ and five horizontal strips of equal width $1/10$ starting from the top — ignore the possibly remaining horizontal strip at the bottom of the top half. An upper line determined by a pebble in the upper rectangle and a pebble in the lower rectangle of the middle vertical strip intersects the bottom horizontal grid line. Choose one of the rectangles. Let it contain $m \le n$ pebbles. Since the area of the rectangle is $1/5 \times 1/10$ it contains $K^2/50$ grid points (plus or minus the grid points on the circumference of length $3K/5$ which we ignore). Place $n - m$ pebbles at positions chosen from $49K^2/50$ grid points outside the rectangle — there are $\binom{49K^2/50}{n-m}$ choices — and place m pebbles at positions chosen from the total of $K^2/50$ grid points in the rectangle — there are $\binom{K^2/50}{m}$ choices. Given n and K, the n pebble positions are determined by m, the position of the rectangle and an index number of $\log \binom{49K^2/50}{n-m} \binom{K^2/50}{m}$ bits. The total description length of the description expressed in bits must be at least the right-hand side of (1). Calculation shows that for large enough n we have $m > n/100$. Since this holds for every one of the 25 rectangles in the upper half, the top square and the bottom squares of the middle column contain at least $n/100$ pebbles each. Each pair of pebbles, one in the top square and one in the bottom square, determine a distinct upper line. The lemma is proven with $C_1 > (1/100) \cdot (1/100) = 1/10^4$. □

Lemma 6. *Let w_1, w_2, w_3, w_4, w_5 be the spacings between the six consecutive intercepts of a sextuplet of upper lines with a horizontal grid line in the bottom* half containing a pebble, and let $D = w_1 + w_2 + w_3 + w_4 + w_5$. Then there is a positive C_2 such that $D > C_2/n^{3-\epsilon/5}$ with ϵ as in the statement of the theorem.

Proof. Place $n-5$ pebbles at positions chosen from the total of K^2 grid points — there are $\binom{K^2}{n-5}$ choices. Choose eight pebbles, P_i ($i = 0, 1, 2, 3, 5, 7, 9, 11$) from among the $n-5$ pebbles — there are at most $\binom{n-5}{8}$ choices — and five new pebbles P_j ($j = 4, 6, 8, 10, 12$) such that $P_1 P_2, P_3 P_4, P_5 P_6, P_7 P_8, P_9 P_{10}, P_{11} P_{12}$ is the sextuplet of upper lines in the theorem, and P_0 is a pebble in the lower half. The coordinates of the five unknown P_j's are determined by (i) the locations of the five intersections of the associated quintuplet of upper lines with the lower half horizontal grid line on which P_0 is located, and (ii) the five unknown distances between these intersections and the P_j's along the five associated upper lines. The grid point positions of the P_j's are uniquely determined if we know the latter distances up to precision $1/4(K-1)$. Relative to the intersection of the known upper line $P_1 P_2$, item (i) uses $5 \log DK + O(1)$ bits. Item (ii) uses $5 \log K + O(1)$ bits. Together these choices form a description of the arrangement. By (1) this implies:

$$\log \binom{K^2}{n-5} + 8 \log n + 5 \log DK + 5 \log K + O(1) \geq \log \binom{K^2}{n} - \delta.$$

A now familiar calculation using (2) yields $5 \log D + O(1) \geq -13 \log n - \delta$, for fixed n and $K \to \infty$. This shows $D > C_2 2^{(2 \log n - \delta)/5}/n^3$ for some positive C_2. Substituting $\delta < (2 - \epsilon) \log n$ proves the lemma. □

Divide lower half horizontal grid lines in consecutive intervals of length D, and choose at most one intersection in every odd interval. Choose constant $C_3 = C_1/(6 \cdot 2) = C_1/12$. By Lemmas 5 and 6 this procedure selects $C_3 n^2$ upper line intersections spaced at least D apart in every lower half horizontal grid line containing a pebble. With A the area of the smallest triange formed by any three pebbles, the forbidden strip associated with an intersection covers a grid line segment of length at least $2A/\sqrt{2} > A$ at each side of an upper line intersection. If

$$2A < D, \tag{3}$$

then the grid points eliminated by the forbidden strips of the $C_3 n^2$ widely spaced upper lines intersections per grid line are all distinct: Pebbles in the lower half can be placed on less than $K(1 - 2C_3 n^2 A))$ grid points per horizontal grid line, and on at most $K(1 - C_3 n^2 D)$ per horizontal grid line otherwise. With

$$B = \min\{2A, D\} \tag{4}$$

and given the horizontal lower half grid line concerned, an x-coordinate of a pebble requires at most

$$\log K(1 - C_3 n^2 B) \quad \text{bits.} \tag{5}$$

Select n horizontal grid lines (to place one pebble per grid line by Lemma 3) chosen from the total of K grid lines — there are $\binom{K}{n}$ choices. Select on everyone of the upper $n/2$ horizontal grid lines a grid point to place a pebble — there are $K^{n/2}$ choices. Finally, select on the lower $n/2$ horizontal grid lines $n/2$ grid points to place the pebbles — there are only $(K(1 - C_3 n^2 B))^{n/2}$ choices by (5) if we do it from top to bottom. Together these choices form a description of the arrangement. By (1) this implies:

$$\log \binom{K}{n} + \frac{n}{2} \log K + \frac{n}{2} \log K(1 - C_3 n^2 B) + O(1) \geq \log \binom{K^2}{n} - \delta.$$

Using (2) with n fixed yields

$$\frac{n}{2} \log(1 - C_3 n^2 B) \geq -\delta - O(1), K \to \infty.$$

The left-hand side

$$\log \left(1 - \frac{C_3 n^3 B/2}{n/2}\right)^{n/2} = \log e^{-C_3 n^3 B/2}, n \to \infty,$$

so that

$$B \leq \frac{2\delta + O(1)}{C_3 n^3 \log e}. \tag{6}$$

Since $\delta < 2 \log n$ in the right-hand side, Lemma 6 shows that $D > B$. Therefore, (4) implies $B = 2A$ so that (6) establishes the theorem. □

Using Lemma 1:

Corollary 3. *If n points are chosen independently and at random (uniform distribution) in the unit square, and A is the least area of a triangle formed by three points, then there is a positive C_4 such that for every positive $\delta < (2 - \epsilon) \log n$ ($\epsilon > 0$), we have $A < C_4 \delta n^3$ with probability at least $1 - 1/2^\delta$.*

The expectation μ_n of A satisfies

$$\mu_n < \sum_{\delta=0}^{\lceil 1.9 \log n \rceil} \frac{B}{2^{\delta+1}} + \frac{1}{n^{1.9}} \frac{C_5}{n^{8/7 - \epsilon'}}$$

since A is upper bounded by $C_5/n^{8/7 - \epsilon'}$ for some positive C_5 for every $\epsilon' > 0$ [18].

Corollary 4. *If n points are chosen independently and at random (uniform distribution) in the unit square, then there is a positive C such that the least area of some triangle formed by three points has expectation $\mu_n < C/n^3$.*

3   Average-Case Analysis of Shellsort

The question of a nontrivial general lower bound (or upper bound) on the average complexity of Shellsort (due to D. L. Shell [37]) has been open for about four decades [16,36]. We present such a lower bound for p-pass Shellsort for every p.

Shellsort sorts a list of n elements in p passes using a sequence of increments $h_1, \ldots, h_p$. In the kth pass the main list is divided in h_k separate sublists of length $\lceil n/h_k \rceil$, where the ith sublist consists of the elements at positions j, where $j \bmod h_k = i - 1$, of the main list ($i = 1, \ldots, h_k$). Every sublist is sorted using a straightforward insertion sort. The efficiency of the method is governed by the number of passes p and the selected increment sequence $h_1, \ldots, h_p$ with $h_p = 1$ to ensure sortedness of the final list. The original $\log n$-pass increment sequence $\lfloor n/2 \rfloor, \lfloor n/4 \rfloor, \ldots, 1$ of Shell [37] uses worst case $\Theta(n^2)$ time, but Papernov and Stasevitch [26] showed that another related sequence uses $O(n^{3/2})$ and Pratt [28] extended this to a class of all nearly geometric increment sequences and proved this bound was tight. The currently best asymptotic method was found by Pratt [28]. It uses all $\log^2 n$ increments of the form $2^i 3^j < \lfloor n/2 \rfloor$ to obtain time $O(n \log^2 n)$ in the worst case. Moreover, since every pass takes at least n steps, the average complexity using Pratt's increment sequence is $\Theta(n \log^2 n)$. Incerpi and Sedgewick [11] constructed a family of increment sequences for which Shellsort runs in $O(n^{1+\epsilon/\sqrt{\log n}})$ time using $(8/\epsilon^2) \log n$ passes, for every $\epsilon > 0$. B. Chazelle (attribution in [35]) obtained the same result by generalizing Pratt's method: instead of using 2 and 3 to construct the increment sequence use a and $(a + 1)$ for fixed a which yields a worst-case running time of $n \log^2 n(a^2/\ln^2 a)$ which is $O(n^{1+\epsilon/\sqrt{\log n}})$ for $\ln^2 a = O(\log n)$. Plaxton, Poonen and Suel [27] proved an $\Omega(n^{1+\epsilon/\sqrt{p}})$ lower bound for p passes of Shellsort using any increment sequence, for some $\epsilon > 0$; taking $p = \Omega(\log n)$ shows that the Incerpi-Sedgewick/Chazelle bounds are optimal for small p and taking p slightly larger shows a $\Theta(n \log^2 n/(\log \log n)^2)$ lower bound on the worst case complexity of Shellsort. Since every pass takes at least n steps this shows an $\Omega(n \log^2 n/(\log \log n)^2)$ lower bound on the worst-case of every Shellsort increment sequence. For the *average-case* running time Knuth [16] showed $\Theta(n^{5/3})$ for the best choice of increments in $p = 2$ passes; Yao [43] analyzed the average case for $p = 3$ but did not obtain a simple analytic form; Yao's analysis was improved by Janson and Knuth [12] who showed $O(n^{23/15})$ average-case running time for a particular choice of increments in $p = 3$ passes. Apart from this no nontrivial results are known for the average case; see [16,35,36].

Results. We show a general $\Omega(pn^{1+1/p})$ lower bound on the average-case running time of p-pass Shellsort under uniform distribution of input permutations for every p.[4] This is the first advance on the problem of determining general nontrivial bounds on the *average-case* running time of Shellsort [28,16,43,11,27,35,36].

---

[4] The trivial lower bound is $\Omega(pn)$ comparisons since every element needs to be compared at least once in every pass.

3.1   Shellsort

A Shellsort computation consists of a sequence of comparison and inversion (swapping) operations. In this analysis of the average-case lower bound we count just the total number of data movements (here inversions) executed. The same bound holds *a fortiori* for the number of comparisons.

The proof is based on the following intuitive idea: There are $n!$ different permutations. Given the sorting process (the insertion paths in the right order) one can recover the correct permutation from the sorted list. Hence one requires $n!$ pairwise different sorting processes. This gives a lower bound on the minimum of the maximal length of a process. We formulate the proof in the crisp format of incompressibility.

Theorem 3. *Let $0 < \epsilon < 1$ and n, p satisfy $p \leq (\epsilon \log n) \log e$. For every p-pass Shellsort algorithm, the average number of inversions (and comparisons) in on lists of n keys is at least $\Omega\left(pn^{1+(1-\epsilon)/p}\right)$ for every increment sequence. The average is taken with all lists of n items equally likely (uniform distribution).*

Proof. Let the list to be sorted consist of a permutation π of the elements $1, \ldots, n$. Consider a $(h_1, \ldots, h_p)$ Shellsort algorithm A where h_k is the increment in the kth pass and $h_p = 1$. For any $1 \leq i \leq n$ and $1 \leq k \leq p$, let $m_{i,k}$ be the number of elements in the h_k-*chain* containing element i that are to the left of i at the beginning of pass k and are larger than i. Observe that $\sum_{i=1}^n m_{i,k}$ is the number of inversions in the initial permutation of pass k, and that the insertion sort in pass k requires precisely $\sum_{i=1}^n (m_{i,k} + 1)$ comparisons. Let M denote the total number of inversions:

$$M := \sum_{k=1}^{p} \sum_{i=1}^{n} m_{i,k} \, . \tag{7}$$

Lemma 7. *Given all the $m_{i,k}$'s in an appropriate fixed order, we can reconstruct the original permutation π.*

Proof. The $m_{i,p}$'s trivially specify the initial permutation of pass p. In general, given the $m_{i,k}$'s and the final permutation of pass k, we can reconstruct the initial permutation of pass k. □

Let M as in (7) be a fixed number. There are $n!$ permutations of n elements. Let permutation π be an incompressible permutation having Kolmogorov complexity

$$C(\pi | n, A, P) \geq \log n! - \log n \, . \tag{8}$$

where P is the decoding program in the following discussion. There exist many such permutations by Lemma 1. Clearly, there is a fixed program that on input A, n reconstructs π from the description of the $m_{i,k}$'s as in Claim 7. Therefore, the minimum length of the latter description, including a fixed program in $O(1)$ bits, must exceed the complexity of π:

$$C(m_{1,1}, \ldots, m_{n,p} | n, A, P) + O(1) \geq C(\pi | n, A, P) \, . \tag{9}$$

An M as defined by (7) such that every division of M in $m_{i,k}$'s contradicts (9) would be a lower bound on the number of inversions performed. How many divisions are there? Choosing a elements out of an ordered list of $a + b$ elements divides the remainder into a sequence of $a + 1$ possibly empty sublists. Hence there are

$$D(M) := \binom{M + np - 1}{np - 1} \tag{10}$$

distinct divisions of M into np ordered nonnegative integral summands $m_{i,k}$'s. Every division can be indicated by its index j in an enumeration of these divisions. This is both obvious and an application of Lemma 2. Therefore, a description of M followed by a description of j effectively describes the $m_{i,k}$'s. We note that clearly $M \geq 1$ by (9). Fix P as the program for the reference universal machine that reconstructs the ordered list of $m_{i,k}$'s from this description. The binary length of this two-part description must by definition exceed the Kolmogorov complexity of the described object.

A minor complication is that we cannot simply concatenate two binary description parts: the result is a binary string without delimiter to indicate where one substring ends and the other one begins. To overcome this problem we encode one of the substrings *self-delimitingly,* see Section 1.1.1.

Encoding the M part of the description self-delimitingly we obtain:

$$\log D(M) + \log M + 2 \log \log M + 1 \geq C(m_{1,1}, \ldots, m_{n,p} | n, A, P).$$

We know that $M \leq pn^2$ since every $m_{i,k} \leq n$. We have assumed $p < n$. Together with (8) and (9), we have

$$\log D(M) \geq \log n! - 4 \log n - 2 \log \log n - O(1). \tag{11}$$

Estimate $\log D(M)$ by[5]

$$\log \binom{M + np - 1}{np - 1} = (np - 1) \log \frac{M + np - 1}{np - 1} + M \log \frac{M + np - 1}{M}$$
$$+ \frac{1}{2} \log \frac{M + np - 1}{(np - 1)M} + O(1).$$

The second term in the right-hand side is bounded as[6]

$$\log \left(1 + \frac{np - 1}{M}\right)^M < \log e^{np-1}$$

---

[5] Use the following formula ([20], p. 10),

$$\log \binom{a}{b} = b \log \frac{a}{b} + (a - b) \log \frac{a}{a - b} + \frac{1}{2} \log \frac{a}{b(a - b)} + O(1).$$

[6] Use $e^a > (1 + \frac{a}{b})^b$ for all $a > 0$ and positive integer b.

for all positive M and $np - 1 > 0$. Since $0 < p < n$ and $1 \leq M \leq pn^2$,

$$\frac{1}{2(np-1)} \log \frac{M + np - 1}{(np - 1)M} \to 0$$

for $n \to \infty$. Therefore, $\log D(M)$ is majorized asymptotically by

$$A = (np - 1) \left(\log \left(\frac{M}{np - 1} + 1 \right) + \log e \right)$$

for $n \to \infty$. Altogether, $A + \log M \geq n \log n - O(n)$. With $p \leq (\epsilon/\log e) \log n$ $(0 < \epsilon < 1)$, this can be rewritten as

$$(np - 1) \log(\frac{M}{np - 1} + 1) \geq (1 - \epsilon)n \log n - O(n) ,$$

and further as

$$\log(\frac{M}{np - 1} + 1) \geq (\frac{1 - \epsilon}{p}) \log n - O(\frac{1}{p}) .$$

The righthand side is positive and asymptotic to the first term for $n \to \infty$. Hence,

$$M = \Omega(pn^{1+(1-\epsilon)/p}) .$$

That is, the running time of the algorithm is as stated in the theorem for every permutation π satisfying (8). By Lemma 1 at least a $(1 - 1/n)$-fraction of all permutations π require that high complexity. Then the following is a lower bound on the expected number of inversions of the sorting procedure:

$$(1 - \frac{1}{n})\Omega(pn^{1+(1-\epsilon)/p}) + \frac{1}{n}\Omega(0) = \Omega(pn^{1+(1-\epsilon)/p}) .$$

This gives us the theorem.   □

Theorem 4. *The average computation time (number of inversions, for $p = o(\log n)$, and comparisons, for $n/2 \geq p = \Omega(\log n)$) in p-pass Shellsort on lists of n keys is at least $\Omega(pn^{1+1/p})$ for every increment sequence. The average is taken with all lists of n items equally likely (uniform distribution).*

Proof. Assume the terminology above. Since for $p = o(\log n)$ ($\epsilon(n) \to 0$ for $n \to \infty$ in Theorem 3) the lower bound on the expected number of inversions of the sorting procedure is at least

$$(1 - \frac{1}{2^n})\Omega(pn^{1+1/p}) + \frac{1}{2^n}\Omega(0) = \Omega(pn^{1+1/p}) ;$$

and for $p = \Omega(\log n)$, the trivial lower bound on the number of comparisons is vacuously $pn = \Omega(pn^{1+1/p})$.   □

Our lower bound on the average-case can be compared with the Plaxton-Poonen-Suel $\Omega(n^{1+\epsilon/\sqrt{p}})$ worst case lower bound [27]. Some special cases of the lower bound on the average-case complexity are:

1. For $p = 1$ our lower bound is asymptotically tight: it is the average number of inversions for Insertion Sort.
2. For $p = 2$, Shellsort requires $\Omega(n^{3/2})$ inversions (the tight bound is known to be $\Theta(n^{5/3})$ [16]).
3. For $p = 3$, Shellsort requires $\Omega(n^{4/3})$ inversions (the best known upper bound is $O(n^{23/15})$ in [12]).
4. For $p = \log n/\log\log n$, Shellsort requires $\Omega(n\log^2 n/\log\log n)$ inversions.
5. For $p = \log n$, Shellsort requires $\Omega(n\log n)$ comparisons; this is of course the lower bound of average number of comparisons for every sorting algorithm.
6. In general, for $n/2 > p = p(n) \geq \log n$, Shellsort requires $\Omega(n \cdot p(n))$ comparisons since every pass trivially makes about n comparisons.

In [36] it is mentioned that the existence of an increment sequence yielding an average $O(n\log n)$ Shellsort has been open for 30 years. The above lower bound on the average shows that the number p of passes of such an increment sequence (if it exists) is precisely $p = \Theta(\log n)$; all the other possibilities are ruled out.

3.2   Conclusion and Open Problems

The average-case performance of Shellsort has been one of the most fundamental and interesting open problems in the area of algorithm analysis. The simple average-case analysis of Insertion Sort (1-pass Shellsort), and similar analyses of Bubble sort, stack-sort and queue-sort are given in the preliminary version of this paper [14] and serve as further examples to demonstrate the generality and simplicity of our technique in analyzing sorting algorithms in general. Some open questions are:

1. Tighten the average-case lower bound for Shellsort. Our bound is not tight for $p = 2$ passes.
2. Is there an increment sequence for $\log n$-pass Shellsort so that it runs in average-case $\Theta(n\log n)$?

Acknowledgement

We thank John Tromp for help with the proof of Theorem 1. We thank Don Knuth, Ian Munro, and Vaughan Pratt for discussions and references on Shellsort.

References

1. G. Barequet, A lower bound for Heilbronn's triangle problem in d dimensions. In: *Proc. 10th ACM-SIAM Symp. Discrete Algorithms*, 1999, 76–81. 40, 41

2. A. Berthiaume, W. van Dam, S. Laplante, Quantum Kolmogorov complexity, *Proc. 15th IEEE Computational Complexity Conference*, 2000, 240–249. 37
3. J. Beck, Almost collinear triples among N points on the plane, in *A Tribute to Paul Erdős*, ed. A. Baker, B. Bollobas and A. Hajnal, Cambridge Univ. Press, 1990, pp. 39–57. 40
4. C. Bertram-Kretzberg, T. Hofmeister, H. Lefmann, An algorithm for Heilbronn's problem, *Proc. 3rd Ann. Conf. Comput. and Combinatorics*, T. Jiang and D. T. Lee (Eds), 1997, pp. 23–31. 40
5. H. Buhrman, T. Jiang, M. Li, and P. Vitányi, New applications of the incompressibility method, pp. 220–229 in *the Proceedings of ICALP'99*, LNCS 1644, Springer-Verlag, Berlin, 1999.
6. G. Cairns, M. McIntyre, and J. Strantzen, Geometric proofs of some recent results of Yang Lu, *Math. Magazine*, 66(1993), 263–265. 40
7. P. Erdős, Problems and results in combinatorial geometry, In: *Discrete Geometry and Convexity*, Annals of the New York Academy of Sciences, 440(1985), 1–11. 40
8. P. Erdős and G. Purdy, Extremal problems in combinatorial theory, In: *Handbook of Combinatorics*, R. L. Graham, M. Grötschel, L. Lovász, Eds., Elsevier/MIT Press, 1995, pp. 861–862. 40
9. M. Goldberg, Maximizing the smallest triangle made by N points in a square, *Math. Magazine*, 45(1972), 135–144. 40
10. R. K. Guy, *Unsolved Problems in Number Theory*, 2nd ed., Springer-Verlag 1994, pp. 242–244. 40
11. J. Incerpi and R. Sedgewick, Improved upper bounds on Shellsort, *Journal of Computer and System Sciences*, 31(1985), 210–224. 47
12. S. Janson and D. E. Knuth, Shellsort with three increments, *Random Struct. Alg.*, 10(1997), 125–142. 47, 51
13. T. Jiang, M. Li, and P. Vitányi, New applications of the incompressibility method II, *Theoretical Computer Science*, 235:1(2000), 59–70.
14. T. Jiang, M. Li, and P. Vitányi, The average-case complexity of Shellsort, Preliminary version, pp. 453–462 in *the Proceedings of ICALP'99*, LNCS 1644, Springer-Verlag, Berlin, 1999. Also: *J. Assoc. Comput. Mach.*, to appear. 37, 51
15. T. Jiang, M. Li, and P. M. B. Vitányi, The Expected Size of Heilbronn's Triangles, *Proc. 14th IEEE Computational Complexity Conference*, 1999, 105–113. 37
16. D. E. Knuth, *The Art of Computer Programming, Vol. 3: Sorting and Searching*, Addison-Wesley, 1973 (1st Edition), 1998 (2nd Edition). 47, 51
17. A. N. Kolmogorov, Three approaches to the quantitative definition of information. *Problems Inform. Transmission*, 1(1):1–7, 1965. 38
18. J. Komlós, J. Pintz, and E. Szemerédi, On Heilbronn's triangle problem, *J. London Math. Soc.*, (2) 24(1981), 385–396. 40, 46
19. J. Komlós, J. Pintz, and E. Szemerédi, A lower bound for Heilbronn's problem, *J. London Math. Soc.*, 25(1982), 13–24. 40
20. M. Li and P. M. B. Vitányi, *An Introduction to Kolmogorov Complexity and its Applications*, Springer-Verlag, New York, 2nd Edition, 1997. 37, 39, 41, 49
21. M. Nielsen, I. Huang, *Quantum Computation and Quantum Information*, Cambridge University Press, 2000. 37
22. D. Mackenzie, On a roll, *New Scientist*, November 6, 1999, 44–48. 37, 41
23. W. Blum, Geometrisch Eingekreist, *Die Zeit*, April 13, 2000 (#16), p. 40. 37
24. D. Mackenzie, Le hasard ne joue pas aux de's, *Courrier International*, December 23, 1999 – January 5, 2000 (#41), p. 477–478. 37
25. A. M. Odlyzko, J. Pintz, and K. B. Stolarsky, Partitions of planar sets into small triangles, *Discrete Math.*, 57(1985), 89–97. 40

26. A. Papernov and G. Stasevich, A method for information sorting in computer memories, *Problems Inform. Transmission*, 1:3(1965), 63–75. 47

27. C. G. Plaxton, B. Poonen and T. Suel, Improved lower bounds for Shellsort, *Proc. 33rd IEEE Symp. Foundat. Comput. Sci.*, pp. 226–235, 1992. 47, 51

28. V. R. Pratt, *Shellsort and Sorting Networks*, Ph. D. Thesis, Stanford Univ., 1972. 47

29. K. F. Roth, On a problem of Heilbronn, *J. London Math Society*, 26(1951), 198–204. 40, 41

30. K. F. Roth, On a problem of Heilbronn II, *Proc. London Math Society*, (3) 25(1972), 193–212. 40

31. K. F. Roth, On a problem of Heilbronn III, *Proc. London Math Society*, (3) 25(1972), 543–549. 40

32. K. F. Roth, Estimation of the area of the smallest triangle obtained by selecting three out of n points in a disc of unit area, *Proc. Symp. Pure Mathematics 24*, AMS, Providence, 1973, pp. 251–262. 40

33. K. F. Roth, Developments in Heilbronn's triangle problem, *Advances in Math.* 22(1976), 364–385. 40

34. W. M. Schmidt, On a problem of Heilbronn, *J. London Math. Soc.*, (2) 4(1972), 545–550. 40

35. R. Sedgewick, Analysis of Shellsort and related algorithms, *Proc. 4th Annual European Symposium on Algorithms*, Lecture Notes in Computer Science, Vol. 1136, Springer-Verlag, Berlin, 1–11. 47

36. R. Sedgewick, Open problems in the analysis of sorting and searching algorithms, Presented at *Workshop on Prob. Analysis of Algorithms*, Princeton, 1997 (http://www.cs.princeton/ rs). 47, 51

37. D. L. Shell, A high-speed sorting procedure, *Commun. ACM*, 2:7(1959), 30–32. 47

38. Tian Zheng Ping, On the problem of Heilbronn type, *Northeast. Math. J.*, 10(1994), 215–216. 40

39. L. Yang, J. Z. Zhang, and Z. B. Zeng, Heilbronn problem for five points, Int'l Centre Theoret. Physics preprint IC/91/252 (1991). 40

40. L. Yang, J. Z. Zhang, and Z. B. Zeng, A conjecture on the first several Heilbronn numbers and a computation, *Chinese Ann. Math.* Ser. A 13(1992) 503–515. 40

41. L. Yang, J. Z. Zhang, and Z. B. Zeng, On the Heilbronn numbers of triangular regions, *Acta Math. Sinica*, 37(1994), 678–689. 40

42. P. Vitányi, Three approaches to the quantitative definition of information in an individual pure quantum state, *Proc. 15th IEEE Computational Complexity Conference*, 2000, 263–270. 37

43. A. C. C. Yao, An analysis of $(h, k, 1)$-Shellsort, *J. of Algorithms*, 1(1980), 14–50. 47

BioInformatics: Databases + Data Mining
(abstract)

CWI, Amsterdam, The Netherlands
arno@cwi.nl

Due to technological advances in, e. g. DNA and protein research, there is a sharp increase in the amount of data generated by molecular biology research. In turn this poses a set of new problems for computer science research. These problems are collectively known as *Bioinformatics*. In this talk, I will focus on two areas in this new field, viz., databases and data mining.

It is well known that DNA can be represented as a string over the alphabet ATCG and that similar observations hold for the other biological macro molecules, RNA and proteins. So, in principle, storing such data in a traditional relational database is straight forward, even though the strings vary in length.

Retrieving such data (querying the database) is, however, far less simple. For, it is not based on criteria such as (sub)string equality but on the *evolutionary similarity* of (sub)strings. This entails that:

- That the strings may contain gaps with regard to each other. That is, a substring that is consecutive in one string may match an ensemble of two or more substrings in the other.
- Character matching is not necessarily character equality. Rather, it is very well possible that a character changes in the course of evolution.

In other words, in principle any two strings match! However, one can compute the probability that two strings derive from the same ancestor in evolution. This probability is based on the existence and length of gaps as well as the frequency of which character changes. Clearly, if one retrieves strings, the most probable strings should be retrieved.

Examples of other requirements on DBMSs are the need for meta data (who discovered this string, when and how), including the need for versioning and the need to store and query 3D molecular structures.

The explosion of new data poses other problems too. An example is one of an embarresment of riches: what to do with all this data? The questions one would want to be answered are, of course, known. But how to answer those questions given the data is far less obvious.

Traditionally in science, data is generated to test a specific hypothesis. In molecular biology, the data is generated because it is assumed that it contains the key to answer important questions. This suggests that data mining techniques may play an important role in this area. And, indeed, there are quite a few examples of succesful applications.

To name a few of the many problems:

V. Hlaváč, K. G. Jeffery, and J. Wiedermann (Eds.): SOFSEM 2000, LNCS 1963, pp. 54–55, 2000.
© Springer-Verlag Berlin Heidelberg 2000

- Gene discovery: which parts of a DNA sequence actually encodes a gene?
- Philogenetic trees: trace back the most likely path of evolution given genomes of species.
- Reconstruct metabolic pathways: determine the processes and their likely order that take place in a cell.
- Drug discovery: one of the holy grails of this area, given all this biomolecular data is it possible to determine likely cures for diseases?

Algorithms for Rational Agents[*]

Amir Ronen

School of Computer Science and Engineering,
The Hebrew University of Jerusalem
amiry@cs.huji.ac.il

Abstract. Many recent applications of interest involve self-interested participants. As such participants, termed agents, may manipulate the algorithm for their *own* benefit, a new challenge emerges: The design of algorithms and protocols that perform well when the agents behave according to their own self-interest.

This led several researchers to consider computational models that are based on a sub-field of game-theory and micro-economics called mechanism design.

This paper introduces this topic mainly through examples. It demonstrates that in many cases selfishness can be satisfactorily overcome, surveys some of the recent trends in this area and presents new challenging problems.

The paper is mostly based on classic results from mechanism design as well as on recent work by the author and others.

1 Introduction

A large part of research in computer science is concerned with protocols and algorithms for inter-connected collections of computers. The designer of such an algorithm or protocol always makes an implicit assumption that the participating computers will act as instructed — except, perhaps, for the faulty or malicious ones. While this assumption seems obvious for "traditional" applications programmed by a single entity, it cannot be taken for granted when considering, for example, applications which are intended to operate on the Internet. Many of these applications involve self-interested participants (e. g. individual users and private companies). Such participants have their *own* goals and preferences and are likely to follow their own self interest. Algorithmic problems that stem from such applications give rise to a new and exciting challenge: The design of algorithms and protocols that perform well when the participants behave selfishly.

Applications that involve self-interested parties emerge from several domains: Participants in an electronic trade pursue their personal profit, users of a wide area network want their own traffic to be optimized and software agents are self-interested by definition. Problems that stem from such applications are essentially different from traditional algorithmic problems. To make this difference

---

[*] This research was supported by grants from the Israeli academy of science and the Israeli ministry of science.

V. Hlaváč, K. G. Jeffery, and J. Wiedermann (Eds.): SOFSEM 2000, LNCS 1963, pp. 56–70, 2000.
© Springer-Verlag Berlin Heidelberg 2000

concrete, consider an imaginary system aimed to utilize resources on the Internet:

Ideally, such a system would function like a regular distributed system. It would efficiently allocate CPU-intensive jobs to CPU-servers, store data in computers with free disk space, extract necessary information from various available databases and combine the services of the many software packages found on the Internet. Beyond many difficult coordination and optimization problems which need to be overcome, such a system faces a major novel challenge: All these resources *belong* to self-interested parties (such as private companies or institutions) and there is no a-priory reason that these parties will allow the system to freely use them, in particular when they are costly. The system may, thus, need to provide some motivation for these owners to "play along". Supplying such motivation is likely to involve some sort of payment. Payment, real or virtual, carries however problems of its own. A payment model which is not carefully designed can easily lead into a situation where manipulating the system's algorithms and protocols can significantly increase the profits of the participants (for example, participants may pretend that they are not capable of performing tasks which are not profitable enough). Such manipulations might severely damage the efficiency of such a system, preventing it to accomplish the purposes which it was designed for. As we shall see, the algorithmic and the monetary aspects of protocols for such systems are tightly coupled. Any solution for an algorithmic problem that involves selfish participants should simultaneously deal with these two aspects. Solving such problems is therefore a difficult and exciting challenge!

Mechanism design is a sub field of game theory and micro economics which deals with the design of protocols for rational agents. Generally, a mechanism design problem can be described as the task of selecting from a collection of feasible games, a game which will yield desirable results for the designer. Specifically, the theory has focused on problems where the goal is to satisfactorily aggregate privately known preferences of several agents towards a "social choice".

An application of this theory within the framework of computer science is by no means straight-forward. There are two main reasons for that:

Different goals. Traditionally, mechanism design theory was developed for applications that arise from economics. Naturally, problems that stem from computer science applications have different goals and assumptions.

Computational complexity. Mechanism design theory ignores the computational aspect of the protocol. This turns essentially all solutions proposed by this theory to be impractical for computationally complex problems.

In recent years, problems which lie on the border of computer science and mechanism design were studied by several researchers. Numerous fundamental result however are yet to be discovered.

This paper is intended to serve as an introduction for this topic. It demonstrates that in many cases selfishness can be satisfactorily overcome, surveys some of the recent trends in this area and presents new challenging problems. The paper is mostly based on classic results from mechanism design as well as on recent work by the author and others.

The rest of this paper is organized as follows: Sections 2 and 3 exemplify mechanism design problems that arise in computer science and demonstrates that they can be handled. Section 4 formally defines mechanism design problems and their valid solutions, describes the celebrated VCG mechanisms and shows some of their properties. Section 5 discusses the computational aspects of mechanisms focusing on the important problem of combinatorial auctions. Section 6 considers problems which cannot be addressed by the standard tools of mechanism design theory. Section 8 surveys recent work on the intersection between computer science and mechanism design and Section 9 describes some fundamental open issues.

2 A Simple Routing Problem

We begin with a problem which has a very simple combinatorial structure:

Consider a communication network consisting of $k > 1$ parallel links between two points s and t. Each link e is owned by a different agent (e. g. a company) and the cost c_e of sending a message along this link is *privately known* to its owner.

A natural requirement from a "traditional" network is to be efficient, i. e. to send each message from s to t along the cheapest link. Clearly, such efficiency cannot be guaranteed in a network where resources are privately owned. We would like however, to construct a protocol that will reach efficiency under reasonable assumptions on the agents' behavior.

2.1 Some Naive Solutions

First, consider a "traditional" algorithmic approach for such a problem: The algorithm first requests from each agent to report its cost. It then chooses the link with the minimal declared cost and routes the message along that link.

Although this approach is "correct" from an algorithmic perspective, it is likely to fail. Clearly, a rational agent will try to avoid being chosen by declaring a very high cost. Since such a strategy has nothing to do with the real cost of the agent, the chosen link will be arbitrary.

It seems therefore unavoidable that a mechanism (a protocol) for such a problem will also be able to *pay* the agents. Such payment however needs to be done carefully.

Consider for example a mechanism which is identical to the previous one except that it pays the chosen agent a fixed amount (say \$100) per message. Such a mechanism may have two potential problems: First, all agents with costs which are higher than \$100 are likely to declare arbitrarily high values. As this may include all agents, a problem similar to the previous might occur. Second, agents with costs which are lower than \$100 are likely to declare arbitrarily small values. This is likely to reduce the efficiency of the network.

An auction may seem a better idea: each agent will declare her cost d_e, the mechanism will select the link with the lowest declared cost and pay the corresponding agent d_e units of currency. Note however that an agent can gain money only if she declares a cost which is higher than her actual cost. Her optimal declaration depends heavily on the declarations of the others. As even the costs of the other agents are not known to her, it is hard to give a convincing prediction of what will happen[1].

Another possible solution is the following multi-rounded protocol: In each round j the mechanism declares a payment p_j starting from a low value and incrementing it. The protocol stops when the first agent accepts the offer. This agent will be payed the p_{j*} units of currency where $j*$ denotes the last round. Although such a protocol is likely to make the right decision and route the message through the cheapest link, it might use a lot of communication. In the next subsection we'll see that we can achieve the same result in a single round!

2.2   A Good Solution

Consider the following solution (hereby called a mechanism) to our routing problem: Each agent is first required to declare its cost. Let d_e denote the declaration of e's agent. Note that it may be falsified. The mechanism selects the link with the minimal declared cost (ties are broken arbitrarily) and pays the owner of this link the minimum among the declared costs of the other agents, i.e. $\min_{e' \neq e} d_{e'}$.

Let us examine some of the properties of this mechanism:

Truthfulness. It is not difficult to see that it is *always* for the benefit of an agent to declare her *true* cost to the mechanism. In a game theoretic language, truth-telling is a dominant strategy. In the literature, a mechanism with this property is called *truthful* or *incentive compatible*. One possible way to prove the truthfulness of this mechanism is to observe that the selected agent is payed an amount that equals the *maximal* (supremum) declaration that will still allow her to win. This can be thought of as if the mechanism offers the agent a payment of 0 if she is not selected and a payment of $\min_{e' \neq e} d_{e'}$ if she is. These two payments do not depend on the agent's declaration. The only thing one must verify is that the agent's benefit is maximized when she declares her true cost. This is obvious since a (truthful) agent is selected iff her costs are lower than the maximal amount that allows her to be selected, i.e. iff her costs are lower than her payment. A rational agent will therefore report her *true* cost to the mechanism.

Participation constraints and zero normalization. Another desirable property of such a mechanism is that the profit of a truthful agent is *guaranteed* to be non-negative. In many cases the agent's participation is voluntary and therefore this property is important. In the literature, a mechanism with this property is said to satisfy *participation constraints*. We shall say that a mechanism is *zero normalized* if an agent who is not selected by the mechanism is always payed zero. In principal, this property implies participation

---

[1] Analysis of such situations under various assumptions do exist in the economic and game theoretic literature.

constraints except for some degenerate mechanisms. From reasons, similar to the truthfulness of the proposed mechanism, it is also zero normalized and in particular satisfies participation constraints.

Specification compatibility. The fact that our mechanism is truthful and satisfies participation constraints has a strong influence on the agent's behavior. A rational agent will choose to cooperate with the mechanism and to reveal her true cost to it. When the agents act rationally, our mechanism makes the *right decision* and selects the link with the minimal cost. We shall call a mechanism *specification compatible* if when the agents report their true input (cost in our case), the problem's specification is met.

The proposed mechanism is likely to make the right decision despite the fact that the "input" of the problem is not known to it and that it is exposed to agents' manipulations!

Definition 1 (good mechanism). We say that a mechanism is *good* if it is truthful, zero normalized, satisfies participation constraints and is specification compatible.

Note that the suggested mechanism is very simple in two perspectives. First, the agents' dominant strategies are straight-forward. Second, it is a single rounded protocol. Throughout this paper we shall mostly seek for good mechanisms.

3   A More Complicated Routing Problem

We now complicate the example in Section 2 and consider a general network topology. Formally:

We have a communication network modeled by a directed graph G, and two special nodes s and t in it. Each link e is owned by a different agent and the cost c_e of sending a message along this link is *privately* known to its owner. The goal of the mechanism is to find the cheapest path from s to t. We will assume for simplicity that the graph is bi-connected.

Note that unlike the previous problem, each possible solution may involve several agents. Despite that, we can construct a good mechanism for this problem as well.

3.1   A Good Mechanism

The mechanism first requires each agent to report its cost to it. Let us denote the declaration of an agent that corresponds to a link e by d_e. According to these declarations, the mechanism selects the cheapest path from s to t. The trick is in the payment function: agent e is given 0 if e is not in the chosen path and $p_e = d_{G|e=\infty} - d_{G|e=0}$ if it is. Here $d_{G|e=\infty}$ denotes the cost of the cheapest path which does not contain e (according to the inputs reported), and $d_{G|e=0}$ is the cost of the cheapest path when the cost of e is assumed to be zero (again according to the reported types).

It is a good exercise to prove the correctness of this mechanisms directly. In fact, the mechanism is a private case of *VCG* mechanisms. Their properties will be proven in Section 4.2.

3.2 Further Comments

The proposed mechanism solves this problem in a central fashion requiring all agents to report directly to it. For many applications, a real *distributed* mechanism is necessary. This is a major open issue which gives rise to many open problems. For example, what is the influence of the network topology on the agents' strategies? How good can a mechanism perform when only local decisions are allowed? Etc.

Many other natural open questions can be asked on such a network. In particular, several problems emerge when considering settings in which messages are coming *stochastically* into the network. This affects both the requirements from the mechanism and the agents' strategies.

Finally, the calculation of the payments of the suggested mechanism hinders an interesting algorithmic problem: Is it possible to do better than calculating the payment of each agent on the chosen path separately?

4 Mechanism Design

The problems that were presented in the previous sections differ from usual algorithmic problems in two main aspects. Firstly, the problems' input was not accessible to the mechanism but was privately held by the participants. Secondly, while the goal of the mechanism was to maximize the efficiency of the network, each participant had a totally different goal which was to maximize her own profit.

Similar problems has been studied for several decades by economists and game theorist within the framework of mechanism design theory. Generally, a mechanism design problem could be described as task of selecting from a collection of feasible games one that will yield results which are desired by the designer. Specifically, the theory focuses on various variants of the canonical problem presented in Section 4.1. An introduction to this field can be found at [18, chapter 23].

As we shall see, the previous examples can all be described as sub-cases of this canonical problem. However, many additional questions emerge when applying mechanism design theory to applications that stem from computer science applications.

4.1 Mechanism Design Problems and Solutions

In this section we shall formally define the canonical problem of mechanism design and its valid solutions.

Definition 2 (The Canonical Problem). A *mechanism design problem* is described by the following:

1. A finite set O of *allowed outputs*.
2. Each agent $i = (1, \ldots, n)$ has a real function $v^i(o \in O)$ called her *valuation* or *type*. This is a quantification of her benefit from each possible output o in terms of some common currency. v^i is *privately* known to agent i. The space V^i of all possible valuation functions is called the *type space* of the agent.
3. If the mechanism's output is o and in addition the mechanism hands an agent p^i units of this currency, then her *utility* u^i equals[2] $v^i(o) + p^i$. This utility is what the *agent* aims to optimize.
4. The goal of the *mechanism* is to select an output $o \in O$ that maximizes the *total welfare* $g(v, o) = \sum_i v^i(o)$.

Let us try to present the example of Section 3 within the framework of the canonical problem. The set of allowable outputs contains all paths from s to t. The valuation of agent e from each possible output o, equals $-c_e$ if e is in the chosen path o, or 0 otherwise. The utility of each agent equals the sum of her valuation from the chosen output and her payment. The goal of the mechanism is to select a path with minimal total cost. Clearly, such a path maximizes the total welfare. This problem can therefore be presented as a sub-case of the canonical problem.

In a direct revelation mechanism, the participants are simply asked to reveal their types to the mechanism. Based on these declarations the mechanism then computes the output o and the payment p^i for each of the agents.

Definition 3 (A mechanism). A *(direct revelation) mechanism* is a pair $m = (k, p)$ such that:

- The *output function* $k(.)$ accepts as input a vector $w = (w^1, \ldots, w^n)$ of declared valuation functions and returns an output $k(w) \in O$.
- The *payment function* $p(w) = (p^1(w), \ldots, p^n(w))$ returns a real vector. This is the payment handed by the mechanism to each of the agents.

A revelation mechanism computes its output according to the type declarations of the agents. As agents may *lie* to the mechanism, it should be carefully designed such that it will be for the *benefit* of each agent to reveal her true type to the mechanism.

Notation: We denote the tuple $(a^1, \ldots a^{i-1}, a^{i+1}, \ldots, a^n)$ by a^{-i}. We let (a^i, a^{-i}) denote the tuple $(a^1, \ldots, a^n)$.

Definition 4 (Truthful mechanism). A mechanism is called *truthful* if truth-telling is a dominant strategy. I. e. for every agent i of type v^i and for every type declaration w^{-i} for the other agents, the agent's utility is *maximized* when she declares her real valuation function v^i.

---

[2] This is called the quasi-linearity assumption.

A simple well known observation called the revelation principle [18, page 871] greatly facilitates the analysis of mechanism design problems. It states that in order to prove or disprove the existence of good mechanisms for a given problem, one can consider only truthful revelation mechanisms.

4.2   VCG Mechanisms

Arguably the most important result in mechanism design is the observation that the canonical problem can be solved by a class of mechanisms called *VCG* (named after Vickrey, Clarke and Groves) [36,1,8]. Intuitively, these mechanisms solve the canonical problem by identifying the utility of truthful agents with the declared total welfare.

Definition 5 (VCG mechanism). A mechanism $m = (k, p)$ belongs to the *VCG* family if:

- $k(w)$ maximizes the total welfare according to w.
- The payment is calculated according to the *VCG formula* ($h^i()$ is an arbitrary function of w^{-i}):

$$p^i(w) = \sum_{j \neq i} w^j(k(w)) + h^i(w^{-i}).$$

Proof. Assume by contradiction that the mechanism is not truthful. Then there exists an agent i of type v^i, a type declaration w^{-i} for the other agents, and $w^i \neq v^i$ such that $v^i(k((v^i, w^{-i}))) + \sum_{j \neq i} w^j(k((v^i, w^{-i}))) + h^i(w^{-i}) < v^i(k((w^i, w^{-i}))) + \sum_{j \neq i} w^j(k((w^i, w^{-i}))) + h^i(w^{-i})$. Let $o = k((v^i, w^{-i}))$ denote the chosen output when the agent is truthful and let $o' = k((w^i, w^{-i}))$. The above inequality implies that $g((v^i, w^{-i}), o) < g((v^i, w^{-i}), o')$. This contradicts the optimality of k.   □

It is worth notify that weighted versions of this method are possible as well (e. g. [28,26]). To date, *VCG* is the only general known method for the construction of truthful mechanisms. Roberts [28] showed that under certain conditions, VCG mechanisms are indeed the only truthful mechanisms. These conditions however are not satisfied for many natural problems.

4.2.1   Clarke's Mechanism.
Clarke's mechanism is a VCG mechanism which satisfies participation constraints and zero-normalization. (It is not feasible to every mechanism design problem, but it is for most of the natural ones.) The mechanism chooses $h^i(w^{-i})$ to be the maximal welfare that can be achieved if agent i would choose not to participate. Formally if there exists a type $\underline{v}^i$ such that for each v^{-i}, $g((\underline{v}^i, v^{-i}), k((\underline{v}^i, v^{-i}))) \leq g((v^i, v^{-i}), k((v^i, v^{-i})))$, then the mechanism defines $h^i(w^{-i}) = g((\underline{v}^i, v^{-i}), k((\underline{v}^i, v^{-i})))$. For the example of Section 3 we can define $\underline{v}^i$ as an infinite cost. In this case the output algorithm never selects a path that goes through this agent's link. The mechanism satisfies participation constraints as the total utility of a truthful agent i equals

$g((v^i, v^{-i}), k((v^i, v^{-i}))) - g((\underline{v}^i, v^{-i})) \geq 0$. It is not difficult to see that the zero normalization condition is also satisfied. The reader is welcome to verify that all the good mechanisms presented so far are Clarke mechanisms.

We shall comment again that an efficient computation of the agents' payments is an interesting algorithmic challenge.

5   The Computational Aspect

The theory of mechanism design does not take into consideration the computational complexity of the mechanism. In recent years, mechanisms have become quite complicated, requiring implementation on computer systems. Consequently, the necessity of a theory that will regard both the computational and the game theoretic aspects of mechanisms became clear to many researchers. In this section we bring as an example, the important problem of combinatorial auctions and briefly survey works that are trying to cope with its computational difficulty.

5.1   Combinatorial Auctions

The problem of combinatorial auctions has been extensively studied in recent years (see e. g. [16,32,7,9,24]). The importance of this problem is twofold. First, several important applications rely on it (e. g. the FCC auction sequence [19] that raised Billions of dollars). Second, it is a generalization of many other problems of interest, in particular in the field of electronic commerce.

The problem: A seller wishes to sell a set S of items (radio spectra licenses, electronic devices, etc.) to a group of agents who desire them. Each agent i has, for every subset $s \subseteq S$ of the items, a number $v^i(s)$ that represents how much s is worth for her. We assume that $v^i(.)$ is privately known to the agent.

We take two standard additional assumptions on the type space of the agents:

No externalities. The valuation of each agent depends only on the items allocated to her, i. e. $\{v^i(s)|s \subseteq S)\}$ completely represents the agent's valuation.

Free disposal. Items have non-negative values. I. e. if $s \subseteq t$ then $v^i(s) \leq v^i(t)$. Also $v^i(\phi) = 0$.

Note that the problem allows items to be complementary, i. e. $v^i(S \cup T) \geq v^i(S) + v^i(T)$ or substitutes, i. e. $v^i(S \cup T) \leq v^i(S) + v^i(T)$ (S and T are disjoint). For example a buyer may be willing to pay \$200 for TV set, \$150 for a VCR, \$450 for both and only \$200 for two VCRs.

When an agent's payment is p^i for a set of items s^i, her overall utility is $p^i + v^i(s^i)$. Note that p^i is always non-positive. This utility is what each agent tries to optimize. For example, an agent prefers to buy a \$1000 valued VCR for \$600 gaining \$400 to buying a \$1500 valued VCR for \$1250.

In a VCG mechanism for such an auction, the participants are first required to reveal their valuation functions to the mechanism. The mechanism then computes, according to the declarations of the agents, an allocation s that maximizes the total welfare. The payment for each of the agents is calculated according to the VCG formula.

Consider however the computational task faced by such a mechanism. After the types are declared, the mechanism needs to select, among all possible allocations, one that maximizes the total welfare. This problem is known to be NP-Complete. Therefore, unless the number of agents and items is very small, such a mechanism is computationally infeasible. Note that even the problem of finding an allocation that approximates the optimal allocation within a reasonable factor is NP-Complete (under the common complexity assumption that RP ≠ Co-NP, see e. g. [32,16]).

5.2   Coping with the Computational Complexity of Combinatorial Auctions

Several researchers in recent years have considered the computational difficulty of combinatorial auctions. Many researchers focused on the algorithmic side of the problem [32,7,9,24,35]. These efforts include various tractable sub-cases where additional limitations where assumed on the agents' valuations and also several heuristics. A truthful mechanism which does not fall into the VCG category was constructed for a sub-case of combinatorial auction at [16].

A recent paper [27] by Nisan and the author studies VCG mechanisms where the optimal algorithm is replaced by by a computationally tractable approximation algorithm or heuristic. The paper shows that it is impossible to construct, in this method, truthful computationally feasible mechanisms that produce reasonable results for combinatorial auctions as well as for many cost minimization problems. Since VCG is the only general method known to date for the construction of truthful mechanisms, there is not much hope for solving mechanism design problems by truthful mechanisms. The paper introduces a slight relaxation of the truthfulness called feasible truthfulness. It shows that under reasonable assumptions on the agents, it is possible to turn *any* VCG-based mechanism into a feasibly truthful one, using an additional appeal mechanism. The resulting mechanism also satisfies participation constraints and zero normalization.

The proposed mechanism may also be used to overcome another problem that emerges from combinatorial auctions — that a full description of the agents' valuation may also be intractable. Thus, it is not clear how to construct an "interface" between the agent and the mechanism [24]. For details see [29].

The results of [27] however have not yet been checked experimentally.

6   Beyond the Canonical Problem: Task Scheduling

The problems that we have presented so far are all sub-cases of the canonical problem and henceforth can be addressed by VCG mechanisms. For many problems that stem from computer science applications this is not likely to be the case. First, in many cases, in particular for task allocation problems, the designer's goal is dependent, not on agents' valuations but on other private parameters such as her capability to perform various tasks. Secondly, even when such a dependency does exist, the objective of the designer may not be to maximize the total welfare.

Nisan and the author studied [26] (a preliminary version appeared at [25]), the following representative problem:

There are k tasks that need to be allocated to n agents. Each agent i's type is, for each task j, the minimum amount of time t_j^i in which she is capable of performing this task. The goal is to minimize the completion time of the last assignment (the make-span). The valuation of an agent i is the negation of the total time she has spent on the tasks allocated to her.

The results of this paper refer to three different models — the "classical" model of mechanism design, a model where the mechanism can use randomization and a model where additional natural verification information is available to the mechanism. In particular the paper shows that when additional verification information is available, the problem can be *optimally* solved. This result remains true even without the (artificial) assumption that the agent's valuation equals the negation of her working time.

Many problems were left open in this paper. In particular it was conjectured that no classical mechanism can approximate this problem by a factor better than the number of agents. However, only a basic lower bound of 2 was proven. The limitations of the model that allows verification are also not known.

7   Revenue Considerations

So far we have treated money only as a mean of motivating the agents to behave well. For many applications however, revenue is a major concern. Very little is currently known about the revenue of truthful mechanisms. In this section we demonstrate that many beautiful open questions can be asked even on a very simple problem — the allocation of a single object. This section is based on [29].

The Problem: A *single object allocation* problem is a mechanism design problem of the following form:

- There are $n + 1$ possible outputs. An output $i > 0$ means that the object is allocated to agent i. 0 means that the object is not allocated to any agent.
- The type of each agent is any strictly positive number.

We shall call a mechanism for this problem *agent-compatible* if it is truthful and satisfies zero-normalization and participation constraints. We shall first characterize these mechanisms.

Definition 6 (proper function). An output function $x\colon R_{++}^n \to \{0, \ldots, n\}$ is called *proper* if for every type vector $t = t^1, \ldots, t^n$, and an agent i such that $i = x(t)$, if $s^i \geq t^i$ then $i = x((s^i, t^{-i}))$.

In other words if an agent wins the object with type t^i she will keep winning when her type increases.

Definition 7 (implied payment). Let x be a proper function. We say that a payment function p is *implied* by x, if $-p^i(t)$ is 0 when $i \neq x(t)$ or equals $\inf\{s^i | i = x((s^i, t^{-i}))\}$ when $i = x(t)$.

In other words i pays zero if she looses or the minimal type that enables her to win the object. It is not difficult to see that the infimum exists.

Theorem 1. *A mechanism for this problem is agent-compatible iff it is of the form $m = (k, p)$ where:*

- $k(.)$ *is proper.*
- $p(.)$ *is implied by k.*

Given a probability distribution on the type space, there are several interesting open questions that emerge. Here are a few examples:

- Does a polynomial algorithm that chooses a mechanism that maximizes the expected revenue exist?
- Given also a risk parameter $0 < r < 1$ and a probability $\hat{p}$, is it possible to find a mechanism that in probability at least $\hat{p}$ generates a revenue of at least $r \cdot \max_i t^i$?
- For the above questions: Each agent-compatible mechanism defines a boolean function of the type space (1 means good, e. g. close to the maximum possible revenue, and 0 means bad). Is the resulting family learnable in the PAC sense?

8   Work on the Border of Computer Science and Mechanism Design

Problems on the border of computer science and mechanism design were studied by several researchers in recent years. This section briefly surveys these works.

Many researchers studied the problem of combinatorial auctions. This line of research is surveyed in Section 5.1. Other cases where mechanism design models were applied to computational problems include resource and task allocation problems [25,39,38], communication networks [5,14,13], multi-agent systems [30,40,4] and others [37,15,6,34,17]. Several aspects of mechanism design were recently studied in [22,21,15,33]. The computational aspect of mechanisms for cost sharing was studied at [5]. This recent paper investigates two ingredients absent from this work — a distributed model and budget balance requirement. These two fundamental aspects are surely to play a significant role in future research in this area. The implementation of mechanism design theory for Internet environments may require new assumptions. This issue is discussed at [31,21].

Another line of research which is related to mechanism design are models which are based on markets [6,10,20,23,23,3]. The main difference between these models and mechanism design is that instead of doing strategic manipulations, the participants are assumed to "honestly response to prices" (i. e. behave as price-takers).

Problems that stem from electronic commerce have a tight relationship with mechanism design and game theory and economics in general. Several papers on these topics can be found at [11,2].

Finally, works in which the author was involved were surveyed in Sections 5.1 and 6.

9   Further Research

This paper demonstrates that in many cases it is possible to design protocols that perform well despite the selfishness of the participants. However, there are numerous directions for further research. I mention some of the most basic ones: The computational power of strategy-proof mechanisms is far from being understood, even in the classical model. Probabilistic models and further relaxation of the concept of dominant strategies are yet to be explored. Concrete connections between mechanism design and computational complexity are yet to be discovered. Moreover, in practice, mechanisms will have to handle additional issues like irrationality and collusive behavior of the agents. Issues like revenue maximization, risk, and budget balance are very important to many applications. In a lot of cases, mechanisms will have to be carried out in a "real" distributed environment. Finally, solution concepts other than dominant strategy implementation (e. g. Bayesian Nash) may be considered.

I am certain that all these issues and a lot of others will provide researchers with many beautiful research problems in the years to follow!

Acknowledgments

I would like to thank Noam Nisan and Inbal Ronen for comments on earlier drafts of this paper.

References

1. E. H. Clarke. Multipart pricing of public goods. *Public Choice*, pages 17–33, 1971. 63
2. *Proceedings of the first ACM conference on electronic commerce (EC99)*, 1999. 68
3. Bernardo Huberman (ed.). *The Ecology of Computation.* Elsevier Science Publishers/North-Holland, 1988. 67
4. Eithan Ephrati. *Planning and consensus among autonomous agents.* PhD thesis, Hebrew University of Jerusalem, Departement of Computer Science, 1993. 67
5. Joan Feigenbaum, Christos Papadimitriou, and Scott Shenker. Sharing the cost of multicast transmissions. In *Thirty-Second Annual ACM Symposium on Theory of Computing (STOC00)*, May 2000. 67
6. Donald F. Ferguson, Christos Nikolaou, and Yechiam Yemini. Economic models for allocating resources in computer systems. In Scott Clearwater, editor, *Market-Based Control: A Paradigm for Distributed Resource Allocation.* World Scientific, 1995. 67

7. Yuzo Fujishima, Kevin Leyton-Brown, and Yoav Shoham. Taming the computational complexity of combinatorial auctions: Optimal and approximate approaches. In *IJCAI-99*, 1999. 64, 65

8. T. Groves. Incentives in teams. *Econometrica*, pages 617–631, 1973. 63

9. R. M. Harstad, Rothkopf M. H., and Pekec A. Computationally manageable combinatorial auctions. Technical Report 95-09, DIMACS, Rutgers university, 1995. 64, 65

10. Brnardo A. Huberman and Tad Hogg. Distributed computation as an economic system. *Journal of Economic Perspectives*, pages 141–152, 1995. 67

11. *Proceedings of The first international conference on information and computation economies (ICE-98)*, 1998. 68

12. Paul Klemperer. Auction theory: a guide to the literature. *Journal of economic surveys*, pages 227–286, 1999.

13. Y.A Korilis, A. A. Lazar, and A. Orda. Architecting noncooperative networks. *IEEE Journal on Selected Areas in Communication (Special Issue on Advances in the Fundamentals of Networking)*, 13(7):1241–1251, September 1991. 67

14. Elias Koutsoupias and Christos Papadimitriou. Worst-case equilibria. In *STACS 99, the 16th Annual Symposium on Theoretical Aspects of Computer Science*, March 1999. 67

15. Ron Lavi and Noam Nisan. Competitive analysis of online auctions. To appear. 67

16. Daniel Lehmann, Liadan O'Callaghan, and Yoav Shoham. Truth revelation in rapid, approximately efficient combinatorial auctions. In *ACM Conference on Electronic Commerce (EC-99)*, pages 96–102, November 1999. 64, 65

17. Kevin Leyton-Brown, Moshe Tennenholtz, and Yoav Shoham. Bidding clubs: Institutionalized collusion in auctions. To appear. 67

18. A. Mas-Collel, Whinston W., and J. Green. *Microeconomic Theory*. Oxford university press, 1995. 61, 63

19. J. McMillan. Selling spectrum rights. *Journal of Economic Perspectives*, pages 145–162, 1994. 64

20. Welleman Michael. Market-oriented programming. Web Page: http://ai.eecs.umich.edu/people/wellman/MOP.html. 67

21. Dov Monderer and Moshe Tennenholtz. Distributed games. To appear in Games and Economic Behaviour. 67

22. Dov Monderer and Moshe Tennenholtz. Optimal auctions revisited. In *Proceedings of the Fifteenth National Conference on Artificial Intelligence (AAAI-98)*, 1998. 67

23. Miller M. S. and Drexler K. E. *The Ecology of Computation*, chapter Markets and Computation: Agoric open systems. North Hollan, 1988. 67

24. Noam Nisan. Bidding and allocation in combinatorial auctions. To appear. 64, 65

25. Noam Nisan and Amir Ronen. Algorithmic mechanism design (extended abstract). In *The Thirty First Annual ACM symposium om Theory of Computing (STOC99)*, pages 129–140, May 1999. 66, 67

26. Noam Nisan and Amir Ronen. Algorithmic mechanism design. *Games and Economic Behaviour*, 2000. To appear. 63, 66

27. Noam Nisan and Amir Ronen. Computationally feasible vcg mechanisms. Submitted to the Second ACM conference on electronic commerce (EC00), 2000. 65

28. Kevin Roberts. The characterization of implementable choise rules. In Jean-Jacques Laffont, editor, *Aggregation and Revelation of Preferences*, pages 321–349. North-Holland, 1979. Papers presented at the first European Summer Workshop of the Econometric Society. 63

29. Amir Ronen. *Solving optimization problems among selfish agents*. PhD thesis, School of Computer Science and Engineering, The Hebrew University of Jerusalem, 2000. 65, 66
30. Jeffrey S. Rosenschein and Gilad Zlotkin. *Rules of Encounter: Designing Conventions for Automated Negotiation Among Computers*. MIT Press, 1994. 67
31. Tuomas W. Sandholm. Limitations of the vickrey auction in computational multiagent systems. In *Proceedings of the Second International Conference on Multiagent Systems (ICMAS-96)*, pages 299–306, Keihanna Plaza, Kyoto, Japan, December 1996. 67
32. Tuomas W. Sandholm. Approaches to winner determination in combinatorial auctions. *Decision Support Systems*, to appear. 64, 65
33. Y. Shoham and Tennenholtz M. Rational computation and the coomunication complexity of auctions. To appear. 67
34. Yoav Shoham and Katsumi Tanaka. A dynamic theory of incentives in multi-agent systems (preliminary report). In *Proceedings of the Fifteenth International Joint Conferences on Artificial Intelligence*, pages 626–631, August 1997. 67
35. Moshe Tennenholtz. Some tractable combinatorial auctions. In *the national conference on artificial intelligence (AAAI-2000)*, 2000. 65
36. W. Vickrey. Counterspeculation, auctions and competitive sealed tenders. *Journal of Finance*, pages 8–37, 1961. 63
37. Nir Vulkan and Ken Binmore. Applying game theory to automated negotiation. To appear. 67
38. W. E. Walsh and M. P. Wellman. A market protocol for decentralized task allocation: Extended version. In *The Proceedings of the Third International Conference on Multi-Agent Systems (ICMAS-98)*, 1998. 67
39. W. E. Walsh, M. P. Wellman, P. R. Wurman, and J. K. MacKie-Mason. Auction protocols for decentralized scheduling. In *Proceedings of The Eighteenth International Conference on Distributed Computing Systems (ICDCS-98)*, Amsterdam, The Netherlands, 1998. 67
40. Gilad Zlotin. *Mechanisms for Automated Negotiation among Autonomous Agents*. PhD thesis, Hebrew University of Jerusalem, Departement of Computer Science, 1994. 67

Simplified Witness Tree Arguments

Thomas Schickinger[*] and Angelika Steger

Institut für Informatik, Technische Universität München
80290 München, Germany
http://www14.in.tum.de/

Abstract. In this paper we survey some results concerning balls-into-bins-games and the power of two choices. We present a unified and rather elementary analysis for models in the parallel as well as in the sequential setting which is based on witness trees.

1 Introduction

For the balanced allocation of resources in a distributed environment randomized strategies often turn out to achieve good results. Among such strategies so-called *balls-into-bins-games* play a major role.

The common characteristics of balls-into-bins-games can be summarized as follows: A set of *jobs* is to be allocated to a set of *processing units* (short: units) in such a way that the maximum load, also called *congestion* at a single unit is minimized. The general strategy for doing this is to first choose a set of d *candidate units* for each job in a random manner. An appropriate protocol then allocates each job to exactly one of its candidate units. Such a protocol depends heavily on the model under consideration, but it should be intuitively obvious that a smaller d reduces the communication overhead within the protocol, but increases the resulting maximum load.

Surprisingly, it turns out that already the cases $d = 1$ and $d \geq 2$ are fundamentally different. For $d \geq 2$ it is often possible to achieve much better results. Consider for example the allocation of n jobs at n units where the jobs arrive sequentially and choose d units uniformly at random. The job is then allocated at a candidate unit with minimum load breaking ties arbitrarily. It is well known that the maximum load for $d = 1$ is about $\ln n / \ln \ln n$ (see e.g. [10] or [17]). It came as quite a surprise when it was shown in [2] that for $d = 2$ the maximum load is exponentially smaller, namely about $\ln \ln n / \ln d$. This phenomenon is often referred to as the *power of two choices* [15].

There is a rather broad literature on this phenomenon. An early application of the power of two choices can be found in PRAM simulations on Distributed Memory Machines (see e.g. [11,8]). Until now many different models for balls-into-bins-games and related problems have been presented and various aspects have been analysed.

---

[*] Supported by DFG-grant Ste 464/3-1.

V. Hlaváč, K. G. Jeffery, and J. Wiedermann (Eds.): SOFSEM 2000, LNCS 1963, pp. 71–87, 2000.

Two main techniques for the analysis of balls-into-bins games have emerged: layered induction and witness trees. In this paper we will concentrate on witness tree proofs since they are applicable to a larger variety of scenarios and often yield results which are more robust against modifications of the model.

Organization of the Paper. This paper is organized as follows. In Sect. 2 we present the basic models for parallel and sequential allocation problems. In Sect. 3 we introduce our generalized proof technique which is based on witness trees. In Sect. 4 and Sect. 5 this technique is applied to parallel and sequential balls-into-bins-games.

2   Two Basic Models

Among the wide variety of different balls-into-bins-games that have been analysed in the literature two fundamentally different models can be distinguished: Parallel and sequential arrival of the jobs. In the sequel we introduce these two variants using classic examples which will also serve as basis for a unified analysis. For simplicity's sake we concentrate on the case when there are exactly n jobs and n units.

2.1   Parallel Arrival

In this model the jobs arrive in parallel and may communicate with the units before they choose their final destination. The communication proceeds in synchronous rounds and the objective is to achieve low congestion using only a small number of communication rounds.

This model and similar variants have achieved much attention in the literature (see e. g. [11,8,9,6,12,13,1,18]). We will consider the model and the algorithm from [18].

A distributed protocol, the so-called *collision protocol* is used to balance the load among the units: Every job chooses $d \geq 2$ candidate units uniformly at random. Then the following steps are repeated until no active, i. e., unassigned jobs remain:

- Every unassigned job j sends a *request* for allocation to its candidate units. (Due to this one-to-one correspondence between candidate units and requests we will use these terms interchangeably.)
- If the number of jobs which want to be allocated at a certain unit exceeds a fixed threshold c then the congestion at this unit is too high and the requests cannot be satisfied. Otherwise the unit sends an acknowledgment to the pending requests. If a jobs receives one or more acknowledgments it is allocated at one of the candidate units that sent them (making an arbitrary choice in case there is more than one possibility) and becomes inactive.

Note that the number of communication rounds for this protocol is not bounded and that, in principle, the protocol may not terminate either. However, it can be shown that for appropriate values of c and t with high probability all jobs are allocated after t rounds. In other word, the protocol finds an assignment with maximum load at most c in at most t time steps.

2.2 Sequential Arrival

In this model the jobs arrive sequentially and each job has to be assigned to a processing unit immediately after its arrival. The arriving jobs may communicate with the units before they choose their final destination. However, the amount of communication should be kept small. Here we focus on the following simple and natural strategy: each job chooses $d \geq 2$ candidate units randomly and checks their current load. Then the job is allocated at a unit with lowest load. This model was introduced in [2], slight variants and improvements can e. g. be found in [2,1,4,19,3]. [14,16,7] consider some related models.

3   A Generalized Approach Using Witness Trees

In this section we introduce the technique that we will later use for the analysis of allocation processes.

3.1   Allocation Graphs

The allocation of the jobs at the units can naturally be modelled by an *allocation graph* $G = (J \cup U, E)$, where J is the set of jobs and U is the set of units. G is bipartite, i. e., the edges in E only connect jobs to units. An edge $e = (j, u)$ corresponds to a job j with candidate unit u. We will also assume that e is labelled with the number $r(e) \in \{1, \ldots, d\}$ of the request which is modelled by e.

3.1.1   Existence of Witness Subgraphs. If high congestion arises in the final allocation then a treelike *witness subgraph* can be found in G. Consider for example the collision protocol for the parallel arrival. Assume that the protocol does not terminate within t rounds. Then there must be at least one job j which survives the tth round. This can only be the case if *all* of its requests are not accepted. In other words, for any candidate unit u of the d candidate units chosen by j there must be c other jobs (which are active in the tth round) which all issue a request that conflicts with job j at unit u. The fact that these $d \cdot c$ jobs are still active in the tth round implies that they must have survived round $t - 1$. We can thus repeat the above argument for each of these $d \cdot c$ jobs[1] yielding $(d \cdot c)^2$ many jobs which must have survived round $t - 2$ and so on.

---

[1] In fact we have to modify the argument a bit because the $d \cdot c$ neighbors of the first job are only adjacent to $(d-1)$ units which are not yet part of the witness subgraph. But we will neglect that for the moment.

The basic idea behind proofs using witness subgraphs is the following: First it is shown, as we sketched before, that high congestion implies the existence of a (large) witness subgraph in the allocation graph. Then such large witness subgraphs are shown to arise with very small probability.

If the witness subgraph were indeed a tree then the analysis would be rather simple. The difficulty of this proof strategy stems from the fact that some of these jobs might actually be identical. That is, instead of $(d \cdot c)$-ary *witness trees* of depth t we get treelike witness graphs where some branches occur multiple times or where cross-edges introduce awkward dependencies. In previous approaches this usually has been taken care of by extracting a witness tree from the witness subgraph using a kind of breadth-first traversal which stops when it runs into cross edges.

3.1.2 Proof Strategy.

In this note we propose a different approach. We directly analyse the *allocation graph*, which is a *random* graph where the randomness comes from the jobs choosing their candidate units randomly. Our method for the analysis of witness trees consists of the following steps:

- First we show that high congestion implies the existence of a large witness subgraph in the allocation graph.
- Then we analyse the structure of the allocation graph and show that it is locally "treelike" with high probability. More precisely, we show that all cycles in a "small" radius can be destroyed by deleting just a few edges.
- In a last step we prove that we can still find a large witness tree after the destruction of the cycles. Such witness trees are then shown to occur with very small probability.

The bounds on the probability will be deduced using the well-known *First Moment Method* which is formulated for our purposes in the following lemma.

Lemma 1 (First Moment Method). *Consider a random graph G defined on an arbitrary probability space. Let N denote the number of subgraphs which satisfy a certain property Q. If $\mathbb{E}[N] = \mathcal{O}(n^{-\alpha})$ for $\alpha > 0$ then*

$$\Pr[\exists H \subseteq G \colon H \text{ satisfies } Q] = \Pr[N \neq 0] = \mathcal{O}(n^{-\alpha}).$$

Proof. Follows directly from Markov's inequality: $\Pr[N \geq 1] \leq \mathbb{E}[N]$.   □

3.2 Multicycles

In this section we introduce a notion which captures the idea that the allocation graph looks "almost like a tree" in a small radius.

Definition 1. A k-multicycle at vertex v of depth at most t is a tree with root v and exactly k cross edges such that the following holds:

- The depth of the tree is at most t.
- All leafs are incident to cross edges.

Obviously, the following simple facts hold for a k-multicycle of depth at most t: The degree of the root is bounded from above by $2k$. The number of vertices is at most $2kt$ and $n - m = 1 - k$.

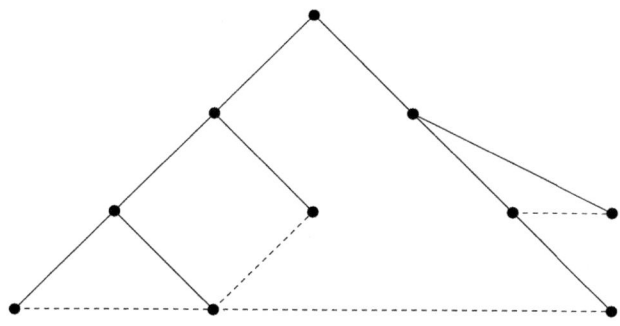

Fig. 1. A 4-multicycle of depth 3

3.2.1 Counting Multicycles.

If the edges in the multicycle occur independently with probability p, the expected number $\mathbb{E}[M_{k,t}]$ of k-multicycles of depth at most t can be estimated quite easily. Consider first the multicycles with exactly s vertices, where $s \leq 2kt$. To bound the number of possible multicycles we first choose the vertices in the multicycle (at most n^s possibilities). Then we fix the edges of the multicycle (at most 2^{s^2} possibilities) and we label the edges with the number of the corresponding request (at most d^{s-1+k} possibilities). As the edges were assumed to occur independently with probability p, each such multicycle occurs with probability exactly p^{s-1+k}. All in all we get

$$\mathbb{E}[M_{k,t}] \leq \sum_{s=1}^{2kt} n^s \cdot 2^{s^2} \cdot d^{s-1+k} \cdot p^{s-1+k} .$$

For our applications we will usually have that $t = \mathcal{O}(\log \log n)$, $d = \mathcal{O}(1)$ and $p = \mathcal{O}(1/n)$. This suffices to show that k-multicycles of depth at most t do not occur with probability $1 - n^{-\alpha}$ for $k \geq \alpha + 2$ due to the First Moment Method.

3.2.2 Turning Graphs into Trees.

The next lemma shows that subgraphs of graphs without large multicycles can be turned into trees by deleting just a small number of edges at the root.

Lemma 2. *Assume that a graph $G = (V, E)$ contains no multicycles of depth at most t with more than k cross edges. Furthermore, consider a subgraph $H = (V', E')$ of G with a root vertex $v \in V'$ where every vertex $w \in V'$ has distance at most t from v in G. Then this subgraph can be turned into a forest by deleting at most $2k$ edges at the root.*

Proof. Traverse H with a BFS starting at v and mark all cross edges C in H. The edges in C together with the paths inside the BFS-tree from the end points of the edges to the root v define a multicycle (which also has root v). Hence, it follows that $|C| \leq k$. The root of the multicycle has degree at most $2k$ and we get a forest $H' \subseteq H$ by deleting all $\leq 2k$ edges at v that belong to the multicycle. $\qquad\square$

3.3   Putting Everything Together

Now we are in a position to give a detailed description of the steps which are used in our analysis method: For an arbitrary load balancing problem we intend to show that the following claims hold for suitable values of l and α.

1. *Finding Witness Trees.* If the maximum load caused by the allocation algorithm is at least l then we can find a witness subgraph T_l. The depth of T_l is bounded from above by a suitable function $t = t(n)$.
2. *Turning Graphs Into Trees.* After the deletion of $2k$ edges at the root of a witness subgraph T_l we can still find a graph $T_{l-k'}$ which is really a tree for suitable constants k and k'.
3. *Counting Multicycles.* Let $\mathcal{M}$ denote the event that the allocation graph contains a k-multicycle of depth at most t. Then $\Pr[\mathcal{M}] \leq \frac{1}{2}n^{-\alpha}$.
4. *Counting Witness Trees.* Let $\mathcal{T}$ denote that event that the allocation graph contains a witness tree $T_{l-k'}$. Then $\Pr[\mathcal{T}] \leq \frac{1}{2}n^{-\alpha}$.

From that we can conclude that the maximum load caused by the allocation algorithm is less than l with probability $n^{-\alpha}$ by the following reasoning: It holds that $\Pr[\mathcal{M} \cup \mathcal{T}] \leq n^{-\alpha}$ by claim 3 and claim 4. Assume that neither $\mathcal{M}$ nor $\mathcal{T}$ occur and that the maximum load is $l' \geq l$. Then we can find a witness subgraph T_l by claim 1. This witness subgraph can be turned into a witness tree $T_{l-k'}$ by claim 2. This yields a contradiction, since we assumed that $\mathcal{T}$ did not occur.

4   Parallel Allocation

Now we turn to the first application of our proof strategy.

4.1   Model and Algorithm

We consider the same model as in [18]: n jobs arrive in parallel and must be allocated at n units. The jobs may communicate with the units in synchronous rounds before their allocation. We try to minimize the maximum congestion executing only few communication rounds. This is achieved using the collision protocol, which we have already described in Sect. 2.1.

We intend to prove the following theorem which is very similar to the result in [18]:

Theorem 1. *Let $\alpha > 0$, $\beta := \alpha + 4.5$ and $2 \leq t \leq \frac{1}{\beta} \ln \ln n$. Assume that n is sufficiently large that $\frac{c}{4e^2} \leq n^{0.1}$. Then the c-collision protocol with $d = 2$ terminates after at most t rounds for the threshold*

$$c = \max\left\{ \left(\frac{\beta t \ln n}{\ln \ln n}\right)^{1/(t-1)}, 5 + 2\alpha, 4e^2 + 1 \right\}$$

with probability at least $1 - n^{-\alpha}$.

4.2   Finding Witness Subgraphs

For the moment we will concentrate on the structure of the witness subgraph and neglect duplication of vertices.

We call a unit *active in round t'* if it still takes part in the collision protocol in round t'. Assume that the collision game does not terminate after t rounds and consider a unit y which is active in round $t + 1$. At time t there are at least $c + 1$ jobs incident to y. These jobs have not been allocated until round t and, thus, the other $d - 1$ units where they are connected to must still be active in round t. Hence, the witness tree exhibits a regular recursive structure (see Fig. 2), i.e., the witness tree T_t for t rounds is composed of $c(d - 1)$ witness trees T_{t-1}. The leafs of the witness tree consist of a single unit since all units are active in round 1. Note that the resulting tree is c-ary but not $(c + 1)$-ary because only the unit at the root has $c+1$ children. We ignore one of its children in order to get a simple regular structure.

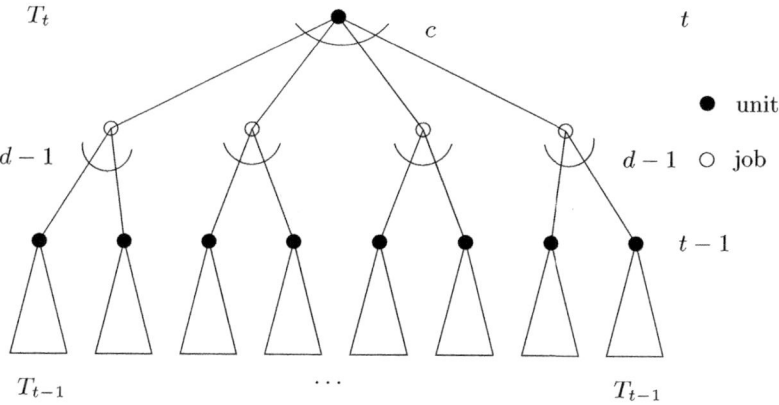

Fig. 2. Witness tree for collision games

Let j_t denote the number of jobs and u_t the number of units in a witness tree T_t. It follows that

$$j_t = c + c(d - 1) \cdot j_{t-1} \quad ; \quad j_1 = 0$$
$$u_t = 1 + c(d - 1) \cdot u_{t-1} \quad ; \quad u_1 = 1 .$$

One easily checks that

$$j_t = \frac{c^t(d - 1)^{t-1} - c}{c(d - 1) - 1} \quad ; \quad u_t = \frac{c^t(d - 1)^t - 1}{c(d - 1) - 1} .$$

We deduce for the number of edges r_t in T_t that $r_t = d \cdot j_t$ since every job has degree d. Furthermore, T_t contains j_t/c units as inner vertices as each such vertex is incident to c jobs.

4.3   Turning Graphs into Trees

Let T_t denote a witness subgraph which certifies that the unit at its root is still active after t rounds of the collision game. Since the root of the witness subgraph has degree c (see Fig. 2) we conclude that we can still find a witness subgraph T_{t-1} after the deletion of $2k$ edges at the root if $c > 2k$. Hence, if there are no k-multicycles and the collision game does not terminate after t rounds then we can find a witness tree T_{t-1}.

4.4   Counting Multicycles

Counting k-multicycles as shown in Sect. 3.2 we obtain

$$\mathbb{E}[M_{k,t}] \leq \sum_{s=1}^{2kt} n^s \cdot 2^{s^2} \cdot d^{s-1+k} \cdot p^{s-1+k} \ .$$

Using the assumptions on d and t and the fact that $p = 1/n$ it follows easily that there are no k-multicycles with probability $1 - \frac{1}{2} n^{-\alpha}$ for $k \geq 2 + \alpha$.

4.5   Counting Witness Trees

Using the values of j_t, u_t and r_t we will now calculate the expected number of witness trees T_t. For simplicity's sake we drop the subscripts of j_t, u_t and r_t.

There are at most n^{j+u} possibilities to choose the vertices. After we have fixed the number of the requests (at most d^r possibilities) every edge occurs with probability $1/n$. Furthermore, we take into account $(1/c!)^{j/c} \cdot (1/(d-1)!)^j$ tree automorphisms. Finally, we deduce that

$$\mathbb{E}[T_t] = n^{j+u} \cdot \left(\frac{d}{n}\right)^r \cdot \left(\frac{1}{c!}\right)^{j/c} \cdot \left(\frac{1}{(d-1)!}\right)^j$$

$$\leq n^{j+u-r} \cdot \left[\frac{e}{c} \cdot \left(\frac{e}{d-1}\right)^{d-1} \cdot d^d\right]^j$$

$$= n \cdot \left[\frac{e}{c} \cdot \left(\frac{e}{d-1}\right)^{d-1} \cdot d^d\right]^{\frac{c^t(d-1)^{t-1}-c}{c(d-1)-1}} \ .$$

To see this note that $j + u - r = 1$ because $j + u$ and r correspond to the number of vertices resp. edges in the witness tree.

For $d = 2$ this expression is similar to the results in [18]. It holds that

$$\mathbb{E}[T_t] \leq n \cdot \left(\frac{e}{c} \cdot 4e\right)^{\frac{c^t-c}{c-1}} \leq n \cdot \left(\frac{4e^2}{c}\right)^{c^{t-1}-1} \ .$$

Similar calculations as in [18] show that $\mathbb{E}[T_t] \leq \frac{1}{2} n^{-\alpha}$. Theorem 1 then follows by the arguments given in Sect. 3.3.

Our analysis also yields a result for the case $d \geq 3$ without much additional effort. Note that

$$\gamma := \frac{c^t(d-1)^{t-1} - c}{c(d-1) - 1} \geq \frac{(c(d-1))^{t-1} - 1}{d} \geq \frac{(c(d-1))^{t-1}}{2d}.$$

Furthermore, it is easy to check that $(d-1)^2/d \geq 1$ and, thus,

$$\gamma \geq \frac{1}{2}c^{t-1}(d-1)^{t-3} \geq (c(d-1))^{t-3}.$$

Hence, we obtain

$$\mathbb{E}[T_t] \leq n \cdot \left[\frac{e}{c}\left(\frac{e}{d-1}\right)^{d-1} \cdot d^d\right]^{(c(d-1))^{t-3}} \leq n \cdot \left[\frac{de^d}{c}\left(\frac{d}{d-1}\right)^{d-1}\right]^{(c(d-1))^{t-3}}$$

$$\leq n \cdot \left[\frac{d \cdot e^{d+1}}{c}\right]^{(c(d-1))^{t-3}}.$$

This enables us to show the following theorem.

Theorem 2. *Let $\alpha > 0$, $\beta := \alpha + 2\ln d + d + 2$ and $2 \leq t \leq \frac{1}{\beta}\ln\ln n$. Then the c-collision protocol with $d \geq 3$ terminates after at most t rounds for the threshold*

$$c = \max\left\{\frac{1}{d-1} \cdot \left(\frac{\beta t \ln n}{\ln\ln n}\right)^{1/(t-3)}, 5 + 2\alpha, de^{d+1} + 1\right\}$$

with probability at least $1 - n^{-\alpha}$.

Using the definition of c and the bound on t we deduce that

$$\mathbb{E}[T_t] \leq n \cdot \left[d^2 e^{d+1} \cdot \left(\frac{\ln\ln n}{\beta t \ln n}\right)^{\frac{1}{t-3}}\right]^{\frac{\beta t \ln n}{\ln\ln n}}$$

$$\leq n \cdot \left[(d^2 e^{d+1})^t \cdot \frac{\ln\ln n}{\beta t \ln n}\right]^{\frac{\beta \ln n}{\ln\ln n}} \leq n \cdot \left[\frac{(d^2 e^{d+1})^{\frac{1}{\beta}}\ln\ln n}{\ln n}\right]^{\frac{\beta \ln n}{\ln\ln n}}$$

$$= n \cdot \frac{(d^2 e^{d+1})^{\ln n}}{n^\beta} = n^{2\ln d + d + 2 - \beta} = n^{-\alpha}.$$

5 Sequential Allocation

5.1 The Classic $d = 2$ Strategy

5.1.1 Model and Algorithm. We consider the same model as in [2]: n jobs are sequentially allocated at n units. Every job chooses d units independently and uniformly at random and is allocated at a unit with minimum load. Ties are broken arbitrarily.

Theorem 3. [2] *For the sequential allocation process with d independent choices it holds that the maximum load is at most $\frac{\ln\ln n}{\ln d} + \mathcal{O}(1)$ with probability $1 - n^{-\alpha}$.*

5.1.2   Finding Witness Subgraphs. For the moment we ignore cross edges and duplication of vertices. Let l denote the load after the allocation of all jobs. We say that a job j is *on level* l' if $l' - 1$ other jobs have been allocated at the same unit as j before j's arrival.

Now we show how a witness tree T_l for a unit x with load l after the allocation of the last job can be constructed. Consider the job j on level l allocated at x. This job has issued requests to $d - 1$ units $y_1, \ldots, y_{d-1}$ different from x and all these units must have had load at least $l - 1$ at the time when j was allocated. Hence, we can find a witness tree T_{l-1} at $y_1, \ldots, y_{d-1}$. Furthermore, we can also find a witness tree T_{l-1} at x certifying that x had load $l-1$ before j was allocated (see Fig. 3). Finally, we define that T_1 consists of single unit and a single job joined by an edge.

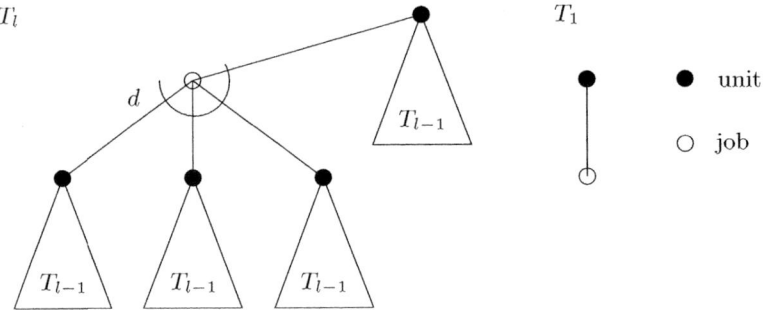

Fig. 3. Witness tree for sequential allocation

We use the variables j_l, u_l and r_l for the witness tree T_l as in the previous section and obtain the following recurrences:

$$j_l = 1 + d \cdot j_{l-1} \quad ; \quad j_1 = 1$$
$$u_l = d \cdot u_{l-1} \quad ; \quad u_1 = 1.$$

We easily deduce that

$$j_l = \frac{d^l - 1}{d - 1} \quad ; \quad u_l = d^{l-1}.$$

Jobs which belong to a T_1 are called *leaf jobs* and we denote their number by h_l. Since a leaf job is allocated on level 1 and each unit contains exactly one such job it holds that $h_l = u_l = d^{l-1}$.

5.1.3   Turning Graphs into Trees. Consider the witness subgraph T_l of a unit u with load l. u contains jobs $j_1, \ldots, j_l$ where j_i is allocated on level i. For $i \geq 2$ it holds that j_i has $d - 1$ incident units different from u with load at least $i-1$ before the insertion of j_i. Hence, it is connected to $d-1$ witness subgraphs T_{i-1} for $i=2,\ldots,l$. Fig. 4 shows this view on the recursive structure of the witness subgraph, where only one of the $d-1$ witness subgraphs T_{i-1} is drawn for each job j_i.

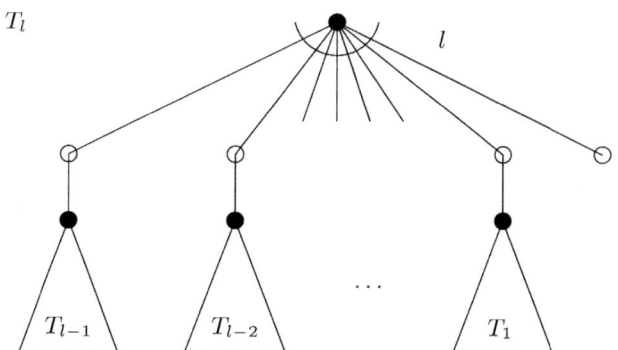

Fig. 4. Different view on witness tree for sequential allocation

From this structure it follows that after the deletion of $2k$ edges at the we can still find a witness tree T_{l-2k}.

5.1.4   Counting Multicycles.

We count multicycles as in Section 3.2:

$$\mathbb{E}[M_{k,l}] \leq \sum_{s=1}^{2kl} n^s \cdot 2^{s^2} \cdot d^{s-1+k} \cdot p^{s-1+k} .$$

As $p = 1/n$ it again follows easily that for $l = \mathcal{O}(\frac{\ln \ln n}{\ln d})$ there are no k-multicycles with probability $1 - \frac{1}{2}n^{-\alpha}$ for $k \geq 2 + \alpha$.

5.1.5   Counting Witness Trees.

In order to show that large witness trees occur with small probability we apply a technique from [19]: We construct the witness tree ignoring jobs on level 1, 2 and 3. If the maximum load after the allocation process amounts to $l+3$ we can find a witness tree T_l which contains only jobs on level 4 and above.

A witness tree is called *active* if its leaf jobs indeed reside on level 4 and above. At any time during the allocation process there are at most $n/3$ units containing at least three jobs. Henceforth, we call these units *heavy*. A witness tree can only be active if all its leaf jobs choose the $d-1$ units which don't belong to the witness tree among the heavy units. This happens with probability $3^{-(d-1)h_l}$. Note that for every job this bound holds deterministically regardless of the random choices of the other jobs. Hence, this probability is independent from the choices of the requests inside the witness tree.

We renounce taking the tree automorphisms into consideration and, thus, we may bound the number of choices for the jobs and units by $n^j \cdot n^u$ and assume that the labelling of the requests for non-leaf jobs is implicit in the order of the chosen vertices. For the labelling of the requests belonging to leaf jobs we have to adjoin the factor d^{h_l}. Each request in the tree occurs independently with probability $1/n$. This leads to

$$\mathbb{E}[T_l] \leq n^{j_l} \cdot n^{u_l} \cdot \left(\frac{1}{n}\right)^{r_l} \cdot d^{h_l} \cdot 3^{-(d-1)h_l} \leq n \cdot 2^{-h_l} = n \cdot 2^{-d^{l-1}}.$$

Choosing $l = \log_d \log_2 n^{\alpha+1} + 2 = \frac{\ln \ln n}{\ln d} + \mathcal{O}(1)$ completes the proof of the theorem.

5.2   Always-Go-Left

5.2.1   Model and Algorithm. In this section we will consider the sequential allocation strategy from [19] which surprisingly still improves on the result from [2] by introducing a slight asymmetry. At first sight this may seem rather unintuitive, but the analysis will show that asymmetry helps in making the witness trees larger and, thus, their occurence already becomes improbable for smaller maximum load.

The n units are divided into d groups of almost equal size, i. e., with $\Theta(n/d)$ units per group. For simplicity's sake we will henceforth assume that each group comprises exactly n/d units.

The unit for the ith request of a job is chosen from the ith group. Then the ball is, as usual, allocated at a unit with minimum load. If there is a draw the unit belonging to the group with the smallest number, i. e., the "left-most" group is selected. In [19] this algorithm is thus called "Always-Go-Left".

Theorem 4. *For $\alpha > 0$ the Always-Go-Left algorithm achieves maximum load at most $\ln \ln n/(d \ln \Phi_d) + \mathcal{O}(1)$ with probability $1 - n^{-\alpha}$.*

The constant Φ_d is defined with the help of generalized Fibonacci numbers. Define $F_d(k) = 0$ for $k \leq 0$, $F_d(1) = 1$, and $F_d(k) = \sum_{i=1}^{d} F_d(k-i)$ for $k \geq 2$. Let $\phi_d = \lim_{k \to \infty} \sqrt[k]{F_d(k)}$, so that $F_d(k) = \Theta(\phi_d^k)$. Then $1.61 \ldots = \phi_2 < \phi_3 < \cdots < 2$.

5.2.2   Finding Witness Trees. The recurrences for the witness trees from Sect. 5.1 must slightly be modified as we have to consider to which of the d groups the units belong. In this section we deviate somewhat from the previous notation and number the groups by $0, \ldots, d-1$ instead of $1, \ldots, d$. The reasons for that will become clear shortly. Let $T_{l,i}$ denote a witness tree for a job on level l which is placed in a unit of group i. The adjacent witness trees are $T_{l,0}, \ldots, T_{l,i-1}, T_{l-1,i}, \ldots, T_{l-1,d-1}$. This recurrence also holds for $l = 1$ if we assume that the trees $T_{0,1}, \ldots, T_{0,d-1}$ are empty. $T_{1,0}$ is defined to consist of a single job and a single unit which are joined by an edge (see Fig. 6 for the general recursive structure and Fig. 5 for the small cases; the numbers correspond to the groups of the units).

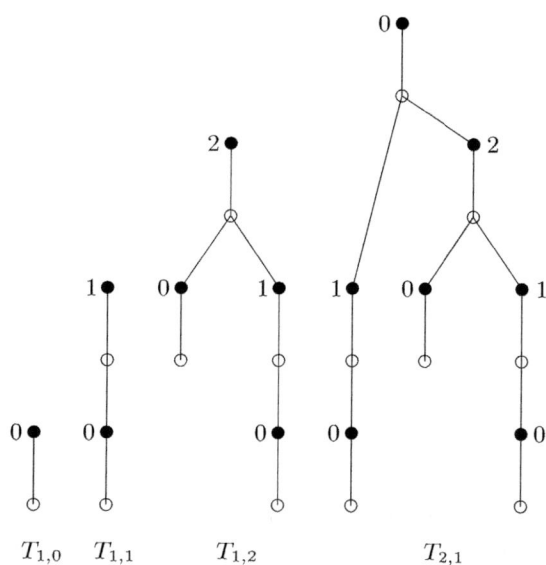

Fig. 5. Small witness trees for always-go-left allocation with $d = 3$

Observe that this construction implies that all leaves are connected to a unit in group 0, i.e., their incident edge is labelled with 0.

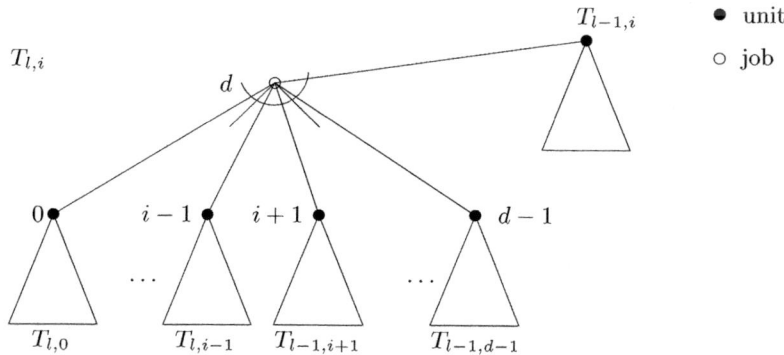

Fig. 6. Witness tree for sequential always-go-left allocation

In order to simplify the recurrence we let $T_x := T_{\lfloor (x+d)/d \rfloor, x \bmod d}$ for $x = 0, 1, \ldots$ and may rewrite the adjacent witness trees of T_x as $T_{x-1}, \ldots, T_{x-d}$.

5.2.3 Turning Graphs into Trees.

By the recursive structure of the witness tree (as presented in Sect. 5.1) it follows that after the deletion of $2k$ edges at the root of a witness tree $T_{l,i}$ we can still find a witness tree $T_{l-2k,i'}$ (with $i' \neq i$) which is at least as large as a $T_{l-2k,0}$ (see Fig. 6 and Fig. 4).

5.2.4 Counting Multicycles.

Multicycles are counted as in Sect. 5.1 for the classic $d = 2$ case

$$\mathbb{E}[M_{k,l}] \leq \sum_{s=1}^{2kl} n^s \cdot 2^{s^2} \cdot d^{s-1+k} \cdot p^{s-1+k}.$$

Note that due to the fact that we choose exactly one unit in each group the probability for the edges changes from $1/n$ to d/n. However, one easily checks that the additional factor d^{s-1+k} is asymptotically negligible and we still obtain that for $l = \mathcal{O}(\frac{\ln \ln n}{\ln d})$ there are no k-multicycles with probability $1 - n^{-\alpha}$ for $k \geq 2 + \alpha$.

5.2.5 Counting Witness Trees.

We get the following recurrences for the witness tree T_x using the same definition for $T_{1,0}$ as for T_1 in Sect. 5.1 (a single unit and a single job joined by an edge):

$$j_x = 1 + \sum_{i=1}^{d} j_{x-i} \quad ; \quad j_{-(d-1)} = \cdots = j_{-1} = 0, \; j_0 = 1$$
$$u_x = \sum_{i=1}^{d} u_{x-i} \quad ; \quad u_{-(d-1)} = \cdots = u_{-1} = 0, \; u_0 = 1.$$

Let h_x denote the number of leaf jobs in T_x. For h_x we deduce the recurrence

$$h_x = \sum_{i=1}^{d} h_{x-i} \quad ; \quad h_{-(d-1)} = \cdots = h_{-1} = 0, \; h_0 = 1.$$

Recall that $F_d(k) = 0$ for $k \leq 0$, $F_d(1) = 1$ and $F_d(k) = \sum_{i=1}^{d} F_d(k-i)$ for $k \geq 2$. Following the argumentation of [19], it holds that $F_d(k) \geq \Phi_d^{k-2}$. Thus, we conclude that $h_x = F_d(x) \geq \Phi_d^{k-2}$.

The next step is to estimate the number of jobs of j_x in comparison to the number of leaves h_x. By induction we prove that $h_x \geq \frac{1}{4} j_x + \frac{1}{4}$.

The basis of the induction is shown as follows: T_0 only contains one job which is a leaf job and, thus, we have $(j - h) = 0$ and $h = 1$. For the trees $T_1, \ldots, T_{d-1}$ we deduce by induction that $j - h = h$. When we compose a tree T_i for $i = 1, \ldots, d-1$ the non-leaf job that connects the trees $T_0, \ldots, T_{i-1}$ is compensated by the tree T_0 which contains one leaf job but no non-leaf job. Hence, for $0 \leq x < d$ it holds that $h_x \geq \frac{1}{2} j_x \geq \frac{1}{4} j_x + \frac{1}{4}$.

Now we prove the induction step. A tree T_x with $x \geq d$ is composed of subtrees $T_{x-d}, \ldots, T_{x-1}$ and contains one additional non-leaf job. Hence, it holds that

$$h_x = \sum_{i=1}^{d} h_{x-i} \geq \frac{1}{4} \sum_{i=1}^{d} j_{x-i} + \frac{1}{4}d \geq \frac{1}{4}(j_x - 1) + \frac{1}{2} = \frac{1}{4}j_x + \frac{1}{4},$$

completing the proof of the induction step.

The expected number of witness trees T_x is estimated as before. We have at most $n^j \cdot (n/d)^u$ possibilities to choose the jobs and the units in the tree. Note that the order of the choices fixes the group where a certain unit belongs to. Hence, we have only n/d instead of n choices per unit. Every edge occurs independently with probability d/n.

As in Sect. 5.1 we call a witness tree active, if for each leaf job the $d-1$ units that do not belong to the witness tree (that is the units in groups $1, \ldots, d-1$) are heavy. For technical reasons we have to strengthen the definition of heavyness and call a unit heavy if it has load at least 80. We claim that the probability that the $d-1$ units are all heavy is bounded from above by $20^{-(d-1-\lfloor d/4 \rfloor)}$. The proof proceeds as follows. Consider an arbitrary distribution of n balls. Let ξ denote the number of groups in which at least $\frac{1}{20}\frac{n}{d}$ units contain at least 80 balls. From $\xi \cdot \frac{1}{20}\frac{n}{d} \cdot 80 \leq n$ we deduce $\xi \leq \lfloor d/4 \rfloor$. That is, at least $d - 1 - \lfloor d/4 \rfloor$ units are choosen in groups with at most $\frac{1}{20}\frac{n}{d}$ heavy units. Hence,

$$\mathbb{E}[T_x] \leq n^j \cdot \left(\frac{n}{d}\right)^u \cdot \left(\frac{d}{n}\right)^r \cdot 20^{-(d-1-\lfloor d/4 \rfloor)h} \leq n \cdot d^{j-1} \cdot 20^{-(d-1-\lfloor d/4 \rfloor)h}$$

$$\leq n \cdot d^{4h-1} \cdot 20^{-(d-1-\lfloor d/4 \rfloor)h} \leq n \cdot 2^{(4 \log_2 d - (d-1-\lfloor d/4 \rfloor) \log_2 20)h}$$

$$\leq n \cdot 2^{-\frac{1}{4}h} \leq n \cdot 2^{-\frac{1}{4}\Phi_d^{x-2}}.$$

A tree $T_{l,i}$ for $i = 0, \ldots, d-1$ is at least as large as a tree $T_{l,0} \equiv T_{(l-1)d}$ and we obtain that

$$\mathbb{E}[T_{ld}] \leq 2^{-\frac{1}{4}\Phi_d^{ld-2}}.$$

This estimate is similar to the bound in [19]. Setting $l := \log_{\Phi_d}(4 \log_2 n^\alpha)/d + 2 = \ln \ln n / (d \ln \Phi_d) + \mathcal{O}(1)$ yields the desired result. (Note that the constants in this section can be significantly improved. In particular, the inequality $h_x \geq \frac{1}{4}j_x + \frac{1}{4}$ is rather weak and can be improved by more careful argumentations.)

6   Conclusion

We have presented a unified view on witness tree proofs for various balls-into-bins games. We feel that the uniform approach for the different models faciliates the understanding of the results and also provides intuitive insight.

References

1. Micah Adler, Soumen Chakrabarti, Michael Mitzenmacher, and Lars Rasmussen. Parallel randomized load balancing. In *Proceedings of the 27th Annual ACM Symposium on Theory of Computing (STOC-95)*, pages 238–247. ACM Press, 1995. 72, 73

2. Yossi Azar, Andrej Broder, Anna R. Karlin, and Eli Upfal. Balanced allocations. In *Proceedings of the 26th Annual ACM Symposium on Theory of Computing (STOC-94)*, pages 593–602, 1994. 71, 73, 79, 82

3. Petra Berenbrink, Artur Czumaj, Angelika Steger, and Berthold Vöcking. Balanced allocation: the heavily loaded case. In *Proceedings of the 32nd Annual ACM Symposium on Theory of Computing (STOC-00)*, pages 745–754, 2000. 73

4. Richard Cole, Alan Frieze, Bruce M. Maggs, Michael Mitzenmacher, Andréa W. Richa, Ramesh K. Sitaraman, and Eli Upfal. On balls and bins with deletions. In *Proceedings of the 2nd International Workshop on Randomization and Approximation Techniques in Computer Science (RANDOM)*, 1998. 73

5. Richard Cole, Bruce M. Maggs, Friedhelm Meyer auf der Heide, Michael Mitzenmacher, Andrea W. Richa, Klaus Schröder, Ramesh K. Sitaraman, and Berthold Vöcking. Randomized protocols for low-congestion circuit routing in multistage interconnection networks. In *Proceedings of the 30th Annual ACM Symposium on Theory of Computing (STOC-98)*, pages 378–388, 1998.

6. Artur Czumaj, Friedhelm Meyer auf der Heide, and Volker Stemann. Improved optimal shared memory simulations, and the power of reconfiguration. In *Proceedings of the 3rd Israel Symposium on Theory of Computing*, pages 11–19, 1995. 72

7. Artur Czumaj and Volker Stemann. Randomized allocation processes. In *Proceedings of the 38th IEEE Symposium on the Foundations of Computer Science (FOCS-97)*, pages 194–203, 1997. 73

8. Martin Dietzfelbinger and Friedhelm Meyer auf der Heide. Simple, efficient shared memory simulations (extended abstract). In *Proceedings of the 5th Annual ACM Symposium on Parallel Algorithms and Architectures (SPAA-93)*, pages 110–119, 1993. 71, 72

9. Leslie Ann Goldberg, Yossi Matias, and Satish Rao. An optical simulation of shared memory. In *Proceedings of the 6th Annual ACM Symposium on Parallel Algorithms and Architectures (SPAA-94)*, pages 257–267, New York, 1994. ACM Press. 72

10. Gaston H. Gonnet. Expected length of the longest probe sequence in hash code searching. *Journal of the ACM*, 28(2):289–304, 1981. 71

11. Richard M. Karp, Michael Luby, and Friedhelm Meyer auf der Heide. Efficient PRAM simulation on a distributed memory machine. In *Proceedings of the 24th Annual ACM Symposium on Theory of Computing (STOC-92)*, pages 318–326. ACM Press, 1992. 71, 72

12. Philip. D. MacKenzie, C. Greg Plaxton, and Rajmohan Rajaraman. On contention resolution protocols and associated probabilistic phenomena. In *Proceedings of the 26th Annual ACM Symposium on Theory of Computing (STOC-94)*, pages 153–162, 1994. 72

13. Friedhelm Meyer auf der Heide, Christian Scheideler, and Volker Stemann. Exploiting storage redundancy to speed up randomized shared memory simulations. In *Proceedings of the 12th Annual Symposium on Theoretical Aspects of Computer Science (STACS-95)*, volume LNCS 900, pages 267–278. Springer-Verlag, 1995. 72

14. Michael Mitzenmacher. Density dependent jump markov processes and applications to load balancing. In *Proceedings of the 37th IEEE Symposium on Foundations (FOCS-96)*, pages 213–223, 1996. 73
15. Michael Mitzenmacher. *On the Power of Two Choices in Randomized Load Balancing*. PhD thesis, 1996. 71
16. Michael Mitzenmacher. On the analysis of randomized load balancing schemes. In *Proceedings of the 9th Annual ACM Symposium on Parallel Algorithms and Arrays (SPAA-97)*, pages 292–301, 1997. 73
17. Martin Raab and Angelika Steger. Balls into bins — a simple and tight analysis. In *Proceedings of the 2nd International Workshop on Randomization and Approximation Techniques in Computer Science (RANDOM-98)*, volume LNCS 1518, pages 159–170, 1998. 71
18. Volker Stemann. Parallel balanced allocations. In *Proceedings of the 8th Annual ACM Symposium on Parallel Algorithms and Architectures (SPAA-96)*, pages 261–269, 1996. 72, 76, 78
19. Berthold Vöcking. How asymmetry helps load balancing. In *Proceedings of the 40th IEEE Symposium on Foundations of Computer Science (FOCS-99)*, pages 131–140, 1999. 73, 81, 82, 84, 85

Software Testing & Diagnostics: Theory & Practice

Vladimír Mařík[1], Luboš Král[1,2], and Radek Mařík[3]

[1] Department of Cybernetics, Czech Technical University
Technická 2, Prague 6, Czech Republic
{marik,kral}@labe.felk.cvut.cz
[2] CertiCon, Shareholders Comp.
Odborů 4, 120 00 Prague 2, Czech Republic
kral@certicon.cz
[3] ProTys Ltd. in control of Rockwell Automation Research Center
Americká 22, 120 00 Prague 2, Czech Republic
rmarik@ra.rockwell.com

Abstract. The introduction into the field of software testing, automated software testing and diagnostics will be given together with explanation of fundamental terminology. The viewpoint of quality theory will be stressed. Presented state of the art basic concepts of software testing, design of tests, their execution and methods of test evaluation will be selected according to their practical usage. The methodology will be demonstrated on case studies developed during practical software testing and diagnostics projects for large international companies in the field of industrial automation and medical instrumentation. The paper will be concluded with a summary of practical experience.

1 Introduction

Software has become necessary to support the majority of products. Its complexity is rapidly growing. This fast-paced software development brings into focus a number of issues that must be addressed in order to keep up with marketing requirements. One of them is a shorter time period during which a product must be identified, designed, developed, tested, and released. The period is dictated by the factor "time to market". On the other hand, the volume of software has already out-stepped possibilities of ad-hoc development and testing in small groups of developers whose successful outcomes depend on heroic individual effort. Such software technology trends together with increasing requirements on reliability of products and requirements to lower risks lead to extremely high demands on the testing phase of software development.

It is widely recognized that transitioning effective processes and technologies, to improve an organization's ability to test software, require a planned approach and a mature methodology. This hot-topic task is common for all software development teams. Much of this framework is considered strategic know-how and is kept secret in the majority of companies. Therefore, waiting for mature commercial solutions could imply the loss of the leading edge in own product technology.

V. Hlaváč, K. G. Jeffery, and J. Wiedermann (Eds.): SOFSEM 2000, LNCS 1963, pp. 88–114, 2000.
© Springer-Verlag Berlin Heidelberg 2000

1.1   The Goal of Testing and SW Diagnostics

Anything written by people has bugs. Not testing something is equivalent to asserting that it's bug-free. Programmers can't think of everything — especially of all the possible interactions between features and between different pieces of software. We try to break software because that's the only practical way we know of to be confident about the product's fitness for use.

The goal of testing and software validation is to support quality assurance: to gather information that, when fed back to programmers, results in avoidance of past mistakes and in better future software. One can go even further towards *software diagnostics*: given a set of complaints and observed software failures, a diagnostic system may search for probable reasons for these and suggest further tests to be performed in order to confirm or reject hypotheses [11]. Finally, the faulty software components should be identified.

It has been shown that the cost of finding and correcting a defect grows dramatically with the length of time the defect exists. That is especially true in the case of design and requirements defects. The testing process must start at the beginning of the overall development, at the stage of the requirements and specification preparation. This minimizes the possible acceptance problems at the beginning of the development. Therefore, we can find the testing activities in each step of the development process. The testing is no more just one step before SW delivery, where only run-time errors can be fixed efficiently.

Another critical issue of testing is maintenance and creation of testing scripts that can be run automatically. The limited flexibility of current commercial solutions in this area often pushes testing activities from automatic back to manual. The testing process breaks down when a testing group creates hundreds of tests scripts to test functionality of a graphical user interface and the interface is changed in later phases of the software development. This requires high levels of resources to constantly rewrite test scripts. Highly skilled testers are spending many hours perfecting specific test scripts and not broadening the test coverage.

1.2   Software Development and Testing

With the advances in object-oriented component based software development it is necessary to define guidelines for software design that will allow for proper testing. It is not obvious how to create a suitable testing environment that enables test aggregations of software components without additional software development. Testing activities cannot be performed without a repeatable software process environment including appropriate scope documents, functional requirements, design and test specifications, as well as a well organized configuration management system. The identification of such a framework creates an essential base for implementation of all testing activities.

It is not an easy task to setup and implement testing process suitable and accepted by software team. There are many aspects like the current software development and testing process maturity, willing of team members to make a change, time and budget issues, etc. that should be taken into account to progress in a reasonable way. It is not sufficient to create a nice abstract model. It is necessary to bring it into a real life. It seems that the success of testing depends mainly on how it is organized. We need a way to describe all workers, activities, artifacts, and workflow that participate in testing process. It cannot be expected to design such process in one step and to implement it in the second one. It is rather long-time goal that must be pursued in many iterations. The most important, but difficult point is to start. One must try to identify the most critical points of the design and to create a skeleton to which detailed solutions could be plugged in.

1.3   Supporting Tools and Methodology

Another key decision is related to tools that are expected to be used for SW design and testing. There are many possible solutions of testing process and they are almost equally good.

A given real tool often implements only a subset of features needed for the whole solution. Sometimes, it can be a very tedious job to implement an unsupported part. Therefore, an abstract model that takes into consideration a specific implementation has much higher chance to be implemented without great overheads. In our case, we started from the view that database oriented approach was the most appropriate. However, it was quickly recognized that it would be too expensive to develop a working process from scratch. A practical software process must also include necessary documentation and people training. Nevertheless, the number of necessary tools is not negligible. For example, the Rational Unified Process contains about ten thousands pages of structured documentation and is supported by about 15 integrated tools. There are many different companies dealing with the issue.

Thus, instead of searching for all classes of structures like documents, subsystems and their interfaces, their relations, the process in which they participate, design constraints, and tools, which they could be manipulated with, we prefer adoption of a framework created by experienced people in the field. That means one can focus on customization of the selected framework for his/her software process environment instead of resource consuming work on identification, building of abstract models, and implementation of tools. The customization also includes building of extensions to fill gaps in the framework.

The important aspect of a framework solution is its openness. Identification of sufficient number of features that would fulfill a given task tends to be very difficult. There is an aspect known as the IKIWISI effect: "I'll Know It When I See It." In other words, the point when users of any system know exactly what they want is not two years before the system is ready but rather a few weeks or months after delivery of the system when they are beyond the initial learning phase. Making the solution (the testing framework) open, we are ready to address these additional requirements.

1.4 Summary

In summary, development teams will not be able to deliver successful software without a clear testing methodology. Having a solid uniform process across the company will lower our risks and allow us to deliver competitive software products to the market within a reasonable time frame. Development communities need to understand and learn how to test their own technologies, and how to build testable products. Utilizing an approach similar to the one identified below will allow us to better meet our customers expectation.

2 Software Development Process

The most important things about a software development process are mainly the following [2]:

- there is a process,
- it is understood,
- it is followed.

We can suppose that there is always a process because even chaos is a kind of process. Having a process in our term means that it is possible to predict in steps what will happen to our developed software.

> "Having the process doesn't mean elaborate process documents. Some of the best projects I have seen had few formal process documents. Conversely, the process document I always point to when someone asks me what is needed came from one of the worst fiasco I have ever seen."

> Boris Beizer [2]

Here, the documents serve only for transmission of the process ideas to the involved persons. Also, quality of the process is kept under control easier if the procedures were discussed before and written to a document.

Of course, the process itself must be understood before is followed. There are different ways how to arrange it (documents, people training, etc.). Anyway, the general training in a process is very often inadequate because what messes things up are the specifics, not the generics. Therefore, some kind of specific process training is important.

If the process is understood, then it should be followed. Here, the human factor can introduce the main problems in process control. A key indicator of a process in trouble is a difference between the official process and what people actually do. This can indicate that the process itself is not well designed for a real work.

2.1   Parts of the Development Process

You can always find in many books (e. g. [13,4]) a set of flowcharts, specifying different process models and their differences between each other. There are mainly mentioned models like waterfall, spiral, stepwise refinements, top-down, bottom-up and etc.

These are often simplified to the process nature, but the process itself in a real world is always more complicated and deformed from its generalization. Also, the process model doesn't determine the success or failure of a software development process. Application, cultural, environmental specifics have a greater influence on process than the theories itself.

Therefore, it is better to pay focus to the process ingredients that should be present and maintained in a good process. The following procedures should characterize the process:

Process road map. Everybody must know where they and their software are in the process at all times. A useful road map divides the process into simple steps that are easy to understand and control.

Process control. There should be effective mechanism by which the participants in the process can learn how to improve those parts of the process with which they are most directly concerned. It means, there is a feedback that can improve the quality of the product and the process itself.

Quantification and metrics. Quantification is the key of objectivity in engineering. In software, metrics is the primary methods for quantification.

Configuration control. We take our product or its part and we have to know at any time: who, what, when, where, why and how. All the history of the project must be kept under the configuration control.

Requirements. These are the documents storing the information about what we are developing to have just only one understanding of the same thing.

Requirement traceability. It means that the requirements can be mapped onto software components and vice versa. Also, if the requirements are structured, there must be registration about all dependencies.

Strategic mores. There are many different strategic objectives (who will use our product, could it be faster, will it make more money), and management decides the relative importance of each. Without quantifying the objectives, no one can fulfill the criteria.

Requirement validation criteria. We need to have satisfaction criteria to know that the requirement was met. Completions of such a requirement can be done only if its pre-conditions were passed.

Responsibility. Who is responsible for what and when.

Exit criteria. How we know that the developed software is really ready for delivery or is ready to go to the next stage of development. What will stop a development and what will save us from never-ending improvements of our product without delivery?

Entry criteria. What is the acceptance criterion for the software to be able to start the development phase? We can have many different phases with different input criteria, so there is no redundancy with exit criteria.

Analysis. Analysis is the engineering process by which a design evolves that fulfills requirements.

Design. That is the core of the development. All the processes are supporting us to have a good design. The design precedes the build, the main coding phase.

Design validation. The design itself should be tested and proved for its correctness.

Coding. Making the working application and testing the units of code.

Integration. The software complexity will grow when its parts are assembled together. Architectural aspects of the final product are taken into account, before the whole application is built up.

Testing. Testing is essential part of the software development and it should affect each part of the software process. The aspects of testing will be introduced later in this chapter.

2.2   Testing as a Part of the Whole Development Process

The earlier the testing starts in the development process and the bugs are discovered, the cheaper is the correction. Herewith, the testing is not a separated process that is started after the real code is produced. The testing should start at the design phase and should be taken into account for all development phases. We can recognize the following activities that should be considered as testing:

Prototyping. Prototype is an incomplete implementation of software that mimics the behavior we think the user needs. The goal is to have something that can be used for basic acceptance tests or as a model for finding the right software solution.

Requirement analysis. The requirements should be checked for logical consistence, for testability and for feasibility. The requirements should be corrected first, mainly in the requirements driven design.

Formal analysis. Not all-possible combinations of situations and states of the software can be tested with the real product. This is often time consuming and hard to prepare a good test set, especially if the algorithm is complex. Therefore, the algorithms are proved for their correctness and design before they are implemented.

Design. Some of the design aspects (like testability, software maintenance, and etc.) will not directly affect the software features, but the software quality. They

Formal inspections are formal, facilitated, peer reviews held for the purpose of efficiently discovering defects in any work product. These include requirement documents, analysis models, design models, plans and tests.

Self-testing. The programmer should be responsible for first tests of the modules or units that he/she developed. The following test phases are not skipped.

2.3   Waterfall Development Process

The classical and often used model of the development life cycle is called water-fall development (see Fig. 1) — also known as 'V' model. The same process is applied in the real projects described bellow. Therefore, we will describe the basic characteristics and phases of this life process.

The classical *waterfall model* of SW development introduces development as a series of phases that are linked into a linear execution, from requirement analysis to product delivery. Testing phase appears at the end of this linear lifecycle. Thus, if waterfall model of software development process is used, the testing phase has no input data until a late phase of development.

Specific activities and deliverables characterize each phase of the software development process. The testing here consists of *verification testing* and *qualification testing*. While the verification testing impacts all phases of the SW development cycle, the qualification testing uses some of the procedures developed during the verification testing and is postponed to the end of the development. The qualification is a formal procedure and serves as a final prove of the software quality.

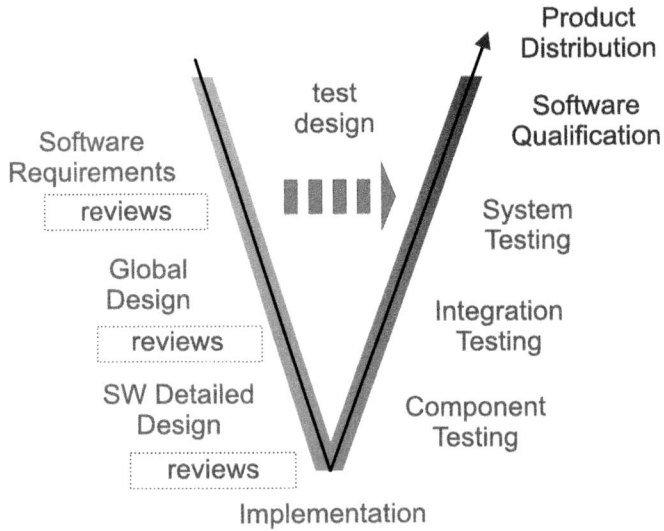

Fig. 1. Software development life cycle

The waterfall development process supports incremental development. The development is divided into increments, where each increment is defined as a sep-arated development life cycle. Therefore, a sequence of verifiable and executable software increments is developed. Each subsequent increment brings additional product functionality. Incremental development enables early and continual quality assessment and user feedback and facilitates process improvements as development progress.

It is generally agreed that *iterative and incremental model* of the development process is much more adequate. On the other hand, management of waterfall model appears to be much easier. Namely, it is very easy to check a progress of the project because of signing off documents. However, one never knows if signed off tasks are solved on the sufficient detailed level. Thus, there is a tendency towards overworked solutions that are very costly and lead into slippage of projects because waterfall model does not support modifications of documents.

Iterative and incremental model does address many of these problems. However, the organizational side of this model is much more demanding than the waterfall's one. Namely, synchronization of versions of documents is not an easy task. It also requires tighter involvement of management structures into the development process. On the other hand, management has better information on what has been done and what can be immediately delivered. From this point of view, waterfall model is very risky because what can be delivered is not known until a very late phase of software development. Furthermore, critical issues of the software development are caught at the starting iterations of the project managed according to iterative and incremental model. Also, solutions of main tasks are known quite soon. In this way, the testing phase of software project can benefit from the development iterations.

2.4   Traditional Development versus Object Oriented

The use of object-oriented development methods (OO) actually increases the quality of software because OO modeling and design can lead to a better system architecture and OO programming languages enforce a disciplined coding style.

Object-oriented SW development methods do not by themselves guarantee the production of correct programs. They are not shields against programmer's mistakes or lack of understanding of a specification. Experience shows that OO software cannot escape to a validation and verification process.

When it comes to testing, the proponents of OO technology sometimes have an amazing trust in some values of the traditional SW engineering methods. They argue that testing OO software is similar enough to testing traditional software that it does not require specific strategies [14]. The OO oriented software systems are presented as so close to applications developed with a traditional method that they could be tested using traditional testing methods.

However, we argue that traditional testing methods can not be applied directly to OO SW since these systems differ on several key issues. Testing must take into account the specifics of the OO development methods, and the structure of OO SW. Some aspects of the OO design, such as encapsulation, inheritance and polymorphism, introduce problems that were not previously found in structured SW, and therefore require adapting the traditional strategies [1].

Metrics show (see Table 1) that despite the conviction of the early adopters of OO methods, the partition of effort in OO life cycles still requires a large amount of time and resources for testing.

Table 1. Partitioning of the SW development process

	Traditional Development [12]	Object-Oriented Development	
		Meyer [12]	Rational Development Process [10]
Requirements & Analysis	20 %	30 %	14 %
Architecture & Design	30 %	50 %	21 %
Implementation	35 %	20 %	42 %
Unit Testing	15 %	10 %	42 %
Integration & Acceptance Testing	15 %	10 %	21 %

In 1988 Meyer estimated [12] that testing would require only ten percent of development time, in favor of an increase of the weight of design and modeling. Here, the more recent life cycle, the Rational development process, recommends scheduling four times more for the testing phase. Software engineers very often devote more than half of their time to implementation and testing. This is almost twice the estimated time suggested by Meyer. As mentioned by [3], reusable components need two to four times more testing than unique components due to their increased level of use.

The main differences of the OO software from the testing point of view are the following:

− There are no global data and data handling is not shared between units. A class contains all the properties that can affect the state of its instance.
− A method is not a testable component, i.e. it can only be tested through an instance of a class. It is no longer possible to consider the subprogram as basic unit of testing. Here, the basic unit is the class construct. The test cases cannot be designed as if the methods were "free-floating" subprograms instead of all being related to an object.
− It is impossible to build either a bottom-up or top-down testing strategy based on a sequence of invocations since the general case comprises no sequential order in which the methods of a class can be invoked.
− Every object carries a state. Furthermore, any method can modify these values. Therefore, the behavior of a method cannot be considered independent of the object for which is defined.

3   Software Quality Metrics

The metric can provide a quantitative assessment of software quality that should be the basis for decisions regarding the software's fitness for use. IEEE Standard 1061-1992 defines a methodology for establishing software quality metrics framework. The bases of this framework are widely used, also during the projects described in this article as practical examples. We will explain the basic ideas of the framework.

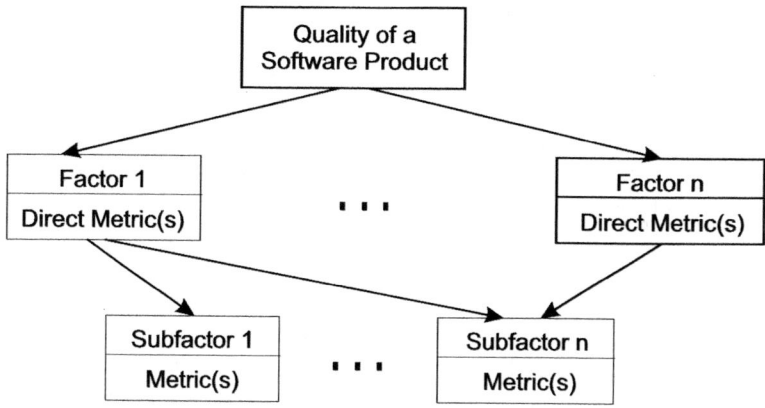

Fig. 2. Software quality metrics framework [8]

The framework is shown in Fig. 2. It is a hierarchy that consists of three levels. At the topmost level are the quality requirements that the software product must meet. These are usually expressed in the customer's way and by using the customer's terms.

The second level of the framework represents specific quality factors that relate to the overall quality requirements. These are the interpretation of the customer's requirements and the complete list can be found in IEEE Standard 1061 [8].

The third level decomposes each quality factor into measurable attributes (sub-factors and metrics). Sub-factors are expressed in terms meaningful to SW engineers and are independent of any one quality factor.

It is important understand what the metrics represent and not just accept them at face value. Therefore, validation of the quality metric should be also done. Its purpose is to gain confidence that the gathered and computed numbers reflect reality. Eventually, begin to use certain metric as predictors of those quality attributes (such as reliability) that cannot be measured during software development.

A number of metrics support the software verification and validation process (here the quality of it). They can be found for example in [13,9,6] and in other sources. We will not explain here the whole set of metrics and their appropriateness of use. We just concentrate on to the following few examples that can help in understanding what the metrics are measuring:

Complexity measures complexity of the code and therefore, also the difficulty of code maintenance, understanding, testing, and etc. There are different complexity measurements, described for example in [13].

Defect metrics are collected from inspection summary reports. Categorizing these metrics by defect type (logic, interface, documentation, and etc.), origin, and severity will identify development areas that need improvement.

Product metrics are measurements that represents the developed product (average size of modules, number of source lines code created, total number of bugs found, and etc.)

Process metrics are intended to reflect the effectiveness of processes (number of person/hours spent on inspections, average amount of rework time, defect correction time, and etc.).

3.1 SW Validation Metrics

The SW validation metrics help to effective plan and manage the testing process and therefore, also help to prepare criteria for software acceptance before delivery. Again, here are a lot of different measurements described in literature. There are two main streams of measurements that can be divided as follows:

– time measures — test estimates, test development time, test execution time, find/fix cycle time, cumulative test time,
– test coverage — code coverage, requirements coverage.

In general, during the metrics preparation and planing, there are some key questions that must be answered to be sure that the things are under control. The metrics should help to generate answers. So, the metrics should be searched for with respect to the following measurements:

– How many tests do we need?
– What resources are needed to develop the required tests?
– How much time is required to execute the tests?
– How much time is required to find bugs, fix them, and verify that they have been fixed?
– How much time has been spent actually testing the product?
– How much of the code is being exercised?
– Are we testing all of the product's features?
– How many defects have been detected in each software baseline?

4 SW Testing

As we mentioned above, the testing in the overall SW development process is not only the executable code verification. It impacts all phases of the development, including the requirements and specifications preparation. Anyway, the code verification is the critical and non-trivial (in the methodology point of view) part of it.

The testing hierarchy is often the same as is shown on the left side of the 'V' model (Fig. 1). Here, the SW components are tested separately before integration (component testing). The whole is tested after integration (integration testing) and in the real environment (system testing). One can find additional testing phases, but these three are the major ones. The software qualification is the process of evaluating software at the end of the development process to ensure compliance with all requirements.

4.1   Test Strategies

A test strategy or test technique is a systematic method used to select and/or generate tests to be included in a test suite. The strategy can give us rules by which we can determine if a given test does or does not satisfy the strategy. In principle, a strategy should be programmable.

A strategy is effective if the tests included by that strategy are likely to reveal bugs in the tested object. A strategy can be effective if results from the combination of the nature of the tests and the nature of the bugs to which those tests are applied. Furthermore, because objects are modified in order to correct their bugs or to enhance their features, the kinds of bugs found in an object change with time, and the effectiveness of strategy changes. It is theoretically possible that a strategy against a specific object improves with time. Realistically, the effectiveness of most strategies degrades with time.

We can recognize the following basic strategies that are often applied:

- *Behavioral test strategies* (called also functional or black box testing) are based on requirements. These tests can, in principle but not in practice, be done in total ignorance of how the object is constructed.
- *Structural test strategies* (also called as glass-box or white-box testing) are derived from the structure of the tested object.
- *Hybrid test strategies* — combination of behavioral and structural strategies

4.2   Tests Automation

There is always a question about the level of automation that should be introduced into a process. Manual process means full flexibility and minimal additional cost of process set up. However, it is very costly if the process is repeated regularly. On the other hand, one must make much effort to establish full automatic process. Maintenance of regular running of automatic process is usually negligible if properly done. However, to be able to create at least partially automatic process, one needs to impose constraints. In fact, these constraints express a model of the world that is automated.

It can be demonstrated on a number of practical examples that the full manual testing of large-scale software projects is very expensive, if not impossible at all, and very frustrating for humans. There are two layers where automation can be very beneficial. At first, one can automate execution of testing. There are many commercial tools that cover this area. The tools are focused mainly on GUI testing and simple functions testing. It is not difficult to create similar tools for sub-system level testing including COM and DLL modules. However, somebody must create scripts to be able to drive testing. This is not an easy task. It can be very annoying activity if scripts must be modified significantly with every small change of functional requirements or software implementation.

4.2.1 Test Scripts Development. Therefore, the second layer suitable for automation is creation of test scripts. Unfortunately, this area is not well theoretically described. As the result, there are only a few tools available on the market. They usually cover only special cases of software systems. Again, it is necessary to impose constraints that serve as input data for creation of scripts. It cannot be expected that functional requirements describing a tested subsystem written in informal English prose will be directly understood by tools generating testing scripts. At present, the only recognized way how to deal with this problem is to transform informal description into formal requirements.

There are basically two classes of formal description used for these purposes. The first class encompasses graphical notations such as UML (Unified Modelling Language from Rational) and OMT (Object Modelling Technique). Unfortunately, it has been reported several times that these notations miss details necessary to describe fully a subsystem interface and its behavior. Furthermore, notations usually do not address consistency of described information. Mainly for large-scale projects it is not reasonable to base formal requirements on these kinds of notations without appropriate supporting consistency checking tools.

On the other hand, much more powerful formal methods belonging to the second class are too abstract. Therefore, they are not generally accepted by people from industry because of a high level of mathematical background necessary to understand and to manipulate with tools. Notwithstanding the fact that available tools are often provided as experimental tools developed at universities. Their user interfaces are often very poor.

Thus, at present we support the idea that the only way to maintain changes in requirements and implementations automatically and to generate thousands of test cases was to use a selected formal method. To start automation in subsequent phases of testing process implies that the remaining initial part must be done manually. Such effort is usually as high as the effort to do the whole testing process manually. Therefore, automation of testing process should begin just behind the informal functional requirement phase. To decrease a burden of developers and testers generating specifications in a formal way we also explored a tool called *Mapper*, generating a kind of formal description of software components.

5   Practical Examples

This section introduces some practical implementation of the processes and methods described above. It is rather true in testing that the theory is often far from the reality and the reality often needs the theoretical backgrounds, but

the presented ones are often too much general. Our examples came from cooperation on SW projects with companies in the area of medical devices (Vitatron
Medical, Medtronic) and in the area of industry automation (Rockwell Automation). The applications for test automation, discussed here, were developed in
C++ under Windows NT operating system.

We want to describe the real working development process that is implemented for production of pacemakers as an example of development life-
supporting devices with extreme care about the final product. Then, we want to
show how to deal with extreme number of test cases that should be generated
to cover SW testing of a complex SW product.

5.1   Testing of Medical Devices

We explain the basic Software Quality Assurance (SQA) and testing strategies
on the development process of pacemakers. In our project, we cooperate with
Vitatron Medical company (Netherlands), producing the most common bradycardia pacemakers.

Herewith, the pacemaker is used to solve problems with an abnormal heart
rate that is less than 60 beats per minute. People with bradycardia have a heart-
beat that is too slow or irregular to meet their body's metabolic demands. Symp-
toms of bradycardia may include dizziness, extreme fatigue, shortness of breath,
or fainting spells.

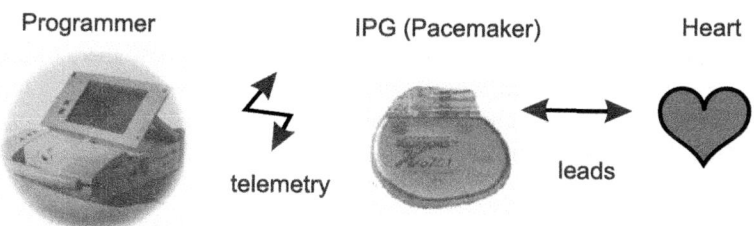

Fig. 3. Pacemaker system overview

The overall system (see Fig. 3) consists of programmer, IPG (Implantable
Pulse Generator = pacemaker) implanted in the human body and leads (connecting the IPG with the patient's heart). The programmer communicates with
the IPG (and vice versa) via telemetry protocol, the communication is wireless.
Doctor uses the programmer to adjust and program different control parameters
of the IPG, i. e. to retrieve diagnostic data from the IPG, analyze the real-time
results of the currently applied therapies and etc. The programmer is based
on standard PC computer including special peripheral devices used for wireless
communications with the IPG. The IPG itself is computer-controlled system,
the programmer's software is written as an object-oriented system.

5.1.1   Development Process. Development of such a medical device consists of the following main phases:

- research phase—a new therapy introduction, clinical studies and clinical proving,
- clinical testing phase,
- new features specification—marketing, medical and technical requirements take place,
- software/firmware development and testing,
- product qualification and distribution.

First, the SQA plan is specified. It contains the general SQA procedures and description of the used standards. These are the procedural rules to be applied and activities to be performed by the SQA engineer(s) and software development team to assure the quality of the software development process, including documentation and the software. Generally, the environment is controlled by the following standards: ISO9001-9003, FDA Guidance for Industry and IEEE standards.

The whole process can be well described by the 'V' development model presented in Fig. 1. As we mentioned in the previous chapters, the verification testing (or just testing) starts with reviews of the SW specifications and designs. First, the SW itself is tested by its components (component testing). It continues with integration testing, where the cooperation of components integrated into one piece of working application is tested. It finishes by testing of the whole product; i. e. the cooperation of the programmer with real IPG (system testing) is verified.

The testing group is not interpersonally mixed with SW developers. The group acts as a separated team located within the SW development. Therefore, the responsibilities are well defined and the knowledge used in the testing is not mixed up with developer's expectations.

5.1.2   Software Verification Testing. The purpose of SW verification testing is to verify the SW functionality and verify that all requirements were successfully implemented. The SW development contains internal cycles to fix all the issues found during the testing phases. Each testing phase starts with searching for critical bugs (test blocking bugs) and continues with deep tests after the critical ones are fixed.

Regression testing is provided for each SW update. SW update can be initiated both by the results of verification testing or by a new product requirement specification. Therefore, we can recognize the following types of regression testing:

- *SW issues are fixed and it is easy to recognize changes in the SW* — verification testing will be focused only on the affected parts of the SW.
- *SW issues are fixed and it is hard to recognize changes in the SW* — all the application must be re-tested again.

— *A new SW requirement was implemented* — the application must be tested as
a whole to prove that the changes have not affected the rest of the product.

The following types of test cases are applied during the verification testing:

a) *Functional (black box) test cases* are created to verify the product against
the specification.
b) *Structural test cases* are created to fully exercise the code.
c) *Interaction test cases* are created to verify interactions between SW modules
(objects).

The structural test cases play an important role mainly during the IPG and
component's testing, due to high code coverage requirements. The functional
and interaction test cases differ in the tested aspects of the SW, as is explained
bellow.

a) Functional test cases. The tests are executed mainly through the user interface of the programmer. The user interface is represented mainly by the graphical
user interface (GUI) of the application. Therefore, the tests are designed as user
actions with defined inputs and verified application outputs.

The test organization structure must be properly chosen at the beginning and
is derived from the structure of the requirement documents. This allows to keep
the tests traceability against requirements simple and understandable. Also, the
test cases can be organized in the same way as the features are specified in the
requirement documents. Therefore, each documented SW feature corresponds to
one test feature. Furthermore, each test feature is divided to test designs with
respect to the test complexity. Each test design stores one or more test cases
that are the main test specifications.

We can identify enormous number of test cases that are needed to verify the
entire application. The number can be in thousands of particular test cases. This
can make impossible to test the application in some reasonable time and repeat
quickly the tests during regression testing. Also, the development cycle can be
radically slowed down and of course, the testing will be really boring.

Therefore, the test automation must be taken into account and majority of
the manual test cases must be automated. Nevertheless, the development of test
cases must be independent of the chosen tests automation tool or strategy. It
must be ensured that the test design will be a common document, allowing freely
switching between different realizations of the tests execution.

The test automation tool is selected in dependency on the controlled SW
interface. We are focused on GUI oriented application. But, for all kinds of
interfaces, the tool should be able to hook the tested application and it should
be able to simulate all the user actions and evaluate the SW response. There
are several tools available on the market like WinRunner, ATF, Rational Robot
and etc.

The currently used test environment for testing of the programmer's software
is shown in Fig. 4. The tested application is running on OS2 machine. The time
for testing is decreased by plugging additional test machines into network. A key

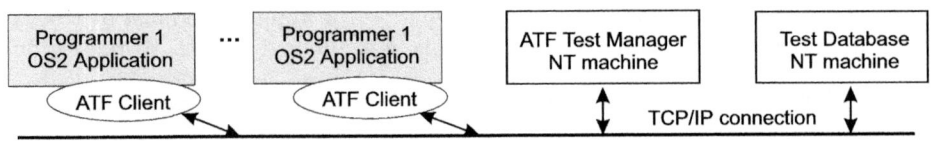

Fig. 4. Environment used for automation of the functional test cases

feature of the test automation and the test scripts development is navigation during test execution. That is how the test script can identify the current status of the application and the GUI objects (currently active window for example) and how to use this information to switch the application to the target state. This knowledge must be stored independently on the test scripts and must be easy maintainable. Following these requirements, the used test automation system is characterized as follows:

– Test scripts are data driven and general.
– Test scripts are navigated through the application by using model of interactions stored in the test database. The model of interactions defines relationships between application widgets and specifies actions to set the desired state of a particular widget.
– The test inputs and the expected test outputs are stored in the test database.

The test cases are reusable for different software products of the same SW family. Just the database information must be updated for every new family product. Thus, the test preparation for a new SW version is reduced mainly to the database maintenance.

c) Interaction Test Cases. The application is written as an object oriented SW based on framework architecture. The intention of the interaction testing is to test the application from inside by driving message oriented application core. Accordingly, all the internal messages must be checked for consistency and correspondence with designed functional scenarios.

The number of interaction test cases is comparable with number of functional tests. Therefore, the test automation should also support the testing process. However, the test automation strategy can not be built-up with using "standardized" application interfaces. This practically disallows implementation of test scripts via testing tool available on the market and forces to develop special supporting tools that will behave similarly as the tools used for functional testing. Herewith, the ideas of the test environment organization stay the same and the tools cost additional development.

5.1.3 Measuring the Testing Effectiveness. We have to define terms 'Defect' and 'Defect Metrics' to be able to measure the test effectiveness. We can say that *defects* are those errors of analysis, design or coding that are passed by the developer to the next stage of the development process. We can recognize *specification defects* (missing or wrong documents) and *implementation defects* (failures in the SW).

In each phase of development we are interested in how many defects are received, how many are introduced, how many are removed, and how many are passed along to the next phase. This is the basic information that is gathered from the process. There are other source code measurements and other information available, but we can use it this to create the basic definition: The testing effectiveness in a specific phase is defined as "Total defects removed in the phase divided by the total defects that have been introduces in that phase."

The process is not much effective if the computed number is close to one. This happens mainly in the first testing phase, where the SW is not yet stable and new errors are introduced with fixing the previous ones. The number should be increased as the product is going to be finished. The SW can still has errors inside, but the process is effective.

5.1.4 Summary. The development of life supporting devices requires formal development process with implemented software configuration management (set of management disciplines performed within the context of the SW development process). The testing of such a device starts at the beginning of the development and is a part of each development phase. The code verification testing requires code that is ready for testing. It means, the code design and development should take the testing into account. This includes interfaces to the testing tools and also development of specifics test automation supporting tools. Therefore, the testing part significantly extends the project planning.

5.2   Automated Creation and Maintenance of Test Cases

A number of authorities from software testing environment have reported that the most difficult part of testing process is creation and maintenance of test cases. It takes time to create a sufficient set of test cases covering the requirements on the product (acceptance testing). It takes even more time to create a reasonable set of test cases exercising the product in a satisfactory way. And only few people respect seriously that the most of time must be spent on keeping this huge set of test cases up to date with the still evolving subject of test.

The Rockwell Automation (Electronic Operator Interfaces) products are man-machine systems. Therefore, their testing is mainly oriented to the testing of the interface between man and machine. A human is a very cooperative and faults tolerant system. Small defects in the man-machine interface are often neglected. Further, the system using the device interface (a human) exhibits only one style, even very rich, of interactions with the device interface.

Testing architecture of one of the projects was even in a worse position. At first, cooperating subsystems were machines. Their tolerance to faults is very low. This implies that the interface should be described in much more precise way. That means, both sides of the interface should be specified. The side called subsystem must constrain clearly all actions expected from calling subsystems.

On the other hand, the calling side should characterize the behavior expected from the called subsystem. It looks quite strange why both sides need to specify the expected behavior. However, the reason is rather simple. The mapping of behaviors is not one-to-one.

We assumed that subsystems would exhibit different complexity. Produced devices would be cost-effective combinations of subsystems. Thus, both sides of an interface can expect more or less complex behavior. All expected pairs should be treated during testing. This is a rather difficult task.

The basic idea is to transform informal human language (English prose) used in software specification requirements into formal one that can be understood by a machine. Using a prover one can validate the following parts of formal description:

- is consistent — in our case it means that both sides of interfaces are compatible,
- specifies the same task as specified by the informal specifications.

Based on the formal description, one can generate a set of test cases assuming given testing strategy. An animator of the formal description, i. e. software that is able to execute formal specifications in a symbolic way, can accomplish the generation of test cases. A number of commercial tools use in their kernels some kind of a formal methods.

Generally, to create a test script we need to know structure and behavior of tested object. Further, a testing strategy must be selected. If done formally, structure and behavior must be described using some notation such as UML or one of formal methods.

We automated only a part of system testing dealing with regression testing of properties available in a hierarchy of software components. Although behavior and properties of software basic components was known, a detailed description of the hierarchical architecture was not available. That was obtained by reverse engineering techniques as it is depicted in Fig. 5.

The test generator generated test cases and created the test suite. Both the reverse engineering tools and the test generator were implemented in Perl. The test suite was generated in Visual Basic. As we can see both tools somehow reflected information about the software structure and system testing strategy. This scheme was able to test a selected set of behaviors of the retrieved software structures.

We extended the scheme to use rule-based expert system able to generate test cases that tested behaviors specific to a given subsets of software structures. The behavior of a given structure combined with testing strategy was coded in the rules. The modified scheme was the following, see Fig. 6.

The test generator was implemented using CLIPS [7]. Therefore, only CLIPS coded representation of test cases were generated. This form was converted into the Visual Basic projects by the test suite generator. We identified two main problems with the rule-based generation of test cases. At first, the rules had to reflect precisely the architecture of the software. There was no connection to the real architecture. The deviations were detected during the testing. That meant,

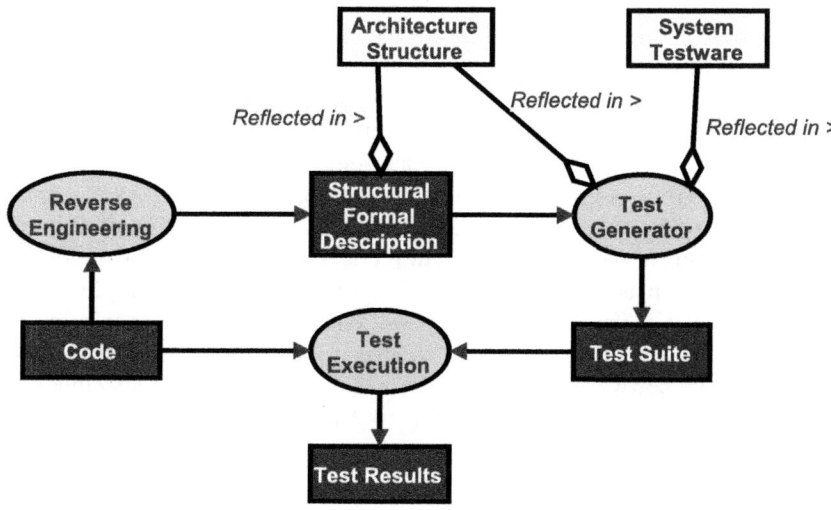

Fig. 5. Testing of Software Structures

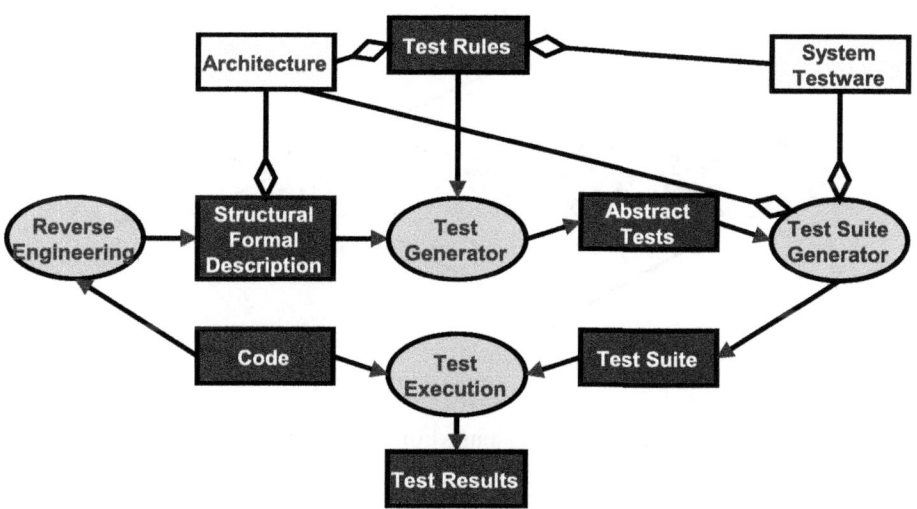

Fig. 6. Knowledge based generation of test scripts

any test failure could be caused by a modification of software architecture, an unexpected behavior of the implementation, or by a bug in a test rule. This is not an environment when developers and testers can trust each other. Therefore, one needs to validate the formal description of the software architecture (the rules) against the original architecture. Further, the formal descriptions of the software architecture and system (or acceptance) testing strategy should be separated.

The only solution we know about is to use formal methods. The formal methods have the power to validate the formal specification against the informal one by proving of so called putative theorems. In other words, the software features that ate represented informally are converted into the formal ones. After that, their approvement is done inside the formal software model. The formal methods can also be used for consistency checking of the formal model. If the formal model is consistent and validated against the informal model, it can be used for automatic generation of test cases. This step is usually performed using animators, in other words, tools able to execute the formal specifications. The developers of the software implementation can use the formal specification too because it is more precise than the informal one. The situation is depicted in Fig. 7.

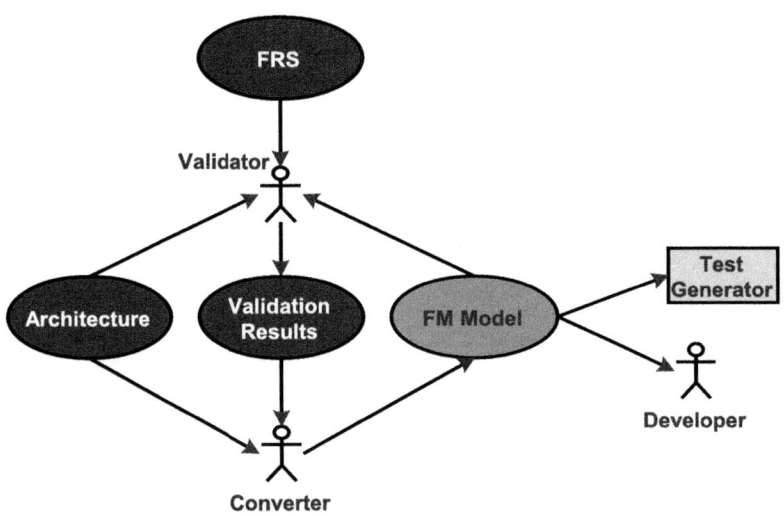

Fig. 7. Testing based on formal methods

Of course, formal methods have their own limits. For example, they are suitable only for applications that can be described by discrete mathematics. They are not suitable for a system implementing, e. g. numerical methods and differential equations.

5.2.1 Experiments. There are other drawbacks of the expert-based system that have appeared when we tried to use it for testing of more complex system.

Originally, the used rules were simple without deep nesting and their number did not exceed 20. When used with more complicated set of rules (e. g. testing of a richer software interface), we have not been capable to drive appropriately combinatorial explosion of all possible test cases. It seems that a suitable solution might be found in theory of planning developed in artificial intelligence field. However, simple planners as STRIPS or WARPLAN are not sufficient because of their low efficiency to find alternative solutions. At present, we are experimenting with advanced interleaved planners using partial-order plan representation and causal links [5,15].

5.3   GUI MAPPER

The GUI Mapper is a prototype of a tool for automatic description of tested software systems and creation of a set of regressive testing scripts. The tool was developed during project with Rockwell Automation Company. It maps the application through its graphical interface and the navigation problem should be solved automatically.

5.3.1   Tool Overview. The GUI Mapper is a tool building a behavioral model of the tested application. At present, only finite state machine is used as the model. No data flow model is considered. The GUI Mapper utilizes general background knowledge about general behavior of applications and minimum knowledge about the given application. In our case, background knowledge supplies information on windows, their structures, and possible actions. For example, it is known that push buttons can be clicked, strings can be entered into edit-boxes etc.

At first, the GUI Mapper updates the model of the application according to available information. Secondly, the Mapper identifies unknown parts of the model and plans activities to discover these parts. The abstract activities are converted into scripts that can be executed by such tool like SQA Robot (GUI based test automation tool from Rational). When the scripts are executed, the application is navigated into an unknown state. The state is carefully described and all related structures are mapped and described. The obtained result serves as input to the next iteration. The iterations continue until all unknown parts of the models are discovered.

Finally, the result model of the application is verified using testing techniques specialized to finite state machines. Any discrepancy between the model and the behavior of the application is resolved by a modification of the model.

5.3.2   Motivation. The tester needs some kind of software specification to create a test plan and to develop test scripts. Software specifications are usually well defined at the system level from the customer point of view. In majority of cases, the specifications are written in a prose language. To automate her/his work, the tester needs more formal specifications. Formality means to follow a given set of accepted rules. Such rules could be utilized by using machine generator and test scripts maintainer. However, an appropriate level of formalism is not generally known. It is even harder to convey such information to developers.

The purpose of the GUI Mapper development was severalfold:

- At first, the Mapper cannot map the tested application blindly because the probability of correct operation on some objects, for instance a secure login into the application, is very low. Therefore, it is necessary to provide minimal information about the application into the Mapper manually. The amount of this information should be kept low. It is not obvious what is that minimum provided information. The development of the Mapper contributed valuable information to this problem.
- Secondly, the GUI Mapper is a machine application and its input must follow a given set of rules. Thus, the set of rules together with the input data represents the formal specifications of the tested application. The Mapper dictates their suitable format.
- Thirdly, the Mapper outputs could serve as a support to developers. The output basically represents both structural and behavioral information about the tested application. This information can be fed back into prose of the software specification. Furthermore, a developer can check if the information produced by the Mapper correspond to the intended implementation.
- At fourth, Mapper output data could serve as input data into the test script generator.
- Finally, the GUI Mapper uses sort of testing methods to map the application. Thus, basic behavior of the tested application is directly tested during the mapping.

One can not expect that the Mapper would be capable to cover the full range of tested software. At first, we mapped GUI based executable applications. Having the basic functionality of the Mapper, we planned to create the extensions for COM and DLL components and similar subsystems.

There are many aspects of software behavior. We started to map behavior of finite state machines and their generalizations, such as those of stream X machines because the majority of software applications could be described using these models.

5.3.3   Methodology Used.

The finite state machine model was built using properties of Windows objects. SQA Robot executed scripts mapping properties of windows and their objects. Majority of object classes of supported objects could be described using SQA Basic functions (test scripting language similar to Basic). It was not difficult to supply additional functions able to describe menu structures of windows and appearance of windows in the system.

In our experimental environment with GUI based applications, automaton state is related to a window and its state. Automaton events correspond to user actions operating the mapped application.

A state is called terminal if all possible events at this state are examined. Otherwise, the state is called non-terminal. The Mapper works in iterations in two modes. In the first mapping mode, the Mapper tries to map the states that can be reached by triggering all possible events starting in non-terminal states. If there is no non-terminal state, the Mapper switches itself into a verification (testing) mode. In the verification mode, the Mapper designs a set of testing scripts verifying that the model and the actual application are equivalent according to finite-state machine behavior. If a verification script detects differences between actual and model automatons, the model is modified, and the Mapper switches back into the mapping mode.

Every state is an abstraction of a corresponding configuration of screen objects. It is valid that any two distinguishable window object configurations are mapped into different states. On the other hand, different states can share the same configuration. In this case, the states can be distinguished by a sequence of transitions starting in these states. It implies that in this case there is a non-empty set of configuration variables that cannot be observed but their values would distinguish the configurations.

Each transition between two states is discovered by one mapping script. At first, the application is brought into a non-terminal state. An event is chosen from the set of admissible events at this input state. The event is sent to the mapped application and a new configuration of window objects is observed. If the configuration corresponds to an already known configuration, the related output states are fetched and the automaton is updated. Notice that an output state might not be unique and the search for output states can result in the whole set. However, only the first such output state is considered. This solution has been implemented as the first approximation of the final solution for debugging purposes.

A special attention must be paid to dependencies between user actions. For example, one is able to open a new file if a project has been already chosen. Passing through the logon window means that the correct password must be written at first and the OK button can be pushed after that, and etc. We investigated manual entries describing such dependencies. We did not detect any obstacle to use it. It can speed up rapidly the mapping process. However, there is a way to detect dependencies automatically. It is based on a very simple idea: a set of testing scripts up to k-level of hidden states is capable to discover dependencies composed from k transitions.

In summary, what is required to specify the application? At first, the Mapper must be provided with the name and the location of the executable. At second, each *editbox* appearing in the application should be supplied with representatives of the categories of their inputs. The current release of the implementation does not use the information on dependencies.

5.3.4 Experiments. We used a standard GUI based application supplied in the SQA Robot tutorial for the development of the Mapper. We mapped namely appearance of windows, pushbuttons, and *editboxes*. The experimental application was described using 26 states and 260 transitions. Thus, the application behavior was obtained in very short time because it was sufficient to run about 4000 mapping and verifying scripts. Using the current generating mechanism the amount of testing scripts is about 30–40 MB.

A modification of the Mapper to map also the rest of used objects is the matter of description tables extensions and related SQA Basic generating strings or functions. The complexity of mapping scripts is very low. Therefore, the speed of their execution is quite high, about 700 mapping scripts in 1 hour. Furthermore, only 260 scripts are already mapping for the chosen example, the others are verifying scripts discovering hidden states.

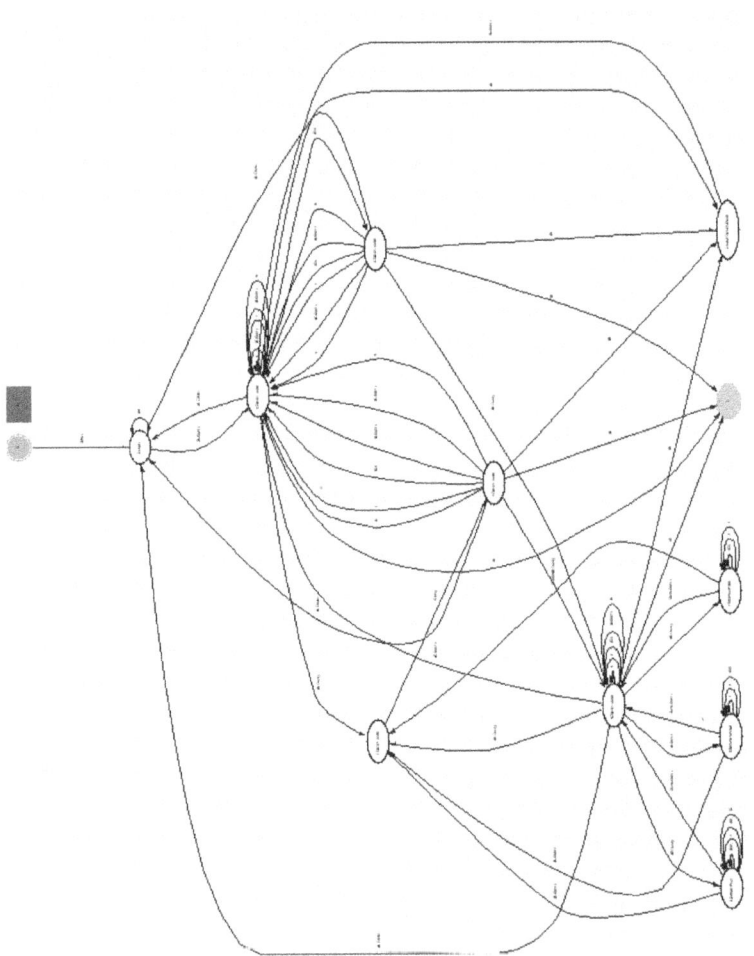

Fig. 8. The GUI application model — 10th iteration

The Fig. 8 depicts an intermediate result of identified finite-state machine models of a GUI based application from the Rational Suite 1.0 tutorial. The application implements ordering and purchasing of audio CD-ROM discs. It has reasonable complexity for demo purposes. Fig. 8 depicts the tenth iteration of the mapping process. Both start end exit states are filled ovals. Non-filled ovals and filled rectangles represent terminal states and non-terminal states, respectively.

6 Conclusion

In this paper we presented an overview of basic issues of software testing. Their complexity, the lack of practical solutions, and necessity to create systematical approach make software testing to be another scientific field of computer science. We guess that software testing will become a fundamental part of software diagnostics dealing not only with testing (searching for consequences) but also with identification of software problem origins (searching for causes).

At present, the major stream of software testing effort is covered by tedious manual work. During the short history of software engineering, there has been a dramatic shift in tester-to-developer ratios (in favor of testers) which indicates that the importance of testing is now recognized, and organizations are now more willing to pay for proper testing. At the same time the number of testers continues to grow, and the time spent on testing and its perceived effectiveness are increasing. Historically, for mainframes, the tester-to-developer ratio was 1:5–10, meaning one tester for every five to ten product developers. The published numbers include:

- Microsoft, 1993 — ratio 2:3,
- Microsoft, 2000 — ratio 1:1,
- Lotus (for 1-2-3 Windows), 1993 — ratio 2:1,
- Average of 4 major companies (Microsoft, Borland, WordPerfect, and Novell), 1993 — ratio 1:2;

more typical ratios are in the range from 1:3 to 1:4.

However, the size of modern software projects is making manual testing impracticable, mainly for regression testing. On the other hand, automation of software testing is still not a mature discipline. A number of unsolved tasks could be addressed by methodologies developed in artificial intelligence such as that of planning. In this paper we demonstrated that there is a way. Nevertheless, whether such algorithms, usually presented on simple abstract examples, are capable to be used as software testing automation tools is still questionable.

Of course, there is also an open space to design software systems including testing features (so called design for testing) as it happens in other activities of human kind.

In a number of practical cases, business managers, but also customers, abandon software quality because of the huge pressure of market competition. Thus, software diagnostics is depreciated, even the majority of automated and decision-making activities is reallocated into software. On the other hand, its importance grows observing a number of software projects failures on one side and successes of projects incorporating software diagnostics features.

References

1. S. Barbey. *Test Selection for Specification-Based Unit Testing of Object-Oriented Software based on Formal Specifications*. PhD thesis, Ecole Polytechnique Federale de Lausanne, Department of Information, 1997. 95
2. Boris Beizer. *Black-Box Testing (Techniques for Functional Testing of Software and Systems)*. John Wiley & Sons, 1995. 91
3. Bob Birs. Testing object-oriented software: a survey. *SunProgrammer — The Newsletter for Professional Software Engineers*, 1(3), 1992. 96
4. Barry W. Boehm. A spiral model of software development and enhancements. *ACM Software Engineering Notes*, 11, 1986. 92
5. David Chapman. Planning for conjunctive goals. *Artificial Intelligence*, 32(3):333–377, 1987. 109
6. Lee Copeland. Object oriented testing. In *Software testing training week*, Amstelveen, 1999. 97
7. Joseph C. Giarratano. *CLIPS — User's Guide (version 6.05)*. International Thompson Publishing, 1997. 106
8. Ieee standard 1061-1992, ieee standard for a software quality metrics methodology, 1993. 97
9. Edward Kit. *Software Testing in the Real World*. Addison-Wesley, 1995. 97
10. P. Kruchten and W. Royce. A rational development process. *CrossTalk*, 9(7), 1996. 96
11. M. Lenz, B. Bartsch-Sporl, H.-D. Burkhard, and S. Wess, editors. *Case-Based Reasoning Technology (From Foundations to Applications)*, volume 1400 of *Lecture notes in artificial intelligence*. Springer-Verlag, 1998. 89
12. B. Meyer. *Object-Oriented Software Construction*. Prentice-Hall, 1988. 96
13. Steven R. Rakitin. *Software Verification and Validation (A Practitioner's Guide)*. Artech House Publishers, 1997. 92, 97, 98
14. J. Rumbaugh, M. Blaha, and F. Eddy W. Premerlani, and W. Lorensen. *Object-Oriented Modeling and Design*. Prentice Hall, 1991. 95
15. Daniel Weld. An introduction to least commitment planning. *AI Magazine*, pages 27–61, 1994. 109

Physical Design of CMOS Chips in Six Easy Steps

Sidney E. Benda

Intel Corp., Colorado Springs Design Center
sidney.benda@intel.com

Abstract. Aimed at software professional not familiar with design processes of semiconductor elements that execute their programs. This paper focuses on algorithms and software involved in a design, layout and verification of CMOS parts. The first section introduces basic building elements of a design — transistor and standard cell — and shows their representation in design database. The design flow is segmented into six distinct steps: design capture, synthesis, floorplanning, placement and routing, extraction and verification.

1   Design Database

Image of physical structures on a chip is typically stored in a form of hierarchically linked lists that can be accessed either programmatically via LISP-like interface or by graphical front-end that allows drawing and manipulation of polygons, transistors, cells and blocks. The database access and manipulation will be shown on examples in the following paragraphs.

1.1   MOS Transistor

Proceeding bottom up in a physical layout of a chip, the smallest circuit unit is a transistor.

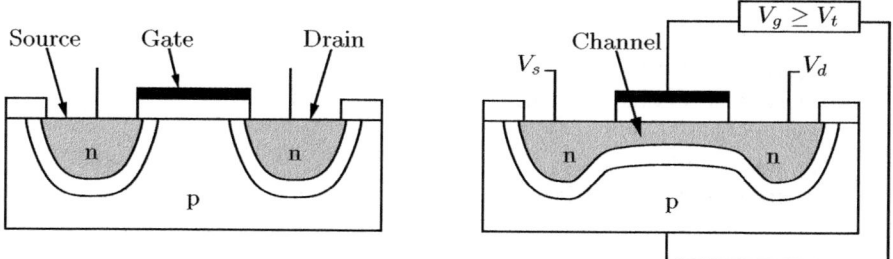

Fig. 1. The cross section of n-channel MOS transistor

V. Hlaváč, K. G. Jeffery, and J. Wiedermann (Eds.): SOFSEM 2000, LNCS 1963, pp. 115–128, 2000.

To fabricate n-channel MOS (Metal Oxide Semiconductor) transistor, p-type substrate is covered with an insulating layer of silicon dioxide. Two windows are cut into oxide to allow diffusion to create two separate n-regions, the *source* and *drain*. A conductive layer of polysilicon is laid on top. When positive voltage greater than *threshold voltage* is applied to the gate, n-type conductive channel is created between the source and drain. To capture footprint of a transistor in a database, we need two rectangles on respective layers "poly" and "diffusion":

```
((objType "rectangle" ((-0.5 -1.0) (0.5 1.0)))
  layer "poly")
 (objType "rectangle" ((-1.0  -0.5) (1.0 0.5)))
  layer "diffusion")
 )
```

1.2   Standard Cell

Although individual transistors can be created in layout of a chip, the usual building unit is a *standard cell* composed of several transistors.

Common standard cell implementing two-input logical function NAND is shown in Fig. 2. The cell uses two n-channel transistors shown in Fig. 1 and two p-channel transistors whose behavior is complementary, i. e. they open when n-channel closes and vice versa. This combination results in low power consumption as the cell dissipates power only while switching. Assuming that low voltage on input/output in logical 0, while high voltage is 1, the truth table for this cell is:

Input A	Input B	Output C
0	0	1
0	1	1
1	0	1
1	1	0

The database record for this cell contains polygons on layers "poly", "diffusion", "metal1" and "contact" as well as properties describing connectivity and location:

```
(objType "cellInst"
 (cellName "NAND")
 (instName "nx1")
 (shapes   ((... list of cell geometries ...)))
 (xy  nil)
 (orient "R0")
 (pins (input "A") (input "B") (output "C"))
 )
```

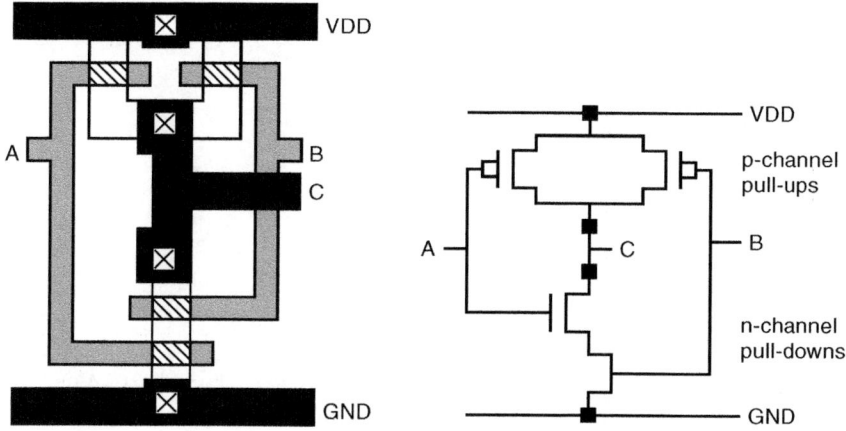

Fig. 2. Layout and schematic of two-input NAND gate

1.3 Design Rules

As indicated in previous discussion of transistor and standard cell, each fabrication process puts several layers on the surface of silicon substrate. Besides diffusion and poly layers used inside cells, there is up to six metal layers for connections. The metal layers are separated by oxide or connected — where necessary — by pseudo-layer called via (cut in oxide). In order to guarantee acceptable yield of CMOS fabrication, each process has set of layer properties and constraints called design rules. The rules are usually grouped into the following three types:

1. *Size rules.* For each layer, there is minimum feature size below which the functionality is not guaranteed. For example, poly width in transistor needs to be at least 0.35 microns, otherwise it may not be able to open the conductive channel.
2. *Separation rules.* Different features on the same layer, e.g. two adjacent wires on the same metal layer must be spaced certain distance so they do not accidentally short.
3. *Overlap rules.* These are necessary for proper function of transistors (poly over diffusion) and for connection between two layers of metal (metal — via overlap).

The set of rules, along with additional physical properties of the process is contained in *technology file* that is integral part of design database. Technology file contains also physical dimensions and properties of the process utilized in latter steps of the physical design:

```
((Technology "pseudoProcess"
   (timeUnit   "ps")
   (capUnit    "fF")
```

```
    (dielectric   3.9)
  )
  (Layer         "metal1"
   (layerNum     8)
   (minWidth     0.35)
   (minSpacing   0.35)
   (pitch        1.0)
   (nomResistance  0.0615)
   (nomCapacitance 6.31e-3)
   (heightFromSub  1.50)
   (nomThickness   0.60)
  )
  (DesignRule       "minSpacing"   ("poly"    "via1" 0.4))
  (DesignRule       "minEnclosure" ("metal1" "via1" 0.2))
)
```

2   Design Capture

The original way of logic design using schematic capture is clearly not feasible in projects containing up to 10^9 elements. The need for higher level structured description led to origin of *hardware description languages* (HDL) such as Verilog and VHDL. The following Verilog code segment is to illustrate several most common HDL constructs:

```
module multiplier(result, op_a, op_b);
parameter size=8;
input [size:1] op_a, op_b;
output [2*size:1] result;
reg [2*size:1] shift_opa, result;
reg [size:1] shift_opb;
always @(op_a or op_b)
begin
 result = 0;
 shift_opa = op_a;    // zero extend left
 shift_opb = op_b;
 repeat (size)
 begin
   #10 if(shift_opb[1]) result = result + shift_opa;
   shift_opa = shift_opa<<1; // logical left  shift
   shift_opb = shift_opb>>1; // logical right shift
 end
end
endmodule
```

The code above multiplies two operands op_a, op_b by repeated shifts of both operands and conditional adding of shifted op_a.

2.1 Modules

The basic building block in Verilog is a module. The complete design is tree of module instances with root in the top-level module. Module header specifies boundary of logic block, direction and size of its ports. *Component instantiation* creates new module instance inside higher level module:

```
module ALU (...);
...
reg  [7:0] OUT1, OUT2;
wire [7:0] A, B;
...
// positional port mapping
multiplier MULT1 (OUT1, A, B);

// named port mapping
multiplier MULT2 (.op_a(A), .op_b(B), .res(OUT2));
endmodule
```

2.2 Data Types

Register data type is declared using keyword reg. This type of variable actually stores data. The net data type is declared as wire. Wire is a physical connection between structural entities of Verilog. It does not store data, only propagates them from register to register. The third data type shown — parameter — is essentially symbolic constant. All three data types can take a form of *bit vector* by specifying its range as [⟨most significant bit⟩ : ⟨least significant bit⟩] .

2.3 Behavior

Most of the operators and control structures in a module body resemble conventional programming languages and therefore do not need to be discussed in detail. The exception is always block. Each of these blocks is sequentially executed inside, but all always blocks run concurrently. The @(...) part of each always block is a list of variables that trigger its execution upon change of their values.

Another important HDL feature is concept of sequencing of events in time. The notation #10 on line 14 in the mutiplier example is *delay specification* indicating that this statement takes 10 time units to execute.

Let it be noted that majority of designs are *synchronous*. In these designs, stages of combinatorial logic feed into register type variables that are synchronized by *clock* signal (Fig. 3).

3 Synthesis

Synthesis is a process in which high-level HDL description of a design is converted into primitives that can be directly laid out on silicon die. There are three tasks performed during synthesis:

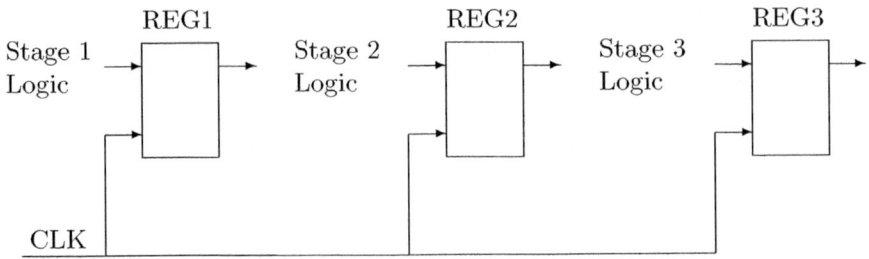

Fig. 3. Example of synchronous logic: Three-stage pipeline

1. Mapping of logic-level HDL constructs onto target library components.
2. Logic optimization attempting to reduce the area and number of components.
3. Selecting sizes of components to meet the timing requirements.

Step 1 is similar to compilation of a high-level programming language. The HDL operators and structures are mapped on logical equations that are subject to Boolean optimization in step 2. Step 3 considers non-zero delay of combinatorial logic components and tries to make sure that overall delay by each logic stage (see Fig. 3) satisfies requirement given by clock rate (i. e. signal delay through logic has to be less than period of the clock). Selecting faster cell to meet timing requirement causes increased power consumption so these two requirements need to be carefully balanced. Synthesis run typically needs to set boundary conditions (external clock rate, set input delay, set load) and take into account various *constraints* imposed by technology (max fanout, max transition).

As an example, let us use dataflow description of a device that selects one of its two inputs A, B by the value of signal SEL:

```
module MUX2(OUT, A, B, SEL);
output OUT;
input  A,B,SEL;
   if (SEL == 1'b0) OUT = A; else OUT = B;
endmodule
```

The module will synthesize into *gate-level netlist* as

```
module MUX2(OUT, A, B, SEL);
output OUT;
input  A,B,SEL;
wire   a1, b1, sel;
   NOT not1(sel,SEL);
   AND and1(a1,A,sel);
   AND and2(b1,B,SEL);
   OR  or1(OUT,a1,b1);
endmodule
```

In Verilog terms, this is structural module that contains nothing else but instances of cells from target library interconnected by wires.

The target library contains standard cells (as described in the intro section) annotated by information on internal cell delays, operating conditions and cell size. In our example, the target library contained only AND, OR and NOT gates while typical production libraries contains hundreds of cells of different functions and sizes, including 2-input multiplexer synthesized above.

4   Floorplanning

Physical representation of modules in design hierarchy can be sorted into several categories:

1. *Bond pads* that represent inputs and outputs of the root module in the design. They are essentially rectangles of metal for soldering of wires during packaging. Their location is always on perimeter of a layout.
2. *Re-used blocks.* Layout of modules like RAM, ROM, register files and others may be imported from previous designs.
3. *Custom blocks.* Typical for analog circuitry (for example A/D converter), layout of some modules need to be created by custom drawing of circuit components.
4. *Standard cell blocks.* These are gate-level netlist modules produced by synthesis as shown in step 2. As opposed to previous three categories which have fixed size, shape and connecting points (*pins*), standard cell blocks (sometimes called *soft blocks*) need to be assigned these properties in the first step of floorplanning.

The second step of floorplanning is placement of defined blocks. There are number of tools available, mostly based on minimizing total length of nets connecting the blocks. There are algorithms [7,11] producing very good results as far as area optimization, yet there is observed lack of algorithm that would factor in a degree of rectilinearity ("number of corners") that results in routing penalties.

Final step of floorplanning creates power/ground grid and performs block level signal routing.

Fig. 4 shows intermediate stage of floorplanning with pad ring in place, unplaced hard blocks (left side) and defined but unplaced soft blocks of standard cells.

5   Placement and Routing

5.1   Placement

A synthesized block contains anything between 10^3 to 10^6 standard cells. The placement algorithm is mapping the set of cells onto *placement grid* while minimizing total net length and congestion. The congestion metric is usually defined

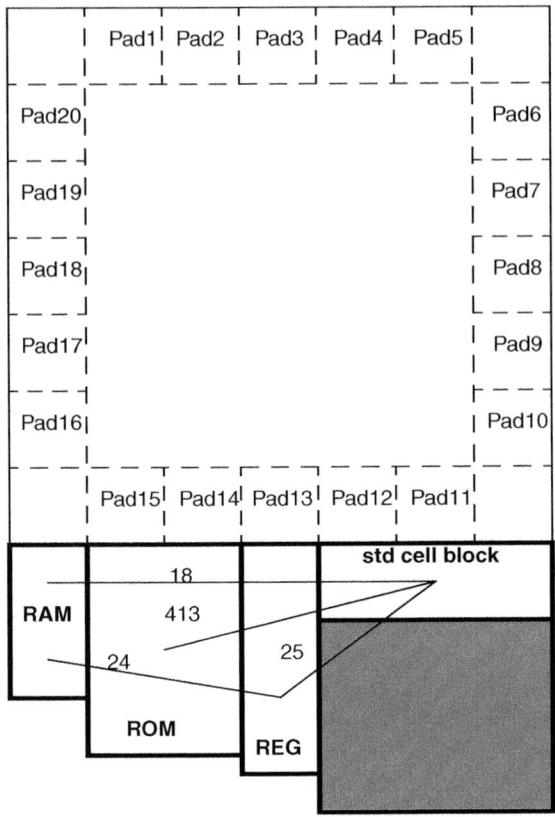

Fig. 4. Design blocks in initialized floorplan with display of connectivity

in terms of net connections per unit of square area [8]. There is significant number of placement algorithms discussed in [10,8] out of which the first usable ones were based on *simulated annealing*: the optimization of a cell placement is analogous to the process of annealing melted material into highly ordered crystalline state. Besides being extremely time-consuming, these algorithms did very little for removing congestion.

Significantly faster are placement tools based on min-cut. The min-cut algorithm slices a block into two halves and swaps cells to minimize number of nets crossing the cut. An alternative is quad-cut in which block is sliced horizontally and vertically into four sections. This is repeated recursively inside the cut sections.

Quadratic method stores the cost of connecting each pair of cells (net length) in connection matrix. The process of net length minimization and proof of existence of non-trivial solution are discussed in [3].

The congestion problem typically happens in sections of combinatorial logic with high connectivity and low porosity of cells. Advanced placement tools allow displaying of *congestion map* — color-coded indication of required number of net connections versus available routing resources. Example of placement congestion map is in Fig. 5. In this design, most connections run in vertical direction with congestion in upper right corner. The congestion removal is accomplished by inserting appropriate amount of white space between cell instances in the congested area.

5.2   Global Route

In the placement phase, the exact location of cell instances and their connecting points has been determined. The task of global routing is to distribute connecting nets over the block as uniformly as possible to avoid routing congestion. The area of a standard cell block is first divided into *switchboxes* — rectangular regions similar to area units used in evaluation of placement congestion. When routing net from one connecting point to another, each switchbox counts number of nets crossing each of its sides. The goal is to find configuration of the nets yielding minimum congestion and minimum total net length. Some global routers show congestion map similar to the one shown in Fig. 5.

5.3   Detail Route

Considering net as n-tuple $(p_1, p_2, \ldots, p_n)$ where p_i is pin of a cell, detail routing is a step that actually creates conductive path connecting together all pins belonging to the net. This is performed for all nets in a given block.

In dark ages of VLSI technology when maximum of two interconnecting metal layers were available, all routing was done in channels — white space between rows of standard cells. Metal 1 used for connections inside cell would represent significant blockage to do much of *over-the-cell routing*. Utilization — in terms of ratio of cell area to total block area — would rarely exceed 50 %. More recent processes use up to six metal layers, which allow much higher utilization (approaching 100 %) with all routing done over the cells.

Detail routing algorithm works on 3-dimensional routing grid extending over the entire routed block. The z-dimension corresponds to each metal layer while x- and y-dimensions specify possible location for horizontal and vertical wires. The pitch of the grid is given by design rule specifying minimum spacing of wires with allowance for adjacent vias (transition from one metal layer to another) that are usually wider than wires. The routing pitch also needs to be considered in construction of standard cells so that when cells are placed, all their pins lie on the routing grid.

The first task of a detail router is to map *blockages* from underlying cells into the routing grid. Space occupied by polygons on "metal1" or "metal2" used in connections inside cells obviously cannot be used for net connections and has to be blocked out of the routing grid (black circles in Fig. 6). This reduces the number of available routing grid vertices on corresponding planes of the routing grid space. The main task of the routing algorithm is to find a path between a pair of points on a net. The areas available for routing are represented as

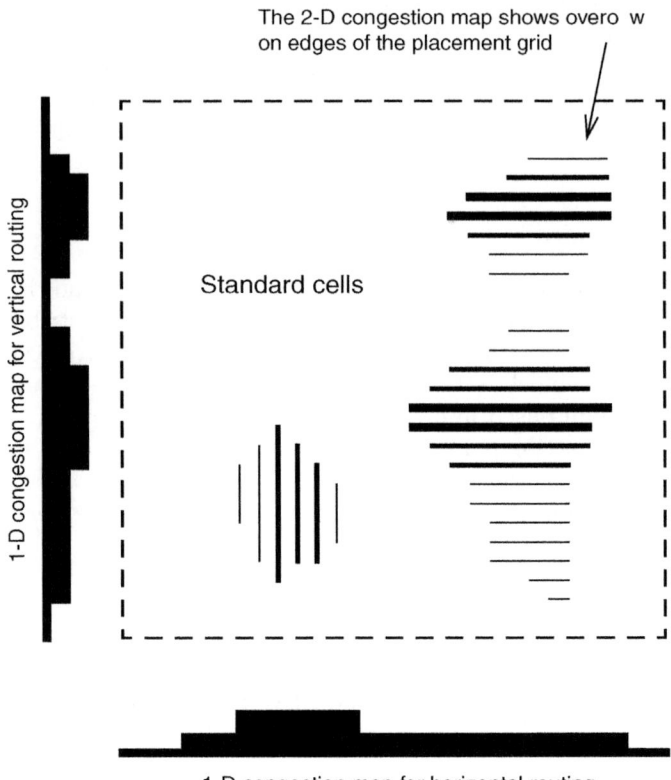

Fig. 5. Placement congestion map

unblocked vertices of the graph (white circles in Fig. 6). The search algorithm for path connecting points S and T in such graph was developed by Lee [5]. It can be visualized as a wave propagating from S to all unblocked adjacent vertices. Labeling these vertices as '1', the algorithm proceeds to propagate wave to all unblocked adjacent vertices '2' and so on, until the target vertex T is reached or no further expansion can be carried out. Due to nature of the search, Lee's maze router is guaranteed to find a solution, if one exists. Soukup [12] modified Lee's algorithm to reduce search time by limiting the wave propagation only in direction towards the target.

A variation of the above algorithms is base for most recent routing tools. However, instead operating on one plane, routing tools work in one more dimension, utilizing all available metal layers. If solution cannot be found on one plane (layer), router uses via to get to one of adjacent planes and continues there.

Unlike global router that considers the entire layout of a block, detail router considers just one switchbox at a time. If we attempt to route entire nets, the first several nets will be easily routable, while routing would get progressively

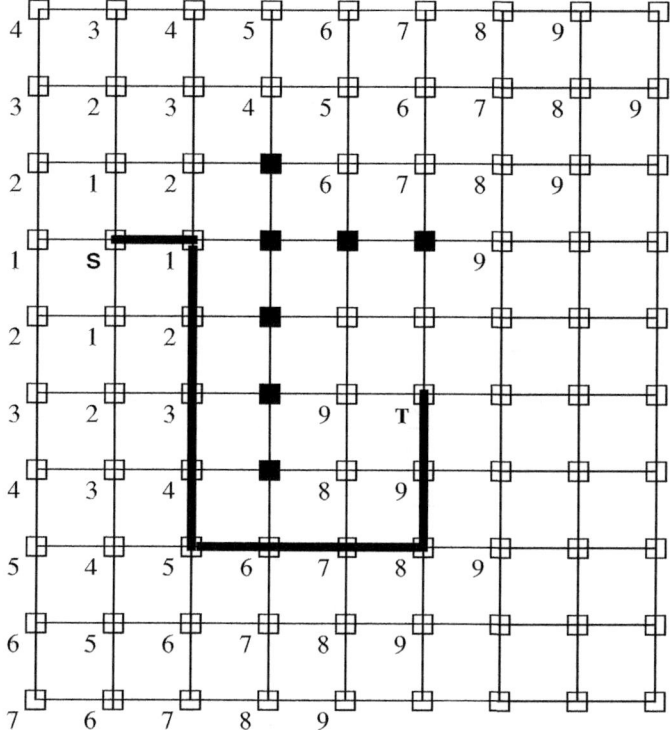

Fig. 6. Maze route between points S and T on one plane

more difficult because of decreasing number of available vertices in routing grid. To even out the chances for every net, detail router first works on individual switchboxes that are connected together later on in several iterative *search and repair* cycles.

On occasions, synthesis step may produce block that is *unroutable* — the internal high connectivity of the block exceeds available routing resources. An efficient placement routability modeling technique is described in [1].

6   Extraction

When all blocks of a design are placed and routed, it is desirable to find out electrical properties of the design before it goes to actual fabrication. More specifically, designer is interested whether his block meets timing specifications so the chip will work at desired speed or clock rate. Signal delays on the chip have two components:

- *Cell delays* caused by finite transition time of transistors. Before synthesis, all the cells in library are characterized and synthesis tool uses these values to select proper cell size or *drive strength*.

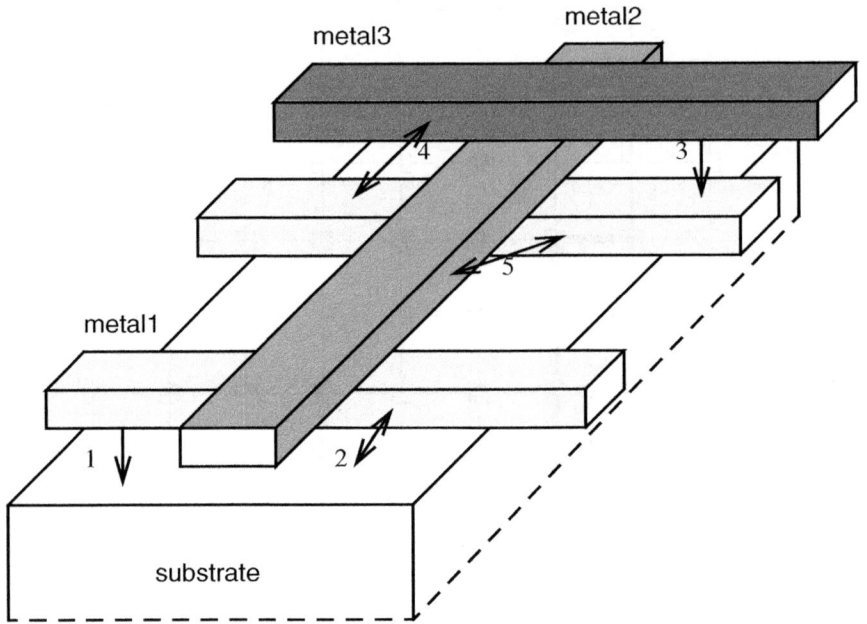

Fig. 7. Coupling capacitance between conductive layers

– *Interconnect delays* caused by parasitic capacitance of nets. This capacitive
  cell load means that every state transition takes time proportional to charg-
  ing/discharging time of related parasitic capacitor.

The second component — parasitic capacitance — is not known at synthesis time
as it depends on placement of cells and specific routing of connected nets. The
synthesis tool makes assumption about placement and estimates capacitance
based on wire model and manhattan distance between cells.

Tools for parasitic extraction can provide fairly accurate values of electrical
properties by traversing the design database. Extraction of net resistance is fairly
simple — it is directly proportional to net length. The capacitance extraction is
more computationally intensive, as suggested by Fig. 7, here limited to three
metal layers for simplicity. Geometry of wires on every conducting layer gives
rise to several types of capacitive coupling, listing just the most dominant ones:

1. wire bottom to substrate,
2. wire side to substrate,
3. wire top to wire bottom on upper level,
4. wire side to wire top/bottom of different layer,
5. wire side to another wire side (the same or different layer).

Thanks to fixed pitch of routing grid and inter-layer distances, capacitance for
unit wire length can be pre-computed for every type of coupling, yet the task of
repeated traversing all nets in the database is extensive.

Extracted values of resistance and capacitance are converted to time units and then back-annotated into gate-level netlist (see Sect. 3). Subsequent simulation using this netlist gives fairly accurate picture of circuit delays. If timing constraints are not met, it is necessary to go back to Step 2 and re-synthesize in order to change driving strength of cells. To avoid potentially infinite loop and speed up the timing closure, recent tools attempt to do synthesis and placement in the same step. This allows for more accurate modeling of parasitics in synthesis time resulting in more accurate sizing of cells.

7   Verification

Before shipping the design to a foundry, the design is subject to at least the following two types of physical verification:

- design rule checking (DRC),
- layout versus schematic (LVS).

7.1   DRC

This is relatively straightforward check of all polygons in a layout against all design rules found in technology file. If no design rules are violated, the layout is manufacturable.

7.2   LVS

The task of LVS is to verify that resulting layout geometries create the circuitry corresponding to the gate-level netlist that was fed into the placement and routing tool. It also examines connectivity by checking for shorted or open nets.

The first part of the LVS input is the netlist itself. Using information from standard cell library, the tool builds a graph GN of the design on transistor level. In GN, nets are nodes of the graph while transistors correspond to edges connecting the nodes.

The layout information from design database requires more extensive processing. The tool is looking for overlapping polygons on diffusion and poly layers — this is indication of presence of a transistor. Computational geometry methods extract the transistors, determine their type and size. Following the transistor connections on metal and via layers, the tool extracts nets. This allows construction of a graph GL following the same rules as when building GN [8].

The final step is matching GL to GN. If the graphs are found isomorphic, the layout was successfully verified. In a case of mismatch, the tool usually provides graphical interface to locate, view and repair the problem.

References

1. E. Cheng. Risa: Accurate and efficient placement routability modeling. In *ICCAD '94 Proceedings*. IEEE Computer Society Press, 1994. 125
2. *Design Compiler Reference Manual*, 1997.
3. K. M. Hall. An r-dimensional quadratic placement algorithm. *Management Science*, 17, 1970. 122
4. P. Kurup and T. Abbasi. *Logic Synthesis Using Synopsys*. Kluwer Academic Publishers, 1997.
5. C. Y. Lee. *An Algorithm for Path Connections and Its Applications*. IEEE Transaction on Electronic Computers. 1961. 124
6. S. Malik and R. Rudell. *Multi-level Logic Synthesis*. ICCAD'92 Tutorial. IEEE Computer Society Press, 1992.
7. H. Murata, K. Fujioshi, S. Nakatake, and Y. Kajitani. Rectangle-packing-based module placement. In *ICCAD '95 Proceedings*. IEEE Computer Society Press, 1995. 121
8. B. Preas and M. Lorenzetti. *Physical Design Automation of VLSI Systems*. The Benjamin/Cummings Publishing Co., Inc., 1988. 122, 127
9. G. Rabbat. *Handbook of Advanced Semiconductor Technology and Computer Systems*. Van Nostrand Reinhold Company Inc., 1988.
10. N. Sherwani. *Algorithms for VLSI Physical Design Automation*. Kluwer Academic Publishers, 1993. 122
11. W. Shi. An optimal algorithm for area minimization of slicing floorplans. In *ICCAD '95 Proceedings*. IEEE Computer Society Press, 1995. 121
12. J. Soukup. Fast maze router. In *Proceedings of 15th Design Automation Conference*, pages 100–102, 1978. 124
13. *Verilog HDL Synthesis Reference Manual*, 1993.
14. *Verilog-XL*, 1996.
15. N. Weste and K. Esraghian. *Principles of CMOS VLSI Design*. Addison-Wesley Publishing Co., 1992.

Analysis Patterns

Ľubor Šešera

SOFTEC
Kutuzovova 23, 831 03 Bratislava, Slovakia
lubor@softec.sk

Abstract. Analysis patterns are patterns used in the analysis phase of
software systems development. Like any other patterns, e. g., design patterns; analysis patterns are recurring combinations of meaningful units
that occur in some context. When comparing to design patterns, however,
analysis patterns are about semantics, i. e., they consist of entities with
their relationships that have some meaning in a domain. In the article
analysis patterns are introduced from three points of view: abstraction,
flexibility and granularity. Then fundamental patterns for modeling an
enterprise are described. Finally, some specializations of these patterns
with applications in real-world projects are shown.

1 Introduction

The concept of pattern was introduced in civil engineering by the architect
Christopher Alexander whose aim was to prefabricate buildings design [1]. Later,
it was adopted by computer scientists. The concept of pattern in software engineering was probably pioneered by Erich Gamma in his dissertation [11]. It
became known to public mainly due to the succeeding book of the Gang of
Four [12].

The Gang of Four book, however, deals with one kind of software patterns
only. These are design patterns of fine-grained granularity. There exist coarse-
grained design patterns called architecture patterns [8]. Furthermore, there are
patterns devoted to other phases of software development, mainly implementation patterns (called idioms) [6] and analysis patterns [10]. Finally, there are
even other kinds of patterns: patterns dealing with the overall process of software development (process patterns) [2], organizational patterns [24], etc. In the
article we focus on analysis patterns.

Despite their different nature, patterns have a common aim: reusability. On
the other hand there is no single definition of pattern. Christopher Alexander
defined pattern as a "solution to a problem in a context". He had in mind
reusability as well. Vlissides added other aspects to pattern: recurrence, teach-
ing, name [25]. Another variation says: "Pattern is a recurring combination of
meaningful units that occur in some context" [9]. The most liberal definition
is given by Fowler: "Pattern is an idea that has been useful in one practical
context and will probably be useful in others". It is worth noting that pattern
is a concept (an "idea") rather than a complete solution (a "component").

V. Hlaváč, K. G. Jeffery, and J. Wiedermann (Eds.): SOFSEM 2000, LNCS 1963, pp. 129–151, 2000.

A definition of pattern is associated with the form in which it is written. Alexander introduced four main parts of a pattern description: context, problem, forces and solution. The Gang of Four uses another but very fixed format: name, purpose, intent, motivation, applicability, structure, etc. In general, a format seems to be essential to patterns. As Fowler states [10]: "Use of an accepted pattern form clearly marks the pattern as something different from the average piece of technical writing". However, some authors, e. g., [10] and [14] dismiss any rigid format. In order to be consistent with the style of this seminar we use a free form of patterns description in the article as well.

As it has been mentioned we focus on analysis patterns. Analysis patterns are newer and less matured than design patterns. Their fatherhood is usually adjudged to Peter Coad [4] or David Hay [14] but they have become known mainly due to the successful book of Martin Fowler [10]. Analysis patterns share the main definition with other kinds of patterns. A more precise definition might be: "Analysis patterns are groups concepts that represent a common construction in business modeling" [10]. The key concept here is semantics. It is the point on which they differ from design patterns. Design patterns are mainly about flexibility and can be applied to any application.

An analysis model of a software system should consist of several kinds of sub-models: a data model, a functional model, a control model, etc. (see, e. g., [15]). However, analysis patterns address data models only.[1] There are two main reasons: (1) it appears that the data model (or the conceptual model) is the primary model in the analysis phase of software development (2) analysis patterns are too "young" to capture other kinds of models. The article reflects the state of the art.

The paper starts with a brief overview of data modeling principles in Section 2. In Section 3 analysis patterns are introduced. As analysis patterns of various authors are of different kinds we characterize a pattern from the three points of view: abstraction, flexibility and granularity. In Section 4 fundamental analysis patterns for modeling an enterprise are given. They are based on Hay's patterns [14]. In Section 5 some specialized enterprise patterns are proposed. Finally, in Section 6 several applications of specialized enterprise patterns from real-world projects in our company are shown.

2   Data Modeling Principles

In software engineering data models are developed using entity-relationship diagrams (ERDs). ERD is a fairly simple modeling language with few elements and their semantic interpretation. Various methods add further elements to basic ERD. Recently, the Unified Modeling Language UML [3] emerged, providing fairly rich ERDs and, most importantly, reasonable standardization. UML is utilized in this article as well.

When developing models with ERD some general principles are used. Most of them have been known and informally used for decades. The first and the best

---

[1] There are few exceptions.

known principles are the low-level techniques of data normalization for relational databases [5]. The other principles include various kinds of abstraction popularized by artificial intelligence (see, e. g., [23]). Finally, software designers have used many techniques and tricks to increase software flexibility. The fundamental of these principles was summarized by the author of this paper in [21].

The principles can be devided into three categories: normalization principles, abstraction principles and flexibility principles.

Normalization principles are used in order to enhance clarity of models and to prevent update anomalies in a database. The main aim is uniqueness: to represent data in such a way that each data is stored in exactly one place. As normalization principles are fairly known we omit them here.

The main purpose of abstraction principles is to enhance reusability of models although they improve clarity and flexibility of models as well. Abstraction principles are of the following kinds:

1. *Abstraction.* Abstraction means generalization of a model in order to focus on essential characteristics.
2. *Aggregation.* Aggragation represents decomposition of the whole to its parts.
3. *Categorization.* Its aim is to group entities into meaningful categories or classes.

Furhermore, abstraction appears in three froms:

- *Substitution.* A more general entity is used instead of a more specialized one.
- *Generalization.* Both general and specialized entities are represented and they are connected with the inheritance relationship.
- *Typing.* Two entities are represented: entity and its type. They are connected with a relationship.

UML provides specific notation for aggregation and generalization but no direct support for the other abstraction principles.[2]

Flexibility principles form the last category of the general data modeling principles. Their purpose is to increase flexibility of the system. Many times they are used hand in hand with the abstraction principles. They include:

1. *Recursion in both forms*: direct and indirect recursion. Recursion in data modeling means a recursive relationship between entities.
2. *Relationships abstraction.* Several relationships between two entities are abstracted to one general relationship represented with a separate entity and its type. Then specific relationships can be defined dynamically.
3. *Attribute abstraction.* Attributes are abstracted to a separate entity so that an attribute list for an original entity can be created dynamically. This technique is seldom used in reality because of its complicated implementation.

General data modeling principles mentioned above will be utilized in designing patterns in the forthcoming sections.

---

[2] To be fair, it can be added using the stereotypes extension mechanism.

3   Points of View on Analysis Patterns

The software community shares the feeling that analysis patterns are groups con-cepts from business modeling that have a recurring nature. Analysis patterns of different authors are fairly different, however. To compare them we introduce three orthogonal points of view by which a pattern can be characterize: abstrac-tion, flexibility and granularity (see Fig. 1).

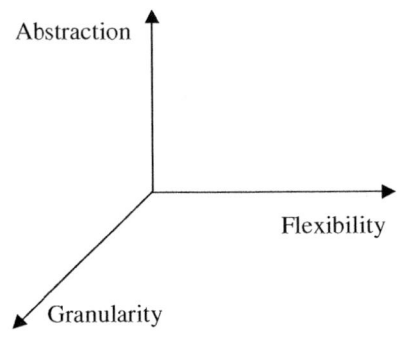

Fig. 1. Points of view

3.1   Abstraction

Let us consider we are developing a system to support maintenance of a gas pipeline network. Maintenance activities on pipelines are triggered by main-tenance orders. The simple representation of such orders is shown in Fig. 2. The pipeline maintenance order is associated with two persons: a preparer and a responsible. The model contains two other entities: a position and a pipeline maintenance order type. These entities are the result of the abstraction principle, typing in particular. Associations between them define constraints on "operat-ing level" [10] entities: a person whose position can be both a preparer and a responsible.

The model in Fig. 2 is suitable for the maintenance of pipeline networks but it is not abstract enough to have a recurring nature. To obtain recurring we abstract the model to any maintenance (Fig. 3). We apply substitution to all entities. Substitution of the maintenance order for the pipeline maintenance order is obvious. Substitution of a party for the person is surprising. The party is a more general term than a person: it includes both persons and organizations. This subsitution is valuable as persons and organizations have many things common in reality: addresses, telephones, bank accounts, etc. In our example this advantage is limited a bit: we can only associate organization with responsibles instead of a person. The model in Fig. 3 can be considered a simple analysis pattern.

We can continue with the abstraction. A maintenance order is a special case of a work order. Thus we can substitute entities for more general ones as in Fig. 4. Other examples of work orders are production orders or emergency orders.

We can even try to abstract work orders. This time the solution is not simple. Martin Fowler came with the concept of an accountability that gave the pattern its name: the Accountability pattern (Fig. 5). Examples of other accountabilities are: a superior (between persons as well as organizations), a manager (person and his organization), a contract (between companies). There are many more one can hardly enumarate. This feature makes an indication of a good pattern: it was abstracted from the real-world case and it is abstract enough to be applicable to many types of problem domains. Some gurus even do not consider models such as in Fig. 4 true analysis patterns as they are not abstract enough.

On the other hand an analysis pattern contrary to a design pattern must have semantics. Semantics decreases with abstraction. That is why the abstraction process must stop on a certain level. For instance, the party *cannot* be abstracted to the "entity", party type to the "entity type" and accountability to the "relationship". Accountability does *not* represent any relationship between two entities.

Analysis patterns of different authors are on different levels of abstraction. For instance, Wolfgang Keller's patterns [16] are restricted to insurance business only. Hay's patterns [14] resulting from abstraction of standard enterprise systems are more abstract. The same level of abstraction is used in the author's patterns [22] and in Fernandez's patterns [9]. The highest level of abstraction is reached in Fowler's patterns [10] who enjoyed showing applications of his patterns in unexpected situations. In the article we use a medium level of abstraction.

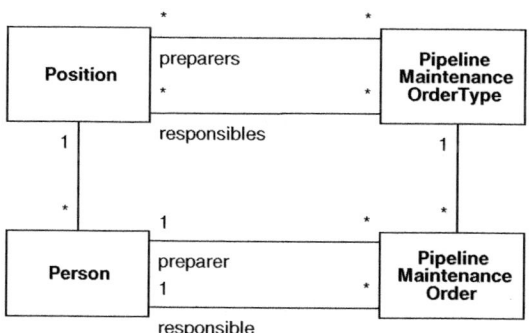

Fig. 2. Pipeline maintenance order

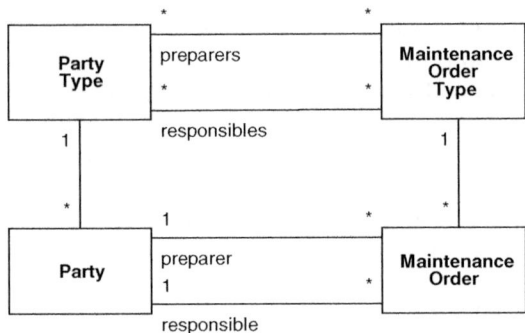

Fig. 3. Maintenance order

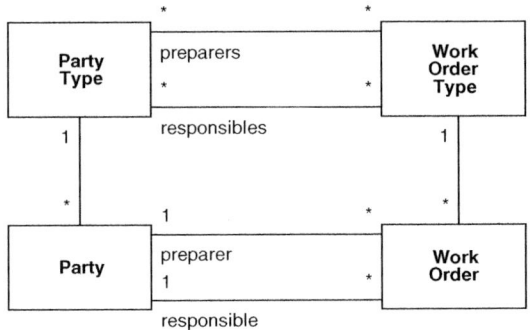

Fig. 4. Work order

3.2   Flexibility

In a classical scheme a company is managed according to an organization hierarchy defining superior-subordinate roles. However, organization hierarchy is a frequent subject of change including adding and removing organization levels. That is why in software system models more flexible representation is utilized based on the direct recursion (Fig. 6).

Simple flexibility that was shown in Fig. 6 works when each responsible has one commissioner at most. When he has more commissioners, new recursive relationships must be added. If there are too many, a fixed set of relationships does not seem to be a good solution. A higher level of flexibility can be obtained by applying the relationships abstraction principle. A new entity is defined representing abstraction of various relationships. To distinguish these relationships the entity is typed. The solution was also applied in the Accountability pattern in Fig. 5. Accountability does not represent a simple substitution only but the relationships abstraction as well. It plays the role of indirect recursion.

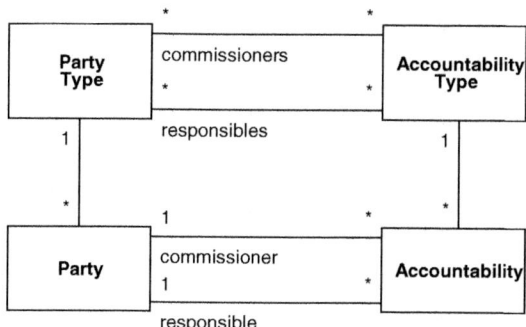

Fig. 5. Accountability

To continue, Fowler's accountability is abstraction of binary relationships only. In work orders, for instance, beside the preparer and the responsible, there can be other roles. As this set of roles does not have to be fixed we can apply relationships abstraction here too. When considering the accountability pattern after introducing the party role entity we obtain the model in Fig. 7.

In reality, however, simple flexibility seems to be sufficient in many cases.

Flexibility is one of the key issues in Fowler's patterns [10] (although he does not mention the model in Fig. 7). In some patterns Hay [14] reaches even the higher level of flexibility (applying the attribute abstraction principle in some cases). Contrary to Fowler, flexibility is not his main topic, however. Flexibility plays an important role in Keller's patterns [16] and the author's patterns [22]. On the other hand, flexibility is not addressed in Fernandez's patterns [9]. He focuses on conceptual models mentioning that flexibility can be added later.

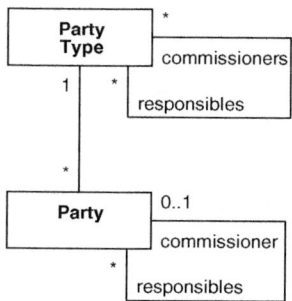

Fig. 6. Simple flexibility

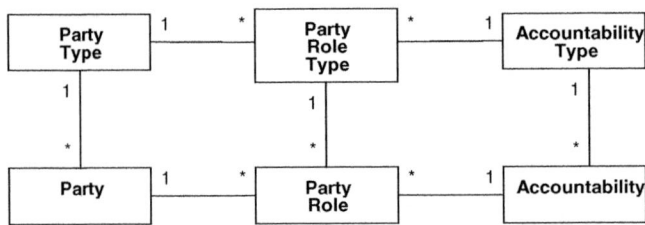

Fig. 7. The more flexible accountability pattern

3.3   Granularity

Granularity is the last dimension we use to characterize analysis patterns.

A fine-grained analysis pattern contains detailed entities and their attributes. Fig. 8 shows an example of a fine-grained pattern of a work order. A work order can be composed of activities performed. These activities are usually ordered (shown with the recursive association). Furthermore, they can be hierarchical (the recursive aggregation). Work orders themselves can be associated, etc. Entities include the most important attributes.

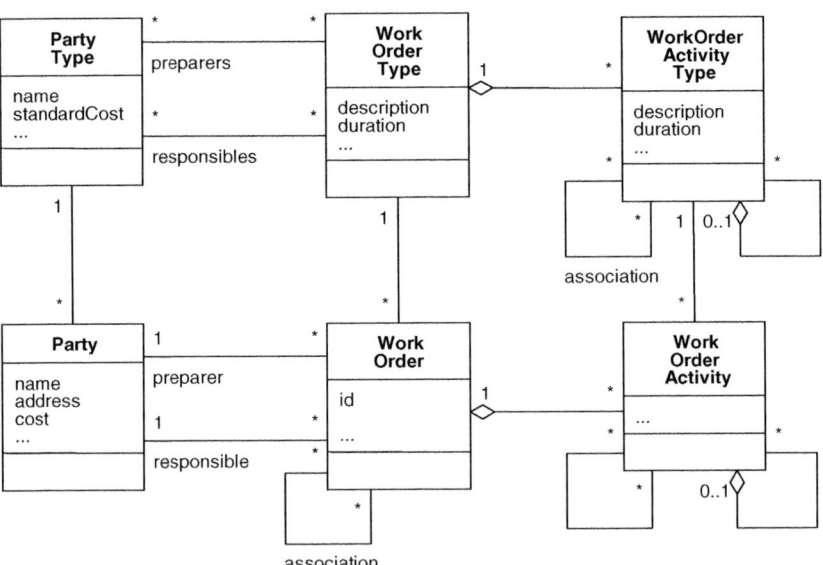

Fig. 8. The fine-grained analysis pattern

As outlined by the previous example, fine-grained analysis patterns are commonly associated with lower level of abstraction. That is why we chose work orders instead of accountabilities.

The middle level of abstraction is represented with the work order in Fig. 4.

Contrary to fine-grained patterns, coarse-grained patterns contains fewer entities. Moreover, an entity usually covers several other detailed entities. A course-grained pattern for our example would be very simple. It would include only two entities, the work order and the party. That is why we broaden the context a bit and we added objects usage and time sheets (Fig. 9).

Entity-relationships diagrams (cardinalities and attributes especially) are not too important in coarse-grained patterns. Many times they are omitted and a pattern is described textually only (see, e. g., Keller's patterns [16]). The other possibility we used is to provide diagrams showing dependences among entities.

Coarse-grained analysis patterns play the similar role in analysis as the architecture patterns in design. They outline a part of a business architecture.

Coarse-grained patterns are provided mainly by Keller [16]. Fowler [10] uses the middle level of granularity. Fine-grained patterns can be found in Hay [14] and other authors [9,22].

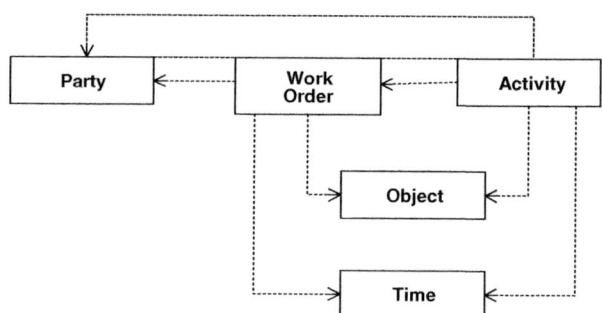

Fig. 9. The coarse-grained pattern

4   Fundamental Patterns for Modeling an Enterprise

A standard enterprise established in a market must include at least[3]:

1. *Parties.* It has an organization structure and employs people.
2. *Objects.* It produces products, uses equipment, owns property, etc.
3. *Activities.* It *produces* products or provides services.
4. *Contracts.* It makes contracts with other enterprises and customers to sell products and/or services and it buys materials and services.

---

[3] For simplicity, we omit other aspects, such as accounting or financial management.

5. *Payments.* It receives money for products and/or services sold and it pays for material and/or services bought.

The coarse-grained pattern showing these fundamental aspects and their dependencies is shown in Fig. 10. In the figure each aspect is represented with an UML package.

Each package can be decomposed to a set of patterns. Patterns presented here have their origin in Hay's patterns [14] except patterns for parties originating from Fowler's patterns [10] and patterns for payments that are our patterns [22]. In the article Hay's patterns are modified slightly.

Modeling even a simple enterprise is a complex task requiring a lot of patterns. For the lack of space we show some of the patterns only. Furthermore, we show several patterns in one diagram.

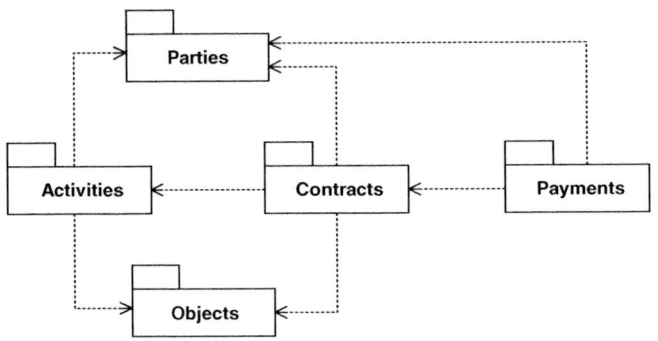

Fig. 10. The coarse-grained pattern for modeling an enterprise

4.1   Parties

The main pattern for representing an organization structure and relationships among employees is the Accountability pattern (Fig. 5). Here, it is not utlizied in all of its endless applications but mainly for representing a superior-subordinate hierarchy.

4.2   Objects

Here the term "object" means abstraction of products, material, equipment and other similar concepts.

The main idea is in distinguishing three kinds of entities: objects, object types and object categories. (VW Golf is an example of the object type, my VW Golf with a serial number XYZ is an example of the object and hatchback is an example of the object category.)

Objects as well as their types can be specialized. Furthermore, they can be either discrete objects or inventory objects.

Objects and their types can be aggregated from other objects. A special kind of aggregation is containment of objects in lots. A lot can contain discrete objects as well as inventory objects.

An object can be associated to other objects to cooperate in fulfilling some function.

It may be important to know a site of certain objects. A site can be represented absolutely (e. g., in geodetic coordinates) or relatively to other objects.

The schematic ERD containg all basic patterns mentioned above is shown in Fig. 11.

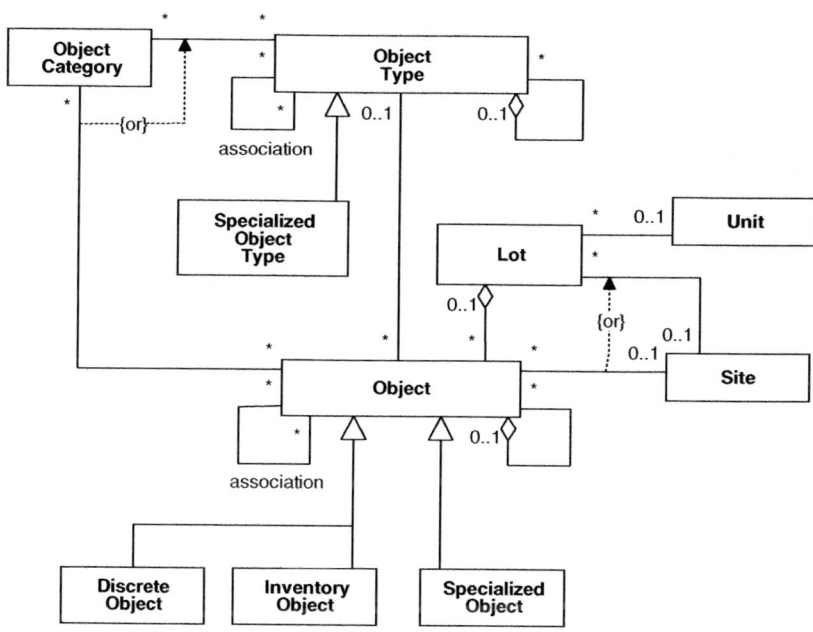

Fig. 11. Objects patterns

4.3   Activities

Activities are represented in a software system in the form of procedures. This form is not captured with ERDs. However, if the system should be flexible, procedures must be parametrized. The section deals with representation of such parameters.

When modeling activities, similar to objects, we distinguish between an activity and its type. The activity type plays the role of prescription or a default rule for the activity.

Similar to objects, activities can be decomposed to lower level activities. Contrary to objects, it is usually important to distinguish between a complex activity and an activity step. Therefore, the pattern uses indirect recursion in the form of the Composite pattern [12].

Activities are associated among themselves. The order in which activities are performed is the most observable example.

Activities are authorized by work orders. A work order is ordered for the main activity type. To fulfil the work order several detailed activities can be performed.

Work orders themselves can be decomposed to lower level work orders.

Work orders are assigned to parties. For flexibility, parties are assigned through work order roles (the relationships abstraction principle). When a detailed watch is required parties can be assigned to activities too.

The first set of activities patterns is shown in Fig. 12.

In activities one is also interested in the time issue. It is concerned with many entities: activities, activities types, work orders, work orders role, etc. To simplify the model they are abstracted to the general entry entity. Any general entry can be associated with a time sheet entry capturing time values. They are of two kinds: a plan and an actual usage.

Similar to time usage, a general entry can have some objects usages. Each usage is of a specific type, its amount is recorded, etc. (Fig. 13).

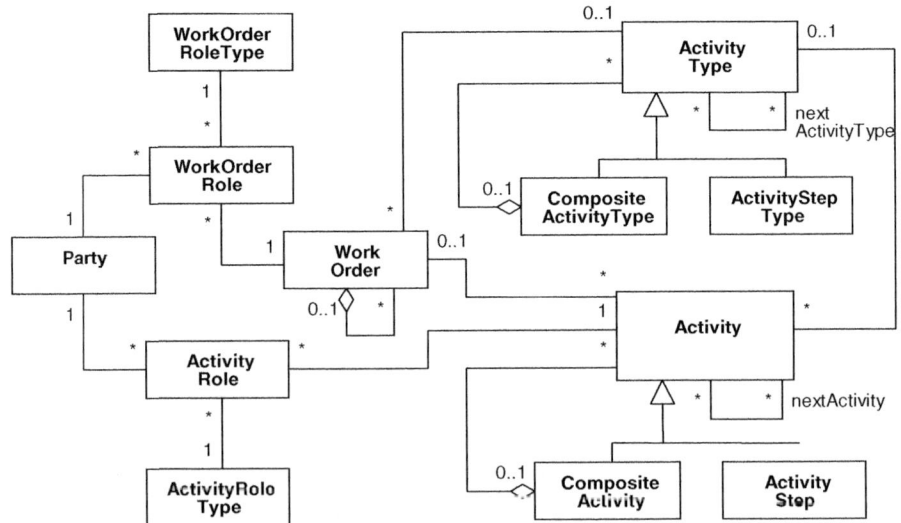

Fig. 12. Activities patterns — part 1

4.4   Contracts

The term "contract" here is the abstraction of various business documents playing a similar role to contracts. Some of the examples are: contracts, orders, invoices, shipping lists, etc.

Similar to objects and activities, contracts can be typed, decomposed to lower level contracts and they can have associated contracts.

A contract usually contains line items. A line item specifies a subject and its quantity. The subject can be an object, an object type, an activity, an activity type, etc.

Contracts are assigned to parties. Mostly, representation of one or two contracting parties, i. e., the buyer or the seller respectively, is sufficient. For flexibility, we utilize the relationships abstraction principle here, too (Fig. 14).

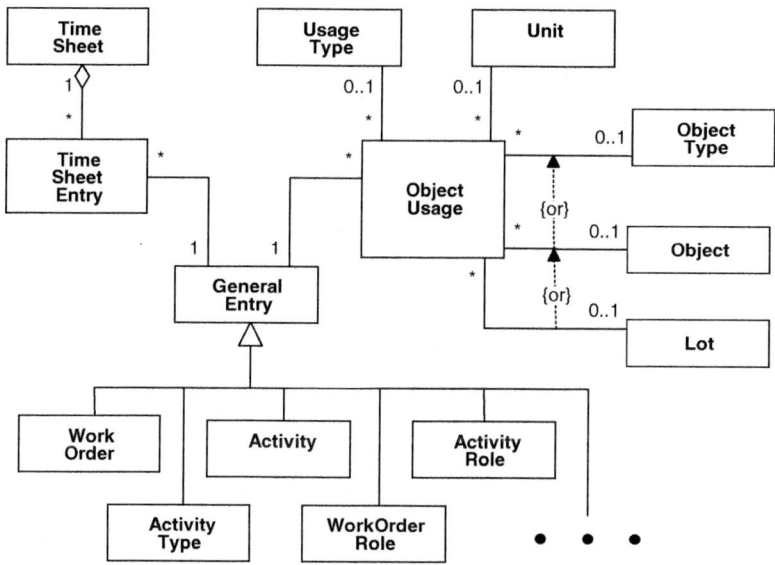

Fig. 13. Activities patterns — part 2

4.5   Payments

The term "payment" is the abstraction of various methods of payments both credits and debits and related documents. Examples include: payment orders, postal orders, credit notices and postal orders returns.

As we are dealing with enterprises, payments are considered via bank accounts. Another side does not necessarily use a bank account, however.

A payment should be associated with a contract to which it is related. This is not always simple because the other side can pay for several contracts in

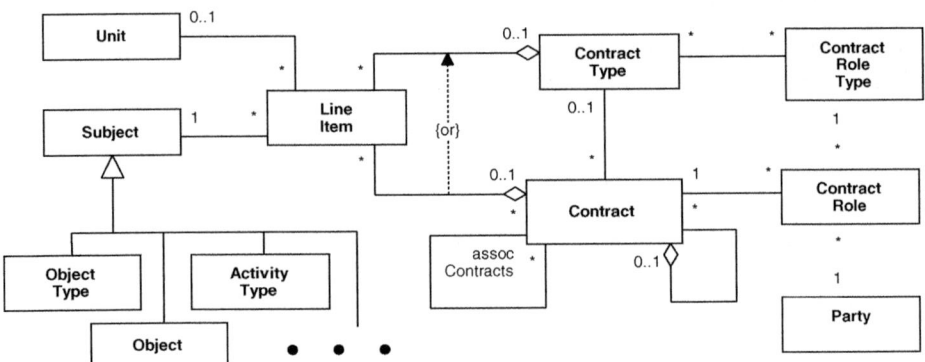

Fig. 14. Contracts

one payment. Therefore the payment in Fig. 15 can be decomposed to payment entries each assignable to one contract only. In reality, design of a decomposition algorithm can be an art itself.

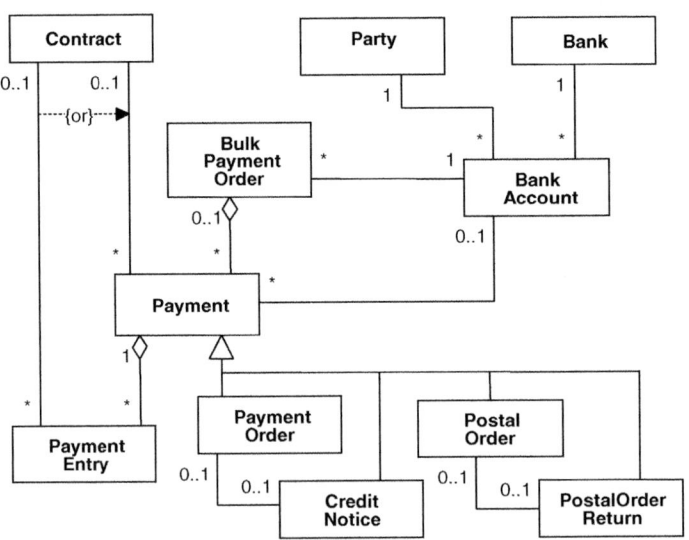

Fig. 15. Payments

5   Some Specialized Enterprise Patterns

Hay's patterns described above are just the fundamental patterns for modeling an enterprise. These patterns can be specialized for some kinds of domains. In this section we show three such patterns that are the result of abstraction of software systems developed in our company.

5.1   Specialization of Object Patterns

Let us consider gas pipeline networks again. It seems they have in common the general idea with some other kinds of networks: electric networks or road networks. Thus we try to abstract their objects to develope a service network pattern.

A service network can be modeled from various points of view in general: (1) point of view of transportation (2) point of view of construction (3) point of view of performing activities (e. g., maintenance) and others. In real-world systems several points of view are needed simultaneously. The transportation point of view is fundamental, however.

From the transportation point of view, a service network consists of two kinds of objects (Fig. 16): service lines and service nodes. A service line starts at one service node and ends (if not recursive) at another service node. Both service lines and service nodes can be typed (and categorized).

Hierarchization is another difference from the fundamental object patterns in Fig. 11. A service node of a specific type can represent the whole lower level service network. On the contrary, a service line cannot be decomposed to the whole network. It can be an aggregation of several service lines (i. e., a multiline) only.

The fundamental network described above can be associated with various network related data. They are of two basic kinds: network related objects and network parameters. Network related objects are, e. g., control objects, monitoring objects, structure objects, service objects and quality improving objects. Network parameters are, e. g., structure, capacity, width, elevation/depth, gradient, etc. Some examples will be shown later.

In general there are two ways network related data are associated with the fundamental network:

1. Distance with regard to a service line object (an absolute distance). This distance is measured from the beginning of the service line object.
2. Distance from a service node (a relative distance).

The absolute and relative distances can be used on different levels of abstraction. The absolute distance is usally associated with a higher level of abstraction. Contrary to the relative distance, it is more understandable but less accurate (it may be difficult to keep it up-to-date when routes of service lines are changed).

5.2 Specialization of Activity Patterns

Service networks are associated with several kinds of activities: from building through control to maintenance. Here we focus on maintenance actvivities. Maintenance patterns can be derived from fundamental activities patterns shown in Fig. 12 and Fig. 13.

Maintenance patterns are very similar to fundamental activities patterns indeed. That is why some differences are shown only.

From the point of view of maintenance, service networks can be structured differently than from the point of view of transportation. They can be decomposed to maintenance areas. Maintenance areas can be hierarchical. Low-level maintenance areas include service network objects (Fig. 17).

Work orders from Fig. 12 used to be on two levels of abstraction: tasks and work orders. Tasks are more general ones. They are specified for a longer period (once a year or once a quarter). A task is associated with a maintenance type and a maintenance area. Work orders are fairly specific. They are associated with a short time period (a day or a week) and specific objects (or low-level maintenance areas).

After performing a maintenance activity its results are put down. When a maintanance result is a defect it becomes the source of another work order or task.

An object usage appears in two forms: an equipment usage and a material usage.

5.3 Specialization of Contracts

Maintenance contracts appear in usual forms: orders, invoices, issue slips, etc. These do not require much specialization of the fundamental contract patterns in Fig. 14. That is why we outline a challenging specialization here. It is from the insurance industry and property insurance systems in particular.

An insurance contract is the main document in the insurance business (Fig. 18). The insurance contract is settled according to a product that plays the role of the contract type in Fig. 14.

A product is associated with some policy. The main parts of a property insurance policy are: object types, risks and tariffs.

An insurance contract is for one or several objects that are of a type allowed by the product. As both several objects can be insured in one insurance contract and each object can be insured against several risks, the insurance contract has parts called assured risks.

An insurance contract can be associated to another insurance contract of the same party. It may be due to a new version of the contract, its supplement, etc.

A premium prescription is another specialization of the general contract from Fig. 14. The premium prescription is generated every relevant payment period of the insurance contract.

Because of the space the whole claim subsystem is omitted in Fig. 18. Basic entities of the claim subsystem can be found, e. g., in [22].

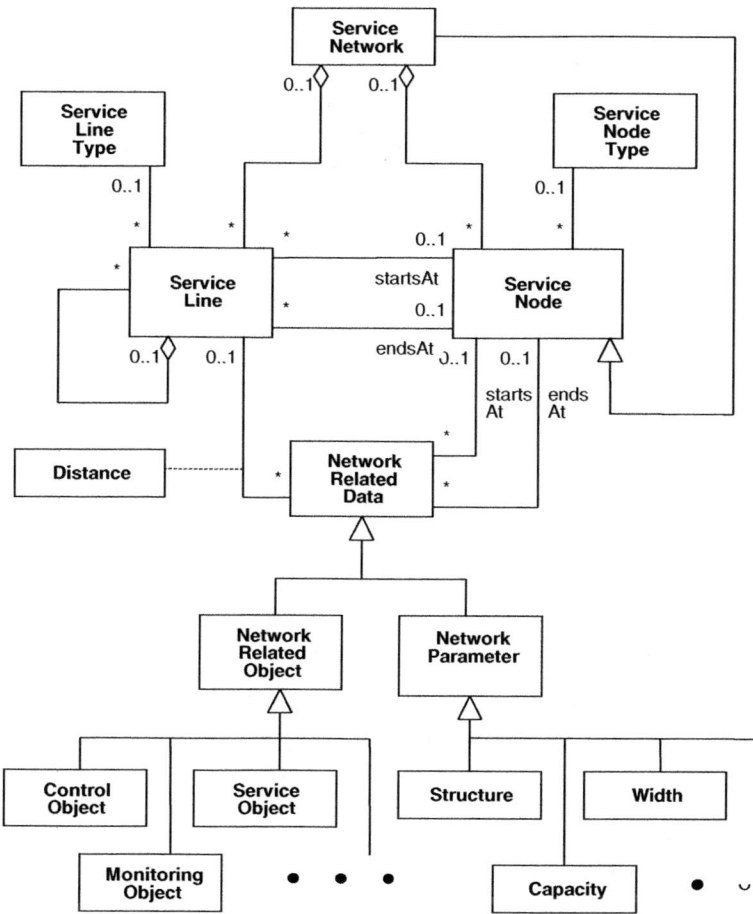

Fig. 16. The service network pattern

6   Some Applications of Enterprise Patterns

6.1   Applications of Object Patterns

In our company we designed two systems of the service network type: the pipeline network [18] and the road network [19].

The pipeline network consists of two levels: (1) a transmission network and (2) a main network. The main network is the result of decomposition of a specific type of service node of the transmission network. For the simplicity one network level is shown in Fig. 19 only.

Both transmission networks and main networks consist of two sublevels: (a) pipelines and (b) service pipes. Service pipes are considered parts of their pipeline.

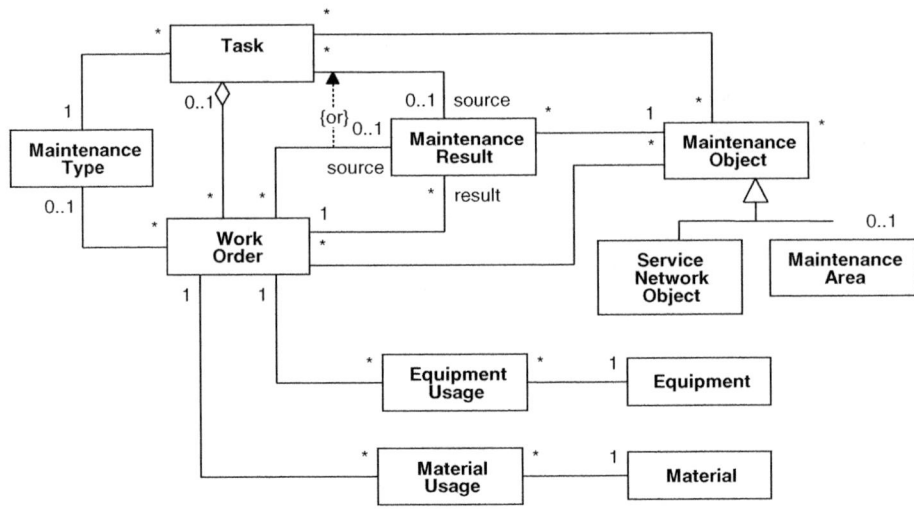

Fig. 17. Maintenance activities on service networks

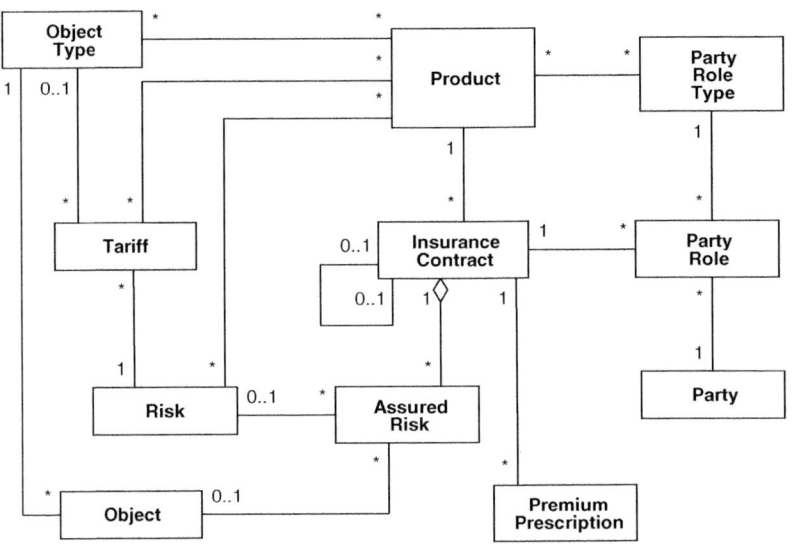

Fig. 18. Property insurance contracts

The basic pipeline network model shown in Fig. 19 is associated with network related data as outlined in Fig. 16. Network related objects are specific to this kind of domain. Examples of control objects are: a gate valve, a pressure regulator and a pressure regulating station. A meter, a manometer and a leak location assembly on the other hand are examples of monitoring objects. To continue, a sleeve and a reduction are examples of structure objects, a pipeline marker is an example of service objects and finally, a syphon pot and a breather are examples of quality improving objects.

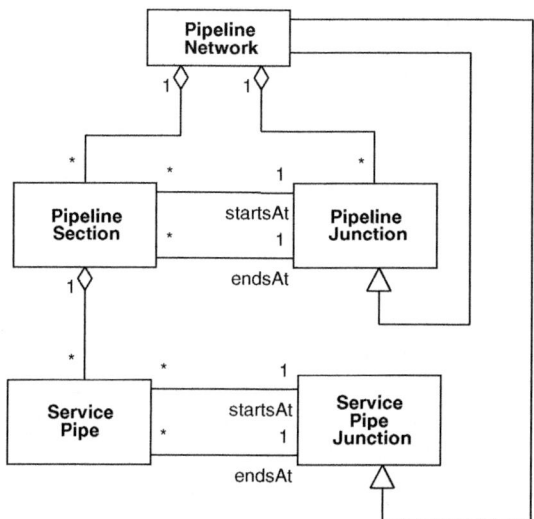

Fig. 19. The gas pipeline network

The road network is the other application of service networks we designed [18]. The model shown is based on the European GDF standard [7].

The road network is modeled on three levels of abstraction (Fig. 20):

1. roads bound with road terminations,
2. road elements bound with intersections[4],
3. basic road elements bound with junctions.

To explain, objects on level 2 can be complex: dual carriageways or complex intersections, respectively. The dual carriageway means that the road element contains two basic road elements. The complex intersection can be seen as consisting of several "smaller" intersections represented with junctions that are connected by basic road elements. (Unlike intersections, the road elements cannot contain junctions, because containing a junction implies there must be an intersection and thus two road elements instead of one.)

Service nodes in the diagram are typed. Types of intersections are, e. g., a crossing, or a roundabout. Types of junctions are, e. g., a bifurcation, a mini-roundabout, etc.

---

[4] The term intersection is taken from [7] an cannot be taken too literally. It contains both rad terminations and road intersections.

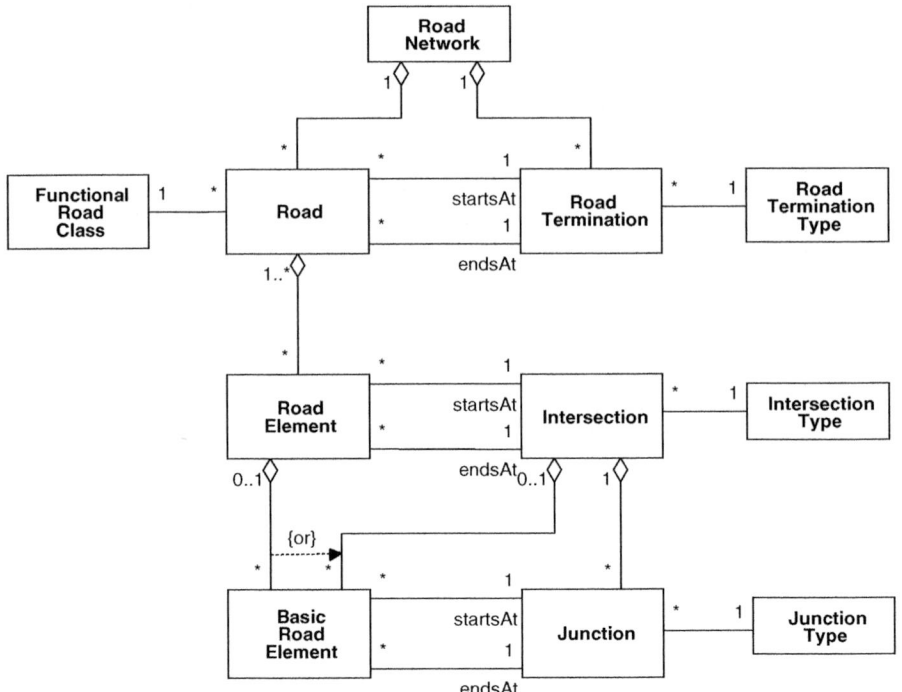

Fig. 20. The road network

Network related data are associated the same way as in the network pattern in Fig. 16. Examples of various types of network related objects are: a trafffic light, a traffic sign (control objects), a thermometer, a camcorder, a balance (monitoring objects), a bridge, a tunnel, an underpass, a wall (structure objects), a signpost, a rest area, a phone, a toll (service objects) and a lighting, a fence, a drainage (quality improving objects).

6.2   Applications of Activities Patterns

Here, an application of the maintenance pattern for the maintenance of gas pipeline networks and road networks should be provided. It is omitted because these models are almost the same as the model of maintenance pattern in Fig. 17. There are some minor differences only. For instance, in gas pipeline networks, pipeline objects are represented in the place of service network objects while in road networks these objects are the road network objects.

6.3   Applications of Insurance Patterns

Our company is devoted to some extent to insurance systems: both to traditional insurance companies [17] and for "public" institutions as the General Health Insurance [13] or the National Labour Office [20].

As the model for traditional insurance is similar to the model shown in Fig. 18 we focus on public insurance and on the National Labour Office in particular.

The National Labour Office collects obligatory unemployment payments. There is no contract between a party and the office: a party only fills a registration form. A party can have several registrations simualtaneously, e. g., when he/she is an employee and a business person in parallel. A type of registration is specified by the registration type entity (Fig. 21).

The registration type specifies policy as well. These include a tariff and a document type.[5] For instance, a businessman declares his/her income once a year (in an individual tax return) while an employee's salary is known each month and an employer sends a monthly statement for all its employees.

Each payment period premium prescriptions are generated on the base of income document. Contrary to traditional insurance, the payment period is fixed (each month) but an amount to pay can vary because it depends on actual salary.

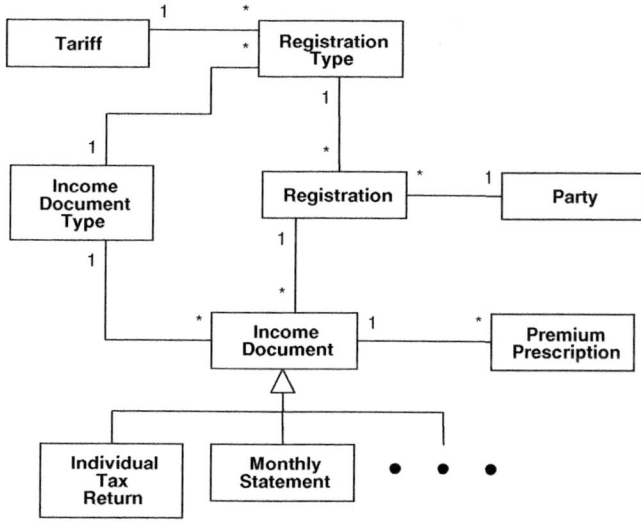

Fig. 21. Unemployment payments

---

[5] Here, the 'powertype' principle [3] is used.

7   Conclusion

In the article, we have shown some principles of organizing and characterizing analysis patterns. Furthermore, we have provided fundamental patterns for modeling an enterprise and have outlined some of their applications. Patterns in general and analysis patterns in particular are further step, next after principles and methods, to discover and capture expertise of software development. As John Vlissides stated [25] main benefits of patterns are:

1. They capture expertise and make it accessible to nonexperts.
2. Their names collectively form a vocabulary that helps developers communicate better.
3. They help people understand more quickly when it is documented with the patterns it uses.
4. They facilitate restructuring a system whether or not it was designed with patterns in mind.

References

1. C. Alexander, S. Ishikawa, M. Silverstein, M. Jacobson, I. Fiksdahl-King, and S. Angel. *A Pattern Language*. Oxford University Press, New York, 1977. 129
2. S. Ambler. *Process Patterns: Building Large-Scale Systems Using Object Technology*. Cambridge University Press, 1999. 129
3. G. Booch, I. Jacobson, and J. Rumbaugh. *Unified Modeling Language User Guide*. Addison-Wesley, 1998. 130, 149
4. P. Coad. *Object Models: Strategies, Patterns and Applications*. Yourdon Press, 1997. 130
5. E. F. Codd. Further normalization of the data base relational model. In *Data Base Systems*, volume 6 of *Courant Computer Science Symposia Series*, Englewood Cliffs, N. J., 1972. Prentice-Hall. 131
6. J. O. Coplien. *Advanced C++ Programming Styles and Idioms*. Addison-Wesley, 1992. 129
7. Comité Européen de Norm. Geographic data files, 1995. ISO NP 14825. 147
8. F. Buschman et. al. *Pattern-oriented Software Architecture*. Wiley, 1996. 129
9. E. B. Fernandez and Y. Xiaohong. *An Analysis Pattern for Reservation and Use of Reusable Entities*. PLoP, 1998. 129, 133, 135, 137
10. M. Fowler. *Analysis Patterns: Reusable Object Models*. Addison-Wesley, Reading, MA, 1997. 129, 130, 132, 133, 135, 137, 138
11. E. Gamma. *Object-Oriented Software Development based on ET+: Design Patterns, Class Library, Tools*. PhD thesis, University of Zurich, 1991. (in German). 129
12. E. Gamma, R. Helm, R. Johnson, and J. Vlissides. *Design Patterns: Elements of Reusable Object-Oriented Software*. Addison-Wesley, Reading, MA, 1995. 129, 140
13. Information system of the general health insurance company, 1996. (in Slovak). 149
14. D. Hay. *Data Model Patterns: Conventions of Thought*. Dorset House, NY, 1996. 130, 133, 135, 137, 138
15. I. Jacobson, G. Booch, and J. Rumbaugh. *The Unified Software Development Process*. Addison-Wesley, 1999. 130

16. W. Keller. *Some Patterns for Insurance Systems.* PLoP, 1998. 133, 135, 137
17. Software system of the Kooperativa insurance company, 1999. (in Slovak). 149
18. A. Micovsky, J. Cerven, and L. Sesera. Object-oriented analysis in the real-world project. *PC Revue*, 3–5, 1997. (in Slovak). 145, 147
19. A. Micovsky, L. Sesera, and V. Zarnovican. Geographic information system of the slovak road administration. In *Highway'98*, Bratislava, 1998. (in Slovak). 145
20. Information system of the National Labour Office, 2000. (in Slovak). 149
21. L. Sesera. General modeling principles: Building blocks of analysis patterns. In *Datasem'99*, 1999. 131
22. L. Sesera. Software systems architectures: Analysis data patterns, 2000. (in Slovak). 133, 135, 137, 138, 144
23. J. F. Sowa. *Conceptual Structures: Information Processing in Mind and Machine.* Addison-Wesley, 1994. 131
24. P. Taylor. *Capable, Productive, and Satisfied: Some Organizational Patterns for Protecting Productive People.* Patterns Languages of Program Design 4. Addison-Wesley, 2000. 129
25. J. Vlissides. Patterns: The top ten misconceptions. *Object Magazine*, 3, 1997. http://www.sigs.com/publications/docs/objm/9703/9703.vlissides.html. 129, 150

Information Society Technologies in Healthcare

Dimitrios G. Katehakis[1], Manolis Tsiknakis[1], and Stelios C. Orphanoudakis[1,2]

[1] Center of Medical Informatics and Health Telematics Applications (CMI-HTA)
Institute of Computer Science,
Foundation for Research and Technology — Hellas (FORTH)
P.O. Box 1385, GR-71110 Heraklion Crete, Greece
{katehaki,tsiknaki,orphanou}@ics.forth.gr
[2] Department of Computer Science, University of Crete,
P.O. Box 2208, GR-71110, Heraklion, Crete, Greece

Abstract. The growing demand for more efficient and effective health-care services, coupled with an implicit requirement for supporting citizen mobility and continuity of care, is currently setting the stage for the exploitation of Information and Telecommunications Technologies in the health sector. The current vision comprises affordable wireless access to healthcare resources and services for all citizens, thus making medical expertise a shared resource wherever and whenever needed. Important areas in which Information Society Technologies are likely to have a significant impact include those of pre-hospital health emergencies, remote monitoring of patients with chronic conditions, and medical collaboration through sharing of health-related information resources. Accessibility to these and other media-rich, user-oriented services, in the context of the emerging Global Information Society, will be supported by a Healthcare Information Infrastructure (HII), which can achieve effective horizontal integration of networked information sources.

1 Introduction

The great challenge in applying information and telecommunications technologies in the health sector is how to be creative in exploiting the opportunities afforded by these emerging technologies, so that peoples' lives may be improved. At the same time, clinically significant and cost-effective, added-value services to the healthcare community ought to be provided, and the potential benefit to be derived from technological advances must also find its way to the scene of an accident, the (virtual) home, and the (virtual) working place of all citizens.

The health sector can serve as the test-bed for assessing the impact which new information and telecommunication technologies will have on our lives. For the past several years, we have witnessed revolutionary technological developments, which afford us a pragmatic look into our digital future. However, the stringent requirements for Quality of Service (QoS) will make the process of change in the health sector evolutionary rather than revolutionary. A plethora of unresolved technical, economic, regulatory, legal, and training issues would have to be settled

V. Hlaváč, K. G. Jeffery, and J. Wiedermann (Eds.): SOFSEM 2000, LNCS 1963, pp. 152–172, 2000.

before the real impact of technological change in this important sector can be fully assessed.

Priorities for the 21st century include a shift toward citizen-centered services, meeting QoS requirements, and a substantially greater emphasis on wellness and prevention. Healthcare professionals will continue to deliver care, but will also be increasingly required to share their knowledge and expertise with other colleagues and citizens in general. The new paradigm provides that informed citizens care for their own health and various cooperating stakeholders, who may also be responsible for the continuity of health services within a region, have an impact on the operation of the healthcare system as a whole. In this context, decentralized healthcare can be supported by integrated services for seamless and personalized information delivery, while services and information must be accessible without (visible) organizational boundaries. Information and Communication Technologies (ICT) support information distribution and sharing for health promotion, pre-hospital health emergency medicine, primary health care, hospital services, rehabilitation, home care and other relevant health services.

The Health Telematics Services that are currently being developed and are partially in use should address the needs of all involved actors. Potential users of such services are: (a) health administrators, and the regional and national health authorities, (b) healthcare professionals, and (c) patients and citizens at large. Specifically,

- For *health administrators* and the regional and national health authorities, continuity of care results in a reduced number of repeated exams, better monitoring and management of healthcare procedures, and better use of available technical and financial resources.
- For *healthcare professionals*, the secure exchange of medical information, for teleconsultation purposes, efficient access to a patient's distributed Electronic Health Record, and the requirement for medical second opinion or updated training, increase the demand for continuing education, and necessitate the design and implementation of increasingly sophisticated information access and management tools.
- For *patients and citizens* in general, one must provide access to information and services anywhere and anytime, while supporting mobility and continuity of care.

Thus, a key challenge facing researchers and technology providers is to provide a technological and organizational framework that can integrate a heterogeneous collection of healthcare resources. This framework will increase information availability and ought to address the demanding information processing requirements of healthcare actors.

2   Application Domain

The healthcare domain is characterized by a hierarchical structure and involves a large number of specialties with different skills and requirements. The geographical distribution of resources is non-uniform and in many cases these are

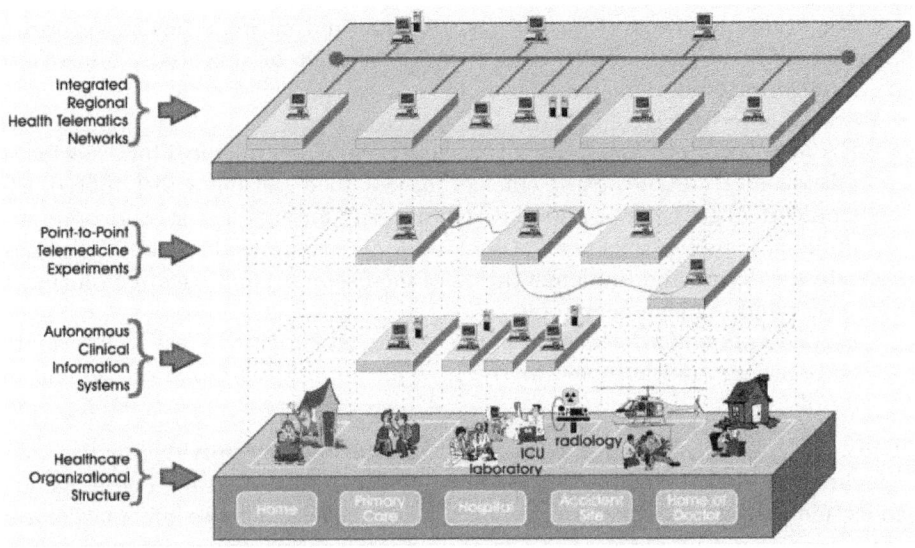

154   Dimitrios G. Katehakis et al.

located in remote and isolated areas. Actors in the healthcare domain possess diverse profiles and often lack adequate education and training in the use of technology. In addition, the large volume of available information is inherently heterogeneous and multimedia in nature, while new information is produced at a very high rate. Finally, paper-based health records and other official documents are frequently illegible, scattered, and largely inaccessible. This makes routine sharing of information and data collection very inefficient, which in turn has an adverse effect on the quality of care.

The primary goal of healthcare networking is to provide support for remote expert consultation based on locally acquired medical data and remote guidance for locally performed medical procedures. Integrated healthcare networks support a set of added-value telematic services, implemented over an advanced telecommunications infrastructure, and supported by different information technologies and related applications. The main goal is to provide different levels of support for remote monitoring, as well as preventive, diagnostic and therapeutic medical procedures. Thus, an integrated healthcare network can be considered as an extended virtual healthcare institution that encompasses available physical and human resources over a wide region, in order to support remote medical procedures and patient management.

Integrated Regional Health Telematics Networks

Point-to-Point Telemedicine Experiments

Autonomous Clinical Information Systems

Healthcare Organizational Structure

Fig. 1. Evolution of the Healthcare Networking Environment (Starting at the Bottom and Moving to the Top)

The four main application areas of telematics in healthcare are: *home care, primary care, hospital care,* and *pre-hospital health emergency medicine.* The traditional environment of autonomous clinical information systems, with point-to-point communication used to conduct telemedicine experiments, results in fragmentation of information and cannot be used to fully exploit the potential of the underlying technologies. Integrated regional health-telematics networks (Fig. 1) are currently at advanced stages of development and aim to provide round the clock services to the citizen, not limited by resource availability constraints.

A fundamental prerequisite for the establishment of a scaleable regional health telematics network is the development of an architecture and tools for the integration of specialized autonomous applications that are supported by a HII. Based on an effective horizontal integration of networked information services, the interoperability of applications and services within a health care institution, the interconnection of different institutions, and the intelligent management of health related information within such an integrated network, can be supported.

2.1   Primary Care

Primary care is usually offered by General Practitioners (GPs) in primary health-care centers, as well as by community doctors. Its mission is to provide primary medical and hospital care, preventive medicine, health promotion and social care. Primary healthcare professionals require the means to manage clinical information in a way which is tailored to their needs.

Storing patient encounter information and examination results are typical uses of primary care clinical information systems. Additional functionalities include the direct acquisition of laboratory and imaging examination results, so that they can be seamlessly integrated into personal health records and be readily available on demand.

2.2   Hospital Care

A number of clinical departments, offering complementary services, cooperate to provide care at a hospital level. Each department has its own needs for keeping health records and for communicating with cooperating departments (both inpatient and outpatient). In a typical information flow scenario within a hospital, a medical or paramedical professional in a requesting department of a hospital (e. g. pathology) may request the examinations (e. g. biochemical, imaging) of certain patients who are being cared for in the clinic. The different clinical information system in which these examinations are stored must then communicate and possibly exchange information in order to respond to such a request.

The communication and sharing of information among autonomous systems with different data (and event) requirements may involve extensions to these systems. The implementation of such extensions may require the agreement of respective vendors, and certainly increases the cost of development. Therefore, interoperability of systems and services, based on relevant standards, ensures the prompt propagation of information and the efficient use (re-use) of software to order medical examinations, access examination results, and manage workflow.

2.3   Home Care

Home care is intended for the remote monitoring of patients with chronic conditions. Typically, healthcare professionals and patients or the elderly at home communicate with each other via videoconferencing. High-speed broadband videoconferencing sessions and high-quality signal transmission between specialized medical instruments (e. g. stethoscope, spirometer) may also be required. In these cases, bandwidth management becomes particularly important.

In certain clinical applications, such as dermatology, it may also be necessary for the healthcare professional to remotely control the pan-tilt motion of the camera viewing the patient at home. Biosignals acquired at the patient's home are transmitted and displayed for viewing on the healthcare professional's monitor.

The monitoring and follow-up of patients at home is currently finding extensive use in cases when, for various reasons, patients cannot be transported to a GP's office or a hospital or in order to reduce costs. In the future, home care activities will be extended to the virtual home and workplace of an increasingly mobile population, as mobility issues are resolved and the "anyone, anywhere, anytime" paradigm becomes a reality.

2.4   Pre-hospital Health Emergency Medicine

The primary tasks of health emergency are: (i) to provide high quality health care services, to the extent possible, at the point of need and (ii) to transfer the victims of accidents and those in some other critical condition to an appropriate healthcare facility. In both cases, it is absolutely essential that the response time is minimized and that the accident victim or patient's condition is monitored closely during transfer to a healthcare facility. Health Emergency Coordination Centers (HECCs) have unique emergency telephone numbers, and need to have access to accurate information regarding the location of an emergency episode, the positioning of ambulances and other mobile units, the qualification of the staff on board, and the availability of healthcare facilities and other resources in the region.

The functional blocks of a health emergency management system are shown on Fig. 2. These include the direct communication of multimedia medical data from mobile units to the HECC, mobile unit tracking and route guidance, resource management at a regional level, and the management of the EHR component related to a specific emergency episode.

Current emergency management systems operate in a sub optimal manner due to the lack or the inadequacy of communication links among the different actors involved. The real issue is not the lack of information and telecommunications technologies, but rather the lack of integration among the different information sources and communication networks. The most important building blocks of such an integrated information infrastructure are the local and the wide are networks (terrestrial, wireless, and mobile), the user terminals for the mobile units, and information systems for the HECC and the positioning of mobile resources.

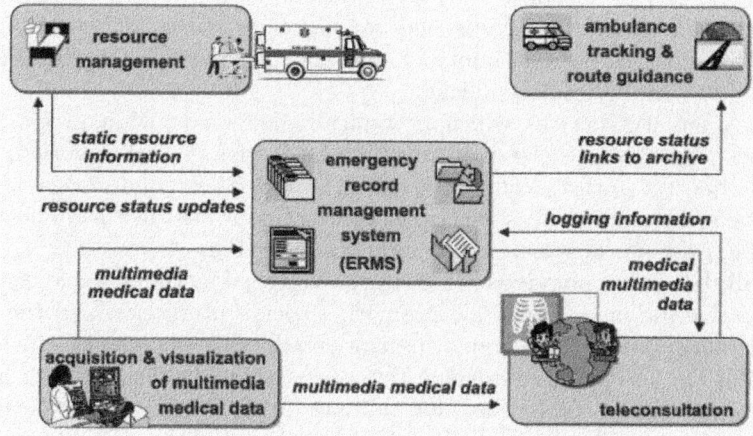

Fig. 2. A Pre-Hospital Health Emergency Management System

3   Health Telematics

Health telematics involves the use of information processing tools and telecommunications to provide the functional and operational framework that allows computers to transfer medical data to one another. Telemedicine, a related term, refers to the use of health-telematics in the remote delivery of healthcare services.

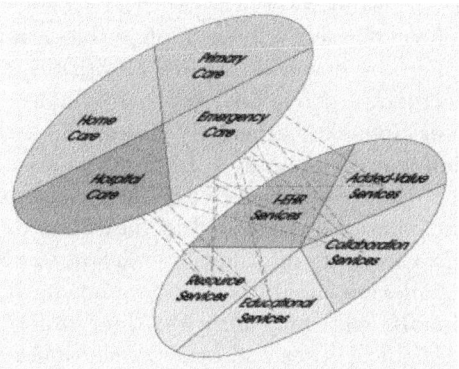

Fig. 3. Healthcare Application Areas and the Five Clusters of Telematic Services

A regional healthcare network supporting integrated user-oriented telematic services to user groups with different needs for information access and QoS requirements presents a significant degree of complexity. This is partly due to the wide spectrum of services that need to be provided and of the requirement for interoperability of telematic services and stand-alone applications. Furthermore, user-oriented telematic services need to be offered in a collaboration environment that ensures the continuity of care and information sharing, under strict security and authorization policies.

The telematic services, which are typically delivered within a regional healthcare network, may be classified into five basic classes: *collaboration, resource, educational, integrated electronic health record (I-EHR),* and *added-value.* These classes of telematic services are applicable to all four healthcare application areas of home, primary, hospital, and emergency care (Fig. 3).

Collaboration services bridge the gap created by the physical distance separating the various users, while promoting social interaction and the exchange of vital information. This type of user-oriented, telematic services includes tele-consultation, and tele-monitoring. *Tele-consultation sessions*, among healthcare professionals, may compensate for the lack of experienced or specialized personnel at remote sites, at the site of an accident, or at primary care facilities. They are intended to address emergencies or to evaluate the severity of a case. *Tele-monitoring* services support patient-physician or physician-physician collaboration for the purpose of delivering healthcare at the home of the patient or monitoring (remotely) a medical examination. Furthermore, as far as community care is concerned, collaboration among user groups that share the same chronic medical condition may provide comfort through the sharing of useful information and experience (special interest groups).

Resource services provide information on the availability of physical resources such as hospital departments, diagnostic modalities, and mobile emergency units, and their characteristics through regional white and yellow page directories. Various sectors of the population and isolated communities benefit from the availability of resource services over the World Wide Web (WWW). In recent years, the Internet-based web technology has stimulated the creation of many such yellow pages by hospitals, health authorities etc., making it possible to get practical information about healthcare providers.

Educational services are especially important for rural regions, where access to information sources is limited. In order to raise public awareness, and to effectively support the continuity of care, healthcare professionals must have access to educational material contained in digital medical libraries. Similarly, the public should have access to information relevant to diseases common in their region. Geographic isolation should not hinder the sharing of knowledge among healthcare professionals, who may improve their practice through interaction with repositories of medical cases and other educational material.

An innovative approach to distance learning, which is based on computer-based training and relies on modern methodologies and WWW technologies, is Web Based Training (WBT) [1]. WBT provides a virtual environment for distance learning by anyone, at any geographic location, and anytime. In a WBT environment, web browsers are used to support 3D reality, video conferencing, chat and other interactive discussion media. Thus, users are able to exchange messages with their tutors and among themselves, while bulletin boards and discussion lists facilitate rich electronic interaction.

I-EHR services support single-point access to clinical information by both patients and physicians. They provide a uniform view of data, which may be configured differently at different locations. This is necessary due to the fact that segments of a patient's electronic health record may be found at different healthcare facilities visited by the patient.

I-EHR services require the existence of an underlying technological infrastructure, in order to facilitate the sharing of patient clinical information. Technological challenges are primarily related to information access and storage. Other problems, not necessarily related to technology, include patient identification, as well as making systems inter-operate not only at the control level, but also at the semantic level. Since confidentiality concerning role-based access to information is important, a number of medico-legal issues remain to be resolved, so that access to the EHR data by authorized healthcare professionals in different institutions may be facilitated. The requirement for shared care and continuity of care makes I-EHR services particularly important.

Finally, **added-value services** extend all the above services and provide specialized support to healthcare professionals. Image processing services, access to specialized indexing and search engines, information filtering and pre-fetching, content-based image indexing and retrieval, and decision support are examples of services that facilitate efficient and effective utilization of the information space.

4   Information Society Technologies

Although relational databases are currently used extensively for storing enterprise data, the Internet is becoming the means for integrating systems. In addition, current advances in wireless technology will soon offer the possibility of creating a telemedicine infrastructure for the wireless world. Consequently, next generation clinical information systems will be capable of managing the distributed segments of the EHR and will be based on technologies that support mobility and provide intelligent and personalized access to information sources.

Technologies for the integration of EHR related information mainly involve *directories* for creating distributed, hierarchical structures of accessible resources, *distributed object computing* to implement advanced modular functionalities, *Internet and Java* to glue pieces of information scattered throughout the world, *portable devices* and *mobile communications* to enable access from anywhere at any time, and *Human Computer Interaction (HCI)* technologies to support universal access.

Directories are specialized databases with a hierarchical information model, which are defined in terms of open, standardized, and vendor-neutral protocols. Important strengths of directory technology are its distributed nature and fast lookup capabilities. In essence, the directory is a distributed database capable of storing, in a hierarchical data model, information about people and objects at various servers or network nodes. It is these servers, which provide the potentially global access to information, made possible by X.500 [2]. Current directory technologies use the Internet standards, conform to a global naming structure, provide public interfaces for directory access (e. g. Lightweight Directory Access Protocol — LDAP), integrate and maintain synchronization with other transitional directories, and support security.

Unlike client/server architectures, where the client discovers and communicates directly with the server, when dealing with **distributed object computing,** communication middleware acts as an extra functional layer between clients and servers. This additional layer allows applications to be developed without knowledge of the location or any given implementation of all external functionalities. The main examples of generic approaches to middleware today are the *Common Object Request Broker Architecture (CORBA)*, standardized by the Object Management Group (OMG) [3], and Microsoft's *Distributed Common Object Model (DCOM)* [4]. Distributed object middleware services include communications, naming and directory services, object life cycle management, security and authentication, notification service, and various development and debugging tools.

The main advantages offered by CORBA include architecture, language and location independence. Furthermore, naming and trading services are also available to act as white and yellow pages respectively. DCOM, like CORBA, adheres to separation of interface from implementation using Microsoft's Interface Definition Language (IDL), which is not compatible with CORBA IDLs. Like CORBA, DCOM provides both static and dynamic bindings for methods, and its interface is language neutral. DCOM objects, also known as ActiveX objects, implement all the interfaces the object supports. **Java** is a programming language similar to C++, easy to learn, efficient, secure, and portable. It produces very compact runtime, which can be used to implement executable content on the web [5]. During the past few years, it has received tremendous support from industry and, consequently, a number of supporting technologies, such as *JDBC, JavaBeans, JavaBlend,* and *Enterprise Java Beans,* have been developed.

Recently, the **Extended Markup Language (XML)** has attracted great attention and is becoming the preferred language for data interchange over the WWW. Requirements best addressed by XML include customizing front-end applications, data mining searches, synthesis of multiple information sources, and electronic commerce-type applications [6]. The Extensible Style Language (XSL), which is a map language that allows transforming XML documents into other language documents, further enables the seamless presentation, and personalization of information.

Research work in the field of **HCI** focuses on the design of User Interfaces (UIs) accessible and usable by different user groups and the propagation of existing guidelines into user-adaptable UI implementations [7]. This work has been driven by the ever-increasing number of computer users, characterized by diverse abilities, skills, requirements, and preferences, as well as the proliferation of technological platforms, giving rise to a variety in contexts of use, thus necessitating the development of self-adapting user interfaces.

The combination of fully distributed, n-tier architecture technologies, together with XML, can support the creation of virtual services and secure access to a diverse set of services, in a single integrated environment. In addition, they can efficiently manage network elements and systems using legacy protocols. In all cases, end users need only access Internet, while all implemented underlying functionalities of the integrated network remain fully transparent to them (Fig. 4). What lies ahead is Internet and wireless technologies: the mobile network evolution has been moving from general packet radio services of 1999, to the GSM evolution of 2000, and the 3rd Generation Mobile System (Universal Mobile Telecommunications System — UMTS) of 2001, continuously enhancing multimedia capabilities, internet access and support for IP-based services [8]. This will allow in the future for service portability and seamless roaming of packet, data based services, and bandwidth on demand.

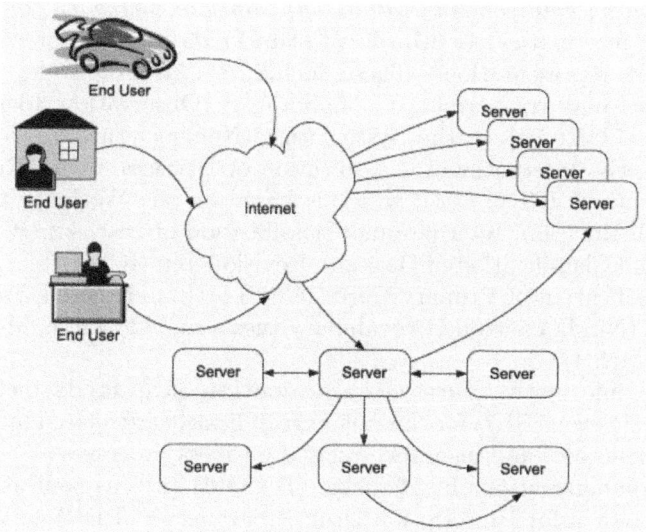

Fig. 4. Schematic Representation of an n-Tier Architecture Over the Internet, Facilitating the Existence of Virtual Environments (home, working place, etc.)

Gradually, more and more devices are being equipped with more processing power and wireless communications capabilities, such as the Infrared Data Association (IrDA) and Bluetooth [9], which allow users to make effortless, wireless and instant connections between various communication devices. This enables more and more appliances to be networked and interoperate, creating new possibilities for home automation and active environment services.

5   Related Work

Work related to the development of a HII falls in two main categories; the first one is associated with *standardization activities* by international standardization bodies, while the second deals with conscious efforts, in the form of *projects or initiatives,* to establish a framework for integrating heterogeneous sources of information into a seamless network of health telematics services.

There are different reasons why standards are needed in the healthcare domain. One such reason is that standards allow computer documentation to be consistent with paper-based medical records. Another reason is that information sharing (communication) among different actors, for the purpose of addressing an end-user's problem, is facilitated by the existence of standards-based integrated environments. This includes all agreements on data and context that needs to be shared, so that decision support is provided and there is a return on investment. Healthcare domain standards can be distinguished into standards for *terminology, data communication,* and *software component interoperability.*

Medical informatics **terminology standards** provide for coding schemes and concept representations. These include the READ codes that describe patient care and treatment [10], Laboratory Observation Identifier Names and Codes (LOINC) [11], the Systematized Nomenclature of Medicine (SNOMED) [12], the International Classification of Diseases, Ninth Revision, Clinical Modification (ICD-9-CM), which is based on the World Health Organization's Ninth Revision, International Classification of Diseases (ICD-9) [13], the International Classification of Diseases, Revision Ten (ICD-10) [14], the International Classification of Primary Care (ICPC) [15], and the National Library of Medicine's (NLM) controlled vocabulary thesaurus, known as Medical Subject Headings (MeSH) [16].

Medical informatics **data communication standards** include those by Health Level Seven (HL7) for the exchange of healthcare related information [17], X12N for insurance and insurance-related business processes [18], Digital Imaging and Communications in Medicine (DICOM) [19], as well as those by the National Council for Prescription Drug Programs (NCPDP) [20], the Institute of Electrical and Electronics Engineers (IEEE) [21], the American Dental Association (ADA) [22], the American Nurses Association (ANA) [23], and the European Standardization Organization CEN/TC251 [24].

The only effort so far at establishing standardized **software component interoperability,** comes from CORBAmed, the Healthcare Domain Task Force (DTF) of the OMG [3]. Standardized object-oriented interfaces, expressed in the Interface Definition Language (IDL), associated with the integration framework of CORBA, that have been adopted so far include services for person identification, accessing clinical observations and imaging, resource access decision, and terminology query. A similar effort by the recently introduced Microsoft Health Users Group [25] is making its initial steps, without having produced any specifications so far. Both types of standards, when utilized, are expected to be particularly important in large hospitals and regional networks, where many kinds of different computers have been installed and cannot be replaced.

Various research and development projects attempt to provide solutions to technical problems associated with the development of a HII. Central element in all these efforts is the Integrated Electronic Health Record (I-EHR), which is the cornerstone of shared care and the point of reference for any exchange of medical information. Currently, three approaches to the I-EHR exist [26]. The most widespread approach relies on *clinical messages* to enable the exchange of information among information systems (e. g. HL7), but it does not scale well when the number of possible system interactions increases. *Clinical data warehouses* offer an alternative way for integrating information, but when used in practice, keeping information up-to-date becomes a real issue [27]. The third approach, that of a federated I-EHR, is based on a common normalized model to map underlying schemas into the overall architecture. Related efforts include that of the STAR [28], GEHR [29], SYNAPSES [30] projects, funded by the European Commission, as well as CEN/TC251 [17], and TeleMed [31] in the USA.

In relation to terminology services, the Unified Medical Language System (UMLS) project [32] of the NLM develops machine-readable 'Knowledge Sources' that can be used by a variety of application programs. This overcomes retrieval problems caused by differences in terminology and by the proliferation of information sources. In the context of the reference architecture, terminology services offered by terminology servers supporting evolving standards will help healthcare professionals and researchers retrieve and integrate electronic biomedical information from a variety of sources.

The real problem with existing standards and recommendations arising from projects/initiatives is that there are many of them, they are difficult to adopt, and they are always in a state of development. Nevertheless, one does not have to wait for standards to be fully developed before attempting to exploit their potential benefits.

6   Architectural Framework

Organizational and procedural context ought to be taken into account when specifying and developing information systems for the healthcare domain. Fundamental principles in developing any architectural framework include the promotion of interoperability, so that development and maintenance costs are kept low, and the use of open standards, so that the potential for compatibility with the rest of the world is sustained. The implementation of scaleable and extensible modular architectures and the provision of high quality services to society is a desirable end result. In order to achieve this result, it is particularly important that the installed infrastructure can continue to evolve and that, as technologies mature, new and improved capabilities can be taken advantage of.

6.1 HYGEIAnet: The Integrated Health Telematics Network of Crete

The development and operation of HYGEIAnet on Crete (Fig. 5) constitute a conscious effort to provide an integrated environment for healthcare delivery and medical training across the island. HYGEIAnet takes advantage of the increasing capacity of terrestrial and mobile communication networks and the development of advanced telemedicine services to provide every citizen of the island with effective healthcare services and to support remote consultation among healthcare professionals in specialized centers, district and regional hospitals, and other points of care.

In the course of designing and implementing this integrated services network, special efforts are being made to meet the requirements of the user groups involved and to use state-of-the-art technology and standards at every stage. Alternative patient, problem, and case-based architectures for the I-EHR have been considered in an attempt to provide transparent access and secure communication of information between and within medical specialty areas, as well as in a variety of situations from community to hospital care across the region. Various strategies for multi-database integration and interoperability were considered in conjunction with the EHR to provide homogeneous access to its distributed segments at all levels of the healthcare system. Advanced multimedia telematics applications such as telecardiology, telepathology, teleradiology, teleophthalmology, etc., supporting synchronous and asynchronous teleconsultation and cooperative diagnostic work between healthcare providers at different locations are currently being developed and will soon become part of the integrated system.

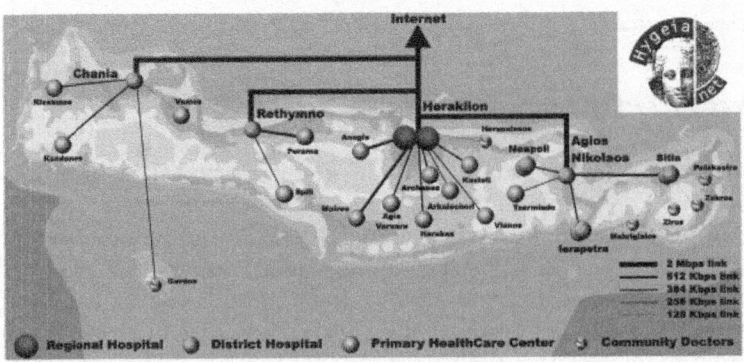

Fig. 5. HYGEIAnet: the Integrated Regional Health Telematics Network of Crete

Short to medium term objectives include the introduction of lifelong electronic health records for all citizens, round-the-clock on-line access to electronic health records and information about best clinical practice, for all authorized actors. Currently, HYGEIAnet includes almost the entire public healthcare system of the Region of Crete, which consists of two Regional Hospitals, including the University Hospital, five general hospitals, fifteen primary healthcare centers, and one hundred and seventeen community doctors. HYGEIAnet also includes pre-hospital emergency services provided by the National Center for Emergency Care.

6.2   HYGEIAnet Reference Architecture

Information technology planners use the term architecture to refer to abstract technical descriptions of systems. Architectures provide the basic framework for the creation, movement, distribution, use, and management of information [33,34]. In particular, a reference architecture model describes a system in terms of basic functional elements and the interfaces among them. It specifies where protocols need to be defined and identifies groups of functionalities, without imposing a specific physical implementation.

A regional healthcare network, providing integrated user-oriented telematic services to user groups with different information and QoS requirements, presents a significant degree of complexity. This is partly due to the wide spectrum of the services provided. Furthermore, interoperability among telematic services and stand-alone applications is critical, since services and applications share data and information. The reference architecture for the HII, that is shown in Fig. 6, guides the development of a health-telematics network for the provision of integrated services [35]. It conforms to the CEN/TC251 Healthcare Information System Architecture (HISA) [36] and offers several middleware services, which can be used to deploy regional and interregional end-user services. Furthermore, it provides a general framework in which healthcare-related information systems may be integrated to provide media-rich services to healthcare professionals, social workers, and the public. It is important to note that the HII provides a conceptual roadmap, since it does not impose any execution platform, and consists of a vast conglomeration of autonomous information systems and supporting services.

The HII consists of three basic components: *applications, enabling* (or *middleware*) *services,* and *network infrastructure.* At the bottom, the **infrastructure layer** provides services that are related to the integration and inter-working of the technological environments. The **application layer** includes the applications that support user activities in the various areas of an organization. These applications are both information sources and/or information access points. Clinical, diagnostic, and administrative information systems, medical libraries, and user-oriented services are all part of the application layer [36]. All applications and services of the application layer are associated with their own data model and user-interface. In the **middleware layer** reside generic and healthcare-specific middleware services. Generic middleware services support the applications with general-purpose facilities, which are common to any information system in any type of business domain [36]. Healthcare-specific middleware services support applications with services related to activities of the healthcare domain.

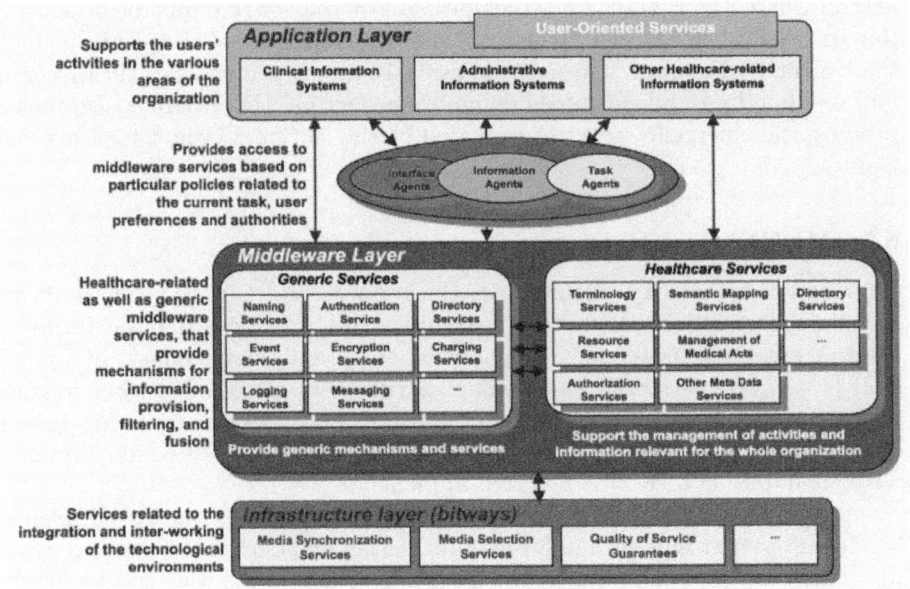

Fig. 6. HYGEIAnet Reference Architecture

System conformance is measured by the capability of an information system to exploit, when necessary, one or more of the common components specified in the reference architecture. The degree of conformance to the reference architecture indicates the capability of the information system to be integrated, from both the functional and information viewpoint, with the rest of the information systems.

6.3   HYGEIAnet Information Infrastructure

The core infrastructure components of HYGEIAnet allow for the secure and hierarchically structured information on end-user *personalized preferences*, the consequent management of all kinds of information resources by means of a *Healthcare Resource Directory (HRD)* and the *Patient Clinical Data Directory (PCDD)*, a central element of the whole infrastructure. Additionally, the *WebOnCOLL* collaboration infrastructure allows for the secure creation and management of virtual workspaces and telemedicine session folders.

The organizational structure, medical services, and personnel of the various healthcare facilities comprise the **regional X.500 directory** of healthcare resources. The directory provides multiple views of the healthcare resources in the region. One view is location-oriented, indexing healthcare resources according to geographic location. Another view follows the healthcare organizational structure, classifying healthcare facilities into tertiary, secondary, and primary ones. Private medical doctors practicing medicine in the region of Crete are also included in the directory and classified according to their specialty and location. In the long term, resource services will be maintained by the individual healthcare facilities and accessed through a concentration service maintained by the regional authorities.

The **PCDD** is a central middleware element of the overall architecture that provides clinical information on the distributed EHR segments maintained by autonomous information systems [37]. Access to detailed information regarding specific healthcare encounters is delivered via role-based authorization privileges and controls. The administration of the healthcare organizations' business rules, for different user-groups, is made via a specially tailored and developed rule-editor [38]. In its current deployment status (as of August 2000), PCDD offers access to various distributed healthcare sites (medical units) in the region of Crete, and to respective distributed clinical information systems (the legacy feeder systems).

The collaboration infrastructure of *WebOnCOLL* is based on virtual workspaces and user profiles [39]. Virtual workspaces implement collections of heterogeneous objects, maintain history data, and support awareness regarding content updates and user interaction. Agents (human users or applications) connected to a workspace may create or add objects into the workspace and are notified of changes in the contents of the workspace or when other agents are connected to the same workspace. User profiles enable the customization of workspaces according to user authorities, tasks, and preferences. User profiles also maintain account information and access information on subscribed services such as personalized information services. The interoperability of *WebOnCOLL* with enabling middleware services of the regional HII ensures availability of accurate resource information and certification of the exchanged data.

6.4   Middleware Services and Components

The initial set of core services supporting the utilization of an I-EHR environment at a regional level, within the framework of the HYGEIAnet Reference Architecture, has been identified and an initial prototype implementation is available providing useful feedback for future enhancements. At present, core services are based on basic infrastructures and include the following:

Authentication services allow access only to authorized end-users. They are implemented by means of a security server that manages the user rights and roles, together with associations to personalized profiles. Its purpose is to certify *the role* and *authority* of both users and services (or applications) within the regional healthcare network. In this context, any patient is able to have complete access to all personal information.

Encryption services are responsible for the secure communication of sensitive personal information over the Virtual Private Network (VPN) of HYGEIAnet, as well as the Internet. The combination of digital signatures for authentication, public key cryptography for recipient authentication, and Secure Socket Layer (SSL) protocols for secure data-transfer, provide the necessary technological framework for secure communication of healthcare related information across the Internet.

Patient identification services allow for the unique association of distributed patient record segments to a master patient index. This is a very challenging task to perform and one of the major barriers in developing a reliable I-EHR environment. This is because no global, unique person identification exists worldwide today. In addition, even for countries that possess one, this is not used internally for identification purposes by clinical or administrative information systems. Apart from person identifiers, identifiers are also needed for providers, locators, devices, etc.

Auditing services are responsible for recording all performed interactions between middleware services and/or end-user applications, directly or indirectly. The logs produced can then be used for both tracing back transactions in time and for charging. They can also be used as a profiler tool for individual server loads, and for the construction of end-user interest profiles by means of data mining techniques.

Resource location services are useful for identifying available resources and the means for accessing them. Examples of resources include pharmacies on-duty, hospitals and clinics, clinical information systems available at a regional level, methods and technologies available for accessing primary information, and protocols for exchanging information with them.

Encounter location services are used for locating primary information found in different patient record segments. In this context, encounter is the term used for describing clinical information that is produced during the communication about the patient, between two or more individuals, at least one of whom is a member of the responsible healthcare team.

Clinical Observation Access Services are required for obtaining primary information directly from specific clinical information systems. This service requires the implementation of standardized gateways for each clinical information system for securely importing/exporting patient record data.

User Profile Services track the long-term interests of users and are used for maintaining personalized settings and preferences [40]. User profiles are made up of terms/keywords to describe interesting information, or examples of interesting information, and are utilized for the selective dissemination of information to their owners. User profiles initially are created according to existing stereotypes that are automatically assigned to them, after gathering some initial user-specific information, and users may actively contribute to the incremental building of their profiles.

Terminology Services have a dual objective: to map and associate existing coding schemes, and to relate the internal semantics of the clinical information systems maintaining primary information. The first objective is accomplished by means of UMLS, while the second requires a conscious effort by clinical information systems developers and people responsible for maintaining I-EHR services up to date.

6.5   Act Management — Workflow Issues

Management of acts involves the coordinated execution of multiple tasks performed by different healthcare actors. Important requirements for the efficient and reliable execution of applications supporting workflow management include deep understanding of the processes to be modeled and workflow automation [11]. The separation of work activities into well-defined tasks, rules, and procedures allows for the modeling of healthcare processes in a rigorous and comprehensive manner. Middleware services, associated with the management of medical acts, facilitate functional integration and coordinate medical procedures in terms of quality, throughput, and reliability [12]. The management of medical acts or workflow requires a process definition stage, a workflow processing environment, and tools to support the run-time interaction.

7   Conclusions

The implementation and operation of Integrated Regional Healthcare Networks, for the provision of cost-effective and clinically meaningful health telematics services, provide many challenges and opportunities for assessing the impact of Information Society Technologies on our lives. The challenges are not only technological, but are also related to various unresolved medical, legal, regulatory, and economic issues. Furthermore, they are enhanced by the complexity of the healthcare application domain, which arises from the physical distribution of available resources, the heterogeneous user profiles, and the diverse requirements of different levels of care in a regional setting. On the other hand, opportunities for applying information and telecommunications technologies, in this rather sensitive and highly visible application domain, exist precisely because there is a need to meet the above challenges for the purpose of supporting continuity and improved quality of care for an increasingly mobile population. The goal is to develop and manage regional health telematics applications in order to support real-time access to services by anyone, anywhere and anytime. This would also require that adequate bandwidth be allocated on demand across different fixed, wireless, and mobile telecommunications networks.

Information Society Technologies support the integration of systems and services at a regional level and facilitate access to medical information by healthcare professionals and citizens, who are thus empowered to care for their own health. Furthermore, they provide support for evidence-based medical practices and contribute toward improving the efficiency of the health sector as a whole.

The definition and adoption of standards, primarily with respect to the functional interfaces between the various system components, represents a fundamental requirement that must be satisfied before different applications, developed by different suppliers, can be integrated and used effectively in health care. Future breakthroughs in optical communication technology, combined with the availability of more powerful and possibly intelligent mobile terminals, will further support continuity of care and prompt care at the point of need, while making medical expertise a shared resource and enabling seamless access to healthcare resources. This will lead to the creation of a virtual distributed healthcare organization. Then, the real challenge will be to make healthcare telematics services accessible by all, at a reasonable cost. At this point, a critical mass needs to be established for the services to become widely available and a conscious effort is required so that a better-informed population can sustain a functioning network of advanced services.

Finally, our duty is to be creative in using the emerging information and telecommunications technologies, so that we may provide support for the delivery of significant and cost effective healthcare services. It is also important that the potential benefit to be derived from technological advances finds its way to the scene of an accident, the (virtual) home, and the (virtual) workplace of all citizens. The adoption of Information Society Technologies in the health sector is a process of change and, therefore, it is likely to be evolutionary rather than revolutionary.

Acknowledgements

The development of the Regional Health Telematics Network of Crete is a long-term goal of the Center of Medical Informatics and Health Telematics Applications (CMI-HTA), at the Institute of Computer Science of the Foundation for Research and Technology — Hellas (ICS-FORTH). The work reported in this article represents a collaborative effort involving all the members of CMI-HTA, whose significant contributions the authors would like to explicitly acknowledge. This work is being supported in part by several R&D projects of the European Commission, the General Secretariat for Research and Technology of the Greek Ministry of Development, and the Greek Ministry of the National Economy.

References

1. Web-Based Training Information Center. http://www.webbasedtraining.com/. 158
2. ITU. Recommendation X.500 — Information technology — Open Systems Interconnection — The directory: Overview of concepts, models, and services, Nov. 1993. 160
3. The Object Management Group. http://www.omg.org/. 160, 162
4. Microsoft COM Technologies. http://www.microsoft.com/com/. 160
5. The Source for Java Technology. http://www.javasoft.com/. 160
6. The World Wide Web Consortium. http://www.w3.org/. 160
7. C. Stephanidis and D. Akoumianakis. Preference-based human factors knowledge repository for designing user interfaces. Int. J. on HCI, 9(3):283–318, 1998. 160
8. M. W. Oliphant. The mobile phone meets the internet. IEEE Spectrum Mag., 36(8):20 28, 1999. 161
9. The Bluetoth Specific Interest Group. http://www.bluetooth.com/. 161
10. The READ Codes. http://www.cams.co.uk/readcode.htm. 162

11. A. W. Forrey, J. M. Clement, G. DeMoor, S. M. Huff, D. Leavelle, and et al.
    D. Leland. Logical observation identifier names and codes (LOINC) database:
    A public use set of codes and names for electronic reporting of clinical laboratory
    test results. *Clin. Chem.*, 42(1):81–90, 1996. 162

12. Systematized Nomenclature of Medicine. http://www.snomed.org/. 162

13. National Center for Health Statistics: Classification of Diseases.
    http://www.cdc.gov/nchs/icd9.htm. 162

14. World Health Organization. http://www.who.int/. 162

15. H. Lamberts, M. Wood, and I. M. Hofman-Okkes, editors. *The International Clas-
    sification of Primary Care in the European Community: With a Multi-Language
    Layer.* Oxford University Press, Oxford, 1993. 162

16. MeSH, National Library of Medicine.
    http://www.nlm.nih.gov/pubs/factsheets/mesh.html. 162

17. Health Level Seven. http://www.hl7.org/. 162, 163

18. X12N. http://www.hipaanet.com/disa_x12n.htm. 162

19. Digital Imaging and Communications in Medicine (DICOM); National Electrical
    Manufacturers Association. http://www.nema.org. 162

20. National Council for Prescription Drug Programs. http://www.ncpdp.org/. 162

21. The Institute of Electrical and Electronics Engineers. http://www.ieee.org/. 162

22. American Dental Association. http://www.ada.org/. 162

23. American Nursing Association. http://nursingworld.org/. 162

24. European Committee for Standardization (CEN), Technical Committee for Health
    Informatics (TC251). http://www.centc251.org/. 162

25. Microsoft Healthcare Users Group — Europe. http://www.mshug-euro.org/. 162

26. J. Grimson, W. Grimson, and W. Hasselbring. The system integration challenge
    in health care. *Communications of the ACM*, 43(6):49–55, 2000. 163

27. W. Hasselbring. Federal integration of replicated information within hospitals. *Int.
    J. Dig. Lib.*, 1(3):197–208, 1997. 163

28. M. Blazadonakis, V. Moustakis, and G. Charissis. Seamless care in the health
    region of Crete: The star case study. In *MIE 97*, pages 157–161, Porto Carras,
    1997. http://www.ics.forth.gr/ICS/acti/cmi_hta/publications/papers.html. 163

29. D. Ingram. The good European health record in healthcare in the new communi-
    cation age. *IOS*, pages 66–74, 1995. 163

30. J. Grimson. A CORBA-based integration using the synapses approach.
    Biomedicine, 2(3):124–138, 1998. 163

31. D. G. Kilman and D. W. Forslund. An international collaboratory based on virtual
    patient records. *Com. of the ACM*, 40(8):111–117, 1997.
    http://www.acl.lanl.gov/TeleMed/Papers/p110-kilman.pdf. 163

32. Unified Medical Language System Documentation, National Library of Medicine.
    http://www.nlm.nih.gov/research/umls/UMLSDOC.HTML. 163

33. Cross Industry Working Team. An architectural framework for the national infor-
    mation infrastructure. White paper, 1994.
    http://www.xiwt.org/documents/ArchFrame.html. 165

34. Cross Industry Working Team. Building the information infrastructure: A progress
    report, 1999. http://www.xiwt.org/documents/BuildingNII.pdf. 165

35. M. Tsiknakis, C. E. Chronaki, S. Kapidakis, C. Nikolaou, and S. C. Orphanoudakis.
    An integrated architecture for the provision of health telematic services based
    on digital library technologies. *Intl. J. on DigLibs.*, 1(3):257–277, 1997.
    http://www.ics.forth.gr/ICS/acti/cmi_hta/publications/papers/1997/
    dglib97/dglib97.html. 165

36. CEN/TC251/WG1/PT1-013: Medical Informatics: Healthcare Information System Architecture, 1995. 165
37. D. G. Katehakis, P. Lelis, E. Karabela, M. Tsiknakis, and S. C. Orphanoudakis. An environment for the creation of an integrated electronic health record in HYGEIAnet, the regional health telematics network of Crete. In *TEPR Procs 1*, pages 89–98, 2000.
    http://www.ics.forth.gr/ICS/acti/cmi_hta/publications/papers/2000/tepr2000/tepr2000.html. 167
38. G. Potamias, D. G. Katehakis, E. Karabela, V. Moustakis, and M. Tsiknakis. Role-based access to patients clinical data: The intercare approach in the region of Crete. In *MIE*, Hannover, 2000. 167
39. C. E. Chronaki, D. G. Katehakis, X. Zabulis, M. Tsiknakis, and S. C. Orphanoudakis. WebOnCOLL: An environment for collaboration in regional healthcare networks. *IEEE Transactions on Information Technology in Biomedicine*, 1(4):257–269, 1997.
    http://www.ics.forth.gr/ICS/acti/cmi_hta/publications/papers/1997/ieee97weboncoll/ieee97weboncoll.html. 167
40. N. J. Belkin and W. B. Croft. Information filtering and information retrieval: Two sides of the same coin? *Communications of the ACM*, 35(12), 1992. 168
41. D. Georgakopoulos et al. An overview of workflow management: From process modeling to workflow automation infrastructure. *Distributed and Parallel Databases*, 3(2):119–153, 1995. 169
42. E. Kaldoudi, M. Zikos, E. Leisch, and S. C. Orphanoudakis. Agent-based workflow processing for functional integration and process re-engineering in the health care domain. In *Procs of EuroPACS*, pages 247–250, Pisa, 1997. 169

Towards High Speed Grammar Induction on Large Text Corpora

Pieter Adriaans[1,2], Marten Trautwein[1], and Marco Vervoort[2]

[1] Perot Systems Nederland BV,
P.O.Box 2729, NL-3800 GG Amersfoort, The Netherlands
{Pieter.Adriaans,Marten.Trautwein}@ps.net
[2] University of Amsterdam, FdNWI,
Plantage Muidergracht 24, NL-1018 TV Amsterdam, The Netherlands
vervoort@wins.uva.nl

Abstract. In this paper we describe an efficient and scalable implementation for grammar induction based on the EMILE approach [2,3,4,5,6]. The current EMILE 4.1 implementation [11] is one of the first efficient grammar induction algorithms that work on free text. Although EMILE 4.1 is far from perfect, it enables researchers to do empirical grammar induction research on various types of corpora.

The EMILE approach is based on notions from categorial grammar (cf. [10]), which is known to generate the class of context-free languages. EMILE learns from positive examples only (cf. [1,7,9]). We describe the algorithms underlying the approach and some interesting practical results on small and large text collections. As shown in the articles mentioned above, in the limit EMILE learns the correct grammatical structure of a language from sentences of that language. The conducted experiments show that, put into practice, EMILE 4.1 is efficient and scalable. This current implementation learns a subclass of the shallow context-free languages. This subclass seems sufficiently rich to be of practical interest. Especially Emile seems to be a valuable tool in the context of syntactic and semantic analysis of large text corpora.

1 Introduction

The current EMILE 4.1 implementation [11] is one of the first efficient and scalable grammar induction algorithms that work on free text. EMILE 4.1 is not perfect, but enables researchers to conduct empirical grammar induction research on different types of corpora. EMILE 4.1 attempts to learn the grammatical structure of such a language from sentences of that language, without any prior knowledge of the grammar apart from the fact that the grammar is categorial (i.e., equivalent to context-free) and shallow [2,3,4]. Theoretically, EMILE learns the correct grammatical structure of a language from sentences of that language in the limit. This and other theoretical concepts used in EMILE 4.1 are elaborated on in Pieter Adriaans' articles on EMILE 1.0/2.0 [2] and EMILE 3.0 [3,5,6].

V. Hlaváč, K. G. Jeffery, and J. Wiedermann (Eds.): SOFSEM 2000, LNCS 1963, pp. 173–186, 2000.

In a *shallow* language every syntactical construction has an example sentence of a length that is logarithmic in the complexity of the grammar as a whole. We believe that natural languages are shallow in this sense. Categorial grammars are based on the assignment of syntactic types to words of the lexicon. A defining characteristic of categorial languages is that expressions of the same type can be substituted for each other in all contexts. This feature forms the basis for the inductive approach of EMILE. For any type in any valid grammar for the language, we can expect context/expression combinations to show up in a sufficiently large sample of sentences of the language. EMILE searches for such clusters of expressions and contexts in the sample, and interprets them as grammatical types. It then tries to find characteristic contexts and expressions, and uses them to extend the types. Finally, it formulates derivation rules based on the types found, in the manner of the rules of a context-free grammar.

In this paper we will focus on the practical aspects of EMILE 4.1 (cf. [11]). With EMILE 4.1 grammar induction experiments can be applied to different types of corpora. Especially Emile seems to be a valuable tool for syntactic and semantic analysis of large text corpora. The experiments show that put into practice EMILE 4.1 is efficient and scalable. The current EMILE 4.1 implementation learns a subclass of the shallow context-free languages that is sufficiently rich to be of practical interest in the context of syntactic and semantic analysis of large corpora.

In comparison to its precursors EMILE 4.1 is better able to handle incomplete samples and uses positive examples only. More information on the precursors of EMILE 4.1 may be found in the above mentioned articles, as well as in the E. Dörnenburg's Master's Thesis [8].

2   The Algorithms of EMILE

This section gives insight into the reasoning underlying the algorithms. Details on the algorithms (like pseudo-code) can be found in [11]. Below, we track the development stages of EMILE, and explain the purpose of each change.

2.1   1-Dimensional Clustering

Semantic types have the property that wherever some expression is used as an expression of a particular type, other expressions of that particular type can be substituted without making the sentence ungrammatical. EMILE uses this property to identify grammatical types. As such, a grammatical type in EMILE is characterized by the expressions that belong to that type, and the contexts in which expressions of that type can appear. The context/expression pair is the principle concept in EMILE. Basically, a context/expression pair is a sentence split into three pairs, for instance,

John (makes) tea .

We say that the *expression* 'makes' appears in the *context* 'John (.) tea', or in terms of formal categorial grammar rules [10]:

$$\text{makes} \Rightarrow \text{John}\backslash\sigma/\text{tea} .$$

A simple clustering technique extracts all possible context/expression combinations from a given sample of sentences, and groups together expressions that appear in the same context. For instance, if we take the sample sentences 'John makes tea' and 'John likes tea', we get the context/expression *matrix* in Tab. 1 from which we can obtain the clusters given in Tab. 2.

Table 1. Context/expression matrix for 1-dimensional clustering

	(.) makes tea	John (.) tea	John makes (.)	(.) tea	John (.)	(.)	(.) likes tea	John likes (.)
John	x						x	
makes		x						
tea			x					x
John makes				x				
makes tea					x			
John makes tea						x		
likes		x						
John likes				x				
likes tea					x			
John likes tea						x		

Table 2. Clusters derived from context/expression matrix

[{'makes', 'likes'}, 'John (.) tea']
[{'John makes', 'John likes'}, '(.) tea']
[{'makes tea', 'likes tea'}, 'John (.)']
[{'John makes tea', 'John likes tea'}, '(.)']

Next, we can group contexts together if they appear with exactly the same expressions. For instance, if we add the sentences 'John makes coffee', 'John likes coffee' to the sample, the relevant part of the context/expression matrix will look like the matrix given in Tab. 3, which will yield the clusters given in Tab. 4.

Table 3. Extended context/expression matrix for 1-dimensional clustering

	John (.) tea	John (.) coffee	John makes (.)	John likes (.)
makes	x	x		
likes	x	x		
tea			x	x
coffee			x	x

Table 4. Clusters derived from extended context/expression matrix

[{'makes', 'likes'}, {'John (.) tea', 'John (.) coffee'}]
[{'tea', 'coffee'}, {'John makes (.)', 'John likes (.)'}]

As stated before, a grammatical type can be characterized by the expressions that are of that type, and the contexts in which expressions of that type appear. Hence the clusters we find here can be interpreted as grammatical types. For instance, the clusters in Tab. 4 correspond to the grammatical types of 'verbs' and 'nouns', respectively.

2.2   2-Dimensional Clustering

The 1-dimensional clustering technique fails to properly handle contexts whose type is ambiguous. For instance, if we add the sentences 'John likes eating' and 'John is eating', the relevant part of the context/expression matrix is given in Tab. 5.

Table 5 shows four distinct grammatical types: noun-phrases ('tea', 'coffee'), verb-phrases ('makes','likes'), 'ing'-phrases ('eating'), and auxiliary verbs ('is') that appear with 'ing'-phrases. The context 'John likes (.)' is ambiguous, since both noun-phrases and 'ing'-phrases can appear in this context. The ambiguity is naturally represented as the context belong to two different types, i.e., we would like to obtain the clustering given in Tab. 6. However, if we proceed as before with the 1-dimensional clustering technique, we get the clusters given in Tab. 7.

In Tab. 7 the ambiguous context 'John likes (.)' is assigned a separate type, which results in a less natural representation. Moreover the separate type prevents us from correctly identifying the so-called *characteristic* expressions, i.e., the expressions that belong to exactly one type. The expected and more natural representation given in Tab. 6 would allow ambiguous contexts and expressions to belong to multiple types.

Table 5. Context/expression matrix for 2-dimensional clustering

	John (.) tea	John (.) coffee	John (.) eating	John makes (.)	John likes (.)	John is (.)
makes	x	x				
likes	x	x	x			
is			x			
tea				x	x	
coffee				x	x	
eating					x	x

Table 6. Expected clusters in context/expression matrix

[{'makes', 'likes'}, {'John (.) tea', 'John (.) coffee'}]
[{'likes', 'is'}, {'John (.) eating'}]
[{'tea', 'coffee'}, {'John makes (.)', 'John likes (.)'}]
[{'eating'}, {'John is (.)', 'John likes (.)'}]

In order to find the desired result, we need a different type of clustering. EMILE 4.1 does a type of *2-dimensional* clustering, namely, it searches for maximum-sized blocks in the matrix. Table 8 shows the matrix of the example, with the maximum-sized blocks indicated by rectangles for visualization purposes. The matrix in this example is carefully arranged. In general blocks do not consist of adjacent context/expression pairs and the rectangles contain a few completely empty rows and columns. (Mentally switch, for instance, the first and last row of the matrix in Tab. 8 to see the effect. Exactly the same blocks are recognized, but the rectangles look a little different and contain two or three empty rows.)

Table 7. Derived clusters in context/expression matrix

[{'makes', 'likes'}, {'John (.) tea', 'John (.) coffee'}]
[{'likes', 'is'}, {'John (.) eating'}]
[{'tea', 'coffee'}, {'John makes (.)'}]
[{'tea', 'coffee', 'eating'}, {'John likes (.)'}]
[{'eating'}, {'John is (.)'}]

Table 8. Context/expression matrix for 2-dimensional clustering

	John (.) tea	John (.) coffee	John (.) eating	John makes (.)	John likes (.)	John is (.)
makes	x	x				
likes	x	x	x			
is			x			
eating					x	x
tea				x	x	
coffee				x	x	

The algorithm to find the maximum-sized blocks is very simple: starting from a single context/expression pair, EMILE randomly adds contexts and expressions whilst ensuring that the resulting block is still contained in the matrix, and keeps adding contexts and expressions until the block can no longer be enlarged. This is done for each context/expression pair that is not already contained in some block. Some of the resulting blocks may be completely covered by other blocks (such as the two 1 × 3 blocks in Tab. 8): once all context/expression pairs have been covered, these superfluous blocks are eliminated.

The total 2-dimensional clustering is efficient (i.e., takes polynomial time in the size of the grammar) as is proven in [11].

2.3   Allowing for Imperfect Data: Using Characteristic Expressions and Contexts

In the previous section, a block entirely had to be contained within the matrix. That is, the clustering algorithm did not find a type unless every possible combination of contexts and expressions of that type had actually been encountered and stored in the matrix. This approach only works if a perfect sample is provided. (With a perfect sample we mean a sample that consists of all and only all sentences of the language that the to be learned grammar generates.) In practical use, we need to allow for imperfect samples. There are many context/expression combinations, which are grammatical but nevertheless will appear infrequently or never: for instance, 'John likes evaporating'.

To allow EMILE to be used with imperfect samples, two modifications have been made to the algorithm. First, the requirement that the block is completely contained in the matrix, is weakened to a requirement that the block is *mostly* contained in the matrix, i.e., exceeds some user-defined tresholds. Specifically, the percentage of context/expression pairs of the block that are contained in the matrix should exceed a treshold, and for each individual row or column of the block, the percentage for that row or column should also exceed a treshold. (The latter treshold should be lower than the former treshold.)

Secondly, the shallowness constraint on languages says that short expressions and contexts contain all grammatical information about a language. Thus initially we can restrict ourselves to short expressions and contexts. The short expressions and contexts that belong to exactly one type are considered to be *characteristic* for that type. EMILE uses these characteristic expressions and contexts to find the long expressions and contexts that also belong to that type. EMILE assumes that any context or expression that appears with a characteristic expression or context, must be itself a context or expression for that type, regardless of length. Thus any (long) context or expression that appears with a known characteristic expression or context of a type, is a context or expression for that type. In the EMILE program, the (long) contexts and expressions identified by the characteristic expressions and contexts are called *secondary* contexts and expressions for that type, as opposed to the *primary* contexts and expressions that are found by the clustering algorithm.

2.4   Finding Rules

After the clustering EMILE transforms the grammatical types found into derivation rules. An expression e that belongs to type $[T]$ yields the rule

$$[T] \Rightarrow e \ .$$

EMILE finds more complex rules, by searching for characteristic expressions of one type that appear in the secondary expressions of another (or the same) type. For example, if the characteristic expressions of a type $[T]$ are

$$\{\text{dog}, \text{cat}, \text{gerbil}\}$$

and the type $[S]$ contains the secondary expressions

$$\{\text{I feed my dog}, \text{I feed my cat}, \text{I feed my gerbil}\}$$

EMILE will derive the rule

$$[S] \Rightarrow \text{I feed my } [T] \ .$$

In certain cases, using characteristic and secondary expressions in this manner allows EMILE to find recursive rules. For instance, a characteristic expression of the type of sentences $[S]$ might be

$$\text{Mary drinks tea} \ .$$

If the maximum length for primary expressions is set to 4 or 5, the sentence

$$\text{John observes that Mary drinks tea}$$

would be a secondary expression for $[S]$, but not a primary or characteristic one. So if there are no other expressions involved, EMILE would derive the recursive rules

$$[S] \Rightarrow \text{Mary drinks tea}$$
$$[S] \Rightarrow \text{John observes that } [S]$$

which would allow the resulting grammar to generate the recursive sentence

John observes that John observes that Mary drinks tea .

The total rule generation step is efficient (requires polynomial time in the size of the grammar) as proven in [11].

3   Experiments

This section presents the results of experiments with the implemented EMILE 4.1 algorithms. The application runs on the Linux operating system (RedHat version 2.2.12-20) with 128 MB RAM. A typical series (with different support percentages) of 8 times 8 experiments on 2000 lines of text data (approximately 100 KB) takes 15.5 hours. On average, we can say that a single run of EMILE processes 100 KB of text data in a quarter of an hour.

3.1   Experiments on a Small Data Set

We conducted several experiments with EMILE 4.1 on a small data set. The underlying grammar for the experiments was equivalent to the following context-free grammar (where the '|' symbol is used to separate alternatives).

$$S \Rightarrow \text{I cannot } V \text{ mail with } N$$
$$V \Rightarrow \text{read | write | open | send}$$
$$N \Rightarrow \text{MS-Mail | MS-Outlook | Mail | Outlook}$$

The purpose of the experiments was to identify the verb (V) and noun (N) categories. The experiments show (Tab. 9) that EMILE learns a correct grammar for small data set under various conditions. When applying EMILE with the default settings (support percentages 70, 70, 91) on the perfect sample of 16 sentences, EMILE induces a perfect grammar that identifies exactly the verb and noun categories. When EMILE is applied with more liberal settings on smaller data sets, EMILE induces the underlying grammar for the intended language.

The first, third and sixth experiments produce a grammar equivalent to the original. The six experiments show that the EMILE program also is able to generalize properly over a very small data sample. Even if only half of the intended sentences are given, EMILE induces the intended grammar when settings are chosen carefully.

3.2   Experiments on Large Data Sets

We experimented with three large data sets. The second series involves a data set of abstracts from the bio-medical (the Medline archive) domain. The final series of experiments is conducted on the Bible, King James version. The first series is an excercise for students.

Table 9. Experiment results on a small data set

A	B	C	D	E	F	G	H	I	J	K
16	70	70	91	229	139	17	2	5	16	yes
12	70	70	91	185	119	53	8	8	12	no
12	30	30	50	185	119	17	2	0	16	yes
8	70	70	91	141	99	53	8	0	8	no
8	40	40	60	141	99	37	5	10	15	no
8	50	50	70	141	99	54	6	15	16	yes

Legend
A = Number of sentences read
B = Primary context support percentage
C = Primary expression support percentage
D = Total support percentage
E = Number of different contexts identified
F = Number of different expressions identified
G = Number of different grammatical types identified
H = Number of different dictionary types identified
I = Number of different Chomsky rules identified
J = Size of generated language
K = Equivalent grammar

3.2.1   A 2000 Sentence Sample.

We conducted an experiment with a group of approximately 30 students. The purpose of the exercise was to reconstruct a specific grammar from a 2000 sentence sample.

The Exercise. The students were given a sample of 2000 sentences randomly generated from the context-free grammar given in Tab. 10 (where the '|' symbol is used to separate alternatives). Using EMILE, and experimenting with the settings, the students were told to find a grammar for the sample.

The Results. On the negative side, the resulting grammars suffer from being oversized (3000 to 4000 rules). Many types appear to be slight variations of one another, all of which are used in the rules, where one variation would suffice. Clearly, the rules-finding algorithm of EMILE would benefit from being optimized to use fewer types or as few types as possible.

On the positive side, the resulting grammars are as powerful as the original grammar, i.e, generates the same constructions as the original grammar). In all cases the resulting grammars manage to capture the recursion of the grammar. In some cases, the grammars are actually stronger than the original grammar (i.e., generated new constructions). Sometimes sentences such as 'John likes the man with the house near the city with the shop' are produced. This is indicative

Table 10. Context-free grammar for 2000 sentence sample

$$[S] \Rightarrow [NP]\,[V_i]\,[ADV] \mid [NP_a]\,[VP_a] \mid [NP_a]\,[V_s]\ \text{that}\ [S]$$
$$[NP] \Rightarrow [NP_a] \mid [NP_p]$$
$$[VP_a] \Rightarrow [V_t]\,[NP] \mid [V_t]\,[NP]\,[P]\,[NP_p]$$
$$[NP_a] \Rightarrow \text{John} \mid \text{Mary} \mid \text{the man} \mid \text{the child}$$
$$[NP_p] \Rightarrow \text{the car} \mid \text{the city} \mid \text{the house} \mid \text{the shop}$$
$$[P] \Rightarrow \text{with} \mid \text{near} \mid \text{in} \mid \text{from}$$
$$[V_i] \Rightarrow \text{appears} \mid \text{is} \mid \text{seems} \mid \text{looks}$$
$$[V_s] \Rightarrow \text{thinks} \mid \text{hopes} \mid \text{tells} \mid \text{says}$$
$$[V_t] \Rightarrow \text{knows} \mid \text{likes} \mid \text{misses} \mid \text{sees}$$
$$[ADV] \Rightarrow \text{large} \mid \text{small} \mid \text{ugly} \mid \text{beautiful}$$

of finding rules such as

$$[NP] \Rightarrow [NP][P][NP_p]$$

as can be induced from the rule for non-terminal $[VP_a]$.

3.2.2   The Bio-medical Domain. The second series of experiments involved bio-medical abstracts, an extremely complex sample. The bio-medical abstracts form a more heterogeneous data set than the Bible in the next section. The abstracts form a total of approximately 150 KB (3000 lines) of free text. The experiments show that each new abstract introduces new words and new sentences (see Fig. 1). The number of different contexts and expressions identified increases linearly with the number of sentences read.

Although the data set is by far not large enough to converge, the experiments already yield some interesting types. Grammatical type [16] in Tab. 11 shows a group of academic institutes; type [94] a group of languages from which the abstracts were translated; type [101] a group of journal issues and type [105] denotes a group of observation-verbs.

3.2.3   The Bible Experiments. The Bible experiments show that on large homogeneous data sets (approximately 6 MB of free text) the number of different sentences and words encountered starts to converge. As a consequence, also the number of different contexts and expressions starts to converge at a higher level. The experiments also identify significant shifts in style. The graph in Fig. 2 depicts a steep increase in sentences and words at Bible book 19.

The Bible experiment shows that the grammar induction starts to converge at a practical data set. This experiment falsifies the conjecture that learning natural language grammars from positive examples only is infeasible.

Table 12 presents a few types for large semantic groups of names that EMILE revealed in the Bible.

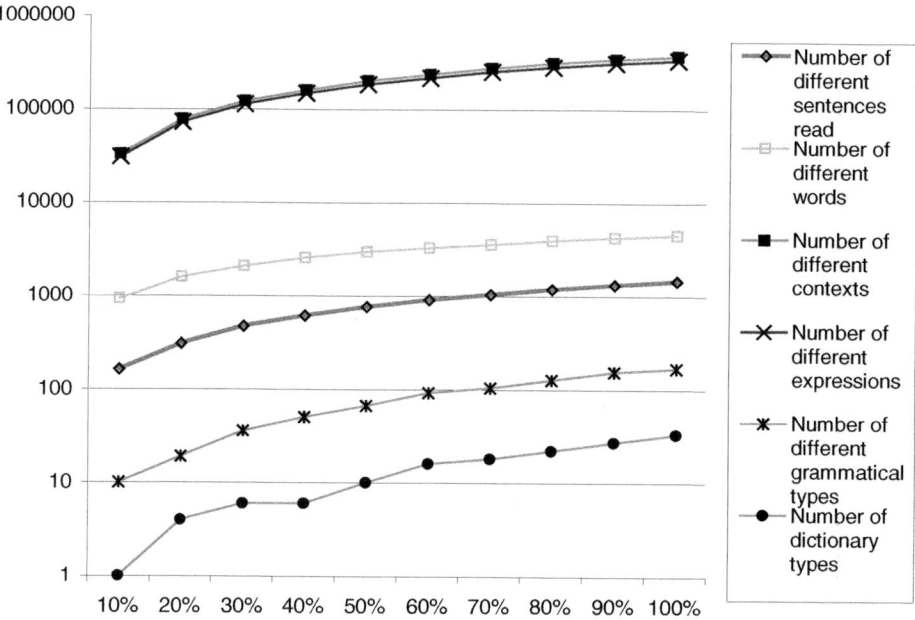

Fig. 1. The Medline experiments

4 Future Developments

Although the initial results with EMILE 4.1 are interesting, there is still a lot of room for improvement. In particular, there should be a better algorithm to transform the grammatical types into a grammar of derivation rules. The current algorithm is a brute-force search with a few basic 'tricks' used to decrease the size of the resulting grammars. The grammars still are larger than necessary, often by a large factor. Additionally, currently the grammars constructed by EMILE are context-free: it may be possible to adapt EMILE to produce more sensible, context-sensitive, grammars.

Furthermore, a better understanding of the potential application domains of EMILE is desirable. The experiments showed that EMILE can be used to extract semantic data from a text. The world wide web is an obvious application domain for EMILE, which has not yet been explored. Currently we are applying EMILE to a large body of different texts and messages: a textbook on Dutch for foreigners, bio-medical data, vocational profiles and archaeological inscriptions. EMILE might be useful as the kernel of a tool that constructs thesauri or knowledge bases from free text. EMILE can be applied to words instead of sentences and learn morphological structures. EMILE might be of help to develop mathematical models of first and second language acquisition.

Table 11. Clusters from the Medline data set

[16] $\Rightarrow$ School of Medicine, University of Washington, Seattle 98195, USA
[16] $\Rightarrow$ University of Kitasato Hospital, Sagamihara, Kanagawa,Japan
[16] $\Rightarrow$ Heinrich-Heine-University, Dusseldorf, Germany
[16] $\Rightarrow$ School of Medicine, Chiba University
[94] $\Rightarrow$ Chinese
[94] $\Rightarrow$ Japanese
[94] $\Rightarrow$ Polish
[101] $\Rightarrow$ 32 : Cancer Res 1996 Oct
[101] $\Rightarrow$ 35 : Genomics 1996 Aug
[101] $\Rightarrow$ 44 : Cancer Res 1995 Dec
[101] $\Rightarrow$ 50 : Cancer Res 1995 Feb
[101] $\Rightarrow$ 54 : Eur J Biochem 1994 Sep
[101] $\Rightarrow$ 58 : Cancer Res 1994 Mar
[105] $\Rightarrow$ identified in 13 cases (72
[105] $\Rightarrow$ detected in 9 of 87 informative cases (10
[105] $\Rightarrow$ observed in 5 (55

Table 12. Clusters from the Bible data set

[76] $\Rightarrow$ Esau | Isaac | Abraham | Rachel | Leah | Levi | Judah | Naphtali | Asher | Benjamin | Eliphaz | Reuel | Anah | Shobal | Ezer | Dishan | Pharez | Manasseh | Gershon | Kohath | Merari | Aaron | Amram | Mushi | Shimei | Mahli |Joel | Shemaiah | Shem | Ham | Salma | Laadan | Zophah | Elpaal | Jehieli
[414] $\Rightarrow$ Simeon | Judah | Dan | Naphtali | Gad | Asher | Issachar | Zebulun | Benjamin | Gershom
[3086] $\Rightarrow$ Egypt | Moab | Dumah | Tyre | Damascus

5   Conclusions

Theoretically, EMILE learns the correct grammatical structure of a language
from sentences of that language in the limit. The current implementation
(EMILE 4.1) is one of the first efficient [2,11] grammar induction algorithms
that work on free text. Although EMILE 4.1 is far from perfect, it enables
researchers to start empirical grammar induction research on various types of
corpora. A big drawback of the current implementation is the overgeneralisation
of types. EMILE almost never finds the simple basic 'sentence is noun-phrase +
verb-phrase' rule when applied to real life data. In most cases it finds thousands
of small variants of this rule in a large body of text. This is obviously an issue
that has to be addressed.

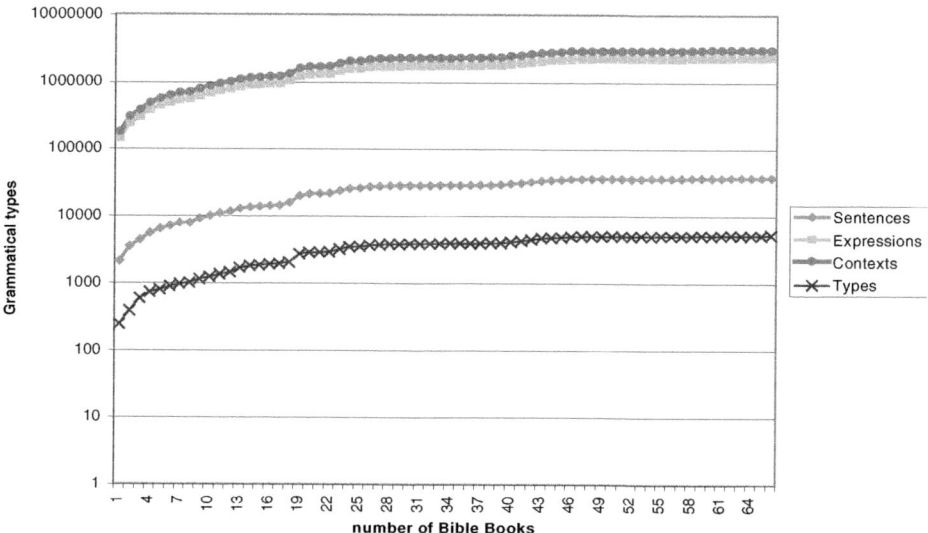

Fig. 2. The Bible experiments

The current EMILE 4.1 implementation learns a subclass of the shallow context-free languages that is sufficiently rich to be of practical interest in the context of syntactic and semantic analysis of large corpora. A very promising observation is that EMILE already starts to converge on data sets of moderate size like the Bible. A better understanding of the prospects of convergence on various types of text is necessary.

References

1. N. Abe, *Learnability and locality of formal grammars*, in Proceedings of the 26th Annual meeting of the Association of computational linguistics, 1988. 173
2. P. W. Adriaans, *Language Learning from a Categorial Perspective*, PhD thesis, University of Amsterdam, 1992. 173, 184
3. P. W. Adriaans, *Bias in Inductive Language Learning*, in Proceedings of the ML92 Workshop on Biases in Inductive Learning, Aberdeen, 1992. 173
4. P. W. Adriaans, *Learning Shallow Context-Free Languages under Simple Distributions*, ILLC Research Report PP-1999-13, Institute for Logic, Language and Computation, Amsterdam, 1999. 173
5. P. W. Adriaans, S. Janssen, E. Nomden, *Effective identification of semantic categories in curriculum texts by means of cluster analysis*, in workshop-notes on Machine Learning Techniques for Text Analysis, Vienna, 1993. 173

6. P. W. Adriaans, A. K. Knobbe, *EMILE: Learning Context-free Grammars from Examples*, in Proceedings of BENELEARN'96, 1996 173

7. W. Buszkowski, G. Penn, *Categorial Grammars Determined from Linguistic Data by Unification*, The University of Chicago, Technical Report 89–05, June 1989. 173

8. E. Dörnenburg, *Extension of the EMILE algorithm for inductive learning of context-free grammars for natural languages*, Master's Thesis, University of Dortmund, 1997. 174

9. M. Kanazawa, *Learnable Classes of Categorial Grammars*, PhD thesis, University of Stanford, 1994. 173

10. R. Oehrle, E. Bach, D. Wheeler (Eds.), *Categorial Grammars and Natural Language Structures*, D. Reidel Publishing Company, Dordrecht, 1988. 173, 175

11. M. R. Vervoort, *Games, Walks and Grammars: Problems I've Worked On*, PhD thesis, University of Amsterdam, 2000. 173, 174, 178, 180, 184

Information Access Based on Associative Calculation

Akihiko Takano, Yoshiki Niwa, Shingo Nishioka, Makoto Iwayama,
Toru Hisamitsu, Osamu Imaichi, and Hirofumi Sakurai

Central Research Laboratory, Hitachi, Ltd.,
Hatoyama, Saitama 350-0395, Japan
{takano,yniwa,nis,iwayama,hisamitu,imaichi,hirofumi}@harl.hitachi.co.jp

Abstract. The statistical measures for similarity have been widely used in textual information retrieval for many decades. They are the basis to improve the effectiveness of IR systems, including retrieval, clustering, and summarization. We have developed an information retrieval system *DualNAVI* which provides users with rich interaction both in document space and in word space. We show that associative calculation for measuring similarity among documents or words is the computational basis of this effective information access with DualNAVI. The new approaches in document clustering (Hierarchical Bayesian Clustering), and measuring term representativeness (Baseline method) are also discussed. Both have sound mathematical basis and depend essentially on associative calculation.

1   Introduction

In this last decade of the twentieth century, we are experiencing an unusual expansion of the information space. The information we can access are literary exploding in amount and variation. Information space we face in our daily life is rapidly losing its coherence of any kind, and this has brought many challenges in the field of information access research.

Individual productivity in this new era can be redefined as a power for recovering order from the chaos this information flood left. It requires the ability to collect *appropriate* information, one to analyze the collected information, and the ability to make proper judgement based on the analysis. This leads to the following three requirements for the effective information access we need in coming century:

- Flexible methods for collecting *relevant* information.
- Extracting *mutual association* (correlation) within the collected information.
- Interaction with user's *intention* (in mind) and the archival system of knowledge.

We strongly believe that the important clue to atack these challenges lies in the metrication of the information space. Once we got proper metrics for measuring

V. Hlaváč, K. G. Jeffery, and J. Wiedermann (Eds.): SOFSEM 2000, LNCS 1963, pp. 187–201, 2000.

similarity or correlation in information space, it should not be difficult to recover some order through this metrics. We looked for a candidate in the accumulation of previous research, and found that the statistical (or probabilistic) measures for the document similarity are the promising candidates. It is almost inspirational when we realize that these measures establish the duality between the document space and word space.

Following this guiding principle, we have developed an information retrieval system *DualNAVI* [19,21,2]. Our experience tells that the associative computation based on mathematically sound metrics is the crucial part to realize the new generation IR technologies.

This paper is organized as follows. In Section 2 we introduce a basic design principle of *DualNAVI*. Two important features, topic word graph and associative search, are also discussed. In Section 3 the new approach in document clustering called Hierarchical Bayesian Clustering is introduced. It is the first clustering algorithm based on probabilistic model. In Section 4 the new method for measuring the representativeness of a term is introduced. Representativeness is the measure to know how informative that the appearance of the term means. It is particularly important when we design an effective feedback by returning informative words to users. These two methods would naturally be employed to realize the new features of *DualNAVI* in the future.

2   *DualNAVI*: Associative Information Retrieval System

2.1   *DualNAVI* Interaction Model

DualNAVI is an information retrieval system which provides users with rich interaction methods based on two kinds of duality, *dual view* and *dual query types*.

Dual view interface is composed of two views of retrieved results: one in document space and the other in word space (See Fig. 1). Titles of retrieved results are listed on the left-hand side of the screen (for documents), and the summarizing information are shown as a "topic word graph" on the right of the screen (for words). Topic word graphs are dynamically generated by analyzing the retrieved set of documents. A set of words characterizing the retrieved results are selected, and the statistically meaningful co-occurrence relations among words are shown as links between them. Connected subgraphs are expected to include good potential keywords with which to refine searches. Two views are tightly coupled with their cross-reference relation: Select some topic words, and related documents which include them are highlighted in the list of documents.

On the other hand, dual query types mean that *DualNAVI* supports two kinds of search facilities. *Document associative search* finds related documents to given set of key documents. *Keyword search* finds related documents to given set of key words. Dual view interface provides a natural way for indicating the key objects for these search methods. Just select the relevant documents or words within the previous search result, and the user can start a new associative search.

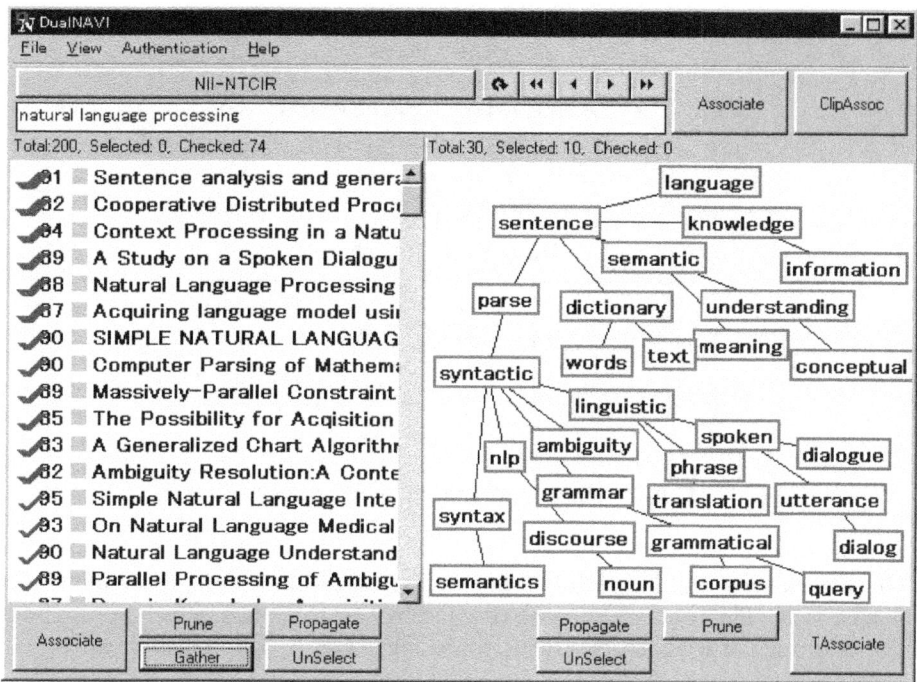

Fig. 1. Navigation Interface of *DualNAVI* (Nishioka et al., 1997)

This enables easy and intuitive relevance feedbacks to refine searches effectively. Search by documents is especially helpful when users have some interesting documents and feel difficult in selecting proper keywords.

The effectiveness of these two types of feedback with *DualNAVI* has been evaluated in [21]. The results were significantly positive for both types of interaction.

2.2   Dual View Bridges Dual Query Types

The dual view and dual query types are not just two isolated features. Dual query types can work effectively only with dual view framework. Figure 2 illustrates how they relate each other. We can start with either a search by keywords or by a document, and the retrieved results are shown in the dual view. If the title list includes interesting articles, we can proceed to next associative search using these found articles as key documents. If some words in the topic word graph are interesting, we can start new keyword search using these topic words as keys.

Another advantage of dual view interface is that the cross checking function is naturally realized. If a user selects some articles of his interest, he can easily find what topic words appear in them. Conversely, it is easy to find related articles by selecting topic words. If multiple topic words are selected, the thickness of

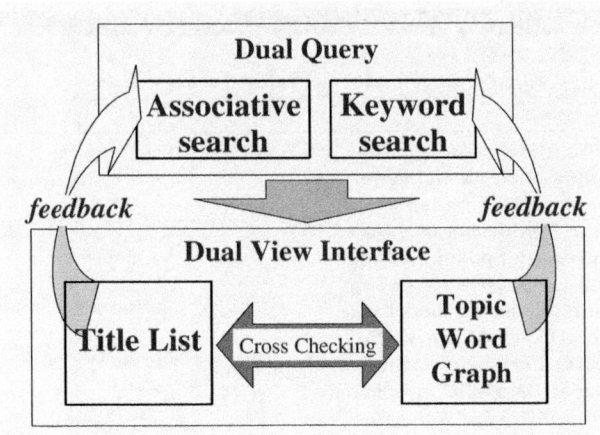

Fig. 2. Dual view bridges Dual query types

checkmark (See Fig. 1) indicates the number of selected topic words included by each article. The user can sort the title list by this thickness, which approximates the relevance of each article to the topic suggested by the selected words.

2.3   Generation of Topic Word Graph

Topic word graphs summarize the search results and suggest proper words for further refining of searches. The method of generating topic word graphs is fully described in [20]. Here we give a brief summary.

The process consists of three steps (See Fig. 3). The first step is the extraction of topic words based on the word frequency analysis over the retrieved set of documents. Next step is the process of generating links between extracted topic words based on co-occurrence analysis. The last step is to assign a xy-coordinates position for each topic word on the display area.

The score for selecting topic words is given by

$$\frac{df(w) \text{ in the retrieved documents}}{df(w) \text{ in the whole database}}$$

where $df(w)$ is the document frequency of word w, i. e. the number of documents containing w. In general, it is difficult to keep the balance between high frequency words (common words) and low frequency words (specific words) by using a single score. In order to make a balanced selection, we adopted the frequency-class method, where all candidate words are first roughly classified by their frequencies, and then proper number of topic words are picked up from each frequency class.

A link (an edge) between two words means that they are strongly related, that is, they co-appear in many documents in the retrieved results. In the link

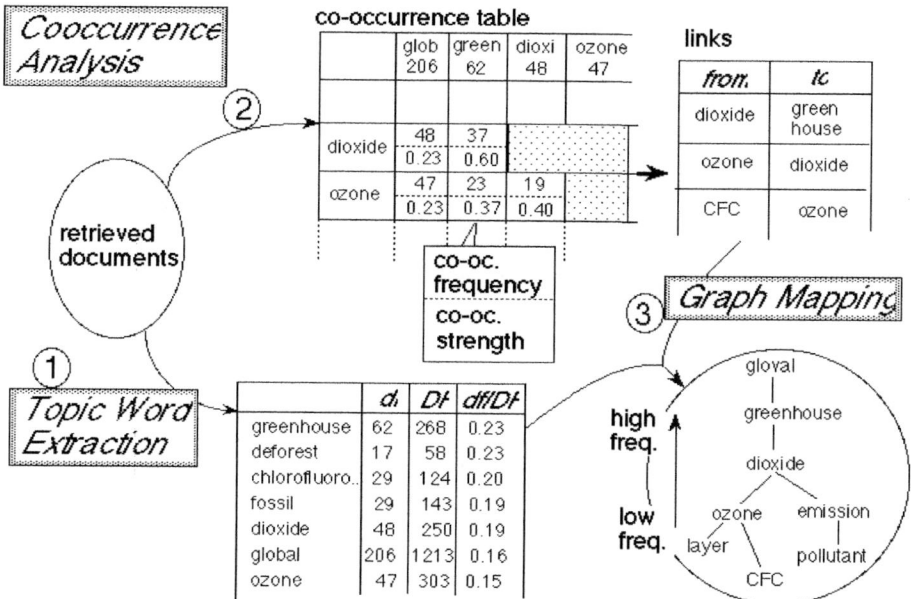

Fig. 3. Generating topic word graph (Niwa et al., 1997)

generation step, each topic word X is linked to another topic word Y which maximizes the co-occurrence strength $df(X \& Y)/df(Y)$ with X among those having higher document frequency than X. Here $df(X \& Y)$ means the number of retrieved documents which have both X and Y. The length of a link has no specific meaning, although it might be natural to expect a shorter link means a stronger relation.

In the last step to give two dimensional arrangement of topic word graphs, the y-coordinate (vertical position) is decided according to the document frequency of each word within the retrieved set. Common words are placed in the upper part, and specific words are placed in the lower part. Therefore, the graph can be considered as a hierarchical map of topics appear in the retrieved set of documents. The x-coordinate (horizontal position) has no specific meaning. It is assigned just in the way to avoid overlapping of nodes and links.

2.4 Associative Search

Associative search is a type of information retrieval method based on the similarity between documents. It is useful when the user's intention cannot clearly be expressed by one or several keywords, but the user has some documents match with his intention. Associative search is also a powerful tool for relevance feedbacks. If you find interesting items in the search results, associative search with these items as search keys may bring you more related items which were not previously retrieved.

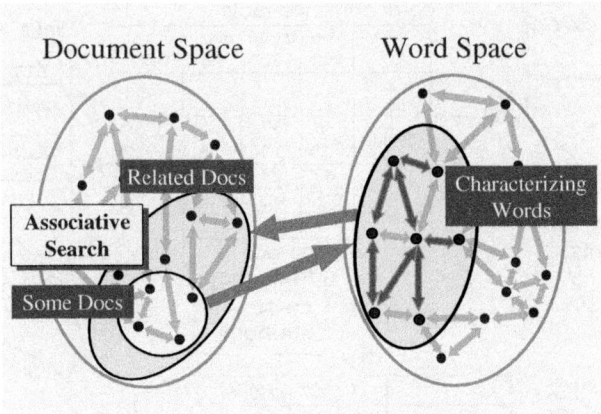

Fig. 4. Associative search

Associative search of *DualNAVI* consists of following steps:

- Extraction of characterizing words from the selected documents. The default number of characterizing words to be extracted is 200. For each word w, which appears at least once in the selected documents, its score is calculated by $score(w) = tf(w)/TF(w)$, where $tf(w)$ and $TF(w)$ are the term frequencies of w in the selected documents, and in the whole database respectively. Then the above number of words of higher score are selected.
- These extracted words are used as a query, and the relevance of each document d in the target database with this query q is calculated by [25]:

$$sim(d, q) = \rho(d) \sum_{w \in q} \sigma(w) \cdot \nu(w, d) \cdot \nu(w, q)$$

where

$$\rho(d) = \frac{1}{\ell + \theta(length(d) - \ell)} \qquad \begin{array}{l} \ell\text{: average document length,} \\ \theta\text{: slope constant} \end{array}$$

$$\sigma(w) = \log \frac{N}{DF(w)}$$

$$\nu(w, X) = \frac{1 + \log tf(w|X)}{1 + \log \left(average_{\omega \in X} \, tf(\omega|X) \right)}.$$

Here $DF(w)$ is the number of documents containing w, and N is the total number of documents in the database.

- The documents in the target database are sorted by this similarity score and the top ranked documents are returned as the search results.

In theory, associative search should not limit the size of the query. The merged documents should be used as the query in associative search from a set of documents. But if we don't reduce the number of the distinctive words in the query, we end up on calculating $sim(d, q)$ for almost all the documents in the target database, even when we request for just ten documents. In fact this extensive computational cost had prevented associative search from being used in the practical systems.

This is why we reduce the query into manageable size in step one. Most common words which appear in many documents are dropped in this step. We have to do this carefully so as not to drop important words within the query. In above explanation, we simply adopt $tf(w)/TF(w)$ for measuring the importance of the words. But it is possible to use any measure for this filtering. In Section 4, we will discuss about the *representativeness* [13] of the words, which is a promising candidate for this purpose. It is a more complex but theoretically sound measure.

Another break through we made for taming this computational cost is to develop a high-speed engine for these generic associative calculation. The computations for realizing above two steps are supported in their most abstract ways:

(a) the method to extract summarizing words from given set of documents, and
(b) the method to collect documents from the target database which are best relevant to the given key document (a set of words).

With these improvement, associative search in *DualNAVI* becomes efficient enough for many practical applications.

2.5   Cross DB Associative Search

This two step procedure of associative search is the key to the distributive architecture of *DualNAVI* system. Associative search is divided into two subtasks, summarizing and similarity evaluation. Summarizing needs only the source DB, and target DB is only used in similarity evaluation. If these two functions are provided for each DB, it is not difficult to realize the cross DB associative search.

Figure 5 shows the structure for the cross DB associative search between two physically distributed *DualNAVI* servers, one for the encyclopaedia and the other for newspapers. User can select some articles in the encyclopaedia and search related articles in other DB's, say newspapers. User can search between physically distributed DB's associatively and seemlessly. We call these set of DB's a "Virtual Database" because it can be accessed as one big database.

3   Hierarchical Bayesian Clustering

Text classification, the grouping of texts into several clusters, has been used as a means of improving both the efficiency and the effectiveness of text retrieval/categorization [15,26,5,27]. For example, to retrieve texts relevant to a user's request, a simple strategy would be to search all the texts in a database by calculating a measure of the relevance of each text to the request. This exhaustive search, however, would require more computation for larger databases. Text

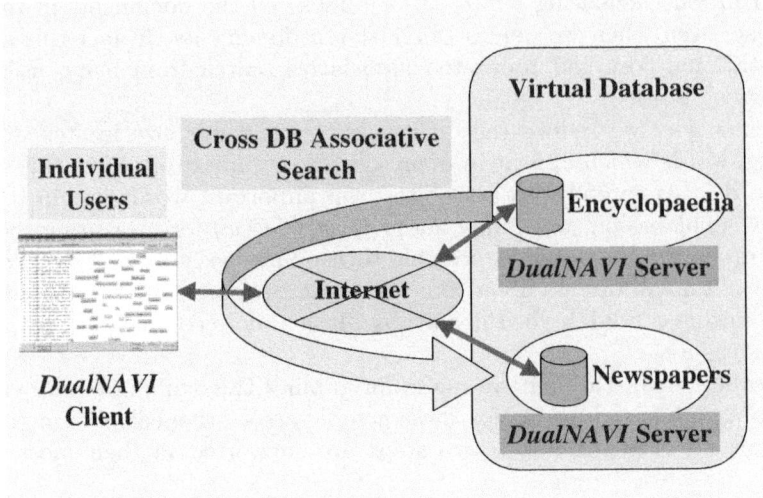

Fig. 5. Cross DB associative search with *DualNAVI*

classification helps to reduce the number of comparisons in an exhaustive search by clustering (grouping) similar texts into clusters in advance and comparing the request with the representative of each cluster. The retrieval/categorization model that incorporates text classification as a preliminary process is often called *cluster-based text retrieval/categorization*.

In this section we explain one algorithm called Hierarchical Bayesian Clustering (HBC) proposed in [14]. It is a hierarchical clustering algorithm that constructs a set of clusters having the maximum Bayesian posterior probability, the probability that the given texts are classified into clusters. Almost all previous algorithms, such as single-link method and Ward's method, use the measure of distance between two objects and merge the closer ones [4,1,10,28]. HBC, however, constructs a set of clusters that has the maximum Bayesian posterior probability, the probability that the given objects are classified into clusters. This maximization is a general form of the well known *Maximum Likelihood* estimation, and we call the algorithm *Hierarchical Bayesian Clustering*.

Probabilistic models are becoming popular in the field of text retrieval/categorization due to their solid formal grounding in probability theory [6,9,16,17]. They retrieve those texts that have larger posterior probabilities of being relevant to a request. When these models are extended to cluster-based text retrieval/categorization, however, the algorithm used for text clustering has still been a non probabilistic one [5]. It is believed that better performance could be obtained by using exactly the same criterion in both clustering and retrieval/categorization, that is, searching for the maximum posterior probability. This assumption has been verified by comparing a probabilistic text categorization using HBC and the same task using non probabilistic clustering algorithms in [14].

3.1   Basic Algorithm for HBC

Like most agglomerative clustering algorithms [4,1,10,28], HBC constructs a cluster hierarchy (also called *dendrogram*) from bottom to top by merging two clusters at a time. At the begining (i.e., at the bottom level in a dendrogram), each datum belongs to a cluster whose only member is the datum itself. For every pair of clusters, HBC calculates the probability of merging the pair and selects for the next merge the best one for which this probability is highest. This merge step takes place $N - 1$ times for a collection of N data. The last merge produces a single cluster containing the entire data set. Figure 6 shows an example of a dendrogram.

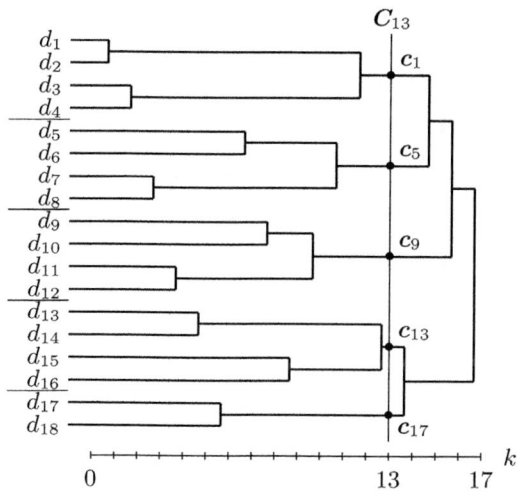

Fig. 6. Example of a dendrogram

Formally, HBC selects the cluster pair whose merge results in the maximum value of the posterior probability $P(C|D)$, where D is a collection of data (i.e., $D = \{d_1, d_2, \ldots, d_N\}$) and C is a set of clusters (i.e., $C = \{c_1, c_2, \ldots\}$). Each cluster $c_j \in C$ is a set of data and the clusters being mutually exclusive. At the initial stage, each cluster is a singleton set; $c_i = \{d_i\}$ for all i. $P(C|D)$ defines the probability that a collection of data D is classified into a set of clusters C. Maximizing $P(C|D)$ is a generalization of *Maximum Likelihood* estimation.

To see the details of merge process, consider a merge step $k + 1$ ($0 \leq k \leq N - 1$). By the step $k + 1$, a data collection D has been partitioned into a set of clusters C_k. That is each datum $d \in D$ belongs to a cluster $c \in C_k$. The posterior probability at this point becomes

$$
\begin{aligned}
P(C_k|D) &= \prod_{c \in C_k} \prod_{d \in c} P(c|d) \\
&= \prod_{c \in C_k} \prod_{d \in c} \frac{P(d|c)P(c)}{P(d)} \\
&= \frac{\prod_{c \in C_k} P(c)^{|c|}}{P(D)} \prod_{c \in C_k} \prod_{d \in c} P(d|c) \\
&= \frac{PC(C_k)}{P(D)} \prod_{c \in C_k} SC(c) \, .
\end{aligned}
\tag{1}
$$

Here $PC(C_k)$ corresponds to the prior probability that N random data are classified into a set of clusters C_k. This probability is defined as follows:

$$
PC(C_k) = \prod_{c \in C_k} P(c)^{|c|} \, .
\tag{2}
$$

$SC(c)$ defines the probability that all the data in a cluster c are produced from the cluster and is defined as

$$
SC(c) = \prod_{d \in c} P(d|c) \, .
\tag{3}
$$

When the algorithm merges two clusters $c_x, c_y \in C_k$, the set of clusters C_k is updated as follows:

$$
C_{k+1} = C_k - \{c_x, c_y\} + \{c_x \cup c_y\} \, .
\tag{4}
$$

After the merge, the posterior probability is inductively updated as

$$
P(C_{k+1}|D) = \frac{PC(C_{k+1})}{PC(C_k)} \frac{SC(c_x \cup c_y)}{SC(c_x)SC(c_y)} P(C_k|D) \, .
\tag{5}
$$

Note that this updating is local and can be done efficiently since all we have to recalculate from the previous step is the probability for the merged new cluster; that is, $SC(c_x \cup c_y)$. As for the factor of $\frac{PC(C_{k+1})}{PC(C_k)}$, we use a well known estimate: the prior probability of a model (in this case, a cluster) is a decreasing function of the model size. For instance, $P(c) \propto A^{-|c|}$ for some constant $A > 1$. According to this estimate,

$$
PC(C) = \prod_{c \in C} P(c)^{|c|} \propto \prod_{c \in C} A = A^{|C|} \, .
\tag{6}
$$

Since the number of clusters $|C|$ decreases one by one as the merge step proceeds, $\frac{PC(C_{k+1})}{PC(C_k)}$ reduces to a constant value A^{-1} regardless of the merged pair. This

Input:
  $D = \{d_1, d_2, \ldots, d_N\}$: a collection of N data;

Initialize:
  $C_0 = \{c_1, c_2, \ldots, c_N\}$: a set of clusters;
  $c_i = \{d_i\}$ for $1 \le i \le N$
  calculate $SC(c_i)$ for $1 \le i \le N$
  calculate $SC(c_i \cup c_j)$ for $1 \le i < j \le N$

for $k = 1$ **to** $N - 1$ **do**
  $(c_x, c_y) = \arg\max_{c_x, c_y} \frac{SC(c_x \cup c_y)}{SC(c_x)SC(c_y)}$
  $C_k = C_{k-1} - \{c_x, c_y\} + \{c_x \cup c_y\}$
  calculate $SC(c_x \cup c_z)$ for all $c_z \in C_k$ where $z \ne x$

Function $SC(c)$
  return $\prod_{d \in c} P(d|c)$

Fig. 7. Hierarchical Bayesian Clustering

means that we can drop the facter for a maximization task. HBC calculates the updated $P(C_{k+1}|D)$ for every merge candidate and merges the one that offers the maximum $P(C_{k+1}|D)$. The HBC algorithm is summarized in Figure 7.

The general framework of HBC is similar to Ward's method, a well known hierarchical clustering algorithm (see [1,10,4] for the algorithm). Whereas Ward's method merges two clusters whose merge causes the least increase in the sum of the distances from each datum to the centroid of its cluster, HBC maximizes the probability that all the members of a cluster actually belong (or are categorized) to the cluster. We think that in application domains like text categorization, HBC would work better than Ward's method because the cluster construction strategy of HBC is more directly related to the task of such applications.

4   Measuring Term Representativeness

Measuring the representativeness (i. e., the informativeness or domain specificity) of a term is essential to various tasks in natural language processing (NLP) and information retrieval (IR). It is particularly important when applied to an IR interface to help a user find informative terms. For instance, when the number of retrieved documents is intractably large, an overview of representative words within the retrieved documents is quite helpful to understand the contents. The topic word graph in *DualNAVI* interface is a good example. Representative measure provides the criterion which words should be selected as topic words. This section introduces a recent development of the new measure of representativeness [12,13].

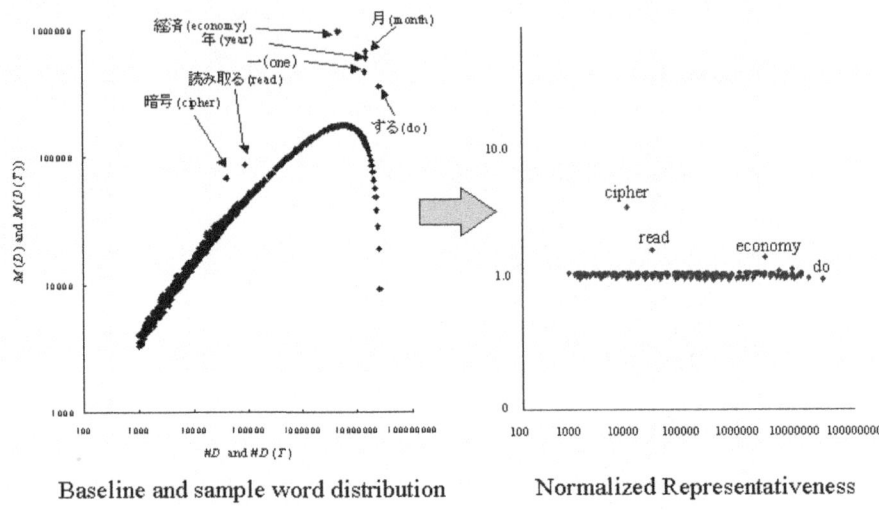

Baseline and sample word distribution   **Normalized Representativeness**

Fig. 8. Normalized Representativeness (Hisamitsu et al., 2000)

Hisamitsu et al. developed a measure of the representativeness of a term by using co-occurrence information and a normalization technique [12]. The measure is based on the distance between the word distribution in the documents containing a term and the word distribution in the whole corpus. Their measure overcomes the following problems which previous measures suffer from:

- Classical measures such as tf-idf [23] are so sensitive to term frequencies that they fail to avoid very frequent non-informative words.
- Methods using cross-category word distributions (such as the χ^2 method) can be applied only if documents in a corpus are categorized [18].
- Most measures in NLP domains cannot treat single word terms because they use the unithood strength of multiple words [3,7].
- The threshold value for being representative is defined in an *ad hoc* manner.

The generic scheme of defining Hisamitsu's measure, called the baseline method [13], is a powerful scheme to define various measures for term representativeness. A characteristic value of all documents containing a term T is normalized by using a baseline function that estimates the characteristic value of a randomly chosen document set of the same size. The normalized value is then used to measure the representativeness of the term T. A measure defined by the baseline-method has several advantages compared to classical measures. Preliminary experiments showed that this measure worked better than existing measures in picking out representative/non-representative terms.

4.1   Baseline Method for Defining Representativeness Measures

The guiding hypothesis on defining term representativeness is as follows:

> For any term T, if the term is representative, $D(T)$, the set of all documents containing T, should have some characteristic *property* compared to the *"average"*.

To apply this hypothesis, we need to specify a measure to obtain some "property" of a document set and the concept of "average". Thus, we converted this hypothesis into the following procedure:

> Choose a measure M for characterizing a document set. For term T, calculate $M(D(T))$, the characterizing value for $D(T)$. Then compare $M(D(T))$ with $B_M(\#D(T))$, where $\#D(T)$ is the number of words contained in $D(T)$, and $B_M(N)$ estimates the value of $M(D)$ when D is a randomly chosen document set of size N.

Here we assume to use the log-likelihood ratio (LLR) for M. The representativeness of a term T, $Rep(T, LLR)$, is defined as a normalization of $LLR(D(T))$ by $B_{LLR}(\#D(T))$:

$$Rep(T, LLR) = 100 \times \left(\frac{\log(LLR(D(T)))}{\log(B_{LLR}(\#D(T)))} - 1 \right). \qquad (7)$$

$Rep(T, LLR)$ (or $Rep(T, M)$ in general) has the following advantages by virtue of its definition:

- Its definition is mathematically clear.
- It can compare high-frequency terms with low-frequency terms.
- The threshold value of being representative can be defined systematically.
- It can applied to n-gram terms for any n.

Figure 8 shows the representativeness of some sample words. It is clear that this measure successfully discards frequent but uninformative terms. We can expect that these measures can be used for automated construction of a stop-word list and improvement of similarity calculation of documents. It is also promising to use these measure for selecting the topical words for topic word graphs or picking up the characterizing words in the first step of associative searches.

5   Conclusions

We have shown how associative calculation, evaluating the similarity among documents, are essential for new generation technologies for the information access. *DualNAVI* which is based on this principle brings a new horizon of the interactive information access. The two important issues related to associative calculation are discussed. Hierarchical Bayesian Clustering succeeded to provide a probablistic foundation of clustering, and is expected to lead to better performance when combined with other methods based on associative calculation. The study on measuring representativeness of terms is a promising recent development for providing mathematically clear criterions for various tasks in associative calculation.

Acknowledgements

This research is partly supported by the Advanced Software Technology Project under the auspices of Information-technology Promotion Agency (IPA), Japan.

References

1. M. R. Anderberg. *Cluster Analysis for Applications*. Academic Press, 1973. 194, 195, 197
2. D. Butler. Souped-up search engines. *Nature*, 405, pages 112–115, 2000. 188
3. K. W. Church, and P. Hanks. Word association norms, mutual information, and lexicography. *Computational Linguistics*, 16(1), pages 22–29, 1990. 198
4. R. M. Cormack. A review of classification. *Journal of the Royal Statistical Society*, 134:321–367, 1971. 194, 195, 197
5. W. B. Croft. A model of cluster searching based on classification. *Information Systems*, 5:189–195, 1980. 193, 194
6. W. B. Croft. Document representation in probabilistic models of information retrieval. *Journal of the American Society for Information Science*, 32(6):451–457, 1981. 194
7. T. Dunning. Accurate method for the statistics of surprise and coincidence. *Computational Linguistics*, 19(1), pages 61–74, 1993. 198
8. R. H. Fowler, and D. W. Dearholt. *Information Retrieval Using Pathfinder Networks*, chapter 12, pages 165–178, 1990. Ablex.
9. N. Fuhr. Models for retrieval with probabilistic indexing. *Information Processing & Retrieval*, 25(1):55–72, 1989. 194
10. A. Griffiths, L. A. Robinson, and P. Willett. Hierarchic agglomerative clustering methods for automatic document classification. *Journal of Documentation*, 40(3):175–205, 1984. 194, 195, 197
11. M. A. Hearst, and J. O. Pedersen. Reexamining the cluster hypothesis: Scatter/gather on retrieval results. In *Proceedings of ACM SIGIR'96*, pages 76–84, 1996.
12. T. Hisamitsu, Y. Niwa, and J. Tsujii. Measuring Representativeness of Terms. In *Proceedings of IRAL'99*, pages 83–90, 1999. 197, 198
13. T. Hisamitsu, Y. Niwa, and J. Tsujii. A Method of Measuring Term Representativeness. In *Proceedings of COLING 2000*, pages 320–326, 2000. 193, 197, 198
14. M. Iwayama and T. Tokunaga. Hierarchical Bayesian Clustering for Automatic Text Classification. In *Proceedings of IJCAI'95*, pages 1322–1327, 1995. 194, 195
15. N. Jardine and C. J. Van Rijsbergen. The use of hierarchic clustering in information retrieval. *Information Storage and Retrieval*, 7:217–240, 1971. 193
16. K. L. Kwok. Experiments with a component theory of probabilistic information retrieval based on single terms as document components. *ACM Transactions on Information Systems*, 8(4):363–386, 1990. 194
17. D. D. Lewis. An evaluation of phrasal and clustered representation on a text categorization task. In *Proceedings of ACM SIGIR'92*, pages 37–50, 1992. 194
18. M. Nagao, M. Mizutani, and H. Ikeda. An automated method of the extraction of important words from Japanese scientific documents. In *Transaction of IPSJ*, 17(2), pages 110–117, 1976. 198
19. S. Nishioka, Y. Niwa, M. Iwayama, and A. Takano. *DualNAVI*: An information retrieval interface. In *Proceedings of JSSST WISS'97*, pages 43–48, 1997. (in Japanese). 188

20. Y. Niwa, S. Nishioka, M. Iwayama, and A. Takano. Topic graph generation for query navigation: Use of frequency classes for topic extraction. In *Proceedings of NLPRS'97*, pages 95–100, 1997. 190

21. Y. Niwa, M. Iwayama, T. Hisamitsu, S. Nishioka, A. Takano, H. Sakurai, and O. Imaichi. Interactive Document Search with *DualNAVI*. In *Proceedings of NTCIR'99*, pages 123–130, 1999. 188, 189

22. H. Sakurai, and T. Hisamitsu. A data structure for fast lookup of grammatically connectable word pairs in japanese morphological analysis. In *Proceedings of ICCPOL'99*, pages 467–471, 1999.

23. G. Salton, and C. S. Yang. On the Specification of Term Values in Automatic Indexing. *Journal of Documentation*, 29(4):351–372, 1973. 198

24. B. R. Schatz, E. H. Johnson, and P. A. Cochrane. Interactive term suggestion for users of digital libraries: Using subject thesauri and co-occurrence lists for information retrieval. In *Proceedings of ACM DL'96*, pages 126–133, 1996.

25. A. Singhal, C. Buckley, and M. Mitra. Pivoted Document Length Normalization In *Proceedings of ACM SIGIR'96*, pages 21–29, 1996. 192

26. C. J. van Rijsbergen and W. B. Croft. Document clustering: An evaluation of some experiments with the granfield 1400 collection. *Information Processing & Management*, 11:171–182, 1975. 193

27. P. Willett. Similarity coefficients and weighting functions for automatic document classification: an empirical comparison. *International Classification*, 10(3):138–142, 1983. 193

28. P. Willett. Recent trends in hierarchic document clustering: A critical review. *Information Processing & Management*, 24(5):577–597, 1988. 194, 195

Cheap Vision — Exploiting Ecological Niche and Morphology

Rolf Pfeifer and Dimitrios Lambrinos

Artificial Intelligence Laboratory, Department of Information Technology,
University of Zurich, Winterthurerstrasse 190, CH-8057 Zurich, Switzerland
{pfeifer,lambri}@ifi.unizh.ch
http://www.ifi.unizh.ch/~pfeifer

Abstract. In the course of evolutionary history, the visual system has
evolved as part of a complete autonomous agent in the service of motor
control. Therefore, the synthetic methodology investigates visual skills
in the context of tasks a complete agent has to perform in a particular environment using autonomous mobile robots as modeling tools. We
present a number of case studies in which certain vision-based behaviors
in insects have been modeled with real robots, the snapshot model for
landmark navigation, the average landmark vector model (ALV), a model
of visual odometry, and the evolution of the morphology of an insect eye.
From these case studies we devise a number of principles that characterize the concept of "cheap vision". It is concluded that — if ecological
niche and morphology are properly taken into account — in many cases
vision becomes much simpler.

1 Introduction

Vision is an enormously large research field. In this paper we focus on robot
vision for navigation purposes. With the growing interest in autonomous robots
in engineering, artificial intelligence, but also biology, there has been a surge of
research in landmark navigation. The reason for this is obvious: Autonomous
robots must, by definition, be able to find their way around. The basic problem
is finding the way to a particular target position. This can be done in many
different ways and there is a considerable literature about this problem [24].
Many of the approaches are based on landmarks and involve visual sensors that
are used for recognizing the landmarks. Recognizing the landmarks typically
(but not always, see below) involves locating it on a map. Once this has been
achieved, the agent decides what to do next, a process that may involve planning.

At a more general level, the basic principle in most of these approaches is
always as follows: Get a visual image from a CCD camera or two CCD cameras
in the case of stereo vision (or perhaps from other sensors, e. g. laser scanners).
In what follows we entirely leave out the stereo vision. The camera delivers
an image normally in the form of a pixel array. This image is then analyzed in
certain ways in order to recover information about the outside world and to build
an accurate model of it. In the navigation case this might be the identification

V. Hlaváč, K. G. Jeffery, and J. Wiedermann (Eds.): SOFSEM 2000, LNCS 1963, pp. 202–226, 2000.

of specific landmarks. This model is taken as the basis to plan the next steps, in the case of a navigation problem, the direction of where to move next. Finally, if we are dealing with a robot, these steps are executed in the real world and the cycle is repeated.

This has been called the sense – think – act approach (sometimes called sense – model – plan – act) [3]. This way of thinking corresponds to our intuitions: We see something and then we react to it. Moreover, it instantiates the standard computer metaphor which is based on input – processing – output. Interestingly enough, natural as the approach may seem, it has not worked in the real world, at least not in general. The reasons have been discussed in the literature and will not be reproduced in detail here (e. g. [3], for a more general perspective on this point [23]). In essence, it is that — because of the high computational requirements — the robots fail to react in real time, and because of the very strict assumptions that have to be made for the algorithms to work (geometry, calibration), they lack the robustness required in the real world. On a more general account, the classical approach is not grounded and does not sufficiently exploit the task-specific system – environment interaction (although more recently this point has been taken up by many researchers). The successful applications of the classical approach to computer vision have been mostly in controlled environments such as in factories where the geometry (distance, orientation) and the possible types of objects are precisely known and the lighting conditions are constant, a situation which hardly occurs in the real world. Moreover, in a factory environment, virtually unlimited amounts of computing power are available.

A completely different approach — "cheap vision" — was proposed by Ian Horswill at the AI Lab of MIT in the group of Rodney Brooks, one of the first proponents of "New Artificial Intelligence". Ian Horswill's robot Polly was one of the first to demonstrate the power of cheap vision and of exploiting task-specific constraints [9,10]. Equipped with only a low resolution vision system with relatively limited computing power, Polly managed to move much faster than most mobile robot systems at the time (for a brief description of Polly, see [23]). For the purpose of giving tours of the research laboratory, there was, for example, no need to recognize specific objects; the robot needed just enough information about the environment to roughly localize itself. In order to do this with a low-resolution vision system, it was exploiting the redundancy contained in a sequence of images. Here, the assumption is that normally subsequent frames from a camera, if taken in quick succession, contain highly redundant information. Another assumption, the so-called ground-plane constraint, supposes that all relevant objects are standing on the ground. If it is further assumed that the ground is relatively homogeneous, it is easy to detect objects by means of simple thresholding methods. If the camera is slightly tilted towards the ground, nearby objects (i. e. those relevant for obstacle avoidance) will be lower in the vertical axis in the image plane than objects further away. Polly beautifully demonstrates that much can be gained by employing principles of "cheap vision".

Turning to nature, our work on modeling vision-based insect navigation strategies has shown that insects also exploit the constraints of their environments in highly interesting ways (for examples, see below). We suspect that this is one of the reasons why there has been a surge of interest in the field of biorobotics. The fact that natural agents exploit environmental constraints comes as no surprise because their visual systems are the result of a long evolutionary process during which — apparently — exploiting constraints has turned out to increase their fitness. In all the work described below, we move back and fourth between biology and engineering, a strategy that has turned out to be highly productive.

Fig. 1. The desert ant *Cataglyphis bicolor* (photograph by R. Wehner)

First, we present two examples of cheap vision that are inspired by biological research in insect navigation, the so-called snapshot model, and the average landmark vector model, and we discuss their implementations in robots, and present some experimental results (Section 2). In this section we demonstrate how the biological ideas can be transferred to the general landmark navigation problem and we discuss an application to indoor navigation as well as an analogue implementation, i.e. an implementation in a robot without software. We then show how optical flow can be used for measuring distance traveled. This is first demonstrated on a ground-based robot and then on a flying one (Section 3). Visual odometry, again, solves some seemingly hard problems in simple ways. The ways in which the specific morphology can be exploited is demonstrated in a case study on evolution of morphology (Section 4). From these case studies, some principles of cheap vision will be summarized (Section 5). Finally, conclusions and speculations on future research are presented (Section 6).

2   Visual Processes in Landmark Navigation Models

The text of this section is largely based on [19]. The systems we describe in this section are all modeled after biological systems, in particular insects. To illustrate our points we use the desert ant *Cataglyphis* (Figure 1) which has been extremely well studied. Typically, insects use a number of navigation strategies in different situations. Experiments have revealed that the desert ants use path integration (dead reckoning), visual landmark navigation, and systematic search (e. g. [31]). Path integration guides the animal to the vicinity of the target location, but is subject to cumulative errors which limits the precision of this strategy. This is why they use visual landmark navigation as they have arrived in the vicinity of the nest with the path integration system. Ants that by means of path integration return to an unmarked target location engage in systematic search around the expected goal position, However, if landmarks are visible, by using visual strategies, they can directly move towards and precisely find the goal.

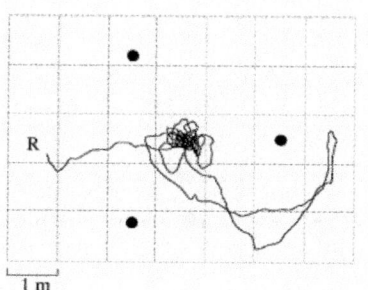

Fig. 2. Landmark navigation experiment with *Cataglyphis*. Ants were trained to locate the center of an array of three landmarks (black cylinders, depicted as circles). The figure shows the trajectory of a single ant that was displaced to a test area with an identical landmark configuration. **R** marks the release point (adapted from [31])

The typical experimental procedure to analyze the visual homing strategies which was used for ants [32,31] and bees [4] is depicted in Figure 2. In a training area, landmarks are positioned close to a target location, e. g., the nest entrance (which is, in essence, a whole in the ground). When the animals have learned to locate this goal, they are displaced to a test area with a somewhat different landmark configuration, where their search path is recorded. The search peak, i. e. the place where the animals search most densely is assumed to be the position where they expect to find the target.

By varying the landmark configuration (e. g. removing a landmark, moving the landmarks further apart, making them bigger) in the test area with respect to the training configuration and observing the changes of the search peak position, properties of the insects' navigation strategies can be inferred. From experiments of this sort Cartright and Collett [ ] derived the idea of the so-called "snapshot model": As the insect leaves the nest it takes a two-dimensional "snapshot" of the visual scene which is stored in a relatively unprocessed manner in its visual memory. When returning from the excursion to the vicinity of the position at which the snapshot was taken, the insect moves in a direction in which the discrepancy between the snapshot and the current sensory stimulation is reduced, until the two views match [ ]. Which aspects of the snapshot (the stored view) and the current sensory stimulation (the current view) are actually compared was derived from experiments with bees, where size and position of the landmarks were varied systematically. The results suggested that no more than the apparent size and the bearing of the landmark, i. e. the angle between the agent's heading direction (its body axis) and the landmark, are considered [ ]. The situation is slightly more complicated but for the present purposes, these comments should suffice. Let us look at how the snapshot model works.

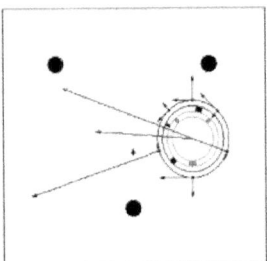 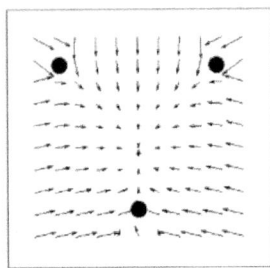 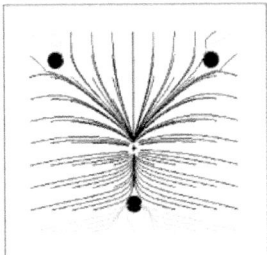

Fig. 3. Simulation of the snapshot model (version with proportional vector contributions) for a configuration of three landmarks (black circles). *Left:* A snapshot (inner ring) taken at the nest position marked with a cross is matched with a current view (middle ring). *Center:* A home vector can be assigned to each point of the plane. *Right:* Trajectories running tangentially to the home vectors. Black trajectories end at the snapshot position, grey trajectories run into one of the landmarks

2.1   The Snapshot Model

The way the snapshot model which was originally proposed by [ ] works, is illustrated in Figure 3. It assumes that views (stored and current) consist of dark and bright sectors corresponding to the landmarks themselves and to the gaps between them. These views are assumed to be aligned with a compass direction. The matching sectors in the two views are found by searching for the closest sector of the same type (dark or bright) in the current view for each sector in the snapshot. Each pair of sectors contributes two vectors to the final movement vector: tangential and radial. A movement in the direction of the tangential vector reduces the angle between the matching sectors; a movement in the direction of the radial vector reduces the difference in their apparent size. Averaging all contributions gives a movement vector pointing approximately to the position of the target (Figure 3, center); a trajectory following these home vectors will approach the location where the snapshot was taken (Figure 3, right), i.e. the target location. Despite this rather simple procedure, homing is highly reliable even for more complex configurations with many landmarks; the algorithm tolerates the occlusion of landmarks and the fusion of landmark sectors.

The snapshot model comes in various alternatives. One is the proportional vector model [14] in which the unit vectors of the original snapshot model have been replaced by vectors that take the disparity between the two patterns (i.e. their difference on the retina) and the distance to the landmark into account. This has several advantages over the original model the details of which do not matter for the current discussion (for details, see [19]). It is this model that we actually use for implementation on the robot. The view-based approach to landmark navigation [8] is very similar and will not be further elaborated.

Fig. 4. The mobile robot *Sahabot 2*

Robot Implementation

Robot hardware. A picture of the robot used for the experiments is shown in Figure 4. The front of the robot is towards the right of the picture. The sensor array in the back contains the polarization elements, the arrays on the side consist of ambient light sensors. The polarized light sensors are only used to get the compass direction (see below). For the visual processing of the experiments

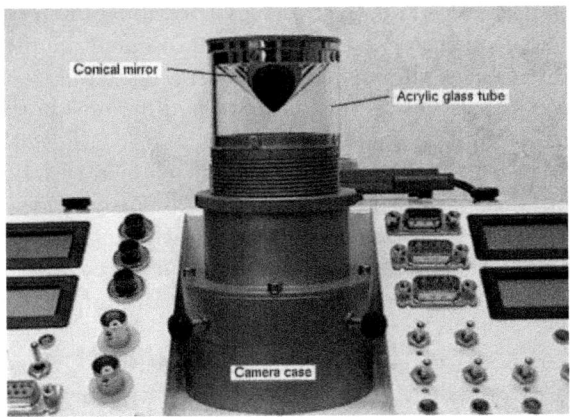

Fig. 5. Detailed view of the 360° camera system of the *Sahabot 2*, consisting of a camera with vertical optical axis (within the case) and a conical mirror that is aligned with the axis of the camera and mounted within an acrylic glass tube

described in this paper, the omnidirectional camera on the front of the robot is employed. It consists of a CCD camera and a conically shaped mirror in the vertical optical axis of the camera (Figure 5). The opening angle of the cone was determined so that the visual field extends 10 degrees around the horizon. Various filters had to be applied to insure proper recording.

Image processing. The image processing preformed on both snapshot and current view was in fact very simple (Figure 6). The camera image (obtained from a situation similar to the one shown in Figure 7) is transformed via a polar mapping into an azimuth-altitude representation which leads to a horizontal "stripe" image. A mean grey value is determined from the transformed image and used to adjust the brightness parameter of the camera in such a way that the mean grey value of the image is kept constant. This is indispensable for the subsequent thresholding operation separating dark and bright regions. The final one-dimensional horizontal view is obtained by counting the number of black pixels within a part of each pixel column (bounded by the two lines shown in the thresholded image).

External compass reference. An important prerequisite of the matching procedure between snapshot and current view is the alignment of both views with respect to an external compass reference. Without proper alignment, the number of mismatches between sectors will increase significantly, resulting in an erroneous home vector. Cataglyphis ants, as other insects, acquire the compass direction from celestial cues, mainly from the polarization pattern of the blue sky (e.g. [30]). On the Sahabot 2 this information is acquired from the polarization sensor array shown in Figure 4 (for details, see e.g. [12]).

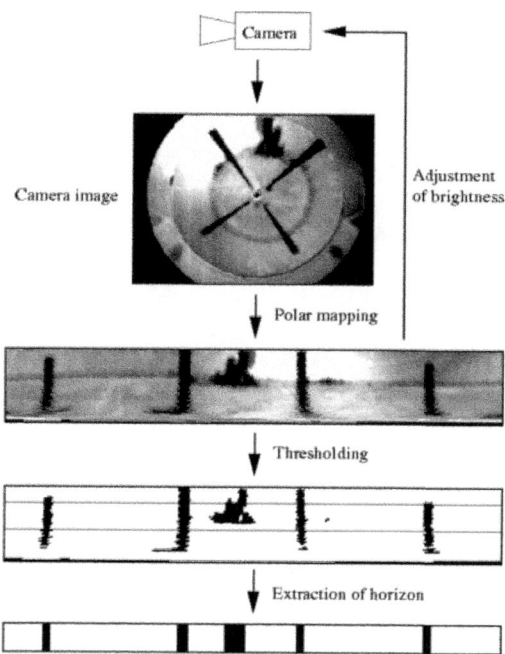

Fig. 6. Image processing for visual homing with the snapshot model. The image from the 360° camera (160 × 120 pixels) is transformed into a polar view (351 × 56). After applying a threshold to each pixel, the segmented horizon (351 × 1) is extracted from the area within the two lines; a pixel in the horizon will be black, if more than 50% of the pixel in the corresponding column are black. The landmark extracted in the center belongs to equipment in the vicinity which was removed for the experiments

Experimental Results. The experiments with Sahabot 2 were performed in one of the habitats of Cataglyphis in the Tunisian part of the Sahara desert in a flat, sandy salt-pan near the town of Maharès. A grid was painted on the desert ground to simplify the alignment of landmarks and robot as well as the registration of the final points of a "trip". Figure 7 shows a typical setup. Black cylinders were used as landmarks; the same type of landmarks were also used for the ant experiments.

At the beginning of each experiment the robot was placed at the starting position within the landmark array. For the experimental runs shown in Figure 8 the landmark array consisted of 3 black cylinders with a height of 80 cm and a diameter of 30 cm, forming an equilateral triangle with 3 m side length. The starting position of the robot is shown as the $(0,0)$ point in the coordinate

Fig. 7. Example of a landmark array used for the experiments with the *Sahabot 2*

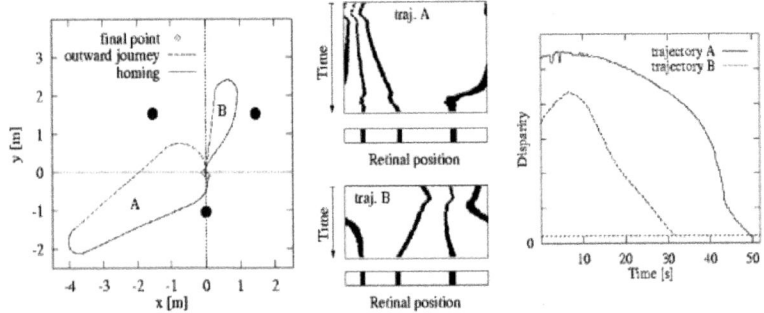

Fig. 8. Visual homing experiment with the robot *Sahabot 2*. *Left:* Two typical trajectories of the robot in an array of three landmarks (black circles). From the end of the preprogrammed outward journey (dashed line) towards the target position $(0,0)$ the robot is guided by the visual landmark navigation algorithm (solid line). *Center:* Transitions of the rotated current view over time towards the snapshots (images underneath each trace) for the two trajectories. *Right:* Time course of disparity between snapshot and current view for the two trajectories. The dashed line depicts the threshold used for terminating the runs

system. Note that the coordinate system is used only to observe the behavior of the robot; the robot itself has absolutely no knowledge of these coordinates.

Data from two of the experiments are visualized in Figure 8. At the beginning, a snapshot was taken at the starting position, processed as described above, rotated by the angle obtained from the polarized light compass, and stored in the form of black and white sectors (Figure 8, center, "retinal position"). After taking the snapshot, the robot had to follow a predefined trajectory indicated by the broken lines in Figure 8 (left) — two examples, A and B are shown. At the end of this outward trip control was handed over to the snapshot algorithm. The development of the rotated current views over time are shown in the center of Figure 8. As soon as the disparity between current view and snapshot view became lower than a threshold, the experiment was stopped (Figure 8, right). A large series of experiments was performed to test the precision and the robustness of the snapshot algorithm in order to assess its plausibility as a potential mechanism employed by the insects, generally with very good results.

2.2   The Average Landmark Vector Model

Even though the snapshot model is very simple, there is — suprisingly — an even more parsimonious method, the "average landmark vector (ALV) model" which can be derived mathematically from the snapshot model [13,14]. In this model, views are characterized by two-component "average landmark vectors", computed as the average (or sum) of unit vectors pointing towards the selected image features (such as edges). Instead of a snapshot image, only the average landmark vector of the target location has to be stored. An image matching procedure as in the snapshot model is not required; in the ALV model, this step is simplified to a subtraction of the average landmark vectors of the current and the target location. Like the snapshot model, the ALV model presumes that the vectors are aligned to the same compass direction. Note the simplicity of the ALV model: only a vector has to be rotated, not an image as in the snapshot model. In terms of information storage, there is also a considerable reduction.

Robot Implementation. Implementation of the ALV model on the Sahabot is straightforward since only the algorithm has to be changed. However, what we would like to demonstrate here, is that the ALV model can also be implemented in analog hardware in a straightforward manner. We only give a rough overview here; the details are provided in [17,18]. Most of the active components are operational amplifiers that are used in standard circuits (as amplifier, comparator, adder, etc.). The sensors, the boards implementing the ALV model, and the motor control boards which are also fully analog, are mounted on a small robot base (Figure 9).

Visual input is provided by a ring of 32 photodiodes (sensor ring in Figure 9) mimicking the ommatidia facing the horizon. The angle between two neighboring diodes is 11.24 degrees. An aperture in front of each diode restricts the opening angle to 8 degrees. The signals of the photo diodes are amplified. Edges of one polarity (clockwise black-to-white) are used as landmark features, detected by thresholding the difference of the signals of two neighboring sensors. Unidirectional lateral inhibition between neighboring edge filters ensures that only one pixel per edge becomes active, a prerequisite of the ALV model. For opening angles smaller than the inter-sensor angles (11.25 degrees) and for sharp visual edges as they are used in the experimental setup, lateral inhibition can be restricted to immediate neighbors.

Fig. 9. The analog robot (height 22 cm, diameter 12.8 cm). The black ring in the center contains 32 photo diodes, the boards above implement the ALV model, the boards below belong to the motor control circuitry. A magnetic compass is mounted on the top of the robot

Fig. 10. Arena used for the experiments with the analog robot

From the outputs of the edge-filters, which deliver binary signals (high constant voltage for an active edge, or 0 V), the robot-centered AL vector is computed. A radial landmark vector is assigned to each edge pixel, and all landmark vectors are added simultaneously. This can be achieved in a simple way by encoding the two components of each landmark vector in two resistors that are connected to the input of two adder circuits.

The home vector is simply the difference of the average landmark vector of the current location and the average landmark vector of the target location. Before the target average landmark vector is stored in two capacitors, it is rotated to world coordinates using a circuit with four analog multipliers. Because the analog robot was conceived for indoor experiments, a magnetic compass is used as an external reference source (polarization cannot be used since there is no polarization pattern indoors that could be used as a global reference). As the robot is returning, the stored vector is rotated back to robot coordinates according to the current orientation of the robot, and subtracted from the current average landmark vector, which yields the home vector in robot coordinates.

The robot uses differential steering. Each of the motors can be controlled by one component of the home vector. The component of the axis on the left side determines the speed of the right motor and vice versa. This arrangement will stabilize a home vector in the frontal direction; if the home vector is pointing to the rear, the robot will automatically turn around, since the opposite direction is unstable. The length of the home vector corresponds to the distance from the goal. Since the home vector components determine the speed of the motors, the robot automatically slows down when it approaches the target location which helps avoid oscillations around the target location.

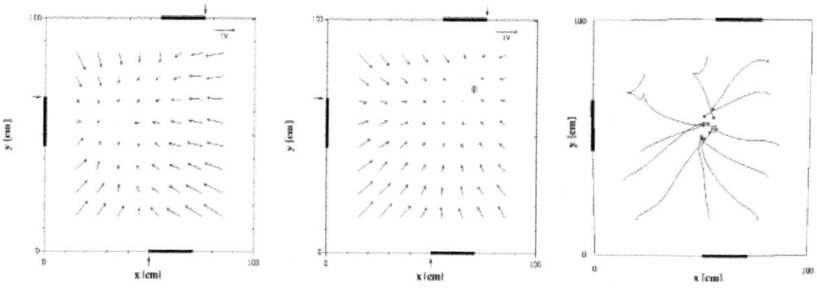

Fig. 11. Visual homing experiment with the analog robot. Three landmarks (depicted by bars) where attached to the walls of the arena. The detectable edges are marked by an arrow. *Left:* Average landmark vector measured for 64 positions on a grid. The vector scaling is shown in the upper right corner (1 Volt). *Center:* Home vector field for the target location marked with the cross-circle. *Right:* Robot trajectories. The cross-circle marks the target location where the AL vector was stored. The final positions of the robot are depicted by dots

2.2.1   Experimental Results. The experiments with the analog robot were conducted in a 1 m by 1 m arena (Figure 10). As landmarks black pieces of paper on the walls were used. Figure 11 (left) shows the average landmark vector voltages measured while the robot was placed at 64 different locations on a grid. The center panel depicts the home vectors from the same positions and the right panel shows some trajectories. The position where the target vector was registered is marked by a circle with a cross. The imprecisions in target location are due to the limited resolution of the system (angles and apertures). The robot is in fact capable of reproducing most of the results obtained from animal experiments.

2.3   Application to Indoor Navigation

A frequent criticism that we hear about the previous models (the biologists and the roboticists get them alike) is that the black cylinders in an otherwise flat environment are too obvious to be realistic. Although there are good reasons to start an investigation with such landmark, the criticism is to a good extent justified. To test if the model would generalize to more realistic situations, Thorsten Roggendorf, a biologist of the University of Bielefeld in Germany, has applied the ALV model to navigation in office environments [27]. Because in this case it was not obvious what the landmarks and the appropriate features would be, some effort hat to be spent on extracting the features. To our surprise, the model worked reasonably well, and within the vicinity of the target position, very well. Figure 12 shows the entrance hall of the department where the model has been tested.

Fig. 12. Indoor environment for experiments with ALV model (entrance hall of our department)

3   Visual Odometry: Measuring Distance with Optical Flow

The text is this section is largely based on [11] from which the details can be gathered. While in the snapshot model and in the ALV model it is not necessary to measure distance — distance to the target is automatically reduced and it stops as the target is reached. For other kinds of models, especially for long-distance navigation, as in the path integration models, distance traveled is required. Under ideal conditions standard odometry using wheel encoders can be employed. However, if conditions are not ideal, for example, if the ground is slippery or sandy, then odometry has to be augmented by some other means (landmarks, other sensors). Also, for flying agents, i.e. insects or flying robots, standard methods cannot be used. The case study to be presented demonstrates how visual odometry can be used for flying robots, again, inspired by biological systems. As we will see, this provides another illustrative example of cheap vision.

Flying insects, for example, have to solve problems of flight control and navigation with their tiny brains (a million times smaller than our own brains). Recent experiments with bees provide evidence that flying insects might be using optical flow induced by egomotion to estimate distance traveled (e.g. [29]. Here is very roughly how the experiments were done.

It is known that bees "report" the location (direction and distance) by a kind of dance to their conspecifics; this is exploited in the experiments. Bees are trained to fly to a particular location through tunnels under various conditions: wide tunnels, narrow tunnels, different types of patterns on the walls of the tunnels. Then their dance is observed from which it can be inferred how far the bees "think" they have traveled. Without going into further detail, it turns out that if bees are flying through narrow tunnels with vertically striped patterns, they report having flown much further than if they have been flying through a wide tunnel with the same pattern. From this, it can be concluded, that they are using something related to optical flow to measure distance traveled.

3.1   The Model

In the model optical flow is measured by so-called Elementary Motion Detectors (EMDs) which represent a particular instantiation of the well-known Reichhardt detectors [26] (for related work, see, for example, [2,20,21,28]). They are depicted in Figure 13 (top-left). They consist of two photoreceptors, high-pass filters, low-pass filters, multipliers, and summation functions. An important feature of this model is that it senses not only image motion but also direction: EMD responses are positive when the image moves in the preferred direction, and negative if it moves in the non-preferred direction (Figure 13, top-right). Since EMD responses indicate self-motion, distance traveled can be measured by accumulating EMD outputs. A wide-field motion detector based on EMDs is shown in Figure 13 (bottom).

3.2   Hardware Implementation, Test Setup, and Flying Robot

For the experiments Iida and Lambrinos developed a panoramic vision system which is shown in Figure 14 (left). It consists of a panoramic mirror, a CCD camera module, and casing components with a total weight of 90 g, light enough so that it can be used on a flying robot. The mirror is based on the panoramic

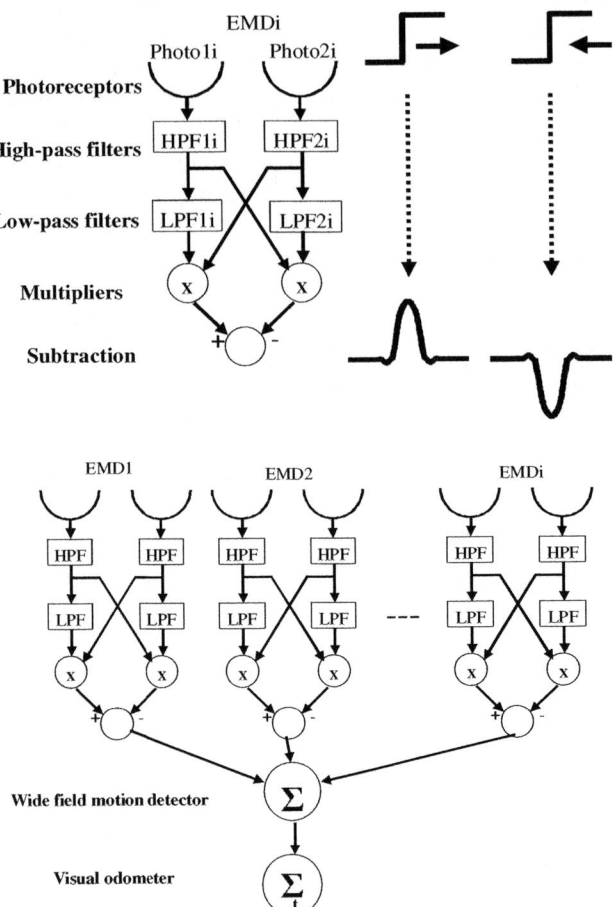

Fig. 13. *Top:* the Reichardt model of elementary motion detection. *Bottom:* the visual odometer based on a wide field motion detector

mirror studies by Chahl and Srinivasan [5] and has a hyperbolic surface that covers an image angle of 360 degrees in the horizontal plane and 260 degrees vertically. (In the Sahabot experiments a conal mirror was used. Because of the obvious advantages in terms of image resolution, the recent versions of the Sahabot also have a hyperbolic mirror.)

First, a set of experiments was conducted under controlled conditions, i.e. where the position of the camera with respect to the patterns in the environment are precisely known (Figure 14, center and right). Typical response patterns are shown in Figure 15. The flying robot is shown in Figure 16, the control architecture in Figure 17.

Fig. 14. Vision system and initial experiment setup. *Left:* The panoramic vision system. *Middle and Right:* This vision system is equipped with the caster-frame on a pair of rails, and an external motor drives the vision system along a straight route at a constant speed Initially walls with black and white stripes were installed along the rails (20 cm width of black and white, 60 cm from vision system)

While the setup of Figure 14 has been deliberately controlled, experiments have been conducted with the flying robot in the entrance hall of our department (Figure 12) which is about 30 m by 30 m and three stories high. Although not entirely "natural" it has not been modified for these experiments. Without going into detail we were surprised at the precision and reliability of the flight control and visual odometry system, given its extreme simplicity (for more detail, cf. [11]).

4   Evolving the Morphology of an Insect Eye: Compensating for Motion Parallax

This paragraph is mostly based on [15]. As the previous example, this one works on the basis of motion detectors. It illustrates another aspect of cheap vision. It demonstrates (a) how the complexity of computation (or neural processing in natural systems) can be strongly reduced by having the right morphology, and (b) the adaptive potential contained in the morphology with respect to visual processing. More generally, it demonstrates that there often is a kind of "balance" between what kind of processing is taken care of by the morphology and what is done neurally. This will become clear, below.

The basic phenomenon of motion parallax is very simple and familiar to everyone. Briefly, when sitting in a train, a light spot, say from a tree or a house, travels very slowly across the visual field if it is towards the front and far away. The closer it gets and the more the spot moves to the side, the faster it moves across the visual field (given the same lateral distance). This phenomenon has been studied in the context of insects. For example, Franceschini et al. ([7]) showed that in the eye of the fly there is a non-uniform layout of the visual axes such that sampling of the visual space is finer towards the front than laterally. If the fly is moving at constant speed the time for a light spot to move from one facet to the next remains essentially the same which implies that at the

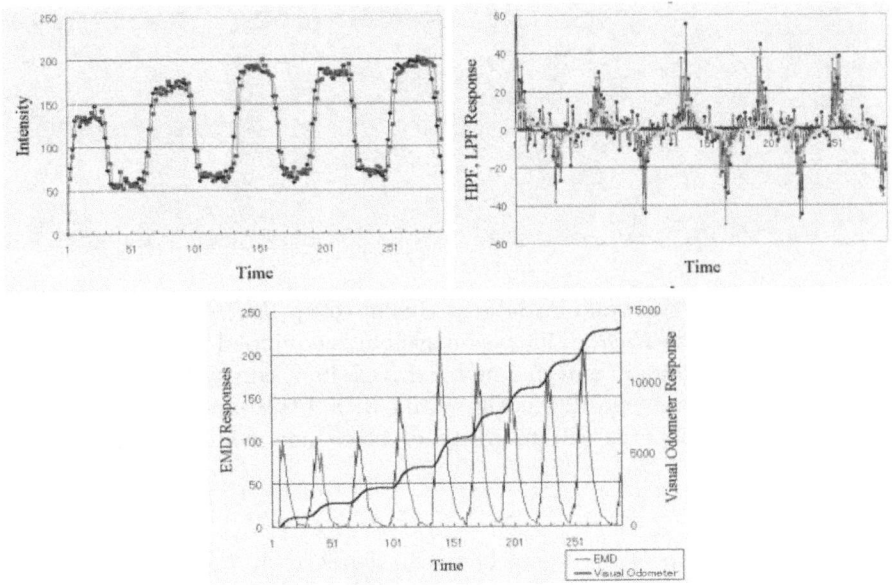

Fig. 15. Typical responses of the EMD and the visual odometer. *Top left:* Photoreceptor activity is calculated directly from the image captured by the CCD camera. Oscillations correspond to the stripe pattern of the walls when the vision system moves horizontally along the corridor. *Top right:* The outputs of high-pass and low-pass filters. The peaks correspond to the edges in the image. *Bottom:* Responses of the wide field motion detectors and the accumulated visual odometer response

neural level a uniform array of elementary motion detectors can be used for the entire eye, i.e. neural processing for motion detection becomes very simple. (It should be mentioned that this is but one example and that insect compound eyes show a big morphological diversity and parameters like the density distribution of individual facets (ommatidia) differ strongly between species and sometimes even between the sexes.). In these experiments, a very simple neural network with delays has been used for motion detection.

Figure 18 (left) shows the robot used for the experiments. The robot consists of a chassis, an on-board controller, and sixteen independently controllable facet units that are all mounted on a common vertical axis. Each facet unit consists of a motor, a potentiometer, two cog-wheels and a thin tube containing a photo diode at the inner end. The angles of the facets of the robot can be adjusted individually under program control. In the experiment the facets are adjusted by means of an evolution strategy [25], a specific kind of evolutionary algorithm. The environment consists of vertical light tubes (a top view is shown in Figure 18, right). The task of the robot is to maintain a critical lateral distance (not too

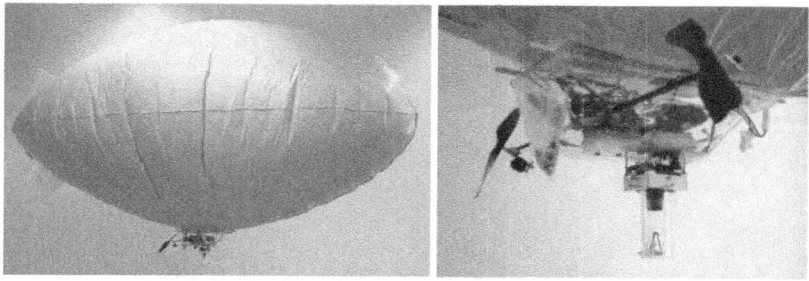

Fig. 16. The autonomous flying robot, Melissa. *Left:* Helium balloon with gondola. The balloon is 2.3m long and has a lift capacity of approx. 400 g. *Right:* Gondola containing 3 motors, a four-channel radio transmitter, a miniature panoramic vision system and image transmitter, and the battery

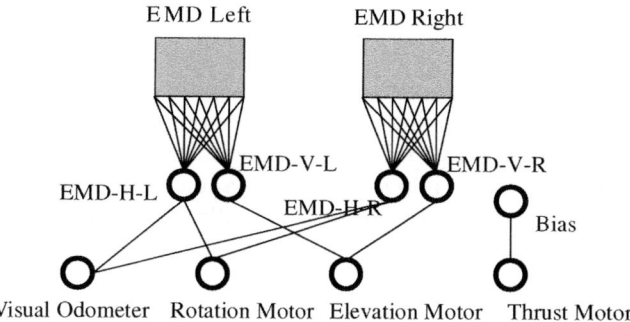

Fig. 17. Sensory-motor control circuit. Outputs of left and right EMD networks provide the vertical (EMD-V-L, EMD-V-R) and horizontal (EMD-H-L, EMD-H-R) image motion values of each side. The horizontally and vertically tuned EMDs are connected to a motor neuron that controls the robot's rotation or elevation, respectively. The outputs of the horizontally tuned EMDs are also used by visual odometer. The thrust motor neuron has a connection to a bias neuron that implements the default move-forward behavior

far away, not too close) to the obstacle which is given by the vertical light tubes. Its fitness is increased if it manages to maintain the critical distance, if not, the angles of the facets are modified by the evolutionary algorithm. The robot experiment takes about 5 to 6 hours until a stable distribution of the facets is achieved. Figure 19 shows the results of some runs with different initial conditions. The head of the robot is towards the right. The result is what one would theoretically expect: a non-uniform distribution which is more densely spaced towards the front. In other words, evolution has found a solution that

Fig. 18. Evolution of "insect eye". *Left: Eyebot:* adjustable facets under control of evolutionary algorithm. *Right:* Experimental setup seen from top

enables the agent to perform its task employing the neural substrate with which it was endowed by the designer. The facets only start at a certain angle; there are none pointing directly forward. This is because the resolution is too low and no information could be acquired within this angle range, which is why evolution could not make use of it. If the obstacle were directly in front of the agent, there would be no motion at all.

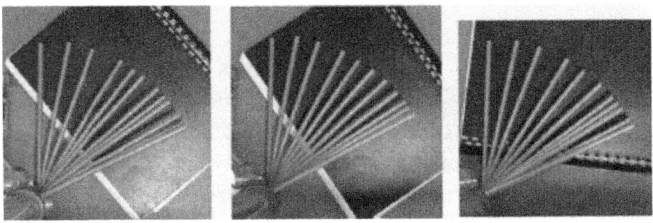

Fig. 19. Result of a typical experiment with the *eyebot*: the facets are more dense towards the front of the robot (which is towards the right)

This is an example of how sensory morphology was not predesigned but emergent from an evolutionary process in which task environment and neural substrate was given. In this case evolution has exploited the potential for adaptation in the morphology of the sensory system. In a very similar set-up [16] has used the adaptation of eye morphology to estimate time-to-contact.

5   Discussion: Cheap Vision

There are a number of points that we would like to raise in this discussion. Before we start, we should perhaps mention that we do not discuss the technicalities of the results of the various case studies. The points to be made here are more of a principled nature to illustrate the idea and the basic ways of thinking behind cheap vision.

A first point is that vision should never be looked at in isolation, but rather in the context of a complete agent that has to perform one or several tasks in the real world. A second, perhaps more obvious one is that the vision system serves multiple purposes. If these points are taken into account, the problems are often dramatically simplified. The perspective taken here requires new ways of thinking.

5.1   Simple Image Processing

The first observation is that the models presented are extremely simple in terms of algorithms: The snapshot model only stores a snapshot (which is essentially a band of black and white stripes, cf. Figure 6) and calculates a movement vector by applying a simple procedure of comparing current view and stored view. The ALV model is even simpler: All that needs to be stored here is one vector! In terms of storage and processing requirements, truly surprising. In the visual odometry model, only a small number of pixels from the visual system are sufficient to perform a simple navigation task, including homing in on a target position and measuring distance traveled [11]. This is very different from traditional optical flow-based methods which are known to be computationally intensive (e. g. [1]. Finally, keeping a constant lateral distance becomes next to trivial if the morphology is right: All that is required is some simple motion detection circuitry — which is the same for the entire eye, to boot — and the proper arrangement of the facets. No distance measurements are required which are often fairly difficult to perform accurately. And, of course, Ian Horswill's robot Polly fits into this picture as well.

This simplicity sharply contrasts with standard vision algorithms. Why then, is this simplicity of algorithms possible? One important reason is that the vision system is not viewed in isolation, but as part of a complete agent.

5.2   Vision as an Aspect of a Complete Agent

This idea suggests that vision never be looked at in isolation but in the context of an entire agent that has to perform a task or a set of tasks. This is in instance of what has been called the "complete agent principle" (e. g. [22,23]). Note, for example, that we have not talked about "object recognition" which is sometimes seen as the most basic purpose of a vision system, and there is certainly a lot of literature about it. For the tasks the agents had to perform this has turned out not to be necessary. It has not even been necessary for landmark navigation, even though the way landmark navigation in the field of autonomous robots is most often performed is via a sense – think – act cycle: recognize the landmark, perform the self-localization (which may require some inferencing), decide what to do next (which may require some planning) and execute the plan or perform the action. Thus, in the standard approach there is a recognition process and a subsequent decision process. In both, the snapshot model and the ALV model, there is no such separation: As the ant (or the robot) is near the landmark it tries to improve the quality of the match by following the vectors calculated from the snapshot (or the ALV) model. As soon as the match has been achieved the ant (or the robot) is at the target location. Thus recognition and action are one and the same thing in this case. The amount of processing required is absolutely minimal compared to the case where a robot (we don't know about ants) has to recognize a landmark. The robots presented do not function according to the sense – think – act principle.

5.3 Sensory-Motor Coupling

One of the consequences of abandoning the sense – think – act cycle is that there is a focus on sensory – motor coupling. As just mentioned, the landmark recognition process is one and the same as moving to the right target position: the sensory and the motor systems are intimately intertwined: they are inseparable. A nice feature of the proportional vector model is that as the robot approaches the target position, it automatically slows down, thus avoiding overshooting. In all the examples presented, the movement of the robot itself is generating just the right sensory inputs the robot needs to perform its task. It is this *generation* of sensory input that is essential, which is why we talk about sensory-motor coupling.

5.4 Cheap Design: Exploitation of Constraints in the System-Environment Interaction

The models presented in this paper instantiate the "principle of cheap design" [22,23] which states that the constraints of the ecological niche and the system-environment interaction can be exploited to make designs more parsimonious. One important constraint that the ants rely on is that as the dead-reckoning system has performed its job, the ant is near the nest. If this assumption does not hold, i.e. if there is no landmark configuration, the ants switch to a fixed search pattern. So, if the assumption (the constraint) does not hold landmark navigation can no longer be applied. Similarly, if the objects in Polly's environment do not stand on the ground, it will fail.

A very clear case of exploitation of the system – environment interaction is the eyebot where the geometry of motion parallax is compensated for by the morphology, i.e. by having the ommatidia more densely spaced towards the front. This example also illustrates that what we normally think would have to be done computationally, the compensation for motion parallax, can be done by appropriate morphology. This is quick and free of charge, and for the task of, for example, estimating time to contact, the only feature required.

5.5   Redundancy of a Complete Agent

Now one might argue that often the constraints do not hold: for example the ant (or the robot) is not near the landmark and so it cannot apply the snapshot model, so visual processing gets much more complicated and a process of landmark recognition may indeed have to be incorporated. While this would represent one possible solution, it may in fact not be the most parsimonious one. If we consider the complete agent, it will always have redundant systems on board that might compensate for the some of the deficiencies. For example, the dead-reckoning system in desert ants provides precisely these constraints. Thus, not only different sensory systems, but other navigation systems altogether take over. In complete agents, vision is not the only possibility. In a sense, the moral of the story is that although vision can be used for many things, it may not provide the best solution for everything. Another example is as that it gets darker vision processing becomes harder and it may be better for other systems to take over (e. g. systems with active sensors, acoustic-based systems or haptic-based systems. These considerations go of course beyond vision proper, but if we want to have the right perspective on vision, we must take the complete agent — which includes other subsystems — into account. This may also greatly simplify the solutions for specific tasks. Again, this is an instance of a design principle (the "redundancy principle") which states that agents should be designed so that the various subsystems provide partially overlapping functionalities.

5.6   Vision: A Multi-purpose System

To illustrate the second point, the fact that the vision system is not only used for object recognition but can be used for many different tasks is well-known and requires little explanation. In the examples given it is used for landmark navigation, measuring distance traveled, speed control, and maintaining constant lateral distance to an obstacle. It should also be noted that in the snapshot and the ALV model obstacle avoidance comes for free: if visual homing is applied, the agent will automatically avoid obstacles (there are some cases where the agent bumps into an obstacle, but in most cases obstacle avoidance works fine). In all examples, extremely little neural processing is required if the constraints are exploited appropriately.

From this discussion it becomes clear that vision cannot be reduced to algorithm only, but it is an aspect of a complete agent.

6   Conclusion

In a series of case studies we have shown that vision problems can often be solved in cheap and efficient ways if we go beyond the algorithm proper and consider the complete agent, its environment, and the tasks it has to perform. Natural systems provide a lot of highly valuable inspiration for cheap vision. It is clear that the systems presented all have their limitations — but then computationally expensive systems do as well. But we need to elaborate the conditions under which the mechanisms function and put some of the work on more sound formal foundations. While formalization at the level of algorithms is typically straightforward to do, it is much harder if the physical reality, morphology, and the like are involved.

There is a lot of related work, especially in the field of biorobotics, where researchers are either generally inspired by biological systems or where they try to model biological systems precisely (e. g. [6]). However, the principles as expressed in the previous section are often not elaborated.

The views expressed in this paper advocate a new look at old problems. The approach of "cheap vision" is entirely compatible with the vast body of research in the neurobiology of vision of many species. But we hope that researchers not only in robotics, artificial intelligence, and computer science, but also in the neurosciences find these perspectives attractive.

Acknowledgments

This work has been partly supported a grant number 20-53915.98 of the Swiss National Science Foundation and the European VIRGO TMR Network. We also thank Václav Hlaváč for his kind invitation and for suggesting the topic for the SOFSEM conference.

References

1. Amidi, O., Kanade, T., Fujita, K. (1998). A visual odometer for autonomous helicopter flight, Intelligent Autonomous Systems, Eds. Y. Kakazu et al. IOS Press, 123–130. 221
2. Borst, A., Egelhaaf, M. (1993). Detecting visual motion: Theory and models, Visual Motion and its Role in the Stabilization of Gaze. F. A. Miles and J. Wallman (eds.), Elsevier Science, 3–27. 215
3. Brooks, R. A. (1991). Intelligence without reason. Proceedings of the International Joint Conference on Artificial Intelligence-91, 569–595. 203
4. Cartright, B. A., and Collett, R. S. (1983). Landmark navigation in bees. Journal of Comparative Physiology, 151, 521–543. 205, 206
5. Chahl, J. S., Srinivasan, M. V. (1997). Reflective surfaces for panoramic imaging. Applied Optics, 36 (31), 8275–8285. 216
6. Chang, C., and Gaudiano, P. (2000) (Eds.). Robotics and Autonomous Systems, special issue: Biomimetic Robotics, 30(1–2), 1–2. 224
7. Franceschini, N., Pichon, J. M., and Blanes, C. (1992). From insect vision to robot vision. Philosophical Transactions of the Royal Society, London B, 337, 283–294. 217
8. Franz, M. O., Schölkopf, B., and Mallot, H. A. (1998). Where did I take that snapshot? Scene-based homing by image matching. Biological Cybernetics, 79, 191–202. 207
9. Horswill, I. (1992). Characterizing adaptation by constraint. In F. J. Varela and P. Bourgine (Eds.), Toward a practice of autonomous systems: Proceedings of the First European Conference on Artificial Life, 58–64. Cambridge, MA: MIT Press. 203

10. Horswill, I. (1993). A simple, cheap, and robust visual navigation system. In J.-A. Meyer, H. L. Roitblat, and S. W. Wilson (Eds.), From animals to animats: Proceedings of the Second International Conference on Simulation of Adaptive Behavior. Cambridge, MA: MIT Press (A Bradford Book). 203

11. Iida, F., and Lambrinos, D. (in press). Navigation in an autonomous flying robot by using a biologically inspired visual odometer. In McKee G. T. and Schenker P. S. (Eds.) Proc. of SPIE Vol 4196, Conf. on Sensor Fusion and Decentralized Control in Robotic Systems III, Boston, MA. 214, 217, 221

12. Lambrinos, D., Maris, M., Kobayashi, H., Labhart, T., Pfeifer R., and Wehner, R. (1997). An autonomous agent navigating with a polarized light compass. Adaptive Behavior, 6, 175 – 206. 208

13. Lambrinos, D., Möller, R., Pfeifer, R., and Wehner, R. (1998). Landmark navigation without snapshots: the average landmark vector model. In N. Elsner, and R. Wehner (Eds.). Proc. Neurobiol. Conf. Göttingen, 30a. Stuttgart: Georg Thieme Verlag. 211

14. Lambrinos, D., Möller, R., Labhart, T., Pfeifer, R., and Wehner, R. (2000). A mobile robot employing insect strategies for navigation. Robotics and Autonomous Systems, special issue: Biomimetic Robotics, 30(1 – 2), 39 – 64. 207, 211

15. Lichtensteiger, L., and Eggenberger, P. (1999). Evolving the morphology of a compound eye on a robot. In: Proc. of the Third European Workshop on Advanced Mobile Robots (Eurobot '99), 127 – 134. 217

16. Lichtensteiger, L. (2000). Towards optimal sensor morphology for specific tasks: evolution of an artificial compund eye for estimating time to contact. . In McKee G. T. and Schenker P. S. (Eds.) Proc. of SPIE Vol 4196, Conf. on Sensor Fusion and Decentralized Control in Robotic Systems III, Boston, MA. 220

17. Möller, R. (1999). Visual homing in analog hardware. In Proc. 2nd European Workshop of Neurmorphic Systems. 211

18. Möller, R. (2000). Insect visual homing strategies in a robot with analog processing. Biological Cybernetics, special issue: Navigation in Biological and Artificial Systems (to appear). 211

19. Möller, R., Lambrinos, D., Roggendorf, T., Pfeifer, R., and Wehner, R. (in press). Insect strategies of visual homing in mobile robots. To appear in: T. Consi, and B. Webb (Eds.). Biorobotics, AAAI Press. 205, 207

20. Mura, F., and Franceschini, N. (1994). Visual control of altitude and speed in a flying agent. Proc. of the 3rd International Conference on the Simulation of Adaptive Behavior: From Animals to Animats, 91 – 99. 215

21. Netter, T., and Franceschini, N. (1999). Towards nap-of-the-earth flight using optical flow. Proc. ECAL'99, 334 – 338. 215

22. Pfeifer, R. (1996). Building "Fungus Eaters": Design principles of autonomous agents. In P. Maes, M. Mataric, J.-A. Meyer, J. Pollack, and S. W. Wilson (Eds.), From animals to animats: Proceedings of the Fourth International Conference on Simulation of Adaptive Behavior, 3 – 12. Cambridge, Ma: MIT Press (A Bradford Book). 221, 222

23. Pfeifer, R., and Scheier, C. (1999). Understanding intelligence. Cambridge, Ma.: MIT Press. 203, 221, 222

24. Prescott, T. J. (1995). Spatial representation for navigation in animats. Adaptive Behaviour, 4(2):85 – 123. 202

25. Rechenberg, I. (1973). Evolutionsstrategie: Optimierung Technischer Systeme nach Prinzipien der Biologischen Evolution [Evolutionary strategies: optimization of

technical systems with principles from biological evolution]. Stuttgart, Germany: Frommann-Holzboog. 218

26. Reichhardt, W. (1969). Movement perception in insects. In W. Reichhardt (Ed.) Processing of optical data by organisms and machines, 465–493. New York: Academic Press. 215

27. Roggendorf, T. (2000). Visual landmark navigation in a natural complex environment (in German). Visuelle Landmarkennavigation in einer natürlichen, komplexen Umgebung. Diploma thesis, Dept. of Theoretical Biology and Biological Cybernetics, Faculty of Biology, University of Bielefeld. 214

28. Srinivasan, M. V., Zhang, S. W., and Bidwell, N. (1997). Visually mediated odometry in honeybees. Journal of Experimental Biology, 200, 2513–2522. 215

29. Srinivasan, M. V., Zhang, S., Altwein, M., and Tautz, J. (2000). Honeybee navigation: nature and calibration of the "odometer". Science, 287, 851–853. 215

30. Wehner, R. (1994). The polarization-vision project: championing organismic biology. In K. Schildberger, and N. Elsner (Eds.). Neural Basis of Adaptive Behaviour. Stuttgart: G. Fischer, 103–143. 208

31. Wehner, R., Michel, B., and Antonsen, P. (1996). Visual navigation in insects: coupling of egocentric and geocentric information. Jounral of Experimental Biology, 199, 129–140. 205, 206

32. Wehner, R., and Räber, R. (1979). Visual spatial memory in desert ants Cataglyphis bicolor (Hymenoptera: Foricidae). Experientia 35, 1569–1571. 205

Hierarchies of Sensing and Control in Visually Guided Agents

Jana Košecká

Department of Computer Science, George Mason University,
Fairfax, VA 22030-4444
kosecka@cs.gmu.edu
http://www.cs.gmu.edu/kosecka

Abstract. The capability of perceiving the environment is crucial for advancing the level of autonomy and sophistication of (semi)autonomous robotic systems and determines the complexity of the tasks robotics agents can achieve. This article reviews some techniques as well as challenges shared by many applications which use visual sensing to guide the action of the robotic agent and require coordination between multiple agents. In order to support hierarchical view of such systems sensing both in the context of low-level control as well as planning and coordination between multiple mobile agents will be considered. Several examples of the design and analysis of these hierarchical hybrid systems will be outlined in the context of Intelligent Highways, namely autonomous driving and coordination between multiple vehicles and mobile robot navigation in indoors man made environments.

1 Introduction

Current new trends in sensing and communication give rise to many applications where computers and computer controlled devices interact with dynamically changing environment. One can encounter complex (semi)autonomous systems in a variety of domains ranging from robot exploration, teleoperation, manufacturing, automated highway systems, air-traffic management systems and coordinated underwater vehicles. The sophistication of the tasks and increase in the autonomy depends to a large extent on the capability of perceiving the environment the agent resides in. The increasing complexity of these systems brings needs for new techniques for their design and analysis as well as utilization of more complex sensors and sensing strategies. Visual sensing is making strides in the domain of embedded systems, partially due the advances in technology and speed of computing. It is now possible to use the vision as a sensor in the control loop of systems operating in unknown and unstructured environments. While the choice of elementary strategies differs across the applications, the presence of multiple sensing and control hierarchies is common to many of these types of systems.

This paper reviews the design and analysis issues of hierarchical hybrid systems and the role of visual sensing in two applications: automated highway

V. Hlaváč, K. G. Jeffery, and J. Wiedermann (Eds.): SOFSEM 2000, LNCS 1963, pp. 227–244, 2000.
© Springer-Verlag Berlin Heidelberg 2000

systems and mobile robot domain. In automated highway applications, the elementary control strategies include automated steering, maintaining safe distance in front of the car ahead, lane change and obstacle detection. These strategies are utilized in the design of inter-vehicle coordination maneuvers so as to assure efficient highway utilization and operation at maximum capacity. In the mobile robot domain visual servoing tasks facilitate relative positioning in indoors man made environment. We also demonstrate how the composition of these elementary strategies enables landmark-based navigation, path following and obstacle detection.

From the control standpoint both of these applications can be viewed as hierarchical hybrid systems. In both cases the low-level strategies will be described in terms of of differential/difference equation and their analysis and design carried out using familiar tools and techniques from Control Theory. For the composition and coordination of these elementary strategies language of finite state machines is chosen. Finite state machine models capture the discrete event aspects of system's behavior and are used for the specification of coordination maneuvers between vehicles in automated highway applications and various goal reaching behaviors in the mobile robot domain. The language enables the specification and composition of elementary strategies, their verification and synthesis of discrete event controller of system behavior.

The presentation of the topics will be organized around two different applications. In the automated highway domain the emphasis will be on dynamic models. Vision-based controller for lateral, longitudinal control and lane change maneuver will be briefly described, followed by examples of inter-vehicle coordination maneuvers. In the domain of mobile robots, where kinematic models are appropriate, we will outline examples of visual servoing techniques for relative positioning tasks and formulate global navigation task as a sequence of relative positioning strategies.

2   Automated Vehicles Control and Coordination

The concept of automated highway arose as a potential solution to the current transportation problems. The main objective of the research carried out as a part California PATH project was to propose a design which would increase safety and throughput of highways by full or partial automation [15]. The automation was suggested both at the level of individual control strategies for automated driving as well as monitoring and coordination of the vehicles. The next section reviews the basic components of the AHS (Automated Highway System) architecture as well as challenges of the overall design.

2.1   Dynamic Vision-Based Control

The employment of the visual sensing in the context of driving is motivated by superior performance of the human visual system to accomplish these types of tasks. It is the availability of the information at the look-ahead distance, which makes the makes the vision sensor favorable choice for driving tasks. The dynamic behavior of the overall system rests on characterizing the dynamic model of the vehicle and the dynamics of the image features. The longitudinal and lateral dynamics of the car can be under some simplifying assumptions decoupled. The respective parts are then used for the controller design. Lateral vehicle dynamics is used for controller design. The linearized model of the vehicle retains only lateral and yaw dynamics, and is parameterized by the current longitudinal velocity. Choosing $\dot{\psi}$ and v_y as state variables the lateral dynamics of the vehicle have the following form:

$$
\begin{bmatrix} \dot{v}_y \\ \ddot{\psi} \end{bmatrix} = \begin{bmatrix} -\frac{c_f+c_r}{mv_x} & \frac{c_r l_r - c_f l_f}{mv_x} - v_x \\ \frac{-l_f c_f + l_r c_r}{I_\psi v_x} & -\frac{l_f^2 c_f + l_r^2 c_r}{I_\psi v_x} \end{bmatrix} \begin{bmatrix} v_y \\ \dot{\psi} \end{bmatrix} + \begin{bmatrix} \frac{c_f}{m} \\ \frac{l_f c_f}{I_\psi} \end{bmatrix} \delta_f .
\tag{1}
$$

The additional measurements provided by the vision system (see Figure 1) are: y_L the offset from the centerline at the lookahead and ε_L the angle between the tangent to the road and the vehicle orientation. Where L denotes the lookahead distance of the vision system as shown in Figure 1. The equations capturing the evolution of these measurements due to the motion of the car and changes in the road geometry are:

$$
\dot{y}_L = v_x \, \varepsilon_L - v_y - \dot{\psi} L
\tag{2}
$$

$$
\dot{\varepsilon}_L = v_x \, K_L - \dot{\psi}
\tag{3}
$$

where K_L represents the curvature of the road. The combined model with state vector $\boldsymbol{x} = [v_y, \dot{\psi}, y_L, \varepsilon_L]^T$, output $\boldsymbol{y} = [\dot{\psi}, y_L, \varepsilon_L]^T$ and control input $\boldsymbol{u} = \delta_f$. The road curvature K_L enters the model as an exogenous disturbance signal $\boldsymbol{w}$. The offset at the lookahead y_L which provides our error measurement. It is obtained by analysis of the image data acquired by a forward looking CCD video camera is mounted inside the passenger compartment. Modeling explicitly the geometric transformation between the image plane and road surface and lane marker detection, y_L can be computed directly from image measurements. This information can be obtained at rate 30 frames per second (lane markers tracking) with a latency of 57 milliseconds [5,8]. Next section outlines briefly the design issues and analysis of the basic control strategies.

2.2 Control

Lateral Control. The design objective of the lateral control is to compute the appropriate steering angle, so as to maintain the desired distance of the vehicle from the center lane. The performance specifications to be achieved are close to human driving and can be characterized in terms of desirable tracking error (0.1 m), maximum allowable error (0.4 m), limited lateral acceleration (0.2 g) and sufficient passenger comfort. Furthermore successful control design should be also robust with respect to the variety of road conditions and car parameters (mass, friction, cornering stiffness etc). Using standard analysis techniques in

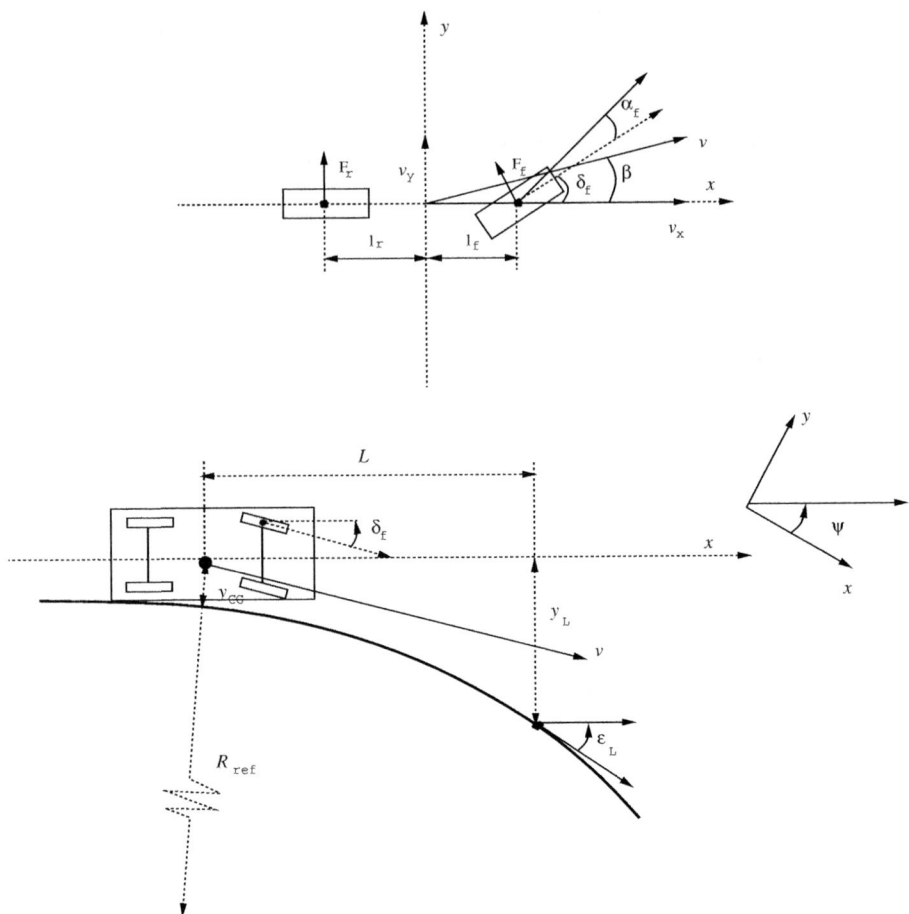

Fig. 1. The vision system estimates the offset from the centerline y_L and the angle between the road tangent and heading of the vehicle ε_L at some lookahead distance L. The motion of the vehicle is characterized by its velocity $\boldsymbol{v} = (v_x, v_y)$ expressed in the vehicle's inertial frame of reference and its yaw rate $\dot{\psi}$. The forces acting on the front and rear wheels are F_f and F_r, respectively, δ_f is the front wheel steering angle, α_f, α_r side slip angles of the front and rear tires, δ commanded steering angle, m total mass of the vehicle, I_ψ total inertia vehicle around center of gravity (CG), l_f, l_r distance of the front and rear axles from the CG, l distance between the front and the rear axle $l_f + l_r$, c_f, c_r cornering stiffness of the front and rear tires

the frequency domain, the stability of the lateral control can be achieved over the entire range of operating speeds. This is possible even in the presence of the delay which is explicitly modeled. The delay can be compensated by the

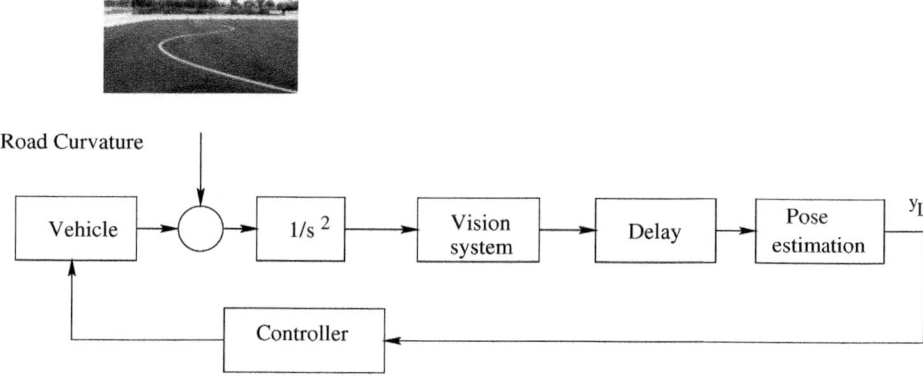

Fig. 2. Block Diagram of the lateral control strategy. Road curvature which is provided as a reference input is estimated by the vision system

Fig. 3. These figures show the view showing the mounted cameras and performance of the lane extraction system on a typical input image

additional phase lead provided by increasing the look-ahead distance. In addition to measurements are obtained from the on-board fiber optic gyro it is possible to design an observer capable of estimating the curvature of the road K_L. This information is used for anticipatory control as a part of the vehicle feedforward control law. Detailed description of the control law can be found in [8].

Lane Change Maneuvers. Lane change maneuvers are accomplished by supplying a reference trajectory, $y_L(t)$, as an input to the lateral control systems. This reference trajectory is a simple fifth order spline which smoothly moves the vehicle from one lane to another. The curvature of the reference trajectory is also supplied as an additive input to the feedforward control law. The actual controller is then identical to the lateral control strategy, which is given this virtual reference trajectory.

Longitudinal Vehicle Control. For the purpose of brake and throttle control for keeping the safe distance in front of the car ahead, both laser radar and vision sensing is used for measuring the distance of the car ahead. The visual sensing in this case combines shape reconstruction (2D planar reconstruction rather than the usual 3D) from stereo/motion with motion estimation, using robust and efficient feature matching methods. The resulting algorithm runs at 3–5 Hz, and frame-rate performance (30 Hz) and performs well over large periods of time.

Fig. 4. Example stereo-pairs from the tracking sequence. The corner features are shown as small crosses, white for those matched over time or in stereo, and black for unmatched features. The black and white circle indicates the position of the fixation point, which ideally should remain at the same point on the lead car throughout the sequence. The white rectangle describes the latest estimate of the bounding box for the vehicle

These elementary strategies constitute the lowest level of control and sensing hierarchy. The standard control theory techniques guide their design and enable their analysis. Presented are examples of vehicle runs at approximately 75 mph, along 7 mile curved oval. In the absence of feedforward control law, the vehicle has some steady state error in the curved section of the track. Figure 5 describes the performance of tested control strategies without and with the feedforward term.

2.3   Vehicle Coordination

The main goal of coordination of multiple vehicles in AHS is to reduce congestion and maximize highway throughput. Towards this end a platooning concept has been explored [15]. The main idea behind the concept is to organize vehicles into closely spaced platoons, where the vehicles travel at high speeds at close distances with respect to each other. The vehicle can operate in two different modes: the follower mode and the leader mode. The switching between the modes is achieved by means of five maneuvers: *join, split, lane change, entry* and *exit*, as demonstrated in Figure 6. Additional lane number information is a part of the mode.

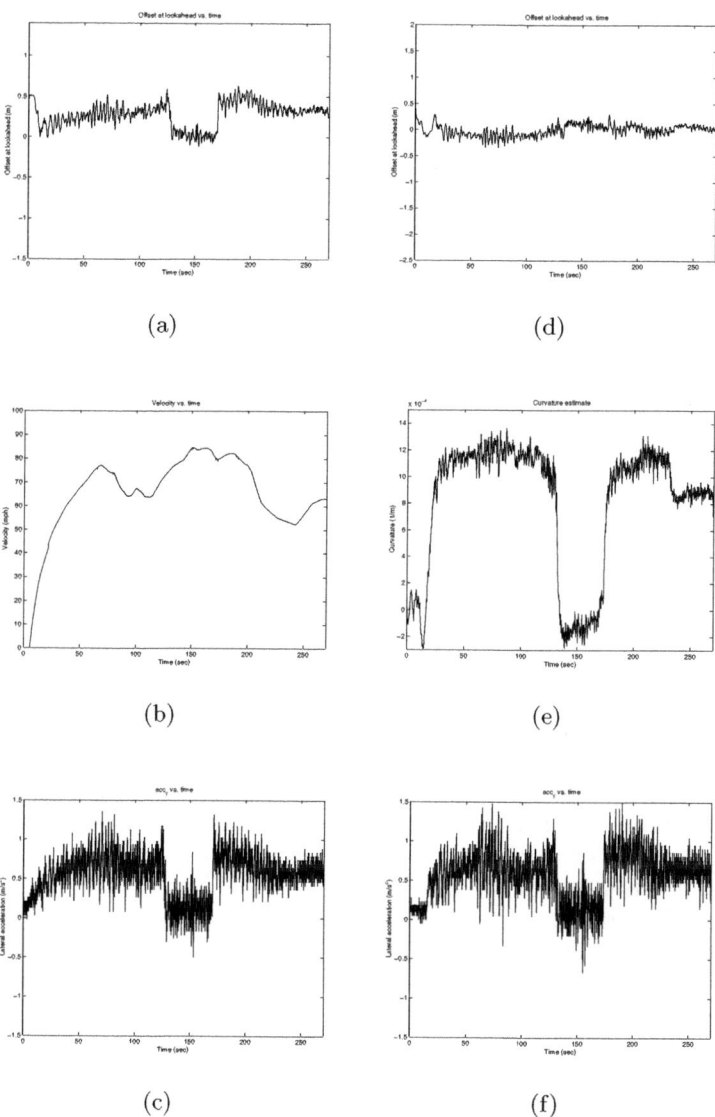

Fig. 5. This figure depicts the performance of the lead-lag controller. Figures a, b and c indicate the offset of the centerline of the road at a distance of 15 meters ahead of the vehicle, velocity profiles used in the runs and the lateral acceleration experienced at the center of gravity of the vehicle. Figures d, e and f demonstrate the effect of the feedforward control term on the overall tracking performance, in particular the offset at the lookahead, the curvature estimate used in the feedforward term and the last row shows the lateral acceleration profile. Notice that the steady state offset in the curved sections was essentially eliminated

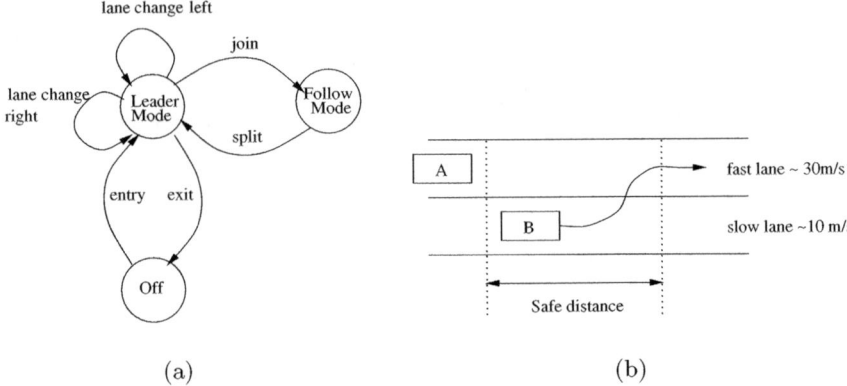

(a)   (b)

Fig. 6. (a) The transitions between different vehicle models, indicate different maneuvers with separately designed communication protocols. (b) An example of an unsafe lane change scenario

The individual maneuvers have associated communication protocols which have been designed in [4]. The coordination protocols exchange information between individual vehicles. When the conditions for the maneuver execution are met, the regulation level executes the appropriate maneuver. For the purpose of discrete verification, the behavior of the continuous controller has been abstracted to the level of finite state machines, which capture the discrete behavior of the sensors and controllers. This enables verification of the logical correctness of the protocols using verification tool COSPAN [3]. In spite of the correctness of the analysis at continuous and discrete event levels of the system, the overall simulation revealed crashes [2].

This indicated that certain aspects of systems behavior were not captured by models at individual levels and proved to be crucial for being able to guarantee safe design. An example of the lane change maneuver of a single vehicle was one such an instance. The basic logic of the *lane change* maneuver protocol first checked whether there is sufficient space in the lane ahead, and provided that the free space would guarantee the safe distance from the neighboring vehicle the maneuver was executed. In case there was no other vehicle in the next lane in sight the maneuver was immediately executed. In the initial state as depicted in Figure 6 (right), the lane change from the slow to fast lane has been enabled. However due to the differences in lane speeds the vehicle was behind was unable to deaccelerate as to prevent the collision with the vehicle ahead. The main cause of this unsafe operation were physical limits of sensors and acceleration and deacceleration limits of the individual vehicles. None of these aspects was captured by the respective levels of hierarchical control system which have been analyzed. This and several other instances of such examples were documented in [2].

Based on these observations alternative techniques for proving the safety of the overall hybrid system design for these particular scenarios have been proposed. In [10] authors advocate the game theoretic approach, where the correctness of the overall hybrid controller can be proved by design, with no need for subsequent verification. Assuming that the designer can determine the control input, all other inputs are considered as disturbance (either discrete or continuous). Given this setting a set of safe initial conditions can be calculated. If the initial conditions of the system are in the safe set the maneuver can be executed, regardless of the disturbances. The advent of this approach has been further explored in the context of other maneuvers as well as other hybrid control problems [14].

3   Mobile Robot Navigation

While the tools and techniques for the analysis of hierarchical hybrid systems developed in the context of AHS are general, the mobile robot domain raises some additional issues and differences. Richness of the future mobile robot environments makes the sensing problem more challenging. This in turn also increases the complexity, level of autonomy as well as variety of robotic tasks. Next section reviews some of the sensing and hierarchical control issues in the context of vision based mobile robot navigation.

3.1   Visual Servoing

In the mobile robot domain we will introduce visual servoing approach which enables formulation of the control objectives using the image measurements directly in the image plane. The overall approach consist of three steps: defining a set of features in the image, specifying their desired goal configuration, and applying a control law that ensures the convergence from any initial configuration to a desired goal configuration in the image. The approach has been originally introduced in [1]. Suppose in general terms that the camera system is considered as a dynamical system $\dot{g} = f(g, u)$ where $u = (\omega, v)$ is the angular and linear velocity $\omega, v \in \mathbb{R}^3$ of the camera system and $g \in SE(3)$ is the pose of the camera. The image feature is typically defined implicitly as a function of pose $h(g, \, \boldsymbol{x}) = 0$. Then given some desired position of the image features, the robot task can be formulated as a regulation of a cost function $J(\, \boldsymbol{x}, \, \boldsymbol{x}_d)$ during the time interval $[0, T]$. Most commonly used control law is a simple gradient based scheme, which is typically sufficient for exponential convergence of the output to zero:

$$u = \arg\min_{u} \dot{\boldsymbol{x}}^T \nabla J \, .$$

Convergence and stability can be assessed using standard control theory techniques. In the next section we will formulate several visual servoing tasks using kinematic models. In the mobile robot domain the speeds are relatively low and dynamic effects are not so prevalent so the use of kinematic models is well justified.

Mobile Robot Kinematics. The kinematic model of the mobile robot used in our experiments is that of a unicycle. Let $p_{fm}(t) = (x, y, z)^T \in \mathbb{R}^3$ be the position vector of the origin of frame F_m from the origin of frame F_f and the rotation angle θ is defined in the counter-clockwise sense about the y-axis, as shown in Figure 7. For the unicycle kinematics, $\theta(t)$ and $p_{fm}(t)$ satisfy:

$$\dot{x} = v \sin \theta$$
$$\dot{z} = v \cos \theta \tag{4}$$
$$\dot{\theta} = \omega$$

where the steering input ω controls the angular velocity $\dot{\theta}$; the driving input v controls the linear velocity along the direction of the wheel. Monocular camera mounted on the mobile robot is facing downward with a tilt angle $\phi > 0$ and the camera is elevated above the ground plane by distance d, as shown in Figure 7. Then the kinematics of a point $q_c = (x, y, z)^T$ attached to the camera frame F_c is given in the (instantaneous) camera frame by:

$$\begin{pmatrix} \dot{x} \\ \dot{y} \\ \dot{z} \end{pmatrix} = \begin{pmatrix} 0 \\ \sin \phi \\ \cos \phi \end{pmatrix} v + \begin{pmatrix} y \sin \phi + z \cos \phi \\ -x \sin \phi \\ -x \cos \phi \end{pmatrix} \omega . \tag{5}$$

An instance of the general visual servoing problem considered here is that of following arbitrarily shaped curve. Detailed treatment of this scenario can be found in [12]. Consider planar ground curve Γ which can be expressed in the camera coordinate system as $\Gamma = (\gamma_x(y, t), y, \gamma_z(y))^T$. Since $\gamma_z(y)$ does not change as a function of time, the dynamics of the ground curve can be expressed using (5) as:

$$\dot{\gamma}_x(y, t) = -(y \sin \phi + \gamma_z \cos \phi) \omega . \tag{6}$$

The shape of the orthographic projection[1] of the ground curve $\tilde{\Gamma} = (\gamma_x(y, t), y)^T$ then evolves in the image plane $z = 1$ according to the following *Riccati-type* partial differential equation.

$$\frac{\partial \gamma_x}{\partial t} = -(y \sin \phi + \gamma_z \cos \phi) \omega + \frac{\partial \gamma_x}{\partial y}(v \sin \phi - \gamma_x \omega \sin \phi) . \tag{7}$$

The above expression captures the dynamics of the ground plane curve. We can the consider a feature function $F = x - \xi_1(y, t)$, which can be directly measured in the image and which we will try to regulate, so as to follow the curve. The relationship between ξ and γ is expressed in caption of Figure 8 in case of orthographic projection. The dynamics of the image curve can be expressed concisely in terms of two vector fields f_1 and f_2 and behaves as a nonlinear system of the form:

$$\dot{\xi} = f_1(\xi)\omega + f_2(\xi)v .$$

---

[1] From the control point of view the perspective and orthographic projection models can be treated as equivalent in this problem.

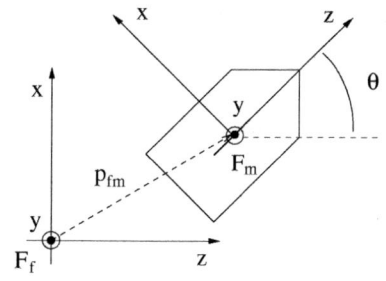

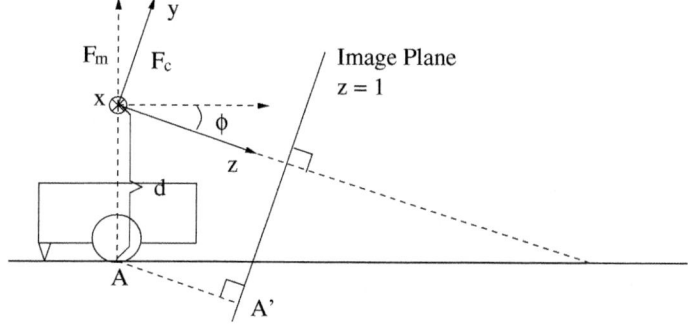

Fig. 7. Model of the unicycle mobile robot and the side-view of the unicycle mobile robot with a camera facing downward with a tilt angle $\phi > 0$

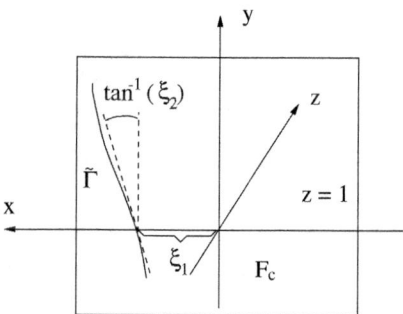

Fig. 8. The orthographic projection of a ground curve on the $z = 1$ plane. Here $\xi_1 = \gamma_x$ and $\xi_2 = \frac{\partial \gamma_x}{\partial y}$

It can be shown that if the given ground curve is a linear curvature curve, the above system is completely controllable and observable and can be globally exponentially tracked given the following control law:

$$v = v_0 + \xi_1 \omega, \quad v_0 > 0$$

$$\omega = \frac{\sin \phi}{1 + \sin^2 \phi \xi_2^2} (v_0 \sin \phi \xi_3 + a\xi_1 + b\xi_2), \quad a, b > 0. \tag{8}$$

Then the partial closed loop system of ξ_1, ξ_2 is linearized and given by:

$$\dot{\xi}_1 = v_0 \sin \phi \xi_2$$

$$\dot{\xi}_2 = -a\xi_1 - b\xi_2. \tag{9}$$

Discussion on control inputs for the general steering problem from one point to another can be found in [12].

Wall Following. A variation of this general strategy can be then used for formulating the wall following as a special case of following a zero curvature curves. The original control law can be used for successful tracking of corridors, while connecting them by virtual circular segments. An example of an image pair of initial and steady state as seen by the camera is shown in Figure 9. The control strategy for following arbitrary curves, can be also used for path following, where the curve will be a virtual one, computed by a path planner.

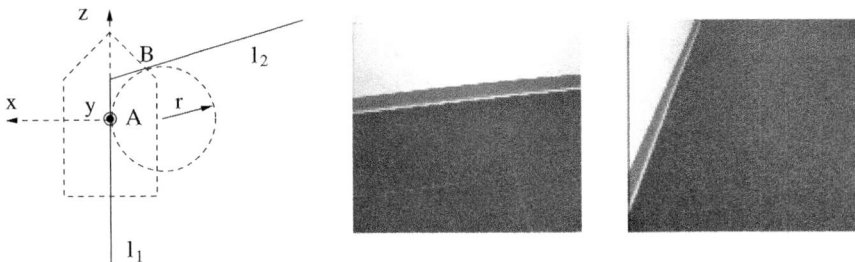

Fig. 9. Piecewise constant curvature curves for wall following. Initial and desired view of the straight line feature. The line corresponds to the intersection of the ground plane and vertical wall plane

Door Servoing. Another relative positioning strategy useful for navigation task is the door servoing strategy. For this control problem we employ an additional degree of freedom: the pan angle ψ of the camera mounted on the turntable. This allows search for the doorway over an extended field of view. The objective of the door servoing task is to position the mobile robot with respect to the doorway so it can pass through it. The control needs to take into account the nonholonomic constraints of the vehicle in slightly different way. The doorway is defined by two points at the same height above the ground plane located at the door frame. An example views of a doorway from an initial and desired configuration is shown in Figure 10. In this scenario the control of the mobile base and the control of the

Fig. 10. Initial and desired view of the doorway features

pan platform are decoupled. Few solutions to this regulation problem have been proposed in [7]. In terms of visual sensing the difficult part of the employment of these strategies in dynamically changing environments is initialization and tracking in the presence of multiple moving objects.

3.2   Composition of Elementary Strategies

Previous section outlined some sensing and control strategies in the mobile robot domain. Together with point-to-point navigation and obstacle avoidance described in [9], different navigation tasks can be formulated. In the presence of manipulators as well as additional sensors (e. g. ultrasound), different low-level controllers and sensing routines can be developed, which constitute basic capabilities of the mobile robot. Combination of these elementary strategies enables accomplishment of bigger variety of tasks. This brings out new needs for specification and composition of the elementary strategies. Similarly as in the intelligent highway scenarios, the discrete event abstractions of the basic control modes need to be established. An example of such model for the mobile robot base is in Figure 11. In addition to the discrete event model of the controlled system (mobile base in this case), discrete event abstractions of the elementary control strategies capture the discrete aspects of continuous behavior such as initialization, failure, change of set point, as depicted in Figure 11. The details of the process can be found in [6]. Similar, robot based schema approach, has been proposed by [11]. Adopting a process view of the elementary control strategies, set of composition operators is introduced, whose semantics is defined in terms finite state machines. The basic composition operators are:

Sequential composition $P = R \, ; \, S$. Process P behaves like R until R terminates and then behaves like S. P terminates when S terminates and has the same termination status as S.

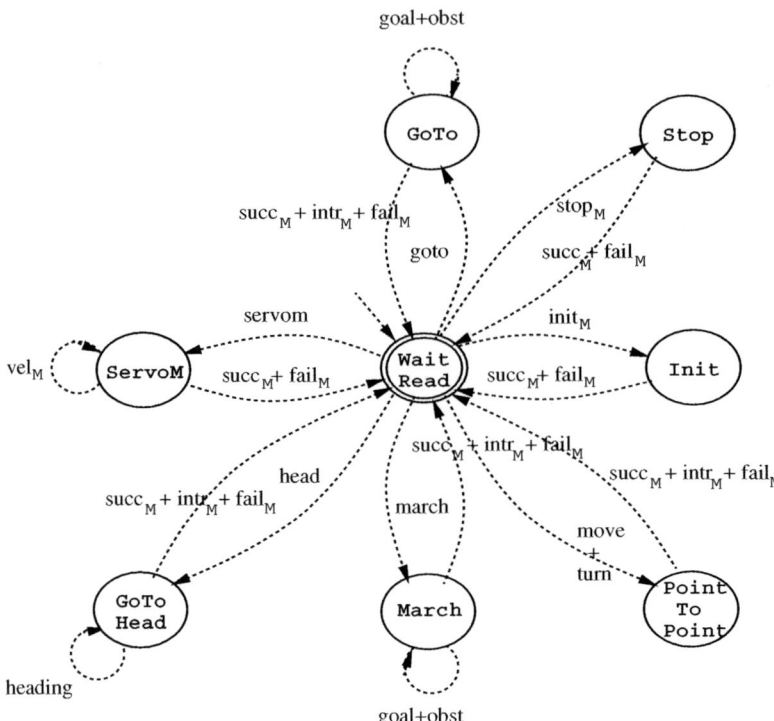

$$\Sigma_C = \{ \text{move, turn, servo}_M, \text{goto, head, march, init}_M, \text{stop} \}$$

$$\Sigma_U = \{ \text{succ}_M, \text{fail}_M, \text{intr}_M, \text{goal}, \text{obst}, \text{vel}_M, \text{heading} \}$$

(a) Mobile base server process and it's modes

GoTo

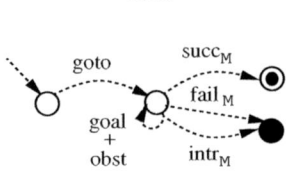

(b) Discrete event abstraction of the elementary control strategy for goal directed navigation

Fig. 11.

Parallel composition $P = R \parallel S$. Process P behaves like R and S running in parallel. P terminates with the termination and status of the last terminated process[2].

Conditional composition $P = R\langle v \rangle : S(v)$. Process P behaves like R until R terminates successfully computing v which is then used to initialize process S.[3] If R fails the composition fails.

Disabling composition $P = R \sharp S$. Disabling composition is similar to parallel but if one of the processes terminates the other process is terminated as well. P has the same termination status as the process that caused the termination of the composition (i. e., the process that finished first).

Synchronous recurrent composition. $P = R\langle v \rangle :; S(v)$ is recursively defined as $R\langle v \rangle :; S(v) = R\langle v \rangle : (S(v) ; (R\langle v \rangle :; S(v)))$. This composition terminates with the failure of process R.

Asynchronous recurrent composition. $P = R\langle v \rangle :: S(v)$ is recursively defined as $R\langle v \rangle :; S(v) = R\langle v \rangle : (S(v) \parallel (R\langle v \rangle :: S(v)))$. This composition terminates with the failure of process R.

Given the composition operators more complex tasks can be expressed in terms of composition of elementary strategies. Such description can be then viewed as specification of a task. Given specification can be automatically translated to the finite state machine representation and using techniques proposed by [13], discrete event supervisor can be synthesized. In addition to the task additional properties of the system can be verified.

In the mobile robot domain the dynamic effects are not so prevalent as in AHS domain, however due to bigger variety and complexity of the tasks it is of importance in some domains that certain notion of task accomplishment can be guaranteed. This rests on global assumptions the sensing strategies make about the environment. Some of these issues will be now demonstrated in the context of global navigation tasks.

3.2.1 Global Navigation. Given a set of relative positioning strategies, the global navigation task can be accomplished as a sequence of relative positioning tasks [7]. That sequence is determined based on topological representation, which is assumed to be given. This topological abstraction is determined by visibility regions associated with individual landmarks and is captured by a *place graph*. A corresponding place graph given a set of landmarks is depicted in Figure 12. Individual nodes in the place graph represent the intersections of the visibility regions of specified landmarks or boundaries leading to landmarks. The edges coming out of the node correspond to the possible servoing strategies that can be applied from a given place. A node is characterized by a set of visible or approachable landmarks, i. e., set of landmarks with respect to which the mobile

---

[2] The composition of parallel processes requires synchronization of the processes in terms of shared events. The exact formulation of this is described in [6].

[3] The variable v is a global variable. We assume shared memory model, which allows the access to a global variable, that may be accessed by multiple processes.

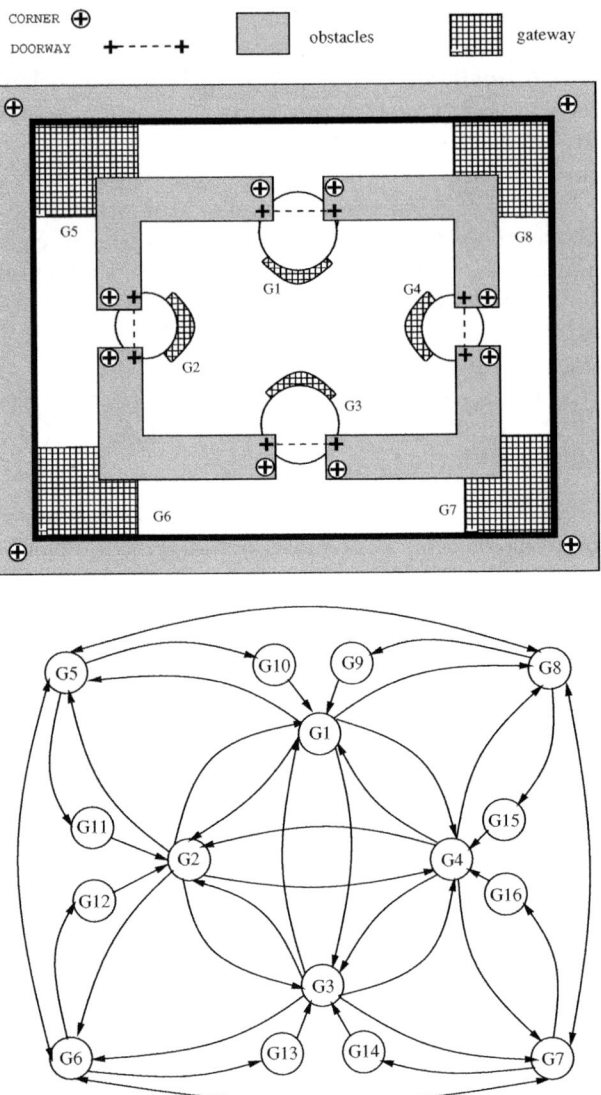

Fig. 12. The gateway regions correspond to the nodes of the place graph. Some of the gateways were omitted for clarity. Place graph corresponding to a set of landmarks chosen in our laboratory. G2 corresponds to the gateway between the door and the boundary of the wall leading to two corner landmarks. The edge between G2 and G5 is labeled by a wall following strategy and the executed path is Figure 8. Some of the gateway nodes and edges were omitted from the graph for clarity

robot can be positioned. In the case every point in the free 2-D configuration space belongs to a certain place, the place graph is fully connected.

What follows is an example of the door servoing task expressed in *task specification language* introduced previously. The initialization of doorway features can be written in a following way:

$$\texttt{InitServo}(door_i) := \texttt{Search}(s) \parallel \texttt{ServoC}$$

where we utilize the degree of freedom of the pan platform. Once the door features are found the actual servoing task can be initiated:

$$\texttt{Servo} := \texttt{Track}(s_d, s) \parallel \texttt{ServoM} \parallel \texttt{ServoC}$$

where $\texttt{ServoC}$ and $\texttt{ServoM}$ are control strategies for mobile base and camera platform and $\texttt{Track}$ is the feature detection and tracking routine which at each instance of time generates appropriate velocity commands to both camera pan platform and mobile base controllers. A single relative positioning task, expressed in task specification language, can be then written as:

$$\texttt{RelPosition}(door_i, s_d) := \texttt{InitServo}(door_i)\langle s \rangle : \texttt{Servo}(s, s_d)$$

where : is the conditional composition operator, which specifies that the first strategy must be completed successfully before the second one can be initiated. By labeling the individual arcs of the place graph by expressions of the above form, we can then generate the global plan as a result of a place graph search.

3.3   Discussion

The outlined approach demonstrates the use of relative positioning strategies with respect to the set of naturally occurring landmarks for global navigation. In general in the domain of mobile robots residing in structured man made environment, the main challenge lies in the proper initialization of the control strategies and acquisition, detection and instantiation of an environment model. These functionalities are central in order to be able to specify and execute more complex goal directed behavior of the robotic agent and move beyond systems, which require hand initialization and are designed specifically for a particular task. In in this article we reviewed mainly deterministic aspects of hierarchical hybrid systems. The need for probabilistic formulations is apparent when in comes to using modeling and interpretation of noisy sensory readings as well as outcomes of robot's actions.

References

1. B. Espiau, F. Chaumette, and P. Rives. A new approach to visual servoing in robotics. *IEEE Transactions on Robotics and Automation*, 8(3):313–326, June 1992. 235

2. D. Godbole and J. Lygeros. Hierarchical hybrid control: A case study. In *Proceedings from IEEE Conference on Decision and Control*, pages 1592–1597, 1994. 234

3. Z. Har'El and R. Kurshan. Cospan user's guide. *AT&T Laboratories*, 1987. 234

4. A. Hsu, F. Eskafi, E. Singh, and P. Varaiya. Protocol desing for an automated highway system. *Discrete Event Dynamic Systems*, 2(1):183–206, 1994. 234

5. J.Malik, P. McLauchlan C. J. Taylor, and J. Košecká. Development of binocular stereopsis for vehicle lateral control. path mou-257 final report. Technical report, Department of EECS, UC Berkeley, 1997. 229

6. J. Košecká and H. Ben-Abdallah. An automaton based algebra for specifying robotic agents. In *Proccedings of the AMAST Real-Time Systems Workshop, Salt Lake City, Utah*, 1996. 239, 241

7. J. Košecká. Visually guided navigation. *Robotics and Autonomous Systems*, 21(1):37–51, July 1997. 239, 241

8. J. Košecká, R. Blasi, C. J. Taylor, and J. Malik. Vision based lateral control of vehicles. In *Conference on Intelligent Transportation Systems, Boston*, 1997. 229, 231

9. J. Košecká and H. I. Christensen. Experiments in behavior composition. *Journal of Robotics and Autonomous Systems*, 19(3/4), 1997. 239

10. J. Lygeros and D. Godbole. Verified hybrid controllers for automated vehicles. *IEEE Transactions on Automatic Control*, 43(4):522–539, 1998. 235

11. D. M. Lyons and A. J. Hendriks. Planning for reactive robot behavior. In *Proceedings of the IEEE International Conference on Robotics and Automation*, pages 2675–2680, 1992. 239

12. Yi Ma, Jana Košecká, and Shankar Sastry. Vision guided navigation of a nonholonomic mobile robot. *IEEE Transactions on Robotics and Automation*, 15(3):521–536, 1999. 236, 238

13. P. J. Ramadge and W. M. Wonham. Supervisory control of a class of discrete event processes. *SIAM J. Contr. Optimization*, 25(1):206–230, 1987. 241

14. S. Sastry, G. Meyer, C. Tomlin, J. Lygeros, , D. Godbole, and G. Pappas. Hybrid control in air traffic management systems. In *Proceedings of the IEEE Conference in Decision and Control*, pages 1478–1483, 1995. 235

15. P. Varaiya. Smart cars on smart roads: problems of control. *IEEE Transactions on Automatic Control*, AC-38(2):195–207, 1993. 228, 232

Recognizing Objects by Their Appearance Using Eigenimages*

Horst Bischof[1] and Aleš Leonardis[2]

[1] Pattern Recognition and Image Processing Group, University of Technology,
Favoritenstr. 9/1832, A-1040 Vienna, Austria
bis@prip.tuwien.ac.at
[2] Faculty of Computer and Information Science,
University of Ljubljana, Slovenia
alesl@fri.uni-lj.si

Abstract. The appearance-based approaches to vision problems have recently received a renewed attention in the vision community due to their ability to deal with combined effects of shape, reflectance properties, pose in the scene, and illumination conditions. Besides, appearance-based representations can be acquired through an automatic learning phase which is not the case with traditional shape representations. The approach has led to a variety of successful applications, e. g., visual positioning and tracking of robot manipulators, visual inspection, and human face recognition.

In this paper we will review the basic methods for appearance-based object recognition. We will also identify the major limitations of the standard approach and present algorithms how these limitations can be alleviated leading to an object recognition system which is applicable in real world situations.

1 Introduction

The goal of computer vision is to find semantic interpretations of images. In particular to localize and name objects contained in a scene and to assess their mutual relationships. The central problem is to recognize known objects reliably, independent of variations in position, orientation, size, and illumination conditions even when those objects are partially occluded. Although quite some information is lost by the image formation process, biological vision systems demonstrate that this task can be accomplished reliably and efficiently even under difficult viewing and illumination conditions.

The study of visual object recognition is often motivated by the problem of recognizing 3D objects given that we only have 2D images. There are two dominating approaches for solving this problem:

---

* H. B. was supported by a grant from the Austrian National Fonds zur Förderung der wissenschaftlichen Forschung (P13981INF) and the K plus Competence Center ADVANCED COMPUTER VISION. A. L. acknowledges the support from the Ministry of Science and Technology of Republic of Slovenia (Project J2-0414).

V. Hlaváč, K. G. Jeffery, and J. Wiedermann (Eds.): SOFSEM 2000, LNCS 1963, pp. 245–265, 2000.

1. One originally popularized by Marr [22] is the 3D reconstructionist approach, i. e., to derive 3D object centered models from the images and to match these models against a set of stored 3D models. One of the most prominent theories along these lines was the "Recognition-By-Components" model by Biederman [7].

2. However, there is converging evidence from neuroscience, psychophysical studies, and computer vision for an approach which is called "image-based", "view-based", or "appearance-based" recognition (see [1]). The key idea of the image-based approach is that object representations encode visual information as it appears to the observer from a specific view point. The problem of object recognition is approached by a sufficiently large memory structure (i. e., trading memory against computation), storing different views of an object seen in the past and comparing the image of the currently viewed object with all the views stored in memory. However, this direct approach will not work in general because the number of all views of all objects to be recognized is too huge. Therefore, the major challenge of this approach is to develop representations that remain stable (invariant) under a variety of viewing conditions.

In this paper we review one such view-based approach that has recently received a lot of attention in the vision community, i. e., *eigenspace methods*. The approach has led to a variety of successful applications, e. g., illumination planning [26], visual positioning and tracking of robot manipulators [27], visual inspection [42], "image spotting" [24], and human face recognition [39,6].

As stressed by its proponents, the major advantage of the approach is that both learning as well as recognition are performed using just two-dimensional brightness images without any low- or mid-level processing. However, there still remain various problems to be overcome since the technique rests on direct appearance-based matching [25]. Therefore, we will also review methods that can perform the eigenspace matching more robustly, in particular, making it insensitive to outliers, occlusions and cluttered background.

The paper is organized as follows: We first motivate the usage of eigenspaces for object recognition by showing its relation to template matching. The major methods for calculating the eigenspaces are reviewed in Section 3. Then we present the standard method for calculating the eigenspace coefficients and determining the pose of the object by using parameterized eigenspaces in Section 4. In Section 5 we review our robust approach of calculating the eigenspace coefficients and demonstrate how it can successfully cope with occluded objects and cluttered scenes. In Section 6 we demonstrate how this method can be embedded in a multiresolution framework such that it can also successfully deal with scaled images. Finally in Section 7 we conclude with a discussion and outline further extensions of the proposed methods.

2   Object Recognition Using Appearance-Based Representations

Let us start our review with the following simple situation which occurs quite often in industrial settings:

We would like to determine where a particular object appears in a scene (for the moment we assume that the illumination is controlled, and that the object can appear only in a single pose and is viewed from a specific direction). A straight forward approach to solve this problem is to take an image of the object as a template[1] $\mathbf{y} = [y_1, \ldots, y_m]^T \in \mathbb{R}^m$. In order to determine the presence or absence of the object in the scene and its position we search for the occurrence of the template in the acquired image $I(x, y) \in \mathbb{R}^{q \times s}$ (of size $q \times s$) by scanning each location in the image and extracting a subwindow of the same size as the template and converting it to a vector $\mathbf{x} \in \mathbb{R}^m$. A match of the template is found when the correlation

$$\rho = \frac{\mathbf{x}^T \mathbf{y}}{\|\mathbf{x}\| \, \|\mathbf{y}\|} > \Theta \tag{1}$$

is above some predefined threshold Θ. If we assume normalized images, i.e., $\|\mathbf{x}\| = \|\mathbf{y}\| = 1$ we can also equivalently look for a match by checking if the sum-of-squared differences $\|\mathbf{x} - \mathbf{y}\|^2 = (\mathbf{x} - \mathbf{y})^T(\mathbf{x} - \mathbf{y}) = 2 - \mathbf{x}^T\mathbf{y}$ is below some threshold.

Now let us suppose that the object can appear in n different poses in the image (e.g., in different orientations). In this case we could acquire a set of templates $\mathcal{Y} = \{\mathbf{y}_1, \ldots \mathbf{y}_n\}$, and perform the matching for each template separately. Of course this might become computationally quite costly if the number of templates is very large. However, we could avoid some of the computations when we assume that there exists a low dimensional representation of the templates in form of an orthonormal transform, i.e., we assume that there exists a set of orthonormal basis vectors $\mathcal{E} = \{\mathbf{e}_1, \ldots \mathbf{e}_p\}$, $\mathbf{e}_i \in \mathbb{R}^m$, $p \ll n$, such that we can approximate each template $\mathbf{y}_i$ in this new basis, i.e., $\mathbf{y}_i \approx \tilde{\mathbf{y}}_i = \sum_{j=1}^{p} a_j(\mathbf{y}_i)\mathbf{e}_j$. In this case we can approximate the sum-of-squared differences by:

$$\|\mathbf{x} - \mathbf{y}\|^2 \approx \left\| \sum_{j=1}^{p} a_j(\mathbf{x})\mathbf{e}_j - \sum_{j=1}^{p} a_j(\mathbf{y})\mathbf{e}_j \right\|^2 = \left\| \sum_{j=1}^{p} (a_j(\mathbf{x}) - a_j(\mathbf{y}))\mathbf{e}_j \right\|^2$$
$$= \|\mathbf{a}(\mathbf{x}) - \mathbf{a}(\mathbf{y})\|^2. \tag{2}$$

The last simplification results from the basis vectors being orthonormal $\mathbf{e}_i^T\mathbf{e}_j = 1$ when $i = j$ and 0 otherwise.

This implies that we can approximately solve the template matching problem by calculating the Euclidean distance of the points $\mathbf{a}(\mathbf{x})$ and $\mathbf{a}(\mathbf{y})$, which is

---

[1] For the ease of notation we will use throughout the paper a simple vector notation which is obtained by lexicographic ordering of the pixel elements of the image in a vector.

computationally cheaper than the original formulation because $p \ll n$. The next question is which are the best basis vectors $\mathcal{E}$? Since we want a good approximation for the $\mathbf{y}_i$ with as few basis functions as possible we are looking for a basis $\mathcal{E}$ which minimizes

$$\sum_{i=1}^{n} \left\| \mathbf{y}_i - \sum_{j=1}^{p} a_j(\mathbf{y}_i)\mathbf{e}_j \right\|^2$$

for any given p. It is well known e.g. [2] that a solution to this problem is given by taking the p eigenvectors with the largest eigenvalues of the covariance matrix $\mathbf{Q} = \sum_{i=1}^{n}(\mathbf{y}_i - \mathbf{c})(\mathbf{y}_i - \mathbf{c})^T$, where $\mathbf{c} = \sum_{i=1}^{n} \mathbf{y}_i$ is the mean vector. This is also known as the Principal Component Analysis (PCA) or Karhunen-Loeve Transform (KLT).

Therefore, we can conclude that we can solve the object recognition problem by taking n different views of each object to be recognized. These images usually encompass the appearance of a single object under different orientations [12], different illumination directions [26], or multiple instances of a class of objects, e. g., faces [39]. In many cases, images not in the training set can be interpolated from the training views [40,31]. Fig. 1 depicts a typical setup using a robot and a turntable for obtaining different views of an object. Fig. 2 shows such a set of images. As can be seen from this example, the sets of images are usually highly

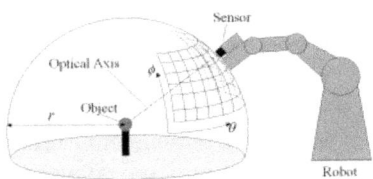

Fig. 1. View sphere for acquiring object training images

correlated. Thus, they can efficiently be compressed using Principal Component Analysis (PCA) [2], resulting in a low-dimensional eigenspace. Fig. 3 shows the 12 eigenimages corresponding to the 12 largest eigenvalues obtained from the set in Fig. 2. The eigenspace coefficients of these views serve then as the representation of the object. When an unknown object is to be recognized we calculate the eigenspace coefficients of the object and then search for the closest point in the eigenspace.

3   Computing the Eigenspace

In this section we review the methods for obtaining the eigenspaces. We first present the standard way of calculating the eigenspace and the present numeri-

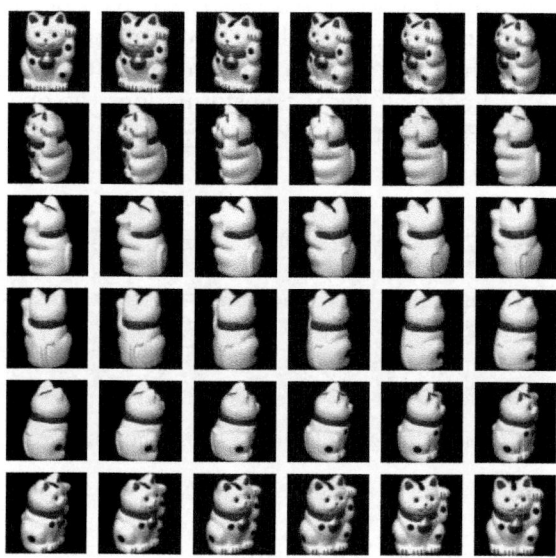

Fig. 2. A set of images obtained by rotating a toy cat on a turntable. This image is taken from the COIL-20 database [28]

cally more efficient procedures. Finally we briefly mention alternative approaches for calculating the eigenspace.

3.1 Standard Eigenspace Calculation

Let $\mathbf{y} = [y_1, \ldots, y_m]^T \in \mathbb{R}^m$ be an individual training image, and $\mathcal{Y} = \{\mathbf{y}_1, \ldots \mathbf{y}_n\}$ be a set of training images. To simplify the notation we assume $\mathcal{Y}$ to have zero mean (i.e., the common mean vector $\mathbf{c} = \sum_{i=1}^{n} \mathbf{y}_i$ has been subtracted). Let $\mathbf{Q}$ be the covariance matrix of the vectors in $\mathcal{Y}$;

$$\mathbf{Q} = \mathbf{Y}\mathbf{Y}^T \tag{3}$$

where $\mathbf{Y}$ is the $m \times n$ matrix obtained by stacking the image vectors columnwise. The eigenvectors $\mathbf{e}_i$ and the corresponding eigenvalues λ_i are determined by solving the well-known eigenstructure decomposition problem:

$$\lambda_i \mathbf{e}_i = \mathbf{Q}\mathbf{e}_i \,. \tag{4}$$

The eigenvectors form an orthogonal basis system, $\mathbf{e}_i^T \mathbf{e}_j = 1$ when $i = j$ and 0 otherwise. We assume that the eigenvectors are ordered in the descending order with respect to the corresponding eigenvalues λ_i. Then, depending on the correlation among the images in $\mathcal{Y}$, only p, $p < n$, eigenvectors are needed to represent the $\mathbf{y}_i$ to a sufficient degree of accuracy as a linear combination of eigenvectors $\mathbf{e}_i$

$$\tilde{\mathbf{y}} = \sum_{i=1}^{p} a_i(\mathbf{y})\mathbf{e}_i \,, \tag{5}$$

where $a_i(\mathbf{y})$ are the coefficients of the eigenspace expansion. The error we make by this approximation is $\sum_{i=p+1}^{n} \lambda_i$ and can be calculated by $\|\tilde{\mathbf{y}}\|^2 - \sum_{i=1}^{p} a_i^2$ [23]. We call the space spanned by the first p eigenvectors the *eigenspace*. It is well known that PCA is among all linear transformations the one which is optimal with respect to the reconstruction error $\|\mathbf{x} - \tilde{\mathbf{x}}\|^2$.

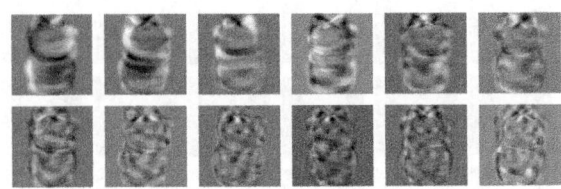

Fig. 3. 12 eigenimages obtained from the images in Fig. 2

3.2 Efficient Eigenspace Calculation

Since the size of the covariance matrix $\mathbf{Q}$ is usually very high (due to the high dimensionality of the image data) e.g., for an image of size 128×128 we get a covariance matrix of size 16384×16384, it is computationally too costly to determine the eigenvectors directly. In general, however, the number of training images n is much smaller than the number of elements m in each image, therefore at most m eigenvectors have an eigenvalue $\lambda > 0$. In addition to that, the eigenvectors must lie in the span of the training vectors. These properties can be used to devise an efficient method for calculating the eigenvectors. Turk and Pentland [39] proposed a method based on these properties. First of all the implicit covariance matrix $\hat{\mathbf{Q}}$ is calculated:

$$\hat{\mathbf{Q}} = \mathbf{Y}^T \mathbf{Y}. \tag{6}$$

Note that the dimension of this matrix is now $n \times n$ instead of $m \times m$. Let $\hat{\mathbf{e}}_i$ and $\hat{\lambda}_i$ be the eigenvectors and eigenvalues of $\hat{\mathbf{Q}}$. It can be shown [39] that the eigenvectors and eigenvalues of $\mathbf{Q}$ can be obtained as:

$$\lambda_i = \hat{\lambda}_i$$
$$\mathbf{e}_i = \hat{\lambda}_i^{-1/2} \mathbf{Y} \hat{\mathbf{e}}_i. \tag{7}$$

An even more efficient algorithm can be obtained by using the Singular Value Decomposition SVD directly on the matrix $\mathbf{Y}$ [25]. These algorithms are especially efficient if we need only $p < n$ eigenvectors which is usually the case.

3.3 Other Methods for Eigenspace Calculation

Many other methods have been proposed to calculate the eigenspaces of a set of samples. One type of methods is based on neural networks (see [4] for a review).

A well studied and thoroughly understood principle component analysis network architecture is the linear autoassociative network, see [11]. This network consists of N input and output units and $M < N$ hidden units, and is trained (usually by back-propagation) to reproduce the input at the output units. All units are linear. Bourlard and Kamp [11] have shown that at the minimum of the usual quadratic error function, the hidden units project the input on the space spanned by the first M principal components of the input distribution. The advantage of such networks is that they can be trained incrementally which is important when the training data is generated on-line.

Another type of efficient eigenspace methods can be classified as "split-and-merge" algorithms. Based on an initial calculated eigenspace, individual images [17] or even complete eigenspaces [35] (build by a separate set of images) are used to update an eigenspace. These methods achieve usually quite a lot of computational savings and/or savings in the memory requirements. The problem with these methods is that in general the obtained representation is no longer optimal (compared to an eigenspace constructed from the full set of images).

4   Standard Approach of Recovering the Coefficients

To recover the parameters a_i during the matching stage, a data vector $\mathbf{x}$ is projected onto the eigenspace

$$a_i(\mathbf{x}) = \mathbf{x}^T \mathbf{e}_i = \sum_{j=1}^{m} x_j e_{i,j} \quad 1 \ldots p. \tag{8}$$

$\mathbf{a}(\mathbf{x}) = [a_1(\mathbf{x}), \ldots, a_p(\mathbf{x})]^T$ is the point in the eigenspace obtained by projecting $\mathbf{x}$ onto the eigenspace. Let us call the $a_i(\mathbf{x})$ coefficients of $\mathbf{x}$. The reconstructed data vector $\tilde{\mathbf{x}}$ can be written as

$$\tilde{\mathbf{x}} = \sum_{i=1}^{p} a_i(\mathbf{x}) \mathbf{e}_i. \tag{9}$$

When projecting the whole training set $\mathcal{Y}$ in that manner, a discrete set of points is obtained. Since consecutive images are strongly correlated (see Fig. 2), their eigenspace coefficients are close to each other. Moreover, we can expect that when the pose of an object varies only slightly that this results in a point close in the eigenspace. Therefore we can assume that all the points belonging to an object lie on a smooth manifold. This manifold can be obtained by interpolating the discrete set of points with e. g., splines (see [25]). We call this representation *parametric eigenspace*. Determining the object pose corresponds then to finding the closest point on this manifold. Note that we can achieve a high resolution in determining the pose by interpolating the manifold. Fig. 4 depicts the manifold obtained from the images of Fig. 2. In this case the manifold is only 1D because we have only one degree of freedom (rotation angle). If we have a setup like in Fig. 1 we would obtain a 2D manifold. In practice, the manifold is stored in memory as a list of p-dimensional points obtained by densely resampling the manifold. Therefore, we are still performing a nearest neighbor search.

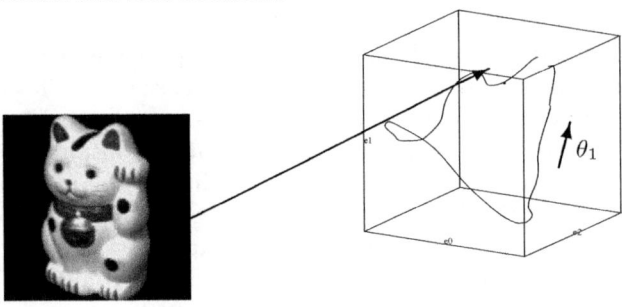

Fig. 4. Parametric eigenspace obtained from the images of the toy cat. Only the first three dimensions of the eigenspace are depicted

5   Robust Recovery of Coefficients

In this section we analyze some of the basic limitations of the current appearance-based matching methods and illustrate them with a few examples. Namely, the way the coefficients a_i are calculated poses a serious problem in the case of outliers and occlusions.

5.1   Non-robustness of Standard Coefficient Recovery

Suppose that $\hat{\mathbf{x}} = [x_1, \ldots, x_r, 0, \ldots 0]^T$ is obtained by setting last $m - r$ components of $\mathbf{x}$ to zero; a similar analysis holds when some of the components of $\mathbf{x}$ are set to some other values, which, for example, happens in the case of occlusion by another object. Then

$$\hat{a}_i = \hat{\mathbf{x}}^T \mathbf{e}_i = \sum_{j=1}^{r} x_j e_{i,j} \; . \tag{10}$$

The error we make in calculating a_i is

$$(a_i(\mathbf{x}) - \hat{a}_i(\hat{\mathbf{x}})) = \sum_{j=r+1}^{m} x_j e_{i,j} \; . \tag{11}$$

It follows that the reconstruction error is

$$\left\| \sum_{i=1}^{p} \left(\sum_{j=r+1}^{m} x_j e_{i,j} \right) \mathbf{e}_i \right\|^2 \; . \tag{12}$$

Due to the non-robustness of linear processing, this error affects the whole vector $\tilde{\mathbf{x}}$. Fig. 8 depicts the effect of occlusion on the reconstructed image. A similar analysis holds for the case of outliers (occlusions are just a special case of spatially coherent outliers). We can show that the coefficient error can get arbitrarily large by just changing a single component of **x**, which proves that the method is non-robust with a breakdown point of 0 %.

The problems that we have discussed arise because the complete set of data **x** is required to calculate a_i in a least square fashion (Eq. 8). Therefore, the method is sensitive to partial occlusions, to data containing noise and outliers, and to changing backgrounds.

Different approaches have been proposed in the literature to estimate the coefficients of the eigenspace projections more reliably: Pentland suggested the use of modular eigenspaces [30] to alleviate the problem of occlusion. Ohba and Ikeuchi [29] proposed the eigen-window method to be able to recognize partially occluded objects. The methods based on "eigen-windows" partially alleviate the problems related to occlusion but do not solve them entirely because the same limitations hold for each of the eigen-windows. Besides, due to local windows, these methods lack the *global* aspect and usually require further processing.

To eliminate the effects of varying background Murase and Nayar [24] introduced the search-window which is the AND area of the object region of all images in the training image set. This was further extended to an adaptive mask concept by Edwards and Murase [13]. However, the assumption on which the method has been developed is rather restrictive; namely, a target object can only be occluded by one or more of the other $M - 1$ target objects, rather than by some unknown background entity.

On the other hand, Black and Jepson [10] proposed to use a conventional robust M-estimator for calculating the coefficients, i. e., they replaced the standard quadratic error norm with a robust error norm. Their main focus was to show that appearance based methods can be used for tracking. Rao [32] introduced a robust hierarchical form of the MDL-based Kalman filter estimators that can tolerate significant occlusion and clutter. The limitations of this approach are similar to those of Black and Jepson. Again, the critical steps are initialization and simultaneous recovery of occluding objects.

In the following sections we review our approach, that successfully solves the problems related to occlusion, cluttered background, and outliers. The major novelty of our approach lies in the way the coefficients of the eigenimages are determined. Instead of computing the coefficients by a projection of the data onto the eigenimages, we apply random sampling and robust estimation to generate hypotheses for the model coefficients. Competing hypotheses are then subject to a selection procedure based on the Minimum Description Length (MDL) principle. The approach enables us not only to reject outliers and to deal with occlusions but also to simultaneously use multiple classes of eigenimages.

5.2   A Robust Method to Calculate the Eigenspace Coefficients

The major novelty of our approach lies [21] in the way the coefficients of the eigenimages are determined. Instead of computing the coefficients by a projection of the data onto the eigenimages (which is equivalent to determining the coefficients in a least squares manner), we achieve robustness by employing *sub-sampling*. This is the very principle of high breakdown point estimation like Least Median of Squares [34] and RANSAC [15]. In particular, our approach consists of a two-fold robust procedure: We determine the coefficients of the eigenspace projection by a robust hypothesize-and-test paradigm using only *subsets* of image points. Each hypothesis (based on a random selection of points) is generated by the robust solution of a set of linear equations (similar to α-trimmed estimators [34]). Competing hypotheses are then selected according to the Minimum Description Length principle.

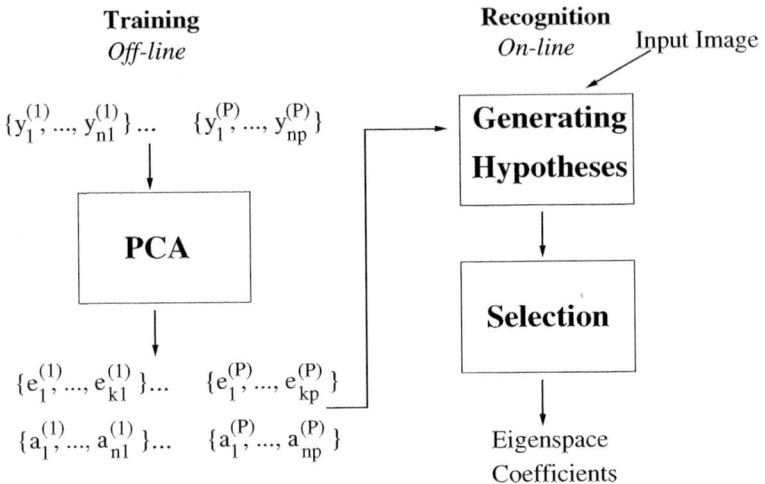

Fig. 5. A schematic diagram outlining the complete robust algorithm

The complete algorithm is shown in Fig. 5. The left side depicts the training (off-line) stage which is the same as for the standard method. The right side of Fig. 5 depicts the recognition (on-line) stage. As input, it receives the output of the training stage (eigenspaces and coefficients for each object) and the image to be recognized. At each location in the image, several hypotheses are generated for each eigenspace. The selection procedure then reasons among different hypotheses, possibly belonging to different objects, and selects those that better explain the data. Thereby, delivering automatically the number of objects, the eigenspace they belong to, and the coefficients (via the nearest neighbor search performed already at the hypotheses generation step). The following subsections detail the hypothesis generation and the selection step.

5.2.1 Generating Hypotheses.
Let us first start with a simple observation. If we take into account all eigenvectors, i.e., $p = n$, and if there is no noise in the data then in order to calculate the coefficients a_i (Eq. 8) we need only n points

$\mathbf{r} = (r_1, \ldots r_n)$. Namely, the coefficients a_i can simply be determined by solving the following system of linear equations (see Fig. 6):

$$x_{r_i} = \sum_{j=1}^{n} a_j(\mathbf{x})e_{j,r_i} \quad 1 \ldots n. \tag{13}$$

However, if we approximate each template only by a linear combination of a subset of eigenimages, i. e., $p < n$, and there is also noise present in the data, then Eq. (13) can no longer be used, but rather we have to solve an over-constrained system of equations in the least squares sense using k data points ($p < k \leq m$). In most cases $k \ll m$. Thus we seek the solution vector $\mathbf{a}$ which minimizes

$$E(\mathbf{r}) = \sum_{i=1}^{k} (x_{r_i} - \sum_{j=1}^{p} a_j(\mathbf{x})e_{j,r_i})^2. \tag{14}$$

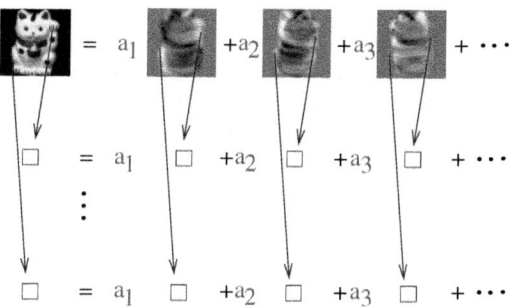

Fig. 6. Illustration of using linear equations to calculate the coefficients of eigenimages

Of course, the minimization of Eq. (14) can only produce correct values for coefficient vector $\mathbf{a}$, if the set of points r_i does not contain outliers, i.e, not only extreme noisy points but also points belonging to different backgrounds or some other templates due to occlusion. Therefore, the solution has to be sought in a robust manner. In particular we use an α-trimmed estimator to solve (14) in a robust manner (see [21] for details). Fig. 7 depicts some of the generated hypotheses for the occluded image in Fig. 8. One can see that 4 out of 8 hypotheses are close to the correct solution.

However, as depicted in Fig. 7 one can not expect that every initial randomly chosen set of points will produce a good hypothesis if there is one, despite the robust procedure. Thus, to further increase the robustness of the hypotheses generation step, i. e., increase the probability of detecting a correct hypothesis if there is one, we initiate, as in [15,3], a number of trials.

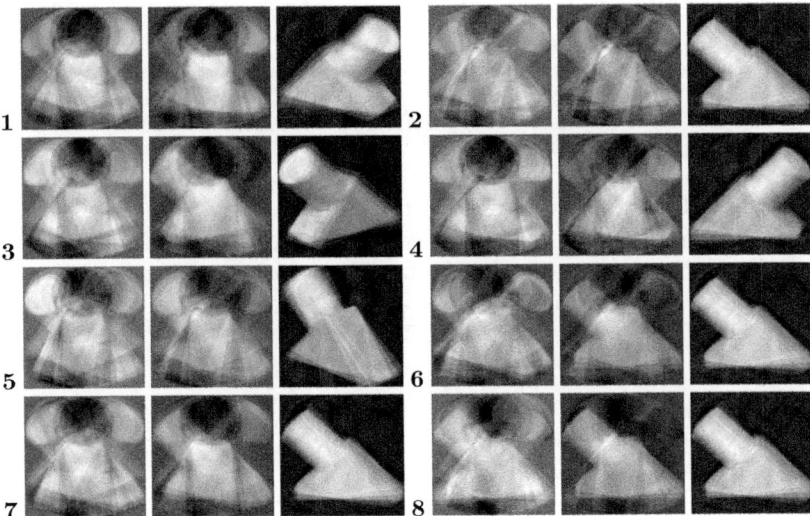

Fig. 7. Some hypotheses generated by the robust method for the occluded image in Fig. 8 with 15 eigenimages; (for each hypothesis (1–8) (from left to right): reconstructed image on the initial set of points, after reduction of 25 % of points with the largest residual error, and the reconstructed image based on the parameters of the closest point on the parametric manifold)

5.2.2   Selection. The task of the selection procedure is to select from the generated hypotheses those that correspond to objects in the scene and to reject superfluous ones. Let us suppose we know that there is only one object in the scene. In this case it is sufficient to check the reconstruction error and choose the hypothesis with the minimum reconstruction error. However, when we have multiple objects in the scene which might even overlap each other we would also like to know the number of object appearing there. In this case we have to use a more involved procedure.

We have proposed a method for solving this problem which is based on the Minimum Description Length principle (MDL) [33]. Basically we select those hypotheses that optimize the following terms:

- the number of pixels that a hypothesis encompasses is large,
- the deviations between the data and the approximation are low,
- while at the same time the number of hypotheses is minimized.

Formalization in terms of the MDL principle leads to an optimization problem whose solution selects the hypotheses which best describe the image. For a detailed derivation which is beyond the scope of this paper see [21].

5.2.3 Experimental Results.

We have extensively tested the robust procedure (see [21] for a detailed analysis) and compared it to the standard method. In the following we present some highlights from this experimental evaluation. We performed all experiments on the standard set of images (Columbia Object Image Library, COIL-20) [28]. Each object is represented in the database by 72 images obtained by the rotation of the object through 360 degrees at 5 degree steps (1440 images in total). We have used 36 images (each $10°$ apart) for training and the rest of the object for testing. Each object is represented in a separate eigenspace, and the coefficients of the eigenspace specify the orientation of the object via nearest neighbor search on the parametric manifold.

Fig. 8 demonstrates that our approach is insensitive to occlusions. One can see that the robust method outperforms the standard method considerably. Note that the blur visible in the reconstruction is the consequence of taking into account only a limited number of eigenimages.

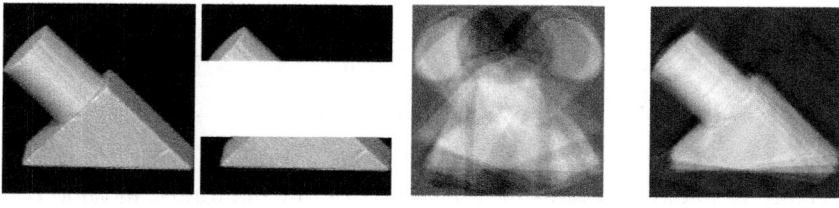

Original image   Occluded image   Reconstructed image Reconstructed image
standard method   robust method

Fig. 8. Demonstration of the effect of occlusion using the standard and robust approach for calculating the coefficients a_i

Fig. 9 demonstrates that our approach can cope with situations when one object occludes another. One can see that the robust method is able to recover both objects. One should note that in this case the selection mechanism based on the MDL principle delivers automatically that there are two objects present in the scene (i. e., we do not need to specify the number of objects in advance).

Table 1 summarizes the results on determining the pose for several objects under salt and pepper noise and occlusions. To generate the table, we used 15 eigenimages and generated 10 hypotheses. The error measure is the median of the absolute orientation error given in degrees. One can clearly see that robust method outperforms the standard method considerably.

Table 2 and Table 3 show results on an object recognition experiments for 50 % Salt and Pepper noise, and for 50 % occlusions. As for the error measure, we used the classification accuracy, and for those objects which have been correctly recognized, we also calculated the median absolute error in the orientation.

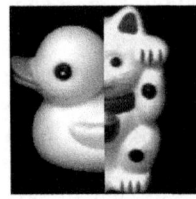 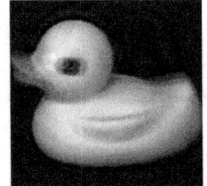 

Two objects   recovered 1st object recovered 2nd object
occluding each other

Fig. 9. Two objects occluding each other

Table 1. Summary of orientation estimation experiments (median of absolute orientation error in degrees)

Method	Salt & Pepper [%]						Occlusions [%]					
	5	20	35	50	65	80	10	20	30	40	50	60
Standard	0	0	0	5	10	10	0	0	5	95	90	90
Robust	0	0	0	0	0	0	0	0	0	0	5	40

These results clearly indicate the superiority of the robust method over the standard method. The higher error rates for the occlusion can be explained by the fact that certain objects are already completely occluded in some orientations.

Table 2. Classification results on images with 50 % Salt & Pepper noise

Method	Recognition Rate	Median absolute orientation error
Standard	46 %	50°
Robust	75 %	5°

6   Extensions

The robust approach outlined above is a step forward for appearance based methods, however, some problems still remain. In particular, the method is sensitive to illumination variations, and scale and in-plane rotation changes are difficult (also computationally expensive) to cope with. This is primarily due to the fact that the approach is based simply on sets of points which neglects the rich local structure of an image.

Table 3. Classification results on images with 50 % occlusion

Method	Recognition Rate	Median absolute orientation error
Standard	12 %	50°
Robust	66 %	5°

However, we can extend our approach to deal also with these issues. We can derive the following property which holds due to the linearity of the equation

$$(f * \mathbf{x})(r_j) = \sum_{i=1}^{p} a_i(f * \mathbf{e}_i)(r_j) \,, \tag{15}$$

where f denotes a filter and $*$ the convolution. This equation states that we can calculate the coefficients a_i from the filtered eigenimages and the filtered input image. As we have demonstrated in [9], the recovered coefficients in filtered and subsampled images remain stable when we use the robust (non-linear) estimation method. Note that the filtering and subsampling destroys the orthogonality property, therefore the standard method based on projections can not be used to recover the coefficients.

We can even go one step further (see also [8]): Let $\mathcal{F} = \{f_1, \ldots f_q\}$ denote a set of linear filters, $f * \mathcal{X} = \{f * \mathbf{x}_1, \ldots, f * \mathbf{x}_n\}$, and $\mathcal{F} * \mathcal{X} = \{f_1 * \mathcal{X}, \ldots, f_q * \mathcal{X}\} = \{f_1 * \mathbf{x}_1, \ldots, f_q * \mathbf{x}_n\}$, filtering of a set of images with a set of filters. Using a set of filters $\mathcal{F}$ we can construct a system of equations

$$(f_s * x)(r_j) = \sum_{i=1}^{p} a_i(f_s * e_i)(r_j) \quad s = 1 \ldots q \,. \tag{16}$$

Based on these observations we can discuss the potential of this approach towards the solution of the following problems:

6.1   Invariance to Scale

Since the coefficients are not affected by filtering and subsampling, we can use a multiresolution approach to calculate the coefficients efficiently: At the training stage, we compute the eigenimages from $\mathcal{Y}$ at the highest resolution, and then we construct an image pyramid of the eigenimages, e. g., a Gaussian $5 \times 5/4$ pyramid, up to a certain level.

At the matching stage, we construct the same pyramid on the input image. Then we start our hypothesize-and-test approach on the lowest resolution. At this level we perform an exhaustive search over all image locations. The selected hypotheses together with their compatible points are down-projected one level in the pyramid. There we update the coefficients on a subset of compatible points which improves the accuracy of the coefficients. This process continues until we reach the level of the highest resolution. This results in considerable savings in computation time because we perform the computationally costly steps (i. e., generating many hypotheses at each image location) on a low resolution, and then we only refine the coefficients on the higher resolutions of the image. What is more, we can also include a scale estimation step (e. g., by a gradient search) while recovering the coefficients. We start at the lowest resolution generating a set of hypotheses for each image location, for each selected hypothesis we estimate the coefficients and the scale, and then propagate the results down one pyramid level where we refine the coefficients and the scale. This process continuous until we reach the highest resolution.

Fig. 10 demonstrates how the multiresolution scale and coefficient estimation algorithm works. On the left side of the image, one can see the pyramid of the original 120 % scaled image. On the right side is the reconstructed image with the currently estimated coefficients (the size of the images has been fixed to reflect the current scale estimate). One can see that during down-projection, the scale and the coefficient estimation improves, until finally the coefficient error as well as the scale error are below 5 %.

Fig. 10. Illustration of the scale and coefficient estimation in a pyramid. On the left side the image pyramid of the original 120 % scaled image is depicted. The right side shows the reconstruction of the image with the estimated coefficients. The size of the image reflects the current scale estimate

In order to test also the robustness of the method, we applied it to the image shown in Fig. 11, where the objects appear at different scales on a complex background and also partially occluded.

Fig. 12 shows the back-projected recovered coefficients of the two cats and ducks when they were occluding each other. Fig. 12(a) shows the result of the non-scaled case, and Fig. 12(b) the result on the 120 % scaled image (the algorithm estimated the scale at 120.93 %). Fig. 12(c) shows the result of the non-scaled duck, and Fig. 12(d) the result on the 120 % scaled duck.

These results demonstrate that we do not loose the robustness of the original method by the multiresolution approach.

Fig. 11. Various objects at different scales on a complex background

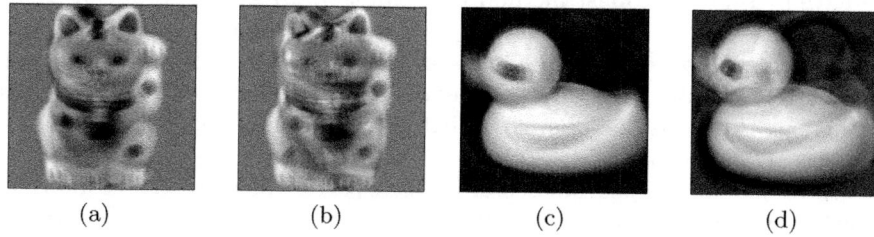

(a)   (b)   (c)   (d)

Fig. 12. Back-projected coefficients for: (a) cat occluded by duck on a complex background (not scaled), (b) 120 % scaled cat occluded by duck on a complex background (c) duck occluded by cat on a complex background (not scaled), (d) 120 % scaled duck occluded by cat on a complex background

6.2 Invariance to In-plane Rotations

Dealing with in-plane rotations of objects, usually requires in the eigenspace approach that rotated copies (e. g. 72 orientations per object for the COIL database) of the object are encompassed into the training set. This results in a huge amount of training data (e. g., for a set of 100 objects $100 \times 72 = 7200$ images have to be in the training set). Using a set of steerable filters, this can be avoided. The steerability condition [37] of the filters provides us with efficient means to calculate the filter responses from a rotated object. In particular, we can use a similar approach to the one we have used for scale estimation [9], i. e., we can simultaneously recover the eigenspace coefficients and the rotation angle.

6.3 Illumination Invariance

While the standard eigenspace methods as well as the original robust approach can not cope with varying illumination conditions, the use of filtered eigenimages offers the possibility to discount the illumination effects. Variations in the illumination are mainly related to three major effects in the images: Changes in the global illumination, highlights, and shadows. Using derivative filters in the estimation of the coefficients helps us discounting the global illumination effects, and the robust coefficient estimation procedure is insensitive to local highlights and shadows. Therefore, we can claim that the estimation of coefficients of eigenimages using local filters and a robust estimation procedure enable an illumination invariant recognition.

7   Discussion and Conclusion

In this paper we have reviewed the basic methods for appearance-based object recognition based on eigenimages. We have demonstrated how eigenimages can be used for object recognition and pose estimation. We have also identified the major limitations of the standard approach i.e, its non robustness. Based on that we have presented a robust method that can cope with these problems.

It is interesting to note that the basic steps of the proposed algorithm are the same as in ExSel++ [38], which deals with robust extraction of *analytical* parametric functions from various types of data. Therefore, the method described in this paper can also be seen as an extension of ExSel++ to *learnable classes* of parametric models.

Up to now we have considered only eigenspaces which are based on principal component analysis as a basis for object representation. We have motivated PCA by its optimality with respect to the template matching problem. However, PCA is not the only choice for appearance based object recognition. Other linear and non linear methods have been proposed for object recognition, in particular:

1. Standard PCA-based methods do not take into account that the correlation between the images (even between the images of views of a single object) may not be significant. As a consequence, the dimensionality of these eigenspaces is usually quite high. This in turn causes that the matching phase which consists of determining the coefficients of an unknown image is not efficient. Namely, such eigenspaces ignore the locally low-dimensional structure of the data. We have developed an algorithm [20] that build automatically multiple low dimensional eigenspaces that solves the above mentioned problems. There has also been some work on mixtures of PCA, cf. [18], or mixture of local linear subspaces [16].However, all these approaches require that both the number of mixture components and the dimensionality of the subspaces is a priori given.
2. Fisher spaces [5] which are based on Fishers linear discriminance analysis have been successfully used for face recognition. This representation is especially useful for object recognition because it optimizes directly the class separation.
3. Kernel PCA [36] computes the PCA in a high-dimensional feature space onto which the input data is nonlinearly mapped. To avoid the computational costs of computing the PCA in this feature space, the fact is used that this computation can be replaced by computing dot products of kernel functions in the input space. This approach is closely related to Support Vector Machines [11].

4. Independent Component Analysis [19] identifies the directions in the input vector space where the signal components are independent random variables or at least as independent as possible. Thus, from a mixture of independent signals ICA can identify the constituents provided that at most one of them is a Gaussian signal and that there are at least as many mixtures as signal sources. This has been used for separating different illuminants in object recognition [14].
5. Poggio and Edelman [31] developed a network, based on the theory of approximation of multivariate functions, that performs nonlinear interpolation between the views. More specifically, they use RBF networks which learn view-based representations from a small set of training views. Results of the recognition task using this object representation appear to be in accordance with the psychophysical experiments [12].

We have further shown in this paper that our method can recover the same eigenimage coefficients irrespective of linear filtering and subsampling of the image. This property has been used to develop an efficient multiresolution algorithm for eigenimage recovery. In contrast to previous approaches of multiresolution eigenimages, this algorithm requires only the calculation of the eigenimages at one resolution. This in turn leads to considerable computational savings at the multiresolution coefficient estimation stage, because the coefficients need not be re-calculated at each level but just refined. We have then demonstrated how this algorithm can be combined with a scale estimation algorithm in order to be able to deal with scaled images. Further, we have discussed that by the same approach can be used to deal with different illuminations and in-plane rotations.

The usage of local filters for the recovery of eigenimage coefficients is particularly interesting because it allows us to switch between the global eigenspace representation and the more local representation using a set of filters. In fact we have demonstrated that we can use both representations in one system [8]. All these should lead to an object recognition system which is fully applicable in real world situations.

References

1. *Object Recognition in Man, Monkey, and Machine.* MIT Press, 1999. 246
2. T. W. Anderson. *An Introduction to Multivariate Statistical Analysis.* New York: Wiley, 1958. 248
3. A. Bab-Hadiashar and D. Suter. Optic flow calculation using robust statistics. In *Proc. CVPR'97*, pages 988–993, 1997. 255
4. P. Baldi and K. Hornik. Learning in linear neural networks: A survey. *IEEE Transactions on Neural Networks*, 6(4):837–858, 1995. 250
5. P. Belhumeuer, J. Hespanha, and D. Kriegman. Eigenfaces vs. fischerfaces: Recognition using class specific projection. In *Proc. ECCV*, pages 45–58. Springer, 1996. 262
6. D. Beymer and T. Poggio. Face recognition from one example view. In *Proceedings of 5th ICCV'95*, pages 500–507. IEEE Computer Society Press, 1995. 246

7. I. Biederman. Recognition by components: A theory of human image understanding. *Psychological Review*, 94:115–147, 1987. 246

8. H. Bischof and A. Leonardis. Recovery of eigenimages from responses of local filter banks. In R. Sablatnig, editor, *Applications of 3D-Imaging and Graph-based Modelling 2000*, volume 142 of *OCG Schriftenreihe*, pages 121–128. Österreichische Computer Gesellschaft, 2000. 259, 263

9. Horst Bischof and Aleš Leonardis. Robust recognition of scaled eigenimages through a hierarchical approach. In *Proc. of CVPR98*, pages 664–670. IEEE Compter Society Press, 1998. 259, 261

10. M. Black and A. Jepson. Eigentracking: Robust matching and tracking of articulated objects using a view-based representation. *International Journal of Computer Vision*, 26(1):63–84, 1998. 253

11. H. Bourlard and Y. Kamp. Auto-association by multilayer perceptrons and singular value decomposition. *Biological Cybernetics*, 59:291–294, 1988. 251

12. H. H. Bülthosf, S. Y. Edelman, and M. Tarr. How are three-dimensional objects represented in the brain? Technical Report A. I. Memo No. 1479, C. B. C. L. Paper No. 9, Massachusetts Institute of Technology, 1994. 263

13. J. Edwards and H. Murase. Appearance matching of occluded objects using coarse-to-fine adaptive masks. In *Proc. CVPR'97*, pages 533–539, 1997. 253

14. H. Farid and E. H. Adelson. Separating reflections and lighting using independent components analysis. In *CVPR99*, pages I:262–267, 1999. 263

15. M. A. Fischler and R. C. Bolles. Random sample consensus: A paradigm for model fitting with applications to image analysis and automated cartography. *Communications ACM*, 24(6):381–395, June 1981. 254, 255

16. B. J. Frey, A. Colmenarez, and T. S. Huang. Mixtures of local linear subspaces for face recognition. In *Proc. CVPR98*, pages 32–37. IEEE Computer Society, 1998. 262

17. P. M. Hall, D. Marshall, and R. R. Martin. Incremental eigenanalysis for classification. TR 98001, Dept. of Computer Science, Univ. of Cardiff, 1998. 251

18. Geoffrey E Hinton, Michael Revow, and Peter Dayan. Recognizing handwritten digits using mixtures of linear models. In G. Tesauro, D. Touretzky, and T. Leen, eds, *NIPS*, volume 7, pages 1015–1022. The MIT Press, 1995. 262

19. A. Hyvärinen and E. Oja. Independent component analysis: algorithms and applications. *Neural Networks*, 13(4–5):411–431, 2000. 263

20. Ales Leonardis and Horst Bischof. Multiple Eigenspaces by MDL (in press). In *Proceedings of ICPR2000*. IEEE Computer Society, 2000. 262

21. Aleš Leonardis and Horst Bischof. Robust recognition using eigenimages. *Computer Vision and Image Understanding*, 78(1):99–118, 2000. 253, 255, 256, 257

22. David Marr. *Vision*. New York: Freeman, 1982. 246

23. B. Moghaddam and A. Pentland. Probabilistic visual learning for object representation. *IEEE Trans. PAMI*, 19(7):696, 1997. 250

24. H. Murase and S. K. Nayar. Image spotting of 3D objects using parametric eigenspace representation. In G. Borgefors, editor, *The 9th Scandinavian Conference on Image Analysis*, volume 1, pages 323–332, Uppsala, Sweden, June 1995. 246, 253

25. H. Murase and S. K. Nayar. Visual learning and recognition of 3-D objects from appearance. *International Journal of Computer Vision*, 14:5–24, 1995. 246, 250, 251

26. H. Murase and S. K. Nayar. Illumination planning for object recognition using parametric eigenspaces. *IEEE Trans. on Pattern Analysis and Machine Intelligence*, 16(12):1219–1227, 1994. 246, 248

27. S. K. Nayar, H. Murase, and S. A. Nene. Learning, positioning, and tracking visual appearance. In *IEEE International Conference on Robotics and Automation*, San Diego, May 1994. 246

28. S. A. Nene, S. K. Nayar, and H. Murase. Columbia object image library (COIL-20). Technical Report CUCS-005-96, Columbia University, New York, 1996. 249, 257

29. K. Ohba and K. Ikeuchi. Detectability, uniqueness, and reliability of eigen windows for stable verification of partially occluded objects. *PAMI*, 9:1043–1047, 1997. 253

30. A. Pentland, B. Moghaddam, and T. Straner. View-based and modular eigenspaces for face recognition. Technical Report 245, MIT Media Laboratory, 1994. 253

31. T. Poggio and S. Edelman. A network that learns to recognize three-dimensional objects. *Nature*, 343:263–266, 1990. 248, 263

32. R. Rao. Dynamic appearance-based recognition. In *CVPR'97*, pages 540–546. IEEE Computer Society, 1997. 253

33. J. Rissanen. *Stochastic Complexity in Statistical Inquiry*, volume 15 of *Series in Computer Science*. World Scientific, 1989. 256

34. P. J. Rousseeuw and A. M. Leroy. *Robust Regression and Outlier Detection*. Wiley, New York, 1987. 254

35. S. Chandrasekaran, B. S. Manjunath, Y. F. Wang, J. Winkler, and H. Zhang. An eigenspace update algorithm for image analysis. Technical Report TR CS 96-04, Dept. of Computer Science, Univ. of California, Santa Barbara, 1996. 251

36. B. Schölkopf, A. Smola, and K. R. Müller. Nonlinear component analysis as a kernel eigenvalue problem. *Neural Computation*, 10(5):1299–1319, 1998. 262

37. E. Simoncelli and H. Farid. Steerable wedge filters for local orientation analysis. *IEEE Trans. on Image Processing*, pages 1–15, 1996. 261

38. M. Stricker and A. Leonardis. ExSel++: A general framework to extract parametric models. In V. Hlavac and R. Sara, editors, *6th CAIP'95*, number 970 in Lecture Notes in Computer Science, pages 90–97, Prague, Czech Republic, September 1995. Springer. 262

39. M. Turk and A. Pentland. Eigenfaces for recognition. *Journal of Cognitive Neuroscience*, 3(1):71–86, 1991. 246, 248, 250

40. Shimon Ullman. *High-level Vision*. MIT Press, 1996. 248

41. V. N. Vapnik. *The Nature of Statistical Learning Theory*. Springer, 1995. 262

42. S. Yoshimura and T. Kanade. Fast template matching based on the normalized correlation by using multiresolution eigenimages. In *Proceedings of IROS'94*, pages 2086–2093, 1994. 246, 248

Information Mining:
Applications in Image Processing

Rudolf Kruse and Aljoscha Klose

Dept. of Knowledge Processing and Language Engineering
Otto-von-Guericke-University of Magdeburg
D-39106 Magdeburg, Germany
rudolf.kruse@cs.uni-magdeburg.de

Abstract. In response to an explosive growth of collected, stored, and transferred data, *Data Mining* has emerged as a new research area. However, the approaches studied in this area are mostly specialized to analyze precise and highly structured data. Other sources of information — for instance images — have often been neglected. The term *Information Mining* wants to emphasize the need for methods suited for more heterogeneous and imprecise information sources. We also claim the importance of fuzzy set methods to meet the prominent aim of to producing comprehensible results. Two case studies of applying information mining techniques to remotely sensed image data are presented.

1 Introduction

With computers and sensor technology evolving at a fast pace, it becomes possible today to generate, collect, store, and transfer huge amounts of data at very low costs. Thus an increasing number of companies and scientific and governmental institutions can afford to build up large archives of data in various forms like numbers, tables, documents, images, or sounds. However, exploiting the information contained in these archives in an intelligent way turns out to be fairly difficult. In contrast to the abundance of data, there is a lack of tools that can transform these data into useful information and knowledge. Although a user often has a vague understanding of his data and their meaning and can usually formulate hypotheses and guess dependencies, he rarely knows where to find the "interesting" or "relevant" pieces of information, or whether (other) interesting phenomena are hidden in the data. It is often hard to say, which methods are best suited to find the needed pieces of information in a fast and reliable way, and how the data can be translated into human notions that are appropriate for the context in which they are needed.

In reply to these challenges a new area of research has emerged, which has been named "Knowledge Discovery in Databases" or "Data Mining". The research in knowledge discovery in databases and data mining combines techniques from a variety of disciplines. Current efforts aim at standardizing the knowledge discovery process and have lead to a number of suggestions for general models. A recent suggestion for such a model, which can be expected to

V. Hlaváč, K. G. Jeffery, and J. Wiedermann (Eds.): SOFSEM 2000, LNCS 1963, pp. 266–285, 2000
© Springer-Verlag Berlin Heidelberg 2000

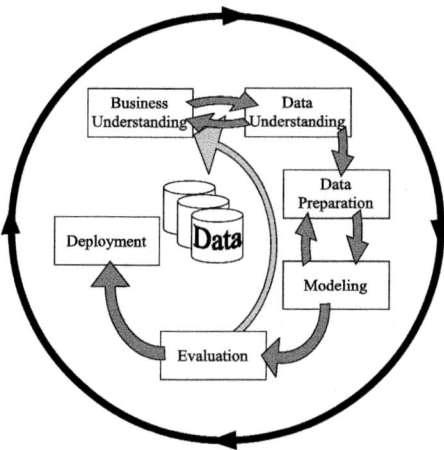

Fig. 1. The CRISP-DM Model

have considerable impact, since it is backed by several large companies like NCR, SPSS and DaimlerChrysler, is the CRISP-DM model (CRoss Industry Standard Process for Data Mining) [3].

The basic structure of this process model is depicted in Figure 1. The *business understanding* and *data understanding* phases are usually strongly human centered and only little automation can be achieved here. These phases serve mainly to define the goals of the knowledge discovery project, to estimate its potential benefit, and to identify and collect the necessary data. In addition, background domain knowledge and meta-knowledge about the data is gathered.

In the *data preparation* step, the gathered data are cleaned, transformed and eventually scaled to produce the input for the *modeling* phase, in which models are constructed from the data in order, for instance, to predict future developments, to build classifiers, or to discover dependencies.

In the *evaluation* phase the results are tested and their quality is assessed. The results can provide new insights into the domain under consideration. The circle in Figure 1 indicates that data mining is essentially an iterative process, in which the evaluation of the results often leads to a re-execution of the data preparation and model generation steps.

1.1 Moving toward Information Mining

Although the standard definition of knowledge discovery and data mining [8] only speaks of discovery in *data*, thus not restricting the type and the organization of the data to work on, it has to be admitted that research up to now concentrated on highly structured data. Usually a minimal requirement is relational data. Most methods (e. g. classical methods like decision trees and neural networks) even demand as input a single uniform table, i. e., a set of tuples of attribute values. It is obvious, however, that this paradigm for mining is hardly applicable to image or sound data or even textual descriptions, since it is inappropriate to see such data as, say, tuples of picture elements.

Another important point to be made is the following: The fact that pure neural networks are often seen as data mining methods, although their learning result (matrices of numbers) is hardly interpretable, shows that in contrast to the standard definition the goal of *understandable* patterns is often neglected. Of course, there are applications where comprehensible results are not needed and, for example, the prediction accuracy of a classifier is the only criterion of success. Therefore interpretable results should not be seen as a *conditio sine qua non*. However, our own experience — gathered in several cooperations with industry — is that modern technologies are accepted more readily, if the methods applied are easy to understand and the results can be checked against human intuition. In addition, if we want to gain insight into a domain, training, for instance, a neural network is not of much help.

Therefore we suggest to concentrate on *information mining*, which we see as an extension of data mining and which can be defined in analogy to the KDD definition given in [8] as follows:

> Information mining is the non-trivial process of identifying valid, novel, potentially useful, and *understandable* patterns in *heterogeneous information sources.* [24]

The term *information* is thus meant to indicate two things: In the first place, it points out that the heterogeneous sources to mine can already provide *information*, understood as expert background knowledge, textual descriptions, images and sounds etc., and not only raw data. Secondly, it emphasizes that the results must be *comprehensible* ("must provide a user with information"), so that a user can check their plausibility and can get insight into the domain the data comes from.

For research this results in the challenges to develop techniques that can extract knowledge from large, dynamic, multi-relational, and multi-medial information sources, and to close the semantic gap between structured data and human notions and concepts, i.e., to be able to translate computer representations into human notions and concepts and vice versa.

The goal of fuzzy systems has always been to model human expert knowledge and to produce systems that are easy to understand. Therefore we expect fuzzy systems technology to play a prominent role in the quest to meet these challenges. In the following we try to point out how fuzzy techniques can help to do information mining.

1.2   Significance of Fuzzy Set Methods in Information Mining

Some well-known analysis methods and tools that are used in data mining are, for instance, statistics (regression analysis, discriminant analysis etc.), time series analysis, decision trees, cluster analysis, neural networks, inductive logic programming, and association rules.

Classical models usually try to avoid vague, imprecise or uncertain information, because it is considered to have a negative influence on an inference process. In contrast to this, natural language, which is a human's most effective tool to structure his experience and to model his environment, is inherently subject to imprecision. The reason for this efficiency despite the inherent vagueness is that for practical purposes full precision is often not necessary and may even be a waste of resources.

Therefore, in order to represent the background knowledge of human experts (e. g. in the business and data understanding phases) and to arrive at understandable data mining results (to be suitable for evaluation), it is absolutely necessary to model linguistic terms and do what Zadeh so pointedly called *computing with words* [39].

Fuzzy set theory provides excellent means to model the "fuzzy" boundaries of linguistic terms by introducing gradual memberships. In contrast to classical set theory, in which an object or a case either is a member of a given set (defined, e. g., by some property) or not, fuzzy set theory makes it possible that an object or a case belongs to a set only to a certain degree [25]. Interpretations of membership degrees include similarity, preference, and uncertainty [5]: They can state how similar an object or case is to a prototypical one, they can indicate preferences between suboptimal solutions to a problem, or they can model uncertainty about the true situation, if this situation is described in imprecise terms. It is obvious that all of these interpretations are needed in applications and thus it is not surprising that they all have proven useful for solving practical problems.

In general, due to their closeness to human reasoning, solutions obtained using fuzzy approaches are easy to understand and to apply. Due to these strengths, fuzzy systems are the method of choice, if linguistic, vague, or imprecise information has to be modeled [24]. However, they also turned out to be worth considering when non-linguistic, but imprecise, i. e., set-valued information has to be modeled.

In data analysis fuzzy sets are used in several ways [1]. We use fuzzy set methods in two ways: As a general and intuitive means to model domain knowledge and problem specific measures, where the extension of classical set theory is most important; and, more specific, we use fuzzy sets to model linguistic terms and use them in fuzzy if-then rules. The antecedent of such a fuzzy rule consists of fuzzy descriptions of input values, and the consequent defines a — possibly fuzzy — output value for the given input. A common way to use such fuzzy rule systems in data analysis is to induce the rules from data. The data driven induction of fuzzy systems by simple heuristics based on local computations is usually called *neuro-fuzzy* [29]. This aspect will be presented in more detail in Section 2.2 in our first case study.

1.3 Images as Heterogeneous Sources of Information

Images can be a natural and rich source of information for humans. In spite of decades of intensive research, machine vision is still far from being competitive to the human visual system. This applies especially to small numbers of images. However, there are many successful applications of automated image processing, including areas with lots of images and strongly repetitive tasks. These tasks often go beyond a manually analyzable scope.

There are several current developments that lead to extreme increases in the number of accessible images. The most important developments are the spreading of the world wide web, and the advances in sensor technology and improved transmission and storage possibilities, as it can be observed in remote sensing.

The world wide web has become an enormous distributed, heterogeneous and unstructured source of information. While its textual parts can more or less be handled with current search engines, the information contained in the images is hardly accessible automatically. Indexing and retrieval of image databases are still in their infancy. Content based image retrieval, where queries are performed by color, texture, and shape of image objects and regions, is a current research topic [7,10,36].

Another area with enormous amounts of data being gathered is remote sensing. Due to technological advances, the analysts of remotely sensed imagery are confronted with huge amounts of data today. Especially the integration of multi-sensor data calls for support of the observer by automatic image processing algorithms.

The following is a list of some prominent examples of such giant image databases (which, however, could easily be extended):

- the classification of (about 5×10^8) stellar objects in about 3 terabytes of sky images reported in the POSS-II sky survey project [8],
- the search for volcanos in about 30.000 radar images of the surface of the Venus in the Magellan study [9], or
- the mosaicing of thousands of high resolution satellite images of the Earth to a large continuous image [11].

An essential aim of information mining in large image databases is to direct the user's attention. For images, traditional data mining techniques will almost always work hand in hand with automatic image processing techniques.

In the following we present two examples which slightly differ from that view: We analyze data that were gathered during image processing. In these applications the aim is to gain insight into and to improve the vision process itself.

2   First Case Study: Analyzing the Machine Vision Process

2.1   Domain and Task

The domain of our studies is the "screening" of collections of high resolution aerial images for man-made structures. Applications of this include remote reconnaissance, or image registration, where man-made structures deliver valuable alignment hints.

The automatic analysis of man-made objects in remotely sensed images is a challenging task. In the framework of structural analysis of complex scenes, a blackboard-based production system (BPI) is presented in [35].

The image processing starts with extracting object primitives (i. e. edges) from the image, and then uses production rules to combine them to more and more complex intermediate objects. The algorithm stops when either no more productions apply or the modeled high level object is detected [33,34].

The following analyses have been done in a cooperation [21]. We considered a concept hierarchy for the screening of runways and airfields. The rules for this concept state that collinear adjacent (short) lines are concatenated to *longer lines*. If their length exceeds a certain threshold they meet the concept *long lines*. The productions used to extend *long lines* allow to bridge larger gaps caused by crossing taxiways or image distortions. If these *long lines* meet certain properties they may be used to generate *runway lines*, which could be part of a runway. Parallel *runway lines* with a given distance to each other are composed to *runway stripes*. In a last step these stripes may be identified as *runways*.

Although we considered only runways, the production net approach can be used for all kinds of stripe-like objects. It can be adapted to a variety of tasks by a number of parameters. The model was developed to be used with image data from different sensors, e. g. visible, infrared, or synthetic aperture radar (SAR). It delivers successful results.

Figure 2a shows an example image with the extracted edge segments, Figure 2b shows the detected runway as a result of applying the production system. The analysis of the process for this image shows that only 20 lines of about 37,000 are used to construct this stripe (see Figure 3a). However, the analyzing system takes all of the lines into account. As the time consumption is at least $O(n^2)$, the processing can take quite a while.

The idea of our analyses was that the production process could significantly be sped up, if only the most promising primitive objects are identified, and the analysis is started with them. The idea is to extract features from the image that describe the primitive objects and train a classifier to decide which lines can be discarded. Due to its suitability for information mining we applied the neuro-fuzzy classifier NEFCLASS to this task. The next section will briefly outline its concepts and appealing features.

2.2   NEFCLASS: A State-of-the-Art Neuro-fuzzy Classifier

When fuzzy systems and neural networks are combined to neuro-fuzzy systems the aim is quite intuitive: We use a fuzzy system to represent knowledge in an interpretable manner and borrow the learning ability of neural networks to determine membership values. The drawbacks of both of the individual approaches — the black box behavior common to neural networks, and the problems to find suitable membership values for fuzzy systems — could thus be avoided. A combination can constitute an interpretable model which can use problem-specific prior knowledge, and which is capable of learning, i. e. capable of being induced

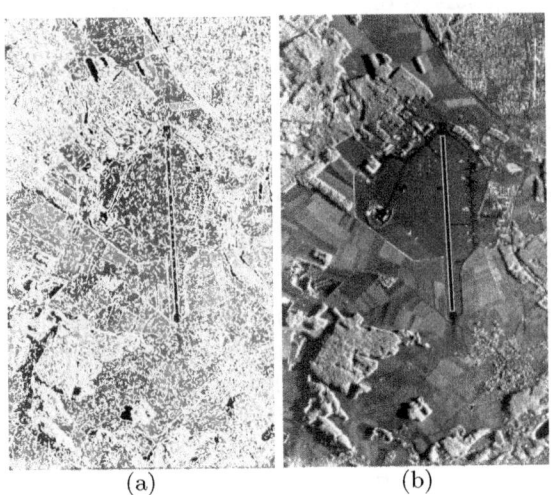

(a)   (b)

Fig. 2. (a) 37,659 lines extracted from SAR image by Burns' edge detector (short segments overlayed in white), (b) runway found by production net

from sample data. This usually implies two phases: induction of the structure (the rule base) and adaptation of the connection weights (the fuzzy sets).

NEFCLASS belongs to the class of structure-oriented approaches that provide (initial) fuzzy sets and thus structure the data space by a multidimensional fuzzy grid. A rule base is created by selecting those grid cells that contain data. This can be done in a single pass through the training data. This way of learning fuzzy rules was suggested in [37] and extended in the NEFCLASS model [29].

After the rule base of a fuzzy system has been generated, the membership functions must be fine-tuned in order to improve the performance. In the NEF-CLASS model the fuzzy sets are modified by simple backpropagation-like heuristics. In the learning phase constraints are used to ensure that the fuzzy sets still fit their associated linguistic terms after learning. For example, membership functions of adjacent linguistic terms must not change position and must overlap to a certain degree [29].

The NEFCLASS model has been continuously improved and extended over the last years, with several implementations for different machine platforms. The most recent version — NEFCLASS-J — has been implemented in Java, which allows platform independence to a large extent. The implementation allows flexible choices, for instance, of the shape of fuzzy sets or the inference functions (conjunction, disjunction) to be used [31]. Additionally, many of the current extensions of the NEFCLASS model are included in this implementation. Most of these extensions address the specific characteristics and problems of real world data and its analysis, like

- symbolic attributes,
- missing values,
- pruning techniques for improved comprehensibility of the rule base,
- unbalanced class frequencies.

The extensions will be outlined in the next few sections. The NEFCLASS-J program is — like the previous versions — publicly available from our web site at http://fuzzy.cs.uni-magdeburg.de.

2.2.1 Symbolic Attributes. Real world data often contains symbolic (class-valued) information. Data mining algorithms that expect numerical (real valued) attributes, usually transform these attributes to a artificial metric scales. However, it would be useful to be able to create fuzzy rules directly from data with symbolic attributes. NEFCLASS has been extended to deal with symbolic data by using mixed fuzzy rules.

Let us consider two attributes x and y, where $x \in X \subseteq \mathbb{R}$ is continuous and $y \in Y = \{A, B, C\}$ is symbolic (categorical). In a fuzzy rule we describe values of x by linguistic terms. We use *lvalue* to denote linguistic terms (like *small*, *approximately zero*, *large*, etc.). In a mixed fuzzy rule using two variables we can have the following situations:

- fuzzy-exact: if x is *lvalue* and $y = A$ then ...
- fuzzy-imprecise: if x is *lvalue* and $y \in \{B, C\}$ then ...
- fuzzy-fuzzy: if x is *lvalue* and y is $\{(A, \mu(A)), (B, \mu(B)), (C, \mu(C))\}$ then ...

In the first two cases the symbolic variable y has a "switching function" for a rule. If y does not assume one of the values noted in the respective y-term of the antecedent, the rule is not applicable at all. But if y does assume any of these values, the applicability of the rule is not restricted by this argument, and the degree of fulfillment only depends on the value for x.

In the third situation, we use a fuzzy set to describe the value that y may assume, by simply attaching a degree of membership to each element of Y using some membership function $\mu\colon Y \to [0, 1]$. By giving some value to $\mu(y)$ we can now restrict the applicability of the rule to any degree between 0 and 1. Obviously case (i) and (ii) are just special cases of case (iii), because we can replace $y = A$ by y is $\{(A, 1), (B, 0), (C, 0)\}$ and $y \in \{A, B\}$ by y is $\{(A, 1), (B, 1), (C, 0)\}$.

Because the elements of Y are not ordered, we cannot easily use a linguistic term to label fuzzy sets like $\{(A, \mu(A)), (B, \mu(B)), (C, \mu(C))\}$. This means the interpretability of the rules is restricted compared to fuzzy rules that just use variables on metric scales [30].

2.2.2 Missing Values. Missing values are common in many applications. Due to problems like high costs, faulty sensors, or errors in recording, some records may have unknown values for some attributes. Trivial pre-processing approaches, like removing incomplete records from the data, or not using attributes with missing values, are not satisfactory as they waste potentially valuable information. More sophisticated methods try to impute — i. e. estimate and replace — the missing values [14,4,28].

For NEFCLASS we use the following simple strategy [31]. If a feature is missing, we do not make any assumptions about its value but assume that any value may be possible. Based on this assumption we do not want to restrict the application of a fuzzy rule to a pattern with missing features. This means a missing value will not influence the computation of the degree of fulfillment of a rule. This can be done by assigning 1.0 as the degree of membership to the missing feature [2], i. e. a missing value has a degree of membership of 1.0 with any fuzzy set. A pattern where all features are missing would then fulfill any rule of the fuzzy rule base with a degree of 1.0, i. e. any class would be possible for such a pattern. The same method of treating missing values can be used in the learning phases. When we encounter a missing value during rule creation, any fuzzy set can be included in the antecedent for the corresponding variable. Therefore we create all combinations of fuzzy sets that are possible for the current training pattern. Similarly, as we have no information about the true value of an missing attribute value, the corresponding fuzzy sets remain unchanged by the fine-tuning heuristic.

2.2.3 Pruning Techniques.

When a rule base is induced from data it often has too many rules to be easily readable, and thus gives little insight into the structures of the data. Therefore, to reduce the rule base, NEFCLASS uses different pruning techniques [29]. The pruning strategies are given in the following list.

- Pruning by correlation: The variable that has the smallest influence on the classification is deleted. To identify this variable statistical measures like correlations and χ^2 tests or information theoretic measures like information gain can be used.
- Pruning by merging: If adjacent rules predict the same class, they can be combined into one rule [23,22]. These methods are especially effective in both, raising generalization ability and reducing the number of rules.
- Pruning by classification frequency: The rule that yields the largest degree of fulfillment in the least number of cases is deleted.
- Pruning by redundancy: The linguistic term that yields the minimal degree of membership in an active rule in the least number of cases is deleted.
- Pruning by fuzziness: The fuzzy set with the largest support is identified and all terms that use this fuzzy set are removed from the antecedents of all rules.

2.2.4 Learning from Unbalanced Data.

In many practical domains — like in ours — the available training data is more or less unbalanced, i. e. the number of cases of each class varies. This causes problems for many classification systems and their associated learning algorithms. This is especially obvious if the classes are not well separated. A typical example is a marketing database, where the task of the classifier is to identify 'good' customers, e. g. to focus mailing activities. A classifier is trained from historical data of 'good' and 'bad' customers. As response rates of mailings are typically pretty small, there are only few positive examples. Moreover, these can be very similar to the negative cases and proper separation is not possible. Classifiers tend to predict the majority class, which is completely reasonable to minimize the error measure, but does not take into account the special semantics of the problem: It is not the same if a good customer is classified as bad or vice versa. A mailing to a bad customer costs merely more than the postage, while ignoring a good customer means a bigger financial loss. A straightforward way to model this asymmetry would be to directly specify the costs of every possible misclassification. This has become possible with NEFCLASS by introducing a matrix M containing the misclassification costs. This is basically a n by $(n+1)$ matrix, where the m_{ij} represent the costs caused if the system classifies a pattern of class i as class j, or as ambiguous ($j = n+1$). The diagonal elements m_{ii} are usually equal to 0, all other elements are set to 1 by default. If the domain bears asymmetries of the classes this matrix allows rather fine and intuitive specification of the errors.

The necessary modifications of the NEFCLASS model were a modification of the performance measures to take into account the misclassification cost matrix, a new learning algorithm to minimize the total costs, and an adaptation of the most important pruning techniques to incorporate the cost matrix. A detailed description of the changes can be found in [21].

These modifications allow to use NEFCLASS in domains with even highly unbalanced class frequencies, where many classifiers fail.

2.3 Application and Results

In the study described in [21] a set of 17 images depicting 5 different airports was used. Each of the images was analyzed by the production net to detect the runway(s) and the lines were labeled as positive if they were used for runway construction or negative else. 4 of the 17 images form the training dataset used to train NEFCLASS. The training set contains 253 runway lines and $31,330$ negatives.

Experiments showed that the regions next to the lines bear useful information. For each line a set of statistical (e. g. mean and standard deviation) and textural features (e. g. energy, entropy, etc.) was calculated from the gray values next to that line.

It needs to be taken into account, that the semantics of misclassifications in this task were asymmetric. The positive lines are the minority class and thus easily ignored by a classifier. However, every missed positive can turn out to be very expensive, as it can hinder successful object recognition. Misclassifying negative lines just increases processing time. With NEFCLASS this could be considered by specifying asymmetric misclassification costs. Thus, the costs of false negatives have empirically been set to 300 times the costs of false positives. After learning, the NEFCLASS pruning techniques were used to reduce

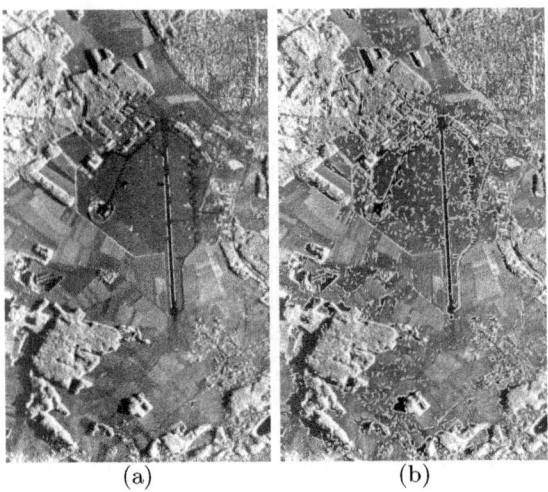

(a)   (b)

Fig. 3. (a) The 20 lines for the construction of the runway (b) 3, 281 lines classified as positive by modified NEFCLASS

the number of rules from over 500 to under 20. The best result was obtained with 16 rules.

The lines from the remaining 13 images were used as test data. The quality of the result could be characterized by a detection and a reduction rate: The detection rate is defined as the ratio of correctly detected positives to all positives. The higher this value is, the higher the probability for a successful recognition is. The average detection rate on the unseen images was 84 %, and varies from 50 % to 100 %. The second measure is the reduction rate, which is defines as the ratio of lines classified as positive to the total number of lines. The lower this value is, the shorter the processing time will be. The average reduction rate on the unseen images was 17 %. For most of the images — even with lower detection rates — the image analysis was successful, as the missed lines are mainly shorter and less important. Figure 9b shows the lines NEFCLASS classified as positive in the example image, which was one of the unseen images. On this image the number of lines was reduced to one tenth, which means a reduction of processing time to under 1 %.

3   Second Case Study: Mining for Images Similarities

3.1   Domain and Task

This second example examines the same image processing algorithm as the first, namely the extraction of runways or other man-made objects from aerial images. However, task and motivation are somewhat different.

The production nets described in Section 2.1 are parameterized by a set of parameters. Typical examples of parameters are thresholds like the maximum length of a gap that may be bridged, or the minimal and maximal distance between two long lines to build a stripe. By these parameters the algorithms can be adapted to the specific image data.

However, the adaptation of the parameters to varying scenarios, different applications and changing image material is not always obvious. Some of these parameters depend on the geometric features of the modeled objects. For example, the exact descriptions of airfields can be taken from maps or construction plans. Thus we can specify intervals, how long or wide runways can be in the real world. Together with knowledge about sensor type, sensor parameters, image resolution and image scaling of a specific image we can determine the parameter values in the pixel domain. These parameters are called *model parameters.*

Other parameter values cannot be derived from this easy accessible image information. Parameters like maximum tolerated deviations from collinearity of lines, or parameters of the (low level) edge detection strongly depend on the image quality (e. g. low contrast, blurred images, low signal-to-noise ratio, partial occlusions). These so-called *tolerance parameters* may also depend on meta data like sensor type and image resolution.

In our case, after fixing all known model parameters to suitable values, there are still more than ten variable parameters for the whole processing chain.

However, human experts with experience and profound knowledge about the algorithms can often find reasonable parameter settings by looking at the image, often with just a few tries. Unfortunately, the experts can hardly explain their intuitive tuning procedure. Therefore, we investigated approaches to support and automate the adaptation of the image processing to changing requirements. We try to discover relationships between image properties and optimal parameters by using data mining techniques.

To analyze the dependencies, we need a set of example images with corresponding optimal parameter values. Our first step was to set up a database of sample images with varying quality and from different sensors. When choosing the images we had to make a compromise. On the one hand, we have to cover a certain variety of images to obtain statistically significant results. On the other hand we can only process a limited number of images due to time restrictions. The optimization implies many iterations of the structural analysis, which can be quite time-consuming, as these images have quite high resolutions. To stay within tolerable processing time spans of several days, we had to limit the database to initially 50 images (Figure 4 shows two examples). However, it may turn out that this data does not contain the necessary information and needs to be extended.

For all images in our database we manually defined a ground truth, i. e. the exact position of the runways. We defined a measure to assess the results of edge detection, i. e. to assess how well extracted line segments match a runway defined in the ground truth.

Fig. 4. Images from the sample database

The structural image analysis was then embedded in an evolutionary optimization loop, and tolerance parameters were determined to maximize the assessment measure [20].

3.1.1   System Identification. Our first suggestion for the problem of finding a suited parameter tuple $p \in P$ for a given image $i \in I$ was to assume a set of suited image features $f_1(i), \ldots, f_n(i) \in \mathbb{R}$ and a function $\phi \colon \mathbb{R}^n \to P$ such that $p = \phi(f_1(i), \ldots, f_n(i))$. If we had appropriate image features, finding ϕ could be understood as a regression or function approximation task, for which a set of standard techniques exists.

We experimented with a set of features that were adopted versions of those that prove to be useful in the line filtering study from Section 2. The results are described in [20]. It turned out, that the ad hoc choice of image features was not satisfactory. The main problem of this approach is that we do not know which image features represent the relevant information for parameter selection. It may even turn out, that such features do not exist or are too complex to be calculated in a reasonable time.

3.1.2   Clustering Images. Another initial idea was to group similar images and then determine a commonly suited parameter tuple for each group. This approach would have several advantages over the parameter regression approach. Most important, by finding optimal parameters not for single images, but for groups of images, we prefer more generally suited parameters and thus avoid optima of very limited local extent. In that way, the parameters will probably be more robust for new images. Determination of parameters for a new image means finding the most similar group and use the corresponding parameters.

The search for groups of objects is a task of cluster analysis [16]. However, from our previous analyses [20] we conclude, that we should avoid to use image features until we know which features reflect relevant information.

The key to our solution is to analyze image 'behavior'. If we find groups of images that behave similar with respect to different parameters — i. e. commonly yield good results for some parameters and commonly worse results for others — we can in a second step analyze what these groups have in common. This may in turn support the finding of hypotheses for suitable image features.

Analyzing the common behavior can be done by applying *the same* set of parameter tuples to *all* images and analyze the assessments of the result. If we use a set of parameter tuples and apply these to each image, we get a corresponding set of assessment values for each image, forming an *assessment vector*, which characterizes image behavior. In that way, we do not directly use the parameter space for analysis, neither do we need image features.

However, an adequate meaning of *similar* has to be defined. We use fuzzy measures to define an appropriate similarity measure. Fuzzy set theory offers a flexible tool to incorporate our knowledge about the domain into this definition. Many standard cluster analysis algorithms rely on numeric (i. e. real valued) data and standard metrics like the Euclidean distance. The use of nonstandard similarity or distance measures makes other cluster methods necessary. Suitable methods are hierarchical clustering [16], or partitioning methods using evolutionary algorithms [6]. Hierarchical clustering algorithms are relatively fast, due to their straightforward mechanism, but they tend to run into local optima and thus can deliver unstable results. Therefore, we decided to use evolutionary clustering algorithms.

3.2   Evolutionary Cluster Analysis

Evolutionary algorithms have been established as widely applicable global optimization methods [12,15,27]. The mimicking of biological reproduction schemes has been successfully applied to all kinds of combinatorial problems. Even many NP-hard problems, for which complete searches for the optimum solution are infeasible, evolutionary algorithms yield near-optimal solutions of satisfying quality. Successful solutions of graph theoretical problems (e. g. the subset sum problem, the maximum cut problem, the minimum tardy problem, and equivalent problems) have been presented [18].

Non-hierarchical, partitioning clustering is a related problem. Evolutionary algorithms have been applied to this problem class for a very long time. One of the earliest experiments on this topic is described in [32], for more recent results see, e. g., [6,17,26].

Evolutionary algorithms are problem independent to a wide extend. However, it is necessary to choose an appropriate scheme to encode potential solutions as *chromosomes*, to define a function to assess the fitness of these chromosomes, and to choose reasonable operators for selection, recombination and mutation.

There are basically two intuitive ways to encode a partitioning of n objects to k clusters:

- Each object o is assigned to a cluster $c(o) \in \{1 \ldots k\}$. A chromosome thus has n genes, the solution space has a cardinality of k^n. Notice, that not all solution are different, and that not all solutions make use of all clusters.

– Each cluster c is represented by a prototype $p(c) \in P$. Each object o is assigned to the cluster with the most similar prototype. The chromosomes thus have k genes, which is smaller than the number of objects (otherwise clustering becomes trivial). The search space cardinality is $|P|^k$. If $P \equiv \{o_i\}$, i. e. only the objects themselves are allowed as prototypes, the search space size is n^k (which is much smaller than k^n in the first encoding). Again, if not constrained explicitly, some of the solutions are identical (i. e. there are only $\binom{n}{k}$ different choices of prototypes).

The fitness must be defined to assess the quality of chromosomes, i. e. the quality of partitionings. We suggest the use of fuzzy sets to define these measure, as it enables us to incorporate our domain specific knowledge (Section 3.3).

As selection operator we chose the tournament selection [13]. When we select parents in the mating phase, we randomly choose two chromosomes from the pool and take the fitter of the two. In comparison to fitness proportional approaches, this algorithm does not depend on the scaling of the fitness function and is thus more robust. Additionally, it is computationally cheap in comparison to rank based selection, which implies sorting of the chromosomes by fitness.

Children are combined from their parents with two-point-crossover of the strings, i. e. two positions in the chromosomes are randomly chosen, the genes in between these positions are copied from one parent to the offspring, the remaining genes are copied from the other parent. This simple operator works fine in our example, as we do not impose any constraints and thus have no need for a repair mechanism. The use of two-point-crossover avoids the positional bias of one-point-crossover [27]. For the mutation of the chromosomes we also used a common approach. We change each of the g genes in a chromosome with a probability of $\frac{1}{g}$, where changing means setting the gene to a new random value [18].

The evolutionary algorithm is randomly initialized with a pool of 400 chromosomes. It then produces — by applying selection, recombination and mutation — new generations of partitions. The algorithm is stopped, when the fitness did not increase for 80 generations or a limit of 1000 generations is exceeded.

3.3   Application and Results

The fitness function of the chromosomes is supposed to measure the quality of the corresponding partitionings. It is common in cluster analysis to measure and to maximize the inner cluster homogeneity, i. e. the similarity between the objects of one cluster. Our objects — the images — are described by their assessment vectors. Thus we have to define a similarity on these vectors. We first considered geometrically motivated measures like linear correlation or cosine between vectors. However, this raises difficulties. Due to the high dimensionalities of the vectors, correlations are near zero and angles near 90° for most pairs of vectors. Furthermore, these measures do not explicitly differentiate between high and low assessment values.

Our goal is a definition of a similarity measure that captures the 'behavior' of the images and groups them accordingly. We suppose that it is more appropriate not to expect images to behave identical for all parameters, but to group images that can be processed with an equal subset of parameters. Thus, high assessment values are more important and must be treated differently than low values.

We can think of the assessment vectors as fuzzy sets, i.e. functions $a_i \colon P \to [0,1]$ that for a given image $i \in I = \{1, \ldots, n\}$ map parameter tuples $p \in P$ to assessment values $a_i(p) \in [0,1]$. This formally satisfies the definition of a fuzzy set. An interpretation of such a fuzzy set a_i could be: "The set of parameters that are suited to process image i."

We can easily create crisp sets $a_{i,crisp}$ with the same meaning by applying a threshold to the assessments, and thus having a binary decision "suited/not suited". If we wanted to define a condition on these crisp sets for a suitable (crisp) prototype $a_{p,crisp}$ for a set $C \subset I$ of images, we could intuitively demand that $a_{p,crisp}$ is a subset of all sets $a_{i,crisp}, i \in C$, i.e. the prototypical parameters are suited for all images. We use fuzzy set operations to apply the same intuitive idea to our assessment fuzzy sets a_i [19].

We used the following measure of (partial) subsethood:

$$s(a, b) = |a \cap b| / |a|,$$

where a and b are fuzzy sets, the intersection $\cap$ is the minimum and the cardinality is defined as $|a| = \sum_x a(x)$.

The subsethood tends to assume higher values for fuzzy sets with small cardinalities. However, we want to find prototypes that also perform well. Thus, for our similarity measure, we multiplied the subsethood by the assessment for the best common parameter, i.e. $\sup_x (a \cap b)(x)$. As a fitness function we took the sum over all similarity values between image and associated (i.e. most similar) prototype.

For our analysis we took the 10 best parameter tuples for each of the 50 images. Thus, we used a total of 500 parameter tuples. The choice of parameters is actually of secondary importance, as long as it ensures adequate coverage of the parameter space. This means, that we should have parameters with good and bad assessments for each image. We then used these 500 parameters in the processing of each of the 50 images and calculated the corresponding vector of 500 assessments.

We used the second partition encoding scheme with the possible prototypes chosen from the set of images. We repeatedly run the evolutionary clustering with values $k \in \{3, \ldots, 30\}$ for the number of clusters. The fitness value reached its maximum after about one to two hundred generations. For all values of k we found identical optimal partitionings for most of the repeated runs. Thus, the search procedure seems to be quite robust and adequate for the problem.

When we analyze the clustering results, we find that the cluster prototypes are stable over the number of clusters, i.e. we do not observe many changes in the most suitable prototypes. Figure 5b shows which images are chosen as prototypes and how many images are assigned to them. We see that the three

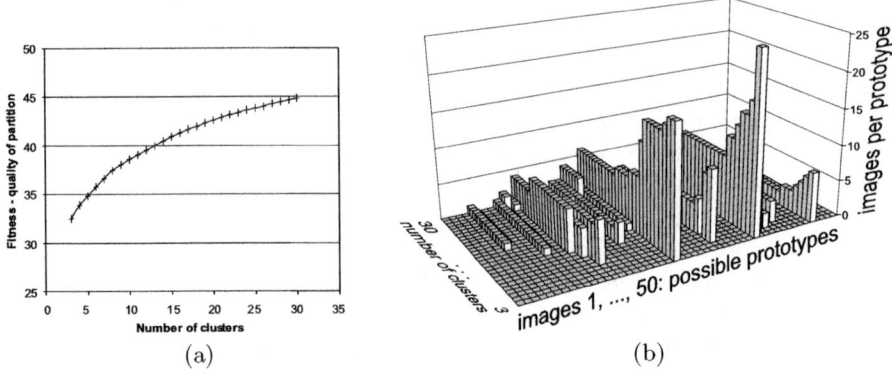

Fig. 5. (a) Fitness value of best partition vs. number of clusters, (b) assignments of images to prototypes

images used as prototypes in case of three clusters seem to be relatively general, as they are also used for higher numbers of clusters. However, the fitness value increases continuously with an increasing number of clusters (see Figure 5a). As the curve does not contain any marked steps, we conclude that the images do not have a natural partitioning (with respect to our similarity measure) that prefers a certain number of clusters. However, the resulting prototypes can be used in further processing or analysis steps.

4   Concluding Remarks

The state of the art in data mining is dominated by purely data-driven approaches, whereas model-based approaches are rare. However, the use of background knowledge and other sources of — in general non-numeric — information, and concentrating on comprehensible models can turn out to be a great benefit.

According to L. A. Zadeh's principle of the incompatibility of precision and meaning [38], precise models often have low interpretability, whereas meaningful models often cannot achieve the same performance. However, many problems have a certain robustness that allows a satisfying trade-off between performance and meaning. In these cases, fuzzy set theory provides a method to formulate knowledge in a way that is interpretable to humans, and still allows efficient computations.

Images can be important sources of information. As the saying goes, "A picture is worth a thousand words". Unfortunately this is not easily scalable: A thousand pictures, for instance, are not necessarily worth a million words — especially human users are easily overwhelmed with too many images. In contrast to numerical data, few — or even single — images are likely to bear interesting information.

Therefore, in image databases, one prominent goal of information mining — as a tool to enable users to understand and access their data — is to guide user attention and to reduce the number of images to the interesting parts. Concerning this goal, we suppose that a variety of techniques is possible and most likely will be necessary. We believe that many amongst these emerging techniques will make use of soft computing. We have shown two examples to support this process, where fuzzy sets and neuro-fuzzy methods have been useful tools model our knowledge about the domain and to get understandable results.

References

1. H. Bandemer and W. Näther. *Fuzzy Data Analysis*. Mathematical and Statistical Methods. Kluwer, Dordrecht, 1992. 269
2. M. Berhold and K.-P. Huber. Tolerating missing values in a fuzzy environment. In Mares, Mesiar, Novak, and Ramik, editors, *Proc. 7th International Fuzzy Systems Association World Congress IFSA'97*, pages 359–362. Academia, Prag, 1997. 274
3. P. Chapman, J. Clinton, T. Khabaza, T. Reinartz, and R. Wirth. The CRISP-DM process model, 1999. available from http://www.crisp-dm.org/. 267
4. A. P. Dempster, N. M. Laird, and D. B. Rubin. Maximum likelihood from incomplete data via the EM algorithm. *Journal of the Royal Statistic Society*, 1(39):1–38, 1997. 274
5. D. Dubois, H. Prade, and R. R. Yager. Information engineering and fuzzy logic. In *Proc. 5th IEEE International Conference on Fuzzy Systems FUZZ-IEEE'96, New Orleans, LA*, pages 1525–1531. IEEE Press, Piscataway, NJ, 1996. 269
6. E. Falkenauer. The grouping genetic algorithms — widening the scope of the GAs. *Belgian Journal of Operations Research, Statistics and Computer Science*, 33:79–102, 1993. 279
7. C. Faloutsos, R. Barber, M. Flickner, W. Niblack, D. Petkovic, and W. Equitz. Efficient and effective querying by image content. *J. of Intelligent Information Systems*, 3(3/4):231–262, 1994. 270
8. U. Fayyad, G. Piatetsky-Shapiro, P. Smyth, and R. Uthurusamy, editors. *Advances in Knowledge Discovery and Data Mining*. AAAI Press / MIT Press, Cambridge, MA, 1996. 267, 268, 270
9. U. Fayyad and P. Smyth, editors. *Image Database Exploration: Progress and Challenges*. AAAI Press, Menlo Park, CA, 1993. 270
10. D. Florescu, A. Levy, and A. Mendelzon. Database techniques for the world-wide web: A survey. *SIGMOD Record*, 27(3):59–74, 1998. 270
11. S. Gibson, O. Kosheleva, L. Longpre, B. Penn, and S. A. Starks. An optimal FFT-based algorithm for mosaicing images, with applications to satellite imaging and web search. In *Proc. 5th Joint Conference on Information Sciences JCIS 2000*, pages 248–251, 2000. 270
12. D. E. Goldberg. *Genetic algorithms in search, optimization and machine learning*. Addison Wesley, Reading, MA, 1989. 279
13. D. E. Goldberg and K. Deb. A comparative analysis of selection schemes used in genetic algorithms. In G. Rawlins, editor, *Foundations of Genetic Algorithms*. Morgan Kaufmann, 1991. 280
14. J. F. Hair, R. E. Anderson, R. L. Tatham, and W. C. Black. *Multivariate Data Analysis, Fifth Edition*. Prentice-Hall, Upper Saddle River, NJ, 1998. 274

15. J. H. Holland. *Adaptation in natural and artificial Systems*. The University of Michigan Press, Ann Arbor, MI, 1975. 279

16. A. Jain and R. Dubes. *Algorithms for Clustering Data*. Prentice Hall, Englewood Cliffs, NJ, 1988. 278, 279

17. D. R. Jones and M. A. Beltramo. Solving partitioning problems with genetic algorithms. In R. Belew and L. Booker, editors, *Proc. 4th Intl. Conf. Genetic Algorithms*, Morgan Kaufmann, Los Altos, CA, 1991. 279

18. S. Khuri, T. Bäck, and J. Heitkötter. An evolutionary approach to combinatorial optimization problems. In *Proc. 22nd Annual ACM Computer Science Conference CSC'94*, pages 66–73, Phoenix, 1994. ACM Press, New York. 279, 280

19. G. J. Klir and B. Yuan. *Fuzzy Sets and Fuzzy Logic*. Prentice Hall, Englewood Cliffs, NJ, 1995. 281

20. A. Klose, R. Kruse, H. Gross, and U. Thönnessen. Tuning on the fly of structural image analysis algorithms using data mining. In Priddy, Keller, and Fogel, editors, *Applications and Science of Computational Intelligence III, Proc. SPIE AeroSense'00*, Orlando, FL, pages 311–321. SPIE Press, 2000. 278

21. A. Klose, R. Kruse, K. Schulz, and U. Thönnessen. Controlling asymmetric errors in neuro-fuzzy classification. In *Proc. ACM SAC'00*. ACM Press, 2000. 271, 275

22. A. Klose and A. Nürnberger. Applying boolean transformations to fuzzy rule bases. In *Proc. EUFIT'99*, 1999. 274

23. A. Klose, A. Nürnberger, and D. Nauck. Some approaches to improve the interpretability of neuro-fuzzy classifiers. In *Proc. EUFIT'98*, pages 629–633, 1998. 274

24. R. Kruse, C. Borgelt, and D. Nauck. Fuzzy data analysis: Challenges and perspectives. In *Proc. 8th IEEE International Conference on Fuzzy Systems FUZZ-IEEE'99, Seoul, Korea*. IEEE Press, Piscataway, NJ, 1999. 268, 269

25. R. Kruse, J. Gebhardt, and F. Klawonn. *Foundations of Fuzzy Systems*. Wiley, Chichester, 1994. 269

26. T. V. Le. Fuzzy evolutionary programming for image processing. In *Proc. Int. Conf. on Intelligent Processing and Manufacturing of Materials*, pages 497–503, Gold Coast, Australia, 1997. 279

27. M. Mitchell. *An introduction to genetic algorithms*. MIT Press, Cambridge, MA, 1998. 279, 280

28. T. M. Mitchell. *Machine Learning*. McGraw-Hill, New York, NY, 1997. 274

29. D. Nauck, F. Klawonn, and R. Kruse. *Foundations of Neuro-Fuzzy Systems*. Wiley, Chichester, 1997. 269, 272, 274

30. D. Nauck and R. Kruse. Fuzzy classification rules using categorical and metric variables. In *Proc. 6th Int. Workshop on Fuzzy-Neuro Systems FNS'99*. Leipziger Universitätsverlag, Leipzig, 1999. 273

31. D. Nauck, U. Nauck, and R. Kruse. NEFCLASS for JAVA — new learning algorithms. In *Proc. 18th Intl. Conf. of the North American Fuzzy Information Processing Society NAFIPS'99*. IEEE Press, New York, NY, 1999. 272, 274

32. V. V. Raghavan and K. Birchard. A clustering strategy based on a formalism of the reproductive process in natural systems. In *Proc. 2nd Intl. Conf. of Research and Development in Information Retrieval*, pages 10–22, 1978. 279

33. R. Schärf, H. Schwan, and U. Thönnessen. Reconnaissance in SAR images. In *Proc. of the European Conference on Synthetic Aperture Radar, Berlin, Offenbach*, pages 343–346, 1998. 271

34. H. Schwan, R. Schärf, and U. Thönnessen. Reconnaissance of extended targets in SAR image data. In *Proc. of the European Symposium on Remote Sensing, Barcelona, September 21th–24th*, 1998. 271

35. U. Stilla, E. Michaelsen, and K. Lütjen. Automatic extraction of buildings from aerial images. In Leberl, Kalliany, and Gruber, editors, *Mapping Buildings, Roads and other Man-Made Structures from Images, Proc. IAPR-TC7 Workshop, Graz*, pages 229–244. R. Oldenbourg, München, 1996. 271

36. N. Vasconcelos and A. Lippman. A bayesian framework for semantic content characterization. In *Proc. Intl. Conf. Computer Vision and Pattern Recognition CVPR*, pages 566–571, 1998. 270

37. L.-X. Wang and J. M. Mendel. Generating fuzzy rules by learning from examples. *IEEE Trans. Syst., Man, Cybern.*, 22(6):1414–1427, 1992. 272

38. L. A. Zadeh. Outline of a new approach to the analysis of complex systems and decision processes. *IEEE Trans. Systems, Man & Cybernetics*, 3:28–44, 1973. 282

39. L. A. Zadeh. Computing with words. *IEEE Transactions on Fuzzy Systems*, 4:103–111, 1996. 269

Contributed Papers

An Automatic Composition Algorithm for Functional Logic Programs

María Alpuente[1], Moreno Falaschi[2], Ginés Moreno[3], and Germán Vidal[1]

[1] DSIC, UPV, Camino de Vera s/n,
46022 Valencia, Spain
alpuente@dsic.upv.es
[2] Dip. Mat. e Informatica, U. Udine,
33100 Udine, Italy
falaschi@dimi.uniud.it
[3] Dep. Informática, UCLM,
02071 Albacete, Spain
gmoreno@info-ab.uclm.es

Abstract. Functional logic languages with a complete operational semantics are based on narrowing, which combines the instantiation of variables with the reduction of expressions. In this paper, we investigate the relationship between partial evaluation and more general transformations based on folding/unfolding. First, we show that the transformations obtained by partial evaluators can be also achieved by folding/unfolding using a particular kind of eurekas which can be mechanically attained. Then, we propose an algorithm (based on folding/unfolding) which starts with the automatic eureka generation and is able to perform program composition, i. e. it is able to produce a single function definition for some nested functions of the original program. This avoids the construction of intermediate data structures that are produced by the inner function and consumed as inputs by the outer function. As opposed to both partial evaluation and (general) fold/unfold transformations, strong correctness of the transformed programs holds w. r. t. goals which contain calls to the *old* function symbols — i. e. from the original program — as well as to the *new* ones — i. e. introduced during the transformation.

1 Introduction

Functional logic programming languages combine the operational methods and advantages of the most important declarative programming paradigms, namely functional and logic programming. The operational principle of such languages is usually based on narrowing. A *narrowing step* instantiates variables in an expression and applies a reduction step to a redex of the instantiated expression. Needed narrowing is the currently best narrowing strategy for first-order (inductively sequential) functional logic programs due to its optimality properties w. r. t. the length of derivations and the number of computed solutions [ ], and it can be efficiently implemented by pattern matching and unification.

The aim of *partial evaluation* (PE) is to specialize a given program w. r. t. part of its input data (hence also called *program specialization*). PE has been

V. Hlaváč, K. G. Jeffery, and J. Wiedermann (Eds.): SOFSEM 2000, LNCS 1963, pp. 289–297, 2000.

widely applied in the field of functional programming [8,13] and logic programming [11,14]. Although the objectives are similar, the general methods are often different due to the distinct underlying computation models. Narrowing-driven PE [3] is the first generic algorithm for the specialization of functional logic languages. The method is parametric w. r. t. the narrowing strategy which is used for the automatic construction of partial trees. The method is formalized within the theoretical framework established in [14] for the PE of logic programs (also known as *partial deduction*), although a number of concepts have been generalized to deal with the functional component of the language (e. g. nested function calls, different evaluation strategies, etc.). This approach has better opportunities for optimization thanks to the functional dimension (e. g. by the inclusion of deterministic evaluation steps). Also, since unification is embedded into narrowing, it is able to automatically propagate syntactic information on the partial input (term structure) and not only constant values, similarly to partial deduction.

The fold/unfold transformation approach was first introduced in [6] to optimize functional programs and then used for logic programs [17]. This approach is commonly based on the construction, by means of a *strategy*, of a sequence of equivalent programs each obtained from the preceding ones by using an *elementary* transformation rule. The essential rules are *folding* and *unfolding*, i. e. contraction and expansion of subexpressions of a program using the definitions of this program (or of a preceding one). Other rules which have been considered are, for example: instantiation, definition introduction/elimination, and abstraction. A transformation methodology for lazy (*call-by-name*) functional logic programs was introduced in [2]; this work extends the transformation rules of [17] for logic programs in order to cope with lazy functional logic programs (based on needed narrowing). The use of narrowing empowers the fold/unfold system by implicitly embedding the instantiation rule (the operation of the Burstall and Darlington framework [6] which introduces an instance of an existing equation) into unfolding by means of unification. [2] also demonstrates that the (inductively sequential) structure of programs is preserved through the transformation sequence $(\mathcal{R}_0, \ldots, \mathcal{R}_n)$, which is a key point for proving the correctness of the transformation system as well as for being effectively applicable.

There exists a large class of program optimizations which can be achieved by fold/unfold transformations and are not possible by using a fully automatic method (such as, e. g. partial evaluation). However, a weak point of the fold/unfold transformation approach is the achievement of the appropriate set of (*eureka*) definitions which make it possible the optimizations to be pursued [6,17,15]. In this paper, we propose an automatic composition algorithm (based on folding/unfolding) which uses a pre-process based on partial evaluation to ascertain the eurekas which guarantee that the optimization will be attained. On the theoretical side, we first prove in Sect. 3 that fold/unfold transformations are able to achieve the effects of PE. A new result w. r. t. both partial evaluation and (general) fold/unfold transformations is that strong correctness of the transformed programs holds w. r. t. goals which contain calls to the *old* function symbols — i. e. from the original program — as well as to the *new* ones — i. e. introduced during the transformation. On the practical side, we define in Sect. 4 an automatic composition algorithm which uses partial evaluation as a (sort of) static analysis phase which delivers the intended eurekas.

2 Preliminaries

We assume familiarity with basic notions from term rewriting [10] and functional logic programming [12]. In this work we consider a (*many-sorted*) *signature* Σ partitioned into a set $\mathcal{C}$ of *constructors* and a set $\mathcal{F}$ of *defined* functions. The set of *constructor terms* with *variables* (e. g. x, y, z) is obtained by using symbols from $\mathcal{C}$ and $\mathcal{X}$. The set of variables occurring in a term t is denoted by $Var(t)$. We write $\overline{o_n}$ for the *list* of objects $o_1, \ldots, o_n$. A *pattern* is a term of the form $f(\overline{d_n})$ where $f/n \in \mathcal{F}$ and $d_1, \ldots, d_n$ are constructor terms. A term is *linear* if it does not contain multiple occurrences of one variable. A term is *operation-rooted* (*constructor-rooted*) if it has an operation (constructor) symbol at the root. A *position* p in a term t is represented by a sequence of natural numbers. (Λ denotes the empty sequence, i. e. the root position). $t|_p$ denotes the *subterm* of t at position p, and $t[s]_p$ denotes the result of *replacing the subterm* $t|_p$ by the term s. We denote by $\{x_1 \mapsto t_1, \ldots, x_n \mapsto t_n\}$ the *substitution* σ with $\sigma(x_i) = t_i$ for $i = 1, \ldots, n$ (with $x_i \neq x_j$ if $i \neq j$), and $\sigma(x) = x$ for all other variables x. id denotes the identity substitution.

A set of rewrite rules $l \to r$ such that $l \notin \mathcal{X}$, and $Var(r) \subseteq Var(l)$ is called a *term rewriting system* (TRS). The terms l and r are called the *left-hand side* (lhs) and the *right-hand side* (rhs) of the rule, respectively. A TRS $\mathcal{R}$ is left-linear if l is linear for all $l \to r \in \mathcal{R}$. A TRS is constructor-based (CB) if each left-hand side is a pattern. In the remainder of this paper, a functional logic *program* is a left-linear CB-TRS. A *rewrite step* is an application of a rewrite rule to a term, i. e. $t \to_{p,R} s$ if there exists a position p in t, a rewrite rule $R = (l \to r)$ and a substitution σ with $t|_p = \sigma(l)$ and $s = t[\sigma(r)]_p$. Given a relation $\to$, we denote by $\to^+$ its transitive closure and by $\to^*$ its reflexive and transitive closure.

The operational semantics of integrated languages is usually based on *narrowing*, a combination of variable instantiation and reduction. Formally, $s \leadsto_{p,R,\sigma} t$ is a *narrowing step* if p is a non-variable position in s and $\sigma(s) \to_{p,R} t$. We denote by $t_0 \leadsto^*_\sigma t_n$ a sequence of narrowing steps $t_0 \leadsto_{\sigma_1} \cdots \leadsto_{\sigma_n} t_n$ with $\sigma = \sigma_n \circ \ldots \circ \sigma_1$ (if $n = 0$ then $\sigma = id$). Narrowing sequences can be represented by a (possibly infinite) finitely branching tree, which is called *narrowing tree*. Modern functional logic languages are based on *needed narrowing* and *inductively sequential* programs.

3 Partial Evaluation via Fold/Unfold

In this section, we recall from [4] the notion of partial evaluation of lazy functional logic programs. Specialized program rules are constructed from narrowing derivations using the notion of *resultant*: given a narrowing derivation $s \leadsto^*_\sigma t$, its associated resultant is the rule $\sigma(s) \to t$. The *(pre-)partial evaluation* of a term s is obtained by constructing a (possibly incomplete) narrowing tree for s and then extracting the specialized definitions (the resultants) from the non-failing, root-to-leaf paths of the tree.

Definition 1 (pre-partial evaluation). Let $\mathcal{R}$ be a TRS and s be a term. Let $\mathcal{T}$ be a finite (possibly incomplete) narrowing tree for s in $\mathcal{R}$ such that no constructor-rooted term has been narrowed. Let $\{t_1, \ldots, t_n\}$ be the terms in the leaves of $\mathcal{T}$. Then, the set of resultants $\{\sigma_i(s) \to t_i \mid s \leadsto_{\sigma_i}^+ t_i, \text{ for } i = 1, \ldots, n\}$ is called a pre-partial evaluation of s in $\mathcal{R}$. The pre-partial evaluation of a set of terms S in $\mathcal{R}$ is defined as the union of the pre-partial evaluations for the terms of S in $\mathcal{R}$.

Given a call s and a program $\mathcal{R}$, there exists in general an infinite number of different pre-partial evaluations of s in $\mathcal{R}$. A fixed rule for generating resultants called an *unfolding rule* is assumed, which determines the expressions to be narrowed (by using a fixed narrowing strategy) and which decides how to stop the construction of narrowing trees (see [1,3] for the definition of concrete unfolding rules).

A recursive *closedness* condition is needed in order to guarantee that each call which might occur during the execution of the resulting program is covered by some program rule. Informally, a term t rooted by a defined function symbol is closed w.r.t. a set of calls S (alternatively, t is S-closed), if it is an instance of a term s in S: $t = \theta(s)$, and the terms in the matching substitution θ are recursively closed by S.

In order to apply a partial evaluator based on needed narrowing and to guarantee that the resulting program is inductively sequential whenever the source program is, we have to ensure that the set of specialized terms contains only linear patterns with distinct root symbols. We note that, whenever the specialized call is not a linear pattern, lhs's of resultants may not be linear patterns either and hence resultants may not be program rules. In order to produce program rules, it is necessary to consider a post-processing renaming transformation which introduces a new function symbol for each specialized call and then replaces each call in the specialized program by a call to the corresponding renamed function. In particular, the lhs's of specialized program rules (which are constructor instances of the specialized terms) are replaced by instances of the corresponding new linear patterns by renaming.

Definition 2 (independent renaming). An independent renaming ρ for a set of terms S is a mapping from terms to terms defined as follows: for $s \in S$, $\rho(s) = f_s(\overline{x_n})$, where $\overline{x_n}$ are the distinct variables in s in the order of their first occurrence, and f_s is a new function symbol, which does not occur in $\mathcal{R}$ or S and is different from the root symbol of any other $\rho(s')$, with $s' \in S$ and $s' \neq s$. We let $\rho(S)$ denote the set $S' = \{\rho(s) \mid s \in S\}$.

Now, the notion of partial evaluation can be formulated as the renaming (using a given independent renaming ρ) of the set of resultants obtained by a pre-partial evaluation. This PE method preserves the structure of programs and it is strongly correct w.r.t. the renamed goals (see [4] for details). Let us illustrate these definitions with an example.

Example 1. Consider the well-known function append to concatenate two lists:[1]

$$\text{append}(\text{nil}, Y_s) \ \rightarrow Y_s \qquad\qquad (R_1)$$
$$\text{append}(X : X_s, Y_s) \rightarrow X : \text{append}(X_s, Y_s) \quad (R_2)$$

and the set $S = \{\text{append}(X_s, Y_s), \text{append}(\text{append}(X_s, Y_s), Z_s)\}$. An independent renaming ρ for S is the mapping:

$$\{ \quad \text{append}(X_s, Y_s) \qquad\qquad\qquad \mapsto \text{app}(X_s, Y_s),$$
$$\text{append}(\text{append}(X_s, Y_s), Z_s) \mapsto \text{dapp}(X_s, Y_s, Z_s) \quad \}.$$

A possible partial evaluation $\mathcal{R}'$ of $\mathcal{R}$ w.r.t. S (under ρ) is:

$$\text{dapp}(\text{nil}, Y_s, Z_s) \ \rightarrow \text{app}(Y_s, Z_s)$$
$$\text{dapp}(X : X_s, Y_s, Z_s) \rightarrow X : \text{dapp}(X_s, Y_s, Z_s)$$
$$\text{app}(\text{nil}, Y_s) \qquad\quad \rightarrow Y_s$$
$$\text{app}(X : X_s, Y_s) \qquad \rightarrow X : \text{app}(X_s, Y_s)$$

In the following, we show that (a subset of) the folding/unfolding transformation rules described in [2] are able to achieve the effects of PE. The proof is not trivial, since: 1) the PE method applies to a single program whereas, in the fold/unfold framework, the programs considered for each transformation step are different, and 2) we do not consider a complete transformation system (such as [2,6]) but three simple rules.

Firstly, we recall from [2] the definition of the transformation rules.

Definition 3. A *transformation sequence* $(\mathcal{R}_0, \ldots, \mathcal{R}_k)$, $k > 0$ is constructed by applying the following transformation rules:

Definition Introduction: We may get program $\mathcal{R}_{k+1}$ by adding to $\mathcal{R}_k$ a new rule (the "definition rule") of the form $f(\overline{t_n}) \rightarrow r$, provided the following conditions hold:
1. $f(\overline{t_n})$ is a linear pattern and $Var(f(\overline{t_n})) = Var(r)$ — i.e. it is non-erasing,
2. f does not occur in the sequence $\mathcal{R}_0, \ldots, \mathcal{R}_k$ (f is *new*), and
3. every defined (old) function symbol occurring in r belongs to $\mathcal{R}_0$.

We say that f is a *new* function symbol, and every function symbol belonging to $\mathcal{R}_0$ is called an *old* function symbol.

Unfolding: Let $R = (l \rightarrow r) \in \mathcal{R}_k$ be a rule where r is an operation-rooted term. Then, $\mathcal{R}_{k+1} = (\mathcal{R}_k - \{R\}) \cup \{\theta(l) \rightarrow r' \mid r \leadsto_\theta r' \text{ in } \mathcal{R}_k\}$.

Folding: Let $R = (l \rightarrow r) \in \mathcal{R}_k$ be a non definition rule, $R' = (l' \rightarrow r') \in \mathcal{R}_j$, $0 \leq j \leq k$, a definition rule[2] and p a position in r such that $r|_p = \theta(r')$ and $r|_p$ is not a constructor term. Then, $\mathcal{R}_{k+1} = (\mathcal{R}_k - \{R\}) \cup \{l \rightarrow r[\theta(l')]_p\}$.

Programs in a transformation sequence constructed by using the previous set of rules are inductively sequential. Moreover, the transformations are strongly correct w.r.t. goals which do not contain new function symbols. The following result represents the main theoretical result of this section.

---

[1] We use "nil" and ":" as constructors of lists.

[2] A *definition rule* maintains its status only as long as it remains unchanged, i.e. once a definition rule is transformed it is not considered a *definition rule* anymore.

Theorem 1. *Let $\mathcal{R}$ be an inductively sequential program, S a finite set of operation-rooted terms, and ρ an independent renaming of S. If $\mathcal{R}'$ is a PE of $\mathcal{R}$ w. r. t. S (under ρ) such that $\mathcal{R}'$ is S'-closed (where $S' = \rho(S)$) then, there exists a transformation sequence starting from $\mathcal{R}$ and ending with $\mathcal{R} \cup \mathcal{R}'$, such that only definition introduction, unfolding and folding steps (in this order) have been performed.*

The following example illustrates how folding/unfolding transformations are able to specialize an input program for a given goal. The main idea is to consider the renaming which is used in the PE process as the (inverted) eurekas which start the transformation process.

Example 2. Consider the program defining the function append of Example 1 as the initial program $\mathcal{R}_0$ of a transformation sequence. In order to mimic the partial evaluation process shown in Example 1, we consider the same independent renaming, ρ, and apply the definition introduction rule twice in order to produce two definition rules for the new symbols of ρ:

$$\mathcal{R}_1 = \mathcal{R}_0 \cup \left\{ \begin{array}{lll} \mathsf{app}(X_s, Y_s) & \rightarrow \mathsf{append}(X_s, Y_s) & (R_3) \\ \mathsf{dapp}(X_s, Y_s, Z_s) & \rightarrow \mathsf{append}(\mathsf{append}(X_s, Y_s), Z_s) & (R_4) \end{array} \right\}$$

Now, by unfolding R_3 (using rules R_1 and R_2, i.e. the original definition of append), we get:

$$\mathcal{R}_2 = \mathcal{R}_0 \cup \left\{ \begin{array}{lll} \mathsf{app}(\mathsf{nil}, Y_s) & \rightarrow Y_s & (R_5) \\ \mathsf{app}(X : X_s, Y_s) & \rightarrow X : \mathsf{append}(X_s, Y_s) & (R_6) \\ \mathsf{dapp}(X_s, Y_s, Z_s) & \rightarrow \mathsf{append}(\mathsf{append}(X_s, Y_s), Z_s) & (R_4) \end{array} \right\}$$

By unfolding R_4 (using rules R_1 and R_2):

$$\mathcal{R}_3 = \mathcal{R}_0 \cup \left\{ \begin{array}{lll} \mathsf{app}(\mathsf{nil}, Y_s) & \rightarrow Y_s & (R_5) \\ \mathsf{app}(X : X_s, Y_s) & \rightarrow X : \mathsf{append}(X_s, Y_s) & (R_6) \\ \mathsf{dapp}(\mathsf{nil}, Y_s, Z_s) & \rightarrow \mathsf{append}(Y_s, Z_s) & (R_7) \\ \mathsf{dapp}(X : X_s, Y_s, Z_s) & \rightarrow \mathsf{append}(X : \mathsf{append}(X_s, Y_s), Z_s) & (R_8) \end{array} \right\}$$

The unfolding of R_8 (using rule R_2) produces:

$$\mathcal{R}_4 = \mathcal{R}_0 \cup \left\{ \begin{array}{lll} \mathsf{app}(\mathsf{nil}, Y_s) & \rightarrow Y_s & (R_5) \\ \mathsf{app}(X : X_s, Y_s) & \rightarrow X : \mathsf{append}(X_s, Y_s) & (R_6) \\ \mathsf{dapp}(\mathsf{nil}, Y_s, Z_s) & \rightarrow \mathsf{append}(Y_s, Z_s) & (R_7) \\ \mathsf{dapp}(X : X_s, Y_s, Z_s) & \rightarrow X : \mathsf{append}(\mathsf{append}(X_s, Y_s), Z_s) & (R_9) \end{array} \right\}$$

Finally, by folding R_6 and R_7 w. r. t. the definition rule R_3 and folding R_9 w. r. t the definition rule R_4, we obtain the desired final program $\mathcal{R}_5 = \mathcal{R}_0 \cup \mathcal{R}'$, where $\mathcal{R}'$ is exactly the program obtained by PE in Example 1.

4   An Automatic Composition Algorithm

The composition strategy was originally introduced in [6,9] for the optimization of pure functional programs. Variants of this composition strategy are the *internal specialization* technique [16] and the *deforestation* method [18]. By using the composition strategy, one may avoid the construction of intermediate data structures that are produced by some function g and consumed as inputs by another function f in a nested expression like $f(g(t))$.

Now, we introduce an algorithm to perform composition:

The Automatic Composition Algorithm

(1) **Partial evaluation phase:** Let $\mathcal{R}$ be an inductively sequential program. As the input of the PE method, we consider the set T of calls which contain the expressions (with nested functions) to be composed. Let $S \supseteq T$ be a finite set of terms and ρ be an independent renaming for S such that the PE $\mathcal{R}'$ of $\mathcal{R}$ w. r. t. S (under ρ) is S'-closed, where $S' = \{\rho(s) \mid s \in S\}$.

(2) **Definition introduction phase:** By repeated application of the definition introduction rule, we add to $\mathcal{R}$ the following set of definition rules: $\mathcal{R}_{def} = \{\rho(s) \to s \mid s \in S\}$. Note that this phase ends with the program $\mathcal{R} \cup \mathcal{R}_{def}$.

(3) **Unfolding phase:** Each definition rule $R = (\rho(s) \to s) \in \mathcal{R}_{def}$ is unfolded (at least once) until a rule whose rhs contains an instance of some term in S is reached. This way, we produce a set of transformed rules of the form: $\mathcal{R}_{unf} = \{\theta(\rho(s)) \to r \mid (\rho(s) \to s) \in \mathcal{R}_{def}\}$, where each term r is obtained by unfolding the corresponding rhs s a number of times (computing the substitution θ). At the end of this phase, we get $\mathcal{R} \cup \mathcal{R}_{unf}$.

(4) **Folding phase:** In order to obtain efficient recursive definitions of the new symbols defined by the rules of $\mathcal{R}_{def}$, we use these rules to fold (if possible) the rhs's of the unfolded rules of $\mathcal{R}_{unf}$. After this process, the set of rules $\mathcal{R}_{unf}$ transforms into $\mathcal{R}_{fold}$, and thus we get $\mathcal{R} \cup \mathcal{R}_{fold}$.

(5) **Post-folding phase:** Finally, we also fold every instance of each term s occurring in the rhs's of the rules of $\mathcal{R}$ by using the appropriate definition rules of $\mathcal{R}_{def}$, which finally produces the transformed program $\mathcal{R}_{post} \cup \mathcal{R}_{fold}$.

There are several important remarks regarding the previous algorithm. A key point is the way in which eureka definitions are derived. The problem of achieving an appropriate set of eureka definitions is well-known in the literature related to fold/unfold transformations [6,15,17]. In our algorithm, we perform a finite, static analysis (by PE) that generates an appropriate set of definition rules at the beginning of the transformation (phases 1 and 2). Termination of the global process is ensured by the closedness condition, which guarantees that the search for regularities during the unfolding process will always succeed, producing efficient and recursive definitions. Observe that this is not generally true for the composition strategy, where the pursued optimization might be frustrated by infinite unfolding.

A relevant property of the programs produced by the automatic composition algorithm is the strong correctness w. r. t. goals containing calls to both the old and the new defined function symbols. This is an improvement w. r. t. the correctness results of the PE method as well as the general fold/unfold techniques: in programs specialized by PE only calls to the new function symbols can be safely executed, whereas in programs optimized by folding/unfolding only goals constructed with the old function symbols are safe (see discussion below). On the other hand, our composition strategy obtains an optimization of the input program which does not reduce its domain of application (as opposed to PE).

The outcome of step 4 of our automatic composition algorithm is a program of the form $\mathcal{R} \cup \mathcal{R}_{fold}$, where $\mathcal{R}_{fold}$ can be seen as an specialization of $\mathcal{R}$ where no calls to old function symbols appear. Since $\mathcal{R}_{fold}$ is self-contained (i. e. every call is covered by the set of rules themselves), then the strong correctness of the PE method ensures that goals which contain calls to the new function symbols can be safely executed in the transformed program. On the other hand, since the algorithm constructs a particular kind of transformation sequence, the strong correctness results of [2] apply. This guarantees that a goal containing old function symbols computes the same set of answer substitutions (and values) in the initial program $\mathcal{R}$ and in the final program $\mathcal{R}_{post} \cup \mathcal{R}_{fold}$, where they (hopefully) run faster.

There is a final remark about the structure of the transformed programs. Looking at their syntax, we distinguish two disjoint set of rules:

- $\mathcal{R}_{fold}$ represents the set of rules defining the new function symbols, where no calls to rules outside from $\mathcal{R}_{fold}$ appear, i. e. the specialized component is "self-contained".
- On the other hand, $\mathcal{R}_{post}$ coincides with the set of rules defining the set of old function symbols. This component is very similar to the original program $\mathcal{R}$, except for certain calls to the old function symbols which have been transformed (by virtue of the folding steps) into calls to functions of the $\mathcal{R}_{fold}$ specialized component.

5   Further Research

We conclude by mentioning some ideas for further research. There are some optimizations which can be achieved by fold/unfold transformations and are not possible by means of PE, e. g. *tupling* [6]. This technique eliminates parallel traversals of identical data structures by merging separate (non-nested) loops together into a new recursive function defined on *tuples* (pairs), thus avoiding the traversal of the involved data structures more than once. Generally, tupling is very complicated and automatic tupling algorithms either result in high run-time cost (which prevents them from being employed in a real system), or they succeed only for a restricted class of programs. Although PE is not able to produce the tupling optimization by itself, we think that it can be also used (with some modifications) as a pre-processing phase for an automatic tupling strategy. Inspired by the analysis of Chin [7], we plan to investigate how to use the PE method as a tupling eureka generator.

References

1. E. Albert, M. Alpuente, M. Falaschi, P. Julián, and G. Vidal. Improving Control in Functional Logic Program Specialization. In G. Levi, editor, *Proc. of Static Analysis Symposium, SAS'98*, pages 262–277. Springer LNCS 1503, 1998. 292

2. M. Alpuente, M. Falaschi, G. Moreno, and G. Vidal. A Transformation System for Lazy Functional Logic Programs. In A. Middeldorp and T. Sato, editors, *Proc. of the 4th Fuji International Symposyum on Functional and Logic Programming, FLOPS'99, Tsukuba (Japan)*, pages 147–162. Springer LNCS 1722, 1999. 290, 293, 296

3. M. Alpuente, M. Falaschi, and G. Vidal. Partial Evaluation of Functional Logic Programs. *ACM Transactions on Programming Languages and Systems*, 20(4):768–844, 1998. 290, 292

4. M. Alpuente, M. Hanus, S. Lucas, and G. Vidal. Specialization of Inductively Sequential Functional Logic Programs. In P. Lee, editor, *Proc. of 1999 International Conference on Functional Programming, ICFP'99, Paris (France)*. ACM, New York, 1999. 291, 292

5. S. Antoy, R. Echahed, and M. Hanus. A Needed Narrowing Strategy. In *Proc. 21st ACM Symp. on Principles of Programming Languages, Portland*, pages 268–279, New York, 1994. ACM Press. 289

6. R. M. Burstall and J. Darlington. A Transformation System for Developing Recursive Programs. *Journal of the ACM*, 24(1):44–67, 1977. 290, 293, 294, 295, 296

7. W. Chin. Towards an Automated Tupling Strategy. In *Proc. of Partial Evaluation and Semantics-Based Program Manipulation, 1993*, pages 119–132. ACM, New York, 1993. 296

8. C. Consel and O. Danvy. Tutorial notes on Partial Evaluation. In *Proc. of 20th Annual ACM Symp. on Principles of Programming Languages*, pages 493–501. ACM, New York, 1993. 290

9. J. Darlington. Program transformation. In J. Darlington, P. Henderson, and D. A. Turner, editors, *Functional Programming and its Applications*, pages 193–215. Cambridge University Press, 1982. 294

10. N. Dershowitz and J.-P. Jouannaud. Rewrite Systems. In J. van Leeuwen, editor, *Handbook of Theoretical Computer Science*, volume B: Formal Models and Semantics, pages 243–320. Elsevier, Amsterdam, 1990. 291

11. J. Gallagher. Tutorial on Specialisation of Logic Programs. In *Proc. of Partial Evaluation and Semantics-Based Program Manipulation, Copenhagen, Denmark, June 1993*, pages 88–98. ACM, New York, 1993. 290

12. M. Hanus. The Integration of Functions into Logic Programming: From Theory to Practice. *Journal of Logic Programming*, 19&20:583–628, 1994. 291

13. N. D. Jones, C. K. Gomard, and P. Sestoft. *Partial Evaluation and Automatic Program Generation*. Prentice-Hall, Englewood Cliffs, NJ, 1993. 290

14. J. W. Lloyd and J. C. Shepherdson. Partial Evaluation in Logic Programming. *Journal of Logic Programming*, 11:217–242, 1991. 290

15. A. Pettorossi and M. Proietti. A Comparative Revisitation of Some Program Transformation Techniques. In O. Danvy, R. Glück, and P. Thiemann, editors, *Partial Evaluation, Int'l Seminar, Dagstuhl Castle, Germany*, pages 355–385. Springer LNCS 1110, 1996. 290, 295

16. W. L. Scherlis. Program Improvement by Internal Specialization. In *Proc. of 8th Annual ACM Symp. on Principles of Programming Languages*, pages 41–49. ACM Press, New York, 1981. 294

17. H. Tamaki and T. Sato. Unfold/Fold Transformations of Logic Programs. In S. Tärnlund, editor, *Proc. of Second Int'l Conf. on Logic Programming, Uppsala, Sweden*, pages 127–139, 1984. 290, 295

18. P. L. Wadler. Deforestation: Transforming programs to eliminate trees. *Theoretical Computer Science*, 73:231–248, 1990. 294

On the Approximation Ratio of the Group-Merge Algorithm for the Shortest Common Superstring Problem*

Dirk Bongartz

Lehrstuhl für Informatik I, RWTH Aachen,
Ahornstraße 55, 52074 Aachen, Germany
bongartz@cs.rwth-aachen.de

Abstract. The shortest common superstring problem (SCS) is one of the fundamental optimization problems in the area of data compression and DNA sequencing. The SCS is known to be APX-hard [1]. This paper focuses on the analysis of the approximation ratio of two greedy-based approximation algorithms for it, namely the naive Greedy algorithm and the Group-Merge algorithm. The main results of this paper are:

(i) We disprove the claim that the input instances of Jiang and Li [4] prove that the Group-Merge algorithm does not provide any constant approximation for the SCS. We even prove that the Group-Merge algorithm always finds optimal solutions for these instances.

(ii) We show that the Greedy algorithm and the Group-Merge algorithm are incomparable according to the approximation ratio.

(iii) We attack the main problem whether the Group-Merge algorithm has a constant approximation ratio by showing that this is the case for a slightly modified algorithm denoted as Group-Merge-1 if all strings have approximately the same length and the compression is limited by a constant fraction of the trivial solution.

1 Introduction

The shortest common superstring problem has been intensively investigated since the early eighties due to its important applications both in data compression and in DNA sequencing. To describe the problem informally assume that we have a set of strings S. The shortest common superstring problem (denoted by SCS in the sequel) is to find one string w that includes all strings in S as substrings.

The SCS has been proven to be NP-complete [2] and also APX-hard [1], i. e. there is no polynomial time approximation scheme for the SCS (unless $P = NP$). Several approximation algorithms have been invented obtaining good approximation ratios and recently a $2\frac{1}{2}$-approximation [5] has been established.

Here we will investigate the Group-Merge algorithm first presented in [3]. This algorithm was conjectured to achieve an approximation ratio of two in [3],

---

* This work was supported by DFG-grant Hr 14/5-1.

V. Hlaváč, K. G. Jeffery, and J. Wiedermann (Eds.): SOFSEM 2000, LNCS 1963, pp. 298–306, 2000.

although only a bound for the approximation ratio of $O(\log n)$ could be established. In a consecutive paper Jiang and Li [4] presented, in contradiction to the conjecture of the 2-approximation, an example which claims that this bound of $O(\log n)$ is really tight.

After giving some preliminary facts and definitions in Section 2, we will disprove this claim in Section 3, and moreover we prove that Group-Merge even computes the optimal solution for this example.

Furthermore, we will show in Section 4 that the Group-Merge algorithm and the well-known Greedy algorithm are incomparable, i.e. there exists an example for which Group-Merge computes a shorter superstring than Greedy and vice versa. In Section 5 we discuss the approximation behavior of a modified Group-Merge algorithm, denoted by Group-Merge-1, under certain constraints.

2   Preliminaries

This section is dedicated to the presentation of some basic notions and observations on shortest common superstrings. A more detailed introduction to the SCS can be found e.g. in [1].

Definition 1. Let S be a finite set of strings over an alphabet Σ. The *shortest (common) superstring* according to this set S is the shortest string w which includes each string $s \in S$ as a substring. We call the set S a *SCS instance*. The *shortest superstring problem* is to find the shortest superstring for a given SCS instance S. For each set of strings S, we define $\|S\| = \sum_{s \in S} |s|$, where $|s|$ denotes the length of a string s.

The trivial solution for finding a superstring of a set S results from concatenating all strings in S and thus leads to a superstring of length $\|S\|$.

Note that we can assume each SCS instance to satisfy the so called substring-freeness property, since strings that are substrings of others do not contribute to the shortest superstring.

There are two ways to measure the performance of approximation algorithms for the SCS, namely with respect to the length of the achieved superstring (*length measure*) or with respect to the difference between the lengths of the achieved superstring and the trivial solution $\|S\|$ (*compression measure*).

Definition 2. Let s, t be strings over an alphabet Σ. If there exist non-empty strings x, y, z, where $s = xy$ and $t = yz$, then we call the string xyz the *merge* of s and t and denote it by $\langle s, t \rangle_{|y|}$. We call y an *overlap* of the strings s and t. If y is the longest string satisfying the above properties, we call it the *maximal overlap*, and denote its length by $\mathrm{ov}(s, t) = |y|$. The corresponding merge is called the *maximal merge*. If the value of $|y|$ is clear from the context we may denote the merge just by $\langle s, t \rangle$.

Now, we present two algorithms both following a greedy approach to compute a approximative shortest superstring. The first one is the well-known Greedy algorithm which has been proven to achieve an approximation ratio of 2 with respect to the compression measure [6] and an approximation ratio of 4 with respect to the length measure [1]. This algorithm performs merges between strings providing a maximal amount of overlap.

Greedy algorithm: Input: $S = \{s_1, \ldots, s_m\}$

(1) Find $s_i, s_j \in S$, $s_i \neq s_j$, for which the maximal overlap $ov(s_i, s_j)$ is maximized over all strings in S.
(2) Obtain s' as the maximal merge of s_i and s_j.
(3) Remove s_i, s_j from S and insert s' into S.
(4) Repeat these steps until $|S| = 1$.

The second algorithm we want to describe here utilizes the greedy approach with respect to the total length of strings covered by a merge. This algorithm was introduced by Li [3] and is denoted as the Group-Merge algorithm.

Here we also consider non-maximal merges and denote by $weight(\langle s, t \rangle)$ the sum of lengths of all strings from S covered by the merge $\langle s, t \rangle$.[1]

Algorithm Group-Merge: Input: $S = \{s_1, \ldots, s_m\}$

(1) Let $T := \emptyset$.
(2) Find $s, s' \in S$ such that $cost(s, s') = \min_{n \in \mathbb{N}} \frac{|\langle s, s' \rangle_n|}{weight(\langle s, s' \rangle_n)}$ is minimized over all pairs of strings in S.
(3) Merge s, s' to $\langle s, s' \rangle_n$. $T := T \cup \{\langle s, s' \rangle_n\}$. Delete all strings covered by $\langle s, s' \rangle_n$ from S.
(4) If $|S| > 0$, then goto Step (2).
(5) If $|T| > 1$, then $S := T$ and goto Step (1), else return the only string in T as the superstring.

The following result is proved in [3,4].

Theorem 1. *Given a set of strings S, if the length of the shortest superstring is n, then the algorithm Group-Merge produces a superstring of length $O(n \log n)$.*

Furthermore we consider a modification of Group-Merge such that the set T is avoided, i. e. merges performed by the algorithm are directly inserted into the set S. This algorithm is also presented in [4] and following their notation we denote it as the **Group-Merge-1** algorithm.

3   A False Lower Bound Example

To establish a lower bound of $\Omega(\log n)$ on the approximation ratio of Group-Merge Jiang and Li [4] presented the following example, which we will denote as the **JL-Example** in the sequel.

---

[1] Note that for technical reasons one has to allow complete self-overlaps here, namely merges of the kind $\langle s, s \rangle_{|s|} = s$, to provide a correct termination of the algorithm.

$$S_0 = \{a^j b^{m-j} \mid 32 \leq j < 64\} = \{a^{32} b^{32}, \ldots, a^{63} b\}$$
$$S_1 = \{a^j b^{m-j} \mid 8 \leq j < 16\} = \{a^8 b^{56}, \ldots, a^{15} b^{49}\}$$
$$S_2 = \{a^j b^{m-j} \mid 2 \leq j < 4\} = \{a^2 b^{62}, a^3 b^{61}\}$$
$$V = \{ccaa, cbca^{13}, cb^2 ca^{60}\}$$

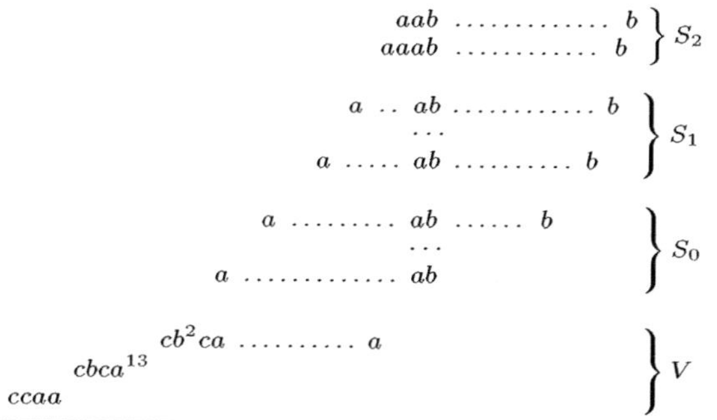

$$
\begin{array}{l}
\left. \begin{array}{l}
aab \ldots\ldots\ldots\ldots b \\
aaab \ldots\ldots\ldots b
\end{array} \right\} S_2 \\[2ex]
\left. \begin{array}{l}
a \ldots ab \ldots\ldots\ldots b \\
\quad \ldots \\
a \ldots\ldots ab \ldots\ldots b
\end{array} \right\} S_1 \\[3ex]
\left. \begin{array}{l}
a \ldots\ldots\ldots ab \ldots\ldots b \\
\quad \ldots \\
a \ldots\ldots\ldots\ldots ab
\end{array} \right\} S_0 \\[3ex]
\left. \begin{array}{l}
cb^2 ca \ldots\ldots\ldots a \\
cbca^{13} \\
ccaa
\end{array} \right\} V
\end{array}
$$

Fig. 1. JL-Example for $k = 3$

Let $\Sigma = \{a, b, c\}$ be the alphabet over which we define the instance for the SCS. Further, let $m = 4^k$, $k \in \mathbb{N}^+$. Then we define the set $S = \bigcup_{i=0}^{k-1} S_i \cup V$, where $S_i = \{a^j b^{m-j} \mid \frac{m}{2^{2i+1}} \leq j < \frac{m}{2^{2i}}\}$ and $V = \{cb^{i-1} ca^{4^i - i - 1} \mid 1 \leq i \leq k\}$.

We want to show here that this example does not lead to the intended result. To obtain a possibility to refer to strings separately, we consider the sets S_i, $(0 \leq i \leq k-1)$ and V to be ordered in the following way.

Definition 3. Let $S_i(j)$ denote the j-th element in the set S_i, namely $S_i(j) = a^{\frac{m}{2^{2i+1}} + j - 1} b^{m - (\frac{m}{2^{2i+1}} + j - 1)}$, for $1 \leq j \leq |S_i|$. Similarly let $V(j)$ be the j-th element in the set V, namely $V(j) = cb^{j-1} ca^{4^j - j - 1}$, for $1 \leq j \leq k$. For simplification denote $S_i(1)$ by $S_i(first)$ and $S_i(|S_i|)$ by $S_i(last)$.

Now, we examine the JL-Example in more detail and describe how one possible shortest common superstring for S can be constructed.

Align all strings included in the sets S_i $(i = 0, \ldots, k-1)$ at the border between a and b. This leads to the superstring $a^{m-1} b^{m-2}$ of these sets with length $2m - 3$. After doing so, merge the string $V(last) = cb^{k-1} ca^{m-k-1}$ with the achieved superstring. We obtain the optimal superstring of S just by concatenating the remaining strings from V with the so far constructed string (see Figure 1).

In [4] it is claimed that Group-Merge behaves on the presented example such that the algorithm would find the merge of $V(last)$ and $S_0(first)$ which covers the complete set S_0 to be of minimal cost, and that all following merges would be of the same kind, i. e. Group-Merge would carry out merges between $V(k-i)$ and $S_i(first)$ covering the complete set S_i successively. In the second iteration of

Group-Merge this would lead to the situation that the only possibility of merging strings is to concatenate them.

An analysis shows, that in this case a superstring of length $O(n \log n)$ is constructed, where n is the length of the optimal solution (see [4]).

We invented that Group-Merge does not produce this above presented superstring. Instead of this, as we will prove, Group-Merge outputs the optimal solution for this example, except in the case $k = 2$, where the achieved superstring is obviously at most twice as long as the optimal one.

We first disprove the claim of [4] that a merge between $V(last)$ and $S_0(first)$ has the minimal cost over all possible merges. This merge has the cost:

$$\text{cost}(\langle V(last), S_0(first)\rangle_{\frac{m}{2}-k}) = \text{cost}(\langle cb^{k-1}ca^{m-k-1}, a^{\frac{m}{2}}b^{\frac{m}{2}}\rangle_{\frac{m}{2}-k}) = \frac{3m+2k}{m^2+2m}.$$

But it is easy to show that a merge of the strings $S_0(last)$ and $S_0(first)$ provides a lower cost except in the trivial case $k = 1$. This merge covers all strings in the set S_0 and has the following cost:

$$\text{cost}(\langle S_0(last), S_0(first)\rangle_{\frac{m}{2}+1}) = \text{cost}(\langle a^{m-1}b^1, a^{\frac{m}{2}}b^{\frac{m}{2}}\rangle_{\frac{m}{2}+1}) = \frac{3m-2}{m^2}.$$

Assume that the claim in [4] holds, then the inequality $\frac{3m+2k}{m^2+2m} < \frac{3m-2}{m^2}$ must hold. An easy calculation shows that this is only the case if $k = 1$, in all other cases we have disproved the claim of [4].

Moreover, we are able to prove that Group-Merge achieves an approximation ratio of 1.25 in the case of $k = 2$ and gives the optimal superstring in all other cases (with respect to this example).

Theorem 2. *The Group-Merge algorithm computes a shortest common superstring if it is set on the SCS instance derived from the JL-Example for all $k \geq 3$.*

Proof. To prove this theorem we have to distinguish several cases each of which needs a technical analysis. Therefore we omit the formal proof here. The main idea is to compare the costs of feasible merges and to show thereby that Group-Merge performs the merges $\langle S_0(last), S_0(first)\rangle$ and $\langle S_1(last), S_{k-1}(first)\rangle$ in its first iteration which results in the optimal superstring presented already in Figure 1 for the case $k = 3$ in the subsequent iteration.   □

Theorem 2 implies that the tightness of the upper bound for Group-Merge remains as an open problem, in particular this includes that a constant bound for the approximation ratio of Group-Merge may be possible.

4   A Comparison between Group-Merge and Greedy

In the following we will compare the two algorithms Group-Merge and Greedy according to their approximation behavior.

Observation 1. *The Greedy and the Group-Merge algorithm are incomparable according to the length of the achieved superstring.*

Proof. To show that Greedy may construct a longer superstring than Group-Merge, consider the SCS instance $S = \{c(ab)^n, (ba)^n, (ab)^nc\}$ (see [1]). The SCS instance $S' = \{(ab)^{\frac{n}{2}}c^{n+1}, c^{n+1}(ab)^{\frac{n}{2}}, (ba)^{\frac{n}{2}}, (ab)^{\frac{n}{2}}(dd)^n\}$ shows that Group-Merge may construct a longer superstring than Greedy.   □

From the second part of this observation we can derive the following theorem.

Theorem 3. *The approximation ratio of the Group-Merge algorithm with respect to the length measure is at least $\frac{6}{5}$.*

Note that this provides one of the best known lower bounds for the approximation of the Group-Merge algorithm, since we have disproved the JL-Example in Section 3.[2] Note also that it would be of great interest to characterize the input sets for which one algorithm performs better than the other, since one might be able to use this knowledge to combine both algorithms and thus to obtain a well-performing approximation algorithm for the SCS.

5 Approximation of Group-Merge-1 with Respect to the Compression Measure

In this section we present a result showing that the algorithm Group-Merge-1 provides a constant approximation with respect to the compression measure if we assume that all strings are of equal length. Note that the resulting restricted SCS remains NP-hard [2] and also arises in the area of DNA fragment assembly. Moreover we will extend this result to SCS instances where the ratio between the lengths of the longest and the shortest string can be bounded by a constant and also transfer these results to the length measure.

Let S_{eq} be the set of SCS instances, where all strings have the same length.

Theorem 4. *Group-Merge-1 is a 12-approximation algorithm with respect to the compression measure for instances from S_{eq}.*

Proof. In this proof we compare the solutions of the Greedy and Group-Merge-1 algorithm to each other, and point out that Group-Merge-1 is at most 6 times worse than Greedy according to the compression of the superstring. The claimed result can simply be inferred by applying the 2-approximation of Greedy with respect to the compression measure [6].

Without loss of generality we assume that Greedy, in the case that there is more than one possible merge to choose, always takes a merge which also appears in the Group-Merge-1 solution if this is possible. This assumption does not influence the analysis since this type of nondeterminism is already taken into account for Greedy's 2-approximation result. In the sequel we will analyze the situation where both solutions differ from each other, i. e. where Group-Merge-1 and Greedy perform different merges.

---

[2] In [3] a remark claims an example providing a lower bound of 1.3. Also the JL-Example as defined in Section 3 provides a lower bound of 1.25 in the case $k = 2$.

So, let δ be the first step in which the Greedy algorithm carries out a merge different from the merge performed by the Group-Merge-1 algorithm in this step. Denote the merge of Greedy at its δth step by $\langle b_\delta, t_\delta \rangle$, the merge of Group-Merge-1 at its δth step by $\langle \overline{b}_\delta, \overline{t}_\delta \rangle$, and the corresponding overlaps by $\mathrm{ov}(b_\delta, t_\delta)$ and $\overline{\mathrm{ov}}(\overline{b}_\delta, \overline{t}_\delta)$, respectively. Note that $\mathrm{ov}(b_\delta, t_\delta)$ always denotes the maximal overlap between the strings b_δ and t_δ, while the overlap denoted by $\overline{\mathrm{ov}}(\overline{b}_\delta, \overline{t}_\delta)$ might not be the maximal one between these strings.

Taking into account the greedy behavior of both algorithms we can establish the following inequalities. Because of the greedy behavior of Greedy:

$$\mathrm{ov}(b_\delta, t_\delta) \geq \overline{\mathrm{ov}}(\overline{b}_\delta, \overline{t}_\delta) \tag{1}$$

$$\frac{|b_\delta| + |t_\delta| - \mathrm{ov}(b_\delta, t_\delta)}{|b_\delta| + |t_\delta|} \geq \frac{|\overline{b}_\delta| + |\overline{t}_\delta| - \overline{\mathrm{ov}}(\overline{b}_\delta, \overline{t}_\delta)}{\|\overline{S}_\delta\|} \tag{2}$$

where $\overline{S}_\delta$ denotes the set of strings from $S \in S_{\mathrm{eq}}$ which are canceled in Group-Merge-1's δth step. Inequality (2) holds due to Group-Merge-1's greedy behavior.

Recall that if Group-Merge-1 finds out a merge to be minimal according to its cost function there are often more than 2 strings covered by that merge. For that reason one merge of Group-Merge-1 often corresponds to a sequence of merges. For instance, let $\langle \overline{w}_j, \overline{w}_k \rangle$ be the merge carried out by Group-Merge-1, and let $\overline{w}_j, \overline{w}_{j+1}, \ldots, \overline{w}_k$ be the series of covered strings, then this merge matches to a sequence of merges $\langle \overline{w}_j, \overline{w}_{j+1} \rangle, \ldots, \langle \overline{w}_{k-1}, \overline{w}_k \rangle$ which we call *internal merges* in the sequel.

From now, let $l_\delta = |\overline{S}_\delta|$. The basic idea of this proof is to estimate the number of merges of Greedy which will be prevented from being selected for the superstring solution by the merge Group-Merge-1 carries out in the δth step.

It is easy to see that each internal merge can prevent at most 3 merges, namely the merges of Greedy corresponding to merges $\langle \overline{w}_i, t \rangle$, $\langle s, \overline{w}_{i+1} \rangle$ (for some strings s and t), and a merge which closes a cycle, e.g. $\langle \overline{w}_{i+1}, \overline{w}_i \rangle$. So, we can estimate the number of merges of Greedy that might be prevented by a merge of Group-Merge-1 by $3 \cdot (l_\delta - 1) < 3 l_\delta$.

The total amount of overlap provided by the merge Group-Merge-1 carries out at step δ, is $OV(\overline{b}_\delta, \overline{t}_\delta) = \overline{\mathrm{ov}}(\overline{b}_\delta, \overline{t}_\delta) + \|\overline{S}_\delta\| - |\overline{b}_\delta| - |\overline{t}_\delta|$.

To estimate $OV(\overline{b}_\delta, \overline{t}_\delta)$ in terms of the overlap provided by Greedy ($\mathrm{ov}(b_\delta, t_\delta)$) we simply have to transform Inequality (2) above which leads to $OV(\overline{b}_\delta, \overline{t}_\delta) \geq \mathrm{ov}(b_\delta, t_\delta) \cdot \frac{\|\overline{S}_\delta\|}{|b_\delta| + |t_\delta|}$.

If we assume that the length of all strings is the same, it follows that the factor $\frac{\|\overline{S}_\delta\|}{|b_\delta| + |t_\delta|}$ in the above equation is equal to $\frac{l_\delta}{2}$.

From this we can directly conclude that the compression achieved by Group-Merge-1 can be at most 6 times worse than the one provided by Greedy, since at most $3 l_\delta$ merges can be prevented by Group-Merge-1 while at least $\frac{l_\delta}{2}$ times the overlap of the Greedy step is achieved. Since this analysis holds for every index δ, the result extends to the whole solutions as well.

Taking into account the 2-approximation of Greedy with respect to the compression measure we have proved that Group-Merge-1 is 12-approximative with respect to the compression measure under the assumption that all strings have the same length.   □

We can transfer this result to the approximation ratio of Group-Merge-1 with respect to the length measure by utilizing the correspondence between the compression and the length measure (similar as in [6]).

Let S be a SCS instance. Denote the length of the shortest superstring by $\mathrm{opt}(S)$, and its compression by $\mathrm{comp}(S)$. It holds that $\mathrm{opt}(S) + \mathrm{comp}(S) = \|S\|$.

Let $S_{a,b}$ be the set of SCS instances, where $\mathrm{comp}(s) \leq \frac{a}{b}\|S\|$, for $a, b \in \mathbb{N}$ and $a < b$. Let L^c denote the set of SCS instances, where the ratio between the length of the longest and the length of the shortest string is limited by a constant c, and let $S_{a,b}^c = S_{a,b} \cap S^c$.

Theorem 5. *Group-Merge-1 is a* $\frac{12b-a}{12(b-a)}$*-approximation algorithm with respect to the length measure for instances from* $S_{a,b}$.

Proof. Let $S \in S_{a,b}$. From Theorem 4 we know that Group-Merge-1 is a 12-approximation algorithm with respect to the compression measure. Let w be the solution computed by Group-Merge-1, then $\frac{\|S\|-\mathrm{opt}(S)}{\|S\|-|w|} \leq 12$. This can be simplified to $\mathrm{opt}(S) \geq 12|w| - 11\|S\|$. Since we assumed $\mathrm{comp}(S) \leq \frac{a}{b}\|S\|$, which implies $\frac{b}{b-a}\mathrm{opt}(S) \geq \|S\|$, we can estimate $\mathrm{opt}(S) \geq 12|w| - \frac{11b}{b-a}\mathrm{opt}(S)$. From that we can conclude $\frac{12b-a}{12(b-a)}\mathrm{opt}(S) \geq |w|$, which completes this proof.   □

We are able to extend these results to instances from S^c and $S_{a,b}^c$.

Corollary 1. *Group-Merge-1 is a* $(12 \cdot c)$*-approximation algorithm with respect to the compression measure for instances from* S^c.

Corollary 2. *Group-Merge-1 is a* $\frac{12cb-a}{12c(b-a)}$*-approximation algorithm with respect to the length measure for instances from* $S_{a,b}^c$.

Acknowledgments

I would like to thank Hans-Joachim Böckenhauer and Juraj Hromkovič for their helpful comments on previous versions of this paper.

References

1. Blum, A., Jiang, T., Li, M., Tromp, J., Yannakakis, M.: Linear approximation for shortest superstrings. In: *Journal of the ACM 41(4)*, pp. 630–647, July 1994. 298, 299, 300, 303
2. Gallant, J., Maier, D., Storer, J. A.: On Finding Minimal Length superstrings. In: *Journal of Computer and System Sciences 20*, pp. 50–58, 1980. 298, 303
3. Li, M.: Toward a DNA sequencing theory. In: *Proc. 31st IEEE Symp. on Foundation of Computer Science*, pp. 125–134, 1990. 298, 300, 303
4. Jiang, T., Li, M.: DNA Sequencing and String Learning. In: *Mathematical Systems Theory 29*, pp. 387–405, 1996. 298, 299, 300, 301, 302

5. Sweedyk, Z.: A 2 1/2-approximation algorithm for shortest superstring. In: *SIAM Journal on Computing 29 (3)*, pp. 954–86, 1999.   298
6. Tarhio, J., Ukkonen, E.: A greedy approximation algorithm for constructing shortest common superstrings. In: *Theoretical Computer Science 57*, pp. 131–145, 1988.   300, 303, 305

Fast Evolutionary Chains

Maxime Crochemore[1], Costas S. Iliopoulos[2*], and Yoan J. Pinzon[2**]

[1] Institut Gaspard-Monge, Université de Marne-la-Vallée
mac@univ-mlv.fr
www-igm.univ-mlv.fr/~mac
[2] Dept. Computer Science, King's College London, London WC2R 2LS, England
{csi,pinzon}@dcs.kcl.ac.uk
www.dcs.kcl.ac.uk/staff/csi
www.dcs.kcl.ac.uk/pg/pinzon

Abstract. Musical patterns that recur in approximate, rather than identical, form within the body of a musical work are considered to be of considerable importance in music analysis. Here we consider the "evolutionary chain problem": this is the problem of computing a chain of all "motif" recurrences, each of which is a transformation of ("similar" to) the original motif, but each of which may be progressively further from the original. Here we consider several variants of the evolutionary chain problem and we present efficient algorithms and implementations for solving them.

Keywords: String algorithms, approximate string matching, dynamic programming, computer-assisted music analysis.

1   Introduction

This paper is focused on string-matching problems which arise in computer-assisted music analysis and musical information retrieval. In a recent article ([4]), a number of string-matching problems as they apply to musical situations were reviewed, and in particular the problem of "Evolution Detection" was introduced and discussed. It was pointed out that no specific algorithms for this problem, either in music or in string-matching in general, exist in the literature. However, it seems that musical patterns, or "motifs" actually "evolve" in this manner in certain types of composition; an actual case is shown by the successive thematic entries shown in the appended Music Example. A more recent example, from Messiaen's piano work, *Vingt Regards sur L'Enfant Jésus*, is given in [3].

A musical score can be viewed as a string: at a very rudimentary level, the alphabet (denoted by Σ) could simply be the set of notes in the chromatic or diatonic notation, or at a more complex level, we could use the GPIR representation of Cambouropoulos [2] as the basis of an alphabet. Although a musical pattern-detection algorithm using approximate matching (allowing the normal

---

* Partially supported by the Royal Society grant CCSLAAR.
** Partially supported by an ORS studentship.

V. Hlaváč, K. G. Jeffery, and J. Wiedermann (Eds.): SOFSEM 2000, LNCS 1963, pp. 307–318, 2000.

edit operations, insertion, deletion and replacement) will detect the occurrence of an evolving pattern in the early stages of its history, once it becomes too different from the original form (past whatever threshold is set by the algorithm or its parameters) it will naturally be rejected. To detect a musical motif which undergoes continuing "evolutionary" change is a more challenging proposition, and is the object of this paper. Musical patterns that recur in approximate, rather than identical, form within a composition (or body of musical work) are considered to be of considerable importance in music analysis. Simple examples are the familiar cases of the standard "tonal" answer in a conventional fugue, or the increasingly elaborated varied reprises of an 18th-century rondo theme; on a more subtle level, the idée fixe in Berlioz's *Symphonie Fantastique* recurs in a wide variety of different forms throughout the four movements of the symphony. In all these cases, each recurrence can be seen as a transformation of the original motif, and each is roughly equivalently "similar" to the original; a measure of this "similarity" will be preset in an algorithm intended to detect the recurrence of the pattern:

$$A \cdots A' \cdots A'' \cdots A''' \cdots \qquad (a)$$

where each of the strings $A', A'', A''', \ldots$ is similar to A within the maximum edit distance preset in the algorithm.

In this paper we are considering the case where each new recurrence of the pattern is based on the previous one rather than on the original form, somewhat in the manner of a "chain":

$$A \cdots (A)' \cdots ((A)')' \cdots (((A)')')' \cdots \qquad (b)$$

where $(X)'$ denotes a string similar to a given string X within the maximum edit distance preset in the algorithm. These two types of pattern-repetition may in practice, of course, be indistinguishable in certain circumstances; in case (b), a variant of the pattern may actually cancel out the effect of a previous variant, so the overall distance from the original may remain within the bounds allowed by an algorithm for detecting patterns in case (a).

This class of musical pattern-repetition is not extremely common, but it does exist, as the musical examples given above demonstrate. As well as the obvious musical-analytical interest in detecting such evolutionary pattern-chains, they have importance in any application where they might be missed in detecting approximate repetitions of a pattern (case (a)). These would include automated music-indexing systems for data-retrieval, in which each variant of a motif needs to be detected for efficient indexing; for obvious reasons, it would be desirable for the original pattern, rather than arbitrarily-selected successive variants, to appear as a term in the index table.

Approximate repetitions in musical entities play a crucial role in finding musical similarities amongst different musical entities. The problem of finding a new type of repetitions in a musical score, called *evolutionary chains* is formally defined as follows: given a string t (the "text") and a pattern p (the "motif"), find whether there exists a sequence $u_1 = p, u_2, \ldots, u_\ell$ occurring in the text t

such that, for all $i \in \{1, \dots, \ell - 1\}$, u_{i+1} occurs to the right of u_i in t and u_i and u_{i+1} are "similar" (i.e. they differ by a certain number of symbols).

There was no specific algorithm for the evolution chain problem in the literature. Landau and Vishkin [11] gave an algorithm (LV Algorithm) for the *string searching with k-differences* problem: given a text of length n over an alphabet Σ, an integer k and a pattern of length m, find all occurrences of the pattern in the text with at most k-differences; the LV algorithm requires $O(n^2(\log m + \log |\Sigma|))$ running time. The LV method uses a complicated data structure (the suffix tree) that makes their algorithm unsuitable for practical use. Furthermore algorithms for exact repetitions are given in [1,6,14], approximate repeats are treated in [12] and quasiperiodicities in [8,9].

Here we present an $O(n^2 m/w)$ algorithm for several variants of the problem of computing overlapping evolutionary chains with k differences, where n is the length of the input string, m is the length of the motif and w the length of the computer word. Our methods are practical as well as theoretically optimal. Here we have also studied and implemented the computation of the longest evolutionary chain as well as the chain with least number of errors in total; both algorithms also require $O(n^2 m/w)$ operations.

Several variants to the evolutionary problem are still open. The choice of suitable similarity criteria in music is still under investigation. The use of penalty tables may be more suitable than the k-differences criterion in certain applications. Additionally, further investigation whether methods such as [11] can be adapted to solve the above problems is needed.

2   Basic Definitions

Consider the sequences $t_1, t_2, \dots, t_r$ and $p_1, p_2, \dots, p_r$ with $t_i, p_i \in \Sigma \cup \{\epsilon\}$, $i \in \{1, \dots, r\}$, where Σ is an *alphabet*, i.e. a set of symbols and ϵ is the empty string. If $t_i \neq p_i$, then we say that t_i *differs* to p_i. We distinguish among the following three types of differences:

1. A symbol of the first sequence corresponds to a different symbol of the second one, then we say that we have a *mismatch* between the two characters, i.e. $t_i \neq p_i$.
2. A symbol of the first sequence corresponds to "no symbol" of the second sequence, that is $t_i \neq \epsilon$ and $p_i = \epsilon$. This type of difference is called a *deletion*.
3. A symbol of the second sequence corresponds to "no symbol" of the first sequence, that is $t_i = \epsilon$ and $p_i \neq \epsilon$. This type of difference is called an *insertion*.

As an example, see Figure 1; in positions 1, 3, 7 and 8 we have "matches", in positions 2, 4 and 8 we have a "mismatch", a "deletion", and an "insertion" respectively. Another way of seeing this difference is that one can transform the t sequence to p by performing insertions, deletions and replacements of mismatched symbols. (Without loss of generality, in the sequel we omit the empty string ϵ from the sequence of symbols in a string).

$$
\begin{array}{ccccccccc}
 & & 1 & 2 & 3 & 4 & 5 & 6 & 7 & 8 \\
\text{String } \tau: & & B & A & D & F & E & \epsilon & C & A \\
 & & | & & | & | & | & & | & | \\
\text{String } \rho: & & B & C & D & \epsilon & E & F & C & A
\end{array}
$$

Fig. 1. Types of differences: mismatch, deletion, insertion

Let $t = t_1 t_2 \ldots t_n$ and $p = p_1 p_2 \ldots p_m$ with $m < n$. We say that p occurs at position q of t with at most k-differences (or equivalently, a *local alignment of p and t at position q with at most k differences*), if $t_q \ldots t_r$, for some $r > q$, can be transformed into p by performing at most k of the following operations: inserting a symbol, deleting a symbol and replacing a symbol. Furthermore we will use the function $\delta(x,y)$ to denote the minimum number operations (deletions, insertions, replacements) required to transform x into y.

$$
\begin{array}{cccccccccccccc}
 & 1 & 2 & 3 & 4 & 5 & 6 & 7 & 8 & 9 & 10 & 11 & 12 & 13 \\
\text{String } t: & A & B & C & B & B & A & D & F & E & \epsilon & F & E & A \\
 & & & & | & & & | & | & & & & & \\
\text{String } p: & & & & B & C & \epsilon & D & \epsilon & E & F & A & F &
\end{array}
$$
Alignment 1

$$
\begin{array}{cccccccccccccc}
 & 1 & 2 & 3 & 4 & 5 & 6 & 7 & 8 & 9 & 10 & 11 & 12 & 13 \\
\text{String } t: & A & B & C & B & B & A & D & F & E & \epsilon & F & E & A \\
 & & | & | & & & & | & & | & & & & \\
\text{String } p: & B & C & \epsilon & \epsilon & \epsilon & D & \epsilon & E & F & A & F & &
\end{array}
$$
Alignment 2

$$
\begin{array}{cccccccccccccc}
 & 1 & 2 & 3 & 4 & 5 & 6 & 7 & 8 & 9 & 10 & 11 & 12 & 13 \\
\text{String } t: & A & B & C & B & B & A & D & F & E & \epsilon & F & E & A \\
 & & & & | & & | & & | & & & & & \\
\text{String } p: & & & & B & C & D & \epsilon & E & F & A & F & &
\end{array}
$$
Alignment 3

$$
\begin{array}{cccccccccccccc}
 & 1 & 2 & 3 & 4 & 5 & 6 & 7 & 8 & 9 & 10 & 11 & 12 & 13 \\
\text{String } t: & A & B & C & B & B & A & D & \epsilon & F & E & F & E & A \\
 & & & & | & & | & & | & & | & & & \\
\text{String } p: & & & & B & C & D & E & F & A & F & & &
\end{array}
$$
Alignment 4

Fig. 2. String searching with k-differences

Let the text $t = ABCBBADFEFEA$ and the pattern $p = BCDEFAF$ (see Figure 2). The pattern p occurs at position 4 of t with at most 6 differences. The pattern p also occurs at position 2 with 7 differences and position 5 with 5 or 4. The alignment (or alignments) with the minimum number of differences is called an *optimal alignment*.

In the sequel we also make use of the following graph-theoretic notions: A *directed graph* $G = (V, E)$ consist of a set V of vertices (nodes) and a set E of edges (arcs). Let $u, v \in V$, then (u, v) denotes the edge between node u and v. A *path* P from v_1 to v_k is a sequence of nodes $P = \langle v_1, v_2, \ldots, v_k \rangle$. P is said to be *simple* iff the nodes are unique. A *cycle* in G is a path such that $v_1 = v_k$. A *directed acyclic graph (DAG)* is a directed graph without cycles. The *in-*

degree d_i^{in} of node i is the number of incoming edges to i. The *out-degree* d_i^{out} of node i is the number of outgoing edges from i. Let $v_s \in V$ be the *source* node and $v_t \in V$ be the *target* node.

Let $c \colon E \to \mathbb{Z}$ be a *cost* function on the edges of G. We will also say *weight* instead of cost. We will write $c(v, u)$ to denote the cost of the edge (v, u). The cost of a path $P = \langle v_1, v_2, \ldots, v_k \rangle$ is defined to be $c(P) = c(v_1, v_2) + \cdots + c(v_{k-1}, v_k)$. The *shortest path* from a node v_s to a node v_t is said to be the minimum $c(P)$ over all possible paths from v_s to v_t.

3   The Evolutionary Matrix

In this section we present a new efficient algorithm for computing the $n \times n$ *evolutionary matrix* D: for a given text t of length n and a given integer m, we define $D(i, j)$ to be the minimum number of differences between $t_{max(1, i-m+1)}, \ldots, t_i$ and any substring of the text ending at position j of t. Informally, the matrix D contains the best scores of the alignments of all substrings of t of length m and any substring of the text. Table 1a shows an example.

Table 1. Evolutionary matrix D and Tick-matrix M for $t = GGGTCTA$ and $m = 3$

		0	1	2	3	4	5	6	7
		ϵ	G	G	G	T	C	T	A
0	ϵ	0	0	0	0	0	0	0	0
1	G	1	0	0	0	1	1	1	1
2	G	2	1	0	0	1	2	2	2
3	G	3	2	1	0	1	2	3	3
4	T	3	2	1	1	0	1	2	3
5	C	3	2	2	2	1	0	1	2
6	T	3	3	3	3	2	1	0	1
7	A	3	3	3	3	2	2	1	0

(a) Matrix D

		0	1	2	3	4	5	6	7
		ϵ	G	G	G	T	C	T	A
0	ϵ	×	×	×	×	×	×	×	×
1	G	×	✓	✓	✓	×	×	×	×
2	G	×	×	✓	✓	✓	×	×	×
3	G	×	×	×	✓	✓	✓	×	×
4	T	×	×	✓	✓	✓	✓	×	×
5	C	×	✓	✓	✓	✓	✓	✓	×
6	T	×	×	×	×	×	✓	✓	✓
7	A	×	×	×	×	×	×	✓	✓

(b) Matrix M

One can obtain a straightforward $\Theta(n^2 m)$ algorithm for computing the evolutionary matrix D by constructing matrices $D^{(s)}[1 \ldots m, 1 \ldots n]$, $1 \leq s \leq n - m$, where $D^{(s)}(i, j)$ is the minimum number of differences between the prefix of the pattern $t_{max(1, s-m+1)}, \ldots, t_s$ and any contiguous substring of the text ending at t_j; its computation can be based on the Dynamic-Programming procedure presented in [13]. We can obtain D by collating $D^{(1)}$ and the last row of the $D^{(s)}$, $2 \leq s \leq n - m$.

Here we will make use of word-level parallelism in order to compute the matrix D more efficiently, similar to the manner used by Myers in [15] and

```
EVOLUTIONARY-DP(t, m, M)  ▷ n = |t|, × = 1, ✓ = 0
 1  begin
 2     D(0...n, 0) ← min(i, m); D(0, 0...n) ← 0  ▷ initialization
 3     for i ← 1 until n do
 4        for j ← 1 until n do
 5           if i < m then
 6              D(i, j) ← min{D(i − 1, j) + 1, D(i, j − 1) + 1, D(i − 1, j − 1) + δ(t_i, t_j)}
 7           else
 8              D(i, j) ← min{D(i − 1, j) + 1 − M(i, j − 1), D(i, j − 1) + 1,
                            D(i − 1, j − 1) + δ(t_i, t_j) − M(i − 1, j − 1)}
 9  end
```

Algorithm 1: EVOLUTIONARY-DP algorithm

Iliopoulos-Pinzon in [10]. But first we need to compute the $n \times n$ *tick-matrix* M: if there is an optimal alignment of $t_{max(1,i-m+1)}, \ldots, t_i$ and any contiguous substring of the text ending at t_j with the property that there is a difference (i. e. insertion, deletion or mismatch) for $t_{max(1,i-m+1)}$, then we set $M(i, j) \leftarrow \times$ otherwise we set $M(i, j) \leftarrow \checkmark$.

Assume that the tick-matrix $M[0 \ldots n, 0 \ldots n]$ is given. We can use M as an input for the EVOLUTIONARY-DP algorithm (see Algorithm 1) to compute the evolutionary matrix $D[0 \ldots n, 0 \ldots n]$ as follows:

Theorem 1. *Given the text t, the motif length m and the tick-matrix M, the* EVOLUTIONARY-DP *algorithm correctly computes the matrix D in $O(n^2)$ units of time.* □

The key idea behind the computation of M is the use of *bit-vector* operations that gives us a theoretical speed up factor of w in comparison to the method presented in [13], where w is the compiler word length; thus on a "64-bit computer word" machine one can obtain a speed up of 64. We maintain the bit-vector $B(i, j) = b_\ell \ldots b_1$ where $b_r = 1$, $r \in \{1 \ldots \ell\}$, $\ell < 2m$, if and only if there is an alignment of a contiguous substring of the text $t_q \ldots t_j$ (for some $1 \leq q < j$) and $t_{i-m+1} \ldots t_i$ with $D(i, j)$ differences such that

- the leftmost $r - 1$ pairs of the alignment have $\Sigma_\ell^{\ell-r-2} b_j$ differences in total,
- the r-th pair of the alignment (from left to right) is a difference: a deletion in the pattern, an insertion in the text or a replacement.

Otherwise we set $b_r = 0$. In other words $B(i, j)$ holds the binary encoding of the path in D to obtain the optimal alignment at i, j with the differences occurring as leftmost as possible.

Given the restraint that the length m of the pattern is less than the length of the computer word, then the "bit-vector" operations allow to update each entry of the matrix M in constant time (using "shift"-type of operation on the bit-vector). The maintenance of the bit-vector is done via operations defined as follows.

```
Tick-Matrix(t, m)  ▷  n = |t|
 1  begin
 2     B[0 ... n, 0] ← max(i, m) 1's; B[0, 0 ... n] ← ε  ▷ initialization
 3     for i ← 1 until n do
 4        for j ← 1 until n do
 5           if i < m then
 6              B(i, j) ← bitmin{shift(B(i − 1, j)) or 1, shift(B(i, j − 1)) or 1,
                            shift(B(i − 1, j − 1)) or δ(tᵢ, tⱼ)}
 7           else
 8              B(i, j) ← bitmin{shiftc(B(i − 1, j)) or 1, shift(B(i, j − 1)) or 1,
                            shiftc(B(i − 1, j − 1)) or δ(tᵢ, tⱼ)}
 9           if lastbit(B(i, j))=1 then M(i, j) ← × else M(i, j) ← ✓
10     return M
11  end
```

Algorithm 2: Tick-Matrix algorithm

- The *shift* operation moves the bits one position to the left and enter zeros from the right, i.e. $shift(b_\ell \ldots b_1) = b_\ell \ldots b_1 0$.
- The *shiftc* operation shifts and truncates the leftmost bit, i.e. $shift(b_\ell \ldots b_1) = b_{\ell-1} \ldots b_1 0$.
- For $x, y, z \in \mathbb{Z}$, the function *bitmin*(x, y, z) returns the integer with least number of 1's, and if there is a draw then it returns the one with the leftmost bits (i.e. the maximum of the two when they are viewed as a decimal integer).
- The *lastbit* operation returns the leftmost bit, i.e. b_ℓ.
- The *or* operation correspond to the bitwise-or operator.

The *shift*, *shiftc*(x), *bitmin*, *lastbit* and *or* operations can be done in $O(m/w)$ time with $\{|x|, |y|, |z|\} < 2m$.

Algorithm 2 computes the matrix $M[0 \ldots n, 0 \ldots n]$.

Example 1. Let the text t be $GGGTCTA$ and $m = 3$, the matrix B (Table 2) is computed to generate the tick-matrix M (Table 1b). Notice that $M(i, j) \leftarrow \times$ if and only if the *lastbit*$(B(i, j)) = 1$ and $M(i, j) \leftarrow \checkmark$ otherwise.

Theorem 2. *The procedure* Tick-Matrix *correctly computes the tick-matrix M in $O(n^2 m/w)$ units of time.* □

Theorem 3. *The* Evolutionary-DP *matrix D can be computed in $O(n^2 m/w)$ units of time.* □

Hence, this algorithm runs in $O(n^2)$ under the assumption that $m \leq w$, where w is the number of bits in a machine word, i.e., in practical terms the running time is $O(n^2)$. Also, the space complexity can be easily reduced to $O(n)$.

Table 2. The Bit-Vector Matrix B for $t = GGGTCTA$ and $m = 3$

		0	1	2	3	4	5	6	7
		ϵ	G	G	G	T	C	T	A
0	ϵ								
1	G	1	0	0	0	1	1	1	1
2	G	11	10	00	00	01	11	11	11
3	G	111	110	100	000	001	011	111	111
4	T	111	101	001	001	000	0001	110	111
5	C	111	011	011	011	001	000	0001	101
6	T	111	111	111	111	110	001	000	0001
7	A	111	111	111	111	101	101	001	000

4   Longest Non-overlapping Evolutionary Chain

The problem of computing the *longest non-overlapping evolutionary chain* (LNO for short) is as follows: given a text t of length n, a pattern p of length m and an integer $k < m/2$, find whether the strings of the sequence $u_1 = p, u_2, \ldots, u_l$ occur in t and satisfy the following conditions:

1. $\delta(u_i, u_{i+1}) \leq k$ for all $i \in \{1, \ldots, \ell - 1\}$,
2. $s_{i+1} - s_i \geq m$ for all $i \in \{1, \ldots, \ell - 1\}$,
3. maximizes ℓ;

where s_i is the starting position of u_i in t.

The method for finding the LNO is based on the construction of the evolutionary matrix D presented in the previous section and the directed graph $G(V, E)$ defined as follows

$$V = \{v_m, \ldots v_n\} \cup \{v_s, v_t\},$$
$$E = \{(v_i, v_j) : D(i, j) \leq k, \; i \geq m, \; j - i \geq m\}$$
$$\cup \{(v_s, v_i) : d_i^{in} = 0, d_i^{out} > 0 \text{ for each } v_i \in V\}$$
$$\cup \{(v_i, v_t) : d_i^{in} > 0, d_i^{out} = 0 \text{ for each } v_i \in V\}.$$

To complete the construction, we define the cost of an edge as follows

$$c(v_i, v_j) = \begin{cases} 0 & \text{if } v_i, v_j \in \{v_s, v_t\} \\ -1 & \text{otherwise.} \end{cases} \tag{1}$$

The problem of finding the LNO is equivalent to the problem of finding a shortest source-to-sink path in G. Let us denote the shortest path of G ($s \leadsto t$) by $P = \langle v_s, u_1, \ldots, u_\ell, v_t \rangle$, where ℓ will be the length of the LNO.

The time complexity for the shortest path problem is known to be $O(|V| \times |E|)$ in the general case. However, our graph G does not have cycles and all the edges are forward (i. e. for each edge $(u, v) \in V$, u appears before v), so G is a *topologically sorted* DAG. Hence, we can compute the shortest path of G in $O(|V| + |E|)$ time. Algorithm 3 shows the algorithm to compute the LNO. Note that the function $G.add\_edge(v_i, v_j, k)$ adds the edge (v_i, v_j) to the graph G, assigning $c(v_i, v_j) = k$.

LNO(t, m, k) $\triangleright$ $n = |t|$, $G(V, E)$, $V = \{v_m, \ldots, v_n\} \cup \{v_s, v_t\}$
1   **begin**
2     $D[0 \ldots n, 0 \ldots n] \leftarrow$ EVOLUTIONARY-DP(t, m, M)
3   **for** $i \leftarrow m$ **until** $n - m$ **do**
4   **for** $j \leftarrow i + m$ **until** n **do**
5   **if** $D(i, j) < k$ **then** $G.add\_edge(v_i, v_j, -1)$
6   **for** $i \leftarrow m$ **until** n **do**
7   **if** $d_i^{in} = 0$ **and** $d_i^{out} > 0$ **then** $G.add\_edge(v_s, v_i, 0)$
8   **if** $d_i^{in} > 0$ **and** $d_i^{out} = 0$ **then** $G.add\_edge(v_i, v_t, 0)$
9     $P=$ SHORTEST-PATH-DAG(G)
10   **return** $P - \{v_s, v_t\}$
11 **end**

Algorithm 3: LNO algorithm

Example 2. Let the text t be $ABCDADCBAD$, $m = 3$ and $k = 1$. Table 3 shows the evolutionary matrix for the given input. Fig. 3 contains the resulting topologically sorted DAG, the shortest path $P = \langle v_s, 3, 7, 10, v_t \rangle$ (shaded edges), spell out the longest non-overlapping evolutionary chain, which is $\{ABC, ADC, AD\}$.

Table 3. The Evolutionary Matrix D for $t = ABCDADCBAD$ and $m = 3$

		1 A	2 B	3 C	4 D	5 A	6 D	7 C	8 B	9 A	10 D
1	A	0	1	1	1	0	1	1	1	0	1
2	B		0	1	2	1	1	2	1	1	1
3	C			0	1	2	2	1	2	2	2
4	D				0	1	2	2	2	2	1
5	A					0	1	2	2	1	2
6	D						0	1	2	2	1
7	C							0	1	2	1
8	B								0	1	2
9	A									0	1
10	D										0

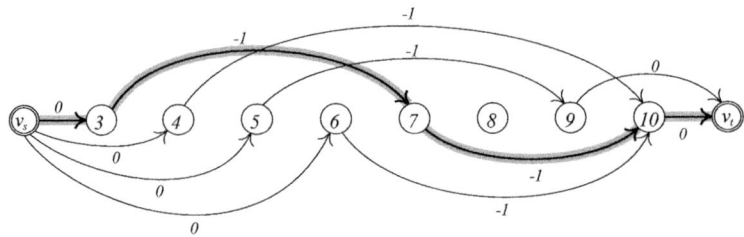

Fig. 3. Graph G for $t = ABCDADCBAD$ and $m = 3$

4.1   Running Time

Assuming that $m \le w$, the time complexity of the LNO algorithm is dominated by the complexity of the EVOLUTIONARY-DP algorithm (see Algorithm 3 line 2). Hence, the overall complexity for the LNO problem will be $O(n^2)$ or $O(n^2/m)$ in the general case. Fig. 4 shows the timing[1] for different values of m and n.

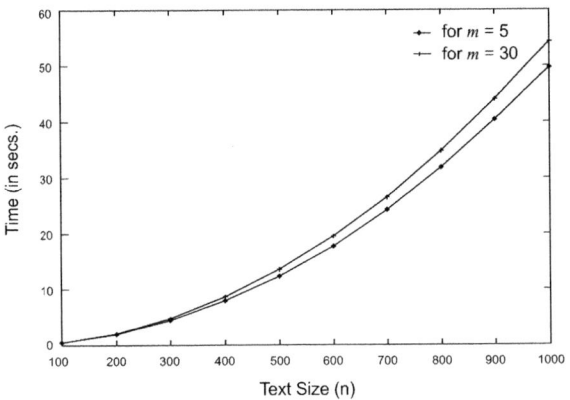

Fig. 4. Timing curves for the LNO Procedure

5   Computing the Longest Nearest-Neighbor Non-overlapping Evolutionary Chain

The problem of computing the *longest nearest-neighbor non-overlapping evolutionary chain* (LNN for short) is as follows: given a text t of length n, a pattern p of length m and an integer $k < m/2$, find whether the strings of the

[1] Using a SUN Ultra Enterprise 300MHz running Solaris Unix.

sequence $u_1 = p, u_2, \ldots, u_\ell$ occur in t and satisfy the conditions for LNO and minimizes

$$d = \sum_{i=1}^{\ell-1} \gamma_i$$

where γ_i is usually the length of the substring (gap) between motif occurrences in the evolutionary chain, i. e. $\gamma_i = f(s_{i+1} - s_i - m)$, where f is a penalty table.

The computation of the LNN can be accomplished by redefining the LNO algorithm (see Algorithm 3). We will use $j - i - m - n+$ instead of -1 in line 5.

6   Computing the Longest Minimum-Weight Non-overlapping Evolutionary Chain

The problem of the *longest minimum-weight non-overlapping evolutionary chain* (LMW for short) is as follows: given a text t of length n, a pattern p of length m and an integer $k < m/2$, find whether the strings of the sequence $u_1 = p, u_2, \ldots, u_\ell$ occur in t and satisfy the conditions for LNO and minimizes

$$e = \sum_{i=1}^{\ell-1} \delta(u_i, u_{i+1}) \,.$$

A slightly modification of the LNO algorithm (see Algorithm 3) will solve the problem, namely, replacing -1 by $-n + D(i,j)$ in line 5.

7   Conclusion and Open Problems

Here we presented practical algorithms for the computation of several variants of the evolutionary chain problem, which are of practical importance.

The problems presented here need to be further investigated under a variety of *similarity* or *distance* rules (see [5]). For example, *Hamming distance* of two strings u and v is defined to be the number of substitutions necessary to get u from v (u and v have the same length).

Finally comparisons of the empirical results obtained and to those that can be obtained from software library of string algorithms (see [7]) should be drawn.

References

1. A. Apostolico and F. P. Preparata, Optimal Off-line Detection of Repetitions in a String, *Theoretical Computer Science*, 22 3, pp. 297–315 (1983).   309
2. E. Cambouropoulos, A General Pitch Interval Representation: Theory and Applications, *Journal of New Music Research* 25, pp. 231–251 (1996).   307
3. E. Cambouropoulos, T. Crawford and C. S. Iliopoulos, (1999) Pattern Processing in Melodic Sequences: Challenges, Caveats and Prospects. In Proceedings of the AISB'99 Convention (Artificial Intelligence and Simulation of Behaviour), Edinburgh, U. K., pp. 42–47 (1999).   307

4. T. Crawford, C. S. Iliopoulos and R. Raman, String Matching Techniques for Musical Similarity and Melodic Recognition, *Computing in Musicology*, Vol 11, pp. 73–100 (1998). 307

5. T. Crawford, C. S. Iliopoulos, R. Winder and H. Yu, Approximate musical evolution, in the Proceedings of the 1999 Artificial Intelligence and Simulation of Behaviour Symposium (AISB'99), G. Wiggins (ed), The Society for the Study of Artificial Intelligence and Simulation of Behaviour, Edinburgh, pp. 76–81 (1999). 317

6. M. Crochemore, An optimal algorithm for computing the repetitions in a word, *Information Processing Letters* 12, pp. 244–250 (1981). 309

7. M. Crochemore, C. S. Iliopoulos and H. Yu, Algorithms for computing evolutionary chains in molecular and musical sequences, *Proceedings of the 9-th Australasian Workshop on Combinatorial Algorithms* Vol 6, pp. 172–185 (1998). 317

8. C. S. Iliopoulos and L. Mouchard, An $O(n \log n)$ algorithm for computing all maximal quasiperiodicities in strings, *Proceedings of CATS'99: "Computing: Australasian Theory Symposium"*, Auckland, New Zealand, Lecture Notes in Computer Science, Springer Verlag, Vol 21 3, pp. 262–272 (1999). 309

9. C. S. Iliopoulos, D. W. G. Moore and K. Park, Covering a string, *Algorithmica* 16, pp. 288–297 (1996). 309

10. C. S. Iliopoulos and Y. J. Pinzon, The Max-Shift Algorithm, submitted. 312

11. G. M. Landau and U. Vishkin, Fast parallel and serial approximate string matching, in *Journal of Algorithms* 10, pp. 157–169 (1989). 309

12. G. M. Landau and J. P. Schmidt, An algorithm for approximate tandem repeats, in *Proc. Fourth Symposium on Combinatorial Pattern Matching*, Springer-Verlag Lecture Notes in Computer Science 648, pp. 120–133 (1993). 309

13. G. M. Landau and U. Vishkin, Introducing efficient parallelism into approximate string matching and a new serial algorithm, in *Proc. Annual ACM Symposium on Theory of Computing*, ACM Press, pp. 220–230 (1986). 311, 312

14. G. Main and R. Lorentz, An $O(n \log n)$ algorithm for finding all repetitions in a string, *Journal of Algorithms* 5, pp. 422–432 (1984). 309

15. E. W. Myers, A Fast Bit-Vector Algorithm for Approximate String Matching Based on Dynamic Progamming, in *Journal of the ACM* 46 3, pp. 395–415 (1999). 311

A Temporal Layered Knowledge Architecture for an Evolving Structured Environment

Cristina De Castro

Centre of Study for Informatics and Telecommunications of the Italian National
Research Council,
V.le Risorgimento 2, Bologna 40136, Italy
phone: +39 051 2093545, fax: +39 051 2093540
cdecastro@deis.unibo.it

Abstract. In this paper a layered architecture is proposed for the representation of an environment that evolves in time. This proposal extends the Layered Knowledge Architecture in [1] and represents the environment by means of a taxonomy of layers. A particular hierarchical graph is defined whose nodes represent a portion of the environment and whose edges represent a path within the environment. Position and cost functions are defined for an efficient path planning.

The proposed architecture is meant to represent and maintain the evolution of the described environment. The concept is defined of *"significant change"*, i.e. a change which alters the cost functions more than a given rate. The idea is exploiting the topological structure of the graph and the consequence of a change on such structure. Necessary and sufficient conditions are stated that assure that a change is significant or not. If a change is significant, a new version of the environment description is produced.

Keywords: structured environment, environment evolution, hierarchical graph connection

Dedication: to Enrico Denti, with deep esteem and gratitude

1   Introduction

The choice of an architecture for the representation of an environment is essential in many applications, ranging from autonomous agents to vehicle navigation systems and the critical problem of *path planning*. In this paper an architecture is proposed for the representation of a structured environment that evolves in time. In particular, an extension is proposed of the *Layered Knowledge Architecture* (LK) in [4]. Such extension deals with the problem of *versioning* the representation of an environment. The topological properties of such environment are exploited in order to recognize all and only the significant changes.

Let us describe the LK model by means of an example. All the concepts will be formalized afterwards. Suppose you must describe an office in a palace with

V. Hlaváč, K. G. Jeffery, and J. Wiedermann (Eds.): SOFSEM 2000, LNCS 1963, pp. 319–326, 2000.

three floors, each floor containing some rooms and each room containing some office furniture, such as chairs, tables, lamps, PCs, etc. In the LK formalism the office is represented by a multi-level graph. At the bottom level, named *Symbolic Layer* in [4], the nodes (*landmarks*) are the pieces of furniture and the edges (*routes*) are the physical paths among them. In the LK formalism, higher level layers can be defined by *aggregation, generalization* or *classification*. In the example, the first layer can be obtained by aggregation, clustering the furniture of the same room. The second knowledge layer (*1-clustered layer*) is obtained by aggregation into rooms. The 1-clustered layer is thus a graph whose nodes are the rooms of the palace and whose edges are the paths connecting the rooms. In the same way, the *2-clustered layer* is obtained by aggregating the rooms of the same floor. In this way a graph is obtained whose nodes are the floors of the palace and whose edges are the stairs. In the *3-clustered layer* all the floors are aggregated in a single node representing the whole office.

Suppose that one chair is moved from a table to another. This type of change does not alter the cost of the navigation from a table to another or from one floor to another. Therefore there is no need of producing a new version of the architecture. On the contrary, if a table and all the furniture around is moved to another room at another floor, the navigation cost for reaching that table may vary deeply. In this case, a new version of the environment description should be produced.

The paper is organized as follows: in Section 2 some related work is compared to the proposed approach. Section 3 describes the LK architecture [4] and the related cost model. Section 4 proposes the temporal extension of such architecture.

2   Related Work

The Knowledge Layered Architecture [4] describes the environment as a hierarchy of graphs. The n-th level graph is derived from the $(n-1)$th level one by applying one of the abstraction primitives: *classification, aggregation, generalization*. In the literature, there are many other interesting hierarchical approaches to path planning, such as [2,3,6], all oriented to a landmark-based navigation. In [2] the hierarchy is built-up by finding out sub-goals for inter-landmark navigation and, at the successive level, a larger goal. The model proposed in [3] contains a control level, a topological level and a geometrical level. The LK approach extends the landmark-based navigation by introducing classification and generalization for a better formulation of path-planning problems.

The extension of the LK formalism to an evolving environment arises from the well known research about temporal information (see [5] for a very rich compendium).

3   The Layered Knowledge Architecture

The main purpose of the Knowledge Layered Architecture is the efficient path planning in a structured environment. A knowledge layer is a meaningful abstraction of the environment, containing only those details which are significant for a specific task. Each layer is obtained from those at the previous level by applying one of the abstraction primitives of classification, generalization and aggregation. Each abstraction primitive describes a specific meta-knowledge of the environment:

- *Meta-knowledge by classification* describes the categories of objects that may be encountered in the environment.
- *Meta-knowledge by generalization* describes hierarchical relationships between categories of objects.
- *Meta-knowledge by aggregation* describes significant clusters of objects.

In the LK formalism, the environment is represented by the *symbolic* layer and *clustered* layers.

3.1   The Symbolic Layer

The symbolic layer is a weakly connected graph whose nodes are the landmarks and whose edges are the physical paths among them, named routes. A landmark l_i is represented by its coordinates in the 3-D space, the origin being the first landmark visited. A route $[l_i \rightarrow l_j]$ is associated to the cost navigation from l_i to l_j. The symbolic layer is denoted by $\mathcal{L}^{(0)} = (L^{(0)}, R^{(0)})$, where $L^{(0)}$ is the set of landmarks and $R^{(0)}$ the set of routes.

3.2   The Clustered Layer

A clustered layer is a weakly connected graph whose nodes are sets of landmarks or sets of clusters and whose edges, named *bridges* are routes connecting sets of landmarks or sets of clusters.

The nodes (1-clusters) of a 1-clustered layer are sets of landmarks and its bridges (1-briges) are routes that connect distinct 1-clusters. If we partition the 1-clusters we obtain a higher level clustered layer, named 2-clustered layer, whose nodes (2-clusters) are sets of clusters of the previous layer and whose edges (2-bridges) are routes connecting distinct 2-clusters. The process can be iterated to the k-th level, obtaining thus the k-clustered layer.

Formally:

Definition 1. Given an oriented graph $\mathcal{L} = (L, R)$, a *clustering* on $\mathcal{L}$ is defined as a partitioning $\xi = \{L_1, \ldots, L_m\}$ of L. The sub-graphs $C_i = (L_i, R_i), i = 1, \ldots, m$ where R_i is the subset of routes connecting nodes of L_i:

$$R_i = \{[l \rightarrow l'] \in R : l \in L_i \wedge l' \in L_i\}.$$

Definition 2. Given an ordered pair of clusters (C_i, C_j), $i \neq j$, we call *bridge* the (possibly empty) set:

$$[C_i, \to C_j] = \{[l \to l'] \in R : l \in L_i \wedge l' \in L_j\} \quad i, j = 1, \ldots, m.$$

Definition 3. The *image* $\mathcal{L}$ *through* ξ is the directed graph $\mathcal{L}^*$ whose nodes are the clusters and whose edges are the bridges that ξ defines on $\mathcal{L}$:

$$\mathcal{L}^* = (C_1, \ldots, C_m, [C_i \to C_j] : [C_i \to C_j] \neq \emptyset, i, j = 1, \ldots, m, i \neq j).$$

For any given graph $\mathcal{L}$, a hierarchical clustering of order n can be defined, by applying first a clustering $\xi = \xi^{(0)}$ to $\mathcal{L} = \mathcal{L}^{(0)}$, then a clustering $\xi^{(1)}$ to $\mathcal{L}^* = \mathcal{L}^{(1)}$ and iteratively a clustering $\xi^{(k)}$ to $\mathcal{L}^{(k)}$, $k = 0, n - 1$.

Definition 4. Let the symbolic layer $\mathcal{L}^{(0)}$ and a nth-level hierarchical clustering $\xi^{(0)}, \ldots, \xi^{(n-1)}$ be given. We name k-*clustered layer*, with $k = 1, \ldots, n$, the weakly connected[1] directed graph $\mathcal{L}^{(k)}$, image of $\mathcal{L}^{(k-1)}$ through $\xi^{(k-1)}$. The vertices are named k-*clusters* and the edges k-*bridges*.

3.2.1 Representation of k-Clusters and k-Bridges.

At the symbolic layer, the landmarks are represented by their coordinates and the routes by their navigation cost. The problem is how to represent the "position" of a k-cluster and the "cost" of a k-bridge. The idea is the following: each 1-cluster $C_h^{(1)}$ of $\mathcal{L}^{(1)}$ can be represented by the coordinates of the barycentre of its landmarks. Let us enote by α_i the coordinates of the i-th landmark. The "position" of a k-cluster $C_i^{(k)}$ of $\mathcal{L}^{(k)}$ can be recursively defined as the barycentre of the positions of the (k-1)-clusters it contains:

$$pos(C_i^{(k)}) = \begin{cases} \alpha_i & \text{if } k = 1 \\ \text{avg}_{C_j \in \mathcal{L}_i^{(k-1)}} \, pos(C_j^{(k-1)}) & \text{if } 2 \leq k \leq n. \end{cases}$$

In the same way, the navigation cost from the cluster $C_i^{(k)}$ to the cluster $C_j^{(k)}$ can be recursively defined as the sum of three costs: the inter-cluster navigation from the cluster $C_i^{(k)}$ to a generic cluster $C_v^{(k-1)}$ at the k-1 layer plus the intra-cluster-navigation from $C_v^{(k-1)}$ to $C_z^{(k-1)}$ plus the inter-cluster navigation from $C_z^{(k-1)}$ to the cluster $C_j^{(k)}$. Considering the symbolic layer, this represents the moving cost from the barycentre of $C_i^{(1)}$ to the first endpoint of the bridge leading from $C_i^{(1)}$ to $C_j^{(1)}$, plus the cost of the route, plus the moving cost from the barycentre of $C_j^{(1)}$ to the second endpoint of the bridge.

Formally, $cost([C_i^{(1)} \to C_j^{(1)}]) = \gamma_{ij}$, otherwise for $k > 1$

$$cost([C_i^{(k)} \to C_j^{(k)}]) =$$
$$\text{avg}_{[C_v^{(k-1)} \to C_z^{(k-1)}] \in [C_i^{(k)} \to C_j^{(k)}]} \, ec([C_v^{(k-1)} \to C_z^{(k-1)}])$$

---

[1] It can be proved that, given a weakly connected directed graph $\mathcal{L}$, $\mathcal{L}^*$ is also a weakly connected directed graph.

where γ_{ij} denotes the navigation cost of the route $[l_i \rightarrow l_j]$ and ec is defined as follows:

$$ec([C_v^{(k-1)} \rightarrow C_z^{(k-1)}]) =$$
$$cost([C_i^k \rightarrow C_v^{(k-1)}]) + cost([C_v^{(k-1)} \rightarrow C_z^{(k-1)}]) + cost([C_z^{(k-1)} \rightarrow C_j^k]).$$

4   Environment Changes and the Delta Method

In this section an extension is proposed of the LK architecture, in order to represent the temporal evolution of the represented environment. The result of an *environment change* is time-stamped with *transaction-time* [5]. In this case *the instant when the environment change is recorded in the knowledge base.*

The considered environment changes (*e. c.*) are:

1. adding a landmark,
2. dropping a landmark,
3. adding a cluster,
4. dropping a cluster.

The consequences of each of the above environment changes are considered, giving great care to the maintainance or the loss of connection.

The concept of *significant environment changes* is defined in the following and necessary and sufficient conditions are stated for their recognition. Depending on the change being significant or not, the e.c. produces a new environment version or a Δ-version, i. e. the description of the change and its timestamp. This technique, here adapted for environment representation, was first proposed in [1] for efficient tuple versioning. In the relational context, the update of an attribute did not produce a new timestamped tuple but only a record containg the updated value and the timestamp.

Let us denote by $(\mathcal{L}^{(k)}, T_z), k = 0, \ldots, n - 1$, the environment description as recorded at transaction time T_z. [2] If the adding of a landmark causes a significant change, a new environment version $(\mathcal{L}^{(k)}, T_w), k = 0, \ldots, n - 1$ is produced, T_w being the transaction-time of the change. If the change does not alter the environment significantly, a triple (l_i, α_i, T_w) and a set $(\{[l_i \rightarrow l_j], \gamma_{ij}\}, T_w)$ are produced. The triple records the landmark symbol, its coordinates and the transaction-time of the change. The set records the symbols and costs of the routes added as a consequence of adding l_i.

4.1   Concept of Significant Environment Change (s. e. c.)

From the recursive expressions of the position $pos(C_i^{(k)})$ of a k-cluster $C_i^{(k)}$ and the cost $cost([C_i^{(k)} \rightarrow C^{(k)}])$ of a k-bridge $[C_i^{(k)} \rightarrow C^{(k)}]$, we can observe that:

---

[2] Recording of a delta or of a new version

- $pos(C_i^{(k)})$ represents the barycentre of the $(k-1)$-clusters contained in $C_i^{(k)}$. By recursion, the barycentre is calculated at the symbolic-layer (base case), the barycentre of the barycentres of the 1-clusters, etc.,
- $cost([C_i^{(k)} \to C^{(k)}])$ can be recursively obtained from the average length of three parts:
  1. lines that connect the barycentre of $C_i^{(k)}$ to $(k-1)$-clusters in the layer below (inter-cluster navigation),
  2. (k-1)bridges between to (k-1)-clusters in the layer below (intra-cluster navigation),
  3. lines that connect the barycentre of $C_j^{(k)}$ to $(k-1)$-clusters in the layer below (inter-cluster navigation).

Notation: $C_{i,T_w}^{(k)}$ is the k-cluster $C_i^{(k)}$ at the time T_w of the environment change; $C_{i,T_z}^{(k)}$ is the k-cluster $C_i^{(k)}$ at the previous instant T_z; $S_{pos}^{(k)}$ represents a chosen threshold.

The considerations above lead to the following consequence: an environment change e. c. is *significant* (s. e. c.) if the barycentre of a k-cluster $C_i^{(k)}$ is varied more than $S_{pos}^{(k)}$. Furthermore, we argue the same condition leads the cost of a k-bridge to vary in a significant way:

$$\left| pos(C_{i,T_z}^{(k)}) - pos(C_{i,T_w}^{(k)}) \right| > S_{pos}^{(k)} . \tag{1}$$

Note that (1) is a sufficient but not necessary condition, since it does not take into account the possible loss of connection that an e. c. may cause. Therefore, *a necessary and sufficient condition for an e. c. to be a s. e. c. is that (1) holds or the e. c. causes loss of connection.* The condition for the loss of connection will be formalized for each type of environment change.

4.2   Analysis of Environment Changes

For each environment change, the following paragraphs discuss these topics:

1. Can the environment change cause loss of connection?
2. If so, what is the condition?
3. On which conditions the environment change moves the barycentre in a significant way?
4. On which conditions a Δ-version must be produced and how is it defined?

4.2.1   Adding a Landmark l_i.
The adding of a landmark can not cause loss of connection: at most it adds connection. Furthermore, if it does not alter too much the barycentre at the symbolic layer, it will not alter the position of the k-cluster. Therefore, given n landmarks $l_1, \ldots, l_n$ at time T_z, if a landmark l_i is added at time T_w, a necessary and sufficient condition for $ADD(l_i)$ to be a s. e. c. is:

$$\left| \frac{\alpha_1 + \cdots + \alpha_n}{n} - \frac{\alpha_1 + \cdots + \alpha_n + \alpha_i}{n+1} \right| > S_{pos}^{(0)} . \tag{2}$$

4.2.2 Dropping a Landmark l_i. Suppose that the landmark l_i is dropped at time T_w. Two situations must be distinguished according to the loss or maintainance of connection at the symbolic layer. The necessary and sufficient condition for the loss of connection is that, after the dropping of l_i, at least a landmark l_j is not connected to any other landmark:

$$\exists l_j \in \{L^{(0)} - \{l_i\}\} : \neg \exists l_k \in \{L^{(0)} - \{l_i\}\} : \exists [l_j \rightarrow l_k] \tag{3}$$

where $[l_j \rightarrow l_k]$ is a route or a path.

Let us now examine the condition of moving the barycentre more than a fixed threshold. If $DROP(l_i)$ does not alter too much the position of the barycentre at the symbolic layer, it can not alter the position of a cluster:

$$\left| \frac{\alpha_1 + \cdots + \alpha_n}{n} - \frac{\alpha_1 + \cdots + \alpha_n - \alpha_i}{n-1} \right| > S_{pos}^{(0)}. \tag{4}$$

In a few words, at the dropping of a landmark l_i, the following algorithm can be applied:

```
if (3) or (4) then
produce (L^(k), T_w), k = 0, ..., n − 1
else produce the Δ version (−l_i, α_i, T_w)
```

4.2.3 Adding a Cluster C_i^k. Similarly to the adding of a landmark, the adding of a cluster can not cause loss of connection. Therefore, such e. c. is significant if and only if it moves the position of the destination cluster at the (k+1)-layer:

$$\left| pos(C_{i,T_z}^{(k+1)}) - pos(C_{i,T_w}^{(k+1)}) \right| > S_{pos}^{(k+1)}. \tag{5}$$

4.2.4 Dropping a Cluster C_i^k. Suppose that the cluster $C_{i,T_z}^{(k)}$ is dropped at time T_w.

As for the dropping of a landmark, two situations must be distinguished according to the loss or maintainance of connection at the symbolic layer. The necessary and sufficient condition for the loss of connection is that, after the dropping of $C_{i,T_z}^{(k)}$, at least a cluster is not connected to any other cluster:

$$\exists C_l^k : \neg \exists C_m^k, \exists [C_l^k \rightarrow C_m^k] \tag{6}$$

where $[C_l^k \rightarrow C_m^k]$ is bridge or a path.

The condition on the barycentre is always the same:

$$\left| pos(C_{i,T_z}^{(k+1)}) - pos(C_{i,T_w}^{(k+1)}) \right| > S_{pos}^{(k+1)}. \tag{7}$$

In a few words, at the dropping of a cluster $C_i^{(k)}$, the following algorithm can be applied:

```
if (6) or (7) then
produce (L^(k), T_w), k = 0, ..., n - 1
else produce the Δ version (C_{i,T_z}^{(k)}, pos(C_{i,T_z}^{(k)}), T_w)
```

4.3 Sequences of "Small" Changes

Suppose that a sequence of small changes appears. Suppose that each change is not significant but the global effect is. In order to control such situation the global navigation cost should be periodically controlled.

5 Conclusion

In this paper a method was proposed for the representation of a structured environment that evolves in time. The topological consequences of a significant class of changes were studied and necessary and sufficient conditions were stated for the production of a new version of the environment description.

References

1. P. Dadam, V. Lum, H. D. Werner. "Integration of Time Versions into a Relational Database System", *Proc. of 10th International Conference on Very Large Databases (VLDB)*, Singapore, 1984. 323
2. Faverjon and P. Tournassoud, "The mixed approach for motion planning: learning global strategies from a local planner", *Proc. of Int. Joint Conf. on Artificial Intell.*, vol. 2, pp. 1131-1137, 1987. 320
3. B. J. Kuipers, R. Froom, W. Lee and D. Pierce, "The semantic hierarchy in robot learning", in *Robot Learning*, J. H. Connel and S. Mahadevan Eds., Kluwer Academic Publishers, pp. 141-170, 1992. 320
4. D. Maio and S. Rizzi, "Layered Knowledge Architecture For Navigation-Oriented Environment Representation", Technical Report CIOC-C. N .R. n. 108, 1996. 319, 320
5. A. Tansel, J. Clifford, V. Gadia, A. Segev, R. T. Snodgrass (eds). *Temporal Databases: Theory, Design and Implementation*. The Benjamin/Cummings Publishing Company, Redwood City, California, 1993. 320, 323
6. S. Timpf, G. S. Volta, D. Pollock and M. J. Egenhofer, "A conceptual model of wayfinding using multiple levels of abstraction", in *Theories and methods of spatio-temporal reasoning in geographic space*, A. U. Frank, I. Campari and U. Formentini Eds., Lecture Notes in Computer Science, 639, Springer-Verlag,1992. 320

On-Line Maximum-Order Induced Hereditary Subgraph Problems

Marc Demange[1], Xavier Paradon[2], and Vangelis Th. Paschos[2]

[1] CERMSEM, Université Paris I, Maison des Sciences Economiques
106-112 boulevard de l'Hôpital, 75647 Paris Cedex 13, France
demange@univ-paris1.fr
[2] LAMSADE, Université Paris-Dauphine
Place du Maréchal De Lattre de Tassigny, 75775 Paris Cedex 16, France
{paradon,paschos}@lamsade.dauphine.fr

Abstract. We first study the competitivity ratio for the on-line version of the problem of finding a maximum-order induced subgraph satisfying some hereditary property, under the hypothesis that the input graph is revealed by clusters. Then, we focus ourselves on two of the most known instantiations of this problem, the maximum independent set and the maximum clique.

1 Introduction

On-line algorithmic is a very active computer science area where one supposes that the instance of a problem is revealed step-by-step and one has, at the end of each step, to irrevocably decide on the part of the final solution dealing with this step.

In this paper, we study an on-line version of the following problem, denoted by HG: given an input-graph G, find a maximum-order subgraph of G verifying a non-trivial hereditary property π. Let $\mathcal{G}$ be the class of all graphs. A graph-property π is a mapping from $\mathcal{G}$ to $\{0, 1\}$ (for $G \in \mathcal{G}$, $\pi(G) = 1$ iff G satisfies π and $\pi(G) = 0$, otherwise). Property π is hereditary if whenever it is satisfied by a graph it is also satisfied by every one of its induced subgraphs; it is non-trivial if it is true for infinitely many graphs and false for infinitely many ones. The property "π: is a clique", or "π: is an independent set" are typical examples of such non-trivial hereditary properties. The maximum clique problem, or the maximum independent set problem are typical examples of hereditary induced subgraph problems.

The on-line version of HG, denoted by LHG is defined as the pair (HG,$\boldsymbol{R}$) where $\boldsymbol{R}$ is a set of rules dealing with:

1. information on the value of some parameters of the final graph,
2. how the final graph is revealed.

An *on-line* algorithm decides at each step which of the vertices revealed during this step will belong to the final solution. The performance of an on-line

V. Hlaváč, K. G. Jeffery, and J. Wiedermann (Eds.): SOFSEM 2000, LNCS 1963, pp. 327–335, 2000.

algorithm **A** is measured in terms of the so-called competitivity ratio c defined, for an instance G and a set $\boldsymbol{R}$, as the ratio of the worst[1] value of the solution computed by **A** on G to $\beta(G)$, where $\beta(G)$ is the value of the solution computed by an optimal off-line algorithm on G.

In this paper, we consider that the input-graph G is revealed per non-empty clusters, i.e., per induced subgraphs of G together with the edges linking vertices of the last revealed cluster to the already revealed ones. In what follows, we denote by $t(n)$ the number of clusters needed so that the whole graph is completely revealed.

Two well-known particular cases of HG are the maximum independent set problem (IS) and the maximum clique problem (Cl). The former is the problem of finding a maximum-size subset $V' \subseteq V$ of a graph $G(V, E)$ such that $\forall (v, u) \in V' \times V'$, $vu \notin E$, while the latter is the problem of finding a maximum-size subset $V' \subseteq V$ of a graph $G(V, E)$ such that $\forall (v, u) \in V' \times V'$, $vu \in E$.

In what follows, we first study LHG. Next we deal with on-line versions of IS and Cl, denoted by LIS and LCl, respectively, under the restrictive case where $t(n) = n$, i.e., when the graph is revealed vertex-by-vertex, and the general one where $t(n) < n$. Finally we study some competitivity preserving reductions for LIS and LCl. The results here are mentioned without detailed proofs, which can be found in [ ].

2   On-Line Maximum-Order Hereditary Subgraph

We consider that G is revealed by $t(n)$ non-empty clusters. In what follows, we suppose that when we deal with approximation, or competitivity ratios, functions of a certain number of parameters of the final graph, the values of these parameters are known from the beginning of the on-line process. In this paper we consider ratios, functions of n and/or $\Delta(G)$, the maximum degree of the final graph.

Theorem 1. *Suppose that HG can be approximately solved by a polynomial time approximation algorithm **FA** achieving approximation ratio*[2] *$\rho(n, \Delta(G))$ (decreasing in n and $\Delta(G)$ for a maximization problem). Then, there exists an on-line algorithm **LA** for LHG achieving $c_{\boldsymbol{LA}}(G) \geq \sqrt{\rho(n, \Delta(G))/nt(n)}$.*

Proof (sketch). Consider Algorithm 1 where $r(n, \Delta(G))$ is a threshold-function specified later.

If $\exists i, |\mathbf{FA}(G_i)| \geq r(n, \Delta(G))$, then

$$c_{\mathbf{LA}}(G) \geq \frac{|S|}{\beta(G)} \geq \frac{r(n, \Delta(G))}{n}. \tag{1}$$

---

[1] Over all the ways G is revealed according to $\boldsymbol{R}$.

[2] The approximation ratio of a polynomial time approximation algorithm **A** for an instance I of an **NPO** problem is the ratio of the value of the solution produced by **A** on I to the value of the optimal solution of I.

$i \leftarrow 1;$
while $|\mathbf{FA}(G_i)| < r(n, \Delta(G))$ **and** $i \leq t(n) - 1$ **do**
  $i \leftarrow i + 1;$
end while
output $S \leftarrow \mathbf{FA}(G_i);$

Algorithm 1: Algorithm **LA**

On the other hand, if, $\forall i \leq t(n)$, $|\mathbf{FA}(G_i)| < r(n, \Delta(G))$, then

$$\beta(G_i) \leq \frac{|\mathbf{FA}(G_i)|}{\rho(n_i)} \leq \frac{r(n, \Delta(G))}{\rho(n, \Delta(G))}. \tag{2}$$

Since we deal with hereditary properties, the restriction of an optimal solution on G in every G_i, forms a feasible solution for G_i; consequently, by expression (2) we get $\beta(G) \leq \sum_{i=1}^{t(n)} \beta(G_i) \leq t(n)r(n, \Delta(G))/\rho(n, \Delta(G))$. Moreover, since $|\mathbf{FA}(G_{t(n)})| \geq 1$, we have $|S| \geq 1$ and this together with the expression for $\beta(G)$ gives

$$\frac{|S|}{\beta(G)} \geq \frac{\rho(n, \Delta(G))}{t(n)r(n, \Delta(G))}. \tag{3}$$

Combining expressions (1) and (3), we get

$$c_{\mathbf{LA}}(G) \geq \min \left\{ \frac{r(n, \Delta(G))}{n}, \frac{\rho(n, \Delta(G))}{t(n)r(n, \Delta(G))} \right\}. \tag{4}$$

Setting $r(n, \Delta(G)) = \sqrt{n\rho(n, \Delta(G))/t(n)}$ one obtains the result claimed. □

Starting from Theorem 1 the following results can be deduced.

Corollary 1. *Let $t(n)$ be a fixed constant. Then $c_{\mathbf{LA}}(G) \geq O(\sqrt{\rho(n, \Delta(G))/n})$. Moreover, if $\rho(n) = O(\log n/n)$ [4], then $c_{\mathbf{LA}}(G) \geq O(\sqrt{\log n}/n)$.*

In the case where ρ depends only in n and is convex one can improve the result of Theorem 1. In [3] we prove the following theorem.

Theorem 2. *When $\rho(n)$ is convex, then $c_{\mathbf{LA}}(G) \geq O(\sqrt{\rho(n/t(n))/nt(n)})$.*

Note that the discussion above can be interpreted in terms of reduction of LHG to HG, transforming any approximation ratio $\rho(n, \Delta(G))$ for HG to a competitivity ratio $(\rho(n, \Delta(G))/(nt(n)))^{1/2}$ for LHG.

3   On-Line Independent Set

3.1   Vertices Arrive One-by-One

We now suppose that vertices arrive one-by-one together with the edges linking them to the vertices already revealed. Once a vertex arrived, an on-line algorithm

```
V ← ∅;
S ← ∅;
for i ← 1 to n do
        V ← V ∪ {v_i};
        E ← E ∪ {v_i v_j : v_j ∈ V};
        if ∀v_j ∈ V, v_i v_j ∉ E then
                S ← S ∪ {v_i};
        end if
end for
output S;
```

Algorithm 2: Algorithm **LS**

has to definitely decide if it will include it in the solution under construction. The simplest such algorithm is Algorithm 2 where we suppose that vertices are indexed in the order of their arrival.

In what follows, dealing with IS, we denote by $\alpha(G)$ the independence number of G. It is easy to see that the set S computed by algorithm **LS** is a maximal independent set. Moreover, it is well-known that maximal independent sets are of size at least $\alpha(G)/\Delta(G)$.

Proposition 1. $c_{\mathbf{LS}} \geq 1/\Delta(G)$.

Theorem 3. *Under the hypothesis that vertices are revealed one-by-one, then, $\forall \epsilon > 0$, no on-line algorithm can guarantee competitivity ratio greater than $1/(\Delta(G) - \epsilon)$.*

Proof (sketch). Choose some $\epsilon > 0$ and set $L = \lceil 1/\epsilon \rceil$. Consider $\Delta \in \mathbb{N}$ and set $n = L(\Delta + 1)$. It could happen that:

- whenever a set S of Δ independent vertices has been revealed but has not been taken in the solution under construction, then the next vertex revealed is the root of a tree of depth 1 having the vertices of S as leaves,
- whenever a vertex v is included in the solution and the number of vertices already revealed is less than $n - \Delta$, then the Δ next revealed vertices together with v form a tree of depth 1 rooted at v,
- suppose that less than, or equal to, $\Delta + 1$ vertices, $v_0, v_1, \ldots, v_\Delta$ remain to be revealed in this order, and that $v_0, \ldots, v_i$, $1 \leq i \leq \Delta - 1$, form an independent set and $v_0, \ldots, v_{i-1}$ have not been included in the solution under construction, whereas v_i is included; then, the subgraph of G induced by $v_0, v_1, \ldots, v_\Delta$ can be a tree T of depth 2 such that:
  - v_i is the root of T,
  - the first level of T consists of $v_{i+1}, \ldots, v_\Delta$ where v_{i+1} is internal and $v_{i+2}, \ldots, v_\Delta$ are leaves,
  - the second level of T consists of leaves $v_0, \ldots, v_{i-1}$;
- the final graph G has no edge other than the ones of the items above.

Remark that the graph so-constructed is of order n and has maximum degree $\Delta(G) = \Delta$.

It is easy to see that $\alpha(G) \geq L\Delta(G) - 1$ and the solution constructed contains no more than L vertices. Then, the competitivity ratio is the one claimed.   □

3.2 Vertices Are Revealed by Clusters

As we have already mentioned, IS is one of the most known instantiations of HG. Consequently, the result of Theorem 1 applies here. The best approximation ratio (in terms of n) is guaranteed by the algorithm of [1] and is of $O(\log^2 n/n)$. Using this ratio in Theorem 1 and Corollary 1 (in other words, considering the algorithm of [1] in place of **FA** in algorithm **LA**), the following results (the proof of which are given in [3]) hold.

Theorem 4. $c_{\mathbf{LA}}(G) \geq O(\log n/n\sqrt{t(n)})$. *When $t(n)$ is a fixed constant, then $c_{\mathbf{LA}}(G) \geq O(\log n/n)$. Function $\log^2 n/n$ being convex (for $n \geq 31$), if $t(n) \leq O(n/\log n)$, then, $c_{\mathbf{LA}}(G) \geq O(\log \log n/n)$.*

4   On-Line Maximum Clique

In what follows, we denote by $\kappa(G)$ the size of a maximum clique of G and, for $V' \subseteq V$, we denote by $G[V']$, the subgraph of G induced by V'.

4.1   Vertices Arrive One-by-One

We suppose here that the final graph does not contain isolated vertices. Let us consider Algorithm 3, where, as in Sect. 3.1, we suppose that vertices are indexed in the order of their arrival. Since the final graph G has no isolated vertices, $|K| \geq 2$. On the other hand, $\kappa(G) \leq \Delta(G) + 1$. Consequently, $c_{\mathbf{LCl}}(G) \geq 2/\Delta(G) + 1$.

```
V ← ∅;
K ← ∅;
for i ← 1 to n do
        V ← V ∪ {vᵢ};
        E ← E ∪ {vᵢvⱼ : vⱼ ∈ V};
        if ∀vⱼ ∈ K, vᵢvⱼ ∈ E then
                K ← K ∪ {vᵢ};
        end if
end for
output K;
```

Algorithm 3:

4.2   Vertices Arrive by Clusters

Of course, Cl being another well-known instantiation of HG, the results of Sect. 3.2 apply identically here. In what follows, we will use polynomial reductions in order to obtain competitivity ratios functions of $\Delta(G)$ for LCl.

4.2.1   Reducing On-Line Clique to (Off-Line) Clique.

By the proof of Theorem 1 and taking into account that $\kappa(G) \leq \Delta(G) + 1$, we get the following theorem.

Theorem 5. *Under the on-line model where vertices arrive by clusters, IS reduces to LCl. This reduction transforms every approximation ratio $\rho(n)$ for IS to a competitivity ratio $O(\sqrt{\rho(\Delta(G))/t(n)\Delta(G)})$ for LCl.*

In [2], we devise a polynomial time approximation algorithm guaranteeing approximation ratio $O(\log^2 \Delta(G)/\Delta(G))$ for Cl. Using this result together with Theorem 5 we get the following corollary.

Corollary 2. *For $t(n)$ a fixed constant, $O(\log \Delta(G)/\Delta(G))$ can be guaranteed for LCl.*

4.2.2   Reducing On-Line Clique to On-Line Independent Set.

Revisit now algorithm **LA**, instantiate algorithm **FA** by the algorithm of [1] and consider that, instead of G_i, the input of **LA** is $\bar{G}_i$ (since G_i is known, so does $\bar{G}_i$). Then, using the complementarity relation: independent set in G_i — clique in $\bar{G}_i$, one can easily deduce the following Theorem 6.

Theorem 6. *There exist a reductions from LCl to LIS (and vice-versa) preserving competitivity ratios, functions of n.*

An immediate consequence of Theorem 6 is that the results of Theorem 4 holds also for LCl.

We now show how a competitivity ratio $c(n)$ for LIS can be transformed into a competitivity ratio $c'(\Delta(G))$ for LCl. Note that n is the cardinality of the final graph.

We shall use the following notations. We set $[V]_i = V_1, \ldots, V_i$ and denote by $(G, [V]_{t(n)})$, an instance of LIS and by $[G]_i$, the graph $G[V_1 \cup \cdots \cup V_i]$. Given an on-line IS-algorithm **LA**, an integer i, a graph H of order $|H|$, the vertices of which are partitioned into i non-empty sets $V_1, \ldots, V_i$, and given $n \in \mathbb{N}$ such that $i \leq t(n)$ and $|H| \leq n$, we denote by $\{\mathbf{LA}_i(H, [V]_i, n)\}$ and by $\{[\mathbf{LA}]_i(H, [V]_i, n)\}$, the set of vertices introduced in the solution computed by **LA** during step i and during steps $1, \ldots, i$, respectively, when the i first vertex-clusters revealed are $V_1, \ldots, V_i$ and the finally revealed graph is of order n. For every instance $(G, [V]_{t(n)})$ of LIS and for every vertex $v \in V$, we denote by $r(v)$ the number such that $v \in V_{r(v)}$. We set $N_v = \{(u \in \{v\} \cup \Gamma(v)) : r(u) \geq r(v)\}$, where $\Gamma(u)$ denotes the set of neighbors of u in G. By $[\Gamma(v)]_i$, we denote the set of neighbors of v in $[G]_i$.

The following non-trivial lemma is proved in [3].

Lemma 1. *Let **LA** be an on-line algorithm for LIS guaranteeing competitivity ratio $c(n)$ when running on a graph of order n (only n is known at the beginning of **LA**). Let $i \le t(n)$ such that $\left| \bigcup_{j=1}^{i} V_j \right| \le n/2$. Then:*

1. *if $\{[\mathbf{LA}]_i([G]_i, [V]_i, n)\} = \emptyset$, then $1/\alpha([G]_i) \ge c(n)$*
2. *if $\{[\mathbf{LA}]_i([G]_i, [V]_i, n)\} \ne \emptyset$, then $1/(n/2) \ge c(n)$.*

Theorem 7. *There exists a reduction from LCl to LIS transforming competitivity ratios $c(n)$ into competitivity ratios $c(\Delta(G) + 1)/2$.*

Proof (sketch). Suppose an algorithm **LISA** achieving competitivity ratio $c(n)$ when running on an instance $(G, [V]_{t(n)})$ of LIS, and consider algorithm **LClA** (Algorithm 4) computing a clique in G. Set $W_v = (\{v\} \cup \Gamma(v)) \cap N_v, \forall v \in V$. Also, observe that, if the output-clique K is computed in line 23 during the ith execution of the **repeat**-loop of line 4, then it contains only vertices of V_i. Clearly, if the **if**-condition of line 22 is true, then **bool1** becomes **true** and the algorithm will finish at the end of this iteration. But if the clique computed contains at least one vertex of V_j for $j < i$, then during the jth iteration, a non-empty clique would have been computed and the algorithm would have finished without ulterior iterations of the **repeat**-loop.

We distinguish two cases whether **bool1** becomes **true** at line 24 or 27 of algorithm **LClA**.

1. *Variable **bool1** Becomes **true** at Line 24.* Then, the clique computed by algorithm **LClA** has been produced at line 23. Consider u and i such that

$$K_{u,i} = K = \left\{ \mathbf{LISA}_i \left([\bar{G}]_i [H_v], [V']_i, \Delta(G) + 1 \right) \right\} \tag{5}$$

while, for $j < i$,

$$\left\{ \mathbf{LISA}_j \left([\bar{G}]_j [H_v], [V']_j, \Delta(G) + 1 \right) \right\} = \emptyset. \tag{6}$$

Expressions (5) and (6) mean

$$\left\{ \mathbf{LISA}_i \left([\bar{G}]_i [H_v], [V']_i, \Delta(G) + 1 \right) \right\} =$$
$$\left\{ [\mathbf{LISA}]_i \left([\bar{G}]_i [H_v], [V']_i, \Delta(G) + 1 \right) \right\}.$$

Moreover, remark that $\left| [\bar{G}]_i [H_v] \right| \le \Delta(G) + 1/2$. Then, using item 2 of Lemma 1, we have $|K| \ge c(\Delta(G) + 1)(\Delta(G) + 1/2) \ge c(\Delta(G) + 1)(|K^*|/2)$, where K^* denotes a maximum-order clique of G.

2. *Variable **bool1** Becomes **true** at Line 27.* Then K contains only one vertex. Let $x \in \text{argmin}\{r(y) : y \in K^*\}$. We partition set W_x into two sets W_x^1 and W_x^2, set W_x^1 containing the first $(\Delta(G) + 1)/2$ revealed vertices of W_x (if $|W_x| < (\Delta(G) + 1)/2$, then $W_x^1 = W_x$, $W_x^2 = \emptyset$). Since $|W_x| < \Delta(G) + 1$ and $K^* \subseteq W_x$, at most one between W_x^1 and W_x^2, includes the half of K^*; let us denote by U_x this set. Remark also that during

Require: a graph G revealed into $t(n)$ clusters $G[V_i]$, $i = 1, \ldots, t(n)$
Ensure: a clique K of G
 1: **bool1** ← **false**;
 2: **bool2** ← **false**;
 3: $i \leftarrow 0$;
 4: **repeat**
 5:     $i \leftarrow i + 1$;
 6:     **for all** $v \in [V]_i$ **do**
 7:         $H_v \leftarrow (\{v\} \cup [\Gamma(v)]_i) \cap N_v$;
 8:         **if** $|H_v| > (\Delta(G) + 1)/2$ **then**
 9:             **if** ¬**bool2 then**
10:                 $H_v \leftarrow \{$the first $(\Delta(G) + 1)/2$ revealed vertices of $H_v\}$;
11:                 **bool2** ← **true**;
12:             **else**
13:                 $H_v \leftarrow H_v \setminus \{$the first $(\Delta(G) + 1)/2$ revealed vertices of $H_v\}$;
14:             **end if**
15:         **end if**
16:         **for all** $j \leq i$ **do**
17:             $V'_j \leftarrow V_j \cap H_v$;
18:         **end for**
19:         $K_{v,i} \leftarrow \mathbf{LISA}_i([\bar{G}]_i[H_v], [V']_i, \Delta(G) + 1)$;
20:     **end for**
21:     $u \leftarrow \mathrm{argmax}\{|K_{v,i}| : v \in \bigcup_{j=1}^i V_j\}$;
22:     **if** $K_{u,i} \neq \emptyset$ **then**
23:         $K \leftarrow K_{u,i}$;
24:         **bool1** ← **true**;
25:     **end if**
26:     **if** ¬**bool1** and $i = t(n)$ **then**
27:         **bool1** ← **true**;
28:         pick a vertex $u \in V_{t(n)}$;
29:         $K \leftarrow \{u\}$;
30:     **end if**
31: **until bool1**;

Algorithm 4: Algorithm **LClA**

one of the executions of the **repeat**-loop, $H_x = U_x$. Since $\forall v \in V$ and $\forall i \leq t(n)$, $\{\mathbf{LISA}_i([\bar{G}]_i[H_v], [V']_i, \Delta(G) + 1)\} = \emptyset$ (a fortiori this remains true also for x), one vertex is sufficient in order that algorithm **LISA** guarantees the competitivity ratio when called on a graph the final order of which is at most $\Delta(G) + 1$. Consequently, from item 1 of Lemma 1: $1/(|K^*|/2) \geq c(\Delta(G) + 1) \implies |K|/|K^*| \geq c(\Delta(G) + 1)/2$.

So, in both cases, on the hypothesis that there exists an on-line algorithm achieving competitivity ratio $c(n)$, the solution computed by algorithm **LClA** guarantees competitivity ratio $c(\Delta(G) + 1)/2$. □

References

1. Boppana, B. B., Halldórsson, M. M.: Approximating maximum independent sets by excluding subgraphs. BIT **32(2)** (1992) 180–196.   331, 332
2. Demange, M., Paschos, V. Th.: Maximum-weight independent set is as "well-approximated" as the unweighted one. Technical Report **163** (1999) LAMSADE, Université Paris-Dauphine.   332
3. Demange, M., Paradon, X., Paschos, V. Th.: On-line maximum-order induced hereditary subgraph problems. Research Note **25** (2000) LAMSADE, Université Paris-Dauphine.   328, 329, 331, 332
4. Halldórsson, M. M.: Approximations via partitioning. JAIST Research Report **IS-RR-95-0003F** (1995) Japan Advanced Institute of Science and Technology, Japan.   329

Quantum Pushdown Automata[*]

Marats Golovkins

Institute of Mathematics and Computer Science
University of Latvia, Raiņa bulv. 29, Riga, Latvia
marats@cclu.lv

Abstract. Quantum finite automata, as well as quantum pushdown automata were first introduced by C. Moore, J. P. Crutchfield [13]. In this paper we introduce the notion of quantum pushdown automata (QPA) in a non-equivalent way, including unitarity criteria, by using the definition of quantum finite automata of [11]. It is established that the unitarity criteria of QPA are not equivalent to the corresponding unitarity criteria of quantum Turing machines [4]. We show that QPA can recognize every regular language. Finally we present some simple languages recognized by QPA, two of them are not recognizable by deterministic pushdown automata and one seems to be not recognizable by probabilistic pushdown automata as well.

1 Introduction

Nobel prize winner physicist R. Feynman asked in 1982, what effects may have the principles of quantum mechanics on computation [8]. He gave arguments that it may require exponential time to simulate quantum mechanical processes on classical computers. This served as a basis to the opinion that quantum computers may have advantages versus classical ones. It was in 1985, when D. Deutsch introduced the notion of quantum Turing machine [6] and proved that quantum Turing machines compute the same recursive functions as classical deterministic Turing machines do. P. Shor discovered that by use of quantum algorithms it is possible to factorize large integers and compute discrete logarithms in a polynomial time [14], what resulted into additional interest in quantum computing and attempts to create quantum computers. First steps have been made to this direction, and first quantum computers which memory is limited by a few quantum bits have been constructed.

For the analysis of the current situation in quantum computation and information processing and main open issues one could see [9].

Opposite to quantum Turing machines, quantum finite automata (QFA) represent the finite model of quantum computation. QFA were first introduced by [13] (measure-once QFA), which were followed by a more elaborated model

---

[*] Research partially supported by the Latvian Council of Science, grant 96-0282 and grant for Ph.D. students; European Commission, contract IST-1999-11234; Swedish institute, project ML2000.

V. Hlaváč, K. G. Jeffery, and J. Wiedermann (Eds.): SOFSEM 2000, LNCS 1963, pp. 336–346, 2000.

of [11] (measure-many quantum finite automata). Since then QFA have been studied a lot, various properties of these automata are considered in [2,3,5,15].

The purpose of this paper is to introduce a quantum counterpart of pushdown automata, the next most important model after finite automata and Turing machines. The first definition of quantum pushdown automata was suggested by [13], but here the authors actually deal with the so-called generalized quantum pushdown automata, which evolution does not have to be unitary. However a basic postulate of quantum mechanics imposes a strong constraint on any quantum machine model: it has to be unitary, otherwise it is questionable whether we can speak about *quantum* machine. That's why it was considered necessary to re-introduce quantum pushdown automata by giving a definition which would conform unitarity requirement. Such definition would enable us to study the properties of quantum pushdown automata.

The following notations will be used further in the paper: z^* is the complex conjugate of a complex number z; U^* is the Hermitian conjugate of a matrix U; I is the identity matrix; ε is empty word.

Definition 1. Matrix U is called *unitary*, if $UU^* = U^*U = I$.

If U is a finite matrix, then $UU^* = I$ iff $U^*U = I$. However this is not true for infinite matrices:

Example 1.

$$U = \begin{pmatrix} \frac{1}{\sqrt{2}} & 0 & 0 & 0 & \dots \\ \frac{1}{\sqrt{2}} & 0 & 0 & 0 & \dots \\ 0 & 1 & 0 & 0 & \dots \\ 0 & 0 & 1 & 0 & \dots \\ \vdots & \vdots & \vdots & \vdots & \ddots \end{pmatrix}$$

Here $U^*U = I$ but $UU^* \neq I$.

Lemma 1. *The matrix U is unitary iff $U^*U = I$ and its rows are normalized.*

This result is very similar to Lemma 1 of [7].

2 Quantum Pushdown Automata

Definition 2. A *quantum pushdown automaton* (QPA)
$A = (Q, \Sigma, T, q_0, Q_a, Q_r, \delta)$ is specified by a finite set of states Q, a finite input alphabet Σ and a stack alphabet T, an initial state $q_0 \in Q$, sets $Q_a \subset Q, Q_r \subset Q$ of accepting and rejecting states, respectively, with $Q_a \cap Q_r = \emptyset$, and a transition function

$$\delta : Q \times \Gamma \times \Delta \times Q \times \{\downarrow, \rightarrow\} \times \Delta^* \longrightarrow \mathbb{C}_{[0,1]},$$

where $\Gamma = \Sigma \cup \{\#, \$\}$ is the input tape alphabet of A and $\#, \$$ are end-markers not in Σ, $\Delta = T \cup \{Z_0\}$ is the working stack alphabet of A and $Z_0 \notin T$ is the stack base symbol; $\{\downarrow, \rightarrow\}$ is the set of directions of input tape head. The automaton must satisfy *conditions of well-formedness*, which will be expressed below. Furthermore, the transition function is restricted to a following requirement:

If $\delta(q, \alpha, \beta, q', d, \omega) \neq 0$, then

1. $|\omega| \leq 2$,
2. if $|\omega| = 2$, then $\omega_1 = \beta$,
3. if $\beta = Z_0$, then $\omega \in Z_0 T^*$,
4. if $\beta \neq Z_0$, then $\omega \in T^*$.

Here ω_1 is the first symbol of a word ω. Definition 2 utilizes that of classical pushdown automata from [10].

Let us assume that an automaton is in a state q, its input tape head is above a symbol α and the stack head is above a symbol β. Then the automaton undertakes the following actions with an amplitude $\delta(q, \alpha, \beta, q', d, \omega)$:

1. goes into the state q',
2. if $d = ' \rightarrow '$, moves the input tape head one cell forward,
3. takes out of the stack the symbol β (deletes it and moves the stack head one cell backwards),
4. starting with the first empty cell, puts into the stack the string ω, moving the stack head $|\omega|$ cells forward.

Definition 3. The *configuration* of a pushdown automaton is a pair $|c\rangle = |\nu_i q_j \nu_k, \omega_l\rangle$, where the automaton is in a state $q_j \in Q$, $\nu_i \nu_k \in \#\Sigma^*\$$ is a finite word on the input tape, $\omega_l \in Z_0 T^*$ is a finite word on the stack tape, the input tape head is above the first symbol of the word ν_k and the stack head is above the last symbol of the word ω_l.

We shall denote by C the set of all configurations of a pushdown automaton. The set C is countably infinite. Every configuration $|c\rangle$ denotes a basis vector in the Hilbert space $H_A = l_2(C)$. Therefore a global state of A in the space H_A has a form $|\psi\rangle = \sum_{c \in C} \alpha_c |c\rangle$, where $\sum_{c \in C} |\alpha_c|^2 = 1$ and $\alpha_c \in \mathbb{C}$ denotes the amplitude of a configuration $|c\rangle$. If an automaton is in its global state (superposition) $|\psi\rangle$, then its further step is equivalent to the application of a linear operator (evolution) U_A over the space H_A.

Definition 4. A linear operator U_A is defined as follows:

$$U_A |\psi\rangle = \sum_{c \in C} \alpha_c U_A |c\rangle .$$

If a configuration $c = |\nu_i q_j \sigma \nu_k, \omega_l \tau\rangle$, then

$$U_A |c\rangle = \sum_{(q,d,\omega) \in Q \times \{\downarrow, \rightarrow\} \times \Delta^*} \delta(q_j, \sigma, \tau, q, d, \omega) |f(|c\rangle, d, q), \omega_l \omega\rangle$$

where

$$f(|\nu_i q_j \sigma \nu_k, \omega_l \tau\rangle, d, q) = \begin{cases} \nu_i q \sigma \nu_k, & \text{if } d = \downarrow \\ \nu_i \sigma q \nu_k, & \text{if } d = \rightarrow . \end{cases}$$

Remark 1. Although a QPA evolution operator matrix is infinite, it has a finite number of nonzero elements in each row and column, as it is possible to reach only a finite number of other configurations from a given configuration within one step, all the same, within one step the given configuration is reachable only from a finite number of different configurations.

We can speak about a *quantum* pushdown automaton only if its evolution operator is unitary. However, evolution operator matrix is infinite, so we need some criteria (well-formedness conditions) to verify its unitarity.

Well-formedness conditions 1.

1. Local probability condition. $\forall (q_1, \sigma_1, \tau_1) \in Q \times \Gamma \times \Delta$

$$\sum_{(q,d,\omega) \in Q \times \{\downarrow, \rightarrow\} \times \Delta^*} |\delta(q_1, \sigma_1, \tau_1, q, d, \omega)|^2 = 1 \,. \tag{1}$$

2. Orthogonality of column vectors condition. For all triples $(q_1, \sigma_1, \tau_1) \neq (q_2, \sigma_1, \tau_2)$ in $Q \times \Gamma \times \Delta$

$$\sum_{(q,d,\omega) \in Q \times \{\downarrow, \rightarrow\} \times \Delta^*} \delta^*(q_1, \sigma_1, \tau_1, q, d, \omega) \delta(q_2, \sigma_1, \tau_2, q, d, \omega) = 0 \,. \tag{2}$$

3. Row vectors norm condition. $\forall (q_1, \sigma_1, \sigma_2, \tau_1, \tau_2) \in Q \times \Gamma^2 \times \Delta^2$

$$\sum_{(q,\tau,\omega) \in Q \times \Delta \times \{\varepsilon, \tau_2, \tau_1 \tau_2\}} |\delta(q, \sigma_1, \tau, q_1, \rightarrow, \omega)|^2 + |\delta(q, \sigma_2, \tau, q_1, \downarrow, \omega)|^2 = 1 \,. \tag{3}$$

4. Separability condition I. $\forall (q_1, \sigma_1, \tau_1), (q_2, \sigma_1, \tau_2) \in Q \times \Gamma \times \Delta, \forall \tau_3 \in \Delta$

$$\sum_{(q,d,\tau) \in Q \times \{\downarrow, \rightarrow\} \times \Delta} \delta^*(q_1, \sigma_1, \tau_1, q, d, \tau) \delta(q_2, \sigma_1, \tau_2, q, d, \tau_3 \tau) +$$

$$+ \sum_{(q,d) \in Q \times \{\downarrow, \rightarrow\}} \delta^*(q_1, \sigma_1, \tau_1, q, d, \varepsilon) \delta(q_2, \sigma_1, \tau_2, q, d, \tau_3) = 0 \,, \tag{4}$$

$$\sum_{(q,d) \in Q \times \{\downarrow, \rightarrow\}} \delta^*(q_1, \sigma_1, \tau_1, q, d, \varepsilon) \delta(q_2, \sigma_1, \tau_2, q, d, \tau_2 \tau_3) = 0 \,. \tag{5}$$

5. Separability condition II. $\forall (q_1, \sigma_1, \tau_1), (q_2, \sigma_2, \tau_2) \in Q \times \Gamma \times \Delta$

$$\sum_{(q,\omega) \in Q \times \Delta^*} \delta^*(q_1, \sigma_1, \tau_1, q, \downarrow, \omega) \delta(q_2, \sigma_2, \tau_2, q, \rightarrow, \omega) = 0 \,. \tag{6}$$

6. Separability condition III. $\forall (q_1, \sigma_1, \tau_1), (q_2, \sigma_2, \tau_2) \in Q \times \Gamma \times \Delta, \ \forall \tau_3 \in \Delta, \ \forall d_1, d_2 \in \{\downarrow, \rightarrow\}, \ d_1 \neq d_2$

$$\sum_{(q,\tau) \in Q \times \Delta} \delta^*(q_1, \sigma_1, \tau_1, q, d_1, \tau) \delta(q_2, \sigma_2, \tau_2, q, d_2, \tau_3 \tau) +$$

$$+ \sum_{q \in Q} \delta^*(q_1, \sigma_1, \tau_1, q, d_1, \varepsilon) \delta(q_2, \sigma_2, \tau_2, q, d_2, \tau_3) = 0 \,, \tag{7}$$

$$\sum_{q \in Q} \delta^*(q_1, \sigma_1, \tau_1, q, d_1, \varepsilon) \delta(q_2, \sigma_2, \tau_2, q, d_2, \tau_2 \tau_3) = 0 . \tag{8}$$

Lemma 2.   *1. The columns system of a QPA evolution matrix is normalized iff the condition (1), i. e., local probability condition, is satisfied.*
  2. The columns system of a QPA evolution matrix is orthogonal iff the conditions (2,4,5,6,7,8), i. e., orthogonality of column vectors and separability conditions, are satisfied.
  3. The rows system of a QPA evolution matrix is normalized iff the condition (3), i. e., row vectors norm condition, is satisfied.

Theorem 1. *Well-formedness conditions 1 are satisfied iff the evolution operator U_A is unitary.*

Proof. Lemma 2 implies that Well-formedness conditions 1 are satisfied iff the columns of the evolution matrix are orthonormal and rows are normalized. In compliance with Lemma 1, columns are orthonormal and rows are normalized iff the matrix is unitary.   □

Remark 2. Well-formedness conditions 1 contain the requirement that rows system has to be normalized, which is not necessary in the case of quantum Turing machine [ ]. Here is taken into account the fact that the evolution of QPA can violate the unitarity requirement if the row vectors norm condition is omitted.

Example 2. A QPA, whose evolution matrix columns are orthonormal, however the evolution is not unitary.

$$Q = \{q\}, \ \Sigma = \{1\}, \ T = \{1\} .$$
$$\delta(q, \#, Z_0, q, \rightarrow, Z_0 1) = 1 , \qquad \delta(q, \#, 1, q, \rightarrow, 11) = 1 ,$$
$$\delta(q, 1, Z_0, q, \rightarrow, Z_0 1) = 1 , \qquad \delta(q, 1, 1, q, \rightarrow, 11) = 1 ,$$
$$\delta(q, \$, Z_0, q, \rightarrow, Z_0 1) = 1 , \qquad \delta(q, \$, 1, q, \rightarrow, 11) = 1 ,$$

other values of arguments yield $\delta = 0$.
  By Well-formedness conditions 1, the columns of the evolution matrix are orthonormal, but the matrix is not unitary, because the norm of the rows specified by the configurations $|\omega, Z_0\rangle$ is 0.

  Even in a case of trivial QPA, it is a cumbersome task to check all the conditions of well-formedness 1. It is possible to relax the conditions slightly by introducing a notion of *simplified* QPA.

Definition 5. We shall say that a QPA is *simplified*, if there exists a function $D : Q \longrightarrow \{\downarrow, \rightarrow\}$, and $\delta(q_1, \sigma, \tau, q, d, \omega) = 0$, if $D(q) \neq d$. Therefore the transition function of a simplified QPA is $\varphi(q_1, \sigma, \tau, q, \omega) = \delta(q_1, \sigma, \tau, q, D(q), \omega)$.

  Taking into account Definition 5, following well-formedness conditions correspond to simplified QPA:

Well-formedness conditions 2.

1. Local probability condition. $\forall (q_1, \sigma_1, \tau_1) \in Q \times \Gamma \times \Delta$

$$\sum_{(q,\omega) \in Q \times \Delta^*} |\varphi(q_1, \sigma_1, \tau_1, q, \omega)|^2 = 1 \,. \tag{9}$$

2. Orthogonality of column vectors condition. For all triples $(q_1, \sigma_1, \tau_1) \neq (q_2, \sigma_1, \tau_2)$ in $Q \times \Gamma \times \Delta$

$$\sum_{(q,\omega) \in Q \times \Delta^*} \varphi^*(q_1, \sigma_1, \tau_1, q, \omega)\varphi(q_2, \sigma_1, \tau_2, q, \omega) = 0 \,. \tag{10}$$

3. Row vectors norm condition. $\forall (q_1, \sigma_1, \tau_1, \tau_2) \in Q \times \Gamma \times \Delta^2$

$$\sum_{(q,\tau,\omega) \in Q \times \Delta \times \{\varepsilon, \tau_2, \tau_1 \tau_2\}} |\varphi(q, \sigma_1, \tau, q_1, \omega)|^2 = 1 \,. \tag{11}$$

4. Separability condition. $\forall (q_1, \sigma_1, \tau_1), (q_2, \sigma_1, \tau_2) \in Q \times \Gamma \times \Delta, \ \forall \tau_3 \in \Delta$

$$\sum_{(q,\tau) \in Q \times \Delta} \varphi^*(q_1, \sigma_1, \tau_1, q, \tau)\varphi(q_2, \sigma_1, \tau_2, q, \tau_3\tau) +$$

$$+ \sum_{q \in Q} \varphi^*(q_1, \sigma_1, \tau_1, q, \varepsilon)\varphi(q_2, \sigma_1, \tau_2, q, \tau_3) = 0 \,, \tag{12}$$

$$\sum_{q \in Q} \varphi^*(q_1, \sigma_1, \tau_1, q, \varepsilon)\varphi(q_2, \sigma_1, \tau_2, q, \tau_2\tau_3) = 0 \,. \tag{13}$$

Theorem 2. *The evolution of a simplified QPA is unitary iff Well-formedness conditions 2 are satisfied.*

Proof. By Theorem 1 and Definition 5. $\qquad \square$

3 Language Recognition

Language recognition for QPA is defined as follows. For a QPA
$A = (Q, \Sigma, T, q_0, Q_a, Q_r, \delta)$ we define $C_a = \{|\nu_i q \nu_k, \omega_l\rangle \in C \mid q \in Q_a\}$,
$C_r = \{|\nu_i q \nu_k, \omega_l\rangle \in C \mid q \in Q_r\}$, $C_n = C \setminus (C_a \cup C_r)$. E_a, E_r, E_n are subspaces of H_A spanned by C_a, C_r, C_n respectively. We use the observable $\mathcal{O}$ that corresponds to the orthogonal decomposition $H_A = E_a \oplus E_r \oplus E_n$. The outcome of each observation is either "accept" or "reject" or "non-halting". The language recognition is now defined as follows: For an $x \in \Sigma^*$ we consider as an input $\#x\$$, and assume that the computation starts with A being in the configuration $|q_0 \#x\$, Z_0\rangle$. Each computation step consists of two parts. At first the linear operator U_A is applied to the current global state and then the resulting superposition

is observed using the observable $\mathcal{O}$ as defined above. If the global state before the observation is $\sum_{c \in C} \alpha_c |c\rangle$, then the probability that the resulting superposition is projected into the subspace E_i, $i \in \{a, r, n\}$, is $\sum_{c \in C_i} |\alpha_c|^2$. The computation continues until the result of an observation is "accept" or "reject".

Definition 6. We shall say that an automaton is a *deterministic reversible pushdown automaton* (RPA), if it is a simplified QPA with $\varphi(q_1, \sigma, \tau, q, \omega) \in \{0, 1\}$ and there exists a function $f : Q \times \Gamma \times \Delta \longrightarrow Q \times \Delta^*$, such that $f(q_1, \sigma, \tau) = (q, \omega)$ if and only if $\varphi(q_1, \sigma, \tau, q, \omega) = 1$.

We can regard f as a transition function of a RPA. Note that the local probability condition (9) is satisfied automatically for RPA.

Theorem 3. *Every regular language is recognizable by some QPA.*

Proof. It is sufficient to prove that any deterministic finite automaton (DFA) can be simulated by RPA. Let us consider a DFA with n states $A_{DFA} = (Q_{DFA}, \Sigma, q_0, Q_F, \delta)$, where $\delta : Q_{DFA} \times \Sigma \longrightarrow Q_{DFA}$. To simulate A_{DFA} we shall construct a RPA $A_{RPA} = (Q, \Sigma, T, q_0, Q_a, Q_r, \varphi)$ with the number of states $2n$. The set of states is $Q = Q_{DFA} \cup Q'_{DFA}$, where $Q_{DFA} \cap Q'_{DFA} = \emptyset$ and Q'_{DFA} are the newly introduced states, which are linked to Q_{DFA} by a one-to-one relation $\{(q_i, q'_i) \in Q_{DFA} \times Q'_{DFA}\}$. Thus Q_F has one-to-one relation to $Q'_F \subset Q'_{DFA}$. The stack alphabet is $T = Ind(Q_{DFA})$, where $\forall i \; Ind(q_i) = i$; the set of accepting states is $Q_a = Q'_F$ and the set of rejecting states is $Q_r = Q'_{DFA} \setminus Q'_F$. As for the function D, $D(Q_{DFA}) = \{\rightarrow\}$ and $D(Q'_{DFA}) = \{\downarrow\}$. We shall define sets R and $\overline{R}$ as follows:

$$R = \{(q'_j, \sigma, i) \in Q'_{DFA} \times \Sigma \times T \mid \delta(q_i, \sigma) = q_j\},$$
$$\overline{R} = \{(q'_j, \sigma, i) \in Q'_{DFA} \times \Sigma \times T \mid \delta(q_i, \sigma) \neq q_j\}.$$

The construction of the transition function f is performed by the following rules:

1. $\forall (q_i, \sigma, \tau) \in Q_{DFA} \times \Sigma \times \Delta \;\; f(q_i, \sigma, \tau) = (\delta(q_i, \sigma), \tau i)$,
2. $\forall (q'_j, \sigma, i) \in R \;\; f(q'_j, \sigma, i) = (q'_i, \varepsilon)$,
3. $\forall (q'_j, \sigma, i) \in \overline{R} \;\; f(q'_j, \sigma, i) = (q_j, i)$,
4. $\forall (q'_j, \sigma) \in Q'_{DFA} \times \Sigma \;\; f(q'_j, \sigma, Z) = (q_j, Z)$,
5. $\forall (q, \tau) \in Q \times \Delta \;\; f(q, \#, \tau) = (q, \tau)$,
6. $\forall (q_i, \tau) \in Q_{DFA} \times \Delta \;\; f(q_i, \$, \tau) = (q'_i, \tau)$,
7. $\forall (q'_i, \tau) \in Q'_{DFA} \times \Delta \;\; f(q'_i, \$, \tau) = (q_i, \tau)_{,,}$.

Thus we have defined f for all the possible arguments. Our automaton simulates the DFA. Note that the automaton may reach a state in Q'_{DFA} only by reading the end-marking symbol $ on the input tape. As soon as A_{RPA} reaches the end-marking symbol $, it goes to an accepting state, if its current state is in Q_F, and goes to a rejecting state otherwise. The construction is performed in a way so that Well-formedness conditions 2 are satisfied. As we know, RPA automatically satisfies the local probability condition (9).

Let us prove, that the automaton satisfies the orthogonality condition (10). For RPA, the condition (10) is equivalent to the requirement that for all triples $(q_1, \sigma_1, \tau_1) \neq (q_2, \sigma_1, \tau_2)$ $f(q_1, \sigma_1, \tau_1) \neq f(q_2, \sigma_1, \tau_2)$.

Let us consider the case when $(q_1, \sigma_1, \tau_1), (q_2, \sigma_1, \tau_2) \in R$. We shall denote q_1, q_2 as q_i', q_j' respectively. Let us assume from the contrary that $f(q_i', \sigma_1, \tau_1) = f(q_j', \sigma_1, \tau_2)$. By rule 2, $(q_{\tau_1}', \varepsilon) = (q_{\tau_2}', \varepsilon)$. Hence $\tau_1 = \tau_2$. By the definition of R, $\delta(q_{\tau_1}, \sigma_1) = q_i$ and $\delta(q_{\tau_2}, \sigma_1) = q_j$. Since $\tau_1 = \tau_2$, $q_i = q_j$. Therefore $q_i' = q_j'$, i.e., $q_1 = q_2$. We have come to a contradiction with the fact that $(q_1, \sigma_1, \tau_1) \neq (q_2, \sigma_1, \tau_2)$. In other cases, proof is straightforward.

The compliance with row vectors norm condition (11) and separability conditions (12) and (13) is proved in the same way.   □

Example 3. Let us consider a language $L_1 = (0, 1)^*1$, for which we know that it is not recognizable by QFA [11]. This language is recognized by a deterministic finite automaton with two states q_0, q_1 and the following transitions: $\delta(q_0, 0) = q_0$, $\delta(q_0, 1) = q_1$, $\delta(q_1, 0) = q_0$, $\delta(q_1, 1) = q_1$. By Theorem 3 it is possible to transform this automaton to the following RPA: $Q = \{q_0, q_1, q_0', q_1'\}$, $Q_a = \{q_1'\}$, $Q_r = \{q_0'\}$, $\Sigma = \{0, 1\}$, $T = \{0, 1\}$, $D(q_0) =\rightarrow, D(q_1) =\rightarrow, D(q_0') =\downarrow, D(q_1') =\downarrow$. By the construction rules, $\forall q \in Q \; \forall \sigma \in \Sigma, \; \forall \tau \in \Delta$

$$f(q_0, 0, \tau) = (q_0, \tau 0) \quad f(q_1, 0, \tau) = (q_0, \tau 1) \quad f(q_0, 1, \tau) = (q_1, \tau 0)$$
$$f(q_1, 1, \tau) = (q_1, \tau 1) \quad f(q_0', 0, 0) = (q_0', \varepsilon) \quad f(q_1', 1, 0) = (q_0', \varepsilon)$$
$$f(q_0', 0, 1) = (q_1', \varepsilon) \quad f(q_1', 1, 1) = (q_1', \varepsilon) \quad f(q_0', 1, 0) = (q_0, 0)$$
$$f(q_1', 0, 0) = (q_1, 0) \quad f(q_0', 1, 1) = (q_0, 1) \quad f(q_1', 0, 1) = (q_1, 1)$$
$$f(q_0', \sigma, Z) = (q_0, Z) \quad f(q_1', \sigma, Z) = (q_1, Z) \quad f(q, \#, \tau) = (q, \tau)$$
$$f(q_0, \tau) = (q_0', \tau) \quad\quad f(q_1, \tau) = (q_1', \tau) \quad\quad f(q_0', \tau) = (q_0, \tau)$$
$$f(q_1', \tau) = (q_1, \tau).$$

Let us consider a language which is not regular, namely,

$$L_2 = \{\omega \in (a, b)^* | \; |\omega|_a = |\omega|_b\},$$

where $|\omega|_i$ denotes the number of occurrences of the symbol i in the word ω.

Lemma 3. *Language L_2 is recognizable by a RPA.*

Proof. Our RPA has four states q_0, q_1, q_2, q_3, where q_2 is an accepting state, whereas q_3 — rejecting one. Stack alphabet T consists of two symbols $1, 2$. Stack filled with 1's means that the processed part of the word ω has more occurrences of a's than b's, whereas 2's means that there are more b's than a's. Furthermore, length of the stack word is equal to the difference of number of a's and b's. Empty stack denotes that the number of a's and b's is equal. Values of the transition function follow: $\forall q \in Q \; \forall \tau \in \Delta$

$$
\begin{aligned}
&f(q, \#, \tau) = (q, \tau) \qquad &&f(q_0, a, Z) = (q_0, Z1) \qquad &&D(q_0) = \;\rightarrow \\
&f(q_0, b, Z) = (q_0, Z2) \qquad &&f(q_0, \$, Z) = (q_2, Z1) \qquad &&D(q_1) = \;\downarrow \\
&f(q_0, a, 1) = (q_0, 11) \qquad &&f(q_0, b, 1) = (q_1, \varepsilon) \qquad &&D(q_2) = \;\downarrow \\
&f(q_0, \$, 1) = (q_3, 1) \qquad &&f(q_0, a, 2) = (q_1, \varepsilon) \qquad &&D(q_3) = \;\downarrow \\
&f(q_0, b, 2) = (q_0, 22) \qquad &&f(q_0, \$, 2) = (q_3, 2) \qquad &&f(q_1, a, Z) = (q_0, Z) \\
&f(q_1, b, Z) = (q_0, Z) \qquad &&f(q_1, \$, \tau) = (q_1, \tau) \qquad &&f(q_1, a, 1) = (q_3, 12) \\
&f(q_1, b, 1) = (q_0, 1) \qquad &&f(q_1, a, 2) = (q_0, 2) \qquad &&f(q_1, b, 2) = (q_3, 21) \\
&f(q_2, a, Z) = (q_3, Z2) \qquad &&f(q_2, b, Z) = (q_3, Z1) \qquad &&f(q_2, \$, Z) = (q_0, Z) \\
&f(q_2, a, 1) = (q_2, \varepsilon) \qquad &&f(q_2, b, 1) = (q_0, 12) \qquad &&f(q_2, \$, 1) = (q_0, 1) \\
&f(q_2, a, 2) = (q_0, 21) \qquad &&f(q_2, b, 2) = (q_2, \varepsilon) \qquad &&f(q_2, \$, 2) = (q_0, 2) \\
&f(q_3, a, Z) = (q_3, Z) \qquad &&f(q_3, b, Z) = (q_3, Z) \qquad &&f(q_3, \$, Z) = (q_3, Z) \\
&f(q_3, a, 1) = (q_3, 1) \qquad &&f(q_3, b, 1) = (q_3, 11) \qquad &&f(q_3, \$, 1) = (q_2, 1) \\
&f(q_3, a, 2) = (q_3, 22) \qquad &&f(q_3, b, 2) = (q_3, 2) \qquad &&f(q_3, \$, 2) = (q_2, 2) \,.
\end{aligned}
$$

$\square$

It is doubtful whether the language L_2 can be recognized with probability 1 by QPA with stack alphabet T containing only one symbol, i.e, by quantum finite one counter automata [12].

Lemma 4. *Pumping lemma for context-free languages. Every context free language L has a positive integer constant m with the following property. If ω is in L and $|\omega| \geq m$, then ω can be written as $uvxyz$, where $uv^k xy^k z$ is in L for each $k \geq 0$. Moreover, $|vxy| \leq m$ and $|vy| > 0$.*

The pumping lemma is from [10], p. 123. Let us consider a language L_3 which is not recognizable by any deterministic pushdown automaton:

Theorem 4. *Language $L_3 = \{\omega \in (a, b, c)^* \mid |\omega|_a = |\omega|_b = |\omega|_c\}$ is recognizable by a QPA with probability $\frac{2}{3}$.*

Proof (Sketch). The automaton takes three equiprobable actions, during the first action it compares $|\omega|_a$ to $|\omega|_b$, whereas during the second action $|\omega|_b$ to $|\omega|_c$ is compared. Input word is rejected if the third action is chosen. Acceptance probability totals $\frac{2}{3}$. By Lemma 4, the language L_3 is not a context-free language (take $\omega = a^m b^m c^m$). Hence it is not recognizable by deterministic pushdown automata. $\square$

Theorem 5. *Language $L_4 = \{\omega \in (a, b, c)^* : |\omega|_a = |\omega|_b \; xor \; |\omega|_a = |\omega|_c\}$ is recognizable by a QPA with probability $\frac{4}{7}$.*

Proof (sketch). The automaton starts the following actions with the following amplitudes:

a) with an amplitude $\sqrt{\frac{2}{7}}$ compares $|\omega|_a$ to $|\omega|_b$,

b) with an amplitude $-\sqrt{\frac{2}{7}}$ compares $|\omega|_a$ to $|\omega|_c$,

c) with an amplitude $\sqrt{\frac{3}{7}}$ accepts the input.

If exactly one comparison gives positive answer, input is accepted with probability $\frac{4}{7}$. If both comparisons gives positive answer, amplitudes, which are chosen to be opposite, annihilate and the input is accepted with probability $\frac{3}{7}$.   □

Language L_4 cannot be recognized by deterministic pushdown automata. (By Lemma 4, take $\omega = a^{m+m!}b^m c^{m+m!}$) It even seems that this language is not recognizable by probabilistic pushdown automata either. In this case this result would be similar to that of [1], where the properties of quantum finite multitape automata are considered.

References

1. A. Ambainis, R. Bonner, R. Freivalds, M. Golovkins, M. Karpinski: Quantum Finite Multitape Automata. *Lecture Notes in Computer Science*, 1999, Vol. 1725, pp. 340–348. 345
2. A. Ambainis, R. Bonner, R. Freivalds, A. Kikusts: Probabilities to Accept Languages by Quantum Finite Automata. *Lecture Notes in Computer Science*, 1999, Vol. 1627, pp. 174–183. 337
3. A. Ambainis, R. Freivalds: 1-Way Quantum Finite Automata: Strengths, Weaknesses and Generalizations. *Proc. 39th FOCS*, 1998, pp. 332–341. 337
4. E. Bernstein, U. Vazirani: Quantum Complexity Theory. *SIAM Journal on Computing*, 26:1411–1473, 1997. 336, 340
5. A. Brodsky, N. Pippenger: Characterizations of 1-Way Quantum Finite Automata. http://xxx.lanl.gov/abs/quant-ph/9903014. 337
6. D. Deutsch: Quantum Theory, the Church-Turing principle and the Universal Quantum Computer. *Proc. Royal Society London, A400*, 1985. pp. 96–117. 336
7. C. Dürr, M. Santha: A Decision Procedure for Unitary Linear Quantum Cellular Automata. *Proc. 37th FOCS*, 1996, pp. 38–45. 337
8. R. Feynman: Simulating Physics with Computers. *International Journal of Theoretical Physics*, 1982, vol. 21, No 6/7, pp. 467–488. 336
9. J. Gruska: Quantum Challenges. *Lecture Notes in Computer Science*, 1999, Vol. 1725, pp. 1–28. 336
10. E. Gurari: An Introduction to the Theory of Computation. *Computer Science Press*, 1989. 338, 344
11. A. Kondacs, J. Watrous: On The Power of Quantum Finite State Automata. In *Proc. 38th FOCS*, 1997, pp. 66–75. 336, 337, 343
12. M. Kravtsev: Quantum Finite One-Counter Automata. *Lecture Notes in Computer Science*, 1999, Vol. 1725, pp. 431–440. 344
13. C. Moore, J. P. Crutchfield: Quantum Automata and Quantum Grammars. http://xxx.lanl.gov/abs/quant-ph/9707031. 336, 337
14. P. W. Shor: Algorithms for Quantum Computation: Discrete Logarithms and Factoring. *Proc. 35th FOCS*, 1994, pp. 124–134. 336

15. M. Valdats: The Class of Languages Recognizable by 1-Way Quantum Finite Automata is not Closed Under Union. *Proc. Quantum Computation and Learning. International Workshop*, 2000, pp. 52 – 64. E-print: http://xxx.lanl.gov/abs/quant-ph/0001005. 337

Use of Dependency Microcontexts in Information Retrieval[*]

Martin Holub

Department of Software Engineering, Faculty of Mathematics and Physics,
Charles University, Prague, Czech republic
holub@ksi.ms.mff.cuni.cz

Abstract. This paper focuses especially on two problems that are crucial for retrieval performance in information retrieval (IR) systems: the lack of information caused by document pre-processing and the difficulty caused by homonymous and synonymous words in natural language. Author argues that traditional IR methods, i. e. methods based on dealing with individual terms without considering their relations, can be overcome using natural language processing (NLP). In order to detect the relations among terms in sentences and make use of lemmatisation and morphological and syntactic tagging of Czech texts, author proposes a method for construction of dependency word microcontexts fully automatically extracted from texts, and several ways how to exploit the microcontexts for the sake of increasing retrieval performance.

1 Introduction

Empirical methods in natural language processing (NLP) employ learning techniques to automatically extract linguistic knowledge from natural language corpora; for an overview of this field see (Brill and Mooney 1997). This paper wants to show their usefulness in the field of information retrieval (IR). A textual IR system stores a collection of documents and special data structures for effective searching. A textual document is a sequence of terms. When analysing the content of a document, terms are the basic processed units — usually they are words of natural language. When retrieving, the IR system returns documents presumed to be of interest to the user in response to a query. The user's query is a formal statement of user's information need. The documents that are interesting for the user (relative to the put query) are relevant; the others are non-relevant. The effectiveness of IR systems is usually measured in terms of *precision*, the percentage of retrieved documents that are relevant, and *recall*, the percentage of relevant documents that are retrieved.

The starting point of our consideration on IR was a critique of word-based retrieval techniques. Traditional IR systems treat the query as a pattern of words to be matched by documents. Unfortunately, the effectiveness of these word-matching systems is mostly poor because the system retrieves only the documents which contain words that occur also in the query. However, in fact, the user

---

[*] This study has been supported by MŠMT (the FRVŠ grant no 1909).

V. Hlaváč, K. G. Jeffery, and J. Wiedermann (Eds.): SOFSEM 2000, LNCS 1963, pp. 347–355, 2000.

does *not* look for the words used in the query. The user desires the *sense* of the words and wants to retrieve the documents containing words having the same sense. In contrast to the word-based approach, a sense-based IR system treats the query as a pattern of the required sense. In order to match this sense by the sense of words in documents, the senses of ambiguous words must be determined. How to take the step from words towards senses? Since an application of word contexts is the only possibility to estimate the sense of words, the way of dealing with word contexts is a central problem in sense-based retrieval. Knowing word contexts we can determine the *measure of collocating*, i. e. the extent to which a pair of words collocates. The knowledge of collocations can be used in IR for several purposes: making up contextual representations of words, resolving word ambiguity, estimating semantic word similarity, tuning the user's query in interaction with the user and quantifying the significance of words for retrieval according to entropy of their contexts.

Section 2 points out that reduction of information caused by text pre-processing makes limits to retrieval performance. Next section is devoted to features of natural language and sense of word contexts. Further part suggests a construction of a dependency micro-context. Then, Section 5 shows connections among contexts, collocations and word similarity and gives several proposals to apply the investigated concepts. Finally, we summarise the results of this study and refer to the project working on an experimental IR textual database.

2   Reduction of Information

We can formulate a self-evident postulate that an IR system cannot provide a larger amount of information than the amount which has been put into the system. This claim is obvious and may seem to be uninteresting. But it concerns the document pre-processing which causes principal limits of retrieval possibilities.

The total information about the contents of a document is given by the document itself. In this sense, IR systems storing full texts do not lose any information about documents. In order to search a textual database effectively, however, the documents are pre-processed and information obtained from them is stored in special data structures enabling effective searching. In these retrieval data structures not all the information contained in original documents is stored. Especially syntactic relations among terms in sentences are lost. Since in retrieval run-time retrieval algorithms work with these retrieval data structures, not with full texts, the amount of information contained in them is crucial for retrieval performance.

According to the amount of information stored in retrieval data structures searched during retrieval, we can roughly divide existing models of IR systems into three levels:

1. systems that recognise only the membership of words in documents,
2. systems that store also the frequencies of words and their positions in documents, and

3. systems that analyse and use word contexts including syntactic relations among words.

The lack of information in the first two types of IR systems caused by reduction of the original documents to mere lists of terms cannot be overcome without dealing with word contexts. The reason for this proposition is that, in fact, not *words* but *senses* of texts are required to be found. But neither a computer nor a human(!) can recognise the sense of a text or even of a word(!) when only a list of the words contained in a document is given.

3 Features of Language

Ambiguity and synonymity of words is a property of natural language causing a very serious problem in IR. Both ambiguous words and synonyms depress the effectiveness of word-matching systems. The direct effect of polysemy on word-matching systems is to decrease precision (e. g. queries about financial banks retrieve documents about rivers). Synonymity decreases recall. If one sense is expressed by different synonyms in different documents, the word-matching system will retrieve all the documents only if all the synonyms are given in the query. Unfortunately, polysemy has another negative effect: polysemy also prevents the effective use of thesauri. Consequently, thesauri cannot be directly used to eliminate the problem with synonyms.

In our opinion, if a retrieval system is not able to identify homonyms and synonyms and to discriminate their senses, ambiguity and synonymity will remain one of the main factors causing 1) low recall, 2) low precision, and 3) the known and inevitable fact that recall and precision are inversely related. There are some evidences that lexical context analysis could be a good way how to eliminate or at least decrease these difficulties — see below.

Word senses are *not* something given a priori. Humans create word senses in the process of thinking and using language. Thinking forms language and language influences thinking. It is impossible to separate them. Word senses are products of their interaction. In our opinion, the effort to represent word senses as fixed elements in a textual information system is a methodological mistake.

Many researchers consider the sense of a word as an average of its linguistic uses. Then, the investigation of sense distinctions is based on the knowledge of contexts in which a word appears in a text corpus. *Sense representations* are computed as groups of similar contexts. According to how wide vicinity of the target word we include into the context we can speak about the *local* context and the *topical context*. The local or *"micro"* context is generally considered to be some small window of words surrounding a word occurrence in a text, from a few words of context to the entire sentence in which the target word appears. The topical context includes substantive words that co-occur with a given word, usually within a window of several sentences. In contrast with the topical context, the microcontext may include information on word order, distance, grammatical inflections and syntactic structure.

In one study, Miller and Charles [6] found evidence that human subjects determine the semantic similarity of words from the similarity of the contexts they are used in. They summarised this result in the so-called *strong contextual hypothesis*: *Two words are semantically similar to the extent that their contextual representations are similar.*

The contextual representation of a word has been defined as a characterisation of the linguistic context in which a word appears. Leacock, Towell and Voorhees [4] demonstrated that contextual representations consisting of both local and topical components are effective for resolving word senses and can be automatically extracted from sample texts. Not only computers but even humans learn, realise, get to know and understand the meanings of words from the contexts in which they meet them. The investigation of word contexts is the most important, essential, unique and indispensable means of understanding the sense of words and texts.

The procedure assigning sense labels to occurrences of a polysemous word is called *word sense disambiguation* (WSD). Researchers dealing with WSD methods often inspect also the way it affects retrieval performance if used in a retrieval model. Krovetz and Croft [3] demonstrated that WSD can improve text retrieval performance. Later, Schütze and Pedersen [7] found a noticeable improvement in precision using sense-based retrieval and word sense discrimination. Towell and Voorhees [8] showed that, given accurate WSD, the lexical relations encoded in lexicons such as WordNet can be exploited to improve the effectiveness of IR systems.

4   Constructing Dependency Microcontexts

Linguistic analysis of an input Czech text consists of a sequence of procedures. Key algorithms used in them are based on empirical methods and on previous statistical processing of training data, i. e. natural language corpora providing statistically significant sample of correct decisions.

For the sake of the construction of word contexts, we use the lemmas of words (i. e. their basic word forms), their part of speech, their analytic function (expressing surface syntactic dependency relations) and the *dependency microcontext structure* (DMCS). See the example of a DMCS given in Figure 1. The edges of the graph are labeled by so called dependency types (see below). The corresponding sentence is: "Kdo chce investovat dvě stě tisíc korun do nového automobilu, nelekne se, že benzín byl změnou zákona trochu zdražen." (Words for translation: Who wants to-invest two hundred thousand crowns in new car, he-does-not-get-frightened that petrol was by-change of-law a-little made-more-expensive.) For more details of the construction of the DMCS see [2].

There are 10 parts of speech in Czech and 18 types of analytic function. However, we will consider only four parts of speech, namely nouns (N), adjectives (A), verbs (V) and adverbs (D), and four types of analytic function, namely subject (Sb), object (Obj), adverbial (Adv) and attribute (Atr), because only these are significant for our purposes.

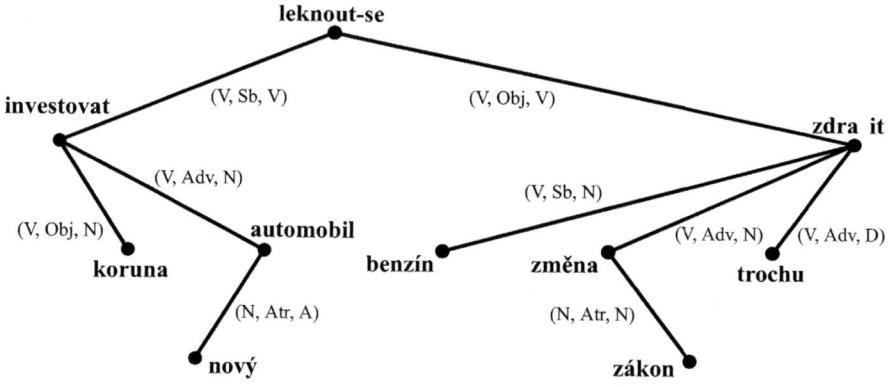

Fig. 1. An example of a DMCS

The construction of the dependency microcontext is based on the identification of *significant dependency relationships* (SDRs) in the sentence. An SDR consists of two words and a *dependency type*. An SDR is a triple $[w_1, DT, w_2]$, where w_1 is a head word (lexical unit), DT is a dependency type and w_2 is a depending word (lexical unit). A dependency type is a triple (P_1, AF, P_2), where P_1 is the part of speech of the head word, AF is an analytic function and P_2 is the part of speech of the depending word. Considering 4 significant parts of speech and 4 analytic functions, we have 64 ($= 4 \times 4 \times 4$) possible distinct dependency types. In Czech, however, only 28 of them really occur. Thus, we have 28 distinct dependency types shown in Table 1: Now we define

Table 1. Dependency types

(N, Atr, N)	(V, Sb, N)	(N, Sb, N)	(A, Adv, A)	(V, Obj, N)
(N, Atr, A)	(V, Sb, V)	(N, Sb, A)	(A, Adv, D)	(V, Obj, V)
(N, Atr, V)	(V, Sb, A)	(N, Sb, V)	(A, Adv, N)	(A, Obj, A)
(N, Adv, N)	(V, Adv, N)	(A, Sb, N)	(A, Adv, V)	(D, Obj, N)
(N, Adv, V)	(V, Adv, V)	(A, Sb, A)	(D, Adv, D)	
(N, Adv, D)	(V, Adv, D)	(A, Sb, V)	(D, Adv, D)	

the *dependency word microcontext* (DMC). A DMC of a given word w is a list of its *microcontext elements* (MCEs). An MCE is a pair consisting of a word and a dependency type. If a word w occurs in a sentence and makes an SDR with another word w_1, i.e. if there is an SDR $[w, DT, w_1]$ or $[w_1, DT', w]$, then w_1 and the dependency type DT or DT' respectively make a microcontext element $[DT, w_1]$ or $[w_1, DT']$ respectively of the word w. The first case implies that w is a head word in the SDR and in the second case the word w is depending. Thus, each SDR $[w_1, DT, w_2]$ in a text produces two MCEs: $[w_1, DT]$ is an element of the context of w_2 and $[DT, w_2]$ is an element of the context of w_1.

5   Applications

5.1   Contexts, Collocations and Word Similarity

A text corpus can be viewed statistically as a sequence of values of a random variable W. The values of W are individual words. When considering significant words only, the same text can be also regarded as a sequence of MCEs as values of a random variable C. The probabilities $p(w_i) = p(W = w_i)$ and $p(c_i) = p(C = c_i)$ can be estimated by the frequencies of occurrences of w_i and c_i in the corpus.

A collocation is a co-occurrence of two words in a defined relation. In order to separate significant collocations from word pairs which occurred merely by a coincidence, we can compute the *measure of collocating* of w_1 and c_1 as the mutual information of the random events $W = w_1$ and $C = c_1$, since the fact that an MCE c_1 appears in a text as a context element of a word w_1 can be regarded as the co-occurrence of the two events. Then, the measure of collocating of w_1 and c_1 is $log \frac{p(w_1, c_1)}{p(w_1) \times p(c_1)}$.

Lin [ ], who has employed a similar method including also the computation of the mutual information, takes into account only 6 dependency types. The model proposed here could be better as it uses a finer distinguishing of relations between words. Lin also suggested an application of collocations or contexts for semantic word similarity computing. His results can be regarded as a proof that sense similarity can be estimated on the basis of context similarity.

If we are able to compute the context similarity measure (*consim*) of each pair of words of the same part of speech, we can make up the *context similarity graphs* (CSGs). Vertexes of these graphs are always the individual lexical units. Words with high *consim* are connected by edges. Since we justifiably expect that these graphs express to some extent also the similarity or at least connection of word senses, we can derive some important relations from their structure. We can ask what a high or low degree of a vertex in CSGs means. Our hypothesis is that lexical units with a high degree are some general or generic terms including some more specialised senses in their sense. Such a term can be replaced with another term with respect to the character of its context. Vice versa, lexical units with a low degree in CSG will be specialised terms, as they occur in a specialised context and thus they are, because of the character of their context, only hardly replaceable with other terms.

5.2   Entropy of Word Context

Having the random variables W and C defined above, we can consider the probability mass function $P(C|w_j) = P(C|W = w_j)$ as a conditional probability of context element given the word w_j. Then we define the *context entropy* of the word w_j as a conditional entropy of context element given the word w_j:

$HC(w_j) = H(C|W = w_j) = -\sum_{c \in CE_j} p(c|w_j) \cdot \log p(c|w_j)$, where CE_j is the set of context elements with the same part of speech as w_j.

A word with too high context entropy will not be much useful for retrieving. Its average context will be too wide, vague, uncertain, fuzzy. On the other hand, the words with low context entropy will have a more certain, more specified, more sharply delimited context, these words will be easily distinguished from other words by the character of their context. The contribution of this quantity to retrieval in texts is obvious: these words should have a "greater weight" for retrieval.

5.3   Using Collocations for Query Tuning

In order to improve retrieval performance by a modification of the query, two methods can be employed. The first is *query expansion* replacing words in the query with a set of words of the same meaning. It should ensure a higher recall. The second is *query refinement*, i. e. specifying the senses of query terms more precisely to avoid ambiguity of the query. Asking a query, the user can be offered collocations of the terms used in the query. Then the user can decrease the vagueness of the (ambiguous) query terms by the choice of collocations that are characteristic for the sense required. It seems to be a good way of refining a query. The user can be also offered a list of words identified by the system as similar to query terms. Then the user can modify the query or even compose an alternative expression for the same query sense. This is a way to decrease or eliminate the negative influence of synonyms in relevant documents.

6   Conclusion

In the presented study, the significance of some empirical NLP methods for information retrieval is shown. It is pointed out that the reduction of information caused by text pre-processing and ambiguity of language as well as synonymy are the two main obstacles preventing retrieval based on sense of the user's query. In order to recapitulate the results of this study and to make them more clear, we can sum up the essential and most important ideas into the following principles:

1. As to retrieval performance, word-based IR systems can be overcome by sense-based ones using effective techniques that are able to identify and compare meanings or senses of words.
2. The amount of information about contents of documents stored in the retrieval data structures is crucial for retrieval performance, and should be maximal.
3. A sense-based IR system must employ a good word sense disambiguation or discrimination algorithm.
4. In order to deal with word senses the investigation of word contexts is necessary.
5. Since the word contexts are to be processed statistically, they should be extracted from a large text corpus.

6. Having the knowledge of word contexts, collocations can be derived and semantic word similarity can be estimated as well. Word contexts are also the fundamental knowledge for WSD or sense discrimination.

7. The construction of the microcontexts can be based on the syntactic relations in the sentence. Then, the closest core of word context can be extracted. The accuracy of this process depends on the quality of the used syntactic parser.

8. Entropy of word contexts can help to determine the importance of lexical units for retrieval, i. e. the capability of terms to discriminate the sense. An occurrence of a term with a more certain context gives a greater amount of information; since the sense is characterised by the context, a more certain context implies a more certain sense.

9. The result of searching or retrieval performance cannot be satisfying if the query is not formulated adequately. The knowledge of collocations as well as the knowledge of word similarity should be employed for tuning of the query in interaction with the user.

10. Uncertainty and vagueness in the text retrieval cannot be eliminated entirely since they are caused primarily by the character of the human thinking necessarily determining also the character of natural language.

We are developing an experimental textual system MATES (MAster of TExt Sources). The main purpose of MATES is to serve as a textual database for experiments with various information retrieval methods. MATES is constructed universally, not only for certain given retrieval algorithms, and it is adapted for the work with Czech language. In the near future, the MATES system should enable us to test the methods proposed here and evaluate their contribution to IR as well. Our long-term goal is to design an efficient IR system using the best methods of natural language analysis. The presented analyses as well as building the experimental textual database MATES are likely to be significant steps towards that goal.

References

1. E. Brill, R. J. Mooney: An Overview of Empirical Natural Language Processing. In: *AI Magazine*, Vol. 18 (1997), No. 4.

2. M. Holub, A. Böhmová: Use of Dependency Tree Structures for the Microcontext Extraction. Accepted for the ACL'2000 conference. 350

3. R. Krovetz, W. B. Croft: Lexical ambiguity and information retrieval. In: *ACM Transactions on Information Systems*, 10(2), 1992, pp 115–141. 350

4. C. Leacock, G. Towell, E. M. Voorhees: Toward building contextual representations of word senses using statistical models. In: B. Boguraev and J. Pustejovsky (editors), *Corpus Processing for Lexical Acquisitions*, 1996, pp 97–113, MIT Press. 350

5. D. Lin: Extracting Collocations from Text Corpora. In: *Computerm '98. Proceedings of the First Workshop on Computational Terminology*. Montreal, 1998. 352

6. G. A. Miller, W. G. Charles: Contextual correlates of semantic similarity. In: *Language and cognitive processes*, 6(1), 1991. 350

7. H. Schütze, J. O. Pedersen: Information Retrieval Based on Word Senses. In: *Proceedings of the Fourth Annual Symposium on Document Analysis and Information retrieval*, pp 161 – 175, Las Vegas, NV, 1995. 350
8. G. Towell, E. M. Voorhees: Disambiguating Highly Ambiguous Words. In: *Computational Linguistics*, March 1998, Vol. 24, Number 1, pp 125 – 145. 350

Some Notes on the Information Flow in Read-Once Branching Programs*

Stasys Jukna[1] and Stanislav Žák[2]

[1] Dept. of Computer Science, University of Frankfurt,
60054 Frankfurt am Main, Germany
jukna@thi.informatik.uni-frankfurt.de
[2] Institute of Computer Science, Academy of Sciences
Pod vodárenskou věží 2, 182 00 Prague 8, Czech Republic
stan@cs.cas.cz

Abstract. In this paper we describe a lower bounds argument for read-once branching programs which is not just a standard cut-and-paste. The argument is based on a more subtle analysis of the information flow during the individual computations. Although the same lower bound can be also obtained by standard arguments, our proof may be promising because (unlike the cut-and-paste argument) it can potentially be extended to more general models.

1   Introduction

In this paper we consider the classical model of (deterministic) branching programs (b. p., for short). The task of proving a super-polynomial lower bound on the size of any b. p. computing an explicit Boolean function is one of the major open problems in complexity theory — such a result would immediately imply that this function needs more than logarithmic space to be computed by a Turing machine. A survey of known lower bounds for branching programs can be found, for example, in [4,5].

Recall that a branching program for a boolean function $f(x_1, \ldots, x_n)$ is a directed acyclic graph. It has one source and its internal nodes have out-degree 2 and are labelled by variables; the two outgoing edges have labels 0 and 1. The sinks (out-degree 0 nodes) have labels from $\{0, 1\}$. If a node has label x_i then the test performed at that node is to examine the i-th bit x_i of the input, and the computation proceeds further along the edge, whose label is the value of this bit. The label of the sink so reached is the value of the function (on that particular input). The *size* of a branching program is the number of nodes in it. The program is *read-once* (1-b. p. for short) if along each computation no bit is tested more than once.

The only known lower bounds method for (unrestricted) branching programs remains the counting argument proposed by Nechiporuk more than 30 years ago. Unfortunately, this argument cannot yield more than quadratic lower bounds. It

---

* Supported by GA ČR, grant No. 201/98/0717.

V. Hlaváč, K. G. Jeffery, and J. Wiedermann (Eds.): SOFSEM 2000, LNCS 1963, pp. 356–364, 2000.

is therefore important to look for alternative, more subtler arguments. As a step in this direction, we have proposed in [2] to take into account the dynamics of the amount of the information about a particular input during the computation on it. For this purpose we have used the language of so-called *windows* of individual inputs at different stages of computation. Roughly speaking, the window of an input $a \in \{0, 1\}^n$ at a given moment of computation on it is the input a itself with some bits "closed" or, as we say, "crossed" $(+)$. Intuitively, the crossed bits are the bits about which the program is uncertain at this moment, whereas the length of the window (the number of non-crossed bits) captures the amount of already collected information.

In [2] we used the well-known Kraft's inequality from information theory to prove that the program cannot be small if the average length of windows is large (we recall this result below; see Theorem 2). We then used this relation between the average length of windows and the program size to prove exponential lower bounds on the size of so-called "gentle" branching programs. Besides that the proof employs a new idea of windows, the bounds themselves are interesting, because (as shown in [2] and [6]) explicit functions, which are known to be hard for all(!) previously considered restricted models of branching programs, can be computed by gentle programs of polynomial size. This fact shows that, apparently, the language of windows captures some aspects of computations which were hidden for us so far. It therefore makes sense to investigate the combinatorial properties of windows in different models of branching programs.

If the program is just a decision tree, then the length of the windows increases by one after each subsequent test. Hence, if the average length of computations is large, the average length of windows is also large, and (by the above mentioned Kraft-type result) the program must be large. However, in a general branching program, some already collected information about the values of some bits may be lost. This may happen when several computation with different values on these bits meet in a node. Thus, in general, the length of windows is not a monotone function, and it is important to better understand their dynamics even in restricted models.

In this paper we consider the following "2-multisym" function. Its input is an $m \times k$ 0-1 matrix, and the function accepts this matrix if and only if each pair of its columns contain 00 or 11 on at least one row (such pairs of bits are "twin-couples"). We show that any 1-b. p., recognizing whether a given matrix is a 2-multisym or not, has exponential size.

Let us stress that (numerically) the obtained lower bound is not interesting at all — it can be obtained by using the standard cut-and-paste techniques for 1-b. p.'s. Our main contribution is an entirely different *proof argument*, which potentially can be extended to more general models. Our proof is based on a so-called "forcing lemma" (Lemma 2) which formalizes an intuitive idea that during the computation on every multisym, for every pair of columns, *both* bits of at least one twin-couple must appear in the window at the same moment, i. e. the program must "see" *both* bits in order to decide whether this couple is a couple of twins or not. Since each multisym has at least $\binom{k}{2} = \Omega(k^2)$ twin-couples, at some moment of the computation on it, at least $h = \Omega(k^2/T)$ bits must appear in the window, where T is the time (i.e. the maximal number of tests along any computation). We then apply the Kraft-type result from [2] (we recall it in the next section) saying that long windows on many inputs imply large program size.

2   Average Length of Windows and the Program Size

In order to capture the flow of information during the computation on a particular input, we have to somehow formalize what bits of a given input a are already "known" by the program at a particular stage of the computation $comp(a)$, and which bits are still "unknown" or were "previously known" but are "forgotten", etc. We can imagine that, during the computation, some bits are closed (and we put, say, a cross $+$ on it) and some bits are open for us (we can see them). After that some already open bits may be closed, and some closed bits may be opened again (after a test on them), etc. This dynamics can be described using so-called "windows" (see [2]). (Here we use a simplified version with only one type of crosses.)

Let P be a branching program, $e = (u, v)$ be an edge in P and $F \subseteq \{0, 1\}^n$ be an arbitrary subset of inputs, the computations on which go through this edge.

The *window* $w(a, e, F)$ of input $a \in F$ at e with respect to the set F is a string of length n in the alphabet $\{0, 1, +\}$ which is defined as follows. We assign a cross $(+)$ to the i-th bit of a if there is a $b \in F$ such that $b(i) \neq a(i)$ and starting from e,

(i)   either the computations on a and b follow the same path until a sink (the bit i is "forgotten"),

(ii) or the first divergence of these two computations is caused by a test on i (the program was not certain about the bit i and tests it again).

The remaining bits of $w(a, e, F)$ are non-crossed (i.e. specified) and their values are the same as in a. The *length* of the window is the number of non-crossed bits.

Remark 1. The smaller is F the larger is the number of non-crossed bits in the windows relative to F.

We have the following general lower bound on the size of branching programs in terms of the average length of windows ([2]).

Let $P = (V, E)$ be a branching program, and $A \subseteq \{0, 1\}^n$ be a set of inputs. A *distribution* of A (among the edges of P) is a mapping $\varphi \colon A \to E$ which sends each input $a \in A$ to some edge of the computation $comp(a)$. (To define such a distribution we just stop the computations $comp(a)$ on particular edges.) Given such a distribution, the *average length* of windows (of inputs from A) is the sum

$$H(A, \varphi) := \frac{1}{|A|} \sum_{a \in A} \ell_a \,,$$

where ℓ_a is the length of the window $w(a, e, F)$ of a at the edge $e = \varphi(a)$ with respect to the set $F := \{b \in A : \varphi(b) = e\}$ of all those inputs, which are mapped to the same edge; we call this set F the *class* of distribution at e.

Theorem 2 (([2])). *Let $P = (V, E)$ be a branching program, $A \subseteq \{0,1\}^n$ a set of inputs and φ be any distribution of these inputs among the edges of P. Then $|E| \geq |A| \cdot 2^{H(A,\varphi)-n}$.*

Thus, in order to prove that a program must be large it would be enough to distribute a large set of inputs A and show that the average length of windows $H(A, \varphi)$ must be large.

The second task (to force long windows) depends on the computed function f. Intuitively, if in order to determine the value $f(a)$ we must "know" the values of some h bits of the input a, then during the computation on this input some of these h bits must all appear in the window. In general, this intuition may be false, but there are situations where it works. To demonstrate this, let us consider the following language of "multisyms."

3   Multisyms

Inputs $a \in \{0,1\}^n$ are $m \times k$ 0-1 matrices with $n = mk$. A *t-trace* (or just a *trace* if parameter t is clear from the context) in a is a set of t bits of a lying on the same row. Such a trace is *monochromatic* if all its bits have the same value. A matrix a is a *t-multisym* if every t-tuple of columns of a contain at least one monochromatic trace.

Intuitively, during the computation on a, for every t-tuple of columns, *all* t bits of at least one monochromatic trace on these columns must appear at least once in the window. It is easy to show that, at least for the case when $t = k$, this is indeed true.

Let SYM be the characteristic function of k-multisyms. That is, SYM accepts an $m \times k$ matrix iff it has at least one monochromatic row.

Proposition 1. *Let P be a branching program computing SYM and A be the set of all k-multisyms. It is possible to distribute the inputs from A among the edges of P so that the average length of windows is at least k.*

Proof. We use the following "stopping rule": stop a computation $comp(a)$ on an input $a \in A$ at the edge e, where the last test on a monochromatic row of a is done. Let $w(a)$ denote the window of a at this edge (with respect to the corresponding class of our distribution). Let i be the index of the monochromatic row whose bit was tested at the edge e, and assume w.l.o.g. that the edge e is a 1-edge (hence, the i-th row is the all-1 row). We claim that all the bits of this row are (non-crossed) in the window $w(a)$.

To show this, assume the opposite, i.e. that $w(a)$ has a cross at some bit $x_{i,j}$. Since, by our stopping rule, no bit of the i-th row is tested after the edge e, this cross could appear only if there is another input $b \in A$ such that $b_{i,j} = 0$, the computation $comp(b)$ reaches the edge e and then follows the computation $comp(a)$ until the sink. Moreover, according to our stopping rule, the test on $x_{i,j}$ was also the *last* test on the monochromatic row along $comp(b)$. Since this test was 1-test, the i-th row of b should be also all-1 row, a contradiction with $b_{i,j} = 0$.

$\square$

We have shown that windows for SYM are long enough, they have length at least k. On the other hand, this function has a trivial b. p. of size $O(n)$. This does not contradict with our general lower bound just because the set A of distributed inputs was too small, $|A| \leq 2m2^{(m-1)k} = m2^{n-k+1}$, and hence, the lower bound $2|P| \geq |E| \geq |A| \cdot 2^{k-n}$ is trivial.

Still, the above example may be suggestive. To increase the size of the distributed set A we could try to consider t-multisyms for some $t < k$. In particular, easy counting shows that, if t is such that $1 + \log \binom{k}{t} \leq m$, then a *constant* fraction of all 2^n inputs are t-multisyms; hence, in this case $|A| \geq 2^{n-c}$ for some constant c. But the problem of forcing long enough windows in this case (when $t \ll k$) turns to a much more difficult task, and so far we were not able to solve it completely.

4   Read-Once Programs for 2-Multisyms

In the rest of the paper we show how this task (of forcing long windows) can be solved for 1-b. p.'s. We show that for such programs the windows must be long even for the case when $t = 2$. In this case the considered language is particularly simple. As before, inputs $a \in \{0,1\}^n$ are $m \times k$ 0-1 matrices with $n = mk$. A *couple* in a is a 2-trace, i. e. a pair (ν, ν') of bits in one row. A couple is a *twin-couple* for an input a if these bits have the same value in a, i. e. if $a(\nu) = a(\nu')$. A pair of columns I, J of a is *covered* if it contains at least one twin-couple. A matrix is a 2-*multisym* (or just *multisym*) if each pair of its columns is covered.

We show that any 1-b. p., recognizing whether a given matrix is a 2-multisym or not, has exponential size. As we already mentioned in the introduction, (numerically) the obtained lower bound is not interesting — it can be obtained by using the standard cut-and-paste techniques for 1-b. p.'s. However, the *proof* itself may be promising to approach the general case. The standard technique for 1-b. p.'s is to stop all the computations after some (fixed in advance) number d of tests and to show that no two of them could be stopped at the same node; hence, we must have at least 2^d nodes. Almost all lower bounds for 1-b.p's were obtained using this argument (a nice exception is an "adversary" argument used in [1]).

In our proof we apply a different argument: we use a more subtle stopping rule, which depends not just on the *number* of tested bits but on the *form* of windows, i. e. on the "form" of already collected information about the input vector. Then the idea is to show that, for every 2-multisym a and for every pair of columns, the bits of at least one twin-couple on these columns must appear *both* in some window along the computation on a. Hence, the new argument has a potential to be extended to more general branching programs (cf. Remark 3 below).

After that we use the following lemma (which holds for arbitrary branching programs). In what follows, by a *natural* window of a multisym a at an edge e we will mean the window $w(a, e, F)$ with respect to the set F of *all* inputs reaching this edge. We say that a couple is non-crossed in a window if *both* its bits are non-crossed in that window.

Lemma 1. *Let P be an arbitrary branching program for multisyms running in time $T = T(n)$. Let a be a multisym. If for each pair of columns at least one of its couples is non-crossed in at least one natural window of a (along $comp(a)$), then at least one natural window along $comp(a)$ has length at least $\binom{k}{2}/T$.*

Proof. Let d be the maximal length of a natural window during $comp(a)$. So, at each edge of $comp(a)$ at most d couples can become newly non-crossed in the window (after the test made at that edge). Since we have at most T edges in $comp(a)$, $d \cdot T \geq \binom{k}{2}$. $\qquad\square$

5   The Forcing Lemma for 1-b. p.'s

The main technical lemma is the following "forcing lemma".

Lemma 2. *Let P be a 1-b. p. computing multisyms, $s(n)$ be any function such that $s(n) \leq m - 2\log n$. Let a be a multisym such that each its natural window along $comp(a)$ is shorter than $s(n)$. Then for every pair of columns of a, at least one couple in these columns is non-crossed in at least one natural window of a.*

Remark 3. If proved without the "read-once" assumption, this lemma would imply a superpolynomial lower bound on branching programs running in super-linear time (via the argument used in the proof of Theorem 4 below). Thus, the problem of proving such a lower bound is reduced to the question of whether also in general the intuition — that (for each pair of columns of each multisym) the program must at least once "see" *both* bits of a twin-couple at the same moment — is correct. This reduction (and not the lower bound itself) is the main message of this paper.

Before we prove this lemma, let us first show how it (together with Theorem 2) implies that multisyms cannot be computed by 1-b. p. of polynomial size.

Theorem 4. *Each 1-b. p. computing 2-multisyms has size at least $2^{\Omega(n^{1/3})}$.*

Proof. Let A be the set of all 2-multisyms. By simple counting, the number of $m \times k$ matrices ($mk = n$) violating this property does not exceed $\binom{k}{2} \cdot 2^{m(k-2)}$ (so many possibilities to choose a pair of "bad" columns) times 2^m (so many possibilities to choose a value in one of these columns and to produce the second column with all values changed to the opposite ones). This number does not exceed $2^n \cdot n^2/2^m$, implying that $|A| \geq 2^n \left(1 - \frac{n^2}{2^m}\right)$, which is at least 2^{n-1} if $m - 1 \geq 2 \log n$. So, we can take $m := n^{1/3}$ and $s(n) := m - 2 \log n$.

We want to prove that for each multisym a there is at least one natural window (along $comp(a)$) longer than $n/3m^2$. To show this, assume that, for some multisym a, all its natural windows along $comp(a)$ have length at most $n/3m^2 < s(n)$. But then, by Lemma 1 and Lemma 2, there must be at least one natural window along $comp(a)$ having length $\binom{k}{2}/n > n/3m^2$. A contradiction.

Now we distribute the multisyms by sending each multisym a to the edge of $comp(a)$ at which natural window is maximal. By Remark 1, the windows with respect to this distribution are not shorter than the natural windows in question. Hence, by Theorem 2, $2|P| \geq |E| \geq |A| \cdot 2^{-n+n/3m^2} \geq 2^{-1+n^{1/3}/3}$.   □

6   Proof of the Forcing Lemma

Let a be a multisym and I, J be a pair of its columns, $I \neq J$. Suppose that each natural window along $comp(a)$ is shorter than $s(n)$. Our goal is to show that both bits of at least one couple in columns I, J appear (i. e. both are non-crossed) in at least one natural window of a. To show this, assume the opposite that for no couple of a in I, J both its bits appear at the same moment in a window.

During the computation on a some bits become non-crossed after the tests on them (these bits appear in the window) but may be crossed (i. e. disappear from the window) later after the computation $comp(a)$ meets a computation on some other input with a different value on these bits. Moreover, both bits of at least one (twin-) couple of a in columns I, J must be tested during the computation on a. Since we assumed that no window of a can contain both these bits, one of them must be crossed somewhere before the test on the second bit. Thus, we can consider the following stopping rule.

Stopping rule: Stop the computation $comp(a)$ at the edge $e = (u, v)$ after which, for the first moment some previously non-crossed bit ν from columns I, J disappears from the window (becomes crossed).

By the definition of crosses, we know that at the node v the computation $comp(a')$ on some other input a' with $a'(\nu) \neq a(\nu)$ joins the computation $comp(a)$. Let b and b' be the partial assignments corresponding to the initial parts of computations $comp(a)$ and $comp(a')$ until the node v. Let $Nask(b)$ ($Nask(b')$) be the set of bits in columns I, J which are not specified in b (resp., in b').

Claim 5. *Nask(b) contains at least* $2 \log n$ *couples in columns* I, J *and* $Nask(b) \subseteq Nask(b')$.

Proof. As $e = (u, v)$ is the *first* edge after which some previously non-crossed bit gets a cross, at most one bit from each of the couples in columns I, J can be tested before v (for otherwise some couple would already appear in the window) and, according to our stopping rule, each of these tested bits must remain in the window until v. But by our assumption, all the windows of a are shorter than $s(n)$. Since we have m couples in columns I, J, no bit of at least $m - s(n) \geq 2 \log n$ of them is tested along $comp(a)$ until the node v, implying that $|Nask(b)| \geq 2 \log n$.

To show the inclusions $Nask(b) \subseteq Nask(b')$, assume that there is a bit $\mu \in Nask(b) \setminus Nask(b')$. Since $\mu \notin Nask(b')$, this bit was tested along $comp(a')$ before the node v, and (since our program is read-once) it cannot be tested after the node v. Moreover, we know that the pair I, J is not covered by the specified bits of b, for otherwise the corresponding twin-couple would be in the window of a at the edge e, by the stopping rule. Extend the (partial) input b as follows. On bits outside I, J take the values of a. On the bit μ' (the second bit of the couple) give the value $a(\mu')$. After that assign the couples, both of whose bits are non-specified, the values 01 and 10 so that all still non-covered pairs of columns I, K and K, J with $K \neq I, J$ become covered; this is possible, since we have at least $2 \log n$ such pairs. In couples in columns I, J with precisely one specified bit, except for the couple (μ, μ'), we assign the opposite value. This way we obtain a partial input, in which μ is the only unspecified bit, and the pair I, J is still not covered by the specified bits. Extend this input to two inputs by setting μ to 0 and to 1. By the construction, both obtained complete inputs reach the same sink (the bit μ is not retested after the node v), but exactly one of them covers the pair I, J, a contradiction.   □

Now take the partial inputs b and b' corresponding to initial segments of the computations $comp_v(a)$ and $comp_v(a')$. Our goal is to extend them to complete inputs c and c' such that $P(c) = P(c')$ and only c is a multisym; this yields the desired contradiction.

We construct the desired extensions c and c' as follows.

1. On bits outside the columns I, J, which are not specified in b', we give both c and c' the values of a; on the bits, where b' is specified, we give c and c' the corresponding values of a and a', respectively.
2. The second bit ν' of the twin-couple (ν, ν') of a is not specified in b and therefore non-specified also in b', by Claim 5. We set $c(\nu') = c'(\nu') := a(\nu)$. This way the pair I, J becomes covered in c but is still uncovered by the (already specified) bits of c'.
3. By Claim 5, we have at least $2 \log n$ couples in I, J both bits of which are specified neither in b nor in b'. Using the same argument as in the proof of this claim, we can set these pairs of bits to 01 and 10 in both c and c' so that all the pairs of columns I, K and K, J with $K \neq I, J$, become covered in c (and in c').
4. What remains are the couples (μ, μ') in columns I, J, precisely one bits of which, say μ, is specified in b. By Claim 5, the second bit μ' is nonspecified in both b and b'. We specify the unspecified bits in such a way that $c'(\mu') = c(\mu') = c'(\mu) \oplus 1$ (see Fig. 1). No twin-couple in c' is produced.

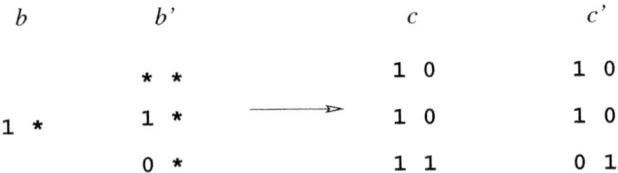

Fig. 1. Specifying the bits in Step 4

Now look at the computations $comp(c)$ and $comp(c')$. By the construction, c is consistent with b and c' is consistent with b'; so, both these computations reach that node v. Since our program is read-once, no of the bits on which both b and b' were specified, are tested along $comp(c)$ after the node v. Since c' can differ from c only in those bits, we have that after the node v both these computations follow the same path until the sink, implying that the program outputs the same value on both inputs c and c'. The input c is a multisym since all the pairs of colums are covered by a twin-couples in it; the pair I, J is covered by the twin-couple (ν, ν') (and, perhaps, by some other twin-couples, arising in Step 4). But this pair of colums remains uncovered in c' because in Step 4 we produced no twin-couple in c', and $c'(\nu) = a'(\nu) \neq a(\nu) = c'(\nu')$. Thus, the program wrongly accepts the input c' which is not a multisym.

The obtained contradiction completes the proof of Lemma 2.   □

References

1. B. Bollig and I. Wegener, A very simple function that requires exponential size read-once branching programs, Inf. Process. Letters **66** (1998), 53–58. 360
2. S. Jukna and S. Žák, On branching programs with bounded uncertainty. In: Proc. of ICALP'98, Springer LNCS **1443** (1998), 259–270. 357, 358, 359
3. E. I. Nechiporuk, On a Boolean function, Soviet Mathematics Doklady **7**:4 (1966), 999–1000. (In Russian).
4. Razborov, A. (1991): Lower bounds for deterministic and nondeterministic branching programs, in: Proc. FCT'91, Springer Lecture Notes in Computer Science **529**, 47–60. 356
5. Wegener, I. (2000): Branching programs and Binary Decision Diagrams: Theory and Applications. SIAM Series in Discrete Mathematics and Applications. 356
6. S. Žák, Upper bounds for gentle branching programs, Tech. Rep. Nr. 788, Inst. of Comput. Sci., Czech Acad. of Sci., 1999. 357

On Vision-Based Orientation Method of a Robot Head in a Dark Cylindrical Pipe*

Marina Kolesnik

GMD — German National Research Center for Information Technology
Schloss Birlinghoven, Sankt-Augustin, D-53754 Germany
kolesnik@gmd.de

Abstract. This paper addresses the problem of navigation of an autonomous robot when it moves in a modern concrete sewer. The robot must keep its orientation within mostly cylindrical sewer pipes. This implies a geometrical constraint on the environment in which the robot operates. We present a hybrid vision system that consists of (a) an optical camera and (b) a laser crosshair projector generating a cross pattern in the camera field of view. The camera acquires the laser footprint projected on the pipe surface. The image of the footprint is the two intersecting curves. The shape of the curves depends on (up to the symmetry of the sewer pipe) a particular robot heading. We describe experiments conducted in the straight pipe segment of the dry sewer test-net. We present an algorithm that recovers instantaneous orientation of the laser projector relative to the pipe axis. We give a strategy for robot self-orientation along the sewer pipe axis.

1 Introduction

About 10 % of Britain's 230,000 km of sewers are likely to need renovation and replacement over the next 10 years [8]. Similarly, about 400,000 km long sewers in Germany are not in a good condition [2]. Maintenance of thousands km of sewers requires their permanent surveying and possibly repair. Sewer pipes are typically inaccessible for humans. These are generally surveyed by mounting a camera and a light either on a sled, which is dragged, or on a tractor, which is driven through the sewer, producing a video record of the pipe's condition. In both cases ground operators who control the vehicle use a cable for guidance and data acquisition. Such a process is both complicated and labour intensive in practice. This motivated a development of new sewer surveying technologies based on machine interpretation of sewer survey videos. Cooper et al. showed how to use a sewer video record to recover the instantaneous orientation of the camera [1]. The method is essentially geared towards old sewers made out of bricks. Pan et al. [6] and Xu et al. [9] argue that the visual appearance of a pipe junction can provide useful information about the pipe's profile in the neighborhood of that junction. They both describe junction detection/description methods based upon

---

* This work was supported by BMBF under the project 02-WK 9702/4

V. Hlaváč, K. G. Jeffery, and J. Wiedermann (Eds.): SOFSEM 2000, LNCS 1963, pp. 365–374, 2000.
© Springer-Verlag Berlin Heidelberg 2000

more traditional techniques such as convolution-based edge detection, thresholding, thinning and profile analysis based on Fourier descriptors. These techniques are effectively used to detect and assess deformations in the pipe joint profiles.

The work reported here is part of the MAKRO project targeted at developing an *autonomous robot for sewer inspection* [3]. The task of such a robot is to travel autonomously through the system of sewer pipes and to *collect* a video record of sewer conditions. The project focuses on typical concrete sewers. The robot consists of a mobile base platform and is equipped with sensors, a light source, a laser crosshair projector and a camera. This work solves the task of robot orientation when it moves along a straight portion of the cylindrical pipe, i. e. the moving robot finds its orientation in real time and continuously corrects its heading so as to stay down in the middle of the pipe.

Robot orientation relies on a hybrid vision system, consisting of two components: (a) an optical camera and (b) a pen-size laser crosshair projector. This design allows using a geometrical constraint, implied by the shape of modern sewer pipes, which are mostly cylindrical with a standard diameter of 60 cm or 30 cm. When illuminated by the laser crosshair projector they give rise to a pair of conic sections whose shape encodes the orientation of the robot head within the pipe. The laser footprints are extracted from the image and their shape is analyzed so as to define an instantaneous orientation of the robot heading. An experimental verification of the orientation algorithm has been carried out in the dry sewer test-net. The robot camera overlooking a long straight portion of the pipe has acquired a number of real images of the laser footprint while the robot heading has been altered to all possible directions.

The paper is organized as follows. In Section 2 we describe geometry of the robot vision system and illustrate the approach with a simulated image of the laser footprint. In Section 3 we present our experimental results and the image processing algorithm, which recovers the robot heading with respect to the pipe axis. We also give the sequence of iterative steps for the robot self-correction. Concluding remarks are made in Section 4.

2   Geometry of the Vision System and Laser Footprint Images

Modern clay and concrete sewers, which constitute over 90 % of the sewage system in Germany are laid out of preformed cylindrical pipe segments. These are joined together into the longer straight pipe portions. The straight portions intersect each other in T-, L- or X- shaped junctions called manhole areas. The latter are regions where humans can access the sewer from outside. MAKRO sewer robot is a snake-like robot composed of 5 equal-sized segments with 1.60 m length in total. The diameter of the robot segments is about 15 cm. The robot moves in a graph-structured environment, characterized by 1) straight portions of the pipe separated by 2) manhole junction areas. A pen-size laser and a camera are fixed on the robot head segment like a stereo rig with maximum possible dis-

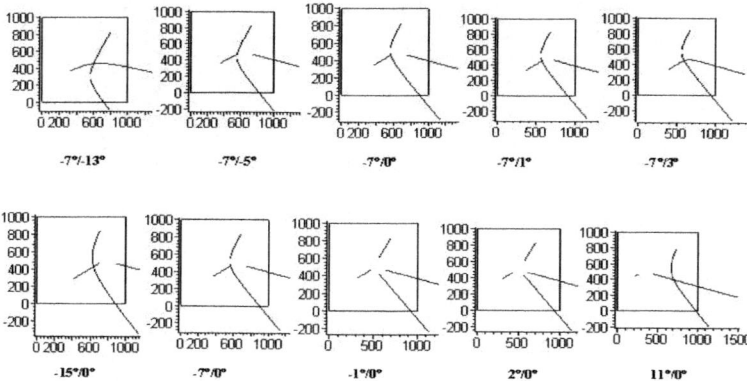

Fig. 1. Ten simulated images of the laser footprints. The camera is located to the left from the laser and below it. The coordinate system is selected in such a way that the x-axis is parallel to the vertical direction of the robot, the z-axis is parallel to the longitudinal axis of the robot head segment, and the y-axis completes the coordinate system. The horizontal/vertical angles under the each plot show the deviations of the laser main beam from the zx/zy coordinate planes. The boxes represent the boarders of the CCD matrix of 1000×1000 pixel size. The gaps in the footprint images occur when the distance from the laser to the 3-D point on the pipe surface exceeds the 20 m distance threshold. The plots in the upper row illustrates the shape variations when the laser rotates downward around the y-axis. The plots in the second row illustrate similar changes when the laser rotates horizontally from left to right around the x-axis

tance (basis) between them. These constitute the robot's two-component hybrid vision system.

The off-the-shelf laser available from LASIRIS ([5], Fig. 2, left) is equipped with a special optical head to project a high quality crosshair from the laser beam. The crosshair is the two perpendicular planar sheets within an accurately known fan angle, which is given by the manufacturer (50 degrees in our case). When the laser-generated two planar sheets are projected on a plane, the laser footprint is a cross. If the laser crosshair is projected onto an ideal cylindrical pipe, its perpendicular planar sheets cut two ellipse segments on the pipe surface. These segments are seen in the image as segments of a conic. i. e. quadratic curves. The 3-D shape of the ellipse segments depends mainly on the direction of the laser beam with respect to the axis of the sewer pipe.

However, *the image* of the laser footprint and, consequently, the shape of the quadratic curves in the image depend on the position of the laser and the camera as well as the distance (basis) between them. The distance plays a crucial role in making the curve shape variations noticeable enough to be recorded. This can be explained by considering an imaginable situation, when the center of the laser

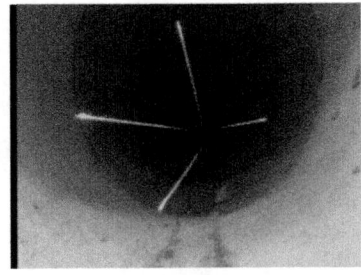

Fig. 2. Left: The LASIRIS laser crosshair projector. Right: The image of the straight pipe segment with the overlaid laser footprint. The laser is well oriented along the pipe axis. The camera and the laser are fixed on the sides of the robot head segment with the camera a little bit higher than the laser. The latter changes the curvature of the horizontal portion of the footprint to the opposite direction when compared to the simulated plots in Fig. 1

projector coincides with the camera optical center. Then the footprint observed by the camera would be always an ideal cross regardless of its actual 3-D shape. A thorough investigation of the shape of the footprint curves in the image made in [1] showed that: 1) the distance $D \approx r/3$ (r is the radius of the cylindrical sewer pipe) between the laser and the camera is enough to record variations in the shape of the laser footprint in the images as a function of the robot heading, and 2) the shape of the laser footprint in the image is uniquely related to the instantaneous robot heading inside the pipe.

Here we present only one simulated result in which the geometrical configuration of the vision system was similar to the actual robot setup used in our experiments. Fig. 1 illustrates the variations in the shape of the laser footprints in the computed images when the robot head executes a vertical downwards (first row) and a horizontal from left to right (second row) motions. The plots clearly show that the shape of a pair of the horizontal and the vertical footprint portions in the image comprises an instantaneous "snapshot" that characterizes the shape of the cylindrical pipe ahead of the robot. The shape of the laser footprints in the image varies depending on the robot heading relative to the pipe axis. The two points of maximum curvature on the horizontal and the vertical portions of the laser footprint in the image are the images of the two most distant 3D points belonging to the corresponding ellipse segments on the pipe surface of which the quadratic curves are the image. The fact that these two points coincide in the image reflects the instance when the most distant 3D point on the pipe surface is common for the two elliptical segments cast by the laser. The latter means that the laser is well oriented along the pipe axis as it is evidenced in the Fig. 2, right.

3   Orientation Algorithm and Experiments

An experiment was carried out in about 20 m long straight portion of the sewer pipe in front of the robot head. The pipe was closed to ensure that no light was coming into the sewer from outside and the robot light was off. The radius of the pipe was equal to 30 cm. The camera and the laser were manually fixed on the sides of the robot head segment with the camera position a little bit below than the laser position and the basis of about 14 cm between them. Their relative orientation ensured approximately parallel direction of the laser main beam and the camera optical axis, although no special tuning was done. In addition, the laser was rotated so that its crosshair appeared to have roughly horizontal/vertical orientation in the image plane. This configuration is similar to the simulated case shown in Fig. 1. Deviations of the robot heading with respect to the pipe axis were characterized in terms of vertical and horizontal deviations defined by the laser footprint curves in the image. Obviously, rotation of the robot around the pipe axis (the axis of symmetry) can not be recovered on the basis of footprint images and must be computed using readings of the robot gyro sensor. We altered the position and the viewing direction of the robot head segment to investigate shape variations in the respective images of the laser footprint.

3.1   Computing the Orientation of the Robot Head

Several image frames (negatives) of the laser footprint acquired by the robot camera with the flashlight off are shown in Fig. 3. We analyze each footprint image as a pair of the horizontal and vertical quadratic curves. For each of the two curves we select the point with the maximum curvature. As it follows from our geometrical construction, these points are the images of the most distant 3-D points of the ellipse segments on the pipe surface. Consequently, if the laser is oriented towards the center of some distant pipe cross-section, the points with maximum curvature on the two curves will eventually coincide. This would mean that the farthest point on each quadratic curve in the image is common for both the vertical and the horizontal portion of the crosshair footprint. If these points do not coincide, than the discrepancy between them in the image characterizes the deviation of the laser beam from the direction of the pipe axis.

We used least squares as a maximum likelihood estimator [7] to fit two polynomials to the pixel sets that constitute the image of the horizontal/vertical portions of the crosshair footprint. Both pixel sets were approximated by quadratic polynomials so as to minimize the following merit function:

$$\xi^2 = \sum_{i=1}^{N} \left[\frac{y_i - \sum_{k=0}^{2} a_k x_i^k}{\sigma_i} \right]^2$$

where a_k are the parameters of the linear approximation, (x_i, y_i) — data set for the horizontal/vertical footprint pixels, (σ_i — the standard deviation associated with the i-th pixel, which we set to the constant value $\sigma = 1$. Let $M_h =$

(X_h, Y_h), $M_v = (X_v, Y_v)$ be the pixel coordinates of the points with the maximum curvature for the horizontal C_h and the vertical C_v curves (fitted polynomials), respectively. Then the values:

$$\Delta_h = X_h - X_v, \quad \Delta_v = Y_v - Y_h \tag{1}$$

characterize the deviation of the laser pointing direction from the "ideal" one, which is to the center of a distant pipe cross-section. We call the vector $\Delta = [\Delta_h, \Delta_v]$ a *correcting rotation*, which indicates the direction in which the robot head segment must be rotated in order to align its heading along the pipe axis. Δ_h indicates the direction of the rotation of the robot head segment around its vertical axis. If $\Delta_h < 0$ than the rotation is to the left; if $\Delta_h > 0$ it is to the right. Similarly, Δ_v indicates the rotation around the horizontal axis, if $\Delta_v < 0$ it is downward, and for $\Delta_v > 0$ it is upwards. The angles of the rotation can be assessed from the camera field of view as follows:

$$\alpha_h = \beta_x(\Delta_h / ImageSizeX), \quad \alpha_v = \beta_v(\Delta_v / ImageSizeY) \tag{2}$$

where α_h and α_v are the angles of rotation in the horizontal and vertical directions, β_h and β_v are the angular values of the camera's field of view, and *ImageSizeX* and *ImageSizeY* are the size of the CCD in pixels in the x and y directions, respectively.

Due to the particular orientation of the laser crosshair and because the quadratic curves C_h and C_v are defined within a limited domain the points with maximal curvature and the extremal values as defined by equation (3) coincide for each curve. Accordingly, considering the horizontal curve $C_h(x)$ as the function defined in the interval R_x and the vertical curve $C_v(y)$ as the function defined in the interval R_y, we denote:

$$M_h = \max_{x \in R_x} C_h(x), \quad M_v = \max_{y \in R_y} C_v(y). \tag{3}$$

It is also faster to look for extremal values instead of the points with maximum curvature.

The following is the sequence of the image processing steps that finds the "correcting rotation" for the robot heading based on a single footprint image:

1. *Histogram based extraction of the footprint points.* A brightness threshold is chosen on the basis of the image histogram. Above-threshold pixels are selected as a binary image of the laser footprint.
2. *Sorting footprint pixels.* Pixels that belong to the horizontal and the vertical footprint portions in the image are collected in the two respective arrays. This step is doable because of the particular orientation of the laser with respect to the CCD matrix.
3. *Fitting quadratic polynomials.* A quadratic polynomial is fitted to the pixels of each array using the least squares. The two polynomials $C_h(x)$ and $C_v(y)$ now approximate the images of the horizontal and the vertical portions of the crosshair footprint.

4. *Recovering the "correcting rotation".* The extremal points M_h and M_v are obtained for each polynomial according to (3). The "correcting rotation" is defined according to (1).

We illustrate the algorithm by applying the above steps to various images of the laser footprint acquired with different robot headings. In the left column of Fig. 3 are the original (negative) images of the different laser footprints. The images in the right column of Fig. 3 show the processed results after having applied the above steps. The last image pair shows a degenerated case of the laser footprint, when the robot heading deviated considerably downward from the pipe axis. Despite the part of the vertical portion of the laser footprint on the upper pipe surface is missing, the same procedure can be applied to derive the "correcting vector" Δ which will take the robot heading towards the pipe axis.

3.2 Self Correcting Algorithm

We now describe a self-correcting algorithm, which takes the robot heading in the desired direction along the sewer pipe axis. The robot corrects its heading in the two consecutive "horizontal" and "vertical" steps. It is not possible to compute precise angular values for the deviation of the robot heading from the pipe axis by analyzing laser footprint images. These angles depend on unknown parameters such as the length of the straight pipe section ahead and the actual position of the robot head within the pipe. Therefore, we perform iterative self-correction of the robot heading based on the analysis of the subsequent image frames. The following steps are used for the robot self correction:

1. Switch light off. Acquire the laser footprint image.
2. Process the laser footprint image to recover the "correcting rotation" vector Δ.
3. Select the rotating angles α_h and α_v according to equation (2).
4. Perform "horizontal" correction by rotating the robot head segment around the robot's vertical axis (the x-axis) in the direction defined by the Δ_h. Perform "vertical" correction by rotating the robot head segment around the robot's horizontal axis (the y-axis) in the direction defined by the Δ_v.
5. Repeat the steps 1–4 till the robot heading converges along the pipe reasonably well.

The algorithm described above is similar to how living beings orient them. The decision about "how to move" in each particular moment is made by assessing actions which will lead closer to a desirable position. This qualitative approach of iterative self-corrections is taken here instead of precise computation of angles and distances.

4   Conclusions

This paper describes a hybrid vision system designed to support the orientation of the autonomous robot for sewer inspection. The orientation approach relies

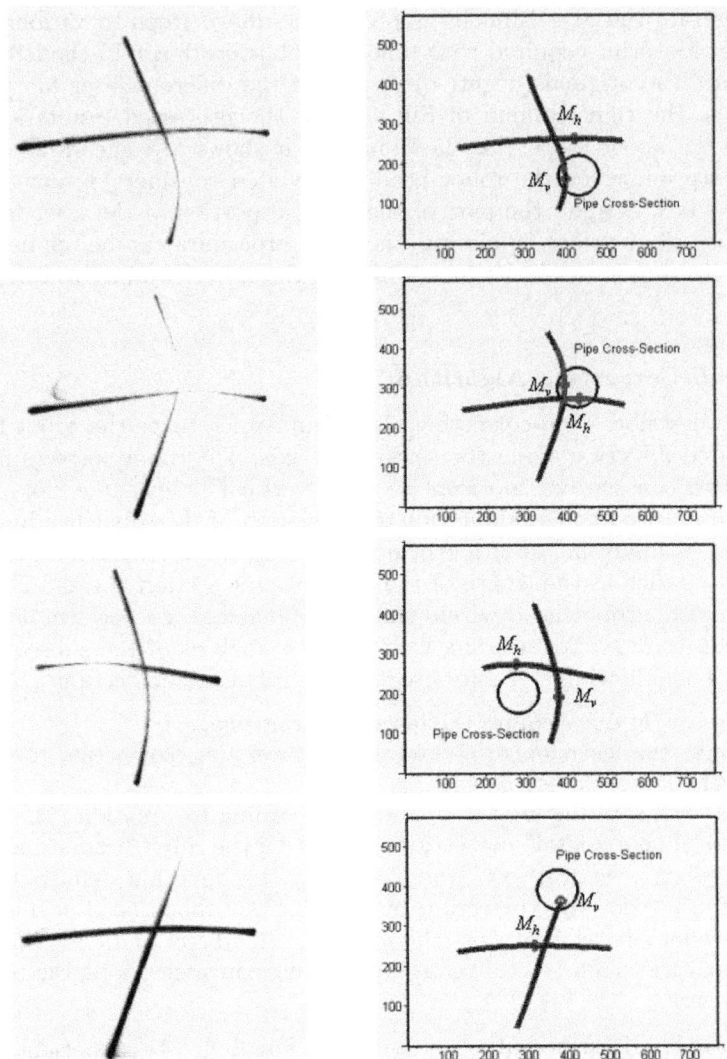

Fig. 3. Negative images of the laser footprint (left column) and their processed results (right column), which show the polynomial fit to extracted pixels and the extremal values for the vertical and the horizontal portions of the footprint. The circles denote approximate locations of a distant pipe cross section ahead of the robot

on the hybrid vision system comprising the laser crosshair projector and the camera, which observes the laser footprint on the surface of the cylindrical pipe. The pen-size laser crosshair projector has low power consumption and can be easily mounted on the relatively small head segment of the sewer robot. The camera records the laser crosshair footprints when the robot light is off. This gives a mostly dark image with a bright laser footprint, which can be processed very fast. An information about the shape of the laser footprint image is used to align robot heading along the pipe axis. The approach meets typical sewer conditions, such as:

1. The robot must operate in a geometrically restricted environment. A priori knowledge about the sewer geometry is the only basic assumption we rely upon.
2. We exploit perfect sewerage darkness to our benefit. The bright laser footprints on the dark background can be easily distinguished in the image plane. There is no need to illuminate the sewer for the robot navigation.

The computation time of the one loop (steps 1 to 4) is about 0.02 sec on the robot's onboard Pentium processor. The orientation algorithm operates real time during robot's motion. It is incorporated into the onboard software block that controls robot operations on its move through the sewer. The tests of the algorithm proved to be successful in taking the robot heading along the axis of a straight cylindrical pipes reliable and fast.

The orientation algorithm neither requires any knowledge of the camera calibration parameters nor is it sensitive to optical distortions. It does not compute accurate values of angles and distances but relies on the iterative approach similar to those one used by living beings. An important objective for our future research is to investigate how the laser-based orientation algorithm can be used for the robot orientation within manhole areas at sewer junctions. It should facilitate robot turns, as well as the robot accessing adjacent pipes.

References

1. D. Cooper, T. P. Pridmore, and N. Taylor. Towards the recovery of extrinsic camera parameters from video records of sewer surveys. *Machine Vision and Applications*, pages 53–63, 1998. 365
2. M. Keding, S. van Riesen, and B. Esch. Der Zustand der öffentlichen Kanalisation in der Bundesrepublik Deutschland. *Ergebnisse der ATV-Umfrage 1990. Korrespondenz Abwasser*, 37:1148–1153, 1990. 365
3. F. Kirchner and J. Hertzberg. A prototype study of an autonomous robot platform for sewerage system maintenance. *Autonomous Robots*, 4:319–331, 1997. 366
4. M. Kolesnik. View-based method for relative orientation in the pipe. In *Proceedings of SPIE, Sensor Fusion: Architecture, Algorithms, and Applications*, volume 3719, 1999. 368
5. Laser crosshair projector LAS-635-15. Commercial product of LASIRIS Inc. 367
6. X. Pan, T. J. Ellis, and T. A. Clarke. Robust tracking of circular features. In D. Pycock, editor, *Roc. British Machine Vision Conference*, pages 553–563, Birmingham. BMVA Press, London. 365

7. W. H. Press, S. A. Teukolsky, W. T. Vetterling, and B. P. Flannery. *Numerical Recipes in C*, pages 656–680. Cambridge University Press, 1996. 369

8. A. Russel and J. Cant. A robotic workout. *Surveyor*, pages 19–21, July 1993. 365

9. Kun Xu, A. R. Luxmoore, and T. Davies. Sewer pipe deformation assessment by image analysis of video surveys. *Pattern Recognition*, 31(2):169–180, 1998. 365

Autonomous Components*

Jaroslav Král and Michal Žemlička

Department of Software Engineering, Faculty of Mathematics and Physics
Charles University, Prague, Malostranské nám. 25, 118 00 Praha 1, CZ
`kral,zemlicka@ksi.ms.mff.cuni.cz`

Abstract. Software systems, especially information systems, tend to be interconnected. The resulting systems must have the structure of a network of autonomous components (NAC). This is the case of the information systems of world-wide companies and/or state administration. We call such system global information systems (GlobIS). GlobIS contain legacy systems, newly developed components, and third party products connected by a powerful middleware. It is shown that the autonomy of components implies that they should communicate asynchronously in the peer-to-peer mode. Practice has shown that the messages in the network should be textual in a language with a complex syntax. The advantages and/or issues of such architecture are discussed. NAC is in software a counterpart of bus architecture in hardware. Many problems of such a software are known from the research of multiagent systems. But there are facts indicating that the components in the above sense do not fit into the concept of software agent completely.

1 Introduction

This paper present the view of a information system analyst and developer looking for tools allowing him to develop his systems more easily. It discusses the techniques orthogonal to the standard object oriented technologies. New SW systems especially the information systems must today work in environment differing substantially from the environment of SW systems ten years ago. The most substantial changes are in the software requirements. It is characterized by the words global economy and information society. The new environment implies new critical requirements like openness, scalability, modifiability, dynamic changes of requirements and/or set of users, integration of legacy systems and third party products etc.

The requirements could not be satisfied ten years ago as the information technology was not mature enough and the demands for global information system were not so strong. Communication facilities were not easily accessible, cheap, and/or powerful enough. The services known now as middleware were very poor, often completely missing. The present middleware enables to use a software architecture allowing to cover critical requirements of a globally used software systems (global information systems, GlobIS). We shall see taht such software must be

---

* Supported by the grant of the Grant Agency of Czech Republic number 201/98/0532.

V. Hlaváč, K. G. Jeffery, and J. Wiedermann (Eds.): SOFSEM 2000, LNCS 1963, pp. 375–383, 2000.

designed as a network of loosely related autonomous components being (almost) complete, applications communicating asynchronously in a peer-to-peer mode. This is typical for the multiagent systems as well [13,3]. It is open whether the similarity indicates a deeper affinity of basic principles.

Modern smart instruments and smart equipments of the mass consumption like household equipments tend to be interconnected. The resulting system must have a structure very similar to the structure of GlobIS.

2   The Need for Autonomous Components

2.1   Global Information Systems

We discuss two cases of GlobIS: the IS of a state administration and the IS of a worldwide company. Worldwide companies are decentralized. They are networks of quite autonomous units — enterprises (NAE).

The common features of the mentioned systems are:

1. A high autonomy of subunits (enterprises, various offices, customers).
2. Open set of end-users (employees, clients making contacts via Internet).
3. Changing set of business partners (business partners of the NAE, enterprises on the territory of the state controlled by the government).
4. Continuous and endless evolution (selling of some divisions of companies, fusions of companies). Changing requirements (changes in laws, changing business conditions).
5. Distributed activities.
6. Subsystems should work also in the case when whole system is out of operation
7. Great projects must be often realized by a consortium of several big companies. Their information systems must be able to support a seamless coordination and cooperation of such autonomous bodies.

It is obvious, that the organizational structure of the NAE and/or state administration should be reflected by the corresponding IS. The feasible system architecture must be (see below) a network of autonomous components (NAC).

2.2   Heterogeneous and Real Time Systems

Modern software is used in equipments. It gives an intelligence to them. Intelligent units can be interconnected quite easily. It is often required that they should be also able to work independently. The software of such autonomous instruments must be designed as a collection of autonomous bodies able to communicate if required. Such software pieces must be often used as black boxes. The only public knowledge is the specification of possibly programmable gates. All the pieces of the software are assumed to be active all the time the whole system is alive (compare real time systems [6]).

2.3   Software Pieces that Should Be Autonomous

The global software systems are rarely built from scratch. Typical situation is that a lot of software must be used without any substantial modification. Typical examples are legacy systems and purchased systems (third party products). Otherwise the development of the system would be too long and too expensive and would require too many changes of the customer organizational structure and the customer business processes. It is often argued that the use of legacy system is a temporal problem, that the legacy systems should be rewritten such that it can be well integrated into the whole system. It appears that it is generally no preferable solution due to the following reasons:

- If an organizational subunit is to be sold, it must be sold with its information system(s). It is easier if the subunits have their autonomous information systems loosely coupled with the information system of the network of enterprises (NAE).
- The use of legacy systems could simplify the development, maintenance, and use of the system as it then the task of the people depending on its quality (see e. g. [1,6]).
- Autonomous components offer better chances to meet security requirements (e. g. application-to-application encryption).
- There is yet another reason not to dissolve any legacy system into the whole system: the organizational subunits may not want to loss their positions and/or political power so they want to have their local information system as autonomous as possible (compare the information system of the state police.
- Critical functions of components should be used even in the situation when the whole system does not work (a special requirement of autonomy).

Let us assume that we have powerful tools to integrate legacy systems. Then we can easily integrate the third party products as well. It simplifies the development of the management level of information system. The management level of such information system should better reflect the fact that managers often want to put ad hoc questions, and that they must look all the time for new tools for data/knowledge presentation, analysis, and discovery. It requires a lot of know-how obtainable via the third party products.

Under the same conditions we can easily integrate newly developed components/applications. If new applications can be integrated easily, then the system can be easily modified and incrementally developed by adding new components. The requirement to use third-party product implies that the components must be ultimately integrated as black boxes. The only knowledge about them is the structures and the meanings of messages that can be addressed to them or obtained from them. It facilitates the modenr SW engineering practices like incremental development.

A real time system must be developed and debugged (i. e. the correctness of answers and their timeliness must be tested) without any presence of the controlled processes. The effective way how to do it is to design the system a set of autonomous components. One component is a simulator of the controlled system. If designed properly the control logic is the same for the case when the simulator is used and when the logic works with the real system. It is good to design the user interface as an autonomous component [5,6].

3   Collaboration of Autonomous Components

It follows from the above requirements that autonomous components should work in parallel and communicate asynchronously in the peer-to-peer mode. The whole system is then a network of autonomous components interconnected by a powerful middleware. The components could be quite complex applications. It has the consequence that the messages for the components must have a quite complex semantics. It implies that messages have a quite complex syntax. Moreover the syntax of the messages for different components must be different as the functions and/or services provided by the components are different. The discussed paradigm differs substantially from the object-oriented one [9].

The tendency to use a complex language for the communication of complex information between complex heterogeneous entities is in fact a long-term tendency. We have languages to define tasks for printers, e. g. postsript and/or pdf formats, for the interchange of information between CASE systems, workflow systems. There are many such languages. Some format standards are very complex. An example is EDI/EDIFACT.

Note that the messages are often commands rather than queries. New applications induce the need for new and new languages. The networks of autonomous components can comprise hundreds of components. The network behaves like a powerful computing device. The format agreements are then difficult to achieve in a centralized way. The protocol defining the structures of messages must be therefore very flexible. The solution is not to agree the standard for the formats of the messages but to standardize the metaformat of messages and to send data together with their metadata, i. e. with marks. solution seems to be XML [12,8]. The structure of messages is given in a framework of markers, which can be to a high degree viewed as the explicit description (parse) of the syntactic structure of the message.

4   Software Engineering Problems

The success of any system based on the architecture of the network of autonomous components depends on the good solution of a number of technical and/or methodological problems and on design skills. Some of them are mentioned above. Let us discuss the most important problems in details:

4.1   User Interface

Any NAC can be used efficiently only in the case when it contains a powerful user interface system (UI). UI should support integrated transparent interface to group of components communicating with the given user. The user should not be aware that the information he is getting is assembled from the messages from several components. WWW browsers have many good properties for such a purpose. But the browsers have no tool powerful enough for the integration of interfaces to several components. Similar problems are solved by database languages (a screen can show data from several tables). The problem is more complex in NAC. In the case of NAC the tables are replaced by the answers of the components. We have, however, no analogy of SQL yet for the case when there is no database.

4.2   Optimization of the System Behavior

It is not difficult to move the components around the underlying computer network to work on different hosts to achieve a better performance of the system (response times or costs). It is possible to clone components (i. e. to make copies of them) and to move the copies to optimize the system behavior.

Similar issues are solved in distributed database system when the system administrator must decide where should reside the data and where their replications. Similar problems are also known from agent theories (e. g. [10,13]). We did not, however, find any theory and any satisfactory implementation allowing to perform the optimization in an automated way.

4.3   Dynamic Reconfiguration of the System

We have seen that the communication of components should be in the language of a very complex syntax[1]. The syntax of the messages can be used to identify the correct addressees. The addressee is any component able to understand the message, i. e. able to parse the syntax of the message.

This schema can be used to identify the components, which will be parts of the given system. The identification (in the sense of configuration control standards like ISO/IEC 12220) of the components can be performed all over the WWW. The chosen components form the system which in turn exists virtually only and can change dynamically. Known problems: Can such a schema be implemented effectively enough? Can the identification of the components be robust enough (i. e. can the identification of components in the sense of configuration control be reliable, e. g. unambiguous, enough)? Can the process of acceptance of components be secure and to what degree it can be automated?

4.4   Multiparty Communication and Collaboration (Communication Protocols)

Suppose that a NAC is very large. Then the majority of task to be supported/solved by it needs the collaboration of some group of components. The problem is

---

[1] Another examples are the languages for the exchange of information between CASE systems (XMI) or between workflow systems (WOMA) and many others.

how to find the components to form the group and how to define the network of their activities and how to verify that the task was finished correctly. It is a generalization of transactions in distributed databases. The generalization is especially in the specification of the network of activities. The task of the group can be specified implicitly in the code of the components. A more flexible solution uses some parts of messages to give information about the structure of the task (compare activity diagrams in UML). It is also possible to have somewhere in the middleware a complete explicit description of the task structure. An almost identical problem is solved by multiagent systems (an example is [13], compare also [11]).

4.5   Programmable Component Interfaces

The autonomous components are used as communicating black boxes. They must be equipped by gates allowing them to communicate. If the component has well known three tier structure then the gate should be part of the application logic. Other solutions like the direct access to component data are risky.

The component gates are usually quite complex programs able to perform syntax analysis (parsing) of incoming messages and to translate the messages into their internal form. It must transform message to be sent from internal form into the external form (now usually in XML). It would be nice if the gates could be designed by any authorized outsider (i. e. by anyone different from the authors of the component), any outsider could program his own gate. It is a problem similar to the problem of programmable user interface.

4.6   The Conceptual Schemata for NAC

The structure of NAC makes sometimes difficult to see the system as one logical entity. The conceptual schema like the schema known from databases is a very useful concept and can solve the problem. The conceptual schema in databases is quite static and usually developed manually. The conceptual schemata for NAC must, however, reflect the dynamics of the system.

There are several classes of users. Each class should have its own schema. There must be several views and each view is temporal only. The schemata must be therefore easily produced and modified. It is possible only in the case when there are tools and methods supporting the generation of the metadata describing the particular conceptual view of the system.

5   Components and Middleware

The properties and services of middleware determine to a high degree the properties of the system [6,4]. The services of the middleware can be in many cases defined or programmed by a system administrator and even by end users (clients). Some services or functions must be provided by the middleware only (e. g. transportation of messages), but the functions can be (partly) modified by system administrator. Many functions are component specific. Some services can be provided either by components or by middleware. The most visible case is the encryption and some security services.

It is important, that the choice where a service will be supported influences the quality of the service (effectiveness, accessibility, quality of solution, etc.). If the encryption is provided as an open service on behalf of middleware only, we obtain a solution near to the client-to-client schema known from Internet, or a server-to-server encryption schema. If the encryption is performed by components we can obtain an application-to-application schema. The solutions are not equivalent. The application-to-application solution is more secure, but it is not too flexible and requires an additional development effort of the application.

The multiparty coordination can be, we hope, based on the principles and attitudes developed by the research of multiagent systems. But the technical realization and the properties like effectivity, security issues (i. e. hacker attack prevention) etc. differs for different solutions.

It is clear from our discussion that the properties and services of the middleware should be specified in requirements specification phase (compare [6]). So the specification of middleware must be a part of the specification of the system. The crucial problem is what should be in middleware and what in components. It is also in the case of the typical problem of multiagent system.

6   Autonomous Components and Autonomous Agents

ACs are different from object oriented components in the sense e. g. [7]. They have many features common with autonomous agents. This is valid for the multiparty communication and/or collaboration and agreements. It is open, however, whether the similarities are not superfluous. The fact that the message formats are standardized by XML on metalevel may be most important difference between NAC and present multiagent systems. The problem what consequences it has is open now.

It is clear that many ideas developed inside the theory of agents can be used in NAC. Besides the collaboration problem we can use results on mobility and cloning. Their identification of addressees (in other words the components that can be members of the network) can use more sophisticated techniques than merely the ability to parse the message or to use an explicit information (address).

A closer look, however, indicates that the problem is solved to some degree conceptually but not from the engineering point of view. For example we are limited in the case of a multiparty coordination by some technical conditions, security issues, and/or by the properties of components. The language of the communication of AC must reflect the needs of existing applications. The messages are commands (e. g. computation of an invoice) rather than knowledge queries.

A particular issue is the design of intelligent and flexible user interface to network of components. The interface must provide control of communication of the changing set of end users having changing needs with varying set of components. The functions implemented by components are given and cannot be changed substantially if ever. The interfaces of components should be modified. Middleware can produce records (log files) of communication.

The application of the results of the theory of agents is a great challenge. But the IS developers need a technically feasible solutions. Mobility and cloning is a topic of agent research. But the authors were unable to find a good engineering mature solution applicable in an on-line automated optimization of the NAC. The most important issue is probably the low understanding of the substantial, if any, differences between networks of the autonomous agents and NAC.

7   Conclusions

NAC is a necessary and very promising paradigm and methodology. It enables an easy adding and replacing of components. It is the only known technique how to support a seamless integration and the use of legacy systems and third party products. It simplifies the incremental development and the modifications of the systems. As we have seen it is the only known solution of the problem of GlobIS The reusability is in principle quite high (it is not the case for object-oriented systems, see [1,2]).

All these advantages are a reality now in spite of the fact that the technology is in its introductory phase. It requires a new way of thinking. We have no good diagramming techniques like UML [9] for it. We do not know what are good software metrics for NAC. No effective SW processes has been developed yet. The integration of the results of agent theory and database research into the NAC paradigm is the question of future.

The importance of the architecture based on AC has been already recognized by practitioners. The academia is somewhat reluctant. There is danger that we repeat the situation with go-to-less programming when we discussed constructs for procedure bodies in the situation when the substantial problem for practitioners was how to develop a complete application.

References

1. CACM, 1995, The Promise and the Cost of Object Technology. A five years Forecast, Comm. Of ACM, Vol. 38. Oct. 1995. 382
2. Finch, L., 1998, http://www.ddj.com/oped/1998/finc.htm. So much OO, So Little Reuse, Dr. Dobb's Web Site, May 1998. 382
3. Fisher, K., Oliveria, E., Štěpánková, O., Multiagent Systems: Which Research for which Applications. To appear. 376
4. Král, J., 1998, Information Systems. Design, Development, Use. Science Veletiny, 357pp. In Czech. 377, 380
5. Král, J., 1998a, Architecture of Open Information Systems. In Evolution and Challenges in Systems Developments, (Wojtkowski, W. G., Wrycza, S., Županič, J., eds.), 7th int. Conf. on Information Systems, Bled, Slovenia, Sept. 21–23., 1998. Plenum Press. 378

6. Král, J., 1999, Middleware orientation — inverese software development strategy. Presented at the ISD'99 conference August 11–13, 1999, Boise, Idaho, U. S. A., to be published by Planum Press. 376, 377, 378, 380, 381

7. Plášil, F., Bálek, D., Janeček, R., 1998, SOFA-DCUP: An Architecture for Component Trading and Dynamic Updating. Proceedings of ICCDS'98, May 4–6, 1998. 381

8. RDF, 1999, http://www.rdf.com/. Resource Description Framework. A Proposal of the W3Cconsorcium. 378

9. UML, 1999, http://uml.systemhouse.mci.com/artifacts. Home page containing links to the proposed standard of UML. 378, 382

10. Weiss, G., 1999, Multiagent systems. A modern Approach to Distributed Artificial Iintelligence, The MIT Press, Cambridge, Mass. 379

11. Winograd, T., Flores, F. C., 1986, *Understanding Computers and Cognition — a New Foundation for Design*, Ablex Publishing Corporation, Norwood, NY. 380

12. XML, 1999, http://www.xml.com/xml/pub/. Extensible Markup Language. A proposal of W3C consortium. 378

13. Ygge, F., Akkermans, H., (2000), Resource-oriented Multicommodity Market Algorithms, Autonomous Agents and Multi-Agent Systems, Vol. 3, 53–71. 376, 379, 380

Parallel Object Server for Fine Grained Objects

Petr Kroha

Fakultät für Informatik, TU Chemnitz
09107 Chemnitz, Germany
kroha@informatik.tu-chemnitz.de

Abstract. In this paper we describe the main features of an implemented parallel object server that we have developed for storing fine grained objects. The motivation was to support a data repository of a CASE tool for a heavy-loaded multi-user environment and to test the suitability of parallel computers for this purpose. We present the results of our experiments concerning the speedup and the load balance of the system.

1   Introduction

In engineering, servers will often be used for management of fine grained objects. It has been proven that the object-oriented DBMSs are in principle more suitable for this purpose than the relational DBMSs [2,6]. The reason is that the normalization of tables in the relational model can cause the splitting of fine structured objects into many tables that must be joined later on again for getting the parts of objects together during the phase of fetching objects [7]. This process of decomposition and the following composition is paid by less performance when we need to use the stored objects as a whole often.

Sequential computers that are currently used as servers have their physical limits of performance. It is difficult to estimate the time point when their limits will be reached, but the usage of parallelism in parallel and distributed systems may be the only possibility to increase the performance of servers in the future. Because of the lack of standard, large variety of parallel computers, and a small demand, there are in principle no object-oriented DBMSs for parallel computers available as commercial products that could be used as a base for a parallel object server.

In this paper we describe some features of our prototype of an object-oriented server OPAS (Object-oriented PArallel Server) running on a parallel computer (shared disk, distributed memory) as a data repository for a CASE tool.

The rest of this paper is organized as follows. Related work will be described in Section 2. In Section 3 we explain what advantages hierarchical data structures may have for parallel processing. Section 4 briefly describes the software architecture designed for the parallel object server. In Section 5, we present the implementation of the prototype in Ada95 and C++. The achieved results and future work are discussed in Section 6.

V. Hlaváč, K. G. Jeffery, and J. Wiedermann (Eds.): SOFSEM 2000, LNCS 1963, pp. 384–391, 2000.
© Springer-Verlag Berlin Heidelberg 2000

2   Related Work

Building a parallel object server concerns many specialized problems that we had to solve during last years. In [8] we described how data have been stored in our first prototype, how buffers are organized, and how efficiently the object manager, the lock manager, and the disk manager have been working. In [10], we introduced the software architecture that has been used and we presented the performance obtained by experiments with the prototype. Specific questions concerning properties of data repositories of CASE tools used in a multi-user environment in software engineering and stored on our parallel server have been discussed in [9].

We did not find any papers concerning specifically object-oriented parallel servers. The research of OODBMSs in a parallel environment seems to be at its very beginning. Thus, we cannot compare our results with other results achieved by other researchers. The key contribution of our project OPAS is that this is the very first attempt in this research direction.

3   Properties of Data Structures

As mentioned above, we focused on processing of fine grained objects specific for computer support of the software development. Data structures of such objects have specific features that may cause some speedup in their parallel processing. For the first attempt we focused our considerations on two groups of hierarchical data structures stored in the data repository of a CASE tool:

- Structured data representing more levels of abstraction, e. g. data stored in trees. They are typical in top-down analysis and bottom-up synthesis.
- Structured data representing only one level of abstraction, e. g. data stored in lists and graphs. Such structures will be used e. g. for representing ER-diagrams, finite state machines, Petri nets, etc.

From the point of view of objects, there are two sources of parallelism:

- Intra-object parallelism — all components of one object can be searched in parallel.
- Inter-object parallelism — objects asked by different users can be searched in parallel.

To get data for our experiments, we have considered the development of two applications (hotel, warehouse). The top-down method of stepwise refinement via decomposition delivered hierarchically organized data. Our test applications generated objects of size between 50 and 500 bytes having the following statistical distribution: 48 % of objects of size 50–100 bytes, 30 % of objects of size 101–150 bytes, 11 % of objects of size 151–200 bytes, and 10 % of objects of size 201–500 bytes.

4   Software Architecture

The software architecture of the parallel server can be seen in Fig. 1. The interface between the object server and its environment is be represented by a dispatcher. It communicates with clients, accepts their queries, and asks some of transaction managers to execute the corresponding tasks.

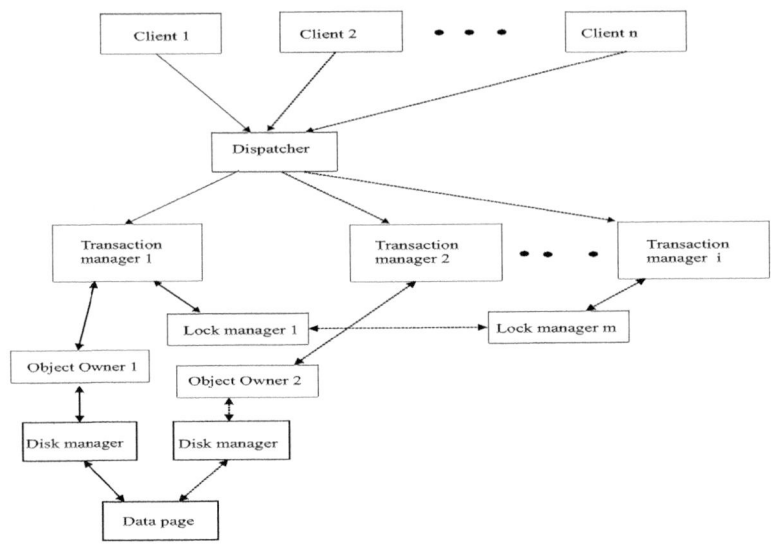

Fig. 1. Architecture of the parallel server

We have used a distributed transaction manager and a distributed lock manager to enable the parallel processing of transactions. Because of the redundancy problem, the concept of a distributed object owner has been introduced. Its components are responsible each for consistency of some subset of objects and each of them cooperate with their own page-oriented disk manager for accessing data on files. Each disk manager has its own page buffer. Object owners represent an interface between transaction managers and disk managers. Each transaction manager checks the consistency of objects by means of the corresponding object owners and controls the synchronization by means of the lock managers. In the first version of the prototype, the simple 2-phase protocol has been used for locking.

For any object fetch a transaction will be started. Transactions will be decomposed on subtransactions according to the concept of intra-object parallelism. As long as there are no synchronization conflicts in processing transactions and as longs as there are enough nodes, transactions are running fully in parallel. Synchronization conflicts occur, if some transactions ask for the same objects. Lock managers will solve them, but this will reduce the degree of overlapping of different queries, of course. However, on real conditions, although users are working on the same project using the same data repository, they are usually not working simultaneously on the same object in software engineering. More details about the software architecture are given in [10].

5   Implementation of Prototypes

5.1   Prototyping in Ada'95 and Its Problems

Debugging parallel programs directly on a parallel computer is a difficult task. Parallel programming on the parallel computer PARSYTEC is enabled by using a specialized library in C++ supported by the specialized operating system PARIX. Because of that we have separated general problems of prototype algorithms from specific problems of using PARSYTEC under PARIX.

In the first step of the design, we have described the prototype in Ada'95 and have used it for debugging and for tuning of the algorithms as a running design specification. Parallel programming is transparent in Ada'95 and it can be done on a Sun workstation. However, the performance features of the prototype has been affected by the run-time support of the Ada environment.

We have represented clients, dispatcher, transaction managers, object owners, lock managers, and disk managers as tasks. To simulate the shared-disk architecture, we have written a disk task. All object owners have to share it having exclusive access. Queries of clients have been written in batch files. Some problems have occurred that are Ada-dependent. Asynchronous communication had to be modeled by using some primitives. Because of the strong type checking in Ada, we had to use a generic package for object buffer and each class has got its own object buffer.

Beside of proving the algorithms we have obtained the supposed dependences between the speed-up and the number of processors used for single- and for multi-user environment.

5.2   Implemented C++-prototype OPAS

After the problems in the Ada-prototype on a Sun machine have been solved, the C++-prototype was written on the parallel computer PARSYTEC/GC Power Plus-128 with operating system PARIX. Our configuration of this computer consists of 64 nodes organized into a 2D lattice. All accesses of its 64 nodes (each if them has two processors) to its shared permanent memory must be synchronized for using 8 access channels. Under PARIX, more than one threads can be started in one node in the context of the node's program. If more than two threads are used in one node, time-sharing will be used.

6   Results, Conclusions, Future Work

As a conclusion, we present some speculative results concerning the used hardware architecture and some experimental results concerning the behavior of our prototype in response to the experimental data.

6.1   Conclusions about the Hardware Architecture

We argue that the shared-disk architecture does not bring significant disadvantages when used as the hardware background for parallel object servers that store data repositories of fine grained objects.

Usually, the shared-nothing hardware architecture will be recommended as the more suitable one [1], but when using it for our purpose, an important question is where the common data repository should be stored:

– If the common data repository is stored distributed and non-replicated on many disks then the responsible processor has to ask other processors to access and send data while processing the query. This increases the overhead.
– If the common data repository is stored distributed and replicated on many disks then it would bring an overhead (because of the checking of consistency) depending very strongly on how often the data will be used and changed.
– If the common data repository is stored on one disk then we have the same problem as in the shared-disk architecture.

When using the shared-disk architecture users are competing for the disk. Usually, there are more channels in the switch which can work in parallel and support more disks. The query GET OBJECT will be processed by one processor which does not have sole access to the data, but it can access to the data directly without asking other processors for help. It seems to be a good solution that the shared, common data repository is stored on the shared disk.

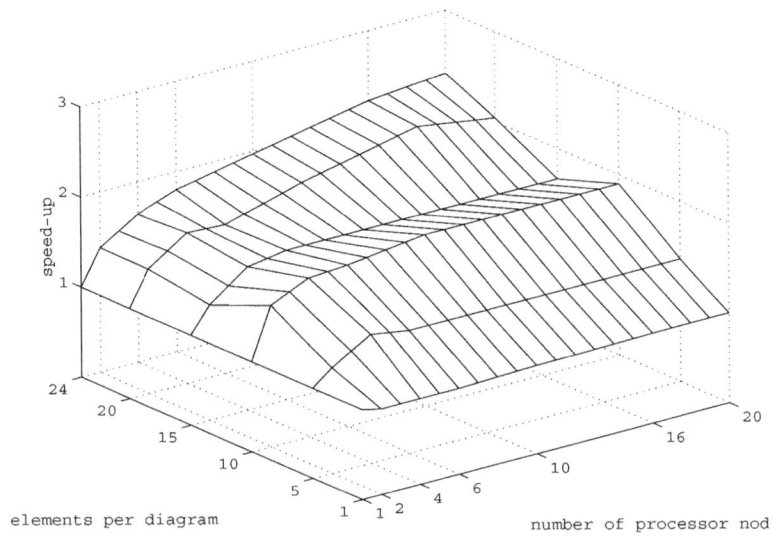

Fig. 2. Intra-object parallelism

6.2   Conclusions about the Prototype Features

In our experiments with the implemented C++-prototype, we investigated at first how the speedup depends on the intra-object parallelism in a single-user environment (Fig. 2). The number of elements per diagram (components of an aggregated object) represents the degree of the intra-object parallelism of the investigated data model. If an object is to be fetched and shown, its data structure has to be synthesized using pointers to its components that can be searched in parallel. We can see that the use of a parallel machine would not bring too much (factor 2.5 for 24 elements in diagram and 20 nodes used). Of course, it depends strongly on the cardinality of aggregation used in classes that are typical for the specific application. For some CAD tools this kind of parallelism can bring perhaps much more speedup.

In the multi-user environment we investigated the inter-object parallelism, i. e. the dependence of the speedup on the number of clients and number of nodes. However, as shown above, there are some additional dimensions expressing the properties of data namely the size of methods and the number of components. Thus, it can be drawn in 3D only using some specific cuts, i. e. additional conditions. Fig. 3 represents a speedup caused by the inter-object parallelism for data structures of objects that would cause the speedup 3 in a single-user environment. Even if the server has implemented a locking mechanism, in this experiment, we supposed that users access different, disjoint objects which is a typical situation when using CASE tools.

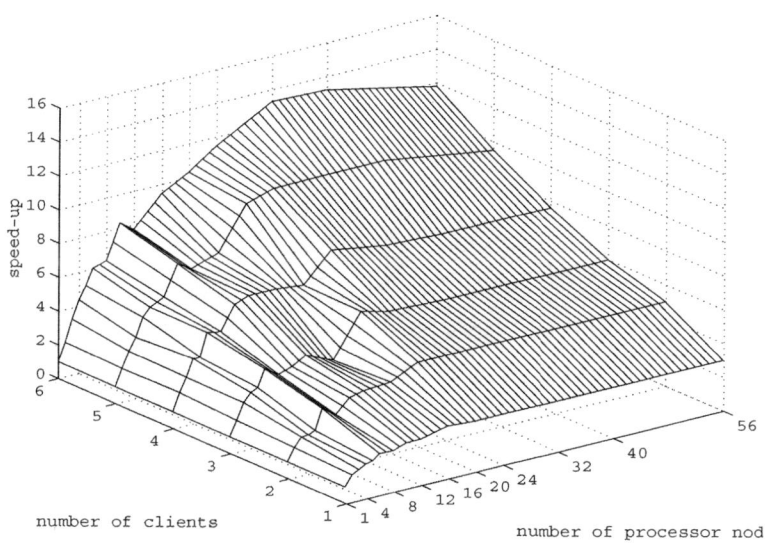

Fig. 3. Inter-object parallelism

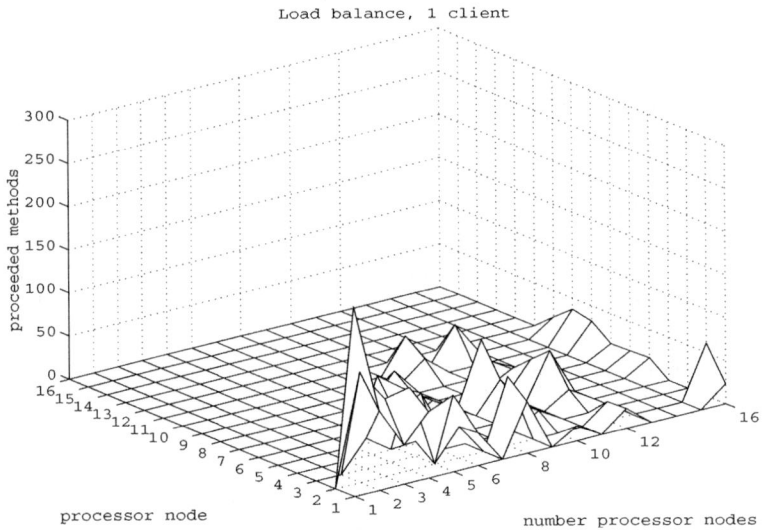

Fig. 4. Load balance for 1 client

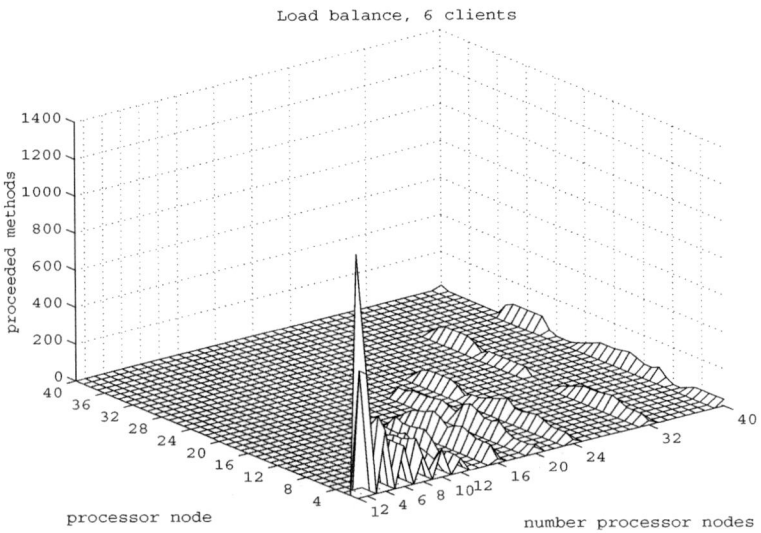

Fig. 5. Load balance for 6 clients

Comparing dependencies on Fig. 4 and Fig. 5 we can see that the load of nodes is good balanced and that the load balance increases with the growing number of clients and nodes.

Our main goals for the future research will concern the reengineering the whole concept and programs into a distributed environment because a cluster of workstations should replace the obsolete parallel computer.

References

1. De Witt, D., Naughton, J. F. et al: ParSets for Parallelizing OODBMS Traversal: Implementation and Performance. In: Proc. 3rd International Conference on Parallel and Distributed Information Systems, pp. 111–120, Austin, September 1994. 388

2. Emmerich, W., Kroha, P., Schäfer, W.: Object-Oriented Database Management Systems for Construction of CASE Environments. In: Marik, V. et al. (Eds.): Proceedings of the 4th Int. Conference DEXA'93, Lecture Notes in Computer Science, No. 720, Springer, 1993. 384

3. Freitag, B., Jones, C. B., Lengauer, Ch. Schek, H. J.: (Eds.): Object Orientation with Parallelism and Persistence. Kluwer Academic Publishers, 1996.

4. Kroha, P.: Translation of a Query in OODBMS into a System of Parallel Tasks. EUROMICRO'92, Microprocessing and Microprogramming 37 (1993), North Holland, 1993.

5. Kroha, P.: Objects and Databases. McGraw-Hill, 1993. 384

6. Kroha, P.: Shortcoming and Extensions of Relational DBMS. In: Adelsberger,H. et al. (Eds.): Information Management in Computer Integrated Manufacturing. Lecture Notes in Computer Science, No. 973, Springer, 1995. 384

7. Kroha, P.: Softwaretechnologie. Prentice Hall, 1997. (In German).

8. Kroha, P., Rosenbaum, S.: Object Server on a Parallel Computer. In: Wagner, R. R. (Ed.): Proceedings of the 8th International Workshop on Database and Expert Systems Applications DEXA'97, IEEE Computer Society, Toulouse, France, 1997. 385

9. Kroha, P., Lindner, J.: Parallel Object Server as a Data Repository for CASE Tools. In: Croll, P., El-Rewini, H.(Eds.): Proceedings of International Symposium on Software Engineering for Parallel and Distributed Systems PDSE'99, Workshop of ICSE'99, pp. 148–156, IEEE Computer Society, Los Angeles, May 1999. 385

10. Kroha, P., Lindner, J.: Parallel Object Server — Architecture and Performance. In: Bench-Capon, T., Soda, G. Tjoa, A. M. (Eds.): Proceedings of the 10th International Conference DEXA'99, Lecture Notes in Computer Science, No. 1677, pp. 450–459, Springer, Florence, Italy, 1999. 385, 387

11. Lindner, J.: Properties of a Parallel Object Server as a Data Repository for CASE-Tools. M.Sc. Thesis, Faculty of Informatics, TU Chemnitz, 1998. (In German).

12. Maier, D.: Making Database Systems Fast Enough For CAD. In: Kim, W., Lochovsky, F. (Eds.): Object-oriented Concepts, Databases and Applications, pp. 573–582, ACM Press 1989.

13. Radestock, M., Eisenbach, S.: An Object Model for Distributed and Concurrent Programming Based on Decomposition. In: [3].

14. Stonebraker, M.: The case for shared nothing. Database Engineering, Vol. 9, No. 1, 1986.

15. Valduriez, P.: Parallel database systems: the case for shared nothing. In: Proc. of the 9th Int. Conf. On Data Engineering, pp. 460–465, Vienna 1993.

Massively Parallel Pattern Recognition with Link Failures

Martin Kutrib and Jan-Thomas Löwe

Institute of Informatics, University of Giessen
Arndtstr. 2, D-35392 Giessen, Germany
{kutrib,loewe}@informatik.uni-giessen.de

Abstract. The capabilities of reliable computations in linear cellular arrays with communication failures are investigated in terms of syntactical pattern recognition.
In particular we consider very fast, i. e. real-time, computations. It is well-known that real-time one-way arrays are strictly less powerful than real-time two-way arrays. Here it is shown that the sets of patterns reliably recognizable by real-time arrays with link failures are strictly in between the sets of (intact) one-way and (intact) two-way arrays. Hence, the failures cannot be compensated in general but, on the other hand, do not decrease the computing power to that one of one-way arrays.

1   Introduction

Nowadays it becomes possible to build massively parallel computing systems that consist of hundred thousands of processing elements. Each single component is subject to failure such that the probability of misoperations and loss of function of the whole system increases with the number of its elements. It was von Neumann [17] who first stated the problem of building reliable systems out of unreliable components. Biological systems may serve as good examples. Due to the necessity to function normally even in case of certain failures of their components the nature developed mechanisms which invalids the errors, they are working in some sense fault tolerant. Error detecting and correcting components should not be global to the whole system because they themselves are subject to failure. Therefore the fault tolerance has to be a design feature of the single elements.

A model for massively parallel, homogeneously structured computers are the cellular arrays. Such devices of interconnected parallel acting finite state machines have been studied from various points of view.

In [3,4] reliable arrays are constructed under the assumption that a cell (and not its links) at each time step fails with a constant probability. Moreover, such failure does not incapacitate the cell permanently, but only violate its rule of operation in the step when it occurs. Under the same constraint that cells themselves (and not their links) fail (i. e. they cannot process information but are still able to transmit it unchanged with unit speed) fault tolerant computations

V. Hlaváč, K. G. Jeffery, and J. Wiedermann (Eds.): SOFSEM 2000, LNCS 1963, pp. 392–401, 2000.
© Springer-Verlag Berlin Heidelberg 2000

have been investigated, e. g. in [5,14] where encodings are established that allow the correction of so-called K-separated misoperations, in [10,11,16,18] where the famous firing squad synchronization problem is considered in defective cellular arrays, and in terms of interacting automata with nonuniform delay in [6,12] where the synchronization of the networks is the main object either.

Recently, this approach has been generalized to more general computations and dynamic defects [8].

Here we are interested in another natural type of defects. Not the cells themselves cause the misoperations but their communication links. It is assumed that each cell has a self-diagnosis circuit for its links which is run once before the actual computation. The results are stored locally in the cells and subsequently no new defects may occur. Otherwise the whole computation would become invalid. A cell with defective links is not able to receive information via at most one of its both links to adjacent cells. Otherwise the parallel computation would be broken into two non-interacting parts and, therefore, would become impossible at all.

In terms of pattern recognition the general capabilities of reliable computations are considered. Since cellular arrays have been intensively investigated from a language theoretic point of view, pattern recognition (or language acceptance) establishes the connection to the known results and, thus, inheres the possibility to compare the fault tolerant capabilities to the non fault tolerant ones.

2   Basic Notions

We denote the integers by $\mathbb{Z}$, the positive integers $\{1, 2, \ldots\}$ by $\mathbb{N}$ and the set $\mathbb{N} \cup \{0\}$ by $\mathbb{N}_0$. $X_1 \times \cdots \times X_d$ denotes the Cartesian product of the sets $X_1, \ldots, X_d$. If $X_1 = \cdots = X_d$ we use the notation X_1^d alternatively. We use $\subseteq$ for inclusions and $\subset$ if the inclusion is strict. Let M be some set and $f \colon M \to M$ be a function, then we denote the i-fold composition of f by $f^{[i]}$, $i \in \mathbb{N}$.

A two-way resp. one-way cellular array is a linear array of identical finite state machines, sometimes called cells, which are connected to their both nearest neighbors resp. to their nearest neighbor to the right. The array is bounded by cells in a distinguished so-called boundary state. For convenience we identify the cells by positive integers. The state transition depends on the current state of each cell and the current state(s) of its neighbor(s). The transition function is applied to all cells synchronously at discrete time steps. Formally:

Definition 1. A *two-way cellular array* (CA) is a system $\langle S, \delta, \#, A \rangle$, where

1. S is the finite, nonempty set of *cell states*,
2. $\# \notin S$ is the *boundary state*,
3. $A \subseteq S$ is the set of *input symbols*,
4. $\delta \colon (S \cup \{\#\})^3 \to S$ is the *local transition function*.

If the flow of information is restricted to one-way (i. e. from right to left) the resulting device is a *one-way cellular array* (OCA) and the local transition function maps from $(S \cup \{\#\})^2$ to S.

A *configuration* of a cellular array at some time $t \geq 0$ is a description of its global state, which is actually a mapping $c_t \colon [1, \ldots, n] \to S$ for $n \in \mathbb{N}$.

The data on which the cellular arrays operate are patterns built from input symbols. Since here we are studying one-dimensional arrays only the input data are finite strings (or words). The set of strings of length n built from symbols from a set A is denoted by A^n, the set of all such finite strings by A^*. We denote the *empty string* by ϵ and the *reversal of a string* w by w^R. For its length we write $|w|$. A^+ is defined to be $A^* \setminus \{\epsilon\}$.

In the sequel we are interested in the subsets of strings that are recognizable by cellular arrays. In order to establish the connection to formal language theory we call such a subset a *formal language*. Moreover, sets L and L' are considered to be equal if they differ at most by the empty word, i. e. $L \setminus \{\epsilon\} = L' \setminus \{\epsilon\}$.

Now we are prepared to describe the computations of (O)CAs. The operation starts in the so-called *initial configuration* $c_{0,w}$ at time 0 where each symbol of the input string $w = x_1 \ldots x_n$ is fed to one cell: $c_{0,w}(i) = x_i$, $1 \leq i \leq n$. During a computation the (O)CA steps through a sequence of configurations whereby successor configurations are computed according to the global transition function Δ. Let c_t, $t \geq 0$, be a configuration, then its successor configuration is as follows:

$$c_{t+1} = \Delta(c_t) \iff \begin{cases} c_{t+1}(1) = \delta\big(\#, c_t(1), c_t(2)\big) \\ c_{t+1}(i) = \delta\big(c_t(i-1), c_t(i), c_t(i+1)\big), i \in \{2, \ldots, n-1\} \\ c_{t+1}(n) = \delta\big(c_t(n-1), c_t(n), \#\big) \end{cases}$$

for CAs and correspondingly for OCAs. Thus, Δ is induced by δ.

An input string w is recognized by an (O)CA if at some time i during its course of computation the leftmost cell enters a final state from the *set of final states* $F \subseteq S$.

Definition 2. Let $\mathcal{M} = \langle S, \delta, \#, A \rangle$ be an (O)CA and $F \subseteq S$ be a set of final states.

1. An input $w \in A^*$ is *recognized* by $\mathcal{M}$ if it is the empty string or if there exists a time step $i \in \mathbb{N}$ such that $c_i(1) \in F$ holds for the configuration $c_i = \Delta^{[i]}(c_{0,w})$.
2. $L(\mathcal{M}) = \{w \in A^* \mid w \text{ is recognized by } \mathcal{M}\}$ is the *set of strings (language) recognized* by $\mathcal{M}$.
3. Let $t \colon \mathbb{N} \to \mathbb{N}$, $t(n) \geq n$, be a mapping and i_w be the minimal time step at which $\mathcal{M}$ recognizes $w \in L(\mathcal{M})$. If all $w \in L(\mathcal{M})$ are recognized within $i_w \leq t(|w|)$ time steps, then L is said to be of *time complexity* t.

The family of all sets which are recognizable by some CA (OCA) with time complexity t is denoted by $L_t(CA)$ ($L_t(OCA)$). If t equals the identity function $id(n) = n$ recognition is said to be in *real-time*, and if t is equal to $k \cdot id$ for an arbitrary rational number $k \geq 1$ then recognition is carried out in *linear-time*. Correspondingly, we write $L_{rt}((O)CA)$ and $L_{lt}((O)CA)$. In the sequel we will use corresponding notations for other types of recognizers.

3   Devices with Link Failures

The defects are in some sense static [16]. It is assumed that each cell has a self-diagnosis circuit for its links which is run once before the actual computation. The result of that diagnosis is indicated by the states of the cells such that cells with intact links can detect whether the links of the neighbors are defective or not. According to the states in the sequel we use the notion *intact or defective cells or neighbors* instead of *cells or neighbors with intact or defective links*. Moreover (and this is the static part), it is assumed that during the actual computation no new defects may occur. Otherwise the whole computation would become invalid. What is the effect of a defective link? Suppose that each two adjacent cells are interconnected by two unidirectional links. On one link information is transmitted from right to left and on the other one from left to right. Now, if both links are failing, then the parallel computation would be broken into two not interacting lines and, thus, would be impossible at all. Therefore, it is reasonable to require that at least one of the links between two cells does not fail.

Suppose for a moment that there exists a cell that, due to a link failure, cannot receive information from its right neighbor. This would imply that the overall computation result (which will be indicated by the leftmost cell) is obtained with no regard to the input data to the right of that defective cell. So all reliable computations would be trivial. In order to avoid this problem we extend the hardware such that if a cell detects a right to left link failure it is able to reverse the direction of the other (intact) link. Thereby we are always concerned with defective links that cannot transmit information from left to right.

Another point of view on such devices is that some of the cells of a two-way array behave like cells of a one-way array. Sometimes in the sequel we will call them OCA-cells.

The result of the self-diagnosis is indicated by the states of the cells. Therefore we have a partitioned state set.

Definition 3. A *cellular array with defective links* (mO-CA) is a system $\langle S, \delta_i, \delta_d, \#, A, m \rangle$, where

1. $S = S_i \cup S_d$ is the partitioned, finite, nonempty set of *cell states* satisfying $S_i \cap S_d = \emptyset$ and $S_d = \{s' \mid s \in S_i\}$,
2. $\# \notin S$ is the *boundary state*,
3. $A \subseteq S_i$ is the set of *input symbols*,
4. $m \in \mathbb{N}_0$ is an upper bound for the *number of link failures*,
5. $\delta_i \colon (S \cup \{\#\})^3 \to S_i$ is the *local transition function for intact cells*,
6. $\delta_d \colon (S \cup \{\#\})^2 \to S_d$ is the *local transition function for defective cells*.

A recognition process has to compute the correct result for all distributions of the at most m defective links. In advance it is, of course, not known which of the links will fail. Therefore, for mO-CAs we have a set of admissible start configurations as follows.

For an input string $w = x_1 \ldots x_n \in A^n$ the configuration $c_{0,w}$ is an admissible start configuration of a mO-CA if there exists a set $D \subseteq \{1, \ldots, n\}$ of defective cells, $|D| \leq m$, such that $c_{0,w}(i) = x_i \in S_i$ if $i \in \{1, \ldots, n\} \setminus D$ and $c_{0,w}(i) = x_i' \in S_d$ if $i \in D$.

For a clear understanding we define the global transition function Δ of mO-CAs as follows: Let c_t, $t \geq 0$, be a configuration of a mO-CA with defective cells D, then its successor configuration is as follows:

$$c_{t+1} = \Delta(c_t) \iff$$

$$\begin{cases} c_{t+1}(1) = \delta_i\big(\#, c_t(1), c_t(2)\big) & \text{if } 1 \notin D \\ c_{t+1}(1) = \delta_d\big(c_t(1), c_t(2)\big) & \text{if } 1 \in D \end{cases}$$

$$\begin{cases} c_{t+1}(j) = \delta_i\big(c_t(j-1), c_t(j), c_t(j+1)\big) & \text{if } j \notin D, j \in \{2, \ldots, n-1\} \\ c_{t+1}(j) = \delta_d\big(c_t(j), c_t(j+1)\big) & \text{if } j \in D, j \in \{2, \ldots, n-1\} \end{cases}$$

$$\begin{cases} c_{t+1}(n) = \delta_i\big(c_t(n-1), c_t(n), \#\big) & \text{if } n \notin D \\ c_{t+1}(n) = \delta_d\big(c_t(n), \#\big) & \text{if } n \in D \end{cases}$$

Due to our definition of δ_i and δ_d once the computation has started the set D remains fixed, what meets the requirements of our model.

4 mO-CAs Are Better than OCAs

The inclusions $\mathrm{L}_{rt}(\mathrm{OCA}) \subseteq \mathrm{L}_{rt}(m\mathrm{O\text{-}CA}) \subseteq \mathrm{L}_{rt}(\mathrm{CA})$ are following immediately from the definitions. Our aim is to prove that both inclusions are strict.

4.1   Subroutines

In order to prove that real-time mO-CAs are more powerful than real-time OCAs we need some results concerning CAs and OCAs which will later on serve as subroutines of the general construction.

4.1.1   Time Constructors. A strictly increasing mapping $f \colon \mathbb{N} \to \mathbb{N}$ is said to be *time constructible* if there exists a CA such that for an arbitrary initial configuration the leftmost cell enters a final state at and only at time steps $f(j)$, $1 \leq j \leq n$. A corresponding CA is called a *time constructor* for f. It is therefore able to distinguish the time steps $f(j)$.

The following lemma has been shown in [1].

Lemma 1. *The mapping* $f(n) = 2^n$, $n \in \mathbb{N}$, *is time constructible.*

A general investigation of time constructible functions can be found, e.g. in [13,2]. Actually, we will need a time constructor for the mapping 2^{2^n}. Fortunately, in [13] the closure of these functions under composition has been shown.

Corollary 1. *The mapping* $f(n) = 2^{2^n}$, $n \in \mathbb{N}$, *is time constructible.*

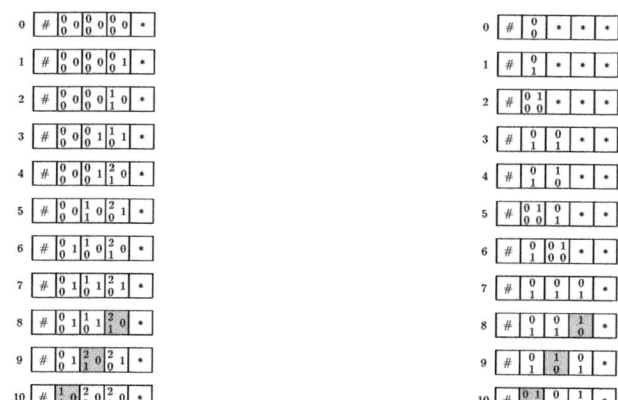

Fig. 1. A binary OCA-counter   **Fig. 2.** A binary CA-shift-right-counter

4.1.2 Binary OCA-Counters.

Here we need to set up some adjacent cells of an OCA as a binary counter. Actually, we are not interested in the value of the counter but in the time step at which it overflows. Due to the information flow the rightmost cell of the counter has to contain the least significant bit. Assume that this cell can identify itself. In order to realize such a simple counter every cell has three registers (cf. Figure 1). The third ones are working modulo 2. The second ones are signaling a carry-over to the left neighbor and the first ones are indicating whether the corresponding cell has generated no carry-over (0), one carry-over (1) or more than one carry-over (2) before. Now the whole counter can be tested by a leftmoving signal. If on its travel through the counter all the first registers are containing 0 and additionally both carry-over registers of the leftmost cell are containing 1, then it recognizes the desired time step. Observe that we need the second carry-over register in order to check that the counter produces an overflow for the first time.

4.1.3 Binary CA-Shift-Right Counters.

For this type of counter we need two-way information flow. It is set up in a single (the leftmost) cell of a CA. Since we require the least significant bit to be again the rightmost bit in the counter we have to extend it every time the counter produces an overflow. Every cell has two registers. One for the corresponding digit and the other one for the indication of a carry-over. The principle is depicted in Figure 2. Details can be found in [9].

4.2 Proof of the Strictness of the Inclusion

Now we are prepared to prove the main result of this section.

Let $L = \{b^n a^m \mid m = 2^{2^n} + 2^n, n \in \mathbb{N}\}$ be a set of strings. The easy part is to show that L does not belong to $\mathrm{L}_{rt}(\mathrm{OCA})$.

Lemma 2. $L \notin \mathrm{L}_{rt}(\mathrm{OCA})$

Proof. In [7] it has been shown that for a mapping $f: \mathbb{N} \to \mathbb{N}$ with the property $\lim_{n\to\infty} \frac{n^{(n+1)^2}}{f(n)} = 0$ the set of strings $\{b^n a^{f(n)} \mid n \in \mathbb{N}\}$ does not belong to $\mathrm{L}_{rt}(\mathrm{OCA})$. Applying the result to L it follows $\lim_{n\to\infty} \frac{n^{(n+1)^2}}{2^{2^n}+2^n} = \lim_{n\to\infty} \frac{2^{(n+1)^2 \cdot \log_2(n)}}{2^{2^n}+2^n} = 0$ and therefore $L \notin \mathrm{L}_{rt}(\mathrm{OCA})$. □

It remains to show that L is real-time recognizable by some mO-CA.

Theorem 1. $L \in \mathrm{L}_{rt}(\text{1O-CA})$

Proof. In the following a real-time 1O-CA $\mathcal{M}$ that recognizes L is constructed. On input data $b^n a^m$ we are concerned with three possible positions of the unique defective cell:

1. The position is within the b-cells.
2. The position is within the leftmost 2^n a-cells.
3. The position is at the right hand side of the 2^nth a-cell.

At the beginning of the computation $\mathcal{M}$ starts the following tasks in parallel on some tracks: The unique defective cell establishes a time constructor $\mathcal{M}_1$ for 2^{2^n} if it is an a-cell. The leftmost a-cell establishes another time constructor $\mathcal{M}_2$ for 2^{2^n} and, additionally, a binary shift-right counter $\mathcal{C}_1$ that counts the number of a's. The rightmost b-cell starts a binary OCA-counter $\mathcal{C}_2$ and, finally, the rightmost a-cell sends a stop signal $*$ with speed 1 to the left.

According to the three positions the following three processes are superimposed.

Case 3. (cf. Figure 3) The shift-right counter is increased by 1 at every time step until the stop signal $*$ arrives. Each overflow of $\mathcal{C}_1$ causes an incrementation (by 1) of the counter $\mathcal{C}_2$. Let i be the time step at which the stop signal arrives at the shift-right counter $\mathcal{C}_1$ and let l be the number of digits of $\mathcal{C}_1$. During the next l time steps the signal travels through the counter and tests whether its value is a power of 2, from which $i = 2^l$ follows. Subsequently, the signal tests during another n time steps whether the value of the binary counter $\mathcal{C}_2$ is exactly 2^n, from which $l = 2^n$ follows. If the tests are successful the input is accepted because the input string is of the form $b^n a^l a^i = b^n a^{2^n} a^{2^l} = b^n a^{2^n} a^{2^{2^n}}$ and thus belongs to L.

Case 2. (cf. Figure 4) In this case the space between the b's and the defective cell is too small for setting up an appropriate counter as shown for case 3. Here a second binary counter $\mathcal{C}_3$ within the b-cells is used. It is increased by 1 at every time step until it receives a signal from the defective cell and, thus, contains the number of cells between the b-cells and the defective cell. Its value x is conserved on an additional track. Moreover, at every time step at which the time constructor $\mathcal{M}_1$ marks the defective cell to be final, a signal is sent to the b-cells that causes them to reset the counter to the value x by copying the conserved value back to the counter track. After the reset the counter is increased by 1 at every time step. Each reset signal also marks an unmarked b-cell.

The input is accepted if exactly at the arrival of the stop signal at the leftmost cell the counter overflows for the first time and all b-cells are marked: Let the

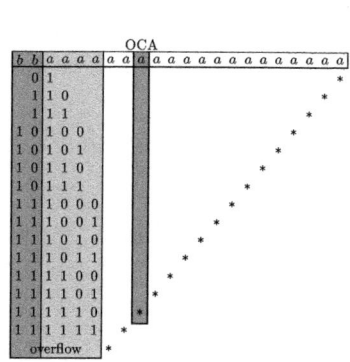
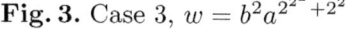

Fig. 3. Case 3, $w = b^2 a^{2^{2^2}+2^2}$

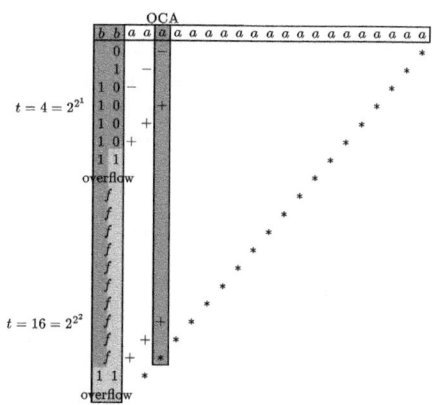

Fig. 4. Case 2, $w = b^2 a^{2^{2^2}+2^2}$

last marking of $\mathcal{M}_1$ happen at time $i = 2^{2^r}$ for some $r \in \mathbb{N}$. The corresponding leftmoving signal arrives at time $2^{2^r} + x$ at the b-cells and resets the counter $\mathcal{C}_3$ to x. The stop signal arrives at time $2^{2^r} + x + s$, for some $s \in \mathbb{N}$, at the counter that has now the value $x + s$. Since the counter produces an overflow it holds $x + s = 2^n$. Moreover, since $\mathcal{M}_1$ has sent exactly r marking signals and all b-cells are marked it follows $r = n$. Therefore, the stop signal arrives at the rightmost b-cell at time $2^{2^r} + x + s = 2^{2^n} + 2^n$ and the input belongs to L.

Case 1. Since the binary counter $\mathcal{M}_3$ within the b-cells is an OCA-counter it works fine even if the defective cell is located within the b-cells. Case 1 is a straightforward adaption of case 2 (here $\mathcal{M}_2$ is used instead of $\mathcal{M}_1$). □

Corollary 2. $\mathrm{L}_{rt}(\text{OCA}) \subset \mathrm{L}_{rt}(\text{1O-CA})$

Without proof we present the following generalization:

Theorem 2. $L \in \mathrm{L}_{rt}(m\text{O-CA})$ *for every constant* $m \in \mathbb{N}$.

Corollary 3. $\mathrm{L}_{rt}(\text{OCA}) \subset \mathrm{L}_{rt}(m\text{O-CA})$ *for every constant* $m \in \mathbb{N}$.

5   CAs Are Better than mO-CAs

In order to complete the comparisons we have to prove that the computational power of real-time mO-CAs is strictly weaker than those of CAs. For this purpose we can adapt a method developed in [15] for proving that certain string sets do not belong to $\mathrm{L}_{rt}(\text{OCA})$. The basic idea in [15] is to define an equivalence relation on string sets and bound the number of distinguishable equivalence classes of real-time OCA computations.

Let $\mathcal{M} = \langle S, \delta, \#, A \rangle$ be an OCA and $X, Y \subseteq A^*$. Two strings $w, w' \in A^*$ are defined to be $(\mathcal{M}, X, Y)$-equivalent iff for all $x \in X$ and $y \in Y$ the leftmost $|x| + |y|$ states of the configurations $\Delta^{[|w|]}(c_{0,xwy})$ and $\Delta^{[|w'|]}(c_{0,xw'y})$ are equal.

The observation is that the essential point of the upper bound on equivalence classes is due to the fact that the input sequences x and y are computationally unrelated. Therefore, we can assume that the cell obtaining the first symbol of w resp. of w' as input is defective and so adapt the results in [15] to 1O-CAs immediately:

Lemma 3. $\{uvu \mid u, v \in \{0,1\}^*, |u| > 1\} \notin L_{rt}(\text{1O-CA})$ *and* $\{uvu \mid u, v \in \{0,1\}^*, |u| > 1\} \in L_{rt}(\text{CA})$.

Corollary 4. $\{uvu \mid u, v \in \{0,1\}^*, |u| > 1\} \notin L_{rt}(m\text{O-CA})$ *for every constant* $m \in \mathbb{N}$.

Corollary 5. $L_{rt}(m\text{O-CA}) \subset L_{rt}(\text{CA})$ *for every constant* $m \in \mathbb{N}$.

Finally, $L_{rt}(\text{OCA}) \subset L_{rt}(m\text{O-CA}) \subset L_{rt}(\text{CA})$ follows for for every constant $m \in \mathbb{N}$.

References

1. Bucher, W. and Čulik II, K. *On real time and linear time cellular automata.* RAIRO Inform. Théor. 18 (1984), 307–325. 396
2. Buchholz, Th. and Kutrib, M. *Some relations between massively parallel arrays.* Parallel Comput. 23 (1997), 1643–1662. 396
3. Gács, P. *Reliable computation with cellular automata.* J. Comput. System Sci. 32 (1986), 15–78. 392
4. Gács, P. and Reif, J. *A simple three-dimensional real-time reliable cellular array.* J. Comput. System Sci. 36 (1988), 125–147. 392
5. Harao, M. and Noguchi, S. *Fault tolerant cellular automata.* J. Comput. System Sci. 11 (1975), 171–185. 393
6. Jiang, T. *The synchronization of nonuniform networks of finite automata.* Inform. Comput. 97 (1992), 234–261. 393
7. Kutrib, M. *Pushdown cellular automata.* Theoret. Comput. Sci. 215 (1999), 239–261. 398
8. Kutrib, M. and Löwe, J.-T. *Fault tolerant parallel pattern recognition.* Cellular Automata for Research and Industry (ACRI 2000), 2000, to appear. 393
9. Kutrib, M. and Löwe, J.-T. *Massively parallel pattern recognition with link failures.* Research Report 0003, Institut für Informatik, Universität Giessen, Giessen, 2000. 397
10. Kutrib, M. and Vollmar, R. *Minimal time synchronization in restricted defective cellular automata.* J. Inform. Process. Cybern. EIK 27 (1991), 179–196. 393
11. Kutrib, M. and Vollmar, R. *The firing squad synchronization problem in defective cellular automata.* IEICE Transactions on Information and Systems E78-D (1995), 895–900. 393
12. Mazoyer, J. *Synchronization of a line of finite automata with nonuniform delays.* Research Report TR 94-49, Ecole Normale Supérieure de Lyon, Lyon, 1994. 393
13. Mazoyer, J. and Terrier, V. *Signals in one dimensional cellular automata.* Theoret. Comput. Sci. 217 (1999), 53–80. 396
14. Nishio, H. and Kobuchi, Y. *Fault tolerant cellular spaces.* J. Comput. System Sci. 11 (1975), 150–170. 393

15. Terrier, V. *Language not recognizable in real time by one-way cellular automata.* Theoret. Comput. Sci. 156 (1996), 281–287. 399, 400

16. Umeo, H. *A fault-tolerant scheme for optimum-time firing squad synchronization.* Parallel Computing: Trends and Applications, 1994, 223–230. 393, 395

17. von Neumann, J. *Probabilistic logics and the synthesis of reliable organisms from unreliable components.* Automata Studies, Princeton University Press 34 (1956), 43–98. 392

18. Yunès, J.-B. *Fault tolerant solutions to the firing squad synchronization problem.* Technical Report LITP 96/06, Institut Blaise Pascal, Paris, 1996. 393

Finitary Observations in Regular Algebras*

Slawomir Lasota

Institute of Informatics, Warsaw University
Banacha 2, 02-097 Warszawa, Poland
sl@mimuw.edu.pl

Abstract. We investigate *regular algebras*, admitting infinitary regular terms interpreted as least upper bounds of suitable approximation chains. We prove that finitary observable contexts are sufficient for observational indistinguishability in a regular algebra. Moreover, assumed all observable sorts to be essentially flat, observational equivalence is also completely characterized by finitary contexts. As a corollary, methods of proving behavioural properties and observational equivalence of standard algebras can be reused in the setting of regular algebras.

1 Introduction

Behavioural semantics of algebraic specifications is widely accepted to capture properly the "black box" character of data abstraction. As a nontrivial example of an algebraic framework where behavioural ideas may be applied, we consider regular algebras, differing from the standard algebras in one respect: they allow one to additionally model infinite regular datatypes, like streams. Regular algebras were introduced in [11,12], and then studied e. g. in [3]. Our starting point here is a more recent paper [2], investigating observational equivalence of regular algebras and the induced behavioural semantics of specification. Regular algebras contain properly continuous algebras [10], intended usually to model infinite datatypes. However continuous algebras are not well suited for behavioural semantics, in particular the requirement of existence of lubs of all (countable) chains seems to be too restrictive (cf. e. g. discussion in [2]).

Our motivation is to analyze applicability of regular algebras as models of behavioural specifications in the process of step-wise development of software systems [7,8]. A crucial role is played here by the concept of observational equivalence: it allows one to consider possibly large class of acceptable realizations of a specification, under the only assumption that the observable behavior of the implementation conforms to the specification requirements. Observational equivalence of regular algebras is defined analogously as in the case of standard algebras, using observational indistinguishability by means of all observable contexts (cf. [2]). However, compared with standard algebras, in regular algebras infinitary contexts are involved too, since the structure is substantially richer: carrier sets are partially ordered and all term-definable mappings have fixed

---

* The work reported here was partially supported by the KBN grant 8 T11C 019 19.

V. Hlaváč, K. G. Jeffery, and J. Wiedermann (Eds.): SOFSEM 2000, LNCS 1963, pp. 402–410, 2000.

points, given by the least upper bounds of appropriate approximation chains. This has a serious impact on complexity of proofs of behavioural properties of regular algebras, including proofs of correctness of implementation step.

In Section 3 we prove that observational indistinguishability in a regular algebra is actually induced by only finitary observable contexts — surprisingly, even when non-trivial approximation chains exist in carrier sets of observable sorts. This makes proofs of behavioural properties of regular algebras substantially easier, and allows one to use proof methods known for standard algebras, like context induction [4] or methods developed in [1].

Finitary contexts are not sufficient for observational equivalence in general. In the following Section 4 we extend the setting of regular algebras with a possibility to have carriers of some sorts essentially unordered (*essentially flat*), which is strongly required in practical examples. We prove that when carrier sets of all observable sorts are essentially flat, the notion of observational equivalence can be characterized by only finitary contexts too. Hence one can prove equivalence of regular algebras e. g. using standard observational correspondences [9].

Results reported here are used in [6] for adaptation of constructor implementation methodology [8] for regular algebras; the results are also contained in Chapter 5 of [5].

2 Preliminaries

2.1 Regular Algebras

Let Σ, Σ' be fixed many-sorted algebraic signatures throughout this paper. We omit introducing classical notions of standard Σ-algebra, homomorphism, subalgebra, congruence, quotient. By $t_{A[v]}$ we denote the value of Σ-term t in algebra A under valuation v. By $|A|$ we denote the many-sorted carrier set of A; by $|A|_s$ the carrier of sort s. For a subset S of sorts of Σ, by $|A|_S$ we denote the carrier sets of sorts from S. All sets are implicitly meant to be many-sorted in the sequel. An *ordered Σ-algebra* is a standard Σ-algebra whose carrier set on each sort s is partially ordered (let $\leq_s^A$ denote the partial order in $|A|_s$) and has a distinguished element $\perp_s^A \in |A|_s$.

The set of *regular Σ-terms* $T_\Sigma^\mu(X)$ over X is defined inductively as usual, with the only additional case: for any $t \in T_\Sigma^\mu(X \cup \{z : s\})_s$ and a distinguished variable z of the same sort s, there is a μ-term $\mu z.t$ in $T_\Sigma^\mu(X)_s$. Similarly, the inductive definition of the value $t_{A[v]}$ of a term under a valuation $v \colon X \to |A|$ in an ordered algebra A needs one more case. For $t \in T_\Sigma^\mu(X \cup \{z : s\})_s$, put:

- $t_{A[v]}^0(\perp) := \perp_s^A$,
- for $i \in \omega$, $t_{A[v]}^{i+1}(\perp) := t_{A[v_i]}$, where $v_i \colon X \cup \{z : s\} \to |A|$ extends v by $v_i(z) = t_{A[v]}^i(\perp)$.

Now, $(\mu z.t)_{A[v]}$ is defined if $t_{A[v]}^i(\perp)$ are defined, for all $i \in \omega$, $t_{A[v]}^i(\perp) \leq_s^A t_{A[v]}^{i+1}(\perp)$, and the least upper bound $\bigsqcup_{i \in \omega} t_{A[v]}^i(\perp)$ exists in $|A|_s$; if so, then

$(\mu z.t)_{A[v]} = \bigsqcup_{i \in \omega} t^i_{A[v]}(\bot)$. An ordered Σ-algebra A is *regular* if it satisfies the following conditions:

- *completeness*: for all $t \in T^\mu_\Sigma(X)$ and $v: X \to |A|$, the value $t_{A[v]}$ is defined,
- *continuity*: for all $t \in T^\mu_\Sigma(X \cup \{y : s\})_{s'}$, $q \in T^\mu_\Sigma(X \cup \{z : s\})_s$ and valuations $v: X \to |A|$, $t_{A[v_i]} \leq^A_s t_{A[v_{i+1}]}$, for $i \in \omega$, and $t_{A[v']} = \bigsqcup_{i \geq 0} t_{A[v_i]}$, where valuation $v': X \cup \{y : s\} \to |A|$ extends v by $v'(y) = (\mu z.q)_{A[v]}$ and $v_i: X \cup \{y : s\} \to |A|$ extends v by $v_i(y) = q^i_{A[v]}(\bot)$, for $i \geq 0$.

As it was proved in [ ], continuity can be equivalently required only for *finitary* terms $t \in T_\Sigma(X \cup \{y : s\})_{s'}$, i.e., those not containing symbol μ. Notice that continuity, as stated above, does not imply even monotonicity of operations in a regular algebra.

By completeness, $\bot^A_s$ is the least element in $|A|_s$.

A regular subalgebra of A is any regular algebra B the carrier of which is a subset of A and such that for all terms $t \in T^\mu_\Sigma(X)$ and valuations $v: X \to |B|$, $t_{B[v]} = t_{A[v]}$. It is easy to see that all operations of B are restrictions of operations of A to $|B|$ and moreover $\bot^B_s = \bot^A_s$ for each sort s. For $Y \subseteq |A|$, by *the subalgebra of A generated by* Y we mean the least regular subalgebra of A whose carrier includes Y.

By a regular Σ-homomorphism $h: A \to B$ we mean any function h such that for all terms $t \in T^\mu_\Sigma(X)$ and valuations $v: X \to |A|$, $h(t_{A[v]}) = t_{B[h \circ v]}$. A regular congruence on A is a kernel of any regular Σ-homomorphism $h: A \to B$ (i.e., $\{(x, x') \mid h(x) = h(x')\}$).

2.2 Observational Equivalence

In the following we concentrate on an observational equivalence induced by a subset of observable sorts; hence throughout this paper let us fix a subset OBS of *observable sorts* of Σ.

In the following, let X denote some OBS-sorted set of variables. By a Σ-*context* of sort s' on sort s we mean any term $\gamma \in T^\mu_\Sigma(X \cup \{z_s : s\})_{s'}$, where z_s is a special, distinguished variable of sort s such that $z_s \notin X$. Note that z_s, for $s \notin OBS$, are the only variables of non-observable sorts appearing in contexts. A special role is played by *observable contexts*, i.e., contexts of observable sort ($s' \in OBS$). For any regular Σ-algebra A, Σ-context γ on sort s, valuation $v: X \to |A|_{OBS}$ and value $a \in |A|_s$, we will write $\gamma_{A[v]}(a)$ for $\gamma_{A[v_a]}$ where v_a extends v by $v(z_s) = a$.

For any A, let A_{OBS} denote its subalgebra generated by (carrier sets of) observable sorts; we call A_{OBS} an *observational subalgebra* of A. The regular congruence $\sim^{OBS}_A$ on A_{OBS} is defined as follows: for any $a, a' \in |A_{OBS}|_s$, $a \sim^{OBS}_A a'$ if and only if for all valuations v into carriers of observable sorts of A_{OBS} and all observable contexts γ, $\gamma_{A[v]}(a) = \gamma_{A[v]}(a')$. The congruence $\sim^{OBS}_A$ is a called *observational indistinguishability* in A; $\sim^{OBS}_A$ is the greatest congruence on A_{OBS} being identity on observable sorts (cf. [2]). The quotient of A_{OBS} by $\sim^{OBS}_A$ represents the observable behaviour of A; $A_{OBS}/\sim^{OBS}_A$ is *fully abstract* in the sense that its indistinguishability is identity. Two regular algebras are taken as equivalent when their behaviours are isomorphic:

Definition 1. Observational equivalence $\equiv_{OBS}$ of regular Σ-algebras is defined by:

$$A \equiv_{OBS} B \quad \text{iff} \quad A_{OBS}/{\sim_A^{OBS}} \cong B_{OBS}/{\sim_B^{OBS}}.$$

$A_{OBS}/{\sim_A^{OBS}}$ will be written shortly $A/{\sim^{OBS}}$, when no confusion can occur.

All definitions concerning observational equivalence are still valid when standard algebras are taken into account instead of regular ones — the only modification required is to restrict contexts γ to only finitary terms $T_\Sigma(X)$ in definition of indistinguishability. We will deliberately overload notation and use symbols $\equiv_{OBS}$, $(\_)_{OBS}$ also for standard algebras. On the other hand, observational indistinguishability in standard algebras will be denoted by $\approx^{OBS}$.

3 Finitary Observations

Roughly, finitary observational contexts are powerful enough for indistinguishability in a regular algebra; the only infinitary regular terms really needed are to denote bottoms $\perp$. The proof of this fact is based on the property that each value of a μ-term is approximated by values of appropriate finitary terms.

For fixed OBS, Let $\mathcal{F}^{OBS}$ denote the set of all observable contexts $\gamma \in T_\Sigma^\mu(X \cup \{z_s : s\})$, such that the only possible μ-subterms of γ are of the form $\mu x.x$. Let $\sim_A^{\mathcal{F}^{OBS}}$ denote the contextual indistinguishability induced in A by only contexts from $\mathcal{F}^{OBS}$.

Theorem 1. *In a regular algebra A, $\sim_A^{OBS} = \sim_A^{\mathcal{F}^{OBS}}$.*

Proof. Assume that two values $a, a' \in |A|_s$ of sort s are distinguished by some regular context $\gamma \in T_\Sigma^\mu(X \cup \{z_s : s\})$ and a valuation v into carriers of observable sorts, i.e., $\gamma_{A[v]}(a) \neq \gamma_{A[v]}(a')$.

Lemma 1 formulated below will be crucial in what follows. Let t_0 be an arbitrary regular Σ-term and let w be an arbitrary valuation. Without loss of generality we can assume that if the same variable x is bound in two different subterms $\mu x.t_1$ and $\mu x.t_2$ of t_0, then these subterms are disjoint and terms $\langle t_1 \rangle_\mu$ and $\langle t_2 \rangle_\mu$ are identical; where for any regular term t, $\langle t \rangle_\mu$ denotes the term obtained from t by replacing each μ-subterm $\mu x'.t'$ with the variable x'. Let $\mu x_1.t_1, \ldots, \mu x_n.t_n$ be all different μ-subterms of t_0, $n \geq 0$. We define inductively $n + 1$ sequences of terms, $\{t_i^j\}_{j \in \omega}$, for $0 \leq i \leq n$, as follows:

$$
\begin{aligned}
t_i^0 &:= \mu x_i.x_i && \text{for } i \geq 1, \\
t_i^{j+1} &:= \langle t_i \rangle_\mu [t_1^j/x_1, \ldots, t_n^j/x_n] && \text{for } i \geq 1, \\
t_0^j &:= \langle t_0 \rangle_\mu [t_1^j/x_1, \ldots, t_n^j/x_n];
\end{aligned}
$$

square brackets denote simultaneous substitution. (Notice that if $t_0 = \mu x_i.t_i$ for some i, then $\langle t_0 \rangle_\mu = x_i$ and $t_0^j = t_i^j$, for $j \geq 0$.) From Theorem 5.2.2 in Section 5.2 in [5] directly follows:

Lemma 1. *Value* $(t_0)_{A[w]}$ *is the l. u. b. of the chain* $\{(t_0^j)_{A[w]}\}_{j \in \omega}$.

Terms t_i^j have no μ-subterms except $\mu x_i.x_i$. Applying the lemma to $t_0 = \gamma$ and $w = v_a$ (i. e., v_a extends v by $v_a(z_s) = a$), we conclude that $\gamma_{A[v]}(a)$ is necessarily the least upper bound of the sequence $\{(\gamma_j)_{A[v]}(a)\}_{j \in \omega}$ and that contexts γ_j are in $\mathcal{F}^{OBS}$. Moreover, for $w = v_{a'}$ we conclude that also $\gamma_{A[v]}(a')$ is the least upper bound of the sequence $\{(\gamma_j)_{A[v]}(a')\}_{j \in \omega}$ induced by the same contexts. Since least upper bounds are different, $\gamma_{A[v]}(a) \neq \gamma_{A[v]}(a')$, the chains differ necessarily on some j, $(\gamma_j)_{A[v]}(a) \neq (\gamma_j)_{A[v]}(a')$; this completes the proof. □

We can easily eliminate each term $\mu x.x$ of observable sort by replacing it with a fresh variable y and extending the valuation by $y \mapsto \bot$. Hence we only need terms $\mu x.x$ of non-observable sorts.

As a corollary, methods of proving behavioural properties of standard algebras (like context induction [4] or methods developed in [1]) can be reused in the framework of regular algebras.

Let $\Sigma(\bot)$ denote signature Σ enriched by a constant symbol $\bot_s$ in each sort s. For a regular Σ-algebra A, let $|A|_{\Sigma(\bot)}$ denote the standard $\Sigma(\bot)$-algebra with carrier sets and operations as in A and with $\bot_s$ interpreted as $\bot_s^A$ in each sort (i. e., by passing from A to $|A|_{\Sigma(\bot)}$, the partial order is forgotten and consequently also the information about values of non-trivial μ-terms). In the sequel, all $\Sigma(\bot)$-terms are called *finitary*.

By Theorem 1 we conclude that observational indistinguishability in a regular algebra A is roughly the indistinguishability in $|A|_{\Sigma(\bot)}$. But observational equivalence of regular algebras is not reducible to observational equivalence of standard $\Sigma(\bot)$-algebras: it *does not* hold

$$A \equiv_{OBS} B \Leftrightarrow |A|_{\Sigma(\bot)} \equiv_{OBS} |B|_{\Sigma(\bot)} \tag{1}$$

(note that on the right-hand side $\equiv_{OBS}$ denotes observational equivalence of standard $\Sigma(\bot)$-algebras). Intuitively, finitary contexts have more distinguishing power in regular algebras than in standard algebras, since the observational subalgebra A_{OBS} of a regular algebra A may be larger than the observational subalgebra $(|A|_{\Sigma(\bot)})_{OBS}$ of the standard $\Sigma(\bot)$-algebra $|A|_{\Sigma(\bot)}$.

Let us find out where the difficulties appear. Since $\sim_A^{OBS}$ is standard $\Sigma(\bot)$-congruence, the forgetful functor $|\_|_{\Sigma(\bot)}$ commutes with observational quotient:

$$|A_{OBS}|_{\Sigma(\bot)}/\sim_A^{OBS} = |A_{OBS}/\sim_A^{OBS}|_{\Sigma(\bot)}. \tag{2}$$

The observational (standard, regular) subalgebras are generated by (finitary, regular) terms, hence $(|A|_{\Sigma(\bot)})_{OBS} = (|A_{OBS}|_{\Sigma(\bot)})_{OBS}$. Moreover $(|A|_{\Sigma(\bot)})_{OBS}$ may be a *proper* subalgebra of $|A_{OBS}|_{\Sigma(\bot)}$ in general—this is why we need another symbol $\approx_A^{OBS}$ to stand for the indistinguishability (by means of $\Sigma(\bot)$-contexts) in $(|A|_{\Sigma(\bot)})_{OBS}$. However, by Theorem 1 $\approx_A^{OBS}$ and $\sim_A^{OBS}$ agree on $(|A|_{\Sigma(\bot)})_{OBS}$, so the implication from left to right holds in (1). On the other hand, from $|A|_{\Sigma(\bot)} \equiv_{OBS} |B|_{\Sigma(\bot)}$, i. e. $(|A|_{\Sigma(\bot)})_{OBS}/\approx^{OBS} \cong$

$(|B|_{\Sigma(\perp)})_{OBS}/{\approx}_{OBS}$ we cannot even conclude (e. g. using (2)) that $|A/_{\sim OBS}|_{\Sigma(\perp)} \cong$ $|B/_{\sim OBS}|_{\Sigma(\perp)}$. But even if we could, this would not guarantee $A/_{\sim OBS} \cong B/_{\sim OBS}$ in general.

Example 1. As a counterexample to (1) (confirming also the last statement), consider two regular algebras, A and A', over Σ containing two sorts, $\{o, n\}$, and two operations: $f : o \to o$, $g : n \to o$; the only observable sort is o.

$$A_o = \{a_0 = \perp_o, a_\infty, a'_\infty\} \cup \{a_i\}_{i=1,2,\ldots}$$
$$A_n = \{a = \perp_n\}$$
$$\perp_o \le a_1 \le \ldots, \; (\bigsqcup_{i=0,1,\ldots} a_i) = a_\infty \le a'_\infty$$

$$f^A(a_i) = a_{i+1}, \; i \ge 0$$
$$f^A(a_\infty) = a_\infty, \; f^A(a'_\infty) = a'_\infty$$
$$g^A(a) = a_\infty$$

A' differs from A only by $g^{A'}(a) = a'_\infty$ (i. e., in particular $|A'| = |A|$). Both A and A' are fully abstract, i. e., their indistinguishabilities are identities. This implies that they are not observationally equivalent, since they are non-isomorphic (e. g. because the equation: $\forall x. \; g(x) = \mu y.f(y)$ is satisfied only in one of them). On the other hand, evidently, $|A|_{\Sigma(\perp)} \cong |A'|_{\Sigma(\perp)}$; an isomorphisms $\sim$ is given by: $\sim_o = \{(a_i, a_i)\}_{i=0,1,\ldots} \cup \{(a_\infty, a'_\infty), (a'_\infty, a_\infty)\}$, $\sim_n = \{(a, a)\}$.

As the example suggests, the reason why (1) does not hold is presence of infinite chains in carrier sets of observable sorts. This will be more apparent in the next section, as our assumption there rules out such chains.

In consequence, the concept of observational correspondence [9] cannot be adopted here using only finitary contexts.

4   Flat Observable Sorts

In many practical situations we need only some sorts of a regular algebra to have upper bounds of approximation chains. In [5] it was argued that the best way to achieve this is to require carrier sets of algebraic sorts to be *essentially flat*. Formally, we say that the carrier set of sort s of a regular Σ-algebra is essentially flat if this algebra is isomorphic (i. e., related via a bijective regular homomorphism) to a regular algebra A whose carrier set of sort s has flat ordering with the least element $\perp_s^A$ ($a \le b$ iff $a = \perp_s^A$ or $a = b$).[1] In consequence, all chains imposed by completeness and continuity in an essentially flat carrier set collapse, namely contain at most two different values.

In practical examples all observable sorts are usually intended to be essentially flat. Besides practical advantages, essentially flat carriers of observable

---

[1]   Evidently, isomorphic regular algebras may have different orders.

sorts imply that finitary observational contexts (and consequently standard correspondences) are sufficient for observational equivalence of regular algebras, in contrast to the negative statement (1) above.

Theorem 2. *For regular algebras A and B with essentially flat carrier sets of observable sorts, $A \equiv_{OBS} B \Leftrightarrow |A|_{\Sigma(\perp)} \equiv_{OBS} |B|_{\Sigma(\perp)}$.*

Proof. Recall from the previous section that the implication from left to right holds for any regular A and B. For the opposite direction, assume $|A|_{\Sigma(\perp)} \equiv_{OBS} |B|_{\Sigma(\perp)}$, i.e., $(|A|_{\Sigma(\perp)})OBS/\approx_A^{OBS}$ and $(|B|_{\Sigma(\perp)})OBS/\approx_A^{OBS}$ are related by an isomorphism of standard $\Sigma(\perp)$-algebras, say i. The proof proceeds in two steps. First, we show that i can be extended to isomorphism between $|A_{OBS}|_{\Sigma(\perp)}/\sim_A^{OBS}$ and $|B_{OBS}|_{\Sigma(\perp)}/\sim_B^{OBS}$.

Recall that $\sim_A^{OBS}$ and $\approx_A^{OBS}$ agree on $(|A|_{\Sigma(\perp)})OBS$ and that observational subalgebra A_{OBS} (resp. $(|A|_{\Sigma(\perp)})OBS$) is generated by regular (resp. finitary) terms with variables of observable sorts. Hence we only need to extend i to abstraction classes of $\sim_A^{OBS}$ of values denoted by infinitary terms in A_{OBS}. We define an isomorphism $i' : |A_{OBS}|_{\Sigma(\perp)}/\sim_A^{OBS} \to |B_{OBS}|_{\Sigma(\perp)}/\sim_B^{OBS}$ as follows: for an arbitrary regular term t with variables of observable sorts and valuation w into carrier sets of observable sorts of A,

$$i'([t_{(A_{OBS})[w]}]_{\sim_A^{OBS}}) = [t_{(B_{OBS})[iow]}]_{\sim_B^{OBS}}. \tag{3}$$

(On observable sorts, i is treated in (3) as if its domain is A, since $\approx_A^{OBS}$ is necessarily identity on OBS.) We need to show the following:

- i' is a well defined function, i.e., its value according to (3) does not depend on a representative of an abstraction class of $\sim_A^{OBS}$,
- i' is a bijective $\Sigma(\perp)$-homomorphism.

For fixed t and w as before, by Lemma 1 in Section 3, $a := t_{(A_{OBS})[w]}$ is the l.u.b. of $\{a_j := t^j_{(|A_{OBS}|_{\Sigma(\perp)})[w]}\}_{j \in \omega}$, for appropriate $\Sigma(\perp)$-terms t^j. Similarly, $b := t_{(B_{OBS})[iow]}$ is the l.u.b. of $\{b_j := t^j_{(|B_{OBS}|_{\Sigma(\perp)})[iow]}\}_{j \in \omega}$. Consider an arbitrary observable context γ (by virtue of Theorem 1 we assume γ to be a finitary $\Sigma(\perp)$-context) together with a valuation v into carrier sets of observable sorts of A. Since carrier sets of observable sorts of A and B are essentially flat, all relevant chains in these sorts are collapsed in A_{OBS} and B_{OBS}. In particular $\{\gamma_{(|A_{OBS}|_{\Sigma(\perp)})[v]}(a_j)\}_{j \in \omega}$ is constant starting from some position. Hence, the value of $\gamma_{(A_{OBS})[v]}(a)$ is equal to a' iff starting from some position, values $\{\gamma_{(|A_{OBS}|_{\Sigma(\perp)})[v]}(a_j)\}_{j \in \omega}$ in the approximation chain are all equal to a'. In a similar way, the value of $\gamma_{(B_{OBS})[iov]}(b)$ is determined by $\{\gamma_{(|B_{OBS}|_{\Sigma(\perp)})[iov]}(b_j)\}_{j \in \omega}$. Moreover, for $j \in \omega$, $b_j = i(a_j)$ and $\gamma_{(|B_{OBS}|_{\Sigma(\perp)})[iov]}(b_j) = i(\gamma_{(|A_{OBS}|_{\Sigma(\perp)})[v]}(a_j))$, since all t^j and γ are finitary. Finally, quotient by the observational indistinguishability $\sim_A^{OBS}$ ($\sim_B^{OBS}$) preserves values of observable contexts, e.g.

$$\gamma_{(|A_{OBS}|_{\Sigma(\perp)}/\sim_A^{OBS})[v]}([a]_{\sim_A^{OBS}}) = \gamma_{(A_{OBS})[v]}(a)$$

(since $\sim^{OBS}$ is identity on OBS, we treat here v as a function into the quotient algebra and moreover we identify carriers of observable sorts of A_{OBS} and $|A_{OBS}|_{\Sigma(\perp)}/\sim_A^{OBS}$). Due to the mentioned facts and since $i'([a]_{\sim_A^{OBS}}) = [b]_{\sim_B^{OBS}}$ by (3), we conclude that i' preserves (up to i) values of observable contexts, i. e.,

$$\gamma_{\left(|B_{OBS}|_{\Sigma(\perp)}/\sim_B^{OBS}\right)[iov]}\left(i'([a]_{\sim_A^{OBS}})\right) = i\left(\gamma_{\left(|A_{OBS}|_{\Sigma(\perp)}/\sim_A^{OBS}\right)[v]}([a]_{\sim_A^{OBS}})\right). \quad (4)$$

Now, consider two indistinguishable values a_1, a_2 in A_{OBS}, $a_1 \sim_A^{OBS} a_2$. By (4) $i'([a_1]_{\sim_A^{OBS}})$ and $i'([a_2]_{\sim_A^{OBS}})$ are also indistinguishable in $|B_{OBS}|_{\Sigma(\perp)}/\sim_B^{OBS}$. But the quotient algebra $|B_{OBS}/\sim_B^{OBS}|_{\Sigma(\perp)}$ is necessarily fully abstract, i. e., any two indistinguishable elements are equal. By (2), $|B_{OBS}|_{\Sigma(\perp)}/\sim_B^{OBS}$ is fully abstract too, hence $i'([a_1]_{\sim_A^{OBS}}) = i'([a_2]_{\sim_A^{OBS}})$ and i' is well defined in (3).

By the very definition, i' is a standard $\Sigma(\perp)$-homomorphism. Moreover, since i is a bijection (hence surjective) on OBS, it follows immediately that i' is surjective. For injectivity, notice that whenever $i'([a_1]_{\sim_A^{OBS}}) = i'([a_2]_{\sim_A^{OBS}})$, by (4) $[a_1]_{\sim_A^{OBS}}$ and $[a_2]_{\sim_A^{OBS}}$ are indistinguishable in $|A|_{\Sigma(\perp)}/\sim_A^{OBS}$, hence equal due to full abstractness of the quotient algebra, similarly as above.

Now we come to the second step of the proof, which fortunately turns out to be immediate. By (2) we conclude that the isomorphism i' relates $|A/\sim_{OBS}|_{\Sigma(\perp)}$ and $|B/\sim_{OBS}|_{\Sigma(\perp)}$. Moreover, by the very definition (3), i' is also a regular Σ-homomorphism. Hence $A/\sim_{OBS}$ and $B/\sim_{OBS}$ are isomorphic. $\qquad\square$

Unlike in Theorem 1, the whole signature $\Sigma(\perp)$ is actually needed in the proof, in order to guarantee that $\perp$'s in all observable sorts are related by i. As a conclusion, we obtain an effective complete proof technique for observational equivalence of regular algebras:

Corollary 1. *Regular algebras with essentially flat carrier sets of observable sorts are observationally equivalent iff they are related by an observational $\Sigma(\perp)$-correspondence [9].*

Acknowledgements

The author is grateful to Andrzej Tarlecki for many fruitful discussions and valuable comments during this work.

References

1. M. Bidoit, R. Hennicker: Behavioural theories and the proof of behavioural properties. *Theoretical Computer Science* 165(1): 3–55, 1996. 403, 406
2. M. Bidoit, A. Tarlecki: Regular algebras: a framework for observational specifications with recursive definitions. Report LIENS-95-12, ENS, 1995. 402, 404
3. I. Guessarian, F. Parisi-Presicce: Iterative vs. regular factor algebras. SIGACT News 15(2), 32–44, 1983. 402

4. R. Hennicker: Context induction: A proof principle for behavioural abstractions and algebraic implementations. *Formal Aspects of Computing*, 3(4):326 – 345, 1991. 403, 406

5. S. Lasota: Algebraic observational equivalence and open-maps bisimilarity. Ph. D. Thesis in Institute of Informatics of Warsaw University, March 2000. Accessible at http://www.mimuw.edu.pl/ sl/work/phd.ps.gz. 403, 404, 405, 407

6. S. Lasota: Behavioural constructor implementation for regular algebras. To appear in *Proc. 7ᵗʰ International Conference on Logic for Programming and Automated Reasoning LPAR'2000*, Springer-Verlag LNAI series. 403

7. D. Sannella, A. Tarlecki: Towards formal development of programs from algebraic specifications: implementations revisited. *Acta Informatica* 25:233 – 281, 1988. 402

8. D. Sannella, A. Tarlecki: Essential Concepts of Algebraic Specification and Program Development. *Formal Aspects of Computing* 9:229 – 269, 1997. 402, 403

9. O. Schoett: *Data abstraction and correctness of modular programming.* Ph. D. thesis, CST-42-87, Department of Computer Science, University of Edinburgh, 1987. 403, 407, 409

10. A. Tarlecki, M. Wirsing: Continuous abstract data types. *Fundamenta Informaticae* 9(1986), 95 – 126. 402

11. J. Tiuryn: Fixed-points and algebras with infinitely long expressions. Part I. Regular algebras. *Fundamenta Informaticae* 2(1978), 102 – 128. 402

12. J. Tiuryn: Fixed-points and algebras with infinitely long expressions. Part II. Muclones of regular algebras. *Fundamenta Informaticae* 2(1979), 317 – 336. 402

Using Consensus Methods for Solving Conflicts of Data in Distributed Systems

Ngoc Thanh Nguyen

Department of Information Systems, Wrocław University of Technology,
Wyb. St. Wyspianskiego 27, 50–370 Wrocław, Poland
thanh@zsi.pwr.wroc.pl

Abstract. By a data conflict in distributed systems we understand a situation (or a state of the system) in which the system sites generate and store different versions of data which refer to the same matter (problem solution, event scenario etc.). Thus in purpose to solve this problem the management system should determine one proper version for the data. The final data version is called a consensus of given versions. In this paper for given conflict situation we propose to solve a consensus problem by determining a consensus function. We present a consensus model, the postulates for consensus choice functions, their analysis and some numerical example.

1 Introduction

Distributed systems consist of autonomous sites and the autonomous feature is the resource of such kind of conflicts that sometimes the information generated by the sites on the same matter is inconsistent. This kind of situations may take place when the system sites realize a common task or solve a common problem.

As the example let us consider a distributed system whose sites' tasks are based on monitoring meteorological situations in their regions, and forecasting, for example, of the speed of wind next day. If the regions occupied by these sites overlap then it is possible that they can generate different (or even contradictory) forecasts for the common towns. Of course at each site these data are consistent from the point of view of database integrity constraints. However, when it is needed to make a forecast for the whole of the country, the management system must create a view of fragments generated by the sites, and in the view there may exist semantic inconsistency of the data.

Generally, it sometimes happens that for the same subject (for example event, fact etc.) the system sites can store different data (for example timestamp, place of occurrence etc.) in their fragments. When a view of these fragments is created we may have two kinds of inconsistency. The first one is related to data integrity because if in the fragments the identifier of an event or a fact is a value of key attribute then in the view to the same key value more than one value of timestamp or occurrence place attribute may correspond. The second kind of inconsistency refers to semantics of data, for the same event or the same

V. Hlaváč, K. G. Jeffery, and J. Wiedermann (Eds.): SOFSEM 2000, LNCS 1963, pp. 411–419, 2000.

fact there may exist more than one timestamp or occurrence place. Therefore the proper timestamp of the event or the occurrence place of the fact is unknown. The reason of this phenomenon is not a mistake of the user who inserts the data to the system, but different results of inference processes on the basis of observations and experimentation, which are made by the system sites, but refer to the same object.

In this paper we propose a tool for resolving semantic conflicts [9], which refer to consistency of data semantics in distributed database systems [3,13]. The tool proposed here consists of consensus methods for data analysis. The version of data, which is a consensus of given versions, should be the most credible one. Generally, consensus of given versions of data (some of which may be contradictory with each other) should be chosen only if these versions refer to the same subject and it is not possible to re-create the proper version on the basis of certain and exact information. Consensus methods, firstly used in social and sociological sciences, are a very good tool for standardising and working out an agreement in solving conflicts. These methods are particularly useful for these systems in which the information uncertainty is assumed but the decision making process is required. Our intention is to present in this work a formal and general model of consensus choice. We define postulates for consensus and present their analysis. This analysis shows how to choose the consensus satisfying fixed properties. A numerical example is also given.

2   Related Works

Consensus theory has arisen in social sciences and has the root in choice theory. A choice from a finite set A of alternatives is based on the choice of some its subset. In the consensus-based researches, however, it is assumed that the chosen alternatives do not have to be included in the set presented for choice. On the beginning of this research the authors have dealt only with simple structures of the set A (named macrostructure), such as linear or partial order. Later with the development of computing techniques the structure of each alternative (named microstructure) have also been investigated. Most often the authors assume that all the alternatives have the same microstructure. On the basis of the microstructure one can determine a macrostructure of the set A. Among others, following microstructures have been investigated: linear orders [1], ordered set partitions [4], non-ordered set partitions [6], n-trees [6]. The following macrostructures have been considered: linear orders and distance (or similarity) functions. Consensus of the set A is most often determined on the basis of its macrostructure by some optimality rules. If the macrostructure is a distance (or similarity) function then the Kemeny's median [1] is very often used to choose the consensus. According to Kemeny's rule the consensus should be nearest to the elements of the set A.

In the field of distributed systems, it seems that consensus methods are very efficient tools for resolving inconsistency of replicated data [5] or for solving the conflicts among experts [11], and agents [7,10]. For fault tolerance many works have used consensus methods for solving this kind of problems. Among others a consensus problem was formulated and solved for asynchronous systems where processors can crash and recover [8]. In [14] the author propose a protocol, which enable tolerance faulty of links by determining consensus of different possibilities of failure. Solving consensus problem in a mobile environment is investigated in [2].

3   Structure of Consensus

3.1   Basic Notions

We assume that some real world is investigated by sites of a distributed system. This real world is represented by a set of objects that may be classified into more than one class (for example, class of cars, class of persons, etc.). The subject of consideration of the distributed system sites is a set of features (relations), which can be possessed by the real world objects.

Thus by a structure of *consensus* we call a relation system

$$Consensus\_Str = (\boldsymbol{X}, \boldsymbol{F}, \boldsymbol{P})$$

where

- $\boldsymbol{X}$ is finite set of carriers, $\boldsymbol{X} = \{X_1, X_2, \dots\}$,
- $\boldsymbol{F}$ is finite set of functions, $\boldsymbol{F} = \{f_1, f_2, \dots\}$, each of them is a function from the Cartesian product of some carriers to a carrier,
- $\boldsymbol{P}$ is finite collection of sets of relations on carriers, $\boldsymbol{P} = \{P_1, P_2, \dots\}$, where $P_i = \{P_i^+, P_i^\pm, P_i^-\}$ and $P_i^+, P_i^\pm, P_i^-$ are relations on carriers from $\boldsymbol{X}$.

The idea of this formalism is relied on including all the information about situations which require consensus choice and all circumstances needed for this process. Following example should give more explanations of above notions.

Example 1. Let us consider a distributed meteorological system where the sites are meteorological stations located in different regions of a country. Each site has to make the forecasting of weather for its towns for next day. Assume that the weather forecast refers to the degree and occurrence time of such phenomena as rain, sunshine, temperature, wind etc. We define above notions as follows (the names of carriers are also used as attribute names):

$$\boldsymbol{X} = \{\, Town, Site, Degree, Time, Temp, Wind\_Speed\}$$

where $Town = \{t_1, t_2, t_3, t_4\}$, $Site = \{s_1, s_2, s_3\}$, $Degree = [0, 1]$, $Time$ — set of time intervals represented by time chronons' identifiers (e. g. [2000-06-15:05a.m.– 2000-06-15:11a.m.] or [5a.m.–11a.m.] if the day is known), $Temp$ — set of intervals of integer numbers representing Celsius degrees, for example $[3°C–6°C]$ or $[(-10°C)-(-1°C)]$, $Wind\_Speed$ — set of integers representing the speed of wind measured in m/s;

$$F = \{ Credibility \}$$

where $Credibility: Site \rightarrow Degree$ is a function which assigns to each site a degree of credibility, because for example in dependence from the modernity of devices the credibility degrees of sites may differ from each other;

$$P = \{ Rain, Sun, Temperature, Wind \}$$

where

$$Rain = \{ Rain^+, Rain^- \} \quad Temperature = \{ Temperature^+, Temperature^- \}$$
$$Sun = \{ Sun^+, Sun^- \} \quad\quad\quad Wind = \{ Wind^+ \}$$

and

$$Rain^+, Rain^-, Sun^+, Sun^- \subseteq Site \times Town \times Time$$
$$Temperature^+, Temperature^- \subseteq Site \times Town \times Temp$$
$$Wind^+ \subseteq Site \times Town \times Wind\_Speed.$$

In this example the relations Sun are presented as follows:

Relation Sun^+

Site	Town	Time
s_1	t_1	8a.m. $-$ 10a.m.
s_1	t_2	7a.m. $-$ 10a.m.
s_1	t_3	9p.m. $-$ 4p.m.
s_2	t_2	5a.m. $-$ 8a.m.
s_2	t_3	8a.m. $-$ 11a.m.
s_2	t_4	7a.m. $-$ 11a.m.
s_3	t_2	8a.m. $-$ 6p.m.

Relation Sun^-

Site	Town	Time
s_1	t_1	7p.m. $-$ 6a.m.
s_1	t_2	6p.m. $-$ 5a.m.
s_1	t_3	5p.m. $-$ 9a.m.
s_2	t_2	4p.m. $-$ 5a.m.
s_2	t_3	7p.m. $-$ 7a.m.
s_2	t_4	8p.m. $-$ 6a.m.
s_3	t_2	8p.m. $-$ 7a.m.

We interpret a tuple (for example $\langle s_1, t_1, [8a.m. - 10a.m.] \rangle$) of relation Sun^+ as follows: according to forecasting of site s_1 in town t_1 it will be sunny during 8a.m.and 10a.m.. Tuple $\langle s_1, t_1, [7p.m. - 6a.m.] \rangle$ of relation Sun^- is interpreted as follows: according to forecasting of site s_1 in town t_1 it will not be sunny during 7p.m.and 6a.m.. It means that in the rest of next day time (viz. from 10a.m.to 7p.m.and from 6a.m.to 8a.m.), site s_1 does not have any grounds to state if it will be sunny in town t_1 or not. Thus the intervals $[10a.m. - 7p.m.]$ and $[6a.m. - 8a.m.]$ can be treated as the uncertainty of site s_1 referring to town t_1.

We give also an example of relations *Temperature*:

Relation *Temperature*$^+$

Site	Town	Temp
s_1	t_1	$12°C-15°C$
s_1	t_2	$16°C-20°C$
s_1	t_3	$10°C-18°C$
s_2	t_2	$7°C-14°C$
s_2	t_3	$11°C-16°C$
s_2	t_4	$11°C-17°C$
s_3	t_2	$14°C-18°C$

Relation *Temperature*$^-$

Site	Town	Temp

We can notice that in relations *Temperature* there is not any uncertainty because for example, for town t_1 site s_1 states that the temperature will be from $12°C$ to $15°C$ (tuple $\langle s_1, t_1, [12°C-15°C]\rangle$), and will not be out side of this interval (tuple $\langle s_1, t_1, (< 12°C) \vee (> 15°C)\rangle$).

3.2   Basis of Consensus

As the foundation of consensus choice we take the set P of relations on the carriers of the relation system. We firstly define a *consensus resource* R as follows:

$$R = \bigcup_{P \in P} R(P)$$

where

$$R(P) = P \cup \{P^{\pm}\} \quad \text{for} \quad P^{\pm} = Dom(P) \setminus \bigcup_{p \in P} p$$

where $Dom(P)$ is the entire Cartesian product of the carriers on which relations P^+ and P^- are defined. In the forecasting system presented above we have, for example, $P = Sun = \{Sun^+, Sun^-\}$, $R(Sun) = \{Sun^+, Sun^-, Sun^{\pm}\}$, $Dom(Sun) = Site \times Town \times Time$ and $Sun^{\pm} = Dom(Sun) \setminus (Sun^+ \cup Sun^-)$.

Next we define a *consensus domain* as a pair of two elements: the first is a set of relations and the second is a relationships between attributes, for example $\langle \{Sun^+, Sun^{\pm}, Sun^-\}, Town \rightarrow Time \rangle$, or $\langle \{Wind^+\}, Town \rightarrow Wind\_Speed \rangle$.

The first component (a subset of consensus resource) of above tuples is called a *consensus basis*, and the second component is called a *consensus subject*. We interpret these components as follows: the consensus basis consists of the part of consensus resource, which is taken into account in consensus choice. It means that sometimes we can take only, for example, relation Sun^+, instead of relations Sun^+, $Sun^{\pm}$ and Sun^-, for consensus choice. Consensus subject, on the other hand, includes requirements, for what is chosen the consensus. For example, subject $Town \rightarrow Time$ in consensus basis $\langle \{Sun^+, Sun^{\pm}, Sun^-\}, Town \rightarrow Time \rangle$ serves to answer such questions as "What is the time of sunshine in town t_2?". It means that in the consensus, if chosen, for a given value of attribute $Town$ there should be only one value for attribute $Time$. This condition is not fulfilled in the relations belonging to the consensus basis. Thus a consensus resource should include all information needed for different choices of consensus, a consensus domain presents a concrete basis from which the consensus should be chosen and the subject to which the consensus refers.

The interpretation of elements of relations P^+ and P^- is given above. Notice that set $P^\pm$ is also a relation on the same carriers as relations P^+ and P^-, and its elements should be interpreted as the uncertainty of system sites. For example, if tuple $\langle s_1, r_1, [0\text{a.m.} - 3\text{a.m.}]\rangle$ belongs to relation $Sun^\pm$ then it means that the site s_1 has no grounds to state if it will be sunny in town t_1 during 0a.m. and 3a.m. or not. The concept of interpretation of relations P^+, $P^\pm$ and P^- is used here in similar way as in agent theory. Notice also that sets P^+, $P^\pm$ and P^- are disjoint from each other, and $P^+ \cup P^\pm \cup P^- = Dom(P)$, thus set $\{P^+, P^\pm, P^-\}$ is a partition of $Dom(P)$.

Relation P^+ is called the positive component of the consensus basis, P^- – negative component and $P^\pm$ – uncertain component. It seems that in practical tasks of consensus choice the most important is positive component, other components (negative and uncertain) do not always have to occur. In the example above, for the subject of wind only positive component is given.

4   Consensus Definition

Let A and B are attribute names, by $Dom(P)_{\{A,B\}}$ we denote the set of all tuples belonging to $Dom(P)$ but restricted to these attributes. The sets of values of these attributes are denoted adequately by V_A and V_B. Let there are given two consensus bases P and P' whose relations are defined on the same carriers, then we define

$$P \cup P' = \{P^+ \cup P'^+, P^\pm \cup P'^\pm, P^- \cup P'^-\}.$$

Definition 1. Let $P = \{P^+, P^\pm, P^-\}$, by a *consensus of domain* $\langle P, A \to B\rangle$ we call a relation $C(P) \subseteq Dom(P)_{\{A,B\}}$ which satisfies the following conditions:

a) for $r, r' \in C(P)$ if $r_A = r'_A$ then $r_B = r'_B$,
b) one or more of the following postulates are satisfied:

$$(\forall a \in V_A)(\exists c \in C(P))\left[(c_A = a) \Longrightarrow \left(\bigcap_{r \in P^+, r_A = a} r_B \subseteq c_B\right)\right], \quad \text{(P1)}$$

$$(\forall a \in V_A)(\exists c \in C(P))\left[(c_A = a) \Longrightarrow \left(\bigcap_{r \in P^-, r_A = a} r_B \not\subseteq c_B\right)\right], \quad \text{(P2)}$$

$$(\forall a \in V_A)(\exists c \in C(P))\left[(c_A = a) \Longrightarrow \left(\bigcap_{r \in P^\pm, r_A = a} r_B \not\subseteq c_B\right)\right], \quad \text{(P3)}$$

$$(\forall a \in V_A)(\exists c \in C(P)) \left[(c_A = a) \Longrightarrow \left(c_B \subseteq \bigcup_{r \in P^+, r_A = a} r_B \right) \right], \qquad \text{(P4)}$$

$$(\forall a \in V_A \; \forall c \in C(P) \; \forall c' \in C(P'))$$
$$[(c_A = c'_A = a) \wedge (c_B \cap c'_B \neq \emptyset) \Longrightarrow \exists c'' \in C(P \cup P')(c''_B = c_B \cap c'_B)], \qquad \text{(P5)}$$

$$(\forall a \in V_A \; \forall b \in V_B)[(\forall r \in C(P)(r_A = a \Longrightarrow b \not\subset r_B)) \Longrightarrow$$
$$\Longrightarrow (\exists P' \; \exists r' \in C(P \cup P'))(r'_A = a \; \wedge \; b \subset r'_B)]. \qquad \text{(P6)}$$

The above postulates require some commentary. The first postulate states that if for some value a of attribute A all the votes in their positive components of consensus basis qualify among others the same value b of attribute B, then this qualification should have also place in the consensus. Postulates P2 and P3 treat in the similar way the negative and uncertain components of consensus basis. According to postulate P4 if any of votes does not qualify a value b of attribute B to a value a of attribute A, then there does not exist any such tuple in the consensus. Postulate P5 requires the consensus to be consistent, that is, if for two bases their consensuses have non-empty common part then this part should be the consensus of the sum of these bases. At last, postulate P6 states that for each tuple belonging to $Dom(P)_{\{A,B\}}$ there should exist a basis whose consensus contains this tuple.

Each of these postulates treated as a characteristic property of consensus choice functions would specify in space C of all consensus choice functions for given consensus domain a region denoted as P_1, P_2, ... and $P6$ respectively. Notice that all regions P_1, P_2, ... and $P6$ are independent, it means $P_i \not\subset P_j$ for all $i, j = 1, \ldots, 6$ and $i \neq j$. Below we present some properties of these postulates.

Theorem 1.
$$P_1 \cap P_2 \cap \ldots P6 \neq \emptyset$$

Theorem 1 states very important property of consensus postulates, namely there should exist at least one consensus function which satisfies all these postulates.

Theorem 2. *If there is defined a metric δ between tuples of $Dom(P)_{\{B\}}$, then for given domain $\langle \{P^+, P^\pm, P^-\}, A \to B \rangle$ the following consensus function*

$$C(P) = \left\{ c \in Dom(P) : \right.$$

$$(\forall a \in V_A) \left[(c_A = a) \Longrightarrow \left(\sum_{x \in P^+} \delta(c_B, x) = \min_{y \in Dom(P)} \sum_{x \in P^+} \delta(y, x) \right) \right] \right\}$$

satisfies dependency $C \in (P_1 \cap P_2 \cap \ldots P6)$.

The second theorem shows very practical property of the consensus postulates, because it shows how to determine a median function which satisfies all these postulates. The proofs of Theorems 1 and 2 are given in report [12].

In above example for consensus domain ($\{$ *Temperature*$^+$, *Temperature*$^-\}$, *Town* $\rightarrow$ *Temp*) the metric δ between tuples $r, r' \in Dom($*Temperature*$)_{\{Temp\}}$ is defined as follows:

$$\delta(r, r') = \delta(r_{Temp}, r'_{Temp}) = |r_{Temp}{}^* - r'_{Temp}{}^*| + |r_{Temp_*} - r'_{Temp_*}|$$

for temperature intervals $[r_{Temp_*}, r_{Temp}{}^*]$ and $[r'_{Temp_*}, r'_{Temp}{}^*]$. Next we use the following algorithm for determining consensus of temperature intervals as the value of the median function defined in Theorem 2:

Given: Relation *Temperature*$^+$ consisting of n temperature intervals $tp_j = [tp_{j_*}, tp_j{}^*]$ for $i = 1, 2, \ldots, n$.

Result: Consensus $tp = [tp_*, tp^*]$ such that

$$\sum_{i=1}^{n} \delta(tp, tp_i) = \min_{tp' \in T} \sum_{i=1}^{n} \delta(tp', tp_i)$$

where T is the set of all temperature intervals.

Procedure: if $n = 1$ then
         $tp := tp_1$; **goto** END;
     else
         {Creating sets with repetitions}
         $X_1 := (tp_{i_*} | i = 1, 2, \ldots, n)$; {of lower values}
         $X_2 := (tp_i{}^* | i = 1, 2, \ldots, n)$; {of upper values}
     end if
     sort sets X_1 and X_2 in increasing order;
     $k := \lfloor (n + 1)/2 \rfloor$; $k' := \lfloor n/2 \rfloor + 1$; { where $\lfloor x \rfloor$ is the greatest integer not greater than x}
     for x in X_1 **do** set integer tp_* such that $x_{k'_*} \geq tp_* \geq x_{k_*}$;
     for x in X_2 **do** set integer tp^* such that $x_{k'}{}^* \geq tp^* \geq x_k{}^*$ and $tp^* \geq tp_*$;
     $tp := [tp_*, tp^*]$
     END.

Using above algorithm to the relation *Temperature*$^+$ given in the example (section 3.2) we should have the following consensus $C($*Temperature*$)$:

Consensus $C($*Temperature*$)$

Town	Temp
t_1	12°C – 15°C
t_2	14°C – 18°C
t_3	10°C – 16°C
t_4	11°C – 17°C

Notice that there does not exist a universal algorithm for all data structures, for each of them a specific algorithm should be worked out.

5   Conclusion

The results of the postulates' analysis show that it is possible to determine a consensus for given conflict situation if the structure of data versions is known. Future works should be concentrated on investigation when a consensus is good enough for a given conflict. As shown above, Theorem 2 enables to calculate a consensus for given conflict situation, but it is not known if this consensus is sensible or not. If it is possible, there should be defined a measure which should inform about the susceptibility to consensus for given situation.

References

1. K. J. Arrow: Social Choice and Individual Values. Wiley New York (1963). 412
2. N. Badache, M. Hurfin, R. Madeco: Solving the Consensus Problem in a Mobile Environment. In: Proceedings of IEEE International Performance, Computing and Communications Conference. IEEE Piscataway NJ (1999) 29–35. 413
3. G. Coulouris, J. Dollimore, T. Kindberg: Distributed Systems, Concepts and Design. Addison Wesley (1996). 412
4. C. Daniłowicz, N. T. Nguyen: Consensus-Based Partition in the Space of Ordered Partitions. Pattern Recognition 21 (1988) 269–273. 412
5. C. Daniłowicz, N. T. Nguyen: Consensus-Based Methods for Restoring Consistency of Replicated Data. In: M. Kłopotek et. al. (eds.): Advances in Soft Computing. Physica-Verlag Heidelberg New York (2000) 325–336. 412
6. W. H. E. Day: Consensus Methods as Tools for Data Analysis. In: H. H. Bock (ed.): Classification and Related Methods for Data Analysis. North-Holland (1988) 312–324. 412
7. E. Ephrati, J. S Rosenschein: Deriving Consensus in Multiagent Systems. Artificial Intelligence 87 (1998) 21–74. 412
8. M. Hurfin, A. Mostefaoui, M. Raynal: Consensus in Asynchronous Systems where Processes Can Crash and Recover. In: Proceedings of Seventeenth IEEE Symposium on Reliable Distributed Systems. IEEE Comput. Soc. Los Alamitos CA (1998). 413
9. M. Kamel: Identifying, Classifying, and Resolving Semantic Conflicts in Distributed Heterogeneous Databases. Journal of Database Management 6 (1994) 20–32. 412
10. N. T. Nguyen: A Computer-Based Multiagent System for Building and Updating Models of Dynamic Populations Located in Distributed Environments, in: E. Kącki (ed.): Proceeding of 5th ICCM. Lodz University of Technology Press (1999) 133–138. 412
11. N. T. Nguyen: Using Consensus Methods for Determining the Representation of Expert Information in Distributed Systems. To appear in: S. Cerri (ed.): Proceedings of 9th International Conference on Artificial Intelligence AIMSA'2000, Lecture Notes on Artificial Intelligence (2000), Springer-Verlag. 412
12. N. T. Nguyen: Consensus Methods for Resolving Conflict Situations in Distributed Information Systems. Reports of Department of Information Systems, series: SPR, No. 29, Wrocław University of Technology (2000). 418
13. T. M. Ozsu: Principles of Distributed Database Systems. Prentice-Hall (1991). 412
14. K. Q. Yan, S. C. Wang, Y. H. Chin: Consensus under Unreliable Transmission. Information Processing Letter 69 (1999), 243–248. 413

Optimisation of Artificial Neural Network Topology Applied in the Prosody Control in Text-to-Speech Synthesis

Václav Šebesta[1*] and Jana Tučková[2**]

[1] Institute of Computer Science, Academy of Sciences of the Czech Republic,
and
Faculty of Transportation, Czech Technical University
vasek@uivt.cas.cz

[2] Faculty of Electrical Engineering, Czech Technical University,
and
Institute of Radioengineering and Electronics,
Academy of Sciences of the Czech Republic
tuckova@feld.cvut.cz

Abstract. Multilayer artificial neural networks (ANN) are often used for the solution of classification problems or for the time series forecasting. An appropriate number of learning and testing patterns must be available for the ANN training. Each training pattern is composed of n input parameters and m output parameters. Number m is usually given by the problem formulation, but the number n may be often selected from a greater set of input parameters. An optimal selection of input parameters is a very important task especially in a situation when the number of usable input parameters is great and the analytical relations between the input and output parameters are not known. The number of neurons in all ANN layers must be generally kept as small as possible because of the optimal generalisation ability.

In this paper we present a possible way for the selection of significant input parameters (the so called "markers"), which are the most important ones from the point of view of influence on the output parameters. These parameters are later used for the training of ANN. A statistical approach is usually used for this reason [5]. After some experience in the ANN application we recognised that the approach based on mathematical logic, i. e. the GUHA method (General Unary Hypotheses Automaton) is also suitable for the determination of markers.

Besides the minimisation of the number of elements in the input layer of ANN, also the number of neurons in hidden layers must be optimised. For this reason standard methods of pruning can be used, described e. g. in [1]. We have used this method in the following applications:

- Optimisation of the intervals between the major overhaul of plane engines by the analysis of tribodiagnostic data. Only selected types of chemical pollution in oil can be taken into account.

---

* Supported by GA AS CR, grant No. A2030801
** Supported by GA CR, grant No. 102/96/K087 and COST 258

V. Hlaváč, K. G. Jeffery, and J. Wiedermann (Eds.): SOFSEM 2000, LNCS 1963, pp. 420–430, 2000.

- Prediction of bleeding of patients with chronic lymphoblastic leukemia. Only a part of parameters about the patient is important from this point of view (see [2]).
- Optimisation of the quality and reliability prediction of artificial resin production in chemical factory. Only a part of the production parameters (times of production phases, temperatures, percentage of components etc.) have straight influence on the product.
- Optimisation of the prosody control in the text-to-speech synthesis. This application is described in the paper.

1 Introduction

A speech signal synthesis is a case of difficult and imperfect processing. Many problems caused by the complexity of speech signals are based on technical, human, physiological, phonological and phonetic properties. We try to minimise the difference between the speech produced by a synthesiser, which is usually more monotonous, and the natural human speech. A speech synthesiser needs three basic parameters for prosody control: fundamental frequency, duration of speech units and their intensity. They are called suprasegmental characteristics and they influence especially on large speech segments (stress units — from word to sentence). A lot of complicated correlation exist among them. It is not possible to determine exact speech properties, because of the speech and language variability. Its processing is usually based on methods of mathematical statistic and logic. ANN and the GUHA method are important parts of available methodology.

The prosodic parameters depend on the speaker's physiology and his or her mental state, on the uttered speech segments and on the universal phonetic properties. If the prosody control part of the synthesiser is based on ANN and this ANN is trained by the natural speech of the speaker, the system will imitate him.

2 Text-to-Speech (TTS) System

The background of our TTS system is in the fundamentals of phonetics, in the linguistic research of the spoken Czech language, in the digital signal processing [13] and in the research of neural network applications. In a conventional synthesiser the prosodic parameters correspond to the grammatical rules of the national language. The Czech system is based upon the concatenation of the elementary speech units — diphones and phonemes of natural speech. Rule-based algorithm for a prosody modelling is based on the stress unit segmentation. Stress unit can be either one or several words. Four different position of stress units can be recognised in Czech language. They are initial (I), medial (M), position before comma (F) and position before full stop, colon, semicolon, question or exclamation mark (FF). Rule-based algorithm use several tens of "melodems", i.e. the typical set of supplements of F_0 for each phoneme or diphone in the stress unit. These supplements can be maximally 5 % in the case I, M and F and 15 % in the case of FF.

The database of the Czech transcribed sounds consists of 5 vowels (a e i o u), 2 diphtongs (au, ou) and 29 consonants (b, c, č, dz, dž, d, ď, f, g, h, ch, j, k, l, m, n, ň, p, r, ř, s, š, t, ť, v, z, ž, glottal plosive, pause). The entire system contains only 441 speech units (diphones) extracted from several hundreds Czech pronounced words. The sampling frequency is 8 kHz.

Diphones are the basic elements in which a speech unit is defined as an interval from the middle of the first speech sound to the middle of the next one. Their parametric description also enables an easy implementation of the prosodic rules. The system runs in real time and most frequently is used as a reading machine for blind people.

The simplified schema of the text-to-speech system is shown in Fig. 1. The speech output from the database represented by frequency F_{FUN} is really monotonous and sounds synthetically. Up to now only the fundamental frequency has been taken into account in the prosody control unit driven by ANN (see [3]). In this paper also the influence of the duration of the speech units is involved. The resulting value of fundamental frequency F_0 is dependent on values F_{FUN}, on the increments of the models for actual diphones and on the increment of fundamental frequency F_{PROS}. The optimal value of this parameter is determined in the unit "prosody control" where either a classical rule-based model or the ANN model designed in the following way can be used.

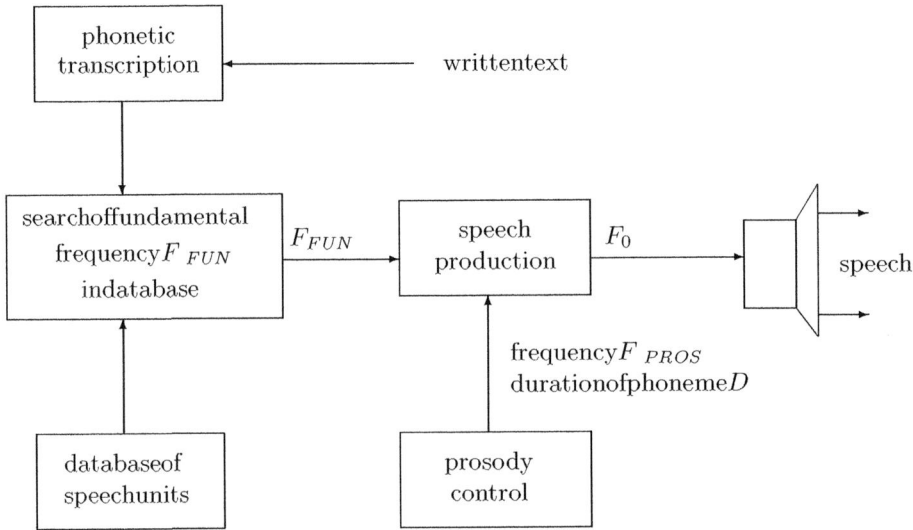

Fig. 1. Simplified scheme of Text-to-Speech system

Experts in phonetics have recommended the basic input parameters as the most important for the prosody control in the Czech language. They are described in Tab. 1. The number and relevancy of the input parameters for prosody control is one of the most discussed problems among the linguistic experts. Their opinion of the relevance of the input parameters are very miscellaneous.

Table 1. Input parameters for ANN which characterise the Czech language

code	characterization of parameters	mode
P_1	End of vowel	Binary
P_2	Beginning of the stress unit	Binary
P_3	Word stress position	Binary
P_4	Intonation pattern type	5 categories
P_5	Number of syllables in a stress unit	integer 0–6
P_6	Number of stress units in the sentence	integer 0–6
P_7	Type of punctual mark in sentence	integer 1–6
P_8	Type of sentence	5 categories
P_9	Type of phoneme on the first left place from the focus place	6 categories[1]
P_{10}	Type of phoneme on the focus place	6 categories[1]
P_{11}	Type of phoneme on the first right place from the focus place	6 categories[1]
P_{12}	Type of phoneme on the second right place from the focus place	6 categories[1]
P_{13}	Type of phoneme on the first left place from the focus place	6 categories[2]
P_{14}	Type of phoneme on the focus place	6 categories[2]
P_{15}	Type of phoneme on the first right place from the focus place	6 categories[2]
P_{16}	Type of phoneme on the second right place from the focus place	6 categories[2]
P_{17}	Relative duration of the phoneme[3][ms]	Real
P_{18}	Number of segments in the phoneme[4]	Real
P_{19}	Type of accent	5 categories
P_{20}	Position of the phoneme in the syllable	3 categories
P_{21}	Word boundaries	3 categories
P_{22}	Phrase boundaries	3 categories
P_{23}	Number of segments in the syllable[5]	Real

[1] fricative, nasal, plosive, semiplosive, vowel, diphtong
[2] vowel, diphtong, sonar consonant, voiced consonant, unvoiced consonant, pause
[3] duration of phoneme divided by the number of syllables in the stress unit
[4] duration of phoneme divided by 12 ms
[5] duration of syllable divided by 12 ms

The first small corpus of natural speech data for this research has been created by a careful choice of available sentences. The database consists only of 27 sentences at present, final version will contain several hundreds sentences.

All types of sentences must be included into the corpus as uniformly as possible. The sentences are read by a professional male TV-speaker. Twenty sentences with 437 diphones create the training set and the other 7 sentences with 136 diphones have been used as a testing set. The success of the prosody control is surely dependent on the labelling of the natural speech signal in the database. By labelling we understand the determination of all speech units, i. e. the decision where diphones or phonemes begin and end. The speech signal was labelled by hand in our case, but an automatic approach is also under construction.

3   Determination of Prosody Parameters by Neural Network

The ANN with one hidden layer was applied for the determination of the increment of fundamental frequency F_{PROS} and speech unit duration. The backpropagation training algorithm with a moment and adaptive learning rate has been used. The sigmoidal activation function in the hidden layer and the linear function in the output layer seem to be optimal, because results express real values of the fundamental frequency increment in Hz and the duration in ms. As it is generally known that a simpler ANN usually has a better generalisation ability, the optimisation of ANN topology has been performed in several steps. We have used the "data mining" procedure based on the GUHA method described in [6, 4] for markers determination.

The GUHA method (General Unary Hypotheses Automaton) can be used for the determination of relations in experimental data. The processed data form a rectangular matrix where the rows correspond to different objects (in our case diphones) and the columns correspond to the different input or output parameters investigated (parameters from P_1 to P_{23} , frequency F_{PROS}. and duration of diphones). The type of data can be either binary (1,0) or categorical or real numbers. In the case of real values of data a corresponding interval of the parameter must be divided into several subintervals and the value of a corresponding attribute is equal to one in only one relevant subinterval. The value is equal to zero in all other subintervals. Attributes are split into antecedents (e. g. input parameters) and succedents (e. g. output parameters). The program generates and evaluates the hypotheses of an association of the form $A \rightarrow S$, where A is an elementary conjunction of antecedents, S is an elementary conjunction of succedents and $\rightarrow$ is a quantifier of implication. The implication quantifier estimates, in a sense, the conditional probability $P(S \mid A)$. The user must specify the number of elements in antecedent and succedent conjunctions and the program in sequence generates all possible hypotheses about the relation between antecedent and succedent. According to the number of the accepted hypotheses we can determine the importance of individual input parameters. Several parameters of the GUHA procedure, e. g. a_{min} and α_{PROS} can determine the "level of hypothesis" (e. g. weak, strong) and also the number of the hypotheses accepted. Also different types of quantifiers can be combined to obtain better knowledge about the relation in data. For more details see [6] or [4].

We have tried at first to find such input parameters that are not generally used in the hypotheses about relations between input and outputs. All 23 input parameters were declared as antecedents, and the fundamental frequency F_{PROS}, and the duration were taken as a succedent. The maximal number of elements in the antecedents conjunction was 3. The total number of verified hypotheses was 1615. The numbers of verified hypotheses are shown in Tab. 2. It can be seen that parameters P_2, P_3, P_9 and P_{13} have a minimal influence on the output parameter.

Table 2. Numbers of hypotheses that the resulting values F_{PROS} and duration depend on the input parameters P_i

Parameter	P_1	P_2	P_3	P_4	P_5	P_6	P_7	P_8
Number of hypotheses about F_{PROS}	29	0	3	168	168	169	39	3
Number of hypotheses about duration	89	9	45	224	260	164	158	50
Total number of hypotheses	92	9	45	293	327	231	178	51
Parameter	P_9	P_{10}	P_{11}	P_{12}	P_{13}	P_{14}	P_{15}	P_{16}
Number of hypotheses about F_{PROS}	44	76	219	242	1	194	172	176
Number of hypotheses about duration	120	169	237	209	52	233	200	192
Total number of hypotheses	120	196	331	315	52	311	265	254
Parameter	P_{17}	P_{18}	P_{19}	P_{20}	P_{21}	P_{22}	P_{23}	total
Number of hypotheses about F_{PROS}	208	344	242	209	216	333	130	500
Number of hypotheses about duration	353	1002	225	252	285	764	684	1443
Total number of hypotheses	447	1100	334	333	371	872	688	1615

The verification (see below) of this elimination of four input parameters have been successful. Therefore we tried to determine some more input parameters which could be deleted. Besides the parameters that have only a limited influence on the output parameters, also some input parameters having serious mutual correlation can be omitted. Their influences on the output parameter can be very similar. Such parameters were looked for in the following step. In this case we took 19 input parameters as antecedents and the same 19 parameters as succedents. The maximal numbers of elements in antecedent and succedent conjunctions were 2.

The total number of verified hypotheses was 3182. The resulting numbers of hypotheses are shown in Tab. 3. The greatest values show the most important mutual correlation between parameters P_{10} and P_{14}, P_{11} and P_{15} and between P_{12} and P_{16}. We decided to omit P_{10}, P_{11} and P_{12} because of a higher total number of hypotheses. This omission caused a further improvement of the practical results proved by listening to synthetic speech. After each reduction of the input parameters a new ANN was trained and our mathematical approach was verified by listening to several training and testing sentences.

Both the steps described were repeated once more. After the next investigation of the relations between the input and output parameters, further reduction of parameters P_1 and P_{13} was proposed and verified by listening. The next proposed reduction from 14 to 13 input parameters (parameter P_{22}) by research of mutual dependencies of the remaining parameters did not give better practical results in the case of all testing sentences. From the mathematical as well as practical points of view the results were better in some sentences but worse in others.

The hidden layer starting from 30 neurons was pruned in a way described in [1] for all variants of input parameters. The resulting numbers of neurons in hidden layer are between 25 and 27.

Table 3. Interesting part of the matrix with the numbers of hypotheses about the mutual dependencies of input parameters P_i

	P_6	P_7	P_9	P_{10}	P_{11}	P_{12}	P_{14}	P_{15}	P_{16}	P_{17}	P_{18}	P_{19}	P_{20}
P_6	...	...	...	...	...	...	...	...	...	...	...	...	...
P_7	...	0											
P_9	...	8	0										
P_{10}	...	44	42	0									
P_{11}	...	45	21	73	0								
P_{12}	...	51	17	54	78	0							
P_{14}	...	43	33	176	56	45	0						
P_{15}	...	42	15	57	210	65	54	0					
P_{16}	...	33	17	44	68	215	46	62	0				
P_{17}	...	31	6	39	29	20	37	24	18	0			
P_{18}	...	23	10	41	39	24	39	32	23	90	0		
P_{19}	...	12	12	23	16	14	17	16	14	10	11	0	
P_{20}	...	...	...	...	...	...	...	...	...	...	...	...	...
Total	424	452	288	716	723	647	645	645	586	411	505	240	386

4 Verification of the Method

After each proposed reduction of the number of input parameters, the multilayer ANN has been proposed and trained by the same set of training patterns as described above with only a reduction of the appropriate input parameters.

Sum square errors after the specified number of iterations (epochs in Matlab) are shown in Table 4. These results show that the optimal number of epochs is approximately 80 or 90. Each epoch has 300 iterations.

The reduction of 23 input parameters to 14 decreases the resulting errors, also in the case of the testing set. It is in accordance with the practical experience in listening to synthetic speech signals. The prosody of these signal sounds is always better than the original prosody.

The last proposed reduction of 14 to 13 parameters decreases the errors in the case of the training set but it does not bring a reasonable benefit in the case of the testing set. It also accords with the real signal, which is for some sentences better but in some cases worse than the previous one. The graphical representation of the learning errors is presented in Fig. 2. The optimal number of the learning epochs can be determined approximately as 80–90 by comparing the values for the training and testing sets.

Table 4. The sum square errors of trained ANN with a different number of input parameters

No. of epochs	Training set		
	23 inputs	14 inputs	13 inputs
1	3.88	6.19	5.80
12	1.27	1.32	1.32
24	1.21	1.13	1.08
48	1.21	1.07	1.08
72	1.14	1.11	1.00
96	1.07	1.02	0.97

No. of epochs	Testing set		
	23 inputs	14 inputs	13 inputs
1	1.06	1.98	1.67
12	0.24	0.36	0.26
24	0.21	0.27	0.22
48	0.24	0.20	0.18
72	0.22	0.24	0.17
96	0.19	0.19	0.17

The original text-to-speech system for PC equipment with the Sound Blaster compatible card for Windows was used for the production of the synthetic speech. The Neural network Toolbox of Matlab, version 4.2 for LINUX and Windows was used for the neural net training.

The relation between the optimal contour of fundamental frequency F_0 (target), frequency determined by a classical method based on the rules from the database (rules), frequency determined by ANN with 23 input parameters (nn-k0), frequency determined by ANN with 14 input parameters (nn-k1) and with

13 input parameters are shown in Fig. 3. for a selected testing sentence, and the same contours for the duration of phonemes are shown in Fig. 4.

It can be seen in both figures that the neural network output is more similar to the target shape of the frequency contour than a rule-based approach. The differences between the contours for 14 and 13 input parameters were negligible for several training and test sentences.

5   Conclusion

The TTS system for the Czech language has been developed in co-operation of the Institute of Phonetics of the Faculty of Arts, Charles University, with the Institute of Radio Engineering and Electronics, Academy of Sciences of the Czech Republic. It is produced by the Cooperative of the Blind (SPEKTRA) in Prague. Our experiments have shown that the ANN approach is better than the standard rule-based system.

Only a mathematical approach to the evaluation, i. e. a simple mean square error between the target and the predicted fundamental frequency contour and duration contour is not the best indicator of the perceived naturalness of speech. It is necessary to judge synthetic sentences by listening. There are some differences between the mathematical results and the listening tests. The physical properties of the acoustic wave, which are perceived as sounds, are transformed several times. First, in the organ of hearing, later at the emergence of neural excitement, and last in the cerebral analysis. Therefore the sounds perceived in listening tests do not correlate completely with the objective properties of the acoustic patterns. The resulting speech has been better in the case of the prosody control by ANN with optimal topology after pruning in comparison with the previous state. Of course, some more improvement of its quality is possible.

In future, we would like to add intensity control too and to increase the number of sentences in database corpus.

References

1. V. Šebesta. Pruning of neural networks by statistical optimization. In *Proc. 6th Schoolon Neural Networks*, pages 209–214. Microcomputer, 1994. 420, 426
2. V. Šebesta and L. Straka. Determination of markers by GUHA method for neural network training. *Neural Network World*, 8(3):255–268, 1998. 421
3. V. Šebesta and J. Tučková. Selection of important input parameters for a text-to-speech synthesis by neural networks. In *Proc. International Joint Conference on Neural Networks IJCNN'99*. Washington, DC, USA, 1999. 422
4. P. Hájek, A. Sochorová, and J. Zvárová. GUHA for personal computers. *Computational Statistics and Data Analysis*, 19:149–153, 1995. 424, 425
5. A. K. Jain, R. P. W. Duin, and J. Mao. Statistical pattern recognition: A review. *IEEE Trans.on PAMI*, 22(1):4–37, 2000. 420
6. P. Hájek, et. al. GUHA method — objectives and tools. *Proc. IXth SOFSEM*. VUT UJEP, Brno, 1982. (in Czech). 424, 425

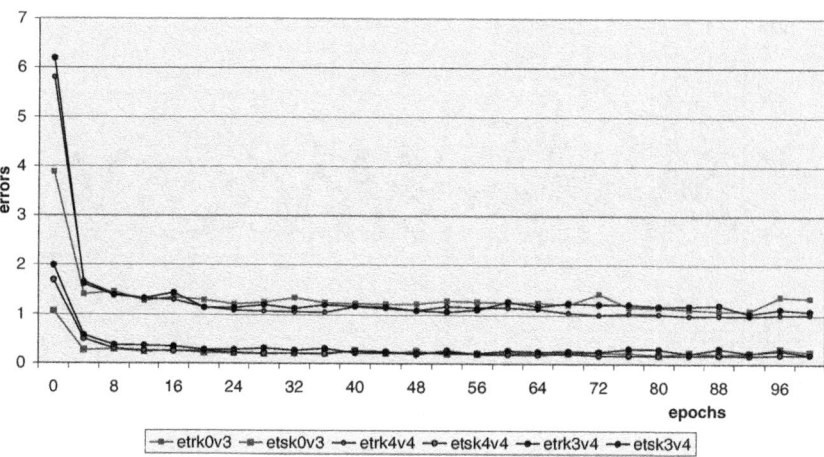

Fig. 2. Sum square errors of trained ANN for training (etrk) and testing (etsk) sets. 0v3 means 23 input parameters, 3v4 means 14 input parameters and 4v4 means 13 input parameters

7. M. P. Reidi. *Controlling Segmental Duration in Speech Synthesis System.* PhD thesis, ETH Zurich, Switzerland.
8. T. J. Sejnowski and Ch. R. Rosenberg. NETtalk: a parallel network that learns to read aloud. Technical Report JHU/EECS-86/01, John Hopkins University.
9. J. Terken. Variation of accent prominence within the phrase: Models and spontaneous speech data. *Computing Prosody,* pages 95–116, 1997.
10. Ch. Traber. *SVOX: The implementation of the Text-to-Speech System for German.* PhD thesis, ETH Zurich, Switzerland, 1995.
11. J. Tučková and P. Horák. Fundamental frequency control in czech text-to-speech synthesis. In *Proc. Third Workshop on ECMS'97.* Toulouse, France, 1997.
12. J. Tučková and R. Vích. Fundamental frequency modelling by neural nets in the czech text-to-speech synthesis. In *Proc. IASTED Int. Conference Signal and ImageProcessing SIP'97,* pages 85–87. New Orleans, USA, 1997.
13. R. Vích. Pitch synchronous linear predictive czech and slovak text-to-speech synthesis. In *Proc. 15th Int. Congress on Acoustics.* Trondheim, Norway, 1995. 421

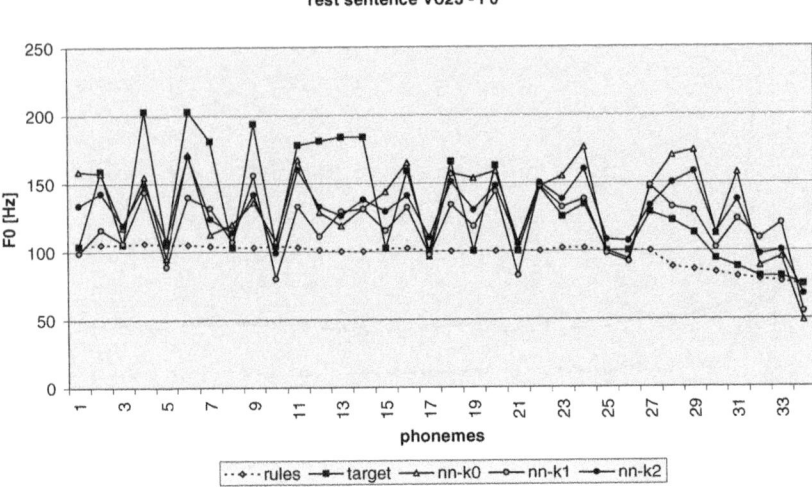

Fig. 3. Frequency contour for selected testing sentence containing 34 phonemes. It is possible to compare target contour, rule-based contour and neural network approach with different numbers of input parameters (nn-k0 23 input parameters, nn-k1 14 input parameters and nn-k2 13 input parameters)

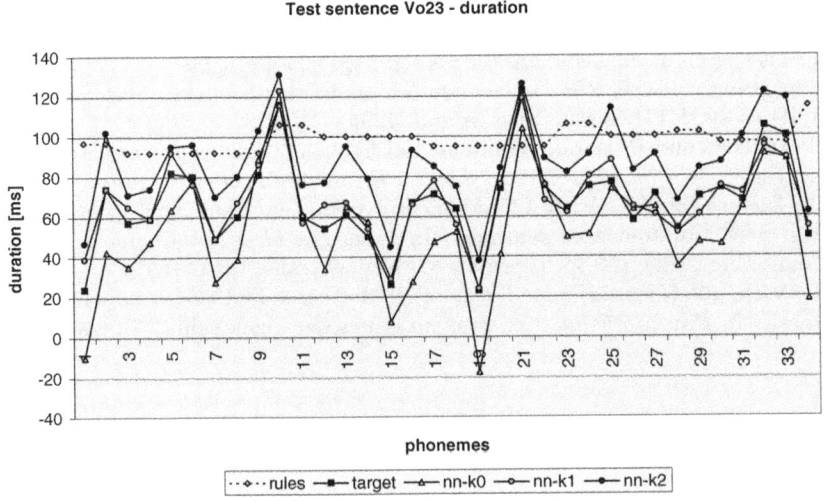

Fig. 4. Duration contour for the same test sentence

Robust Implementation of Finite Automata by Recurrent RBF Networks[*]

Michal Šorel[1] and Jiří Šíma[2]

[1] Institute of Information Theory and Automation
Academy of Sciences of the Czech Republic
Pod vodárenskou věží 4, 182 07 Prague 8, Czech Republic,
michal.sorel@centrum.cz
[2] Institute of Computer Science, Academy of Sciences of the Czech Republic,
Pod vodárenskou věží 2, 182 07 Prague 8, Czech Republic,
and Institute for Theoretical Computer Science (ITI), Charles University, Prague
sima@cs.cas.cz

Abstract. In this paper a recurrent network, which consists of $O(\sqrt{m \log m})$ RBF (radial basis functions) units with maximum norm employing any activation function that has different values in at least two nonnegative points, is constructed so as to implement a given deterministic finite automaton with m states. The underlying simulation proves to be robust with respect to analog noise for a large class of smooth activation functions with a special type of inflexion.

1 RBF and Perceptron Neural Networks

The so-called *radial basis functions* (RBF) were first introduced in the context of interpolation problems [22] which are now one of the main research fields in numerical analysis. These functions were later exploited in the design of feedforward neural networks [3,18,21,23] which are called *RBF networks* and represent an important alternative to the classical *perceptron networks* [17]. Unlike the perceptrons that classify unbounded halfspaces, the RBF units are localized around centers in the areas of bounded width. Hence, also the learning heuristics for RBF networks may be different and their application fields are usually complementary to that of perceptrons [9].

The computational properties of traditional perceptron networks seem to be well understood now. The computational power of the finite recurrent discrete-time neural networks with saturated-linear activation function increases with the Kolmogorov complexity of real weight parameters [2]. For example, such networks with integer weights (corresponding to binary-state networks with threshold units) are equivalent to finite automata [14], while those with rational weights can simulate arbitrary Turing machines [12,24]. In addition, finer descriptive measures were introduced for the so-called *neuromata* which are binary-state neural networks implementing finite automata. A size-optimal neuromaton with

---

[*] Research supported by GA AS CR Grant B2030007.

V. Hlaváč, K. G. Jeffery, and J. Wiedermann (Eds.): SOFSEM 2000, LNCS 1963, pp. 431–439, 2000.

$\Theta(\sqrt{m})$ perceptron units can be constructed as to simulate a given deterministic finite automaton with m states [11,12]. Similarly, a regular language described by a regular expression of length d can be recognized by a size-optimal neuromaton with $\Theta(d)$ perceptrons [20]. These neuromaton constructions were generalized for analog-state recurrent neural nets with a large class of sigmoidal activation functions so that the respective simulations are stable in a sense that potentially infinite computations are robust with respect to the analog noise [15,20,25].

One motivation for analog implementations of neuromata issues from real-world applications in which partial prior knowledge (i.e. several automaton transitions) is known which should be refined and completed by training data. However, most of the learning heuristics (e.g. gradient methods) operate in an analog state space and hence, the analog neuromaton implementation can serve as an initial network configuration for the underlying learning procedure. The resulting transition rules may be extracted after the neuromaton is adapted to training data. This approach has widely been applied [4,5,7,16,19,20,27,28], especially for second-order neural nets which are also related to recurrent RBF networks [6]. The analog implementations of neuromata offer other advantages besides their use in gradient-based training algorithms; they also permit analog VLSI implementation, the foundations necessary for the universal approximation theories, the interpretation of outputs as posteriori probability estimates, etc. [20].

Unlike the perceptron networks, the computational capabilities of recurrent RBF networks have not been fully analyzed yet. Partial theoretical results along this direction have been achieved for hybrid recurrent networks consisting of both the RBF and perceptron layers which exhibited successful experimental results for inductive inference of regular grammars [6,8].

This paper investigates the issue of implementing deterministic finite automata by recurrent RBF networks. In Section 2, the recurrent RBF network of size $O(\sqrt{m \log m})$ units with maximum norm employing any activation function that has different values in at least two nonnegative points, is constructed which simulates a given deterministic finite automaton with m states. Thus the recurrent RBF networks prove to be at least as powerful as finite automata and hence, they can be called the *RBF neuromata*. In Section 3, the underlying simulation is shown to be stable for more practical imprecise analog representations of binary states for a large class of smooth activation functions with a special type of inflexion which includes the most common Gaussian activation function. Finally, some open problems are mentioned in Section 4.

2   Construction of RBF Neuromata

We will first specify the model of a *recurrent RBF network*. The network consists of s *RBF units* indexed as $1, \ldots, s$, which are connected into a generally cyclic oriented graph called *architecture* where each edge (i, j) leading from unit i to j is labeled with real parameter c_{ji}. Denote by $c_j = (c_{ji_1}, \ldots, c_{ji_{n_j}}) \in \mathbb{R}^{n_j}$ the *center* of RBF unit j where $i_1, \ldots, i_{n_j}$ are all the n_j incoming units incident to j. Each RBF unit j is also associated with its real positive *width* parameter $b_j > 0$.

The computational dynamics of the recurrent RBF network determines the evolution of the *network state* $y^{(t)} = (y_1^{(t)}, \ldots, y_s^{(t)}) \in \mathbb{R}^s$ for discrete time instants $t = 0, 1 \ldots$ as follows. At the beginning of the computation, the network is placed in an *initial state* $y^{(0)} \in \mathbb{R}^s$. At discrete time $t \geq 0$, the *excitation* $\xi_j^{(t)} = \|x_j^{(t)} - c_j\|/b_j \geq 0$ of unit j is proportional to the distance between the corresponding *input vector* $x_j^{(t)} = (y_{ji_1}^{(t)}, \ldots, y_{ji_{n_j}}^{(t)}) \in \mathbb{R}^{n_j}$ and its center c_j, where the *maximum norm* $\|x\| = \|x\|_\infty = \max_{i=1,\ldots,n} |x_i|$ for $x = (x_1, \ldots, x_n) \in \mathbb{R}^n$ will be exploited in our construction. At the next time instant $t+1$, an *activation function* $\sigma \colon \mathbb{R} \longrightarrow \mathbb{R}$ is applied to $\xi_j^{(t)}$ only for the RBF units $j \in \alpha_{t+1}$ from a given subset α_{t+1} in order to determine their new *states (outputs)* $y_j^{(t+1)} = \sigma(\xi_j^{(t)})$ in parallel whereas the remaining ones do not change their states, i.e. $y_j^{(t+1)} = y_j^{(t)}$ for $j \notin \alpha_{t+1}$. A typical example of the activation function is the *Gaussian function* $\sigma_G(\xi) = e^{-\xi^2}$.

For the RBF neuromaton recognizing a language $L \subseteq \{0,1\}^\star$ over binary alphabet an input/output protocol is defined as follows. For a general activation function producing real outputs an *analog representation* $r \colon \{0,1\} \longrightarrow \mathbb{R}$ such that $r(0) \neq r(1)$, is introduced to encode the binary values 0 and 1 by the real states $r(0)$ and $r(1)$ of RBF units, respectively. The analog representation will also be used for Boolean vectors, i.e. $r(z_1, \ldots, z_n) = (r(z_1), \ldots, r(z_n))$ for $z \in \{0,1\}^n$, $n \geq 1$. Thus a binary input string $w = w_1 \ldots w_k \in \{0,1\}^k$, $k \geq 0$ is presented bit after bit to the RBF neuromaton by means of an *input unit* j_{inp} whose state $y_{j_{inp}}^{(\tau(i-1))} = r(w_i)$ is externally set (and e.g. clamped), regardless of the RBF network computational dynamics, to the respective input-bit representation $r(w_i)$ at time instant $\tau(i-1)$ where an integer constant $\tau \geq 1$ is the *time overhead* for processing a single input bit. Then an *output unit* j_{out} signals at time τk whether the input word w belongs to language L, i.e. $y_{j_{out}}^{(\tau k)} = r(1)$ for $w \in L$ and $y_{j_{out}}^{(\tau k)} = r(0)$ for $w \notin L$. Similar definitions of language recognition by perceptron neuromata appeared in [1,12,24,26].

In the following lemma the implementation of a universal NAND gate over multiple literals by the RBF unit with an analog representation of Boolean values is presented which is used for the RBF neuromaton construction in the subsequent theorem.

Lemma 1. *Assume a real function σ is defined in at least two different non-negative points $0 \leq \xi_1 < \xi_2$ so that $\sigma(\xi_1) \neq \sigma(\xi_2)$. Let $n \geq 1$ be an integer and $I \subseteq \{1, \ldots, n\}$. Denote by $g \colon \{0,1\}^n \longrightarrow \{0,1\}$ a Boolean function defined as $g(z_1, \ldots, z_n) = NAND(\tilde{z}_1, \ldots, \tilde{z}_n)$ where $\tilde{z}_i = z_i$ for $i \in I$ and $\tilde{z}_i = \bar{z}_i$ for $i \notin I$ are literals. Then the n-input RBF unit with the center $c = (c_1, \ldots, c_n)$ such that $c_i = c$ for $i \in I$ and $c_i = \bar{c}$ for $i \notin I$ and width $b > 0$ where*

$$c = \frac{\xi_2 \sigma(\xi_2) - \xi_1 \sigma(\xi_1)}{\xi_2 - \xi_1}, \quad \bar{c} = \frac{\xi_2 \sigma(\xi_1) - \xi_1 \sigma(\xi_2)}{\xi_2 - \xi_1}, \quad b = \frac{|\sigma(\xi_2) - \sigma(\xi_1)|}{\xi_2 - \xi_1}, \quad (1)$$

employing the maximum norm and activation function σ, computes g within the analog representation $r(0) = \sigma(\xi_1)$ and $r(1) = \sigma(\xi_2)$, i.e. for any $z \in \{0,1\}^n$

$$\sigma\left(\frac{\|r(z) - c\|}{b}\right) = r(g(z))\,. \tag{2}$$

Proof. It follows from (1) that

$$|\sigma(\xi_1) - \bar{c}| = |\sigma(\xi_2) - c| = b\xi_1 < b\xi_2 = |\sigma(\xi_1) - c| = |\sigma(\xi_2) - \bar{c}|\,. \tag{3}$$

Further denote by $a = (a_1, \ldots, a_n) \in \{0,1\}^n$ a Boolean vector so that $a_i = 1$ for $i \in I$ and $a_i = 0$ for $i \notin I$ which is the only input that yields $g(a) = 0$. Hence, for any $1 \le i \le n$ either $a_i = 1$ and $c_i = c$, or $a_i = 0$ and $c_i = \bar{c}$. Thus for $z = a$ it holds $\sigma(\|r(a) - c\|/b) = \sigma(b\xi_1/b) = \sigma(\xi_1) = r(0)$ according to (3). On the other hand, for any $z \in \{0,1\}^n$, $z \ne a$ there exists $1 \le i \le n$ such that either $z_i = 1$ and $c_i = \bar{c}$, or $z_i = 0$ and $c_i = c$ which gives $\sigma(\|r(z) - c\|/b) = \sigma(b\xi_2/b) = \sigma(\xi_2) = r(1)$ due to (3). □

Theorem 1. *Let σ be a real function that assigns different values $\sigma(\xi_1) \ne \sigma(\xi_2)$ to at least two nonnegative points $0 \le \xi_1 < \xi_2$ which establish the analog representation $r(0) = \sigma(\xi_1)$ and $r(1) = \sigma(\xi_2)$. Given a deterministic finite automaton with m states, an equivalent RBF neuromaton of size $O(\sqrt{m \log m})$ units with maximum norm and activation function σ, can be constructed that recognizes the same regular language for the analog representation r within the time overhead $\tau = 3$ per each input bit.*

Proof. Set Q of m states of a given deterministic finite automaton can be enumerated so that each $q \in Q$ is binary encoded within $\lceil \log_2 m \rceil$ bits. The underlying transition function $\delta \colon Q \times \{0,1\} \longrightarrow Q$ producing the new automaton state $q_{new} = \delta(q_{old}, z) \in Q$ from an old one $q_{old} \in Q$ and a given input bit $z \in \{0,1\}$ can be viewed as a vector Boolean function $f_\delta \colon \{0,1\}^{\lceil \log_2 m \rceil + 1} \longrightarrow \{0,1\}^{\lceil \log_2 m \rceil}$ in terms of binary encoding of states. It can be shown by techniques from [10] that any vector Boolean function $f \colon \{0,1\}^n \longrightarrow \{0,1\}^p$ can be implemented by an optimal-size Boolean circuit of depth 3 with $\Theta(\sqrt{p2^n})$ gates computing NAND functions over multiple literals. According to Lemma 1 the underlying NAND gates can be realized by RBF units with the maximum norm and activation function σ within the analog representation r. Hence, the automaton transition function f_δ can be implemented by a three-layered feedforward RBF network of size $O(\sqrt{m \log m})$ units which is used for constructing the respective RBF neuromaton as follows.

The inputs to the first layer are taken from the third-layer units storing current neuromaton state within analog representation r and from a single external input unit j_{inp} which is updated by encoding the next bit of input string $w = w_1 \ldots w_k$ once every $\tau = 3$ time instants. In the beginning, the third-layer units encode the initial automaton state $q_0 \in Q$ and $y_{j_{inp}}^{(0)} = r(w_1)$ represents the first input bit. Set α_t of RBF units which update their states at time instant $1 \le t \le \tau k$ corresponds to the ℓth layer for $t = \tau(i-1) + \ell$ when the ith bit w_i

of the input string is being processed. This means that the binary encoding of new state is computed in the period of 3 parallel updates in which layer after layer takes its part. Finally, at time instant τk, the input string w of length k is read and accepted iff the third-layer units encode an accepting automaton state which is indicated by an additional bit in the binary encoding of automaton states corresponding to the output unit j_{out} whose state $y_{j_{out}}^{(\tau k)} = r(1)$ iff w is accepted. This completes the desired construction of the RBF neuromaton. □

3   Robust RBF Neuromata

In Section 2 the RBF neuromaton is implemented only for precise analog representations of binary values assuming noise-free operations over real numbers. However, the infinite precision of real number representation is far from being realistic and an analog noise (e. g. rounding errors) could deteriorate the RBF neuromaton computations. Therefore, in this section the underlying construction is analyzed to find out conditions under which the respective RBF neuromaton is robust when the analog representation of binary values 0 and 1 is released to be within specific disjoint small intervals around real states $r(0)$ and $r(1)$, respectively.

For the robust RBF neuromaton construction it suffices to show that the implementation of NAND gates by RBF units according to Lemma 1 preserves the prescribed precision of analog representation. More precisely, the underlying computation of Boolean function g by an RBF unit (with activation function σ defined in a sufficiently large domain) is said to be ε-stable, $0 < \varepsilon < (r(0)+r(1))/2$, if for every binary input $z \in \{0,1\}^n$ and for any $x \in \mathbb{R}^n$ of its analog representations within precision ε, i. e. $\max_{i=1,\ldots,n} |r(z_i) - x_i| = \|r(z) - x\| \le \varepsilon$, the output precision of RBF unit is preserved:

$$\left| \sigma\left(\frac{\|r(z) - c\|}{b}\right) - \sigma\left(\frac{\|x - c\|}{b}\right) \right| \le \varepsilon. \tag{4}$$

A large class of differentiable activation functions for which Lemma 1 provides a robust implementation of NAND gates by RBF units will be characterized.

Theorem 2. *Let σ be a real function that is differentiable within sufficiently large neighborhoods of two positive points $0 < \xi_1 < \xi_2$ where $\sigma(\xi_1) \ne \sigma(\xi_2)$. Then the computation of g by the RBF unit in Lemma 1 is ε-stable ($\varepsilon \le \xi_1 b$) if*

$$\forall \xi \in D(\xi_1, \xi_2, \varepsilon) = \left[\xi_1 - \frac{\varepsilon}{b}, \xi_1 + \frac{\varepsilon}{b}\right] \cup \left[\xi_2 - \frac{\varepsilon}{b}, \xi_2 + \frac{\varepsilon}{b}\right] \quad |\sigma'(\xi)| \le b \tag{5}$$

and it is not ε-stable if $|\sigma'(\xi)| > b$ for all $\xi \in D(\xi_1, \xi_2, \varepsilon)$.

Proof. First suppose that σ satisfies (5) and let $z \in \{0,1\}^n$ and $x \in \mathbb{R}^n$ be such that $\|r(z) - x\| \le \varepsilon$. It follows from the triangular inequality that

$$\|r(z) - c\| - \|r(z) - x\| \le \|x - c\| \le \|r(z) - c\| + \|x - r(z)\|. \tag{6}$$

Then divide (6) by $b > 0$ and recall from the proof of lemma 1 that $\|r(z) - c\|/b$ equals either ξ_1 for $z = a$, or ξ_2 for $z \neq a$ which together with $\|r(z) - x\| \leq \varepsilon$ implies $\|x - c\|/b \in D(\xi_1, \xi_2, \varepsilon)$. Therefore by the mean value theorem there exists $\zeta \in D(\xi_1, \xi_2, \varepsilon)$ such that

$$\sigma\left(\frac{\|r(z) - c\|}{b}\right) - \sigma\left(\frac{\|x - c\|}{b}\right) = \sigma'(\zeta)\left(\frac{\|r(z) - c\|}{b} - \frac{\|x - c\|}{b}\right) \qquad (7)$$

that yields the desired (4) since $|\sigma'(\zeta)| \leq b$ from (5) and $|\|r(z) - c\| - \|x - c\|| \leq \varepsilon$ according to (6).

On the other hand, suppose $|\sigma'(\xi)| > b$ for all $\xi \in D(\xi_1, \xi_2, \varepsilon)$ and let $z \in \{0, 1\}^n$. Choose $x_0 = r(z) + \varepsilon(r(z) - c)/\|r(z) - c\|$. Clearly $\|r(z) - x_0\| = \varepsilon$ and thus $x_0 \in \mathbb{R}^n$ is an analog representation of z within precision ε. In addition, $\|r(z) - c\| - \|x_0 - c\| = \varepsilon$ which implies $\|x_0 - c\|/b \in D(\xi_1, \xi_2, \varepsilon)$ since $\|r(z) - c\|/b \in \{\xi_1, \xi_2\}$. Therefore again by the mean value theorem (7) there exists $\zeta_0 \in D(\xi_1, \xi_2, \varepsilon)$ such that

$$\left|\sigma\left(\frac{\|r(z) - c\|}{b}\right) - \sigma\left(\frac{\|x_0 - c\|}{b}\right)\right| = |\sigma'(\zeta_0)|\frac{\varepsilon}{b} > \varepsilon \qquad (8)$$

which means that the computation of g is not ε-stable according to (4). □

Condition (5) that characterizes the differentiable activation functions for which the presented RBF neuromaton is robust includes parameter b which is defined in (1) by the function values again. In the following lemma a useful characterization of smooth functions, which implies (5), is formulated. Namely, these functions must have a special type of an inflexion point at which either the increasing function changes from convex to concave part, or conversely for the decreasing one.

Lemma 2. *Let σ be a real function that has the continuous derivative within $(\alpha, \beta) \subseteq [0, \infty)$. Assume that there exist $\xi_0 \in (\alpha, \beta)$ with $\sigma'(\xi_0) \neq 0$ and $\Delta > 0$ such that σ is either convex within $(\xi_0 - \Delta, \xi_0)$ and concave within $(\xi_0, \xi_0 + \Delta)$ if $\sigma'(\xi_0) > 0$, or concave within $(\xi_0 - \Delta, \xi_0)$ and convex within $(\xi_0, \xi_0 + \Delta)$ when $\sigma'(\xi_0) < 0$. Then there exist $\alpha < \xi_1 < \xi_2 < \beta$ and $\varepsilon > 0$ such that $\sigma(\xi_1) \neq \sigma(\xi_2)$ and for any $\xi \in D(\xi_1, \xi_2, \varepsilon)$: $|\sigma'(\xi)| \leq b = |\sigma(\xi_2) - \sigma(\xi_1)|/(\xi_2 - \xi_1)$ (which corresponds to condition (5) in Theorem 2).*

Proof. Suppose that $\sigma'(\xi_0) > 0$ while for $\sigma'(\xi_0) < 0$ the argument is similar. Since σ' is continuous there exists $0 < \Delta' < \Delta$ such that $\sigma'(\xi) > 0$ for all $\xi \in (\xi_0 - \Delta', \xi_0 + \Delta')$. According to the assumption, σ' is nondecreasing within $(\xi_0 - \Delta', \xi_0)$ and nonincreasing within $(\xi_0, \xi_0 + \Delta')$, and hence σ' has its maximum at ξ_0. Without loss of generality there exists $\gamma > 0$ such that either $\sigma'(\xi) = \sigma'(\xi_0)$ for all $\xi \in (\xi_0 - \gamma, \xi_0 + \gamma)$ (shift ξ_0 appropriately), or $\sigma'(\xi) \neq \sigma'(\xi_0)$ for all $\xi \in (\xi_0 - \gamma, \xi_0) \cup (\xi_0, \xi_0 + \gamma)$. In the former case set $\xi_1 = \xi_0 - \gamma/2$, $\xi_2 = \xi_0 + \gamma/2$, and $\varepsilon = \gamma/4$ for which $\sigma(\xi_1) \neq \sigma(\xi_2)$ and $\sigma'(\xi) = (\sigma(\xi_2) - \sigma(\xi_1))/(\xi_2 - \xi_1)$, i.e. $|\sigma'(\xi)| = b$ for any $\xi \in D(\xi_1, \xi_2, \varepsilon)$ since σ' is positive and constant there. In the latter case choose $u > 0$ within $\sigma'((\xi_0 - \Delta', \xi_0)) \cap \sigma'((\xi_0, \xi_0 + \Delta'))$ which is a nontrivial interval excluding $\sigma'(\xi_0)$. Then there exists $\xi_1 \in (\xi_0 - \Delta', \xi_0)$ and $\xi_2 \in (\xi_0, \xi_0 + \Delta')$ such that $\sigma'(\xi_1) = \sigma'(\xi_2) = u$ due to σ' is continuous. Again $\sigma(\xi_1) \neq \sigma(\xi_2)$ because σ is increasing within $(\xi_0 - \Delta', \xi_0 + \Delta')$. Moreover $\sigma'(\xi) > u$ for all $\xi \in (\xi_1, \xi_2)$ and therefore

$$u(\xi_2 - \xi_1) < \int_{\xi_1}^{\xi_2} \sigma'(\xi)d\xi = \sigma(\xi_2) - \sigma(\xi_1), \tag{9}$$

which implies $0 < \sigma'(\xi_1) = \sigma'(\xi_2) = u < (\sigma(\xi_2) - \sigma(\xi_1))/(\xi_2 - \xi_1)$ and thus there exists $\varepsilon > 0$ such that $|\sigma'(\xi)| < b$ for any $\xi \in D(\xi_1, \xi_2, \varepsilon)$ because σ' is continuous. □

For example, if σ has the first three derivatives and there exists an inflexion point $\xi_0 > 0$ such that $\sigma''(\xi_0) = 0$ and $\sigma'(\xi_0)\sigma'''(\xi_0) < 0$, then the type of this inflexion corresponds to that described by the assumption of Lemma 2. This can be used for checking that the most common Gaussian activation function $\sigma_G(\xi) = e^{-\xi^2}$ can be employed for the robust RBF neuromaton implementation according to Theorem 1. Namely, $\xi_0 = 1/\sqrt{2}$ is the required inflexion point, i. e. $\sigma_G''(\xi_0) = 0$ and $\sigma_G'(\xi_0)\sigma_G'''(\xi_0) < 0$. In addition, it also follows from Theorem 2 that $\xi_1 = \sqrt{\ln(4/3)}$, $\xi_2 = \sqrt{\ln 4}$, i. e. $r(0) = 3/4$, $r(1) = 1/4$ are valid parameters for the corresponding 0.2-stable RBF neuromaton computations.

4   Conclusions and Open Problems

In the present paper, the recurrent RBF network with maximum norm has been exploited for implementing a given deterministic finite automaton within a relatively small network size. For the precise analog representation of binary values a corresponding simulation works for almost any activation function (Section 2). In addition, for a large class of differentiable activation functions, which are characterized in detail, this implementation has proved to be robust with respect to the analog noise in a sense that it preserves a prescribed precision of the underlying representation (Section 3). It follows that the recurrent RBF networks are efficient and reliable analog computational devices that are at least as powerful as finite automata and thus comparable to perceptron networks [15,20,25].

It would be interesting to generalize the construction of the RBF neuromaton for general norms including the Euclidean one. Another challenge for further research is to prove the upper bounds on the computational power of analog recurrent RBF networks, e. g. to show that they are able to simulate Turing machines as it is known for analog perceptron networks [12,13,24].

References

1. Alon, N., Dewdney, A. K., Ott, T. J. Efficient simulation of finite automata by neural nets. *Journal of the ACM*, **38**, 495–514, 1991.   433

2. Balcázar, J. L., Gavaldà, R., Siegelmann, H. T. Computational power of neural networks: A characterization in terms of Kolmogorov complexity. *IEEE Transactions of Information Theory*, **43**, 1175–1183, 1997. 431

3. Broomhead, D. S., Lowe, D. Multivariable functional interpolation and adaptive networks. *Complex Systems*, **2**, 321–355, 1988. 431

4. Das, S., Mozer, M. C. A unified gradient-descent/clustering architecture for finite state machine induction. In J. Cowan, G. Tesauro, and J. Alspector, editors, *Neural Information Processing Systems*, **6**, 19–26, 1994. 432

5. Frasconi, P., Gori, M., Maggini, M., Soda, G. A unified approach for integrating explicit knowledge and learning by example in recurrent networks. In *Proceedings of the IEEE International Joint Conference on Neural Networks IJCNN'91*, Seattle, vol. **I**, 881–916, IEEE Press, New York, 1991. 432

6. Frasconi, P., Gori, M., Maggini, M., Soda, G. Representation of finite state automata in recurrent radial basis function networks. *Machine Learning*, **23**, 5–32, 1996. 432

7. Giles, C. L., Miller, C. B., Chen, D., Chen, H. H., Sun, G. Z., Lee, Y. C. Learning and extracting finite state automata with second-order recurrent neural networks. *Neural Computation*, **4**, 393–405, 1992. 432

8. Gori, M., Maggini, M., Soda, G. Inductive inference with recurrent radial basis function networks. In *Proceedings of the International Conference on Artificial Neural Networks ICANN'94*, Sorrento, Italy, 238–241, Springer-Verlag, 1994. 432

9. Haykin, S. *Neural Networks: A Comprehensive Foundation*. Prentice-Hall, Upper Saddle River, NJ, 2nd edition, 1999. 431

10. Horne, B. G., Hush, D. R. On the node complexity of neural networks. *Neural Networks*, **7**, 1413–1426, 1994. 434

11. Horne, B. G., Hush, D. R. Bounds on the complexity of recurrent neural network implementations of finite state machines. *Neural Networks*, **9**, 243–252, 1996. 432

12. Indyk, P. Optimal simulation of automata by neural nets. In *Proceedings of the Twelfth Annual Symposium on Theoretical Aspects of Computer Science STACS'95*, vol. **900** of LNCS, 337–348, Springer-Verlag, Berlin, 1995. 431, 432, 433, 437

13. Kilian, J., Siegelmann, H. T. The dynamic universality of sigmoidal neural networks. *Information and Computation*, **128**, 48–56, 1996. 437

14. Kleene, S. C. Representation of Events in Nerve Nets and Finite Automata. In C. E. Shannon and J. McCarthy, editors, *Automata Studies*, vol. **34** of *Annals of Mathematics Studies*, 3–41, Princeton University Press, NJ, 1956. 431

15. Maass, W., Orponen, P. On the effect of analog noise in discrete-time analog computations. *Neural Computation*, **10**, 1071–1095, 1998. 432, 437

16. Manolios, P., Fanelli, R. First-order recurrent neural networks and deterministic finite state automata. *Neural Computation*, **6**, 1155–1173, 1994. 432

17. Minsky, M. L., Papert, S. A. *Perceptrons*. MIT Press, Cambridge, MA, 1969. 431

18. Moody, J. E., Darken, C. J. Fast learning in networks of locally-tuned processing units. *Neural Computation*, **1**, 281–294, 1989. 431

19. Omlin, C. W., Giles, C. L. Training second-order recurrent neural networks using hints. In D. Sleeman and P. Edwards, editors, *Proceedings of the Ninth International Conference on Machine Learning*, 363–368, San Mateo, CA, Morgan Kaufman Publishers, 1992. 432

20. Omlin, C. W., Giles, C. L. Constructing deterministic finite-state automata in recurrent neural networks. *Journal of the ACM*, **43**, 937–972, 1996. 432, 437

21. Poggio, T., Girosi, F. Networks for approximation and learning. In *Proceedings of the IEEE*, **78**, 1481-1497, 1990. 431

22. Powell, M. J. D. Radial basis functions for multivariable interpolation: A review. In J. C. Mason and M. G. Cox, editors, *Proceedings of the IMA Conference on Algorithms for the Approximation of Functions and Data*, RMCS, Shrivenham, UK, 143–167, Oxford Science Publications, 1985. 431

23. Renals, S. Radial basis function network for speech pattern classification. *Electronics Letters*, **25**, 437–439, 1989. 431

24. Siegelmann, H. T., Sontag, E. D. Computational power of neural networks. *Journal of Computer System Science*, **50**, 132–150, 1995. 431, 433, 437

25. Šíma, J. Analog stable simulation of discrete neural networks. *Neural Network World*, **7**, 679–686, 1997. 432, 437

26. Šíma, J., Wiedermann, J. Theory of neuromata. *Journal of the ACM*, **45**, 155–178, 1998. 432, 433

27. Tiňo, P., Šajda, J. Learning and extracting initial mealy automata with a modular neural network model. *Neural Computation*, **7**, 822–844, 1995. 432

28. Zeng, Z., Goodman, R., Smyth, P. Learning finite state machines with self-clustering recurrent networks, *Neural Computation*, **5**, 976–990, 1993. 432

MDBAS — A Prototype of a Multidatabase Management System Based on Mobile Agents

Richard Vlach, Jan Lána, Jan Marek, and David Navara

Department of Software Engineering
Faculty of Mathematics and Physics, Charles University
Malostranské nám. 25, 118 00 Praha 1, Czech Republic
vlach@ksi.ms.mff.cuni.cz
jmar5300@ss1000.ms.mff.cuni.cz
{jan.lana,david.navara}@st.mff.cuni.cz

Abstract. Mobile agent technology brings new possibilities in developing distributed applications. We used mobile agents for building a prototype of a multidatabase management system called MDBAS. The system integrates a set of autonomous databases distributed over a network, enables users to create a global database scheme, and manages transparent distributed execution of users' requests and procedures including distributed transactions. Developing the system, we have emphasized easy and flexible administration together with efficient execution. We have implemented a dynamic optimization algorithm for distributed query processing. Additionally, a unique feature of MDBAS is the capability to transparently manage mobile execution of database procedures. Technically, our solution is based on Java-based mobile agents that exploit JDBC API for access to underlying databases. In this paper, we present the architecture of MDBAS, glance at the implementation and its difficulties, and discuss design and implementation alternatives.

1   Introduction

Mobile agents have a unique ability to transport themselves from one system in a network to another. The ability to travel allows mobile agents to move to a system that contains services they want to interact with and then to take an advantage of being in the same host or network as the service [5]. Bringing new promising possibilities for distributed systems development, mobile agent technology is attractive especially in information retrieval in widely distributed heterogeneous environments, network management, electronic commerce and mobile computing.

Whether and how the mobile agent paradigm can solve or improve some database and information retrieval problems is investigated in [10]. Upon some basic distributed computing models adapted to the mobile agent paradigm, a set of frameworks for distributed database access over the World-Wide Web were proposed and tested [11,7]. Mobile agents were efficiently used for distributed query processing [4]. Recently, a basic research into efficient execution strategies

V. Hlaváč, K. G. Jeffery, and J. Wiedermann (Eds.): SOFSEM 2000, LNCS 1963, pp. 440–449, 2000.
© Springer-Verlag Berlin Heidelberg 2000

for mobile database procedures querying distributed databases was presented in [12].

In the field of distributed database systems, we can determine several classes of systems operating over a distributed database [13]. The identifying characteristic of *multidatabase systems* is that the component databases have no concept of cooperation. A *multidatabase management system* is the software that provides for the management of this collection of autonomous databases and enables transparent access to it. Based on a topology in which a multidatabase management system connects component databases, we can distinguish two basic architectural types. First, the *star architecture* employs one central node that connects databases according to the client/server model. This is currently the most common solution, with easy and flexible administration, offering access tools for a wide range of heterogeneous data sources. However, impossibility of transferring data directly between different database sites reduces usage of optimization methods that can significantly decrease the response time for a global request. Second, the *fully interconnected architecture* enables establishing a connection between arbitrary two components and applying full optimization of data transmission. On the other hand, complex administration, namely in case of heterogeneous databases, is the main disadvantage of this approach.

In this paper, we describe a design and implementation of a multidatabase management system that combines efficient execution of fully interconnected architecture with easy and flexible administration [6]. Our solution is technically based on Java technology which is widely considered as a powerful application development tool in network-centric computing [8]. We have used Java-based mobile agents implemented in ASDK [1] and already established Java database connectivity application interface (JDBC API) [9,3] supported by all major database vendors.

Description of MDBA, comprising its architecture, performance principles, and implementation difficulties, is presented in Section 2. Alternatives to system design and implementation are discussed in Section 3. Finally, Section 4 concludes the paper.

2 Description of MDBAS

MDBAS provides a user with functionality that is expected from a multidatabase management system. To assure operability of the system, the component databases are required to support at least SQL92 ANSI Entry level and they must be accessible via a JDBC driver. A global user can use a set of statements to join (or disjoin) multiple databases into the system, find out their local scheme, create and drop local tables, manage a global scheme, perform typical SQL statements, define and execute procedures, and manage global transactions.

A component database can be connected in either the read-only or read-write mode. As the name suggests, the read-only mode allows the system to read the database data but denies updating them or changing the database scheme. The read-write mode permits data updates and scheme changes as well as managing system's temporary database structures. The read-write databases are internally used for integrating partial results of a global query result. Therefore, to promote the distributed query processing, at least one database must be connected in the read-write mode.

The global scheme, i. e., tables that a user can use, consists of tables from the joined databases and global virtual tables defined by the user. Any global virtual table is defined as a global view by an SQL SELECT or UNION statement in which any table of the current global scheme, including already defined global virtual tables, can be used. Potential conflicts in names of tables from different databases are prevented by usage of database-alias prefixes. After the global scheme is set up, the user can work with it without any notion of distribution and location of processed data. Note that underlying mobile agent nature of the system is hidden to the user. So, the user has no means of controlling individual agents. Transparent distributed execution of user's requests and procedures is fully ensured by the system.

The SQL statements SELECT, UNION, UPDATE, INSERT, DELETE operate over the global scheme with the only reasonable restriction that manipulation statements can not affect virtual tables. MDBAS supports features such as GROUP BY, ORDER BY constructs, aggregation functions in queries, inserting a global query result, manipulation statements with global scheme conditions, and several others. Transaction management COMMIT and ROLLBACK statements are supplemented with the PREPARECOMMIT statement to allow to participate MDBAS in a distributed transaction of a higher level.

Additionally to individual SQL statements, a user can define and execute a procedure. Inspired by SQL3, we have developed a simple interpretable programming language providing database procedure basis such as loop and if-then-else control structures, opening queries and fetching individual rows, working with variables and expressions, binding them to SQL statements. In principle, a procedure can execute any SQL statement that can be submitted by a user as an individual request including statements over virtual tables from the global scheme.

2.1   MDBAS's Architectural Blocks

The functionality of MDBAS is accomplished by mobile or stationary agents that communicate to one another via messages. Therefore, each of functional units, which can be identified in the system, must run an agent server to provide agents with the runtime environment. In our implementation, we used *Tahiti* agent servers delivered with ASDK packages. MDBAS comprises functional units of two types:

- the *Central* unit forming the core of the system,
- multiple *Workplace* units serving as database access points.

There is just one Central in the system. The Central acts as a distributed database server. It stores information about the system, accepts user's requests, starts and manages their execution. Additionally, the Central usually stores the program codes of all agents regardless the site on which they will operate later.

The Workplaces are the ports from which incoming agents access the databases through the JDBC API that is the borderline between uniformly designed global system and possibly heterogeneous databases. A Workplace can connect one or more databases. To gain the best results of global execution optimization, it is beneficial to place a Workplace to the same site as a database or, still advantageous, to a site providing fast database access.

To establish a Workplace, just a general agent server with appropriate configuration parameters and a proper JDBC driver must be installed at that site. The additional Workplace's functional codes come as agents. Note that the individual databases remain totally unaware of the global system existence and keep their full autonomy. The only inevitable information, which the global system must hold to be able to work with a database, is the URL of the related Workplace.

The logical concept of functional units does not require their distribution to different sites. If advantageous, for example for administration purposes, several Workplaces can run on the same machine. Moreover, it is possible to combine the Central and one of the Workplaces such that both of them run the same agent server. However, to keep the comprehensibility of this paper, we assume that they are separated.

The following are the basic types of agents operating on functional units and short description of their responsibility:

- The *Master* stationary agent is the organization chief of the system. There is just one agent of this type. It is located at the Central. The Master takes care of global information of the system, manages joining and disjoining remote databases through Workplaces, establishes user sessions, and provides an http gate to the system.
- A *Manager* stationary agent is created by the Master at the Central to handle one user's session. The main role of the Manager is to create and control Workers and Runners to execute individual user's requests. Additionally, the Manager coordinates global transactions.
- A *Porter* stationary agent is a permanent resident of a Workplace. It is created by the Master to control access to a database for all the time the database is joined in the system. The Porter is responsible for providing incoming Workers with database connections, executes simple database statements, manages possible temporary database structures, and takes part in a global transaction as a local participant.
- A *Worker* agent is designed to perform database operations. Workers usually operate in a tightly cooperating group created by a Manager to carry out one user's non-procedural request. Created at the Central and equipped with mission information, a Worker migrates to the proper Workplace, asks the Porter for a database connection, and accomplishes its database tasks.
- A *Runner* agent executes a user procedure. The Runner interprets the procedure code and exploits migration and data prefetching into Buffer agents to achieve a better response time than that of stationary execution.

- A stationary *Buffer* agent, created by a Runner and acting on behalf of it, loads remote data required by a procedure at the most advantageous site.
- The *Permeability* agent, located at the Central, controls its slaves to measure the permeability of the links between joined Workplaces. The permeability information is used by the Runner to find out an efficient migration sequence.

There are two ways how a user communicates with MDBAS. In the first one, a user running a web browser connects directly to the Master which submits the requests to the appropriate Manager. After the Manager acquired the results from slave agents, it generates a HTML reply page that is returned through the Master to the user.

The second way of communication is more sophisticated but much more efficient in case of a large sized reply. The user can develop a Java application that accesses MDBAS via a preinstalled MDBAS Client Package. The advantage of using the Client Package consists in the ability to communicate directly to the agents that gather the data at Workplaces. In contrast to the http access, the reply's data are directly delivered to the user's site instead of passing them through the Manager and the Master at the Central.

The Client Package shields the user from direct communication with a dynamic set of cooperating agents that process the current request. Its outer structure and user interface is very similar to the simplified JDBC. Its hidden structure copies the states of the Central and regularly checks the evaluating process. Therefore, the user can see just global scheme and does not need to take care of agents that process their partial queries or to check if they are working properly and to dispose them when they finish their tasks.

2.2　Processing Requests

At the beginning, a user asks the Master to open a session. The Master creates a Manager that becomes a user's communication partner. From that time, the Manager receives user's requests and arranges their execution. However, as the Master keeps information about the global system, it parses and preprocesses requests received by the Manager. Moreover, the Master is engaged namely in carrying out *administrative requests* which comprise joining and disjoining databases or defining the global database scheme and procedures. Whereas a defining request just changes the global information, joining or disjoining a database implies creation or disposing a Porter at the related Workplace.

In case of a *database query request*, the Master identifies and substitutes the global virtual objects in the query and prepares a preoptimized Select-tree structure describing a distributed execution plan. The nodes in the Select-tree represent SELECT or UNION database operations that hierarchically, towards the root, combine data gathered from component databases to produce the final result. According to the Select-tree, the Manager creates one Worker for each tree node and supervises their cooperation in the inherited arrangement. While any leaf Worker has its execution destination determined by the component database it accesses, the Manager uses dynamic optimization to dispatch any of non-leaf Workers to the Workplace such that the amount of remote data that must be fetched from son-Workers (i. e., Workers that are closer to leaves) is minimized. The result obtained by the root Worker is delivered to the user. The tree in an example of simple query processing captured in Fig. 1 has only two layers. Generally, the more complex query, the more layers appear in the tree.

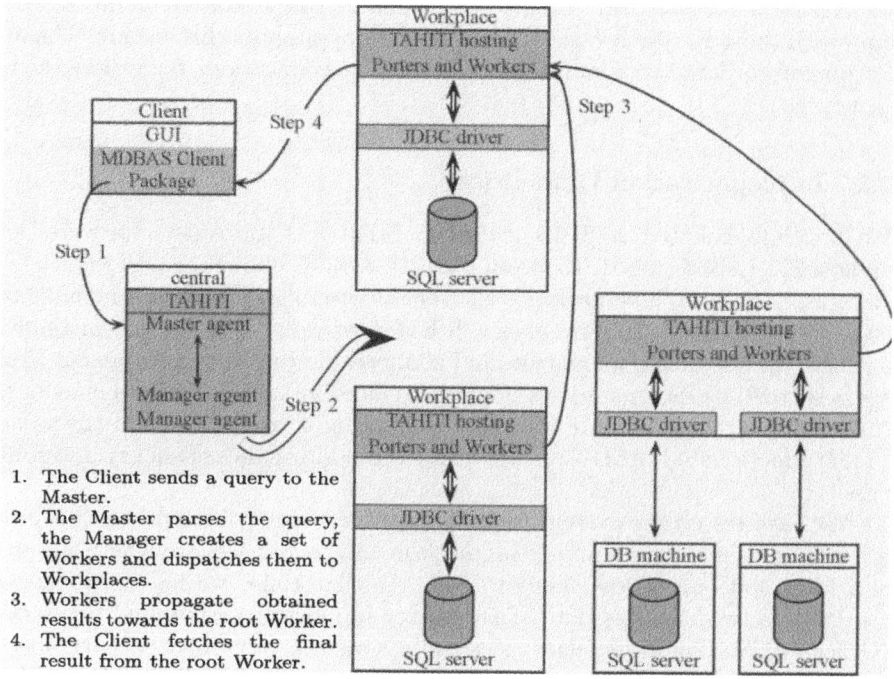

1. The Client sends a query to the Master.
2. The Master parses the query, the Manager creates a set of Workers and dispatches them to Workplaces.
3. Workers propagate obtained results towards the root Worker.
4. The Client fetches the final result from the root Worker.

Fig. 1. Schematic processing of a simple query

In our implementation, when a non-leaf Worker combines partial results, it uses SQL capability of a component read-write database. First, it downloads results of remote son-Workers and inserts them into temporary tables. Second, to obtain the result, it submits its SQL operation to the database engine.

A *database manipulation request* is processed in a very similar way as above. The data for the associated query, if any, are prepared first. Then, the root Worker executes the manipulation statement. Processing a *request invoking a procedure*, the Manager receives the procedure code from the Master and creates a Runner which is responsible for code execution. The Runner is equipped with the recent information about network permeability to be able to properly apply an efficient execution strategy. In MDBAS, we have implemented a variant of the Sure Migration strategy exploiting migration as well as possibility to establish fetch buffers for remote result sets [12]. The main idea of this strategy is to start execution at the Central and use migration only if it can be guaranteed that migration gives better response time than non-mobile execution. Inside a procedure, any non-SQL statement is executed by the Runner itself. The majority of SQL statements are submitted to the Manager. The rest of them, namely some kinds of manipulation requests, can be submitted directly to a proper Porter to carry them out.

To involve a database into a distributed transaction, the associated JDBC driver must support the distributed transaction extension. In case of *transaction management requests*, the Manager coordinates the 2-phase commit algorithm only with those Porters whose JDBC connections support this feature. The other Porters are ordered to commit or rollback their connections regardless the consequences.

2.3   Implementation Difficulties

We have implemented MDBAS using Java (JDK 1.1) and Aglets Software Development Kit (ASDK ver. 1.0.3) from IBM [1]. ASDK, one of the well-known agent systems, is a set of Java packages that enable users to deploy and manage their own mobile agents and agent servers. It has provided us with an easy installation, intuitive and flexible deployment, and comfortable runtime environment (Tahiti agent server). Unfortunately, we sometimes faced an unpredictable behavior that caused lower reliability. Additionally, comparing to newer tools of the same or similar functionality, ASDK may reveal worse performance efficiency and robustness [11].

We have tested the system with database servers of different vendors on different platforms: Oracle and Postgresql on Linux, Sybase Anywhere, Interbase and Microsoft Access on Windows NT. At that time, we had only one Oracle database with appropriate JDBC driver supporting distributed transactions (Oracle 8.1.6). The other databases could simulate capability to participate in a global transaction under a strong optimistic assumption that if the local processing does not fail during execution, the local participant is assumed to be in the ready-to-commit state.

In general, the most significant difficulties were connected to JDBC access. Since MDBAS does not take into account specific features of component databases, we have sometimes met problems with column naming (collisions with reserved words), automatic type conversions (database specific types to Java and backward), value conversions (e. g., different handling of strings that were longer than expected), and slight differences between expected behavior according to the SQL92 standard and real database behavior (MS Access's handling of views). Moreover, there were significant differences in the JDBC access speed. For example, inserting rows in Postgresql is about 10 times faster than in Interbase although non-JDBC performance is comparable. Consequently, since inserting a row is one of the most often used operation during global query evaluation, this non-proportionality in speed can reduce query optimization adequacy.

3   Discussion on Design and Implementation Alternatives

Developing the system, we discussed several issues that brought out alternatives to the presented system design and implementation. The most essential ones are now rephrased.

The first inevitable topic is a *level of mobility* applied in the system. At one *mobile extreme*, having the Master as the only stationary agent, any user's request can be carried out by just one mobile agent that cruises the databases, connects them on its own, and builds up the reply step by step. Obviously, besides the other reasons, this approach decreases the performance by decreasing the level of execution parallelism. Still staying near the mobile extreme, keeping the maximal parallelism of the current approach, we could design a smaller group of agents that use their mobility instead of sending messages to deliver gathered data. However, as [11], [7] and our experiments prove, due to migration overhead it is more efficient to send the same amount of data by a message than to let a mobile agent deliver them on its own. The important consequence with the general validity is that implementing a distributed algorithm into mobile agents, the better performance is guaranteed by creating stationary agents (at the beginning or in progress) communicating via messages than exploiting mobility. Application of this idea leads us to another *stationary extreme* in which only stationary agents are used. Even procedure execution can be implemented in this way. In general, this approach reduces the advantageous features of mobile agent technology only to that of easy end flexible installation of a functional code to remote sites. However, for some types of problems the usage of mobility is quite natural. Then, it is rather a question for software engineers whether to prefer performance efficiency to design and implementation ease. Considering the pros and cons in the context of our system, we have decided to prefer performance in case of evaluating a global query while preferring design and implementation ease in case of mobile procedures.

The second topic is probably the most debatable one. The question is *how to integrate partial query results* during distributed query execution. Our approach (see Section 2.2) advantageously employs the underlying database engines that are optimized for typical SQL operations. Disadvantageously, besides administration difficulties with read-write databases, the lack of read-write databases in the system significantly reduces query optimization possibilities. An alternative to our approach is proposed in [7]. For the above purpose, they suggest to use specialized agents with SQL capabilities. Then, on the one hand, combining partial results is possible at any site running an agent server, on the other hand, processing larger data may cause problems as well as performance efficiency is rather questionable in this case. Finally, in accordance with the prototype nature of our system, we have decided to give up looking for the optimal solution in this field and applied the presented straightforward solution.

Another discussed topic pertinent to agent technology was that of *task distribution* especially in case of stationary agents running on one site. In general, one multithreaded (possibly multifunctional) task running on a site can be implemented either as *one multithreaded agent* or as a *set of cooperating agents*. Considering performance, the multithreaded agent variant exploiting native Java thread synchronization and direct method invocation outperforms the multi-agent variant using constructs based on inter-agent messaging. Applying the multifunctional idea into our system, we could join up functionality of the Master and Managers on the Central, or Workers and Porters on Workplaces. On the other hand, suitable distribution of a naturally multithreaded task into more or less autonomous pieces can simplify design, architecture comprehensibility and maintenance. Our final solution preferring functional distribution reflects the observation that in context of the global system the performance gains of the multithreaded variant can be treated as negligible. However, inner multithreading is widely used inside functional blocks namely in order to increase execution parallelism and for controlling mechanisms.

4   Conclusion

In this paper, we have presented a mobile agent based prototype of a multi-database management system. The system, called MDBAS, provides a user with powerful functionality, easy administration and efficient execution. A user of the system can join and disjoin multiple autonomous databases, define global virtual tables, process typical SQL statements, define and execute procedures. The system transparently manages distributed execution including distributed transactions.

The functionality of the system is accomplished by a set of cooperating agents that operate on functional units of two types: a unique Central and multiple Workplaces. While the Central forms the core of the system and acts as a distributed database server, the multiple Workplaces are intended to be the ports from which agents arriving from the Central can access the component databases with a high data transmission rate. This basic framework reveals two important features. First, heterogeneity of individual databases can be hidden under the uniformly designed Workplaces. Second, the right integration code comes to Workplaces as mobile agents when needed instead of pre-installing it locally. Inherently, besides flexible administration, this framework gives full opportunity for applying optimization algorithms for distributed execution of users' requests. Additionally to a simple algorithm optimizing distributed query processing, we have implemented an efficient strategy for executing procedures, which are transparently carried out by mobile agents.

In addition to specific features, for example mobile procedures, MDBAS comprises many of advantageous ideas that can be separately found in existing multidatabase management systems. Although the prototype nature of the system allowed us to lay aside some other serious issues, especially more sophisticated security control, we are of the opinion that MDBAS is a valuable example of the proficient application of mobile agent technology in the field of distributed databases.

References

1. ASDK homepage. http://www.trl.ibm.co.jp. 441, 446
2. D. Chess, C. Harrison, and A. Kershenbaum. Mobile agents: Are they a good idea? Technical report, IBM Research Division, T. J. Watson Research Center, Yorktown Heights, New York, 1995.
3. Java Technology homepage. http://java.sun.com/. 441
4. R. Jones and J. Brown. Distributed query processing via mobile agents. http://www.cs.umd.edu/~keleher/818s97/ryan/paper.html. 440
5. D. B. Lange and M. Oshima. *Programming and Deploying Java Mobile Agents with Aglets*. Addison-Wesley, 1998. 440
6. MDBA homepage. http://www.ms.mff.cuni.cz/~dnav5337/mdba/. 441
7. S. Papastavrou, G. Samaras, and E. Pitoura. Mobile agents for WWW distributed database access. In *Proc. 15th International Conference on Data Engineering (ICDEE99)*, Sydney, 1999. http://ada.cs.ucy.ac.cy/~cssamara/DBMS-Agents/Paper/mobpaper.ps. 440, 447
8. E. Pitoura and G. Samaras. *Data Management for Mobile Computing*. Kluwer Academic Publishers, 1997. 441
9. G. Reese. *Database Programming With JDBC and Java*. O'Reilly & Associates, 1997. 441
10. A. Sahuguet. About agents and databases (draft). CIS-650, http://www.cis.upenn.edu/~sahuguet/Agents/Agents_DB.pdf, 1997. 440
11. G. Samaras, M. D. Dikaiakos, C. Spyrou, and A. Liverdos. Mobile agent platforms for web databases: A qualitative and quantitative assessment. In *Proc. ASAMA'99*, 1999. 440, 446, 447
12. R. Vlach. Efficient execution strategies for mobile procedures querying distributed databases. In *Proc. DOA'00*. IEEE, 2000. To be published. http://aglaja.ms.mff.cuni.cz/~vlach/papers/doa00.ps. 441, 445
13. M. T. Özsu and P. Valduriez. *Principles of Distributed Database Systems*. Prentice Hall, 2nd edition, 1999. 441

Computing the Dimension of Linear Subspaces

Martin Ziegler[1*] and Vasco Brattka[2]

[1] Heinz Nixdorf Institute, Fachbereich 17
University of Paderborn, 33095 Paderborn, Germany
ziegler@uni-paderborn.de
[2] Theoretische Informatik I, Informatikzentrum
FernUniversität, 58084 Hagen, Germany
vasco.brattka@fernuni-hagen.de

Abstract. Since its very beginning, linear algebra is a highly algorithmic subject. Let us just mention the famous Gauss Algorithm which was invented before the theory of algorithms has been developed. The purpose of this paper is to link linear algebra explicitly to computable analysis, that is the theory of computable real number functions. Especially, we will investigate in which sense the dimension of a given linear subspace can be computed. The answer highly depends on how the linear subspace is given: if it is given by a finite number of vectors whose linear span represents the space, then the dimension does not depend continuously on these vectors and consequently it cannot be computed. If the linear subspace is represented via its distance function, which is a standard way to represent closed subspaces in computable analysis, then the dimension does computably depend on the distance function.

1 Introduction

Computational aspects of linear algebra are mostly studied with respect to their algebraic complexity, that is, in machine models capable of processing in unit time real numbers. Digital computers can however work on finite information like integers or floating point numbers as approximation of reals. The common implicit believe (or hope) is that, as precision increases, program's approximate output tends to the desired exact result.

We investigate computational aspects of linear algebra from the somewhat different point of view of computable analysis, which offers a precise framework for treating computability aspects of real number computations based on Turing machines. Starting with Turing's own famous paper [9] real number computations have been investigated using his machine model. Later on, the theory has been further developed by Grzegorczyk [4], Lacombe [6], Pour-El and Richards [8], Kreitz and Weihrauch [10], Ko [5] and many others. We have essentially adopted Weihrauch's approach [10], the so-called *Type-2-Theory of Effectivity*, which allows to express computations with real number, continuous functions and subsets in a highly uniform way.

---

* Work partially supported by DFG Grant Me872/7-3

V. Hlaváč, K. G. Jeffery, and J. Wiedermann (Eds.): SOFSEM 2000, LNCS 1963, pp. 450–458, 2000.
© Springer-Verlag Berlin Heidelberg 2000

In constructive analysis [1], as well as in computable analysis closed subsets are often represented by distance functions, which, roughly speaking, plays
the role of continuous substitutes for characteristic functions (cf. [2] for a survey). Such representations of sets by distance functions can also be considered
for constructions of data structures for solid modeling and other CAD applications (cf. [7]). If it appears that the result of a computation with sets is a linear
subspace, one is interested in computing the dimension and a basis of this space.
Our main result proves that both is possible.

The following section contains a short introduction to computable analysis
and the notions used there. Section 3 presents our computability results on
the dimension of linear subspaces.

2   Computable Analysis

In this section we briefly present some basic notions from computable analysis
(based on the approach of Type-2 theory of effectivity) and some direct consequences of well-known facts. For a precise and comprehensive reference we refer
the reader to [10]. Roughly speaking, a partial real number function $f :\subseteq \mathbb{R}^n \to \mathbb{R}$
is computable, if there exists a Turing machine which transfers each sequence
$p \in \Sigma^\omega$ that represents some input $x \in \mathbb{R}^n$ into some sequence $F_M(p)$ which
represents the output $f(x)$. Since the set of real numbers has continuum cardinality, real numbers can only be represented by infinite sequences $p \in \Sigma^\omega$
(over some finite alphabet Σ) and thus, such a Turing machine M has to compute infinitely long. But in the long run it transfers each input sequence p into
an appropriate output sequence $F_M(p)$. It is reasonable to allow only one-way
output tapes for infinite computations since otherwise the output after finite time
would be useless (because it could possibly be replaced later by the machine). It
is straightforward how this notion of computability can be generalized to other
sets X with a corresponding *representation*, that is a surjective partial mapping
$\delta :\subseteq \Sigma^\omega \to X$.

Definition 1 (Computable functions). Let δ, δ' be representations of X, Y,
respectively. A function $f :\subseteq X \to Y$ is called (δ, δ')-*computable*, if there exists
some Turing machine M such that $\delta' F_M(p) = f\delta(p)$ for all $p \in \text{dom}(f\delta)$.

Here, $F_M :\subseteq \Sigma^\omega \to \Sigma^\omega$ denotes the partial function, computed by the Turing
machine M. It is straightforward how to generalize this definition to functions
with several inputs and it can even be generalized to multi-valued operations
$f :\subseteq X \rightrightarrows Y$, where $f(x)$ is a subset of Y instead of a single value. In this case
we replace the condition in the definition above by $\delta' F_M(p) \in f\delta(p)$.

Already in case of the real numbers it appears that the defined notion of
computability sensitively relies on the chosen representation of the real numbers. The theory of *admissible* representations completely answers the question
how to find "reasonable" representations of topological spaces [10]. Let us just
mention that for admissible representations δ, δ' each (δ, δ')-computable function
is necessarily continuous (w. r. t. the final topologies of δ, δ').

An example of an admissible representation of the real numbers is the so-called *Cauchy representation* $\rho :\subseteq \Sigma^\omega \to \mathbb{R}$, where, roughly speaking, $\rho(p) = x$ if p is an (appropriately encoded) sequence of rational numbers $(q_i)_{i\in\mathbb{N}}$ which converges rapidly to x, i.e. $|x_i - x_k| \leq 2^{-k}$ for all $i > k$. By standard coding techniques this representation can easily be generalized to a representation of the n-dimensional Euclidean space $\rho^n :\subseteq \Sigma^\omega \to \mathbb{R}^n$ and to a representation of $m \times n$ matrices $\rho^{m\times n} :\subseteq \Sigma^\omega \to \mathbb{R}^{m\times n}$.

If δ, δ' are admissible representations of topological spaces X, Y, respectively, then there exists a canonical representation $[\delta, \delta'] :\subseteq \Sigma^\omega \to X \times Y$ of the product $X \times Y$ and a canonical representation $[\delta \to \delta'] :\subseteq \Sigma^\omega \to C(X,Y)$ of the space $C(X,Y)$ of the total continuous functions $f\colon X \to Y$. We just mention that these representations allow evaluation and type conversion (which correspond to an utm- and smn-Theorem). Evaluation means that the evaluation function $C(X,Y) \times X \to Y$, $(f, x) \mapsto f(x)$ is $([[\delta \to \delta'], \delta], \delta')$-computable and type conversion means that a function $f\colon Z \times X \to Y$ is $([\delta'', \delta], \delta')$-computable, if and only if the canonically associated function $f'\colon Z \to C(X,Y)$ with $f'(z)(x) := f(z,x)$ is $(\delta'', [\delta \to \delta'])$-computable. As a direct consequence we obtain that matrices $A \in \mathbb{R}^{m\times n}$ can effectively be identified with linear mappings $f \in \mathrm{Lin}(\mathbb{R}^n, \mathbb{R}^m)$.

Lemma 1. *The correspondence between matrices and vector space homomorphisms is effective. This means that the mappings*

$$\mathrm{Lin}(\mathbb{R}^n, \mathbb{R}^m) \to \mathbb{R}^{m\times n}, \; (x \mapsto A \cdot x) \mapsto A$$
$$\mathbb{R}^{m\times n} \to \mathrm{Lin}(\mathbb{R}^n, \mathbb{R}^m), \; A \mapsto (x \mapsto A \cdot x)$$

are $([\rho^n \to \rho^m], \rho^{m\times n})$- *and* $(\rho^{m\times n}, [\rho^n \to \rho^m])$-*computable, respectively.*

Since a mapping like rank: $\mathbb{R}^{m\times n} \to \mathbb{R}$, which associates to each matrix $A \in \mathbb{R}^{m\times n}$ the dimension of its image, can only take finitely many different values, it is necessarily discontinuous and thus not $(\rho^{n\times m}, \rho)$-computable. Later on we will see that this mapping has a weaker computability property: given the matrix A we can at least find an increasing sequence of values which converge to rank(A). To express facts like this precisely, we will use two further representations $\rho_<, \rho_> :\subseteq \Sigma^\omega \to \mathbb{R}$. Roughly speaking, $\rho_<(p) = x$ if p is an (appropriately encoded) list of all rational numbers $q < x$. (Analogously, $\rho_>$ is defined with $q > x$.) It is a known fact that a mapping $f :\subseteq X \to \mathbb{R}$ is (δ, ρ)-computable, if and only if it is $(\delta, \rho_<)$- and $(\delta, \rho_>)$-computable [10].

Occasionally, we will also use some standard representation $\nu_\mathbb{N}, \nu_\mathbb{Q}$ of the natural numbers $\mathbb{N} = \{0, 1, 2, \dots\}$ and the rational numbers $\mathbb{Q}$, respectively. Moreover, we will also need a representation for the space $\mathcal{L}^n$ of linear subspaces $V \subseteq \mathbb{R}^n$. Since all linear subspaces are non-empty closed spaces, we can use well-known representations of the hyperspace $\mathcal{A}^n$ of all closed non-empty subsets $A \subseteq \mathbb{R}^n$ (cf. [2,10]). One way to represent such spaces is via the distance function $d_A\colon \mathbb{R}^n \to \mathbb{R}$, defined by $d_A(x) := \inf_{a\in A} d(x, a)$, where $d\colon \mathbb{R}^n \times \mathbb{R}^n \to \mathbb{R}$ denotes the Euclidean metric of $\mathbb{R}^n$. Altogether, we define three representations $\psi^n, \psi^n_<, \psi^n_> :\subseteq \Sigma^\omega \to \mathcal{A}^n$. We let $\psi^n(p) = A$, if and only if $[\rho^n \to \rho](p) = d_A$. In other words, p encodes a set A w. r. t. ψ^n, if it encodes the distance function d_A w. r. t. $[\rho^n \to \rho]$. Analogously, let $\psi^n_<(p) = A$, if and only if $[\rho^n \to \rho_>](p) = d_A$ and let $\psi^n_>(p) = A$, if and only if $[\rho^n \to \rho_<](p) = d_A$. One can prove that $\psi^n_<$ encodes "positive" information about the set A (all open rational balls $B(q, r)$ which intersect A can be enumerated), and $\psi^n_>$ encodes "negative" information about A (all closed rational balls $\overline{B}(q, r)$ which do not intersect A can be enumerated). It is known that a mapping $f :\subseteq X \to \mathcal{A}^n$ is (δ, ψ^n)-computable, if and only if it is $(\delta, \psi^n_<)$- and $(\delta, \psi^n_>)$-computable [10]. We mention that

a) the operation $(f, A) \mapsto f^{-1}(A) \subseteq \mathbb{R}^n$ is $([\rho^n \to \rho^m], \psi^m_>, \psi^n_>)$-computable,
b) the operation $(f, B) \mapsto \overline{f(B)} \subseteq \mathbb{R}^m$ is $([\rho^n \to \rho^m], \psi^n_<, \psi^m_<)$-computable.

Together with Lemma 1 we obtain the following computability facts about kernel and image of matrices.

Lemma 2. *Given an $m \times n$ matrix A, its kernel can effectively be approximated from outside and its image can effectively be approximated from inside. More precisely, the mappings*

$$\ker : \mathbb{R}^{m \times n} \to \mathcal{A}^n, \ A \mapsto \{x \in \mathbb{R}^n : A \cdot x = 0\}$$
$$\mathrm{img} : \mathbb{R}^{m \times n} \to \mathcal{A}^m, \ A \mapsto \{A \cdot x : x \in \mathbb{R}^n\}$$

are $(\rho^{m \times n}, \psi^n_>)$- and $(\rho^{m \times n}, \psi^m_<)$-computable, respectively.

Finally, we will also use the notion of an *r. e. open* set $U \subseteq \mathbb{R}^{m \times n}$, which is a set such that there exists a $(\rho^{m \times n}, \rho)$-computable function $f : \mathbb{R}^{m \times n} \to \mathbb{R}$ with $\mathbb{R}^{m \times n} \setminus U = f^{-1}\{0\}$. Given a representation δ of X, we will say more generally that a subset $U \subseteq Y \subseteq X$ is δ-*r. e. open* in Y, if $\delta^{-1}(U)$ is r. e. open in $\delta^{-1}(Y)$. Here a set $A \subseteq B \subseteq \Sigma^\omega$ is called *r. e. open* in B, if there exists some computable function $f :\subseteq \Sigma^\omega \to \Sigma^*$ with $\mathrm{dom}(f) \cap B = A$. Intuitively, a set U is δ-r. e. open in Y, if and only if there exists a Turing machine which halts for an input $x \in Y$ given w. r. t. δ, if and only if $x \in U$. It is known that a set $U \subseteq \mathbb{R}^{m \times n}$ is $\rho^{m \times n}$-r. e. open in $\mathbb{R}^{m \times n}$, if and only if it is r. e. open. If a set $U \subseteq X$ is δ-r. e. open in X, then we will say for short that it is δ-*r. e. open.*

3   Computing the Dimension

In this section we will discuss the problem to determine the dimension of a given linear subspace. We will see that in our setting this question is somehow related to the problem to determine a basis of a given linear space. First we note that we can compute the determinant of a matrix $A = (a_{ij}) \in \mathbb{R}^{n \times n}$ using the well-known formula $\det(A) = \sum_{\sigma \in \mathcal{S}_n} \mathrm{sign}(\sigma) \prod_{i=1}^n a_{\sigma(i)i}$, where $\mathcal{S}_n$ denotes the set of all permutations $\sigma : \{1, \dots, n\} \to \{1, \dots, n\}$. Since addition and multiplication are computable on the real numbers and by applying certain obvious closure schemes we can deduce:

Lemma 3. *Given an $n \times n$ matrix we can compute its determinant:*

$$\det \colon \mathbb{R}^{n \times n} \to \mathbb{R}, \ A \mapsto \det(A)$$

is $\left(\rho^{n \times n}, \rho\right)$-computable.

Now we can test a tuple $(x_1, \ldots, x_n) \in \mathbb{R}^{m \times n}$ with $n \leq m$ for linear independence by searching for a non-zero determinant of the $n \times n$ sub-matrices of $(x_1, \ldots, x_n)$. Using this idea we can define a function $f \colon \mathbb{R}^{m \times n} \to \mathbb{R}$ by $f(A) := \sum_{S < A} |\det(S)|$, where the sum is over all $n \times n$ sub-matrices S of A. Thus f has the property that a tuple $(x_1, \ldots, x_n)$ is linearly independent, if and only if $f(x_1, \ldots, x_n) > 0$. Since f is computable by the previous lemma, this proves the following:

Lemma 4. *The property "linear independence", i. e. the set*

$$\{(x_1, \ldots, x_n) \in \mathbb{R}^{m \times n} : (x_1, \ldots, x_n) \text{ linearly independent }\}$$

is r. e. open.

Now we are prepared to investigate computability properties of the rank mapping rank: $\mathbb{R}^{m \times n} \to \mathbb{R}$ which maps a matrix A to the dimension of its image. Since the image of the rank mapping contains finitely many different values, the rank mapping cannot be continuous for $n, m \geq 1$. Nevertheless, we can approximate the rank from below. Using the previous lemma we can systematically search for a maximal linearly independent tuple among the column vectors of the matrix A and we can determine an increasing sequence of numbers $k \in \mathbb{N}$ in this way which converges to $\mathrm{rank}(A)$.

Proposition 1. *The rank of a matrix can be approximated from below:*

$$\mathrm{rank} \colon \mathbb{R}^{m \times n} \to \mathbb{R}, \ A \mapsto \mathrm{rank}(A)$$

is $\left(\rho^{m \times n}, \rho_<\right)$-computable, but neither $\left(\rho^{m \times n}, \rho_>\right)$-computable, nor continuous.

The linear span mapping which maps a matrix A to the linear span of its column vectors has similar properties as the rank mapping. If we know a basis of a linear subspace, we can even obtain complete information about its span.

Proposition 2. *The linear span mapping*

$$\mathrm{span} \colon \mathbb{R}^{m \times n} \to \mathcal{A}^m, \ (x_1, \ldots, x_n) \mapsto \bigcap \{V \in \mathcal{L}^m : x_1, \ldots, x_n \in V\}$$

is $(\rho^{m \times n}, \psi_<^m)$-computable, but neither $(\rho^{m \times n}, \psi_>^m)$-computable nor continuous. Restricted to linear independent inputs $(x_1, \ldots, x_n) \in \mathbb{R}^{m \times n}$ the linear span mapping is even $(\rho^{m \times n}, \psi^m)$-computable.

Proof. The first property follows directly from Lemma 2 since span$(A) =$ img(A). It is easy to see that the linear span mapping is not continuous in the zero matrix $A = 0$. Finally, we have to prove that the linear span mapping is $(\rho^{m \times n}, \psi_{>}^{m})$-computable, restricted to linear independent inputs. If $n = m$, then this is trivial since span$(x_1, \ldots, x_m) = \mathbb{R}^m$ for linearly independent $(x_1, \ldots, x_m)$. For the case $n < m$ we will again use the function $f : \mathbb{R}^{m \times (n+1)} \to \mathbb{R}$, defined by $f(A) := \sum_{S < A} |\det(S)|$, where the sum is over all $(n+1) \times (n+1)$ submatrices S of A. As we have seen, f is computable and $(x_1, \ldots, x_n, x)$ is linearly independent, if and only if $f(x_1, \ldots, x_n, x) \neq 0$. Especially, we can deduce

$$\text{span}(x_1, \ldots, x_n) = \{x \in \mathbb{R}^m : f(x_1, \ldots, x_n, x) = 0\},$$

provided that $(x_1, \ldots, x_n)$ is linearly independent. Using type conversion we can show that $g : \mathbb{R}^{m \times n} \to C(\mathbb{R}^m, \mathbb{R})$ with $g(x_1, \ldots, x_n)(x) := f(x_1, \ldots, x_n, x)$ is $(\rho^{m \times n}, [\rho^m \to \rho])$-computable. Moreover, as we have already stated, it is known that $C(\mathbb{R}^m, \mathbb{R}) \to \mathcal{A}^m, h \mapsto h^{-1}\{0\}$ is $([\rho^m \to \rho], \psi_{>}^{m})$-computable. Thus, span, restricted to linearly independent inputs, is $(\rho^{m \times n}, \psi_{>}^{m})$-computable. □

As we have seen, the dimension of a linear subspace cannot be computed from a tuple of vectors whose linear span generates the subspace. In general the information included in such a tuple does not suffice to determine upper bounds on the dimension. If we additionally supply negative information about the linear subspace, the dimension operator becomes computable. As a preparation we first prove that the set with the zero-space as single point is r.e. open in the set of linear subspaces w.r.t. negative information.

Lemma 5. *The set* $\{\{0\}\} \subseteq \mathcal{A}^n$ *is* $\psi_{>}^{n}$*-r.e. open in* $\mathcal{L}^n$.

Proof. We note that it is known that given a $\psi_{>}^{n}$-name p of a subspace V, we can effectively find a $[\nu_{\mathbb{N}} \to \nu_{\mathbb{Q}}^{2}]$-name q of a function $f : \mathbb{N} \to \mathbb{Q}^2$ such that $\mathbb{R}^n \setminus V = \bigcup_{k=0}^{\infty} B(c_k, r_k)$, where $(c_k, r_k) := f(k)$ (cf. [2]). In other words, we can effectively represent V by a sequence of open rational balls, whose union exhausts the exterior of V. For a set $V \in \mathcal{L}^n$ we obtain

$$V = \{0\} \iff V \cap S^{n-1} = \emptyset$$

where $S^{n-1} := \partial B(0,1) = \{(x_1, \ldots, x_n) \in \mathbb{R}^n : x_1^2 + \ldots + x_n^2 = 1\}$ denotes the unit sphere of the n-dimensional space $\mathbb{R}^n$. Since S^{n-1} is compact, we can conclude

$$V \cap S^{n-1} = \emptyset \iff (\exists m) \; S^{n-1} \subseteq \bigcup_{k=0}^{m} B(c_k, r_k).$$

Since S^{n-1} is a recursive compact set, i.e. there exists some computable s such that $\psi^n(s) = S^{n-1}$, we can deduce that we can even effectively find an m with the property above, if such an m exists. This proves that there exists a computable function $f :\subseteq \Sigma^\omega \to \Sigma^*$ such that $p \in \text{dom}(f)$, if and only if $\psi_{>}^{n}(p) = \{0\}$, for all $p \in (\psi_{>}^{n})^{-1}(\mathcal{L}^n)$. □

Now we are prepared to prove the following main result of our paper.

Theorem 1. *One can compute the dimension of a given linear subspace:*

$$\dim\, :\subseteq \mathcal{A}^n \to \mathbb{R}, \ V \mapsto \dim(V)$$

is $(\psi_<^n, \rho_<)$- and $(\psi_>^n, \rho_>)$-computable. It is in particular (ψ^n, ρ)-computable.

Proof. First of all, it is known that given a $\psi_<^n$-name p of a subspace V, we can effectively find a $[\nu_\mathbb{N} \to \rho^n]$-name q of a function $f : \mathbb{N} \to \mathbb{R}^n$ such that the image $f(\mathbb{N})$ is dense in V (cf. [2]). We claim that if $\dim(V) = k$, then there exists a tuple $(i_1, \ldots, i_k) \in \mathbb{N}^k$ such that $(f(i_1), \ldots, f(i_k))$ is a basis of V. If $(x_1, \ldots, x_k) \in \mathbb{R}^{n \times k}$ is an arbitrary basis of V, then there exist an open neighbourhood U of $(x_1, \ldots, x_k)$ which only consists of tuples of linear independent vectors (by Lemma 4 linear independence especially is an open property). Since $f(\mathbb{N})$ is dense in V, there exists a tuple $(i_1, \ldots, i_k) \in \mathbb{N}^k$ such that $(f(i_1), \ldots, f(i_k)) \in U \cap V^k$. This proves the claim. Thus, we can use the name q to search for tuples $(i_1, \ldots, i_m) \in \mathbb{N}^m$ of maximal size m such that $(f(i_1), \ldots, f(i_m))$ is linear independent. In this way we can produce an increasing sequence $m_1, m_2, \ldots$ of natural numbers. Lemma 4 guarantees that the whole procedure is effective and the claim proved before guarantees that the sequence converges to $\dim(V)$.

We note that it is known that the intersection operation $\mathcal{A}^n \times \mathcal{A}^n \to \mathcal{A}^n$, $(A, B) \mapsto A \cap B$ is $([\psi_>^n, \psi_>^n], \psi_>^n)$-computable (cf. [10]). If we can find some linear subspace U of $\mathbb{R}^n$ with $U \cap V = \{0\}$ and $\dim(U) = n - m$, then we can conclude $\dim(V) + \dim(U) = \dim(U \oplus V) \leq n$ and thus $\dim(V) \leq m$. On the other hand, if $\dim(V) \leq m$, then there exists always such a subspace U. Thus, to guarantee $\dim(V) \leq m$, it suffices to find $n - m$ linear independent vectors $x_1, \ldots, x_{n-m}$ such that $\mathrm{span}(x_1, \ldots, x_{n-m}) \cap V = \{0\}$. If such vectors exist, then there exist also rational vectors $x_1, \ldots, x_{n-m} \in \mathbb{Q}^n$ with the same property, since linear independence is an open property by Lemma 4, the test on equality with $\{0\}$ is open by Lemma 5, the linear span mapping (by Proposition 2) and intersection are continuous (w. r. t. the final topology of $\psi_>^n$). Thus, we can produce a decreasing sequence of natural number $m_1, m_2, \ldots$ by searching for a minimal m and linear independent rational vectors $x_1, \ldots, x_{n-m} \in \mathbb{Q}^n$ with the property above. The considerations above together with Lemma 4, Proposition 2 and Lemma 5 show that the whole procedure is effective and that the sequence converges to $\dim(V)$. □

Using the same method as in the proof before, we can construct a basis of a linear subspace as a set w. r. t. $\psi_<^n$. If we know the dimension in advance, then by virtue of Lemma 4 we can determine a basis directly by representing its vectors.

Corollary 1. *One can effectively find a basis of a given linear subspace. More precisely, the multi-valued mapping*

$$\mathrm{basis}\, :\subseteq \mathcal{A}^m \rightrightarrows \mathcal{A}^m, \ V \mapsto \big\{ \{b_1, \ldots, b_n\} \subseteq \mathbb{R}^m : (b_1, \ldots, b_n) \text{ basis of } V \big\}$$

is $\left(\psi^m_<, \psi^m_<\right)$- and $\left(\psi^m, \psi^m\right)$-computable. If $n := \dim(V)$ is known in advance,

$$\text{basis}' :\subseteq \mathcal{A}^m \rightrightarrows \mathbb{R}^{m \times n}, \ V \mapsto \{(b_1, \dots, b_n) \in \mathbb{R}^{m \times n} : (b_1, \dots, b_n) \text{ basis of } V\}$$

is even $\left(\psi^m_<, \rho^{m \times n}\right)$-computable.

We can also effectively compute complementary spaces.

Corollary 2. *Given a linear subspace* $V \subseteq \mathbb{R}^m$, *one can effectively find a linear subspace* $U \subseteq \mathbb{R}^m$ *such that* $V \oplus U = \mathbb{R}^m$. *More precisely, the multi-valued mapping*

$$\text{compl} :\subseteq \mathcal{A}^m \rightrightarrows \mathcal{A}^m, \ V \mapsto \{U \in \mathcal{L}^m : V \oplus U = \mathbb{R}^m\}$$

is (ψ^m, ψ^m)-*computable.*

4 Conclusion

Computations with sets find an increasing interest in computable analysis, cf. for instance [3,7,12,11,2]. One of the motivations is to find suitable data structures for solid modeling and other practical applications of computations with sets [7]. We have presented a result which shows that the dimension of a linear subspace can be computed, provided that the subspace is represented via its distance function. This result can be considered as a starting point of "computable linear algebra". Many interesting questions in this field still remain open.

References

1. Errett Bishop and Douglas S. Bridges. *Constructive Analysis*, Springer, Berlin, 1985. 451
2. Vasco Brattka and Klaus Weihrauch. Computability on subsets of Euclidean space I: Closed and compact subsets. *Theoretical Computer Science*, 219:65–93, 1999. 451, 452, 455, 456, 457
3. Xiaolin Ge and Anil Nerode. On extreme points of convex compact Turing located sets. In Anil Nerode and Yu. V. Matiyasevich, editors, *Logical Foundations of Computer Science*, vol. 813 of *LNCS*, 114–128, Berlin, 1994. Springer. 457
4. Andrzej Grzegorczyk. On the definitions of computable real continuous functions. *Fundamenta Mathematicae*, 44:61–71, 1957. 450
5. Ker-I Ko. *Complexity Theory of Real Functions*. Progress in Theoretical Computer Science. Birkhäuser, Boston, 1991. 450
6. Daniel Lacombe. Les ensembles récursivement ouverts ou fermés, et leurs applications à l'Analyse récursive. *Comp. Rend. Acad. des Sci. Paris*, 246:28–31, 1958. 450
7. Andrè Lieutier. Toward a data type for solid modeling based on domain theory. In K.-I Ko, A. Nerode, M. B. Pour-El, K. Weihrauch, and J. Wiedermann, eds, *Computability and Complexity in Analysis*, vol. 235 of *Informatik Berichte*, pages 51–60. FernUniversität Hagen, August 1998. 451, 457
8. Marian B. Pour-El and J. Ian Richards. *Computability in Analysis and Physics*. Perspectives in Mathematical Logic. Springer, Berlin, 1989. 450

9. Alan M. Turing. On computable numbers, with an application to the "Entschei-dungsproblem". *Proceedings of the London Mathematical Society*, 42(2):230–265, 1936. 450

10. Klaus Weihrauch. *Computable Analysis*. Springer, Berlin, 2000. 450, 451, 452, 453, 456

11. Ning Zhong. Recursively enumerable subsets of R^q in two computing models: Blum-Shub-Smale machine and Turing machine. *Theoretical Computer Science*, 197:79–94, 1998. 457

12. Qing Zhou. Computable real-valued functions on recursive open and closed subsets of Euclidean space. *Mathematical Logic Quarterly*, 42:379–409, 1996. 457

Author Index

Lecture Notes in Computer Science

For information about Vols. 1–1878
please contact your bookseller or Springer-Verlag